FIFTH EDITION

Direct Instruction Mathematics

Marcy Stein
University of Washington Tacoma

Diane Kinder
University of Washington Tacoma

Kristen Rolf
University of Washington Tacoma

Jerry Silbert
National Institute for Direct Instruction

Douglas W. Carnine
Professor Emeritus, University of Oregon

330 Hudson Street, NY NY 10013

Director and Portfolio Manager: Kevin M. Davis
Content Producer: Janelle Rogers
Executive Development Editor: Linda Bishop
Portfolio Management Assistant: Anne McAlpine
Executive Field Marketing Manager: Krista Clark
Executive Product Marketing Manager: Christopher Barry
Procurement Specialist: Carol Melville
Full Service Project Management: Katrina Ostler, Cenveo®
Publisher Services

Cover Designer: Carie Keller
Cover Image: Rob Van Esch/Offset.com
Composition: Cenveo® Publisher Services
Printer/Binder: LSC Communications
Cover Printer: LSC Commuicatons
Text Font: 10/12 Times LT Pro

Every effort has been made to provide accurate and current Internet information in this book. However, the Internet and information posted on it are constantly changing, so it is inevitable that some of the Internet addresses listed in this textbook will change.

Library of Congress Cataloging-in-Publication Data

On file with the Library of Congress.

2   18

Student Edition
ISBN 10: 0-13-471122-x
ISBN 13: 978-0-13-471122-5

Enhanced eText
ISBN 10: 013457673X
ISBN 13: 978-0-13-457673-2

To Wes Becker, a leader in showing how science can serve education.

To Zig Engelmann, the designer of Direct Instruction, whose impact in the field of education continues to inspire us.

Preface

Mathematics instruction continues to be challenging for many teachers in American schools. Although the goals of current approaches to mathematics instruction are reasonable, often the methods for achieving those goals are lacking. The need for improvement in mathematics instruction has been well documented by national, even international, evaluations. Moreover, research also has suggested that many teachers are ill-prepared to meet the needs of a diverse student population. We have received numerous requests from teachers who found their preparation to teach mathematics to be inadequate. Teachers were particularly vocal about the lack of specific guidance in how to support students who have difficulty learning mathematics. This text provides teachers with the information needed to design supplemental mathematics instruction and to evaluate and modify the commercially developed programs currently available to them.

Although we have found the procedures suggested in this book effective, we do not claim they are panaceas. Implementing our suggestions requires hard work on the part of the teacher. It is our hope that the systematic procedures and teaching strategies recommended here will stimulate the development of even better instructional practices.

NEW TO THIS EDITION

This is the first edition of *Direct Instruction Mathematics* designed as an interactive eText. We provide you with point-of-use videos and the opportunity to self-assess your learning as you read each chapter. Look for the clickable icons in the margins to watch the videos. Look for Apply What You Learned to find the checkmark icons and launch self-assessment questions at the end of each chapter.

Our Pearson eText* includes the following new features:

- Learning Outcomes for each chapter
- Sections on Conceptual Understanding for each topic
- Apply What You Learned sections in each chapter with feedback links
- More than 100 printable teaching formats
- The alignment of teaching strategies with Common Core State Standards (CCSS)
- Links to videos of teaching demonstrations for many teaching formats
- Links to a supplemental math facts program including math facts worksheets and assessments
- Topics appropriate for adult learners working on basic skills
- New content in the following areas: probability, data analysis, statistics

ORGANIZATION OF THIS EDITION

Direct Instruction Mathematics provides teachers with evidence-based teaching strategies that can be used to supplement mathematics instruction for students from preschool through grade 8. The teaching strategies also are relevant for older students and adult learners who are struggling with

---

*Please note that eText enhancements such as video clips and Apply What You Learned quizzes are only available in the Pearson eText and not other third-party eTexts such as CourseSmart or Kindle.

basic skills. The text outlines procedures that can be used to evaluate and then modify the commercially developed math programs used in most schools. Most importantly, the text gives teachers systematic procedures for addressing both conceptual understanding and procedural fluency for critical topics in K–8 mathematics aligned with the Common Core State Standards (CCSS).

The new edition includes an updated chapter on research, video links to teaching demonstrations for many of the teaching formats, and new content related to probability and data analysis. Finally, *Direct Instruction Mathematics* contains Instructional Sequence and Assessment Charts that can serve as the basis for designing diagnostic tests as well as for constructing goals and objectives for the design of Individualized Education Plans (IEPs).

The book is organized into three parts: Part I, Perspective; Part II, Basic Concepts and Skills; and Part III, Extended Concepts and Skills. Part I is composed of three chapters. Chapter 1 outlines the components of the Direct Instruction approach to mathematics instruction—instructional design, instructional delivery, and instructional language. Chapter 2 provides an updated brief review of relevant research on effective mathematics instruction. Chapter 3 provides a framework for evaluating commercially developed mathematics instructional materials.

The Basic Concepts and Skills (Part II) and Extended Concepts and Skills (Part III) are the heart of the book. Each chapter covers a specific topic: counting, symbol identification and place value, basic facts, addition, subtraction, multiplication, division, problem solving, measurement, time, money, fractions, decimals, percent, ratio, probability, data analysis, geometry, and pre-algebra. These chapters include suggestions for introducing critical concepts and procedures for teaching specific skills.

SPECIAL FEATURES OF THIS EDITION

Each chapter in the fifth edition of *Direct Instruction Mathematics* includes the following special features:

- Learning Outcomes
- Conceptual understanding sections
- Printable teaching formats
- Videos of teachers demonstrating teaching formats
- Diagnosis and remediation sections
- Apply What You Learned

In addition to the features mentioned above, the fifth edition now includes links to worksheets and tests for a math facts program and a glossary of terms used throughout the text.

ACKNOWLEDGMENTS

Foremost among the many people to whom we are grateful are the Direct Instruction teachers who prove every day that math failure is not inevitable. We also are grateful to Zig Engelmann, whose melding of logical analysis and empiricism has resulted in the development of numerous highly effective mathematics programs. Many of the procedures described in this book were derived from *DISTAR Arithmetic, Connecting Math Concepts, Corrective Mathematics, Essentials for Algebra,* and *Core Concepts in Mathematics* authored by Engelmann and his colleagues. Special thanks go to Bernadette Kelly whose suggestions and ideas contributed greatly to this text. We also would like to acknowledge and thank the reviewers who inspired us in our revision decisions: Bridget Kelley, Western Washington University; Mary Ann Nelson, University of Florida; Jennifer Neyman, Gonzaga University; Cynthia T. Shamberger, Fayetteville State University; and Sean Wachsmuth, Minnesota State University, Mankato.

In addition, we would like to thank everyone involved in producing the videos included in this edition: Lori Agar, Tom Edwards, Paul Lovelady and his crew, Tristan Marcum, Tonya Middling, Joe Query, Michaela Query, and Susan Templin. We also would like to thank the following people for their contributions to the production of the text: Deena Beard, Donna Braboy, Austin Campbell, Courtney Leininger, and Tatiana Wolfe. Finally, we would like to thank our families and friends for their support.

Brief Contents

Contents

Formats for Teaching Major Skills

continued

CHAPTER

1

Direct Instruction

LEARNING OUTCOMES

1.1 Discuss the areas that comprise mathematical proficiency according to the National Research Council.

1.2 Outline the features of instructional design that are essential to mathematics instruction.

1.3 Discuss the four features of instructional delivery that are characteristic of Direct Instruction.

1.4 Explain the importance of explicitly teaching students mathematics vocabulary and concepts.

MATHEMATICAL PROFICIENCY

According to the National Research Council (2001), mathematical proficiency is represented by competency in five areas: conceptual understanding, procedural fluency, strategic competence, adaptive reasoning, and productive disposition. Many mathematics textbooks used in teacher preparation discuss the philosophy and theory of mathematics instruction and provide instructional activities, but few outline with specificity the means by which teachers can translate these areas into explicit instruction. *Direct Instruction Mathematics* provides teachers with a comprehensive blueprint to organize and teach specific content for major mathematical topics that appear in elementary and middle school. The textbook also provides teachers with strategies to address the needs of struggling learners. Each chapter in this text provides specific recommendations to promote conceptual understanding (teaching language concepts and providing visual representations) and procedural fluency (teaching explicit strategies). Embedded in the chapters are recommendations to promote adaptive reasoning (asking students to explain their answers) and to determine strategic competence (monitoring student performance).

Regarding a productive disposition, research has suggested that when students experience success, they develop positive self-concepts (Stebbins, St. Pierre, Proper, Anderson, & Cerra, 1977). More specifically, research in the area of Direct Instruction (see Chapter 2) leads us to conclude that well-designed instruction that promotes student mathematical proficiency, as outlined in this text, will yield productive dispositions.

In this chapter, we provide a detailed discussion of three critical components—instructional design, instructional delivery, and instructional language—that are essential to understanding how *Direct Instruction Mathematics* addresses the five proficiency areas mentioned above. Building mathematics instruction with these components as the foundation will ensure that students acquire, retain, and generalize new learning in as humane, efficient, and effective a manner as possible.

INSTRUCTIONAL DESIGN

To effectively teach mathematics, teachers must construct the kinds of lessons and develop the specific teaching procedures that best meet the needs of their students. Throughout the chapters in this text, we emphasize five essential instructional design features to assist teachers in designing mathematics instruction and in evaluating and modifying the commercial programs that have been adopted for use in their school or district. The learning theory underlying these features is elaborated in detail in *Theory of Instruction* (Engelmann & Carnine, 1991) and serves as the foundation for Direct Instruction programs. The website for the National Institute for Direct Instruction (NIFDI) provides detailed information about the commercially available Direct Instruction programs. Throughout this text we discuss the following features that represent instructional design elements essential to well-designed mathematics instruction:

1. Sequence of skills and concepts
2. Explicit instructional strategies
3. Preskills
4. Example selection
5. Practice and review

Before designing instruction or modifying it, teachers must clearly identify the objectives they want to teach. Most commercial programs specify student objectives for each instructional unit. However, not all objectives are written so that teachers can determine when they have been met. The objectives should be stated as specific, observable behaviors and include both accuracy and rate criteria, if possible. For example, a clear first-grade objective for single-digit addition is: "Given 25 single-digit addition problems, students will correctly solve at least 22 in 1 minute with no more than one error." Poorly stated objectives contain vague descriptions of student behavior that are difficult to measure, such as "Students will understand the concept of addition."

Teachers can use the Instructional Sequence and Assessment Charts found at the beginning of most chapters in this book as a guide to selecting important grade-level objectives. These charts, aligned with national Common Core State Standards for Mathematics (CCSSM) (National Governors Association Center for Best Practices & Council of Chief State School Officers, 2010), offer a sequence of instruction based on the difficulty level of the given problem types. Teachers can use the charts to help prioritize objectives, deciding which problem types to teach and in which sequence. Teachers of students who perform poorly should focus their instruction on higher-priority skills, those that are used more frequently, or those that are prerequisites for more advanced skills.

Once the teacher has determined the types of problems students should be able to work when they have completed the unit, the teacher must decide on appropriate levels of mastery. Both accuracy and fluency must be considered when specifying levels of mastery. Unfortunately, there is little research available on determining accuracy and fluency criteria. Generally, teachers should provide supervised practice until students reach an 85% to 90% accuracy level for worksheet assignments containing a review of previously introduced types of problems. A fluency criterion usually depends on the relative complexity of the problem type. Most educators agree that students who work problems with relative fluency are more likely to retain strategies over a longer period of time. We present more detail about fluency criteria in the section on progress monitoring later in this chapter.

Sequence of Skills and Concepts

The order in which information and skills are introduced affects the difficulty students have in learning them. Sequencing involves determining the optimum order for introducing new information and strategies. Following are three general guidelines for sequencing the introduction of new skills:

1. Teach preskills for a strategy before teaching the strategy.
2. Teach easy skills before more difficult ones.
3. Separate the introduction of information or strategies that students are likely to confuse.

Generally, the more steps in a strategy and the greater the similarity of the new strategy to previously taught strategies, the more likely students will have difficulty. For example, in column subtraction, problems that require a regrouping strategy are more difficult than problems that do not. But not all problems that require regrouping are of equal difficulty. A problem such as 3,002 − 89 is significantly more difficult than a problem such as 364 − 128, largely due to the presence of zeros.

One of the preskills we recommend teaching for regrouping with zeros in problems like the one above is hundreds-minus-one problems (300 − 1 = 299). That preskill should be taught prior to introducing problems such as 3,002 − 89, which requires renaming 300 tens as 299 tens. This example of identifying and teaching the appropriate preskills illustrates the first sequencing guideline.

$$\begin{array}{r} 299 \\ 30\cancel{0}^{1}2 \\ - \quad 89 \\ \hline \end{array}$$

The instruction of easier skills before more difficult ones is the second sequencing guideline. For example, before teaching students to add fractions with unlike denominators, we recommend teaching students the easier skill of adding fractions with like denominators. Although this guideline may seem obvious, many commercially available programs disregard its importance.

The third sequencing guideline is to separate the introduction of information and strategies that are likely to be confused. The more similar two skills are, the more likely students are to confuse them. For example, because young students are likely to confuse identification of the numerals 6 and 9, those numerals should not be introduced consecutively. Likewise, the skip-counting series for 6s and 4s are quite similar in that they both contain 12, 24, and 36 (6, **12**, 18, **24**, 30, **36** and 4, 8, **12**, 16, 20, **24**, 28, 32, **36**). Introducing these series consecutively is likely to cause confusion for some students.

Explicit Instructional Strategies

Research suggests that teaching students explicit instructional strategies increases their performance in mathematics. (See Chapter 2 for this research.) According to Archer and Hughes, explicit instruction is "instruction that is systematic, direct, engaging, and success-oriented" (2011, p. vii). In addition to being explicit, well-designed instructional strategies must be generalizable. That is, a well-designed instructional strategy will apply to a range of different types of problems. For example, many programs introduce fractions to students using a single representation, such as a cookie, divided into thirds or fourths (1/3 or 2/4). When students are introduced to improper fractions (5/4), they often are unable to generalize the fraction concept. Students cannot conceptualize 5/4 (1 ¼) if prior visual representations have been limited to one whole. A well-designed strategy for teaching students fraction concepts is one that applies to both proper and improper fractions. (See Chapter 13.)

Some commercially developed mathematics programs suggest that students generate a number of alternative strategies for the same problem. Rather than developing a conceptual foundation that highlights mathematical relationships, the introduction of alternative strategies often confuses instructionally naive students. Teachers should select the most generalizable, useful, and explicit strategies to teach their students—strategies that draw attention to the relationships among the mathematical skills and concepts being taught.

As mentioned previously, this text provides teachers with explicit instructional strategies to teach content expected to be taught in elementary and middle school classrooms. The strategies are translated into teaching procedures using teaching formats or scripts that provide specific teacher wording, examples, and often error-correction procedures. Formats are designed so that teacher explanations are clear and unambiguous so teachers do not have to worry if the explanation they provide one day is consistent with explanations they've given previously.

The teaching formats represent a carefully designed instructional sequence reflecting the gradual release of responsibility from teacher to student. Most of the formats consist of four parts: a structured board presentation, a structured worksheet presentation, a less structured worksheet presentation, and supervised practice. A characteristic of the formats is the use of frequent questioning that allows teachers to continuously check for student understanding and increases student engagement. This text provides links to teaching formats for the instructional strategies discussed in each chapter. In addition, some of the formats are accompanied by video demonstrations.

Preskills

As mentioned previously, instruction should be sequenced so that the requisite component skills of a strategy are taught before the entire strategy is introduced. The component skills, therefore, can be called preskills. For example, to solve a percent problem (What is 23% of 67?), the student must be able to (a) convert percent to a decimal ($23\% = .23$), (b) solve multiplication problems with multi-digit factors ($.23 \times 67$), and (c) place the decimal point correctly in the product (15.41).

$$
\begin{array}{r}
67 \\
\times\ .23 \\
\hline
201 \\
134 \\
\hline
15.41
\end{array}
$$

The necessary preskills for many strategies may have been taught earlier or in previous grades. Nonetheless, to ensure that students have mastered the preskills before introducing a new instructional strategy, teachers should test students on those preskills. Each chapter in this text identifies critical preskills for the strategies presented so that teachers can design tests to determine whether the preskills have been mastered or must be taught.

Example Selection

Selecting examples involves constructing or choosing appropriate problems to be used during teaching demonstrations and student practice. Two guidelines are particularly helpful in assisting teachers in selecting appropriate examples. The first example selection guideline is simply to include only problems that students can solve by using a strategy that has been explicitly taught. For example, if students have been taught a regrouping strategy for solving subtraction problems without zeros, but they have not yet been taught to solve problems with zeros, the teacher should not give them a problem such as $3,004 - 87$. As mentioned previously, teaching students to rename in problems containing zeros requires additional instruction in specific preskills.

The second guideline is ultimately to include not only examples of the currently introduced type (introductory examples) but also examples of previously introduced problem types that are similar (discrimination examples). The purpose of including previously introduced problem types is to provide students with practice in determining when to apply the new strategy and when to apply previously taught strategies. For example, after students learn how to regroup from ones to tens in column addition, their practice examples should include problems that require regrouping and problems that do not. Working a set of discrimination problems encourages students to examine the problems more carefully to determine when to apply the regrouping strategy instead of reverting to the rote behavior of just "putting one on top of the tens column." The importance of including discrimination examples cannot be overemphasized. Unless previously taught problem types are included, students will likely forget or misapply earlier taught strategies.

Practice and Review

Providing sufficient practice for initial mastery and adequate review for retention is an essential aspect of instructional design. Two guidelines are fundamental in helping teachers provide practice and review. First, teachers must provide massed practice (Dunlosky, Rawson, Marsh,

Nathan, & Willingham, 2013) on an individual skill until mastery is reached. Students demonstrate mastery on a particular skill when they can work problems accurately, fluently, and independently. Following this guideline requires that teachers monitor their students carefully and frequently to determine if and when mastery has been achieved. If students have not mastered a skill in the time originally allotted, teachers will need to provide additional practice opportunities.

Second, teachers must provide systematic review of previously introduced skills. Once students have reached a specified level of mastery on a given skill, the teacher can gradually decrease the amount of practice on that skill. But practice should never entirely disappear. The skill should be reviewed systematically over time to ensure retention. Reviewing a skill systematically over time is called distributed practice. Distributed practice is a hallmark of all Direct Instruction programs.

The review of previously introduced skills requires deliberate planning, because many commercial programs do not provide an opportunity for that review. Often, review is naturally provided because the newly taught skill serves as a component skill for a more advanced problem type. For example, as subtraction problems with regrouping are mastered, those problems are integrated into word problems, thereby providing practice on the component skill.

In Chapter 3 we illustrate how the instructional design features discussed in this chapter contribute to a framework for evaluating published mathematics programs.

INSTRUCTIONAL DELIVERY

Once teachers have planned their mathematics instruction using the five essential instructional design features discussed above, they need to integrate instructional delivery features into their teaching plans. While the instructional design focuses on what to teach, instructional delivery addresses issues of implementation, that is, how best to teach. Four features are included in this section on instructional delivery:

1. Progress monitoring
2. Presentation techniques
3. Error-correction procedures
4. Diagnosis and remediation

Progress Monitoring

A major goal of progress monitoring is to determine whether students have mastered the material. A second goal of progress monitoring is to determine whether students are progressing at an optimal rate. One research-based approach to monitoring student progress that assists teachers in determining an optimal rate is curriculum-based measurement, or CBM (Fuchs, Fuchs, & Hamlett, 2015). CBM offers an alternative both to informal observations, which tend to lack consistency, and to achievement tests, which are administered too infrequently to help teachers make instructional decisions.

Shinn and Walker (2010) explain that CBM has two distinctive features that separate it from other curriculum-based assessments: First, the recommended CBM procedures are as reliable and valid as most standardized achievement tests; second, the procedures are designed to be administered frequently enough to provide teachers with ongoing performance data.

One of the strongest advantages of using CBM is that by monitoring progress frequently, teachers can identify and remedy problems by making instructional changes before students fall too far behind their peers. Likewise, teachers can use CBM data to accelerate instruction. The National Center for Intensive Intervention (NCII) offers educators online tools and resources to assist them in implementing progress monitoring.

Presentation Techniques

A major aspect of Direct Instruction involves attention to a group of teaching or presentation techniques. How skillfully a teacher presents instruction significantly affects both the student's rate of learning and the student's self-concept. The relationship between success and self-concept, a primary tenet in the Direct Instruction approach to teaching, was articulated by Engelmann as long ago as 1969:

> The sphere of self-confidence that can be programmed in the classroom has to do with the child's ability to stick to his guns, to have confidence in what he has learned, and to approach school tasks with the understanding that he is smart and will succeed. For a child to maintain such an impression of himself, he must receive demonstrations that these descriptions of himself are valid. If he finds himself failing in school, displeasing the teacher, feeling unsure about what he has learned, he must reevaluate himself and perhaps conclude that he is not a complete success. (p. 68)

The presentation techniques addressed here capture those skills needed for effective teacher-directed group instruction. Several factors contribute to a successful teacher-directed lesson. For example, the length of a teacher's explanation or demonstration affects the likelihood that students will be attentive. Teachers should make explanations brief and concise. The more time the teacher spends talking, the fewer opportunities for student involvement. Teachers working with primary-grade and lower-performing students in the upper grades should structure their presentations so that students are required to answer frequent questions.

Because teachers cannot call on every individual student to answer each question, unison responses should be incorporated into the teacher-directed lessons. Unison responses ensure that all of the students in the classroom actively participate in the lesson. Two very specific presentation skills promote effective use of unison responses: appropriate use of signals and pacing.

Signals A signal is a cue given by the teacher that tells students when to respond in unison. The effective use of signals allows participation by all students, not just the highest-performing students who, if allowed, tend to dominate the activity.

To signal a unison response, the teacher (a) gives directions, (b) provides a thinking pause, and (c) cues the response. For example, when presenting an addition fact task, the teacher might say, "Listen. Get ready to tell me the answer to this problem: 4 + 6." After the directions comes the thinking pause. The duration of the thinking pause is determined by the length of time the lowest-performing student needs to figure out the answer. (If one student takes significantly longer to answer than the other students in the group, the teacher should consider providing extra individual practice for that student.) For easier questions (simple tasks involving review of previously taught skills), the thinking pause may be just a split second, while for more complex questions the thinking pause may last longer. Carefully controlling the duration of the thinking pause is a very important factor in maintaining student attention.

The final step in the signaling procedure is the actual cue to respond. A cue or signal to respond may be a clap, finger snap, hand drop, touch on the board, or any similar type of action. This procedure can be modified for use with most tasks. On tasks calling for a long thinking pause, the teacher would say, "Get ready" an instant before signaling. The purpose of the get-ready prompt is to let the students know when to expect the cue to respond. Since the length of thinking pauses varies with the difficulty of the question, a prompt is needed; students may not know when to respond following a pause. Therefore, to elicit a group response in which each student has an equal opportunity to respond, the cue "Get ready" is given. An auditory signal (snap, clap, etc.) is necessary for teacher-directed worksheet tasks, since students are looking at their worksheets and cannot see a silent hand signal from the teacher.

The essential feature of a good signal is its clarity. The signal must be given so that students know exactly when they are expected to respond. If a signal is not clear, students cannot respond in unison. The teacher can use the student responses to evaluate the clarity of her signals. A repeated failure to respond together usually indicates that the signals are unclear or that the teacher has not provided adequate thinking time.

Giving individual turns (also called individual tests) is an essential part of any instructional activity in which students are asked to respond in unison. Using only unison responses, a teacher can never be absolutely certain whether each student has produced a correct response independent from the responses of nearby students. Giving individual turns helps teachers verify that all students are participating appropriately in the activity.

The teacher should give individual tests only after all the students in the group appear to be answering correctly during unison practice. Calling on a student who has not had enough practice to master the task may needlessly embarrass the student in front of his peers. Since individual tests are time-consuming, they should not be given to every student after every task. As a general rule, turns should be given to all lower-performing students each time a new or difficult task is presented. Higher-performing students, on the other hand, can be tested less often.

Pacing   Anyone who has observed young children watching TV shows or playing video games can attest to the role that pacing plays in maintaining attention. Teachers should be familiar enough with their material to present it in a lively, animated manner and without hesitation. Teachers who are well practiced with their instructional materials not only can teach at a livelier pace but also can focus their attention more fully on student performance.

Throughout this text, we have included videos of teaching demonstrations to illustrate instructional delivery skills. For each video, we have identified a "watch-for" that highlights the implementation of a specific presentation technique. For example, for the following video, note that the watch-for calls attention to Tristan's use of signals and pacing.

Format 5.12: Expanded Notation
Watch for Tristan's use of clear signals and lively pacing.

Error-Correction Procedures

The first step in correcting errors made by students during group instruction is to determine the cause of the error. Teachers must decide if the error resulted from inattentiveness or from a lack of knowledge. Teachers can determine whether student errors were caused by inattentiveness by checking where the students were looking or what the students were doing when the question was asked.

Teachers should correct students who respond late or don't respond at all during tasks requiring unison responding. For these errors teachers should inform the students that because not all students responded (or because some students failed to respond on signal), they have to repeat the task. Teachers should not direct any attention to the students who made the errors but should praise students who performed well and attended to the task.

Most error corrections follow a three-step procedure of model, test, and delayed test. If an error occurs when the teacher is presenting a strategy, the teacher would model the correct response or ask leading questions from the strategy so that students can generate the correct response. Next, the teacher would test the students by presenting the same task again—this time providing no assistance. The teacher then would return to the beginning of the original task and present the entire task again, the delayed test. The function of a delayed test is to check whether the student remembers the correct responses when starting from the beginning of the task.

Specific recommendations are outlined in each chapter for corrections of errors students are likely to make for a given topic. Specific teacher wording often can be found in the teaching formats provided within each chapter along with additional recommendations to ensure that the corrections are effective.

Diagnosis and Remediation

Diagnosis is determining the cause of a pattern of errors; remediation is the process of reteaching the skill. Diagnosis and remediation, as used in this text, are not the same as a simple error correction. An error correction immediately follows the mistake a student makes during teacher-directed instruction and requires minimal diagnosis because the teacher knows exactly what question the student missed.

A diagnosis, on the other hand, consists primarily of an analysis of the errors students make on independent work. The first decision to make in diagnosing errors is determining whether the errors are "can't-do" or "won't-do" problems. Won't-do problems occur when students have the necessary skills but are careless, do not complete their work, or are inattentive. A diagnosis of won't-do errors requires a remediation that focuses on increasing student motivation. A diagnosis of can't-do problems requires a remediation that focuses on the student's confusion or skill deficit.

The teacher diagnoses can't-do errors by examining the missed problems on worksheets and/or by interviewing the students about how they worked the problems they missed. The following basic steps apply to diagnosing and remedying errors on most types of problems:

1. Diagnosis: Analyze worksheet errors and hypothesize what the cause of the errors might be.
2. Confirmation: Interview the student to determine the cause of the errors if it is not obvious.
3. Remediation: Provide reteaching through board and/or worksheet presentations.
4. Assess: Test the student on a set of problems similar to the ones on which the original errors were made.

An error usually is of three basic types: a fact error, a component-skill error, or a strategy error. Students often miss problems only because they don't know their basic math facts. Basic facts are the addition and multiplication facts formed by adding or multiplying any two single-digit numbers and their subtraction and division corollaries.

Component skills are previously taught skills that are integrated as steps in a lengthier problem-solving strategy. Below is an example of an addition problem with renaming that a student missed due to a component-skill error:

$$\begin{array}{r} 2 \\ 67 \\ +25 \\ \hline 1 \end{array}$$

Note that in the incorrectly solved problem, the student knew to rename but did not know the component skill related to place value for renaming appropriately (12 equals 1 ten and 2 ones). To remedy this component-skill error, the teacher would present instruction only on the component skill of expanded notation. Once the student mastered the component skill, the teacher would give students addition problems similar to the one originally missed.

A strategy error occurs when the student demonstrates that she does not know the sequence of steps required to solve the particular type of problem. In the following example, the student subtracts the denominator from the numerator when instructed to convert an improper fraction to a mixed number, indicating that the student does not have a viable strategy for reducing improper fractions. To remedy this problem, the teacher must teach the entire strategy of rewriting fractions to the student.

$$\frac{13}{6} = 7 \qquad \frac{15}{2} = 13$$

The diagnosis and remediation procedures recommended here are designed to increase instructional efficiency by helping teachers determine exactly how much additional teaching is necessary to bring students to mastery. If a teacher determines that student errors are due to deficient math fact knowledge, it is unnecessary to reteach lengthy problem-solving strategies. Similarly, if an error pattern reflected in a student's independent work is related to a single component skill, then the teacher would reteach only that skill and not the entire instructional strategy. These diagnosis and remediation procedures can save teachers valuable instructional time by focusing on only those skills that require remediation.

INSTRUCTIONAL LANGUAGE

Attention to the need for instruction in discipline-based language has recently been extended to the area of mathematics as evidenced by the CCSSM. Mathematical language practices required by the CCSSM include engaging students in mathematical reasoning, developing viable arguments, and critiquing the reasoning of others—high expectations for math students and their teachers. These higher-level language skills require that students understand basic mathematics concepts and are able to use appropriate mathematics vocabulary.

Attention to language has always been fundamental to Direct Instruction teaching (Engelmann, Carnine, & Steely, 1991). For example, in a first-grade mathematics class asking students if "3 is fewer than 5" may be problematic if students were taught the concept of "less than" and not the term "fewer." Consistency in language contributes to clarity of instruction, and that clarity of instruction is especially important for English language learners and students with math disabilities.

Sequencing Guidelines Applied to Language Instruction

The three sequencing guidelines discussed earlier (see Sequence of Skills and Concepts) are particularly relevant to a discussion of mathematics language. Below are three examples of the application of these guidelines to the math language instruction.

Teach Preskills of a Strategy Before the Strategy   Teachers should consider what vocabulary is necessary to teach prior to teaching a concept and what vocabulary can be taught after the concept is introduced. Vocabulary terms that appear in the teaching formats should be taught prior to the introduction of the format. For example, in teaching the equality rule—"we must end with the same number on this side and the other side of the equal"—the terms "end with," "side," "equal," " same," and "other" are used. Therefore, the meaning of these terms should be taught prior to the introduction of the equality rule.

Teach Easy Skills Before More Difficult Ones   Although precise terminology is critical to mathematics, it is not necessary to teach precise, mathematically correct definitions initially; rather it is important to provide students with the language that will permit them to take part in math instruction. For example, the following definition for the area of a rectangle, although correct, contains difficult vocabulary concepts and initially is not very useful to students: "To find the area of a rectangle, multiply the length times the width resulting in an answer of square units." In contrast, applying the guideline of "easy before more difficult," we recommend introducing the area of a rectangle as "the number of squares it takes to cover the rectangle." Using student-friendly math vocabulary, appropriate to students' age and skill level, results in clear communication and promotes understanding.

Separate the Introduction of Information or Strategies That Are Likely to Be Confused   The third sequencing guideline emphasizes separating confusing content. Teaching the concept first and later attaching more precise terminology to the concept reduces possible confusion. For example, teaching students the concepts of fractions using the more student-friendly terms "top numeral" and "bottom numeral" (rather than "numerator" and "denominator") allows students to focus on the concept rather than on the new terminology. The application of this guideline prevents most students from confusing the two parts of a fraction.

While teaching students mathematics language concepts is critical to mathematics proficiency, it is beyond the scope of this book to provide detailed instructional recommendations for all math-related vocabulary. Teachers can find more information on how to teach specific vocabulary in *Direct Instruction Reading* (Carnine, Silbert, Kame'enui, Slocum, & Travers, 2017). In this text, we address mathematics language by including an online glossary for teachers, presenting specific instructional procedures for teaching critical concepts, and ensuring that all teaching formats adhere to the instructional design guidelines outlined above.

APPLY WHAT YOU LEARNED

 Click on the √ to answer the questions online.

1. What are the areas that comprise mathematical proficiency according to the National Research Council?

2. Outline the essential features of instructional design.

3. Describe the four features of instructional delivery characteristic of Direct Instruction.

4. Describe how the Direct Instruction sequencing guidelines are applied to mathematical language.

Research Support for Direct Instruction Mathematics

By Kaitlyn Bundock and Timothy Slocum

LEARNING OUTCOMES

2.1 Discuss the rationale for improving U.S. math instruction.

2.2 Compare the differences between di and DI and the research support for each.

2.3 Outline three research-based recommendations for improving math instruction.

THE NEED FOR EXCELLENT MATH INSTRUCTION

Mathematical competence is important for living successfully in modern American society. It is a gateway to higher education as well as to success in many other career paths (Child Trends Databank, 2015). For example, studies have found that students who take higher-level math courses in high school are more likely to graduate from college (Adelman, 1999; Attewell & Domina, 2008). Our increasingly technological workplace raises the stakes for math proficiency—those with strong math skills can access numerous exciting career options in the new economy, while those who have weak math skills can be limited to fewer and less desirable career options. A great deal of evidence points to the conclusion that math competence is related to level and quality of employment (Finnie & Meng, 2006; Murnane, Willett, Braatz, & Duhaldeborde, 2001; Tyler, 2004). Further, the relationship between high school students' math skills and their later earnings has grown stronger since 1976 (Murnane, Willett, & Levy, 1995; Reyna & Brainerd, 2007). During the 1990s, growth in employment in the math-intensive sectors of science and engineering tripled that in other areas of the economy (National Science Board, 2008). And the personal implications of mathematical proficiency are not limited to employment; math skills are required in everyday life for selecting purchases, managing finances, and understanding interest rates (Kirsch, Jungeblut, Jenkins, & Kolstad, 2002). Math skills are related to patients' health behaviors and outcomes, their understanding of medical issues, and their implementation of treatments (Reyna & Brainerd, 2007).

In addition to its impact on individual outcomes, mathematic competence is increasingly recognized as being important for the economic success of the nation (Reyna & Brainerd, 2007). As the National Mathematics Advisory Panel (NMAP) stated in 2008:

> The eminence, safety, and well-being of nations have been entwined for centuries with the ability of their people to deal with sophisticated quantitative ideas. Leading societies have commanded mathematical skills that have brought them advantages in medicine and health, in technology and commerce, in navigation and exploration, in defense and finance, and in the ability to understand past failures and to forecast future developments. (p. 29)

Many states have responded to the importance of math proficiency by increasing demands for the number and level of mathematics courses required for high school graduation (National Mathematics Advisory Panel, 2008; Rasmussen et al., 2011). As a result, poor math skills can be a considerable barrier to receiving a high school diploma (Rasmussen et al., 2011).

Current Performance of U.S. Math Students

Despite an increased focus on enhancing the rigor of K–12 mathematics instruction in recent years, the math performance of students in the United States continues to be substandard. The National Assessment of Educational Progress (NAEP) measures the performance of American students in a variety of content areas (National Center for Education Statistics [NCES], 2015). Students in grades 4 and 8 are assessed in mathematics every 2 years. The 2015 NAEP results revealed that 49% of fourth graders and 57% of eighth graders failed to meet proficiency standards. This represents a worse performance than was seen only 2 years earlier. The situation is dire for underrepresented groups. For example, 87% of Black and 81% of Hispanic eighth graders were not proficient in math in the 2015 assessment (NCES, 2015). The National Mathematics Advisory Panel commented in 2008:

> There are large, persistent disparities in mathematics achievement related to race and income—disparities that are not only devastating for individuals and families but also project poorly for the nation's future, given the youthfulness and high growth rates of the largest minority populations. (p. xii)

Similarly, students with disabilities experience very poor math outcomes. From 5% to 8% of U.S. students are identified as having learning disabilities in math (Bryant, 2005; Fuchs et al., 2008; Jitendra & Star, 2011; Judge & Watson, 2011). Results on the NAEP indicate that 84% of fourth-grade students with disabilities and 92% of eighth-grade students with disabilities were not proficient in mathematics (NCES, 2015). These results are consistent with research showing that 95% of students with disabilities rank in the lowest 25th percentile on standardized math assessments throughout all grade levels (Gersten et al., 2012; Judge & Watson, 2011). International comparisons consistently show that American students lag behind other industrialized countries in math proficiency. The Organization for Economic Cooperation and Development (OECD) administers the PISA test every 3 years in 65 countries to evaluate 15-year-olds' performance in reading, mathematics, and science (OECD, 2014a). The 2012 PISA math results indicate that the United States ranked 27th among the 34 OECD member nations assessed (OECD, 2014b). Additionally, U.S. math scores were below the average of math scores calculated from all 65 countries assessed, and 25% of students in the United States tested below the basic proficiency level established by the PISA. The 2015 PISA focused primarily on science, although data related to mathematics were obtained. The overall mathematics results indicate that students in the United States continued to perform below average compared to the other industrialized nations (OECD, 2016). The results of the PISA indicate that U.S. students struggle with real-world math problems, mathematical modeling, geometry, and mathematical literacy.

When the math results of all U.S. students are considered together, they reveal a nationwide need for instruction that improves the performance of students from all demographic groups. The National Council of Teachers of Mathematics (NCTM) published an "Agenda for Action" in 1980, calling for a shift in mathematics education toward an emphasis on problem solving, cooperative learning, the use of manipulatives, and alternative ways of assessing students; these recommendations, however, were not based on research (NCTM, 1980). The NCTM later released "Principles and Standards for School Mathematics" in 2000 (NCTM, 2000). This guide presents a vision of mathematics education, as well as guidelines for educators, and includes principles (foundational precepts for quality mathematics instruction) and content and process standards.

By far the most important policy development in response to poor math outcomes is the Common Core State Standards for Mathematics (CCSSM). Produced by the National Governors Association and the Council of Chief State School Officers in 2009, these standards were intended to raise educational achievement by creating a coherent and consistent sequence of standards that build to high-level achievement (Dingman, Teuscher, Newton & Kasmer, 2013; National Governors Association & Council of Chief State School Officers, 2012).

The majority of states have adopted the CCSSM, which are consistent with the NCTM principles and standards. The CCSSM represent four main shifts in math education: changes to the grade level in which certain math content is taught; adjustments made to the number of grade levels certain math topics span; shifts in emphasis on certain math topics; and development of the Standards for Mathematical Practice, which focus on problem-solving across the standards (Dingman et al., 2013; National Governors Association & Council of Chief State School Officers, 2012). The CCSSM are more rigorous than the previous standards that were in place in the majority of states, in part because one of the goals reflected in the CCSSM is that students master higher-level algebra by the end of high school (Dingman et al., 2013; Schmidt & Houang, 2012). As such, math concepts that are foundations for algebra are introduced at earlier grades, and they tend to be emphasized across a larger number of grade levels to provide more in-depth coverage (Schmidt & Houang, 2012). The changes in content associated with the CCSSM, in particular the increases in rigor, require educators to pay greater attention to effective teaching practices in mathematics. When mathematics instruction is highly effective, many students will meet the CCSSM standards and realize the benefits of high-level math competence. But if mathematics instruction is not effective, the higher standards represented by CCSSM will simply impose a barrier to school success and graduation. Therefore, these high standards increase the consequences of the quality of instruction. Now more than ever, it is imperative that mathematics instruction enable a wide range of students—including those at risk for failure in math—to achieve high levels of proficiency.

RESEARCH ON DIRECT INSTRUCTION

Direct instruction is a research-based approach to instruction that has been shown to be highly effective across many academic domains, including mathematics. This book is, of course, concerned with using this method to teach mathematics. The specific meaning of the term "direct instruction" is somewhat complicated, however. When stated in lowercase letters, direct instruction is an instructional strategy that includes:

1. Content presented in small steps.
2. Explicit teacher modeling or explanation.
3. Guided student practice with gradually faded support.
4. Use of feedback including explicit corrections of errors.
5. Independent practice including cumulative review.

These strategies also have been termed "explicit instruction," "effective instruction," and "systematic teaching" (Archer & Hughes, 2011; Rosenshine & Stevens, 1986).

When the term is written as a proper noun with capital letters ("Direct Instruction"), it primarily refers to instructional programs that include all the features of direct instruction (note the lowercase) and also have additional instructional design features, as described in Chapter 1, that make them even more effective for teachers and students. Commercially developed Direct Instruction (capital letters) programs organize the content around generalizable strategies that students can use to solve a wide variety of problems, and they implement detailed principles of clear communication to ensure that these generalizable strategies are conveyed effectively to students—including those at risk. Direct Instruction programs also include features to increase student engagement such as unison student responding and signals to coordinate those responses.

Explicit or direct instruction has been supported by hundreds of studies that describe the specific teacher behaviors that are most closely associated with strong academic outcomes. In 1986, Brophy and Good reviewed more than 200 publications that examined correlations between particular teacher behaviors and student achievement and derived the following recommendations:

- Students should receive frequent opportunities to respond to questions, and they should get clear feedback about the correctness of their responses.
- Skills should be mastered to overlearning, with new ones gradually phased in while old ones are being mastered.
- Both progress through the curriculum and pacing within specific activities should be brisk, producing continuous progress achieved with relative ease (small steps, high success rate).
- Individual progress should be closely monitored so that all students, especially struggling students, are checked, receive feedback, and achieve mastery.

Rosenshine and Stevens (1986) reviewed dozens of experimental studies in which teachers learned to use specific teaching techniques and student achievement was measured. Based on this research, they recommended that teachers:

- Present new material in small steps, with student practice after each step.
- Give clear and detailed instructions and explanations.
- Provide a high level of active practice for all students.
- Ask a large number of questions, check student understanding, and obtain responses from all students.
- Guide students during initial practice.
- Provide systematic feedback and corrections.
- Provide explicit instruction and practice for seatwork exercises and, where necessary, monitor students during seatwork.

For teaching academic subjects and improving student outcomes, large bodies of research converge upon the Direct Instruction model, which incorporates the above techniques.

Direct Instruction programs also have been subjected to extensive research. Project Follow Through, a federal education project, was implemented beginning in the late 1960s and was the largest organized experiment in the history of education. It involved nearly 100,000 students in 170 communities across the country and cost nearly $1 billion (Watkins, 1997). The goal of Project Follow Through was to identify models of instruction that could close the gap in academic achievement between economically disadvantaged students and those from higher-income families. Researchers tested nine instructional models including Direct Instruction. Each was implemented in at least three schools, and each model school was paired with a similar control school. Outcome measures included three domains: (a) basic academic skills such as word knowledge, spelling, and math computations; (b) cognitive outcomes such as reading comprehension, math concepts, and math problem solving; and (c) affective outcomes such as responsibility and self-esteem.

Figure 2.1 summarizes the overall results of Project Follow Through. This figure clearly shows that Direct Instruction was the only model that demonstrated large positive effects in all three domains. These data indicate that Direct Instruction can be effective with students who are economically disadvantaged and that it can improve not only basic skills but also complex cognitive and affective outcomes (Engelmann, Becker, Carnine, & Gersten, 1988; Stebbins, St. Pierre, Proper, Anderson, & Cerva, 1977).

Figure 2.2 illustrates the math performance of third-grade students from each of the nine major models on the math subtest of the Metropolitan Achievement Test. The graph shows that students taught using the Direct Instruction model significantly outperformed students taught using the other models. In fact, the Direct Instruction students performed close to the 50th percentile, an outstanding feat considering the 50th percentile is the median for students of all income levels in the United States (Gersten & Carnine, 1984; Stebbins et al., 1977).

FIGURE 2.1   Direct Instruction was found to be highly effective for improving basic skills, cognitive skills, and affective outcomes in project follow through. Based on data from Stebbins et al. (1977)

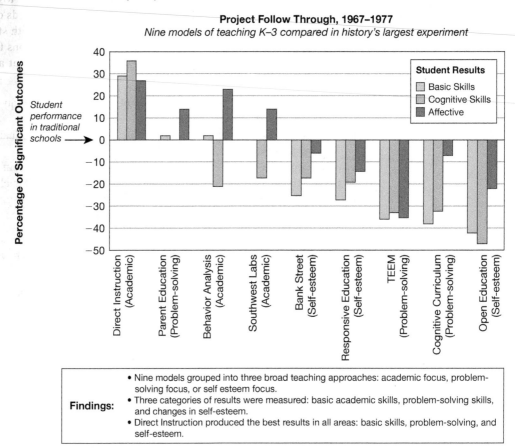

Project Follow Through, 1967–1977
Nine models of teaching K–3 compared in history's largest experiment

Findings:
- Nine models grouped into three broad teaching approaches: academic focus, problem-solving focus, or self esteem focus.
- Three categories of results were measured: basic academic skills, problem-solving skills, and changes in self-esteem.
- Direct Instruction produced the best results in all areas: basic skills, problem-solving, and self-esteem.

FIGURE 2.2   Direct Instruction was found to be highly effective for improving math performance in low-income students. Based on data from Stebbins et al. (1977)

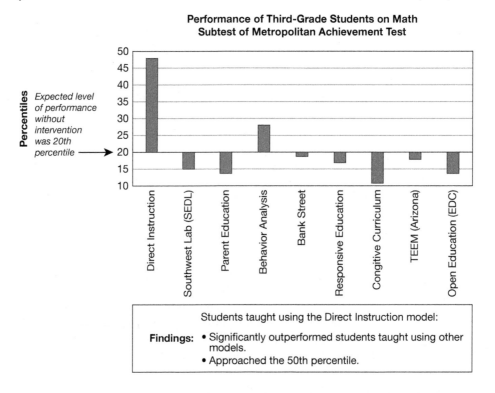

Performance of Third-Grade Students on Math Subtest of Metropolitan Achievement Test

Findings:
Students taught using the Direct Instruction model:
- Significantly outperformed students taught using other models.
- Approached the 50th percentile.

A great deal of research has been conducted on Direct Instruction since the time of Follow Through:

- Adams and Engelmann (1996) conducted a meta-analysis of research studies in which one group received Direct Instruction while a comparable control group was taught with other methods. The work identified 37 such studies and found that, on average, they favored Direct Instruction by a very large margin (*effect size* = .87). Further, across these studies, Adams and Engelmann found 33 individual comparisons between a Direct Instruction group and comparison group on a measure of math performance. On average, these comparisons favored the Direct Instruction groups by an even larger margin (effect size = 1.11).
- Borman, Hewes, Overman, and Brown (2002) performed a meta-analysis of 29 comprehensive school reform models based on 232 individual studies. They concluded that "the combined quantity, quality, and statistical significance of evidence from three models, in particular, set them apart from the rest" (p. 3). One of these models was Direct Instruction.
- In a similar review, the American Institutes for Research conducted an independent review of 24 prominent school reform models; it also concluded that Direct Instruction was one of only three models with strong evidence of positive effects on achievement (Herman et al., 1999).
- The American Federation of Teachers (AFT) issued a series of research reviews that identified (a) promising programs for teaching reading and language arts (AFT, 1998a), (b) effective school reform models (AFT, 1998b), and (c) effective remedial reading programs (AFT, 1999). In each case, Direct Instruction was one of a small number of models that were found to be well supported by research.

Taken together, the large and diverse body of research on Direct Instruction strongly supports its effectiveness for teaching a wide variety of academic subjects to diverse learners including those who are at risk for academic failure.

RESEARCH RECOMMENDATIONS FOR MATH INSTRUCTION

In response to an increased emphasis on the importance of mathematics for individual and national success, along with the need to address consistently poor student outcomes, President George W. Bush commissioned the National Mathematics Advisory Panel (NMAP) in 2006. Composed of respected education and mathematics experts, the panel was charged with recommending ways "to foster greater knowledge of and improved performance in mathematics among American students" based on "the best available scientific evidence" (NMAP, 2008, p. xiii). The panel's 2008 final report was based on a review of 16,000 research publications and policy reports as well as public testimony from 110 individuals. This report provides recommendations on curricular content, learning processes, teacher preparation, instructional practice, instructional materials, assessment, and research policies and mechanics (NMAP, 2008). With respect to instructional practice, the panel's recommendations for advancing student performance in mathematics included the use of explicit instruction, defined as:

- Clear teacher modeling of problem types using an array of examples.
- Extensive student practice of strategies and skills.
- Provision of opportunities to think aloud.
- Extensive feedback.

All of these elements of instruction are consistent with Direct Instruction. The panel's recommendations confirm that the components of Direct Instruction are in fact highly effective for mathematics instruction. The same components identified in early research on direct instruction and built into the Direct Instruction programs are found in a careful examination of the research on effective math instruction.

More recent studies conducted by Slavin and his colleagues (Slavin & Lake, 2008; Slavin, Lake, & Groff, 2009) also found these instructional practices effective for improving student achievement in mathematics. Slavin and Lake (2008) reviewed 87 studies conducted with students in grades K–6. They compared approaches that focused on (a) mathematics curricula, (b) computer-assisted instruction, and (c) instructional process programs. Instructional process programs, they explained, are characterized as approaches that "focus on teachers' instructional practices and classroom management strategies rather than on curriculum or technology" (p. 430). For example, cooperative learning and direct instruction would be considered to be instructional process programs. The authors then categorized the studies they reviewed as having strong, moderate, limited, or insufficient evidence of effectiveness based on the quality and significance of the results of each study. The studies showing the strongest evidence of effectiveness were all instructional process programs, with the exception of one computer-assisted instructional program being included in the moderate effectiveness category. The limited evidence of effectiveness category included only mathematics curricula programs. These results indicate that instructional process programs such as direct instruction have a greater potential to improve student performance than curricular or computer-assisted instructional programs do alone (Slavin & Lake, 2008).

Slavin and colleagues (2009) replicated this study with programs implemented in middle and high schools and found similar results. The primary implication from these two studies is that instructional process programs, such as direct instruction, are among the most promising methods to improve student achievement in mathematics at any grade level (Slavin & Lake, 2008; Slavin et al., 2009).

The Institute for Educational Sciences (IES) is the research arm of the U.S. Department of Education. Its mission is to provide scientific evidence to support practice and policy. The IES produces practice guides to provide usable information to educators. These practice guides are developed by a panel of leading researchers and are carefully reviewed for their scientific validity. The IES practice guide *Assisting Students Struggling with Mathematics* (Gersten, Beckmann et al., 2009) outlines specific recommendations to design and implement mathematics interventions including:

- Screening all students to identify those at risk of math failure.
- Using explicit and systematic instruction during intervention.
- Instructing students to solve word problems based on common underlying structures.
- Dedicating approximately 10 minutes of any intervention session to help students build fluent basic arithmetic fact retrieval.
- Monitoring students' progress.
- Including motivational strategies within interventions.

Again, these recommendations are closely aligned with Direct Instruction. In particular, the IES practice guide reported strong evidence in support of the recommendation that:

> Instruction during the intervention should be explicit and systematic. This includes providing models of proficient problem solving, verbalization of thought processes, guided practice, corrective feedback, and frequent cumulative review. (p. 21)

The NMAP, the IES practice guide, and the work of Slavin and colleagues were focused mainly on students without disabilities. Gersten, Chard et al. (2009) conducted a meta-analysis that evaluated the results of 42 interventions conducted with students with learning disabilities in math. Of all of these interventions, Gersten and colleagues determined that the two instructional components that resulted in statistically significant increases in effect sizes were teaching students to use heuristics and the use of explicit instruction. The key elements of explicit instruction identified by the authors included teacher demonstrations of step-by-step processes to solve problems, the application of the strategies to a specific set of problems, and the requirement that students then use a specific step-by-step protocol to solve problems (Gersten, Chard et al., 2009).

While the particular purposes, methods, populations, and results of these various research syntheses differ, their recommendations converge on the use of an explicit and systematic approach to instruction that incorporates explicit teacher modeling, extensive student practice with feedback, and assessment of student progress. These recommendations give strong support to *Direct Instruction Mathematics.*

APPLY WHAT YOU LEARNED

 Click on the √ to answer the questions online.

1. Why should improving U.S. mathematics instruction be a priority?

2. Describe the differences between direct instruction and Direct Instruction.

3. Outline three research-based recommendations for improving math instruction.

Curriculum Evaluation and Modification

LEARNING OUTCOMES

3.1 Discuss the critical components of a curriculum adoption process.

3.2 Outline major topics that should be included in a curriculum evaluation.

3.3 Describe recommendations for modifying mathematics curricula.

In this chapter, we present a framework for evaluating and modifying commercially developed mathematics programs. We derived this Mathematics Curriculum Framework from the Direct Instruction principles of instructional design that we outlined in Chapter 1 and the research findings outlined in Chapter 2.

Given the role that instructional programs play in the classroom, especially for teachers who have not been well prepared to teach mathematics, the quality of commercially developed mathematics programs should be closely scrutinized. We designed the framework outlined here to help teachers evaluate mathematics programs—both to select new programs and to modify the mathematics programs available to them. While the Mathematics Curriculum Framework is not exhaustive, it will help teachers focus their curriculum evaluation efforts and identify areas in mathematics programs that can easily be enhanced to foster student success.

THE CURRICULUM ADOPTION PROCESS

Curriculum materials should reflect a high degree of instructional integrity, include well-designed content, develop ideas in depth, and clarify the relationships among topics. Commenting on the role that curriculum likely played in the results of the 2002 Trends in International Mathematics and Science Study (TIMSS), Schmidt and colleagues (2002) stated, "The curriculum itself— what is taught—makes a huge difference" (p. 12).

While the term "curriculum" technically is not synonymous with "program," in this chapter we use the terms "curriculum materials" and "instructional programs" interchangeably to refer to those commercially developed mathematics programs used by both general and special education teachers.

Many educators are surprised to learn that most publishers do not routinely evaluate the effectiveness of their programs, either during development or while in use (Jobrack, 2011; Reys, Reys, & Chavez, 2004). Because research is costly, publishers tend not to invest in extensive research on their programs. Given the limited availability of scientific evidence of the effectiveness of math instructional programs, educators need to examine programs carefully prior to purchasing and implementing them in their classrooms.

The process of choosing a curriculum is critical to the selection of high-quality instructional materials. Educators should employ a systematic framework for both adopting and evaluating instructional materials. Stein, Stuen, Carnine, and Long (2001) described some of the critical features of a systematic adoption process for the selection of literacy programs. Not surprisingly, these features also should be present when selecting mathematics programs. Although a thorough discussion of the adoption process is beyond the scope of this chapter, we have highlighted the features from Stein and colleagues that we believe are essential to conducting an effective curriculum adoption in the area of mathematics. These features include time allocation, committee responsibilities, and the screening process.

Time Allocation and Committee Responsibilities

A major consideration in the adoption of curriculum materials is allocating sufficient time for the work of an adoption committee. Many curriculum adoption committees meet only after school for brief periods of time. But meaningful and thorough examination of instructional materials requires large blocks of uninterrupted time. Therefore, curriculum adoption committees must be given adequate release time to review the materials and discuss findings and questions with their colleagues. During this time educators on the adoption committee would review research, generate screening and evaluation criteria, screen all submitted programs, thoroughly evaluate three to four of those programs, deliberate, and then select a program.

Teachers in schools or districts often are given the opportunity to vote on the selection of a mathematics program from a short list generated by an adoption committee. Given that the adoption committee members are given adequate time to evaluate the mathematics programs thoroughly, we recommend that the final selection of an instructional program rest with the adoption committee. To feel comfortable with a committee decision, however, teachers should be kept informed at all stages of the adoption process. Therefore, adoption committee members must communicate regularly and effectively with the groups they represent.

Members of mathematics curriculum adoption committees are often selected based on seniority and knowledge of mathematics. But additional factors also should be considered when forming the committees. Committees should include individuals representing a range of grade levels, those representing both special and general education students, and those with excellent communication skills.

Screening Process

To expedite the task of evaluating instructional programs, we recommend that the adoption committee first screen all the programs submitted for consideration. Evaluating programs thoroughly requires a substantial time commitment, and screening will reduce the number of programs that the committee must evaluate.

The first step in the screening process is to determine the criteria that will be used. **Table 3.1** illustrates an example of criteria that we believe will facilitate the screening process. The criteria include questions that address two important areas: Evidence of Effectiveness and Critical Content. On the form, there are two columns next to each evaluation question. One column is designated for comments to record brief answers to the evaluation questions. The second column is designated for examples that support the comments that are made in the evaluation.

The questions under Evidence of Effectiveness direct evaluators to determine if the program has been systematically evaluated in controlled research studies that have been published in the scientific literature. In addition to published research, evidence of whether the program has been field-tested is considered in this section as well. Several resources are available to assist teachers in finding evidence-based instructional programs. For example, Hughes, Powell, Lembke, and Riley-Tillman (2016) discuss the concept of evidence-based

TABLE 3.1 Mathematics Curriculum Framework: Screening Criteria Form

Evaluation Questions	Comments	Examples
A. Evidence of Effectiveness		
1. Is there published evidence of the effectiveness of the program? 2. Is there evidence that the program has been field-tested with large groups of students?		
B. Critical Content		
1. Is the content taught using explicit strategies? 2. Does the instruction follow a logical sequence? 3. Are there sufficient practice opportunities for mastery distributed across the grade level?		

practices and provide their readers with resources that may be used when evaluating instructional programs.

The questions under Critical Content can be used to compare how different programs teach important skills or concepts. We recommend that for screening purposes, evaluators compare two skills from each program they are considering in two grade levels (one early grade and one later grade). By comparing how programs teach these skills, evaluators can get a sense of the overall program design. The questions selected for screening purposes are similar to those that form the more comprehensive set of evaluation questions that appear in the Mathematics Curriculum Framework, which we discuss below.

TOPICS FOR CURRICULUM EVALUATION

On the following pages we present details about our Mathematics Curriculum Framework for examining commercially developed mathematics programs (see **Table 3.2**). The framework consists of two sections: General Program Design and Specific Content Design. As in the screening form, this form has two columns corresponding to each evaluation questions: Comments, and Examples. The Examples column is included so that evaluators can provide specific references to program examples that illustrate and support their comments. These examples are necessary if evaluators are to engage in objective discussions about program quality with other committee members.

General Program Design

The following questions are included in the General Program Design section of Table 3.2:

1. Does the program provide a logical sequence of skills and concepts?
2. Are objectives stated as observable and measurable behaviors?
3. Does the program integrate conceptual understanding, procedural fluency, and problem solving in a coherent manner?

Does the Program Provide a Logical Sequence of Skills and Concepts? The purpose of the General Program Design criteria is to provide evaluators with a clear overview of the program. The questions in this section address design features relevant to all levels. To answer these questions, we recommend that evaluators examine the scope and sequence of each level as well as sample lessons in grades K–8.

When examining the scope and sequence of a program, it is helpful to establish if the program is organized using a spiral or strand design. In programs using a spiral design, many

TABLE 3.2 Mathematics Curriculum Framework: Evaluation Form

Evaluation Questions	Comments	Examples
A. General Program Design		
1. Does the program provide a logical sequence of skills and concepts?		
2. Are objectives stated as observable and measurable behaviors?		
3. Does the program integrate conceptual understanding, procedural fluency, and problem solving in a coherent manner?		
B. Specific Content Design		
1. Strategy Instruction		
a) Are the steps in the target strategy explicitly outlined?		
b) Is the strategy of intermediate generalizability—not too narrow or too broad?		
2. Preskills		
Are the necessary preskills identified and taught prior to introducing the strategy?		
3. Example Selection		
a) Are introductory examples provided for initial mastery?		
b) Are there opportunities for discrimination practice?		
4. Practice and Review		
a) Does the program provide sufficient opportunities for practice when new skills are introduced (massed practice)?		
b) Does the program provide opportunities for cumulative review (distributed practice)?		

Note 3.1:
Consult the Instructional Sequence and Assessment Charts for Chapters 4–18. These charts provide a logical sequence of instruction for each chapter topic and corresponding performance indicators that can serve as examples of observable and measurable objectives. (Link to Chapter 4, **Instructional Sequence and Assessment Chart**, for example.)

topics are introduced at each level and repeated across many levels. Typically, programs that use a spiral design lack adequate initial instruction and review to promote student mastery. Lessons in these programs usually cover a different topic each day. Schmidt et al. (2002) referred to programs organized using a spiral design as "a mile wide and inch deep" (p. 12).

Recently, more instructional programs are being organized using a strand design (Snider, 2004). These programs present fewer topics over a longer period of time and have a pronounced focus on student mastery. A unique feature of strand design is that lessons are organized around multiple topics. For example, a single lesson at the fourth-grade level might include some work on multiplication facts, subtraction with regrouping, fraction analysis, and measurement.

Are Objectives Stated as Observable and Measurable Behaviors? Program objectives help teachers determine exactly what students should be able to do as a result of the instruction provided. The objectives should contain a statement of a measurable behavior. Many programs contain objectives that describe teacher behavior but not student behavior. For example, we found objectives similar to this one in several mathematics programs: "Review telling time." Note that the objective identifies what the teacher is to do but not what the students do. Alternatively the following time-telling objective is stated as a measurable behavior: "Students will express time as minutes after the hour."

Note 3.2:
Consult Chapter 13, **Skill Hierarchy Chart**, for an example of how instruction on fractions is integrated in and across grade levels. Note how the relationships among fraction topics are interwoven into a coherent sequence.

Does the Program Integrate Conceptual Understanding, Procedural Fluency, and Problem Solving in a Coherent Manner? Coherence in this framework refers to the extent to which the content of the program is integrated within and across grade levels and to the balance and integration of instruction that addresses conceptual understanding, procedural fluency, and problem solving. Research has identified program coherence as a common characteristic of the curricula used in the top-performing countries participating in international assessments such as the TIMMS. Consequently, one of the recommendations of the National Mathematics Advisory Panel directly addresses program coherence:

> A focused, coherent progression of mathematics learning, with an emphasis on proficiency with key topics, should become the norm in elementary and middle school mathematics curricula. Any approach that continually revisits topics year after year without closure is to be avoided. (NMAP, 2008, p. 22)

Specific Content Design

The Specific Content Design section of the Mathematics Curriculum Framework is divided into four main sections: Strategy Instruction, Preskills, Example Selection, and Practice and Review. The evaluation questions for each section are discussed below.

Strategy Instruction Instructional strategies may be the most important component of a mathematics program. We recommend that evaluators select three to four different skills or concepts for each grade level and use the evaluation questions specified to examine how systematically the skills or concepts are taught.

We recommend that evaluators conduct a skill trace when evaluating instruction strategies. A skill trace involves locating every instance where the target strategy appears in the program. The skill trace helps evaluators isolate the instructional strategy to best evaluate its explicitness and generalizability. The skill trace for each of the target skills then can be used to answer the following questions:

Note 3.3:
Consult the teaching formats in Chapters 4–18 for examples of explicit strategy instruction. **Click here** to review **Format 10.8: Correct Estimated Quotients with Two-Digit Divisors** as an example. See how clearly it illustrates the level of explicitness typical of Direct Instruction.

a. Are the steps in the target strategy explicitly outlined?
b. Is the strategy of intermediate generalizability—not too narrow or too broad?

To determine the explicitness of a strategy, evaluators should examine where in the program the strategy is first introduced and determine whether the program clearly articulates the steps that students follow to solve a problem (either a computation problem or word problem). When evaluating instructional strategies, evaluators should pretend that they do not already know how to solve the problem and follow the steps in the strategy as specified in the teacher's manual. By doing this, evaluators can more easily determine whether the steps in the strategy are explicit and useful.

A well-designed, efficient strategy should reliably lead students to the solution of a range of related problem types. Teachers should not spend valuable instructional time teaching a narrow strategy, one that is of limited use. For example, the shortcut for finding 1/3 of 9, dividing 9 by 3, works only when the fraction in the problem has a 1 in the numerator. Low-performing students are likely to overgeneralize this strategy when asked to find 2/3 of 9 and answer incorrectly. Similarly an overly broad strategy can lead to confusion. "Guess and check" is one such strategy in that it provides little guidance to students in solving problems.

Note 3.4:
Click here to consult **Format 13.3: Writing Numerical Fractions** for an example of a generalizable strategy that promotes conceptual understanding of both proper and improper fractions.

Preskills The explicit strategies discussed above all require the integration of component skills that when put together comprise the steps in the generalizable strategy. As mentioned in Chapter 1, these component skills also may be referred to as preskills. Often mathematics programs introduce preskills and the strategy in which they are embedded simultaneously. Most students need time to master the requisite preskills prior to being introduced to a strategy that requires their application. For example, a commercial program may introduce estimation at the same time that it introduces long division with a strategy requiring the use of estimation. Determining whether the necessary preskills for a given strategy have been identified and taught will help evaluators compare programs.

Note 3.5:
Consult "Preskills" in the section on Two-Digit Divisors in Chapter 10 for a discussion of the preskills required prior to introducing double-digit division and corresponding recommendations for teaching those preskills.

This text includes a discussion of the requisite preskills for each instructional strategy presented in Chapters 4–18. These discussions may be embedded in the introduction to specific instructional content, have its own dedicated section within a chapter, and/or may be presented in its own unique teaching format.

Example Selection The types of examples used to teach specific content are critical to ensuring students successfully apply the strategies they are taught. Evaluating the examples provided in a program involves determining not only the number of examples initially provided but also the quality of those examples. The following two questions are important to consider when evaluating example selection:

a. Are introductory examples provided for initial mastery?
b. Are there opportunities for discrimination practice?

Introductory examples are examples that provide practice only on the newly introduced skill. For example, when students are introduced to addition with renaming from the ones column to the tens column, they should be given only practice examples that require renaming from the ones column to the tens column. The question of whether there are sufficient numbers of introductory examples can only be answered using information about student performance. (Did students master this skill with the number of introductory examples available?)

Discrimination practice refers to including a set of practice examples that requires students to determine when to apply a strategy and when not to. For example, after providing initial practice on addition with renaming, the program should give students the opportunity to practice renaming using a set of examples in which some problems require renaming and some do not. Without discrimination practice, some students will try to apply the renaming strategy indiscriminately to any multi-digit addition problem they encounter.

Evaluators will need to compare programs with respect to the number and type of examples (introductory and discrimination) provided. We recommend evaluators err in selecting programs with more rather than fewer examples. Reducing the number of practice examples presented is far easier for the teacher than creating additional examples for students who need more practice.

Specific recommendations for example selection are embedded throughout Chapters 4–18. These recommendations can be found in the initial discussion of instructional content, corresponding instructional formats, and/or recommendations for remediation.

Note 3.6:
Consult "Complex Renaming Problems" in the section on Multi-Digit Subtraction in Chapter 8 and Part E of **Format 8.3: Subtraction with Renaming** for an example of appropriate example selection.

Practice and Review One of the features of a well-designed mathematics program is the presence of adequate and systematic review for the strategies introduced. Well-designed programs include two types of practice and review. First, the program should provide practice that is adequate for students to initially learn the content (massed practice). The section above on example selection addresses appropriate examples for such practice.

The second type of practice and review is distributed practice, practice over time so that students do not forget what they have learned. Distributed practice also can be referred to as cumulative review, as discussed in Chapter 1. Cumulative review in instructional programs is the presence of repeated opportunities for practice throughout a specific grade level. Cumulative review is related to the notion of strategic integration in that the review of newly introduced strategies is integrated and reviewed with previously introduced strategies.

By examining the practice examples available for several strategies, evaluators can determine the extent to which a program provides these types of review. Distributed practice may occur in isolation as simple independent review activities or embedded in related, more sophisticated content. For example, evaluators should inspect whether a program provides massed practice when initially introducing long division and whether the program includes opportunities for distributed practice (cumulative review) throughout the grade level, either as a set of independent computation problems or as a component of solving word problems.

The following questions from Table 3.2 are relevant to practice and review:

a. Does the program provide sufficient opportunities for practice when new skills are introduced (massed practice)?
b. Does the program provide opportunities for cumulative review (distributed practice)?

MODIFYING MATHEMATICS CURRICULUM

The evaluation criteria based on Direct Instruction design principles outlined in this chapter can be applied to curriculum modification. Note that while no individual instructional program will meet the needs of all students, adopting programs that require less modification is undoubtedly preferable as those programs require fewer changes and save teachers time.

TABLE 3.3   Mathematics Curriculum Framework: Modification Form

Evaluation Questions	Potential Problems	General Modification Guidelines
A. General Program Design		
1. Does the program provide a logical sequence of skills and concepts?	Skills are not presented in a logical sequence.	Determine missing skills from the instructional sequence and assessment charts in the related chapter and reorder the sequence of instruction.
2. Are objectives stated as observable and measurable behaviors?	Objectives are lacking, vague, and/or not measurable.	Generate measurable and observable objectives.
3. Does the program integrate conceptual understanding, procedural fluency, and problem solving in a coherent manner?	Program lacks one or more of the following and/or fails to integrate: conceptual understanding, procedural fluency, or problem solving.	Determine what aspects of the instruction are missing and provide supplemental instruction or reconsider the choice of instructional program.
B. Specific Content Design		
1. Strategy Instruction		
a) Are the steps in the target strategy explicitly outlined?	The steps in the recommended strategy are not clearly outlined.	Choose explicit instructional strategies from the teaching formats available in the related chapter.
b) Is the strategy of intermediate generalizability—not too narrow or too broad?	The strategy applies only to a limited type of example; the strategy is too broad and not specific enough to apply or too narrow and applies to a limited type of example.	Analyze the examples for which the strategy applies and decide whether it is worthwhile to present to students. If not, choose alternate strategies from the related chapter.
2. Preskills		
Are the necessary preskills identified and taught prior to introducing the strategy?	The preskills are neither clearly identified nor taught.	Outline the steps in the available strategy. Using that outline, determine where (or whether) the preskills required for that strategy are introduced. Supplement preskill instruction when necessary.
3. Example Selection		
a) Is there a sufficient number of practice examples for initial mastery?	Only a few examples are used to introduce a strategy.	Add practice examples to ensure student mastery on the strategy.
b) Are there opportunities for discrimination practice?	The practice examples represent only the newly introduced problem type.	After students master a new strategy, provide discrimination practice that involves working related problems, for example, working subtractions problems with and without renaming.
4. Practice and Review		
a) Does the program provide sufficient opportunities for practice when new skills are initially introduced?	Program includes limited numbers of examples when new skills are introduced.	Provide additional examples on the newly introduced skill for students to practice.
b) Does the program provide opportunities for cumulative review?	Once a unit is complete, little cumulative review is provided.	Provide distributed practice by including practice on the skills introduced in that unit across the grade level.

Some features of the math instruction in commercial programs may be easier to modify than others. For example, the instructional strategies in a given program may be well designed, but the program may fail to provide sufficient practice and review opportunities. In that case, the modification is simply for teachers to supplement the programs by adding more practice examples during initial instruction (massed practice), then building in more systematic review throughout (cumulative review). In contrast, if a commercial program is fragmented and lacks strategic integration of critical skills and concepts, then curriculum modification will be onerous and time-consuming.

Table 3.3 on the previous page is based on the evaluation criteria outlined previously in Table 3.2 and is designed to address insufficiencies identified through the evaluation process. This table focuses not on the presence or absence of critical instructional design features but on the recommendations for modification that the evaluation questions suggest. For example, if an evaluator finds that the program being evaluated has not identified and/or taught the preskills required for a particular instructional strategy, the recommendation would be to identify those preskills and teach them prior to introducing the strategy. Following each evaluation question on Table 3.3, we have presented potential problems and suggested general modifications.

Importantly, we wrote this text to serve as a resource for the modification of commercial programs. Chapters 4–18 are organized to permit teachers to access explicit strategies accompanied by specific teaching procedures. Additionally, the chapters identify the preskills corresponding to those strategies and provide detailed guidelines for selecting appropriate examples for instruction. Finally, the text provides specific recommendations for designing high-quality practice and review.

APPLY WHAT YOU LEARNED

 Click on the √ to answer the questions online.

1. How was the Mathematics Curriculum Framework, presented in this chapter, derived?

2. What are some critical features of a well-designed curriculum adoption process?

3. Describe the evaluation criteria represented in the Mathematics Curriculum Framework.

4. How can this text be used to modify existing math instruction?

4

Counting

LEARNING OUTCOMES

4.1 Identify four different types of counting skills and discuss the importance of each.

4.2 Contrast the use of pictorial representations and manipulatives to introduce counting.

4.3 Outline instructional strategies to teach counting, including rote counting, counting from numbers other than one, and skip counting.

SKILL HIERARCHY

Counting skills not only are important in and of themselves, but they are also important prerequisite skills for many problem-solving strategies. The Instructional Sequence and Assessment Chart outlines a recommended instructional sequence for the following counting skills: rote counting, rational counting, counting from a number other than one, skip counting, and ordinal counting.

Rote counting is identifying number names in sequence (1, 2, 3, 4, 5, 6). We suggest that during kindergarten students are taught to count to 100; first grade students to 1,000; and second grade students into the thousands.

Rational counting involves coordinating counting with the touching of objects to determine the quantity of a particular group. Rote counting is a prerequisite skill for rational counting. We recommend that students be able to rote count to 10 before rational counting is introduced. Initial rational counting exercises involve counting a single group of objects. Later exercises involve counting two groups of objects, a prerequisite skill for early addition.

Counting from a number other than one is also a prerequisite skill for addition. For example, students begin with 6 and then count 7, 8, 9. In early addition problems such as 6 + 3, students would be taught to say 6, extending the pronunciation for a few seconds, and then count markers for the second addend: *sssiiixxx*, 7, 8, 9.

INSTRUCTIONAL SEQUENCE AND ASSESSMENT CHART

Note: For performance indicators involving writing, if a student fails the written test, the teacher should check student performance orally.

Grade Level	Problem Type	Performance Indicator
K	Counting by ones from 1 through 30	Verbal test: teacher asks students to count to 30.
K	Counting a group of lines	Teacher writes four lines, asks how many lines. Repeat with seven lines, five lines.
K	Counting two groups of lines	Teacher writes | | | | | | | | | and asks, "How many lines all together?"
K	Counting from a number other than 1	Verbal test: teacher asks students to begin counting at 6, at 11, at 8.
K	Ordinal counting first through tenth	Verbal test: teacher draws 10 lines on board, asks the students to touch third line and seventh line.
K	Counting backward from 10 to zero	Verbal test: teacher asks students to count backward from 10 to zero.
K	Counting by ones from 1 through 100	Write the number that comes next: 26, _____, _____, 29, _____ 46, _____, _____, 49, _____
K	Skip counting by 10	Verbal test: teacher asks students to count by 10s to 100.
1	Skip counting by 2, 5, 100	Fill in the missing numerals: 2, 4, 6, _____, _____, _____, _____ 5, 10, 15, _____, _____, _____, _____ 100, 200, 300, _____, _____, _____, _____, _____, _____, _____, _____
1	Counting by ones 100 to 999	Write the numeral that comes next: 599, _____ 299, _____ 499, _____ 699, _____ 889, _____ 704, _____ 349, _____ 509, _____
2	Skip counting	Fill in the missing numerals: 9, 18, 27, _____, _____, _____, _____, _____, _____, _____, _____ 4, 8, 12, _____, _____, _____, _____, _____, _____, _____, _____ 7, 14, 21, _____, _____, _____, _____, _____, _____, _____, _____ 3, 6, 9, _____, _____, _____, _____, _____, _____, _____, _____ 8, 16, 24, _____, _____, _____, _____, _____, _____, _____, _____ 6, 12, 18, _____, _____, _____, _____, _____, _____, _____, _____
2	Counting by ones 1,000 to 9,999	Write the numeral that comes next: 3,101, _____ 2,529, _____ 5,499, _____ 7,308, _____ 3,999, _____ 7,999, _____

Skip counting is counting in which the students say multiples of a base number. For example, when counting by fives, students say 5, 10, 15, 20, 25, 30. We recommend that skip counting by tens be taught early to facilitate teaching rote counting to higher numbers. From skip counting, students learn that 40 follows 30; therefore, they more easily learn to say 40 after 39. Similarly, they learn to say 50 after 49, 60 after 59.

Skip counting by tens is taught after students can rote count to 30. Skip counting by twos and fives is taught later in first grade. Other skip-counting series are taught in second grade. Learning the skip-counting series in early grades also facilitates solving basic multiplication problems. For example, 2×3 involves skip counting by twos three times and results in 6 (see Chapter 9, "Multiplication").

Ordinal counting, counting associated with position, is introduced when the students have mastered rational counting. Ordinal counting is taught because of the common use of ordinal numbers. Teachers often use ordinal numbers in directions ("Touch the third problem.").

CONCEPTUAL UNDERSTANDING

Many commercial programs do not differentiate between teaching rote counting and teaching rational counting. We recommend teaching rote counting without the use of manipulatives or visual representations prior to teaching rational counting (see Instructional Procedures for teaching Rote Counting). However, we recommend using pictorial representations of objects when introducing rational counting. Teachers can better monitor student performance during group instruction if the students are touching and counting pictures, as opposed to managing the students' use of manipulatives. As soon as students are proficient in counting pictures of objects, they can more easily apply their skills to different types of manipulatives.

INSTRUCTIONAL PROCEDURES

The teaching procedures for the major counting skills appear in this section. The skills are listed in their relative order of introduction. Rote counting by ones to 30 is discussed first. Rational counting is discussed next. Rational counting would be introduced when students can rote count to about 10. Thereafter, daily lessons would include both rote and rational counting exercises. After students learn to count one group of objects, they count two groups of objects and determine the total quantity. Next, procedures for teaching students to count from numbers other than one, to ordinal count, to rote count between 30 and 100, to rote count between 100 and 999, and to skip count are discussed.

Rote Counting by Ones to 30

On the first day of instruction, the teacher tests the students to determine how high they can rote count without error. The teacher pretests the students individually simply by asking them to count as high as they can. The teacher records the highest number to which each student counts. The performance of the group determines which new numbers are introduced. The teacher notes the lowest number correctly counted to by members of the group and adds the next two or three numbers in the counting sequence. For example, if a student counts to 11 on the pretest, the new part would be 11, 12, 13 (the last number said correctly on the pretest, 11, and the next two numbers, 12 and 13). The teacher should test students at the beginning of each lesson to determine whether new numbers can be introduced. If the students count correctly, the teacher introduces several new numbers. If the students make errors, the teacher repeats the format with the previously introduced numbers.

The format for introducing new numbers in the counting sequence appears in **Format 4.1: Introducing New Numbers**. The teacher first tests students on previously introduced numbers (1–10). Next, the teacher models counting from 1 to 13, then models just the new part, 11, 12, 13 (see step 2 in **Format 4.1**). In step 3, the teacher leads the students in saying the new part. When introducing new numbers, during both the model and lead (steps 2 and 3), the teacher should emphasize the new numbers by saying them in a louder voice so that students are always hearing a correct answer. When the students appear able to say the new part by themselves, the teacher tests (step 4), then has them say the entire counting series from 1 through the new part (step 5). The students should repeat the counting sequence until they say it correctly several times in a row. Providing sufficient practice for students to count correctly several times is important to facilitate retention. Teachers should not forget to provide individual turns, as well. Finally, teachers should give a delayed test to ensure that students have mastered the sequence. **Summary Box 4.1** outlines the critical steps in the teaching format.

The teacher often must provide practice for students in counting at a lively pace. To do this, she uses a model-lead-test presentation, modeling how fast she wants the students to count. Counting at a lively pace helps keep students attentive. In future lessons, as the students become more proficient, the rate should be increased. Some students may need 15 to 20 repetitions before they can say a new part of the counting sequence correctly. If teachers provide adequate repetition during the first weeks of instruction, they will find that they save time in later weeks. When students can count familiar numbers at a lively pace, the teacher introduces new numbers in the counting sequence.

When presenting a counting task, the teacher must be quite careful not to give the students inappropriate cues. For example, some teachers have a tendency to count quietly when students are supposed to be counting alone (steps 4 and 5). Sometimes teachers just move their lips, inappropriately prompting the students to say the next number, precluding them from answering independently. If a teacher finds that a number of students can count correctly with the group but cannot perform the counting task individually, the teacher might be prompting unnecessarily during group instruction.

Correcting Errors Teachers must be careful to correct all student errors. If students leave out a number (counting 1, 2, 3, 4, 6), they should be stopped immediately and the teacher should model the "hard part" by saying four numbers, beginning with two numbers before the missed number (3, 4, 5, 6). Next, the teacher should lead the students on the hard part, test them on the hard part, and then have them begin counting again from 1, which will serve as a delayed test.

The teacher should be quite careful when making this correction. If a counting error is corrected inappropriately, students may become quite confused. The mistake teachers should avoid is saying the skipped number after the student has made the error. For example, the student says, "1, 2, 3, 4, 6," and the teacher says, "5." What the student hears is "1, 2, 3, 4, 6, 5." The teacher can avoid this mistake by saying "stop" when a student makes an error and then modeling the entire hard part. The teacher should repeat a rote counting exercise until students can respond correctly to the complete series multiple times without errors. If the teacher does not immediately correct the errors and provide sufficient practice, students are less likely to remember the sequence the next day.

Mastering rote counting requires even more practice for struggling students. One way to prevent students from becoming frustrated while practicing counting is to spend only 2 to 3 minutes on rote counting tasks at any one time and present those counting tasks several times during a lesson. This distributed practice tends to be more effective than spending 10 to 15 minutes on counting all at once. Also, counting practice should not be restricted to the instructional time allotted for mathematics. The teacher may have students practice counting when they are lining up for recess, just before they go to lunch, during opening exercises in the morning, or during

---

SUMMARY BOX 4.1

Rote Counting: Introducing New Numbers into a Counting Sequence

1. Teacher tests students on the previously introduced counting sequence.
2. Teacher models counting sequence, emphasizing new part.
3. Teacher models and tests students on the new part of the sequence until students can say the new part correctly three times in a row.
4. Teacher tells students the number they will be ending with.
5. Teacher tests students from the beginning of the sequence through the new part.
6. Teacher practices new counting sequence frequently throughout the day.

the last 5 minutes of class. Finally, the teacher should treat counting as a fun exercise. One way this can be done is to incorporate game-like activities into counting exercises; for example, have students count one time with their hands on their knees, the next time with hands on their heads, and so on.

Rational Counting: One Group

Rational counting is the one-to-one correspondence of touching objects while counting. We recommend that teachers initially use lines or illustrations of objects to teach rational counting skills for reasons of efficiency. The preskill for rational counting is rote counting. The initial exercises in rational counting can begin when the students can rote count to 10.

Format 4.2: Rational Counting has two parts. In Part A, the teacher touches lines as the students count and then asks what number they ended with. In Part B, the students count illustrations of objects on their worksheets. The objects in the illustrations in Part B should be spaced sufficiently so that the students do not become confused about which object they are touching. The students begin the task by pointing at, not touching, the first object. The teacher signals by saying, "Get ready," and then claps. If the students are already touching the first object, they might touch the second object when they hear the clap. The teacher claps at about 1-second intervals. Note that clapping too fast or at an unpredictable rate might result in coordination errors.

Monitoring student performance is particularly critical in this format. Since coordinating touching and counting is the key behavior, listening to the students count is not sufficient. When the skill is first taught, the teacher must repeat the task until he has watched each student touch objects while counting. If students do not begin at the first picture, they will make mistakes. Note that during step 1 of Part B, the teacher demonstrates that counting can be done from left to right or right to left. However, to facilitate monitoring, we recommend that all students count from left to right.

Correcting Errors   Students may make coordination or rote counting errors. If a student makes a coordination error, saying the number before touching the object, the teacher tells the student to count only when touching an object. The teacher then repeats the task, saying, "Go back to the first object and *point* to it." The teacher checks that students are pointing correctly and then repeats the task. As with all corrections, after an error is made, a student should repeat the task until she performs it correctly several times in a row. If a student has difficulty coordinating counting and pointing, the teacher can slow the cadence and prompt the student by taking the student's hand, counting with her, and moving the student's index finger from object to object. The teacher may need to repeat this procedure several times before retesting the student by having her touch and count the objects without assistance. If students make many rote counting errors (counting 1, 2, 3, 5, 6), the teacher should delay rational counting and provide extra practice on rote counting.

Practice and Review   Exercises in counting objects on worksheets should be done daily for several weeks. After students can quickly and accurately count lines and pictures of objects, they may be given manipulatives to count. Initially, the objects can be arranged in a row, which makes counting manipulatives easier. Counting objects in rows is like counting pictures in rows. After students can count objects in rows, objects can be placed more randomly in front of students.

Rational Counting: Two Groups

Counting two groups of lines is introduced when students are able to count a single group of six to eight lines. The format for counting two groups of lines teaches students the function of the word "all" and prepares them for addition. When students first add, they count two groups of lines—"all" of the lines. The format for counting two groups appears in Format 4.3: Counting Two Groups of Lines. In Part A, the teacher draws two groups of lines on the board and has the students count the lines in the first group, count the lines in the second group, and then count all of the lines in both groups. Part B is a worksheet exercise in which the students count two groups of objects on their worksheets.

Correcting Errors   The error students are likely to make in Part A occurs when they are asked to count all of the lines. After counting the lines in the first group, a student is likely to say "one" for the first line in the second group instead of continuing to count. To correct, the teacher models and tests students on that step and then repeats from step 2. For example, if in counting the lines in this diagram ||||| ||, the student counts 1, 2, 3, 4, 1, 2, the teacher models correct counting by saying, "When we count *all* of the lines, we keep on counting. My turn: 1, 2, 3, 4, 5, 6." The teacher then tests the students on counting all of the lines and repeats steps 2–5. Counting all of the lines independently in step 5 serves as a delayed test for the original task.

Practice and Review   Once students are proficient at counting one group of pictures, many practice opportunities can be provided for counting manipulatives and classroom objects. Students can count the windows in the room, the students at each table, or the pencils in a box as the teacher points or touches. Paired practice can be provided by having one student drop objects or counters into a container while another counts. Roles then are reversed as the other student removes objects one at a time while the first student counts. Students can count, rearrange, and recount the same group of objects.

Once students are proficient at counting two groups of pictures, they can be given practice counting two groups of objects. Teachers can pose questions that prepare students for later problem-solving applications. For example, the teacher arranges a group of three girls and a group of five boys at the front of the class. "How many girls in this group?" "How many boys in this group?" "Now let's count all of the children." "How many children in all?"

Counting from Numbers Other Than One

Counting from numbers other than one saves time when teaching rote counting to higher numbers. If students can start at numbers other than one, teachers can focus on the new parts of the number sequences. For example, if students can count to 32 and the teacher is introducing rote counting to 35, the teacher would have students practice counting from 30 (30, 31, 32, 33, 34, 35) rather than starting from one. A second reason for teaching counting beginning at a number other than one is that this counting skill is a preskill for the early addition strategy. Students solve a problem such as $4 + 3 = \square$ by starting to count from 4 and then counting each line in the second group: 5, 6, 7.

|||

the second group: 5, 6, 7.

Format 4.4: Counting from Numbers Other Than One shows how to teach students to count beginning from a number other than one. This format is introduced when students can rote count to about 15. The format contains two parts. The first part teaches students the meaning of the term "get it going." (When the teacher says, "Get it going," the students say the designated number, holding the number as long as the teacher signals; (4 is said, "ffoouurr.") The signal used is quite different from signals used in other rote counting tasks. To prompt the students to say the number for a longer time, the teacher signals by moving her hand in a circular motion. (See picture of hand signal.) The students are to begin saying the number as the teacher begins the signal (moving her finger) and to stop saying the number when the teacher stops the signal (dropping her hand). The purpose of this get-it-going signal is to better enable the students to respond in unison.

When presenting Part B, the teacher should present a set of at least three examples. Initially, the examples all should be less than 10. The exercise is repeated until students respond correctly to the *entire set*, which increases the likelihood that they can generalize the skill to other numbers. Responding correctly to an entire set requires that the teacher repeat all of the examples in the set until the students can respond to them consecutively with no errors. Students will need several repetitions before they master an entire set. If high expectations are maintained initially, the amount of practice needed to master subsequent sets will be reduced.

Format 4.4A/B: Counting from Numbers Other Than 1
Watch how Michaela demonstrates the get-it-going signal and uses it to teach counting from a number other than one.

Correcting Errors Sometimes students make the error of starting over at 1—for example, "ffoouurr, 1, 2, 3, 4." The teacher corrects by modeling and then leading the students several times emphasizing the next number in the sequence. However, if the students continue to make errors, the teacher can introduce a procedure in which she counts quickly from 1 to the get-it-going number and then signals for the students to join her. For example, the teacher would say, "I'll start counting and when I signal, you count with me: 1, 2, 3 (signal), ffoouurr, 5, 6, 7, 8, 9." The teacher responds with students several times then tests them for mastery. After the students begin responding correctly to several consecutive examples, they no longer need the prompt of beginning the sequence at 1.

Ordinal Counting

Ordinal counting involves saying the number associated with a relative position, such as first, second, third, fourth, fifth, and sixth. Ordinal counting is introduced when students can rote count to 15 and can count a group of objects. A model-lead-test-delayed test procedure is used to introduce ordinal counting. Teachers may introduce ordinal counting by having children participate in a race, after which the teacher discusses the positions of the runners: "Who came in first? Who came in second?" The teacher would then model and test various ordinal counting sequences.

Counting by Ones from 30 to 100

The procedure for counting by ones from 30 to 100 should demonstrate the relationship between each tens grouping; that is, each decade has a sequence in which the numerals 0, 1, 2, 3, 4, 5, 6, 7, 8, 9 appear in the ones column: 40, 41, 42, 43, 44, 45, 46, 47, 48, 49. Two preskills related to counting higher numbers are rote counting beginning at a number other than one and skip counting by tens (10, 20, 30, 40, 50, 60, 70, 80, 90, 100), which is discussed later in the chapter.

The format for counting numbers from 30 to 100 is similar to **Format 4.1: Introducing New Numbers** for introducing new numbers in the early counting sequence with two modifications. First, the new part begins at a tens number ending in 7 and continues through the next tens number ending in 2 (27, 28, 29, 30, 31, 32). Starting at a higher number (28 or 29) gives students too little time to prepare for transition to the next decade. Starting at the beginning of the decade (21, 22) makes the task time-consuming. Second, instead of testing the students on counting from one, the teacher has them count from a number approximately 10 to 20 numbers lower than the new part in order to save additional time.

The first exercises should teach students to count from the thirties to the forties. Counting from the forties to the fifties and higher should be introduced several days later or whenever students master the lower numbers. After students practice counting through a new decade for 2 days, the examples are modified daily to promote generalization. For example, students might count from 27 to 42 one day, from 25 to 47 the next, and from 27 to 49 the next.

Counting Backward

Once students can count to 50, counting backward can be introduced. Counting backward is an important preskill for some beginning subtraction strategies. Students initially learn to count backward from 5, then they are introduced to counting backward from increasingly higher numbers. A beginning exercise may have the teacher write a number line from 0 to 5:

The teacher models, leads, and tests on counting backward while touching the numerals on the number line. Numerals then may be erased one at a time; each time the students count backward from 5. Ideally, the teacher provides delayed tests throughout the day. If students perform the sequence correctly the next day with no visual prompt, two or three more numbers may be added to the counting backward sequence.

Counting Between 100 and 999

Students are usually taught to count from 100 through 999 during first grade. First, students are taught to count by hundreds from 100 to 1,000. This hundreds skip-counting series is usually quite easy for students to learn, requiring only a few days of practice. Once students can count by ones through 99 and by hundreds from 100 to 1,000, the teacher can introduce counting by ones in the hundreds numbers. We recommend using a three-stage procedure. In the first stage, the teacher has students count a single decade within a single hundred (350–359). The teacher uses a model-lead-test-delayed test procedure on four to five sets of examples each day. Examples similar to the following set are presented daily until students demonstrate mastery:

350, 351, 352, 353, 354, 355, 356, 357, 358, 359

The second stage introduces students to making the transition from one decade to the next. An example set should include several series extending from a number with 5 in the ones column to the next number in the counting sequence that has 5 in the ones column (325–335). Examples similar to those below are presented daily until students demonstrate mastery. Lower-performing students may require 2 to 3 weeks of practice.

785, 786, 787, 788, 789, 790, 791, 792, 793, 794, 795

The third stage focuses on the transition from a hundreds series to the next hundreds series. The example set should include several series extending from a hundreds number ending with 95 to the next number in the counting series that has a 5 in the ones column (495–505). A daily lesson would include examples like the following:

495, 496, 497, 498, 499, 500, 501, 502, 503, 504, 505

Practice and Review   After the students have mastered transitioning from a hundreds series to the next, review can be provided through written worksheets in which the teacher writes a numeral on a worksheet with 10 spaces following it. The students are to fill in the next 10 numerals. For written exercises, teachers should be careful to use number sequences that involve only those numbers students can write accurately from dictation.

Skip Counting

Skip counting refers to counting each number of a specified multiple. When a student skip counts by fives, the student says, "5, 10, 15, 20, 25, 30, 35, 40, 45, 50." When skip counting by eights, the student says, "8, 16, 24, 32, 40, 48, 56, 64, 72, 80." Throughout this book, we refer to a skip-counting sequence as a *count-by series*. Knowledge of the count-by series for multiples of 2, 3, 4, 5, 6, 7, 8, 9, and 10 is an important preskill for the memorization of basic multiplication and division facts. Students should learn to count 10 numbers for each series except fives: 2 to 20, 3 to 30, 4 to 40, 6 to 60, and so on. Students should learn to count by fives to 60 because telling time requires this skill. Teachers also may want to teach counting by twenty-fives to 100 as a prerequisite to counting money.

We recommend introducing the tens count-by series first because knowledge of this series is a preskill for rote counting to 100. Counting by tens is typically introduced after students can rote count by ones to about 30, usually several months into kindergarten. The next count-by series, the twos, is not introduced until the students have mastered counting by tens. This may be several weeks later. Thereafter, a new series may be introduced when students can say each of the previously introduced series accurately and fluently.

We suggest teaching the count-by series cumulatively in the following sequence: 10, 2, 5, 9, 4, 25, 3, 8, 7, 6. This order is designed to separate those count-by series that contain many of the same numbers. For example, several numbers in the fours series also appear in the eights series: 4, 8, 12, 16, 20, 24. Students may begin counting by fours and switch to eights when they come to 16, 24, or 32 (4, 8, 12, 16, 24, 32, 40). The chances of making that error are reduced when the two series are not introduced consecutively.

Format 4.5A:
Count-By

Watch Michaela's clear point-and-touch signal.

Format 4.5B:
Count-By

Watch how Michaela corrects Jerone's error and brings the group to mastery.

Format 4.5: Count-By includes two parts. Part A demonstrates to students that they end up with the same number whether they count by ones or count by another number such as twos or fives. It is also intended to show that counting by a number other than one can save time.

Part B is designed to teach students to memorize the various count-by series and includes a review of previously introduced count-by series. Two or three previously taught series should be reviewed daily.

When teaching the count-by series, the teacher uses a model-lead-test-delayed test procedure, saying the numbers of the new series alone, saying the numbers of the new series with the students, and finally having the students say the numbers themselves. Teachers will need to adjust how many numbers in a given series they introduce based on their students' performance. Teachers working with instructionally naive students may introduce only the first three numbers of a series (9, 18, 27), while teachers working with more experienced students might introduce five or six numbers (9, 18, 27, 36, 45).

On the second day of instruction on a series, the teacher tests the students on the part of the series taught during the previous lesson. If the students make an error, the teacher repeats the model-lead-test-delayed test procedure from steps 2 and 3 of Part B. If the students know the part of the series previously taught or require just a couple of practice opportunities to say the previously taught part correctly, the teacher introduces the next several numbers of the count-by series. For example, if students have been previously taught the nines series to 36 (9, 18, 27, 36), the new part would include 45 and 54. The teacher uses a model-lead-test-delayed test procedure beginning with 9 and emphasizing the new part (9, 18, 27, 36, <u>45</u>, <u>54</u>).

Practice and Review   As with any rote counting task, adequate repetition must be provided for student mastery. A teacher may have to lead lower-performing students five to ten times through a series until they can say it fluently without errors. When leading students, the teacher should initially lead with a strong voice, particularly when saying difficult parts of a counting sequence. The purpose of using a voice emphasis is to ensure that all students are hearing the correct response and to prevent them from following the lead of students who may be responding incorrectly. A brisk rhythm should be established by the teacher's tapping his foot or clapping his hands to make mastering the series easier. Additional practice on previously taught series also can be provided through peer tutoring or other partner practice activities. A new series is introduced only when students know all of the previously introduced series.

Correcting Errors   Count-by errors are corrected by following the model-lead-test-delayed test correction procedures. When the teacher hears an error, he immediately stops the students, models the hard part (the two numbers just before the missed number and the one number following the missed number), leads the students on the hard part several times, tests the students on the hard part, and then has them say the entire series from the beginning. For example, if students count "8, 16, 24, 32, 40, 48, 54," the teacher stops them as soon as he hears 54 instead of 56. Next, he models, leads, and tests on the hard part: 40, 48, <u>56</u>, 64. After students perform acceptably on the test of the hard part, the teacher has the students count from the beginning, which serves as a delayed test.

SUMMARY BOX 4.2

Skip Counting: Introducing a New Count-by Series

1. Teacher writes part of the new count-by series on the board and models saying the series. (The teacher determines how much of the series to introduce at once based on previous performance of the students.)
2. Teacher leads the students in reading the new series from the board.
3. Teacher gradually erases numbers in the series as students practice saying the series.
4. Teacher tests students on saying the series from memory.
5. Teacher alternates practice with previously introduced series and the new series as a delayed test.

APPLY WHAT YOU LEARNED

 Click on the √ to answer the questions online.

1. Identify four different types of counting skills and discuss the importance of each.

2. Contrast the use of pictorial representations and manipulatives to introduce counting.

3. When counting from 1 to 10, a student counts "5, 6, 7, 9." Immediately after the student says "9," the teacher says "8" to correct her. What is the problem with this correction? What *should* the teacher say and do? Give specific teacher wording.

4. Two days ago, the teacher introduced rote counting to 16. At the beginning of today's lesson, the teacher tests the students and they can all count to 16. What should the teacher do for the rote counting exercise today? What if the students had not been able to count to 16?

5. The teacher tells the students to count to 45. A student counts correctly until 39 and then says 50. What should the teacher say to correct the error?

6. When counting this group of lines, | | | | |, a student ends up with 8. What are two possible causes of the error? How would the correction procedures differ?

Format 4.1
INTRODUCING NEW NUMBERS

TEACHER	STUDENTS
1. You are going to count and end up with 10. What number will you end up with?	10
Start at 1, get ready, count.	1, 2, 3, 4, 5, 6, 7, 8, 9, 10
2. I'm going to count and end up with 13. What am I going to end up with?	13
Yes, 13. Listen: 1, 2, 3, 4, 5, 6, 7, 8, 9, 10, *11, 12, 13. (Quickly count to 10 and then emphasize 11, 12, 13.)* Listen to the new part: *11, 12, 13.*	
3. When I drop my hand, say the new part with me. *(Extend pronunciation of 10.)* Teeennn *(drop hand and respond with students),* 11, 12, 13.	11, 12, 13
Again. Teeennn *(drop hand),* 11, 12, 13.	11, 12, 13
(Repeat until students respond correctly several times in a row.)	
4. Say the new part all by yourselves: teeennn *(drop hand).*	11, 12, 13
5. Now you're going to count and end up with 13. What number will you end up with?	13
Starting at 1, get ready, count.	1, 2, 3, 4, 5, 6, 7, 8, 9, 10, 11, 12, 13
(Give individual turns.)	

Format 4.2
RATIONAL COUNTING

TEACHER	STUDENTS
Part A: Structured Board Presentation	
1. *(Draw four lines on the board.)*	
My turn. Every time I touch a line, I count. Watch. *(Touch lines at 1-second intervals.)* 1, 2, 3, 4.	
What number did I end with?	4
(Repeat step 1 with seven lines.)	
2. *(Draw six lines on the board.)* Every time I touch a line, you count.	
(Point to left of line.) Get ready.	1, 2, 3, 4, 5, 6
(Touch lines from left to right at 1-second intervals as students count.)	
(If students count before you touch a line, tell them:	
Watch my finger. Count *only* when I touch a line.*)*	
3. What number did we end with?	6
4. So, how many lines are there?	6
5. *(Repeat steps 2–4 with three lines, then seven lines. Give individual turns to several students.)*	
Part B: Structured Worksheet Presentation	

Sample worksheet item:

1. *(Hold up a worksheet, and point to a group of objects.)*	
We're going to count all the objects. Watch me count. *(Touch the objects from left to right and count.)* 1, 2, 3, 4, 5.	
Watch me count again. *(Touch objects from right to left and count.)* 1, 2, 3, 4, 5.	
2. Everyone, hold your finger over the first picture. *(Check to see that all students are pointing to but not touching the appropriate picture.)*	
Each time I clap, you touch an object and say the number. Get ready. *(Clap one time per second. Count with students while monitoring their touching.)* 1, 2, 3, 4, 5	1, 2, 3, 4, 5
3. All by yourselves, you're going to count the pictures. Hold your finger over the first picture. *(Check.)* Get ready. *(Clap one time per second.)*	1, 2, 3, 4 ,5
How many lines are there?	5
4. *(Repeat steps 2 and 3 with other examples. Give individual turns to several students.)*	

Format 4.3
COUNTING TWO GROUPS OF LINES

TEACHER	STUDENTS
Part A: Structured Board Presentation	
1. *(Write the following lines on the board.)*	
Here are two groups of lines. *(Touch the first group.)* Here is the first group. *(Touch the second group.)* Here is the second group.	
2. Let's count the lines in the first group. *(Touch as students count.)*	1, 2, 3, 4, 5
How many in the first group?	5
3. Let's count the lines in the second group. *(Touch as students count.)*	1,2,3
How many in the second group?	3
4. Now let's count all the lines. You count the lines in the first group, and then you keep on going and count the lines in the second group. *(Touch as students count.)*	1, 2, 3, 4, 5, 6, 7, 8
5. How many lines in all?	8
(Repeat with additional examples.)	
Part B: Structured Worksheet Presentation	
a. ||| |||| b. ▢▢▢▢▢ ▢▢	
c. 🐾🐾🐾 🐾🐾🐾🐾🐾 d. ○○○○○ ○○○	
1. Touch a. *(Check.)*	
2. Touch the first group of lines. I'll clap. You count the objects in the first group. Put your finger over the first line. *(Pause and check.)* Get ready. *(Clap at 1-second intervals.)* How many in the first group?	3
3. *(Repeat step 2 with the second group.)*	
4. Now you're going to count all the lines. Start counting with the first group. Put your finger over the first line. *(Pause and check.)* Get ready. *(Clap at 1-second intervals.)*	1, 2, 3, 4, 5, 6, 7
5. How many in all?	7
6. *(Repeat steps 1–5 with b, c, and d. Be sure to give individual turns.)*	

Format 4.4
COUNTING FROM NUMBERS OTHER THAN 1   (See Video A/B)

TEACHER	STUDENTS
▶	
Part A: Preskill—Get-It-Going Signal	
1. "Get it going" means to say a number for as long as I move my finger.	
2. *(Hold up hand.)* My turn. I'm going to get 4 going.	
(Move hand in circular motion, saying ffoouurr with extended pronunciation. After several seconds, drop hand and stop saying 4.)	
3. *(Repeat step 2 with the numbers 6 and 9.)*	
4. Let's do it together. We have 4. How many do we have?	4
Get it going: ffoouurr.	ffoouurr
5. You have five. How many do you have?	5
Get it going: ffiivve	ffiivvee
(Repeat step 5 with the numbers 7 and 3.)	
Part B: Oral Presentation	
1. We're going to get it going and count. My turn. We have four. Get it going.	
(Signal by moving hand in circular motion. After 2 seconds, drop hand.) Ffoouurr, 5, 6, 7, 8, stop. *(Count at a rate of about two numbers a second.)*	
2. Get it going and count with me. You have 4. How many do you have?	4
Get it going: Foouuurr, 5, 6, 7, 8.	Ffoouurr,
	5, 6, 7, 8
3. All by yourselves. You have 4. Get it going.	ffoouurr, 5, 6, 7, 8
4. *(Repeat steps 1–3 with the numbers 7 and then 3. Give individuals turns.)*	

Format 4.5
COUNT-BY   (See Videos in Parts A and B)

TEACHER	STUDENTS
▶	
Part A: Introducing the Count-by	
1. *(Draw lines in groups of two on the board.)*	
‖ ‖ ‖ ‖ ‖	
Let's find out how many lines we have. I'll touch and you count.	1, 2, 3, 4, 5, 6, 7, 8, 9, 10
How many lines are there? *(Write 10 next to the last group.)*	10

continued

Format 4.5 *(continued)*
COUNT-BY

TEACHER	STUDENTS
Now I'll show you a fast way to count those lines. *(Circle each group of two lines with your finger. For each group, ask, "How many lines in this group?" After asking about all five groups, ask, "How many lines are in each group?")*	
When we count groups of 2, we count lines the fast way.	
2. Let's figure out the numbers we say when we count by 2. Count the lines in the first group. *(Point to each line as students count.)*	1, 2
Yes, there are two lines, so I write 2 above the first group. *(Write 2 above the first group.)*	
Count the lines in the first and second groups.	1, 2, 3, 4
You counted four lines so far, so I'll write 4 above the second group. *(Write it.)*	
(Continue to have the students count each successive group from the beginning, writing the appropriate numeral above each group, such as the following:	
2 4 6 8 10	
|| || || || ||	
When the students have finished, the lines should look like the above example.)	
3. Now you know what numbers to say when you count by 2. Let's count the lines again, but this time we'll count by 2. *(Point to each numeral as students count.)*	2, 4, 6, 8, 10
4. How many did you end up with when you counted by 2?	10
5. *(Point to the 10 written next to the last group.)* How many did you end up with when you counted the regular way?	10
See, the fast way really does work.	

▶

Part B: Structured Board Presentation

1. *(Write the following numerals on the board.)* 6, 12, 18, 24, 30	
Today we are going to learn to count by 6.	
2. I will say the first few numbers in the series: 6, 12, 18, 24, 30.	
3. Say this part with me as I touch each numeral. Get ready. *(Signal)*	6, 12, 18, 24, 30
4. Say the series by yourselves. Get ready. *(Signal.)*	6, 12, 18, 24, 30
(Give individual turns to several students.)	
5. *(Erase one of the numerals in the series.)* Say the sixes again, including the missing number.	6, 12, 18, 24, 30
(Repeat step 5, erasing another numeral each time, until students can say the series without help.)	
6. *(Alternate previously learned count-by series with practice on new series.)*	

Symbol Identification and Place Value

LEARNING OUTCOMES

5.1 Discuss the relationship between numeral identification and place value and why place value is critical to mathematical understanding.

5.2 Explain the importance of introducing place value charts prior to introducing manipulatives when teaching place value concepts.

5.3 Describe the general teaching procedures for reading and writing numerals.

5.4 Explain how to teach students to read and write numerals beyond 20.

SKILL HIERARCHY

Symbol identification and place value are addressed together in this chapter because a numeral has a different value depending on the column in which it is placed. For example, 4 in 483 has the value of 400 but 4 in 64 has the value of 4. Symbol identification, especially reading and writing numerals accurately, along with a strong conceptual understanding of place value concepts prepares students for more advance computation and problem solving.

The Instructional Sequence and Assessment Chart provides a recommended progression of skills that is designed to integrate critical place value concepts with numeral reading and writing skills. Numeral identification and the concept of numeral/object correspondence form the foundation of the Instructional Sequence and Assessment Chart. Numeral/object one-to-one correspondence requires students to write the numeral that corresponds to the number of objects in a group or, conversely, draw a group of lines to show the number represented by a numeral.

Place value concepts are introduced through the following instructional activities: reading and writing tens, hundreds, thousands, and millions numerals; expanded notation; and column alignment. In reading multi-digit numerals, students translate each digit into a value according to its position and then identify the entire numeral. Writing numerals requires the reverse—breaking into parts rather than putting parts together.

Expanded notation and column alignment are critical to reading and writing multi-digit numerals. Expanded notation problems with hundreds numerals involve rewriting a numeral by identifying its components:

$$342 = 300 + 40 + 2$$

When teachers see that students can read and write hundreds numerals, they then introduce column alignment problems with hundreds numerals:

$$342 + 8 \text{ is rewritten as } 342$$
$$+8$$

The Instructional Sequence and Assessment Chart lists specific skills, indicating their relative order of introduction. Note that many of the tasks in kindergarten and first grade require teachers to test students individually. In later grades, only tasks requiring students to read numerals need be tested individually.

INSTRUCTIONAL SEQUENCE AND ASSESSMENT CHART

Grade Level	Problem Type	Performance Indicator
K	Reading numerals zero through 10	Read these numerals: 4 2 6 1 7 3 0 8 5 9 10
K	Writing numerals zero through 10	Write these numerals: 4 2 6 1 7 3 0 8 5 9 10
K	Writing members of set (lines) to represent a numeral	4 6 ____ ____
K	Writing a numeral to represent members of a set	☐ ☐ ⎮⎮⎮ ⎮⎮⎮⎮⎮⎮⎮
K	Reading teen numerals	Read these numerals: 15 11 13 12 17 19 14 16 18
K	Writing teen numerals	Write these numerals: 15 11 13 12 17 19 14 16 18
K–1	Reading numerals from 20 to 99	Read these numerals: 64 81 44 29
K–1	Writing numbers from 20 to 99	Write these numerals: 47 98 72 31
1	Column alignment: Rewriting horizontal addition and subtraction problems	Rewrite the following problems vertically: 85 + 3 = _____ 4 + 25 = _____ 37 − 2 = _____
1	Expanded notation	63 = _____ + _____ 92 = _____ + _____
2	Reading and writing numerals between 100 and 999 except those with a zero in the tens column	Read: 320, 417, 521 Write seven hundred fifteen _____ Write four hundred thirty-six _____ Write three hundred fifty _____
2	Reading and writing numerals between 100 and 999 with zero in tens column	Read: 502, 708, 303 Write four hundred eight _____ Write seven hundred two _____ Write three hundred three _____

2	Rewriting horizontal equations; one numeral is a hundreds numeral	$305 + 8 + 42 =$ _____ $428 - 21 =$ _____ $31 + 142 + 8 =$ _____
2	Expanded notation with hundreds numerals	$382 =$ _____ $+$ _____ $+$ _____ $417 =$ _____ $+$ _____ $+$ _____ $215 =$ _____ $+$ _____ $+$ _____
3	Reading and writing thousands numerals between 1,000 and 9,999 with no zeros in hundreds or tens column	Read: 3,248; 7,151; 1,318 Write five thousand three hundred fourteen _____ Write two thousand six hundred forty-three _____ Write one thousand one hundred forty-one _____
3	Reading and writing thousands numerals between 1,000 and 9,999 with a zero in the hundreds column	Read: 7,025; 8,014; 2,092 Write five thousand seventy-two _____ Write one thousand forty _____ Write six thousand eighty-eight _____
3	Reading and writing thousands numerals between 1,000 and 9,999 with zeros in the hundreds and/or tens columns	Read: 7,025; 2,002; 1,409 Write six thousand eight _____ Write nine thousand four _____ Write five thousand two _____
3	Column alignment: Rewriting horizontal problems	$35 + 1,083 + 245 =$ _____ $4,035 - 23 =$ _____ $8 + 2,835 =$ _____
4	Reading and writing all thousands numerals between 10,000 and 999,999	Read: 300,000 90,230 150,200 Write two hundred thousand _____ Write ninety thousand four hundred _____ Write one hundred thousand two hundred _____
4	Reading and writing numerals between 1 million and 9 million	Read: 6,030,000 5,002,100 1,340,000 Write seven million _____ Write three million, eighty thousand _____ Write eight million, six hundred thousand _____
5	Reading and writing numerals between 10 million and 999 million	Read: 27,400,000 302,250,000 900,300,000 Write ten million _____ Write forty million two hundred thousand _____

CONCEPTUAL UNDERSTANDING

In this chapter, we introduce reading and writing numerals using place value charts so that students can see how the numerals represent their respective values. These charts are used both by the teacher to introduce place value concepts and by the students as they practice independently. Once students have mastered these place value skills, the charts are no longer necessary but can be reintroduced when correcting errors.

Although many commercial programs recommend introducing place value concepts using manipulatives, we recommend delaying the use of manipulatives until after students demonstrate their ability to read and write numerals using place value charts. The manipulatives used in this way provide students with further evidence of the value of the numeral and increase the chances that students are using the manipulatives correctly.

INSTRUCTIONAL PROCEDURES: SYMBOL IDENTIFICATION

This section addresses skills typically taught during kindergarten and early first grade. These skills are prerequisites for the equality-based strategies that provide a conceptual understanding of addition and subtraction. The skills, listed in the order they are discussed in this section, are as follows:

1. Numeral identification (zero through 10)
2. Numeral writing (zero through 10)
3. Symbol identification and writing $(+, -, \square, =)$
4. Equation reading and writing
5. Numeral/object correspondence

Numeral Identification

Numeral identification tasks usually begin when students can rote count at least to 10. The reason for delaying numeral identification is to avoid the potential confusion that could occur between counting and recognizing numerals. Students who enter school knowing how to count can begin learning to identify numerals immediately.

The sequence in which numerals are introduced is important. A basic guideline in sequencing the introduction of numerals is to separate similar-looking and similar-sounding numerals. Students are likely to confuse 6 and 9 because they look similar; likewise, students may have difficulty discriminating 4 and 5 because they sound alike, both beginning with the same sound. Therefore, a good sequence of introduction would separate both pairs of numerals by several lessons. One possible sequence for introducing numerals 0 to 10 is 4, 2, 6, 1, 7, 3, 0, 8, 5, 9, 10. Note the separation of 6 and 9; 1, 0, and 10; and 4 and 5. This sequence is included as an example and is certainly not the only sequence that will minimize student errors.

A second sequencing guideline is to introduce new numerals cumulatively. A new numeral is not presented until students have demonstrated mastery of the previously introduced symbols. Teachers working with students who enter school with little or no previous knowledge of numerals can generally introduce new symbols at a rate of one new symbol each three to five lessons.

Format 5.1: Introducing New Numerals consists of a model in which the teacher points to the numeral and tells the students the name of the numeral; a test in which the teacher asks the students to identify the new numeral; and discrimination practice in which the teacher asks students to identify the new numeral and previously introduced numerals.

In this format, the teacher first writes a set of numerals on the board. Each of the previously introduced numerals is written once. The new numeral is written several times to ensure that the student attends to the *appearance* of the numeral rather than its position on the board. The most important part of the introduction is the discrimination practice in step 2 of the format. Note that the presentation of the numeral follows an **alternating pattern**: new numeral, one previously introduced numeral, new numeral, two previously introduced numerals, new numeral, three previously introduced numerals, and so on. The time the student has to remember the new numeral is gradually increased by interspersing practice with more familiar numerals. This pattern is designed to help students better remember a new or difficult numeral. Individual turns are given after the teacher presents the discrimination practice. If, when given an individual turn, a student misidentifies or does not respond, the teacher models and tests the new numeral and uses the alternating pattern as a delayed test, focusing on that numeral and previously identified numerals.

Format 5.1: Introducing New Numerals

Watch how Michaela uses a clear point-and-touch signal along with individual turns to ensure all students are responding and have mastered the new numeral.

FIGURE 5.1   Point and touch signal

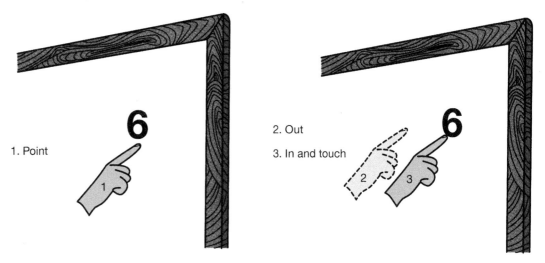

A clear point-and-touch signal is essential for presentation of this format. The features of a good point-and-touch signal are illustrated in **Figure 5.1**. When signaling, the teacher points under the numeral (not touching the board), making sure that no student's vision is blocked by any part of the teacher's hand or body. After pointing under the numeral for 1 to 2 seconds, the teacher signals by moving her finger away from the board and then back toward it, touching under the numeral. The out-and-in motion is done crisply with the finger moving away from the board (about 6 inches) and then immediately moving back to the board. When the finger touches below the numeral, the students are to respond. The out-and-in motion should be done the same way every time it is used. Any hesitation or inconsistency makes unison responding difficult because the students cannot tell when they are supposed to answer.

As with rote counting, the numeral identification tasks are more efficiently taught if presented for 3 to 5 minutes at several different times during the lesson rather than in one long session. Numeral identification also can be practiced at various times of the day. Many teachers put the symbols on a bulletin board or wall in the room. The teachers then ask the students to identify the symbols during early morning exercises, before going to recess or lunch, or at other opportune times. The practice provided by these brief tasks, interspersed throughout the day, can make a great difference in how quickly low-performing students learn to identify symbols.

Numeral Writing

Numeral writing is an important skill in and of itself and also reinforces numeral identification. As a general rule, a new numeral can be introduced into numeral writing exercises several lessons after it first appears in a numeral identification format. As noted in numeral identification, symbols are introduced cumulatively. Instructionally naive students will be ready to practice writing a new numeral every three to five lessons. There are three basic stages in teaching students to write single-digit numerals:

1. Tracing numerals written on worksheets
2. Copying numerals
3. Writing numerals from dictation

For worksheet tracing exercises, we recommend that dots and dashes be used to prompt the students in writing the numerals.

During the first several lessons, the teacher leads the students through tracing, monitoring them quite carefully and, if necessary, moving the students' hands to help them make the lines. The students say the name of the numeral each time they write it. When the students are able to trace a numeral without assistance, the teacher introduces copying. In initial copying exercises, dashed lines and dots appear for the first numeral but only dots for the remaining numerals.

When students can do this exercise, a more sophisticated copying exercise is introduced in which no dots or dashed lines are used as prompts. The students should practice writing each numeral many times each day for the first week the symbol is introduced. The number of repetitions can be gradually reduced as student performance improves.

The third and final stage of numeral writing includes numeral dictation exercises in which the teacher says a number and the students write the numeral. Some students find dictation exercises quite difficult in that they have to remember not only what a numeral looks like but also how to write it. The prerequisites for introducing a numeral in dictation exercises are being able to identify and copy the numeral.

In a numeral dictation exercise, the teacher follows the same alternating pattern used in numeral identification tasks. For example, if students have learned to write 4, 2, 6, 1 and are being introduced to 7 in a dictation exercise, the sequence of examples presented by the teacher might be 7, 4, 7, 6, 1, 7, 4, 2, 6, 7. The worksheet on which the students are to write the numerals should have blank spaces or boxes large enough to write each symbol.

Monitoring student writing is important when presenting numeral dictation exercises. The teacher should check the responses of all low-performing students after each numeral is written. The responses of higher-performing students can be checked after every second or third numeral. As soon as the last student has finished writing a symbol, if no mistakes were made, the teacher should dictate the next numeral. Too much time between tasks can result in off-task behavior.

Correcting Errors   The correction procedure for errors involves a model-test-alternating pattern procedure. The teacher shows the students how to write the numeral, has the students copy it, and then alternates between having students write the missed numeral and other numerals, which serves as the delayed test.

Teachers must be careful in setting reasonable criteria for neatness. Students with little prior writing experience may require many months of practice before they consistently write numerals neatly. The teacher should gradually increase criteria for legibility and neatness. In initial exercises, writing a reasonable facsimile of a numeral is the critical student behavior. If a student writes a numeral backward, the teacher may respond by acknowledging that the correct numeral was written but address the positioning: "Good. That is a 4, but here's how to write it." Note that the correction is made in a positive manner.

Symbol Identification and Writing

The symbols for plus, minus, equal sign, and empty box are taught with the same procedures used for teaching numerals. An empty box can be introduced as "how many," which facilitates reading equations; for example, $6 + 5 = \square$ is read: "Six plus five equals how many?"

Introduction of the various symbols should be interspersed throughout the lessons in which numerals are introduced. The first symbol would be introduced after several numerals; subsequent symbols would be introduced after two to three additional numerals had been introduced.

Equation Reading and Writing

Equation reading and writing are prerequisite skills for problem solving and learning math facts. Children may have difficulty reading a problem such as $6 - 3 = \square$, even though they can identify each symbol in isolation. When they read a problem, they must connect the numerals and symbols together. Reading and writing number sentences requires considerable practice.

Equation reading is introduced when the students can identify numerals and symbols accurately and fluently. If students have not received adequate practice to quickly identify numerals when they appear in isolation, they will have much difficulty reading equations.

Because the procedure for teaching the reading of equations is quite straightforward, a format is not included. The teacher simply writes several equations on the board and follows a model-lead-test-delayed test procedure:

$$4 + 3 = \square \qquad 7 - 3 = \square$$

The teacher *models* reading the first equation at a rate of about a numeral or symbol each second. Reading at a faster rate should be avoided initially, since it may encourage guessing. The teacher then *leads* by responding with the students as they read the statement. Lower-performing students may need 10 or more repetitions. When the students can read the statement by themselves, the teacher *tests* the group and then individuals. The teacher gives a delayed test using previously introduced examples before introducing subsequent statements.

Equation reading is practiced daily for several weeks. It can be discontinued when addition is introduced, since the addition formats begin with the students reading an equation.

Equation writing requires students to write equations dictated by the teacher; for example, "Listen: Four plus three equals how many? Say that . . . Write it." Equation writing is introduced when the students can read equations with relative ease and are fluent in writing numerals and symbols during dictation exercises.

Format 5.2: Equation Writing involves the students repeating a statement at a normal rate, then repeating the statement at a slow rate, and finally writing the statement. The purpose of having students say the statement slowly is to help young students who write slowly remember the latter part of the statement as they are writing the earlier part.

Correcting Errors   A common error is writing a numeral or symbol out of order. As soon as the teacher notices an error in a written equation, she points to each symbol while saying the correct statement. For example, if a student writes 6 + $\square$ = 2 for 6 + 2 = $\square$, the teacher says "6" and points to 6; says "plus" and points to +; says "2" and points to the box that the student has written. The teacher immediately says, "This is not 2. Let's try the problem again." The teacher has the student cross out or erase the problem, then repeats the equation, has the student say the equation, and then has the student write the equation. The teacher provides a delayed test by dictating similar equations or returning to the missed equation at a later time.

Numeral/Object Correspondence

This section includes two types of one-to-one correspondence tasks. In the first task, the student identifies a symbol and then writes the appropriate number of lines; for example, the student identifies the numeral 2 and then draws two lines under the 2. For the second, the student counts the number of lines or other objects and writes the numeral that represents the number of objects; for the task below, the student writes a 2 in the box.

Both tasks are component skills for the equality-based strategies students are taught to solve addition and subtraction in which they write and count lines. Therefore, these tasks should be taught relatively early in the instructional sequence. Both one-to-one correspondence skills can be introduced within a short period of time, since they usually are easy for students to learn. As soon as the students learn to identify a new numeral, teachers should incorporate it into these tasks.

Identifying a Number and Drawing Lines   Prior to introducing tasks in which the students draw lines to correspond to a numeral, the teacher may need to provide practice for lower-performing students in simply drawing lines. The teacher gives students a piece of paper with a series of dots about 1/4 inch apart and 1/2 inch above a horizontal line. The teacher then models how to draw lines. This initial exercise is followed by an exercise in which students write a line each time the teacher claps.

Students may write crooked lines or crowd them together—for instance, \/\/\. Either error may cause overlapping or crossed lines, which makes accurate counting difficult. The teacher should carefully monitor and correct by modeling and then, if necessary, guiding the student's pencil as the student makes the lines. When students can draw lines as the teacher claps, the teacher introduces an exercise in which the students also count as they draw lines. When the students can count and draw lines as the teacher claps, exercises with numerals can be introduced.

Format 5.3: Identifying a Symbol and Drawing Lines teaches students to draw lines for numerals. In the format, students first identify a numeral, state that the numeral tells them to draw a certain number of lines, and then draw the lines. Since most students readily learn this skill, they require only two to four lessons before teachers can include this type of task on independent worksheets. Note that a how-many box is included as an example in the teacher presentation because students must understand that not every symbol tells them to draw lines.

If students make errors on independent worksheet items, the teacher should test them to determine the cause of the error. Did the student identify the numeral correctly? If not, the misidentification caused the error. If the student identified the numeral correctly, the error resulted from a line drawing error, which is corrected by reviewing **Format 5.3**.

Counting Objects and Writing a Numeral   Writing a numeral to represent a set of objects is an integral part of the conceptual strategy we recommend for teaching addition. This strategy involves drawing lines for each addend, counting all of the lines, drawing that number of lines under the box on the other side of the equals, and finally writing the numeral for those lines (the sum) in the box (see below). Note that a more detailed explanation of this initial strategy designed to teach conceptual understanding of addition is provided in Chapter 7.

$$4 + 2 = \boxed{6}$$

|||| || |||||

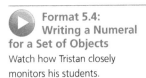

**Format 5.4:
Writing a Numeral
for a Set of Objects**
Watch how Tristan closely
monitors his students.

Format 5.4: Writing a Numeral for a Set of Objects begins with an explanation of the function of the objects under a box: "The objects under a box tell what numeral goes in the box." The students are then told to count the objects under the box and write the numeral for the number they end up with. If students have mastered the necessary preskills of rational counting and numeral writing, they will have little difficulty. After practicing this skill in two or three lessons, tasks of this kind can be included on worksheets as independent activities.

The two mistakes students might make on this task are miscounting the objects and writing the wrong numeral. Often it is not clear by looking at a worksheet how a student derived an answer. In this case, the teacher should ask the student to work several items while counting aloud so that the cause of the error can be identified and an appropriate correction provided. If the student cannot correctly count objects in several problems, the teacher should provide practice on object counting (see Chapter 4). If a student writes the wrong numeral, the teacher needs to provide practice in numeral identification and numeral dictation. Mistakes involving mechanics such as writing a numeral backward are not critical. However, the teacher should have the student rewrite the backward numeral. As mentioned earlier, some students need months of practice writing numerals before they consistently write them in the correct form.

Practice and Review

Once students are proficient with drawing lines for a symbol and writing a numeral for a group of objects, the tasks may be extended to similar tasks using manipulatives. For example, rather than drawing lines for a symbol, students may be provided with counters or other objects. They place the appropriate number of objects in a space below or next to each numeral. Students can work in pairs to check one another's work by reading each numeral and counting the corresponding objects.

A large display can also be provided at a workstation with numerals and an empty box below each numeral. A variety of objects could be made available with the display (10 each of pencils, identical plastic toys, blocks, etc.). Students can create sets of objects for each numeral, placing the correct number of similar objects in each box. Other students then can check the sets and create different sets for each numeral. The purpose of these types of activities is to provide additional independent practice opportunities.

INSTRUCTIONAL PROCEDURES: PLACE VALUE

Three skills related to place value discussed in this section are: (1) reading and writing numerals, (2) expanded notation, and (3) column alignment. The teaching procedures discussed for reading and writing numerals address the following: teens, tens, hundreds, thousands, and millions. The teaching procedures are quite similar for reading and writing numerals. In reading numerals, the students identify the numerals in each column (two tens and four ones) and their value (two tens equal 20) and then combine the values to read the entire numeral (20 and 4 = 24). In writing numerals, students first expand the number into its component parts (24 = two tens and four ones) and then write each component.

Variations in the teaching procedures are needed with teen numerals and numerals with zero. With teen numerals, students say the ones number first (16 is read "sixteen," not "teensix") but write the tens numeral first (in writing 16, students write the 1, then the 6). Numerals with zeros are difficult because students must omit the zeros when reading (306 is read "three hundred six," not "three hundred zero six") but include them when writing, even though the students don't hear them. Instructions in reading and writing numerals should be carefully coordinated. Students should be introduced to numeral identification first and then to numeral writing for those types of numerals.

Reading and Writing Teen Numerals

Reading Teen Numerals
Reading teen numerals is introduced when the students can read all numerals between zero and 10. Regular teens are introduced before irregular teens. The numerals 14, 16, 17, 18, and 19 are regular teens. The irregular teens are 11, 12, 13, and 15. Note that 14 is regular because it is pronounced *four*teen. But 12 is not pronounced *two*teen, and 15 is not pronounced *five*teen, so they are considered irregular.

Format 5.5: Reading Teen Numerals Using Place Value Concepts is constructed in three parts. In Part A, a structured board exercise, the teacher makes a chart on the board with spaces for the tens and ones columns. The teacher tells the students that they read one 10 as "teen" and models reading teen numerals. Then the students read them. On the first day of instruction, examples are limited to regular teen numerals: 14, 16, 17, 18, and 19. The next day, one irregular teen is introduced. A new irregular teen is introduced each day unless students have difficulty with previously introduced teens. When a new irregular teen is introduced, the teacher alternates between the new numeral and previously introduced numerals (13, 14, 13, 16, 18, 13, 17, 14, 19, 13) to provide practice and facilitate retention.

Part B is a less structured exercise in which the students read teen numerals without prompting. Part B is presented daily for several weeks. Part C is a worksheet exercise designed to emphasize place value concepts. In Part C, the students are shown pictures of counters and instructed to circle the appropriate numeral. After writing teen numerals has been introduced, students can write the appropriate numeral rather than circle it.

Writing Teen Numerals
Writing teen numerals is introduced when students can read teen numerals accurately and fluently. As in the procedure for reading teen numerals, regular teen numerals (14, 16, 17, 18, and 19) are introduced first, then irregular teen numerals (11, 12, 13, and 15). Irregular teens can be introduced about two days after regular teens. If students have no or little difficulty, a new irregular teen can be taught each day.

Format 5.6: Writing Teen Numerals Using Place Value Concepts has four parts. Part A, a preskill, contains a model-test procedure for teaching students to tell the component parts of a teen numeral: 14 equals a 1 for the teen (10) and a 4. Part B is a structured board presentation. The teacher refers to the place value chart on the board and writes the digits in the appropriate columns. Part C is a structured worksheet exercise in which the teacher prompts the students as

FIGURE 5.2   Teen numerals worksheet

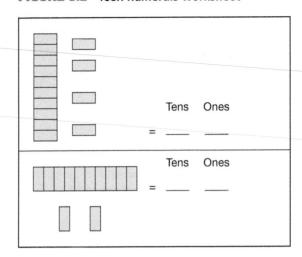

they write numerals. Part D is an independent dictation exercise in which the teacher says teen numbers and the students write them. If students are able to read the words fluently, the dictation exercise can be replaced with a written worksheet in which students write the numerals indicated by written words.

Practice in writing teen numerals is continued daily for several weeks to facilitate mastery. The place value chart is included in writing exercises only for the first several weeks and then dropped.

Practice and Review

The worksheet exercise in **Figure 5.2** contains pictures of a group of 10 objects and several single objects. The students are to fill in numerals in the tens and ones columns. This exercise, which reinforces the place value concept, can be introduced after students become proficient in writing dictated numerals.

Additional worksheets to reinforce place value may include pictures of groups of common objects, such as a bundle of pencils, a box of 10 crayons, and single objects. Finally, students can be presented with groups of manipulative objects—for instance, a bundle of 10 toothpicks with six single toothpicks, a bouquet of 10 flowers and individual flowers—or, if students know the value of dimes and pennies, a dime and nine pennies. Students write the teen numeral for each example.

Reading and Writing Tens Numerals

Reading Numerals 20–99   Reading numerals from 20 through 99 is introduced when students can read teen numerals accurately and fluently. Students also should be able to count by ones and skip count by tens to 100 (10, 20, 30, 40, 50, 60, 70, 80, 90, 100). **Format 5.7: Reading Tens Numerals Using Place Value Concepts** is designed to teach students to read numerals between 20 and 99.

Parts A and B utilize piles of 10 blocks to emphasize the place value concept for tens numbers. In Part A, the teacher draws several sets of 10 blocks. The teacher then has the students count by tens to figure out the total number of blocks and verifies the tens place value (five tens equal 50).

In Part B, the teacher uses a model-test procedure to facilitate memorization of the various place value facts for tens numbers. Some students can be expected to have difficulty with translating two tens, three tens, and five tens, since the names for these numbers are irregular. While four tens equal forty and eight tens equal eighty, two tens do not equal "twoty."

Parts C and D involve reading numerals in the place value chart. In Part C, the teacher instructs students to start reading in the tens column. She asks students to identify the numeral in the tens column and its value. Finally, the teacher asks students to read the entire numeral.

In Part D, students read numerals with no prompting from the teacher. If students have a lot of difficulty with Part D, they may have transitioned too quickly from Part C to Part D. The teacher should return to the structured board presentation and provide additional practice. When students demonstrate mastery, the teacher can continue to the less structured format in Part D. When students can correctly identify the numerals using a place value chart, the teacher should eliminate the prompt of the chart and have students read numerals without it. About a fourth of the examples in Part D should be teen numerals to provide the appropriate discrimination practice.

In Part E, the student is to select the numeral that represents a group of blocks. The worksheet shows diagrams with sets of 10 and individual blocks. The students determine the total by first counting the piles of 10. Then they figure out what number the groups of 10 equal (three tens equal 30). Finally, they count the single blocks, starting with the tens number they ended with (31, 32, 33, 34), which requires that students have mastered the preskill of counting from different numbers.

Writing Numerals 20–99 Writing numerals for 20 through 99 is introduced after students can read these numerals. The procedures for teaching students to write these numerals appear in Format 5.8: Writing Tens Numerals Using Place Value Concepts. Parts A and B are preskills. Part A teaches the student to say the composite parts of the numeral (97 is 90 and 7). Part B teaches the students to tell how many tens in a tens number (50 is five tens). Part C introduces writing numerals from 20 through 99 using a place value chart. The teacher says a number and has the students say its component parts. For example, the teacher asks how many tens in 84 and writes 8 in the tens column. The teacher then says, "Eighty equals 8 tens. Listen: 84 equals 80 and what else?" After the students say "4," the teacher writes the 4 in the ones column. Part D has the same steps as Part C, except the students write the numerals. Part E is a dictation exercise. The teacher dictates numbers, and the students write the appropriate numerals in the place value chart.

About a third of the examples in Part D should be teen numbers. As with reading numerals, if students make frequent mistakes with the less structured exercise, they have moved too quickly from the prompted to the unprompted task. The teacher should then return to the structured board presentation (Part C) before returning to Part D. When students respond confidently to several consecutive examples in Part D, the teacher then can present the dictation exercise in Part E.

Teachers working with struggling students can expect these students to have reversal problems, specifically with numerals ending in 1. For example, students may write 31 as 13, 71 as 17, or 21 as 12. To remedy these reversal problems, the teacher presents Parts B, C, and D from Format 5.6: Writing Teen Numerals Using Place Value Concepts for one or two lessons concurrently with Format 5.8: Writing Tens Numerals Using Place Value Concepts, excluding all tens numerals ending with 1 (21, 31, 41, 51). The purpose of excluding those tens numerals is to ensure that students master the easier numerals before reintroducing numerals that students have reversed.

After the students write teen and tens numerals without assistance for several days, the teacher can begin working directly on the reversal problem. She would return to Part E of Format 5.8: Writing Tens Numerals Using Place Value Concepts but include minimally different examples, focusing on the discrimination between tens and teen numerals like 13 and 31, 17 and 71. Part E may have to be reviewed daily for several weeks for students who are confused. Note that minimally different pairs are used only for struggling students, not for younger students learning the skill for the first time.

Reading and Writing Hundreds Numerals

Reading Numerals 100–999 Reading hundreds numerals is usually taught during second grade. Students should be able to read and write numerals for numbers below 100 prior to the introduction of numerals from 100 to 999. The teaching procedure is very similar to that used for teaching students to read tens numerals. The procedures for reading hundreds appear in Format 5.9: Reading Hundreds Numerals Using Place Value Concepts. In Part A, the

FIGURE 5.3 Worksheet exercise for reading hundreds numerals

Circle the correct numeral:			
three hundred sixty-two	320	362	360
four hundred eighty-six	48	468	486
two hundred seventy-one	217	270	271
nine hundred thirty-two	732	932	923

teacher introduces the hundreds column using a place value chart, explaining that numerals in that column tell how many hundreds. The teacher then leads students in reading numerals. He points to the digit farthest to the left, asks what column it is in, and then asks what number the digit represents: "What column does this numeral start in?. . . How many hundreds do we have?. . . What do five hundreds equal?" The teacher then does the same for each remaining digit in the numeral. "How many tens do we have?. . . What do four tens equal?. . . How many ones do we have?. . . What do eight ones equal?" A slight modification of the basic procedure is used for numerals with a 1 in the tens column. This modification involving a prompt appears at the end of Part A of Format 5.9. In Part B, the students read the numerals without that prompt.

Daily exercises in reading numerals are continued for several weeks. Thereafter, practice in reading numerals is incorporated into the formats for teaching computation strategies in which the first step always involves reading the problem. Practice also can be provided through worksheet exercises like that in **Figure 5.3** where students read numerical words and then circle the correct numeral. Obviously, such written exercises are appropriate only for students who can decode the words.

The sequence in which hundreds numerals are introduced is important. Hundreds numerals that do not include a zero in the tens column should be introduced first. Numerals with a zero in the tens column are difficult because the student says nothing for the zero. These more difficult examples would be introduced in Part A about a week after introducing the easier numerals. A slight modification to the format is required. In step 3 of Part A, the teacher would say, "We have zero tens, so we don't say anything when I point to the numeral zero." For example, for 608, students say "600" when the teacher points to 6, remain quiet when the teacher points to 0, and then say "8" when the teacher points to 8.

When presenting exercises to teach students to read hundreds numerals with a zero in the tens column, the teacher would include several sets of examples like these: 38, 308, 380; 42, 420, 402; 703, 730, 73. Note that each set contains three minimally different numerals: a tens numeral and two hundreds numerals. The hundreds numerals include the same digits that appear in the tens numeral plus a zero. In one of the hundreds numerals, the zero appears in the tens column, and in the other hundreds numeral, the zero appears in the ones column. Minimally different examples, such as those above, are introduced only after students have been systematically taught to read hundreds numerals with zeros. Students who correctly read minimally different sets of examples have demonstrated mastery of this skill.

Writing Numerals 100–999 Students usually have more difficulty learning to write hundreds numerals than to read them. The sequence in which hundreds numerals are introduced in writing tasks is the same sequence recommended for reading numerals. We recommend that hundreds numerals be introduced in two stages. During the first stage, hundreds numerals with a zero in the tens column should be excluded; 248 would be acceptable, but 208 would not be. Two hundred eight is troublesome because no tens number is heard. During the second stage, numerals with a zero in either the tens or the ones column may be used.

Format 5.10: Writing Hundreds Numerals Using Place Value Concepts includes the procedures for teaching students to write hundreds numerals without a zero in the tens column. In Part A, the teacher guides the students in writing numerals for numbers through 999. For example, for writing 486, the teacher asks students to say the first part of the number (400) and points out that since it's a hundreds number, they are to start writing the numeral in the hundreds column. The teacher asks how many hundreds and has the students write the numeral (4) in the hundreds column. The teacher then asks what column comes next (tens). This question is designed to remind students that they must always write a numeral in the tens column. The teacher has the students say the tens number (80), asks how many tens in that number (8), and has the students write that numeral (8) in the tens column. The ones column is completed next. The students write 6 in that column.

Part B is a supervised practice exercise in which numbers are written as words and students must write the numerals. Teachers working with students struggling with decoding may read the words to the students. Daily practice continues for several weeks. A place value chart is incorporated into exercises for the first several weeks and then should be eliminated.

Note that several tens numbers are included in Part B to reinforce the concept of proper column alignment. The first digit in a tens number is written in the tens column, while the first digit in a hundreds number is written in the hundreds column.

Hundreds numbers with a zero in the tens column are introduced in writing exercises after students can accurately write three-digit numerals without a zero in the tens column. For numbers with a zero in the tens or ones column, step 3 in Part A of Format 5.10 must be modified. For example, after the students indicate that they do not hear a tens number, the teacher asks, "So what do we write in the tens column?" "Zero." "Write a zero in the tens column." The teacher then proceeds to step 4.

Examples would be the same as for exercises focusing on reading numerals with a zero in the tens column; minimally different sets such as 902, 92, 920; 48, 480, 408; and 702, 72, 720 should be used. Note that for the tens numbers, once students identify the tens column as the column they start writing in (step 2), they can simply write the numeral.

Reading and Writing Thousands Numerals

Reading Numerals 1,000–9,999 Thousands numerals are usually introduced during third grade. Format 5.11: Reading Thousands Numerals Using Place Value Concepts introducing students to reading thousands numerals is fairly simple. Students are taught that the numeral in front of the comma tells how many thousands. They read that numeral, say "thousand" for the comma, and then read the rest of the numeral. For example, in reading 3,286, students say "3," then "thousand" for the comma, and finally "286."

Students should practice reading 8 to 10 numerals in this format. The sequence in which thousands numerals are introduced should be carefully designed. We recommend that thousands numerals be introduced in this sequence:

1. Numerals between 1,000 and 9,999 without zeros in the tens or hundreds column
2. Numerals between 1,000 and 9,999 that have zeros in the tens and/or hundreds column
3. Numerals between 10,000 and 99,999
4. Numerals between 100,000 and 999,999

We recommend not including numerals with zeros in the tens or hundreds column initially, since students may mistakenly develop the misrule that thousands have something to do with the number of zeros in a numeral rather than the number of places. When numerals with zeros are introduced, the teacher should pay careful attention to example selection. A fourth of the numerals should have a zero in the hundreds and a zero in the tens columns, a fourth should have a zero in just the hundreds column, another fourth should have a zero in just the tens column, and a final fourth should have no zeros at all. A sample set of examples might include 2,000, 2,058, 2,508, 2,815; 7,002, 7,020, 7,200, 7,248; and 9,040, 9,400, 9,004, 9,246.

During fourth grade, students should be introduced to thousands numerals between 1,000 and 9,999 that do not have a comma because some reference materials that students encounter will have thousands numerals written without a comma. In presenting thousands numerals without a comma, the teacher tells the students that when a numeral has four digits, it is a thousands numeral and then presents a list that includes a mix of thousands and hundreds numerals.

Writing Numerals 1,000–9,999 We recommend teaching writing thousands in the same sequence as identified previously for teaching reading thousands. Because teaching writing thousands is very similar to teaching writing hundreds, we do not include a separate format. Please see Format 5.10: Writing Hundreds Numerals Using Place Value Concepts for those teaching procedures. The only change needed to that format is adding a thousands column in the place value chart and adjusting examples accordingly. Note that initially, all numerals in the teaching examples would have a digit other than zero in the hundreds and tens columns. Subsequently, numerals with a zero in the hundreds column and/or the tens column would be introduced.

Numerals with a zero in the hundreds column are difficult because students may omit the zero. Students often will write the numeral four thousand eighty-five as the numbers they hear: four thousand, eighty, and five (4, 85). The teaching procedure for writing numerals must be designed to reinforce the place value concept of writing digits in each of the thousands, hundreds, tens, and ones columns. Writing numerals with a zero in the hundreds or tens column may be introduced about a week after the easier examples are taught. Just as with reading thousands numerals, sets of minimally different examples should be presented in numeral writing exercises: 4,028, 4,208, 4,218, 4,280; 6,200, 6,002, 6,020, 6,224; 5,090, 5,900, 5,009, 5,994.

Practice in writing thousands numerals should be continued daily for several weeks. Practice can be provided through worksheet exercises similar to those in Figure 5.3 for reading hundreds. Students read number words and then write the appropriate numerals.

Reading and Writing Millions Numerals

Millions numerals are usually taught during late fourth grade and early fifth grade. Reading millions can be taught using a procedure similar to that used for reading thousands. The teacher instructs students to identify millions by examining the number of commas in the numeral. Students are taught that when two commas appear, the numerals in front of the first comma signify millions, while the numerals in front of the second comma signify thousands. The teacher initially prompts students by having them say the number a part at a time. See **Summary Box 5.1**.

Example selection for reading millions numerals should include a mix of millions numerals and thousands numerals so that the students receive practice in discriminating what to do when there are two commas instead one comma. Writing millions numerals is taught by using a blank line for each digit in the number and placing the two commas correctly for students:

_____, _____ _____ _____, _____ _____ _____

The teacher leads the students through writing the numerals, focusing on each comma as she did when teaching reading millions. "Listen. 5 million, 203 thousand, 450. How many million?. . . Write 5 in the millions space before the millions comma. . . 5 million, 203 thousand. How many thousands?. . . Write 203 in the spaces before the thousands comma . . . Listen. 5 million, 203 thousand, 450. Write the rest of the numeral."

Numerals with zeros in either the hundred thousands, the ten thousands, or the thousands, such as 3,064,800; 2,005,000; or 8,000,124; are especially difficult for students to write. These numerals are introduced in writing exercises only after the students can write easier numerals and can read millions numerals. Again, as with thousands numerals, minimally different sets should be used (6,024,000; 6,204,000; 6,024; 6,240,000; 6,240). The sets should include a

---

SUMMARY BOX 5.1

Symbol Identification: Reading Millions

1. Teacher asks students to identify how many commas are in the numeral.
2. Teacher asks what the numeral in front of the first comma tells about and has students identify that numeral.
3. Teacher asks what the numerals in front of the second comma tell about and has students identify that numeral.
4. Teacher asks students to identify the entire numeral.

mixture of millions and thousands numerals. Multiple practice opportunities to read and write millions numerals are necessary in order for students to develop mastery. This practice should be provided through oral and worksheet exercises over a period of several months.

Expanded Notation

Expanded notation involves rewriting a numeral as an addition problem composed of the numerals that each digit represents. For example, the numeral 3,428 is rewritten as 3,000 + 400 + 20 + 8, or vertically as:

$$
\begin{array}{r}
3{,}000 \\
400 \\
20 \\
+\quad 8 \\
\hline
\end{array}
$$

The sequence in which expanded notation problems are introduced parallels the sequence in which students are taught to read and write numerals: teens, hundreds, thousands, then millions.

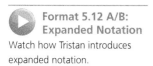

Format 5.12 A/B: Expanded Notation
Watch how Tristan introduces expanded notation.

The initial teaching procedure for expanded notation is included in Part A of Format 5.12: Expanded Notation. The teacher has students identify the number they hear in each place. For example, the teacher asks, "Do you hear a hundreds number in 362? What hundreds number? Do you hear a tens number in 362? What tens number? Do you hear a ones number in 362? What ones number?" After students can accurately identify the values for a complex number, they should have relatively little trouble saying a number as an addition problem (362 = 300 + 60 + 2), which is the focus of Part B. In Part C, students practice writing the numerals as addition problems. Finally, in Part D, students are given independent worksheet problems for which they apply their expanded notation skills.

Column Alignment

Column alignment involves writing a series of numerals so that the appropriate digits are vertically aligned. Column alignment is important because it is a prerequisite for advanced computation and for solving word problems in which the numerals do not appear in a column. For example, "Pearl has 4,037 marbles. She gives 382 marbles to her younger brother. How many does she have left?" Column alignment exercises also test students' understanding of place value. For example, students who try to solve the word problem about Pearl's marbles by writing the problem as:

$$
\begin{array}{r}
4{,}037 \\
-\quad 382 \\
\hline
\end{array}
$$

not only will arrive at the wrong answer but also will have demonstrated that they do not have a clear understanding of place value.

Column alignment tasks usually involve numerals with different numbers of digits written as horizontal problems. The complexity of these column alignment tasks increases as the number of digits increases. Initially, exercises should involve adding tens numbers and ones numbers (32 + 5 + 14); later, hundreds, tens, and ones (142 + 8 + 34); then thousands, hundreds, tens, and ones (3,042 + 6 + 134 + 28).

The strategy we recommend to teach column alignment involves teaching students to rearrange the order of the numerals. The numeral with the most digits is written first, and the other numerals are written underneath. The purpose of writing the largest numeral first is to establish the columns. Format 5.13: Teaching Column Alignment involves a simple model-test procedure in a structured worksheet format. The teacher introduces students to the rule about writing the numeral with the most digits first and then guides the students in determining which column to begin writing the other numerals. The structured worksheet exercise is presented for several lessons. Thereafter, practice on about five problems daily should be given on independent worksheets for several weeks.

APPLY WHAT YOU LEARNED

 Click on the √ to answer the questions online.

1. The numerals below are representative of various types. Tell the type each numeral illustrates. List the order in which the types would be introduced.

    836; 13; 18; 305; 64; 5,024; 5,321

2. Two teachers are introducing reading hundreds numerals. Below are the examples each included in their lessons. Which set is more appropriate? Tell why.

    Teacher A: 306, 285, 532, 683, 504

    Teacher B: 724, 836, 564, 832, 138

3. Explain the importance of introducing place value charts prior to introducing manipulatives when teaching place value concepts.

4. Construct a set of six to eight examples to be used in presenting Format 5.11: Reading Thousands Numerals Using Place Value Concepts, Part B, including zeros in the hundreds and/or tens column.

5. The teacher is presenting a task in which the numerals 4, 2, and 5 appear. When the teacher points to 4 and asks, "What numeral?" a student says, "5." What is the correction procedure?

6. A student writes a 7 in an empty box over a group of five lines. Tell two possible causes of this error. How could you determine the exact cause? Describe the correction procedure.

7. During a test of writing numerals, a student writes a 2 as a 5. What should the teacher do?

8. Below is a worksheet item done independently by a student. The item required the student to write the appropriate number of lines to represent a numeral. Note the errors made by the student and describe the probable cause. Describe the correction procedure.

2	5	6	4	3	7
||	||||	||||||	|||||	|||	|||||||

9. When reading numerals, a student identifies 71 as 17. What is the correction procedure?

10. During the supervised practice for writing hundreds numerals, students make frequent errors (some students write 38 for three hundred eight). How should the teacher respond to these errors?

Format 5.1
INTRODUCING NEW NUMERALS   (See Video)

TEACHER	STUDENTS
Note: This format is used with each new symbol. In this example, we assume that the numerals 1, 4, 6, and 2 have been introduced and that the numeral 7 is being introduced. *(Write the following numerals on the board.)*	

7   2

4   6   7

7   1

TEACHER	STUDENTS
(Model and test. Point to 7.)	
1. **This is a seven. What is this?** *(Touch 7.)*	7
(Discrimination practice.)	
2. **When I touch it, tell me what it is.** *(Point to 2, pause a second.)* **What numeral?** *(Touch 2.)*	2
(Repeat step 3 with these numerals: 7, 1, 6, 1, 7, 2, 1, 6, 7, etc.)	
3. *(Individual turns: Ask individual students to identify several numerals.)*	

Format 5.2
EQUATION WRITING

TEACHER	STUDENTS
(Give students paper and pencil.)	
1. **You are going to write an equation. First you'll say it. Listen: Six plus two equals how many? Listen again. Six plus two equals how many? Say that.**	Six plus two equals how many?
To correct: Respond with students until they can say the statement at the normal rate of speech.	
2. **Now we'll say it the slow way. Every time I clap, we'll say a part of the statement.** *(Respond with the students.)* **Get ready.** *(Clap.)* **Six**	Six
(Pause 2 seconds; clap.) **plus**	plus
(Pause 2 seconds; clap.) **two**	two
(Pause 2 seconds; clap.) **equals**	equals
(Pause 2 seconds; clap.) **how many?**	how many?
(Repeat step 2 until students appear able to respond on their own.)	
3. **Now I'll clap and you say the statement by yourselves.**	Six plus two equals how many?
(Pause.) **Get ready.** *(Clap at 2-second intervals.)*	
4. **Now write the problem.**	Students write 6 + 2 = □
5. *(Repeat steps 1–5 with three more equations, e.g., 8 − 3 = □; 4 + 5 = □; 7 − 2 = □.)*	

Format 5.3
IDENTIFYING A SYMBOL AND THEN DRAWING LINES

TEACHER	STUDENTS
1. **Everybody touch the first numeral on your worksheet.** *(Hold up worksheet and point to 4.)*	
What is it?	4

4	6	▣	2

continued

Format 5.3 *(continued)*
IDENTIFYING A SYMBOL AND THEN DRAWING LINES

TEACHER	STUDENTS
A 4 tells you to make four lines. What does a 4 tell you to do?	Make 4 lines.
Each time I clap, draw a line and count.	1, 2, 3, 4
(Signal by clapping once each 2 seconds.)	
How many did you end up with?	4
Yes, 4.	
2. Touch the next symbol. What is it?	6
A 6 tells you to make six lines. What does a 6 tell you to do?	Make 6 lines.
Each time I clap, draw a line and count.	1, 2, 3, 4, 5, 6
(Signal by clapping once each two seconds.)	
How many did you end up with?	6
Yes, 6.	
3. Touch the next symbol. What is it?	box
Does a box tell you to draw lines? No. A box does not tell you to draw lines.	
Does a box tell you to draw lines?	no
So are you going to draw lines?	no
4. Touch the next symbol. What is it?	2
What does 2 tell you to do?	Make two lines.
Do it.	
Get ready to count the lines. Get ready. *(Signal by clapping once each 2 seconds.)*	1, 2
How many did you end up with?	2
(On subsequent days use step 4 wording to provide additional examples.)	

Format 5.4
WRITING A NUMERAL FOR A SET OF OBJECTS   (See Video)

TEACHER	STUDENTS

(Give students a worksheet similar to the one above.)

TEACHER	STUDENTS
1. Everybody, here's a rule: The objects under a box tell what numeral goes in the box. Get ready to count the objects under this box. *(Point to the first set of objects on the worksheet and pause while the students point to the first line.)* Count as I clap. Get ready. *(Clap each second.)*	1, 2, 3
How many objects are under this box?	3
So what numeral are you going to write in the box?	3
Write that numeral.	
2. *(Repeat step 1 for additional examples.)*	

Format 5.5
READING TEEN NUMERALS USING PLACE VALUE CONCEPTS

TEACHER	STUDENTS
Part A: Structured Board Presentation	

(Write the following chart on the board.)

tens	ones
1	4
1	6
1	7
1	8
1	9

1. *(Point to the tens column.)* This is the tens column. *(Point to the ones column.)* This is the ones column.

2. These numerals all start with one ten. When we have *one* ten in the tens column, we say *teen*. Listen to me read the numerals. *(Point to 14)* 14 *(Point to 16)* 16 *(Point to 17)* 17 *(Point to 18)* 18 *(Point to 19)* 19

3. Your turn to read these numerals. *(Point to numerals in random order as students read.)*

4. *(Give individual turns to several students to read two numerals.)*

Part B: Less Structured Board Presentation

1. *(Write 14 on the board. Point to 14.)* What numeral?   14

2. *(Repeat step 1 with 19, 17, 18, 16.)*

Part C: Worksheet

(Give students worksheets with problems such as these.)

A.   B.

12 14 4 10   8 18 10 17

continued

Format 5.5 *(continued)*
READING TEEN NUMERALS USING PLACE VALUE CONCEPTS

TEACHER	STUDENTS
1. Look at picture A. The big pile has 10 blocks in it. The small pile has 4 blocks in it. I'll count: 10 *(pause)*, 11, 12, 13, 14. How many blocks?	14
2. There are 14 blocks. Put a circle around the numeral 14. *(Check student work.)*	
3. Look at picture B. The big pile has 10 blocks in it. Start with 10 and count. Get ready.	10, 11, 12, 13, 14, 15, 16, 17
4. How many blocks are there?	17
5. Circle the numeral 17.	
(Repeat steps 4–6 with other examples.)	

Format 5.6
WRITING TEEN NUMERALS USING PLACE VALUE CONCEPTS

TEACHER	STUDENTS
Part A: Preskill—Components of Teen Numbers	
1. You're going to write teen numerals. Remember, the ending "teen" tells you the numeral has one ten in the tens column.	I write a 1 for the teen and a 9.
Listen: 16. Write a 1 for the teen and then a 6. Listen: 19. What do I write for 19	I write a 1 for the teen and a 4.
Listen: 14. What do I write for 14?	
2. Your turn. 14. What do you write? *(Monitor students as they write.)*	A 1 for the teen and a 4.
3. *(Repeat step 2 with 16, 19, 17, 18.)*	
4. *(Give individual turns to several students on step 3.)*	
Part B: Structured Board Presentation	
1. *(Write the following place value chart on the board.)*	

tens	ones

2. *(Point to the tens column.)* This is where we write a 1 for the ten.	
Remember, for one ten we say "teen." What do we say for one ten?	Teen
3. What do I write for 14? *(Write the numeral on the chart.)*	A 1 for the teen and a 4.
4. *(Repeat step 3 with 17, 19, 16, 18.)*	
5. *(Call on students.)* Read each numeral on the chart. *(Point as students read.)*	

Part C: Structured Worksheet—Dictation

(Give students a worksheet similar to the one below.)

	tens	ones
a.		
b.		
c.		
d.		

TEACHER	STUDENTS
1. Touch the space for problem a. You're going to write 14. What number?	14
2. What do you write for 14?	A 1 for the teen and a 4.
3. Write 14. *(Monitor students as they write.)* Read the numeral you just wrote.	14
4. *(Repeat steps 1–3 for 16, 19, 14, 17, 18.)*	
Part D: Less Structured Worksheet—Dictation	
1. *(Give students a worksheet with a place value chart.)* You're going to write 14 on the first line. What are you going to write? Write 14.	14
2. *(Repeat step 1 with 16, 18, 19, 17.)*	

Format 5.7
READING TENS NUMERALS USING PLACE VALUE CONCEPTS

TEACHER	STUDENTS
Part A: Preskill-Counting by tens	
(Show students a diagram like the following.)	
1. Each pile has 10 blocks. How many blocks in each pile?	10
2. Count by 10 each time I touch a pile. *(Touch piles.)*	10, 20, 30, 40, 50
3. How many blocks in all?	50
Right, five tens equal 50.	
(Repeat steps 2 and 3 with two tens and four tens.)	
Part B: Preskill-Tens Facts	
1. *(Erase board from Part A.)* Let's practice with groups of 10. Listen. Three tens equal 30. What do three tens equal?	30
2. What do two tens equal?	20
(Repeat with five tens, three tens, six tens, eight tens, and four tens until students can respond correctly to all examples.)	
3. *(Present individual turns on step 2.)*	
Part C: Structured Board Presentation	
(Write the following place value chart on the board.)	

tens	ones
4	6

continued

Format 5.7 *(continued)*
READING TENS NUMERALS USING PLACE VALUE CONCEPTS

TEACHER	STUDENTS
1. *(Point to tens column.)* What column?	tens column
(Point to ones column.) What column?	ones column
2. How many tens?	4
What do four tens equal?	40
3. How many ones?	6
What is 40 and 6?	46
So what does the whole numeral say?	46
(Repeat steps 2 and 3 with 52, 38, 93, 81.)	

Part D: Less Structured Board Presentation

(Write the following place value chart on the board.)

tens	ones
7	2

1. What does this whole numeral say?	72
2. *(Repeat step 1 with 95, 20, 16, 31, 47, 50, 12.)*	
3. *(Give individual turns to several students.)*	

Part E: Less Structured Worksheet

43   30   40   34

1. *(Hold up student worksheet.)* Let's find out how many blocks are in this picture. How many piles of tens are there?	3
2. What do three tens equal?	30
3. But we're not done. *(Point to four remaining blocks.)* We have to count these blocks. *(Point to tens group.)* We have 30 blocks here. Start counting at 30 then touch these blocks as we count. *(Count 30, 31, 32, 33, 34.)*	30, 31, 32, 33, 34
4. How many blocks in the picture?	34
Put a circle around the numeral 34.	
5. *(Provide students with similar problems on worksheets for additional practice.)*	

Format 5.8
WRITING TENS NUMERALS USING PLACE VALUE CONCEPTS

TEACHER	STUDENTS
Part A: Preskill—Expanded Notation	
1. Say this number: 84.	84
2. Eighty-four equals 80 and 4. What does 84 equal?	80 and 4
What's the first part of 84?	80
3. Eighty-four equals 80 and what else?	4
4. *(Repeat steps 1–3 with 72, 95, 88, 43.)*	
Part B: Preskill—Tens Facts	
1. Twenty has two tens. How many tens in 20?	2
2. How many tens in 40?	4
3. *(Repeat step 3 with 80, 30, 60, 20, 50.)*	
4. *(Give individual turns to several students.)*	
Part C: Structured Board Presentation	
(Write the following place value chart on the board.)	

tens	ones

TEACHER	STUDENTS
1. I want to write some big numerals. When we write big numerals, we write the tens first. Then we write the ones. What do we write first?	the tens
What do we write next?	the ones
2. Listen: 84. What is the first part of 84?	80
3. How many tens in 80?	8
So I write 8 in the tens column. *(Write 8 in the tens column.)*	
Eighty equals eight tens.	
4. Listen: Eighty-four equals 80 and what else?	4
So I write 4 in the ones column. *(Write 4 in the ones column.)*	
5. What numeral did I just write?	84
6. How many tens in 84?	8
How many ones in 84?	4
7. *(Repeat steps 2–6 with several examples.)*	
Part D: Structured Worksheet Presentation	
(Give students the following place value chart.)	

	tens	ones
a.		
b.		
c.		
d.		
e.		
f.		

TEACHER	STUDENTS
1. Touch a. Next to a, you are going to write 79.	79
What are you going to write?	

continued

Format 5.8 *(continued)*
WRITING TENS NUMERALS USING PLACEVALUE CONCEPTS

TEACHER	STUDENTS
2. What is the first part of 79?	70
How many tens in 70?	7
Write 7 in the tens column.	
3. Seventy-nine equals 70 and what else?	9
Write 9 in the ones column.	
4. What numeral did you write?	79
5. How many tens in 79?	7
6. How many ones in 79?	9
7. *(Repeat steps 1–6 with 45, 19, 84, 76, and 12.)*	
Part E: Less Structured Worksheet—Dictation	
(Have students write a–f on a piece of paper similar to below.)	
a. _____ b. _____ c. _____ d. _____ e. _____ f. _____	
1. You're going to write a numeral on each line.	
2. Touch line a.	
3. You're going to write 49. What are you going to write?	49
4. Write 49.	Students write 49.
5. *(Repeat steps 2–4 with 73, 20, 99, 14, 51, 42, 61, 17.)*	

Format 5.9
READING HUNDREDS NUMERALS USING PLACE VALUE

TEACHER	STUDENTS
Part A: Structured Board Presentation	
(Show students a diagram like the following.)	
hundreds | tens | ones 5 | 4 | 8	
(Point to appropriate column as you say the following.)	
1. This is the hundreds column.	
This is the tens column.	
This is the ones column.	
Tell me the names of the columns. *(Point to the columns, starting with hundreds; repeat until students are firm.)*	hundreds, tens, ones

TEACHER	STUDENTS
2. The first thing we do when we read a numeral is identify the column the numeral starts in. *(Point to 5 in 548.)*	
What column does this numeral start in?	hundreds
How many hundreds do we have?	5
What do five hundreds equal?	500
3. *(Point to 4.)* What column is this?	tens
How many tens do we have?	4
What do four tens equal?	40
4. *(Point to 8.)* What column is this?	ones
How many ones do we have?	8
What do we say?	8
5. Let's read the whole numeral. When I touch each numeral, you tell me what it says.	
(Point to 5, pause a second, touch 5.)	500
(Point to 4, pause a second, touch 4.)	40
(Point to 8, pause a second, touch 8.)	8
6. Say the whole numeral.	548
7. *(Repeat steps 2–6 with 697, 351, 874, 932, all written in place value charts.)*	
Note: When presenting examples with a 1 in the tens column, present the following steps instead of steps 3, 4, and 5 in the format.	
The following example shows how to teach the number 514.	
What column is this?	tens
How many tens do we have?	1
How many ones do we have?	4
We have one 10 and four ones, so what do we say?	14
Let's read the whole numeral. *(Point to 5.)* What do we say for this?	500
(Point to 14.) What do we say for these?	14
Say the whole numeral.	514

Part B: Less Structured Board Presentation

1. *(Write the following chart on the board.)*

hundreds	tens	ones
4	4	6

2. Now we are going to read the numerals without saying the parts first.

This time when I point, you are going to tell me the whole numeral. *(Point to 446 and then pause 2–3 seconds.)* — 446

3. *(Repeat step 2 with 249, 713, 321, 81, 720, 740.)*

4. *(Give individual turns to several students.)*

Format 5.10
WRITING HUNDREDS NUMERALS USING PLACE VALUE CONCEPTS

TEACHER	STUDENTS
Part A: Structured Worksheet Presentation—Dictation	
(Give students a worksheet with a place value chart as illustrated.)	

	hundreds	tens	ones
a.			
b.			
c.			
d.			
e.			

TEACHER	STUDENTS
1. You are going to write hundreds numerals. Touch the hundreds column. Touch the tens column. Touch the ones column. *(Monitor responses.)*	
2. What's the first part of 648?	600
So what column do you start writing in?	hundreds
How many hundreds in 600?	6
Write 6 in the hundreds column.	
3. What column comes next?	tens
Do you hear a tens number in 648?	yes
How many tens?	4
Write 4 in the tens column.	
4. What column comes next?	ones
Do you hear a ones number in 648?	yes
How many ones?	8
Write 8 in the ones column.	
5. We finished. How many hundreds in 648?	6
How many tens in 648?	4
How many ones in 648?	8
Read the numeral you wrote.	648
6. *(Repeat steps 2–5 with 326, 463, 825, 253, 866.)*	

TEACHER	STUDENTS

Part B: Supervised Practice

(Give students a worksheet like the one below.)

	hundreds	tens	ones
a. two hundred sixty-one			
b. four hundred eighteen			
c. eight			
d. nine hundred sixty-two			
e. forty-eight			
f. four hundred eighty			
g. twelve			
h. nine hundred seven			
i. forty-one			
j. three hundred ninety-seven			

TEACHER	STUDENTS
1. The instructions tell you to write the numerals.	
2. Item a. Read the words.	
3. Write the numeral. *(Monitor responses.)*	two hundred sixty-one
4. *(Repeat steps 2 and 3 with a few examples and then have them complete the rest of the worksheet independently.)*	

Format 5.11
READING THOUSANDS NUMERALS USING PLACE VALUE CONCEPTS

TEACHER	STUDENTS
Part A: Structured Board Presentation	
1. When a big number has one comma, the comma tells about thousands. Here's the rule: The numeral in front of the comma tells how many thousands. What does the numeral in front of the comma tell?	how many thousands
2. *(Write 6,781 on the board.)* What numeral comes in front of the comma?	6
So what is the first part of the numeral?	6 thousand
3. *(Point to 781.)* Get ready to read the rest of the numeral.	781
4. Now you are going to read the whole numeral. *(Point to 6, then comma, then 781.)*	6,781
5. *(Repeat steps 2–4 with these numerals: 2,145; 3,150; 5,820; 6,423.)*	
6. *(Give individual turns to several students.)*	
Part B: Less Structured Board Presentation	
1. *(Write 3,820 on the board.)* Read this numeral.	3,820
To correct: Repeat steps 2–4 from Part A.	
2. *(Repeat step 1 with 9,270; 3,174; 3,271; 9,563; 4,812.)*	
3. *(Give individual turns to several students.)*	

Format 5.12
EXPANDED NOTATION
(See Video A/B)

TEACHER	STUDENTS
▶	
Part A: Expanded Notation	
1. Count by hundreds to 900. Get ready, count.	100, 200, 300, 400, 500, 600, 700, 800, 900
Now count by tens to 90. Get ready, count.	10, 20, 30, 40, 50, 60, 70, 80, 90
2. Listen to this number: 428. Do you hear hundreds in 428?	Yes
What hundreds number?	400
3. Listen again: 428. Do you hear a tens number in 428?	Yes
What tens number?	20
4. Listen again: 428. Do you hear a ones number in 428?	Yes
What ones number?	8
5. $428 = 400 + 20 + 8$. Say it with me. $428 = 400 + 20 + 8$	$428 = 400 + 20 + 8$
Say it by yourselves.	$428 = 400 + 20 + 8$
6. *(Repeat steps 2-5 with 362, 624, and 139.)*	
7. *(Give individual turns on steps 2–5 to several students.)*	
Part B: Structured Board Presentation	
1. Listen to this number: 624. Say the number.	624
2. Now listen to me say 624 as an addition problem: $600 + 20 + 4$	
3. Your turn. Say 624 as an addition problem.	$600 + 20 + 4$
4. *(Repeat step 3 with 528, 55, 871, 29, and 314.)*	
Part C: Structured Worksheet	
1. Listen. Say 472 as an addition problem.	$400 + 70 + 2$
I'll write 472 as an addition problem. *(Write on the board $400 + 70 + 2$.)*	
2. Listen. Say 528 as an addition problem.	$500 + 20 + 8$
Write 528 as an addition problem. *(Monitor student responses.)*	
3. *(Repeat step 2 with 94, 427, 35, 53, and 266.)*	
Part D: Supervised Practice	
(Give the students worksheets with problems like the following. Have students write each numeral on the worksheet as an addition problem. Monitor students' responses.)	
a. 624 = _____ + _____ + _____	
b. 386 = _____ + _____ + _____	

Format 5.13
COLUMN ALIGNMENT

TEACHER	STUDENTS
(Give students the following worksheet.)	

a. 42 + 361 + 9   361
            42
          + 9	

b. 7 + 604 + 32	
1. Touch problem a. I'll read it. 42 + 361 + 9. Problem a has been rewritten in a column. When we write column problems we write the largest numeral first, followed by the rest of the numerals. Touch the column problem. *(Check.)* The largest numeral is on top. What is that numeral?	361
Then the next largest numeral is written below. What numeral is that?	42
The smallest numeral is on the bottom. What is the smallest numeral?	9
2. Touch problem b. *(Check.)* Read the problem.	7 + 604 + 32
3. You are going to write the numerals in a column. You will write the largest numeral first. What is the largest numeral?	604
Write it and then cross out 604 in the row problem. *(Check.)*	
4. What is the next largest numeral?	32
What column does 32 start in?	tens
Write 32 and cross it out in the row problem. *(Check.)*	
5. Now get ready to write the smallest numeral. What is the smallest numeral?	7
What column will you start writing in?	ones
Write 7 and cross it out in the row problem. *(Check.)*	
6. Have you crossed out all the numerals in the row problem?	yes
What kind of problem is this?	addition
Write in the sign. You are done writing the problem. Now work it. *(Check.)*	
7. *(Repeat steps 2–6 with four more problems.)*	

Basic Facts

LEARNING OUTCOMES

6.1 Discuss the sequencing guidelines for introducing fact series.

6.2 Discuss the role that relationship activities play in teaching math facts to students.

6.3 Describe two types of relationship activities and how they promote efficient math fact mastery.

6.4 Discuss the components essential for promoting fact mastery.

6.5 Outline the procedures for setting up a math facts mastery program.

There are 380 basic arithmetic facts: 100 addition, 90 subtraction, 100 multiplication, and 90 division. Basic addition facts include all possible combinations in which each of the **addends** is a whole number under 10. Basic subtraction facts include all possible combinations in which the **subtrahend** and the **difference** (a and b in $c - a = b$) are one-digit numbers. **Tables 6.1** and **6.2** include all the basic addition and subtraction facts.

TABLE 6.1 Basic Addition Facts

	Addends									
Addends	**0**	**1**	**2**	**3**	**4**	**5**	**6**	**7**	**8**	**9**
0+	0	1	2	3	4	5	6	7	8	9
1+	1	2	3	4	5	6	7	8	9	10
2+	2	3	4	5	6	7	8	9	10	11
3+	3	4	5	6	7	8	9	10	11	12
4+	4	5	6	7	8	9	10	11	12	13
5+	5	6	7	8	9	10	11	12	13	14
6+	6	7	8	9	10	11	12	13	14	15
7+	7	8	9	10	11	12	13	14	15	16
8+	8	9	10	11	12	13	14	15	16	17
9+	9	10	11	12	13	14	15	16	17	18

Note: Problems are formed by a numeral (addend) from the column on the left, a numeral (addend) from the row on top, and their intersection; the numerals for 7 + 6 = 13 are boxed.

TABLE 6.2 Basic Subtraction Facts

	Subtrahends									
Minuends	0	1	2	3	4	5	6	7	8	9
1−	1	0								
2−	2	1	0							
3−	3	2	1	0						
4−	4	3	2	1	0					
5−	5	4	3	2	1	0				
6−	6	5	4	3	2	1	0			
7−	7	6	5	4	3	2	1	0		
8−	8	7	6	5	4	3	2	1	0	
9−	9	8	7	6	5	4	3	2	1	0
10−		9	8	7	6	5	4	3	2	1
11−			9	8	7	6	5	4	3	2
12−				9	8	7	6	5	4	3
13−					9	8	7	6	5	4
14−						9	8	7	6	5
15−							9	8	7	6
16−								9	8	7
17−									9	8
18−										9

Note: Problems are formed by a numeral (**minuend**) from the column on the left, followed by a numeral (subtrahend) from the top row, and, finally, the difference, which is the intersection; the numerals for 13 − 7 = 6 are boxed.

TABLE 6.3 Basic Multiplication/Division Facts

÷/×	0	1	2	3	4	5	6	7	8	9
0	0	0	0	0	0	0	0	0	0	0
1	0	1	2	3	4	5	6	7	8	9
2	0	2	4	6	8	10	12	14	16	18
3	0	3	6	9	12	15	18	21	24	27
4	0	4	8	12	16	20	24	28	32	36
5	0	5	10	15	20	25	30	35	40	45
6	0	6	12	18	24	30	36	42	48	54
7	0	7	14	21	28	35	42	49	56	63
8	0	8	16	24	32	40	48	56	64	72
9	0	9	18	27	36	45	54	63	72	81

Note: Problems are formed by a numeral from the column on the left, a numeral from the top row, and their intersection; the row and column for the numerals 6 and 7 intersect at 42; these boxed numerals form 6 × 7 = 42 and 42 ÷ 6 = 7.

Basic multiplication facts include all possible combinations in which each of the **factors** is a single-digit number (in $a \times b = c$, a and b are single digits). Basic division facts include all possible combinations in which the **divisor** and **quotient** are single-digit numbers (in $c \div a = b$, a and b are single-digit numbers and a does not equal 0). **Table 6.3** includes all basic multiplication and division facts.

SKILL HIERARCHY

Basic facts should be introduced in a carefully planned sequence. New sets of facts should be introduced systematically to avoid potential confusion. **Figures 6.1, 6.2, 6.3,** and **6.4** suggest

FIGURE 6.1 Sequence of addition facts

Plus-one format is Format 6.1.
Series-saying format is Format 6.2.
Three-number format is Format 6.3.

Sets of New Facts	Relationship Formats
A. 2 + 1, 3 + 1, 4 + 1, 5 + 1	Plus-one, series saying
B. 6 + 1, 7 + 1, 8 + 1, 9 + 1	Plus-one, series saying
C. 2 + 2, 3 + 2, 4 + 2, 5 + 2	Series saying
D. 6 + 2, 7 + 2, 8 + 2, 9 + 2	Series saying
E. 3 + 3, 4 + 4, 5 + 5, 6 + 6	Series saying
F. 2 + 3, 3 + 3, 4 + 3, 5 + 3	Series saying
G. 6 + 3, 7 + 3, 8 + 3, 9 + 3	Series saying
H. 1 + 2, 1 + 3, 1 + 4, 1 + 5	Three numbers—addition (1, 2, 3) (1, 3, 4) (1, 4, 5) (1, 5, 6)
I. 1 + 6, 1 + 7, 1 + 8, 1 + 9	Three numbers—addition (1, 6, 7) (1, 7, 8) (1, 8, 9) (1, 9, 10)
J. 2 + 4, 2 + 5, 2 + 6	Three numbers—addition (2, 3, 5) (2, 4, 6) (2, 5, 7) (2, 6, 8)
K. 2 + 7, 2 + 8, 2 + 9	Three numbers—addition (2, 7, 9) (2, 8, 10) (2, 9, 11)
L. 3 + 4, 3 + 5, 3 + 6	Three numbers—addition (3, 4, 7) (3, 5, 8) (3, 6, 9)
M. 3 + 7, 3 + 8, 3 + 9	Three numbers—addition (3, 7, 10) (3, 8, 11) (3, 9, 12)
N. 7 + 7, 8 + 8, 9 + 9, 10 + 10	Series saying
O. 1 + 0, 2 + 0, 3 + 0...9 + 0	Series saying
P. 0 + 1, 0 + 2, 0 + 3...0 + 9	Three numbers—addition (1, 0, 1) (2, 0, 2)
Q. 5 + 4, 6 + 4, 7 + 4	Series saying
R. 7 + 6, 8 + 6, 9 + 6	Series saying
S. 4 + 5, 4 + 6, 4 + 7	Three numbers—addition (4, 5, 9) (4, 6, 10) (4, 7, 11)
T. 6 + 7, 6 + 8, 6 + 9	Three numbers—addition (6, 7, 13) (6, 8, 14) (6, 9, 15)
U. 7 + 4, 8 + 4, 9 + 4	Series saying
V. 7 + 7, 8 + 7, 9 + 7	Series saying
W. 9 + 8, 8 + 9, 4 + 8	Three numbers—addition (8, 9, 17) (8, 4, 12)
X. 6 + 5, 7 + 5, 8 + 5, 9 + 5	Series saying
Y. 7 + 8, 7 + 9, 4 + 9	Three numbers—addition (7, 8, 15) (7, 9, 16) (9, 4, 13)
Z. 5 + 6, 5 + 7, 5 + 8, 5 + 9	Three numbers—addition (5, 6, 11) (5, 7, 12) (5, 8, 13) (5, 9, 14)

FIGURE 6.2 Sequence of subtraction facts

Series-saying format is Format 6.2.
Three-number format is Format 6.3.

Sets of New Facts	Relationship Format
A. 3 − 1, 4 − 1, 5 − 1, 6 − 1	Series saying
B. 7 − 1, 8 − 1, 9 − 1, 10 − 1	Series saying
C. 4 − 2, 5 − 2, 6 − 2, 7 − 2	Series saying
D. 8 − 2, 9 − 2, 10 − 2, 11 − 2	Series saying
E. 1 − 0, 2 − 0, 3 − 0, 4 − 0, 5 − 0, 6 − 0, 7 − 0, 8 − 0, 9 − 0	Three numbers—subtraction (1, 0, 1) (2, 0, 2) (3, 0, 3) (4, 0, 4) . . .
F. 1 − 1, 2 − 2, 3 − 3, 4 − 4, 5 − 5, 6 − 6, 7 − 7, 8 − 8, 9 − 9	Three numbers—subtraction (1, 1, 0) (2, 2, 0) (3, 3, 0) (4, 4, 0) . . .
G. 6 − 3, 8 − 4, 10 − 5, 12 − 6	Three numbers—subtraction (6, 3, 3) (8, 4, 4) (10, 5, 5) (12, 6, 6)
H. 5 − 3, 6 − 3, 7 − 3, 8 − 3	Series saying
I. 9 − 3, 10 − 3, 11 − 3, 12 − 3	Series saying
J. 3 − 2, 4 − 3, 5 − 4, 6 − 5	Three numbers—subtraction (3, 2, 1,) (4, 3, 1) (5, 4, 1) (6, 5, 1)
K. 7 − 6, 8 − 7, 9 − 8, 10 − 9	Three numbers—subtraction (7, 6, 1) (8, 7, 1) (9, 8, 1) (10, 9, 1)
L. 5 − 3, 6 − 4, 7 − 5	Three numbers—subtraction (5, 3, 2) (6, 4, 2) (7, 5, 2)
M. 8 − 6, 9 − 7, 10 − 8, 11 − 9	Three numbers—subtraction (8, 6, 2) (9, 7, 2) (10, 8, 2) (11, 9, 2)
N. 6 − 3, 7 − 4, 8 − 5, 9 − 6	Three numbers—subtraction (6, 3, 3) (7, 4, 3) (8, 5, 3) (9, 6, 3)
O. 10 − 7, 11 − 8, 12 − 9	Three numbers—subtraction (10, 7, 3) (11, 8, 3) (12, 9, 3)
P. 14 − 7, 16 − 8, 18 − 9	Three numbers—subtraction (14, 7, 7) (16, 8, 8) (18, 9, 9)
Q. 8 − 4, 9 − 4, 10 − 4, 11 − 4	Series saying
R. 12 − 6, 13 − 6, 14 − 6, 15 − 6	Series saying
S. 9 − 5, 10 − 6, 11 − 7	Three numbers—subtraction (9, 5, 4) (10, 6, 4) (11, 7, 4)
T. 13 − 7, 14 − 8, 15 − 9	Three numbers—subtraction (13, 7, 6) (14, 8, 6) (15, 9, 6)
U. 10 − 4, 11 − 4, 12 − 4, 13 − 4	Series saying
V. 14 − 7, 15 − 7, 16 − 7	Series saying
W. 17 − 8, 17 − 9, 12 − 8	Three numbers—subtraction (17, 9, 8) (12, 8, 4)
X. 11 − 5, 12 − 5, 13 − 5, 14 − 5	Series saying
Y. 15 − 8, 16 − 9, 13 − 9	Three numbers—subtraction (15, 8, 7) (16, 9, 7) (13, 9, 4)
Z. 11 2 6, 12 2 7, 13 2 8, 14 2 9	Three numbers—subtraction (11, 6, 5) (12, 7, 5) (13, 8, 5) (14, 9, 5)

FIGURE 6.3   **Sequence of multiplication facts**

Series-saying format is Format 6.2.
Three-number format is Format 6.3.

Sets of New Facts	Relationship Format
A. Any problem with a one	Series saying
B. $5 \times 2, 5 \times 3, 5 \times 4, 5 \times 5$	Series saying
C. $2 \times 2, 3 \times 2, 4 \times 2, 5 \times 2$	Series saying
D. $2 \times 5, 3 \times 5, 4 \times 5, 5 \times 5$	Three numbers—multiplication
E. $2 \times 2, 2 \times 3, 2 \times 4, 2 \times 5$	Three numbers—multiplication
F. Any problem with a zero	Series saying
G. $5 \times 6, 5 \times 7, 5 \times 8, 5 \times 9$	Series saying
H. $2 \times 6, 2 \times 7, 2 \times 8, 2 \times 9$	Series saying
I. $6 \times 5, 7 \times 5, 8 \times 5, 9 \times 5$	Three numbers—multiplication
J. $6 \times 2, 7 \times 2, 8 \times 2, 9 \times 2$	Three numbers—multiplication
K. $2 \times 0, 3 \times 0, 4 \times 0, 5 \times 0$	Series saying
L. $0 \times 6, 0 \times 7, 0 \times 8, 0 \times 9$	Three numbers—multiplication
M. $9 \times 2, 9 \times 3, 9 \times 4, 9 \times 5$	Series saying
N. $4 \times 2, 4 \times 3, 4 \times 4, 4 \times 5$	Series saying
O. $2 \times 9, 3 \times 9, 4 \times 9, 5 \times 9$	Three numbers—multiplication
P. $2 \times 4, 3 \times 4, 4 \times 4, 5 \times 4$	Three numbers—multiplication
Q. $9 \times 6, 9 \times 7, 9 \times 8, 9 \times 9$	Series saying
R. $4 \times 6, 4 \times 7, 4 \times 8, 4 \times 9$	Series saying
S. $6 \times 9, 7 \times 9, 8 \times 9, 9 \times 9$	Three numbers—multiplication
T. $6 \times 4, 7 \times 4, 8 \times 4, 9 \times 4$	Three numbers—multiplication
U. $3 \times 6, 3 \times 7, 3 \times 8, 3 \times 9$	Series saying
V. $6 \times 6, 6 \times 7, 6 \times 8, 6 \times 9$	Series saying
W. $6 \times 3, 7 \times 3, 8 \times 3, 9 \times 3$	Three numbers—multiplication
X. $7 \times 6, 8 \times 6, 9 \times 6$	Three numbers—multiplication
Y. $7 \times 7, 8 \times 7, 9 \times 7$	Series saying
Z. $7 \times 8, 8 \times 8, 9 \times 8$	Three numbers—multiplication

FIGURE 6.4   **Sequence of division facts**

Three-number format is Format 6.3.

Sets of New Facts	Relationship Format
A. Any number divided by one	Three numbers—division (8, 1, 8) (4, 1, 4) (7, 1, 7)
B. Any number divided by itself	Three numbers—division (3, 1, 3) (9, 1, 9) (8, 1, 8) (2, 1, 2)
C. $10 \div 5, 15 \div 5, 20 \div 5, 25 \div 5$	Three numbers—division (2, 5, 10) (3, 5, 15) (4, 5, 20) (5, 5, 25)
D. $4 \div 2, 6 \div 2, 8 \div 2, 10 \div 2$	Three numbers—division
E. $10 \div 2, 15 \div 3, 20 \div 4, 25 \div 5$	Three numbers—division
F. Zero divided by any number	
G. $4 \div 2, 6 \div 3, 8 \div 4, 10 \div 5$	Three numbers—division
H. $30 \div 5, 35 \div 5, 40 \div 5, 45 \div 5$	Three numbers—division
I. $12 \div 2, 14 \div 2, 16 \div 2, 18 \div 2$	Three numbers—division
J. $30 \div 6, 35 \div 7, 40 \div 8, 45 \div 9$	Three numbers—division
K. $12 \div 6, 14 \div 7, 16 \div 8, 18 \div 9$	Three numbers—division
L. $18 \div 9, 27 \div 9, 36 \div 9, 45 \div 9$	Three numbers—division
M. $8 \div 4, 12 \div 4, 16 \div 4, 20 \div 4$	Three numbers—division
N. $18 \div 2, 27 \div 3, 36 \div 4, 45 \div 5$	Three numbers—division
O. $8 \div 2, 12 \div 3, 16 \div 4, 20 \div 5$	Three numbers—division
P. $54 \div 9, 63 \div 9, 72 \div 9, 81 \div 9$	Three numbers—division
Q. $24 \div 4, 28 \div 4, 32 \div 4, 36 \div 4$	Three numbers—division
R. $54 \div 6, 63 \div 7, 72 \div 8, 81 \div 9$	Three numbers—division
S. $24 \div 6, 28 \div 7, 32 \div 8, 36 \div 9$	Three numbers—division
T. $18 \div 3, 21 \div 3, 24 \div 3, 27 \div 3$	Three numbers—division
U. $36 \div 6, 42 \div 6, 48 \div 6, 54 \div 6$	Three numbers—division
V. $18 \div 6, 21 \div 7, 24 \div 8, 27 \div 9$	Three numbers—division
W. $42 \div 7, 48 \div 8, 54 \div 9$	Three numbers—division
X. $49 \div 7, 56 \div 7, 63 \div 7$	Three numbers—division
Y. $56 \div 8, 64 \div 8, 72 \div 8$	Three numbers—division

orders for introducing addition, subtraction, multiplication, and division facts. Each figure lists about 25 sets of facts, each set composed of three or four facts. The sets are lettered in their order of presentation. The facts in Set A would be introduced first, followed by the facts in sets B, C, D, and so on. Across from each set of facts is the relationship format recommended for introducing the facts. For example, in Figure 6.2 for subtraction facts, the teacher presents the Set G facts using the three-number subtraction format. For the 6 − 3 fact, the teacher writes

$$\underline{\qquad} - \underline{\qquad} = \underline{\qquad}$$

in Part A. The teacher writes blanks for only one statement because only one subtraction statement, 6 − 3, can be generated from the numbers 6, 3, and 3. The teacher presents Part A with all four sets of numbers and then presents Part B with the same four sets of numbers. While the teacher is introducing the new set of facts, memorization exercises on the previous sets continue. Each relationship exercise, as illustrated with Set G for subtraction, is presented for several days before the facts are introduced into mastery exercises.

In constructing these sequences, three guidelines were followed: (a) easier facts are introduced first, (b) related facts are introduced together, and (c) the reverse of specific series of facts is taught relatively soon after the initial series was presented. Note that these sequences illustrate just one possible order for introducing facts and are not intended to represent the only acceptable sequence for teaching facts.

In most commercial math programs, addition facts are introduced first, followed by subtraction, multiplication, and division facts. The question of exactly when to introduce the other facts is a difficult one. For example, should subtraction facts be introduced while students are still learning addition facts (and, if so, when?), or should subtraction facts be introduced only after students have mastered all addition facts? Similar questions can be raised about multiplication and division facts.

Unfortunately, little experimental research has been done to answer questions about sequencing the introduction of facts. In our observations of lower-performing students, we have found that students have more difficulty when a set of addition facts and the inverse subtraction facts are introduced concurrently. Consequently, we recommend introducing related subtraction or division facts for a particular set a month or more after the original addition or multiplication set has been introduced. More specifically, teachers might begin introducing subtraction facts when the students have learned about half of their addition facts. The teacher then alternates between introducing sets of addition and subtraction. Following this recommendation, teachers first introduce addition sets A through M and then introduce subtraction Set A. Thereafter, the teacher alternates between addition and subtraction fact sets. Addition Set N is followed by subtraction Set B, which is followed by addition Set O, then subtraction Set C, and so on.

The question of when to introduce multiplication is of particular importance. Many students will not have mastered all basic addition and subtraction facts at the time a program calls for the introduction of multiplication. We recommend teaching multiplication facts beginning in third grade, even though addition and subtraction facts may not have been completely mastered. Knowledge of basic multiplication facts is a critical prerequisite for more advanced operations and should be mastered no later than the end of third grade. We recommend that teachers devote extra time to fact instruction for students who have not mastered the basic addition and subtraction facts by third grade. For example, two practice sessions might be conducted daily, one focusing on addition and subtraction facts and one focusing on multiplication and, later, division facts.

For upper-elementary and middle school students who did not master basic addition and subtraction facts by the end of third grade, we recommend presenting multiplication and division facts before returning to addition and subtraction. The reason for this recommendation is that these students are likely to have some type of finger strategy that allows them to compute addition and subtraction facts correctly. (More advice on the use of fingers appears at the end of the chapter.) On the other hand, these students are likely to have no viable strategy for figuring out multiplication and division facts. Teaching multiplication and division facts first allows the teacher to present a wider range of operations during the school year. After multiplication and division facts are mastered, the teacher can go back and work on addition and subtraction facts.

CONCEPTUAL UNDERSTANDING AND ORGANIZATION

Three different types of instructional activities designed for teaching basic facts are recommended in this text. These three types include activities that promote conceptual understanding, emphasize relationships among facts, and facilitate mastery. The activities to promote conceptual understanding involve demonstrations of the operations, similar to those we have included in Chapters 7 through 10.

Relationship activities are exercises designed to teach the relationships among various facts. One way of teaching these relationships is by presenting facts in a series, such as the plus ones $(3 + 1, 4 + 1, 5 + 1,$ etc.), fours $(4 + 5, 4 + 6, 4 + 7,$ etc.), and the plus doubles $(2 + 2, 3 + 3, 4 + 4,$ etc.). Another way of teaching these relationships is through the introduction of fact families. Fact families are sets of three related numbers that generate four facts. Following are examples of fact families constructed from three related numbers:

Addition and Subtraction Using 3, 5, 8	Multiplication and Division Using 3, 5, 15
$3 + 5 = 8$	$3 \times 5 = 15$
$5 + 3 = 8$	$5 \times 3 = 15$
$8 - 3 = 5$	$3\overline{)15} = 5$
$8 - 5 = 3$	$5\overline{)15} = 3$

Note how using the **commutative property** of addition $(3 + 5 = 8,$ so $5 + 3 = 8)$ and multiplication $(3 \times 5 = 15,$ so $5 \times 3 = 15)$ greatly reduces the memorization load for students. Instead of memorizing each fact individually $(5 + 3 \; and \; 3 + 5)$, students can be taught that if they know one fact, they also know the reverse. Instructional procedures based on the commutative property are discussed later.

Our recommendations for grouping facts into sets of fact families appear in Figures 6.2 through 6.5. These sets form the basis for organizing instruction. The teaching formats for the relationship activities listed in these figures are discussed in the next section.

INSTRUCTIONAL PROCEDURES: RELATIONSHIP ACTIVITIES

Because the activities to promote conceptual understanding of the major operations are presented in the chapters for each respective operation, this chapter focuses only on relationship and mastery activities. The teaching procedures for the relationship activities include (a) presenting facts in a related series $(3 \times 1, 3 \times 2, 3 \times 3)$ and (b) introducing number fact family exercises that utilize inverse relationships between addition and subtraction and between multiplication and division $(4 + 2 = 6, 2 + 4 = 6, 6 - 4 = 2, 6 - 2 = 4)$. The purpose of teaching relationship activities is to make fact memorization easier and more efficient. Following a discussion of the teaching procedures for relationship activities, mastery activities are outlined.

Plus-One Facts

Prior to introducing basic addition facts, teachers should teach students a strategy to figure out plus-one facts. (Students who know 30 or more facts do not need to receive instruction on this preskill.) Prior to instruction in facts, students most likely have been using picture representations or concrete objects to solve simple equations. **Format 6.1: Plus-One Facts** not only teaches plus-one facts but also begins teaching students that numbers are related in systematic ways. Plus-one facts, which should be introduced in kindergarten, are taught through the application of this rule: *When you plus one, you say the next number.* From the rule, students learn that the first addend is systematically related to the sum:

$$6 + 1 = 7 \qquad 9 + 1 = 10$$

To prepare students for the plus-one rule, the term *next number* is taught in Part A of the format. At first, the teacher counts several numbers, holding the last number for several seconds ("3, 4, 5, sssiiixxx"). The students say the next number, 7. After presenting several examples in which the teacher says a series of numbers and asks students the next number (step 2), the teacher presents examples in which she says just a single number, not a series of numbers (step 3), and the students say the next number. A common error made by students is that they continue counting rather than stopping at the next number. The teacher should stop students immediately if they say more than the next number, model saying just the next number, then repeat the same example before presenting additional examples.

Part B should not be introduced until students have mastered the next number skill taught in Part A. In Part B, the teacher presents the plus-one rule, models several examples, and then tests. As a prompt, the teacher emphasizes the first addend, stretching it out for several seconds, and de-emphasizes the words *plus one* (in *sssiiixxx* plus one, the *plus one* is said quietly so that students can make the six–seven counting association).

In Part C, the teacher presents the plus-one facts without any prompting. The teacher initially should pause for 2 to 3 seconds before signaling for a response so that the students have time to figure out the answer. After several days of practice, the teacher can decrease the pause to a second. The teacher continues to provide practice on plus-one facts until students can respond instantly to any plus-one problem.

Series Saying

Series saying, one of the major relationship activities, involves teaching the students to say a consecutively ordered set of fact statements. Series saying prompts students to notice the counting relationship among facts, as indicated by the circled numerals in the following series:

$$\begin{aligned} 6 + 2 &= 8 \\ 7 + 2 &= 9 \\ 8 + 2 &= 10 \end{aligned}$$

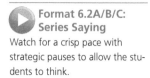

Format 6.2A/B/C: Series Saying

Watch for a crisp pace with strategic pauses to allow the students to think.

Series saying may be incorporated into instruction for any of the four types of basic facts: addition, subtraction, multiplication, and division. **Format 6.2: Series Saying** illustrates the series saying format for an addition series. Note that the same format can be used to present other series.

There are four parts to the series-saying format. In Part A, students read the consecutively ordered statements. In Part B, the teacher erases the answers and the students read the statements. In Part C, the teacher erases everything and requires the students to say the series from memory. Part D is a drill on randomly presented facts. The teacher writes the fact questions on the board without the answers. Note that the facts are written in random order and vertically. The facts are written in random order so the students will not memorize the order of the answers. The vertical presentation is intended to help students transition from relationship activities to mastery activities.

Teaching students to read statements (Part A) in a rapid, crisp fashion is critical for student success. If students cannot *read* the series of statements accurately and quickly, they will have difficulty saying the series from memory and remembering facts during the random drill (Part D). Providing adequate practice is essential to enable the students to say the series of statements at a fast rate.

The teacher should set a quick, rhythmic pace for saying the statements to help the students memorize them. There should be a slight pause between each statement. The correction for slow pacing is to keep leading (responding with the students) at a brisk pace and gradually fade the lead so that the students are saying the statements independently. The teacher must be careful to provide the adequate repetition in an engaging manner. Teachers working with lower-performing students may find that several days of practice on Parts A and B are needed before continuing on to Parts C and D. Teachers working with higher-performing students may be able to present all parts in a day or two.

Three-Number Fact Families

The other major format designed to demonstrate the relationships among facts is taught through the introduction of three-number fact families. These are sets of three numbers from which students can be taught to generate four statements, either addition and subtraction or multiplication and division. For example, given the numbers 3, 4, and 7, students are taught to construct the addition statements $3 + 4 = 7$ and $4 + 3 = 7$. Later, students learn to construct the subtraction statements based on the same three numbers: $7 - 4 = 3, 7 - 3 = 4$.

There are two formats for teaching number families. **Format 6.3: Three-Number Fact Families: Addition and Multiplication** teaches students to use the commutative properties of addition (if $a + b = c$, then $b + a = c$) and multiplication (if $a \times b = c$, then $b \times a = c$). The second, **Format 6.4: Three-Number Fact Families: Subtraction and Division**, teaches students to generate subtraction statements from addition statements and division statements from multiplication statements. Using the commutative property as the basis for generating fact families is extremely important in that it greatly reduces the number of facts students need to memorize. For every fact that students learn, they can derive the answer to the inverse fact quickly and easily by using the commutative property. Note that the term *commutative property* is not explicitly taught initially, only the function of the property.

Format 6.3 consists of three parts. In Part A, students are taught how to construct a pair of addition statements from a set of three numbers. For example, given 2, 5, and 7, the students construct $2 + 5 = 7$ and $5 + 2 = 7$. One member of each pair has been previously presented in a series-saying format. The second member of each pair is the reverse fact. For example, if students have been taught the plus-two facts ($5 + 2$, $6 + 2$, etc.), the new facts would be the two-plus facts ($2 + 5$, $2 + 6$, etc.). In Part B, the students are orally tested on the new "reversed" facts. Part C is a worksheet exercise in which the students are given a diagram like this:

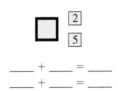

They are asked to fill in the sum (called the "big number") and generate two addition statements.

Format 6.4 demonstrates how facts can be related across operations. It is used to generate subtraction facts from addition facts and division facts from multiplication facts. The teacher demonstrates how to generate the subtraction or division statements. For example, after constructing $3 + 4 = 7$ and $4 + 3 = 7$, students are taught to generate the subtraction statements of $7 - 4 = 3$ and $7 - 3 = 4$.

The format for subtraction and division facts includes two parts. Although examples in **Format 6.4** illustrate subtraction, the same format can be used to introduce division facts. In Part A, the teacher demonstrates how three related numbers such as 3, 5, and 8 can generate two subtraction statements. The teacher first has the students add the two smaller numbers (3 and 5), then points out that two subtraction statements can be made. The teacher introduces the rule: *When you subtract, you always start with the big number,* which helps avoid errors like $3 - 8 = 5$. Part B is a worksheet exercise in which the students construct four statements, two addition and two subtraction, from three numbers.

INSTRUCTIONAL PROCEDURES: COORDINATING MASTERY AND RELATIONSHIP ACTIVITIES

Mastery activities are designed to facilitate fact memorization. The activities we have identified for building mastery require the following components: designing a coherent sequence for introducing facts as previously discussed, coordinating relationship activities with memorization activities, establishing specific performance criteria that indicate when new facts can be introduced, providing intensive and systematic review, and implementing record-keeping procedures

---

for monitoring student performance and increasing motivation. As a general rule, new sets of facts should be presented in relationship exercises before appearing in mastery exercises. The teacher introduces a set of facts through a relationship exercise and then provides practice to develop mastery on that set of facts.

Memorization Activities

Practice to promote memorization of basic facts can be provided in a number of ways: paired practice in which students work with each other, teacher-directed practice in which the teacher presents facts to a group, worksheet exercises, flash card exercises, fact games, and computer-based activities. Memorization exercises should be cumulative; that is, newly introduced facts receive intensive practice, while previously introduced facts receive less intensive, but still systematically planned, practice.

Performance Criteria

Mastery is demonstrated by students' ability to accurately and fluently recall facts. Students should practice a new set of facts until they can answer each member of the new set and members of previously introduced sets quickly and correctly. Most teachers use written performance tasks to determine mastery. The criterion for written exercises depends on the students' motor coordination. That is, rate criteria for written work should be based on the speed with which students can write numerals. Obviously, a student who writes numerals slowly will not be able to complete a worksheet as quickly as a student whose fine motor skills are more developed and is able to write numerals more quickly. Our basic recommendation is that the criterion be set at a rate that is about two-thirds of the rate at which the student can write digits. A student's writing ability can be easily determined by giving a 1-minute timed test. The student is instructed to write the numerals 1 through 9 as many times as he can. It is appropriate to provide several practice trials before the timing. The student's writing rate is determined by counting the number of digits written during this 1-minute period. By multiplying that number by $2/3$, the teacher can estimate how many digits a student should be able to write as answers during a 1-minute fact timing. For example, a student who writes 60 digits in 1 minute should write 40 digits in 1 minute in a fact timing ($60 \times 2/3 = 40$).

Intensive Practice and Systematic Review

As previously stated, in addition to providing intensive practice on new facts, the teacher must provide practice on previously taught facts. Unless earlier introduced facts are systematically reviewed, students are likely to forget them. We recommend that daily practice of new facts be followed immediately by review of previously introduced facts. (See the section titled "Instructional Procedures: Two Fact Mastery Programs" for more detail.)

The amount of time allocated to fact practice must be sufficient. We recommend that teachers allocate at least 15-20 minutes per day for basic fact–learning activities throughout the entire school year. This time allotment is much more than what is provided in most classroom schedules. Teachers should keep in mind that work on basic math facts is time well spent. Students who know facts will be able to compute efficiently and are more likely to achieve success in later problem-solving activities.

Record-Keeping Procedures

Record-keeping is needed to monitor student progress so that the teacher knows when a student needs additional practice and when a student is ready to progress to the next set of facts. This system should involve a minimum of paperwork so that little time is taken from actual fact practice. A motivational system should be integrated with the record-keeping procedure. The motivation system must be carefully designed so that students see a clear relationship between working hard and receiving recognition for their work. Details about increasing motivation appear later in the chapter.

INSTRUCTIONAL PROCEDURES: TWO FACT MASTERY PROGRAMS

Two examples of fact mastery programs are presented in this section. The first program is designed for teachers working with homogeneous groups of students who are all performing near the same instructional level. The second program is designed for teachers working with heterogeneous groups, groups composed of students performing at different levels, or for one-to-one tutoring.

Homogenous Group Program

The homogenous group program consists of teacher-directed instruction with students completing daily exercises on a fact worksheet. In this program, the teacher first presents an exercise in which the students orally practice newly introduced facts. The oral exercise is followed by a written exercise on which the students are timed.

Materials   This program requires specially prepared sequences of worksheets for each type of fact: addition, subtraction, division, and multiplication. A worksheet is prepared for each set listed in Figures 6.1 through 6.4. Each worksheet is divided into two parts. The top half of the worksheet should provide practice on new facts, including facts from the currently introduced set and from the two preceding sets. More specifically, each fact from the new set should appear four times. Each fact from the set introduced just earlier should appear three times, and each fact from the set that preceded that one should appear twice. If this pattern were applied to sets, each containing four facts, the top part of the worksheet would have 36 facts: 16 new facts (4×4), 12 facts from the previously learned set (4×3), and 8 facts from the set before that (4×2).

The bottom half of the worksheet should include 30 problems. Each fact from the currently introduced set should appear twice. The remaining facts are taken from previously introduced sets. All previously introduced facts appear just one time. Note that at the beginning of a fact program, students will not know many facts; therefore, facts from previous sets may appear several times on the bottom half of the worksheet. Only when 30 facts have been introduced can each fact appear just once. On the other hand, after more than 30 facts have been introduced, review should be planned so that each fact appears at least once every second or third worksheet.

Figure 6.5 is a sample worksheet for introducing facts according to the above guidelines for worksheet construction. The new set consists of $5 + 6, 5 + 7, 5 + 8$, and $5 + 9$. Each of these facts appears four times in the top half. The previously introduced set includes $7 + 8, 7 + 9$, and $4 + 9$, each presented three times. Finally, the next earlier introduced set includes $6 + 5$, $7 + 5, 8 + 5$, and $9 + 5$, each presented twice. The top half of the worksheet has 33 facts. The bottom half of the worksheet includes the four facts from the new set, each written twice, along with previously introduced facts, each appearing just once.

Note 6.1:
Math facts worksheets designed according to the recommendations described above and based on the sequences listed in Figures 6.1 through 6.4 can be found at [http://depts.washington.edu/spedtrac/direct-instruction/resources-for-teachers/]

FIGURE 6.5 Sample worksheet

5 +6	8 +5	5 +8	6 +5	7 +9	5 +7	4 +9	5 +6	7 +8	5 +9	7 +9
5 +8	7 +5	5 +7	7 +8	5 +6	5 +8	4 +9	5 +9	4 +9	7 +9	5 +7
8 +5	5 +6	5 +9	6 +5	5 +7	7 +5	5 +8	9 +5	7 +8	5 +9	9 +5

5 +8	6 +4	7 +5	4 +7	5 +6	9 +8	7 +9	5 +9	4 +8	5 +7
8 +9	7 +8	8 +5	5 +6	8 +7	9 +5	7 +7	5 +8	8 +4	4 +9
9 +7	6 +7	5 +9	7 +4	6 +9	4 +6	5 +7	9 +4	6 +5	6 +8

Pretesting   Before beginning instruction, teachers should determine which type of fact to start with (addition, subtraction, multiplication, division) and where students should be placed in that fact program.

Groups with students who know few facts start at Set A. Students who know more facts begin at later points. To determine the set at which students might begin, the teacher administers a written pretest that includes the basic facts with the easier facts listed at the top. The teacher allows students 2 minutes to work as many problems as they can. A teacher with 10 or more students in a group must compromise when selecting a starting point. As a general rule, we recommend a point lower than the average starting point for the students in the group. If pretesting results indicate a wide range in students' math facts skills, we recommend using the heterogeneous group program. Visit the link mentioned above to find available pretests.

Daily Practice   The teacher begins the lesson with a group exercise in which the students orally practice the facts on the top half of the worksheet. The teacher instructs the students to touch the first problem. After allowing a brief time for students to think about the answer, the teacher says, "Get ready," and signals for students to respond. After the students respond, the teacher repeats the procedures for the following facts. "Next problem" (pause). "Get ready" (signal). "Next problem" (pause). "Get ready" (signal).

The teacher repeats this procedure with each fact in the first row of the worksheet and repeats the row until students are able to answer each fact quickly and correctly. This may take several repetitions of the entire row. The same procedure may be repeated with each subsequent row on the top half of the worksheet.

Timed Test   The timed test is done on the bottom half of the worksheet. The teacher sets a specified time. A minute and 15 seconds is a realistic goal for upper-elementary students. The teacher allows the students a minute or two to study the bottom half of the worksheet, then tells them to get ready for the test. The teacher tells the students how much time they have and when to start. At the end of the specified time, the teacher says, "Stop," has the students trade papers, and reads the answers. Students are to mark all mistakes, write the total number correct at the top of the page, and then return the worksheet to its owner.

Performance Criteria   After the lesson, the teacher inspects the students' papers and records the number of facts each student answered correctly on the written timed test. In the next lesson, the teacher either repeats the same worksheet or presents the worksheet for the next set of facts. The teacher presents the next worksheet if three-quarters or more of the students answered 28 of the 30 facts correctly. The teacher repeats the same worksheet if fewer than three-quarters of the students answered 28 facts correctly. Keep in mind that students generally need anywhere from 3 days to 2 weeks to master a set. During this time, the teacher should keep presenting the relationship exercises for the new fact set and encourage the students.

Summary   The advantage of the homogenous group program is that it allows the teacher to coordinate the presentation of relationship activities and memorization exercises. Also, the program makes monitoring the performance of the students relatively easy. The disadvantage of this program is that it does not allow individual students to progress at optimal rates. However, if only one or two students are performing at a much lower rate than other students in the group, the teacher could provide extra practice for those students.

Heterogeneous Group Program

The heterogeneous group program is designed for teachers working with a group of students who demonstrate significant differences in their knowledge of facts. This system also can be adapted for use in tutoring programs (peer tutoring, cross-age tutoring, or tutoring by adult volunteers).

Materials   Before the school year begins, teachers should make booklets for each type of fact—addition, subtraction, division, and multiplication—consisting of the worksheets for each fact set. The same worksheets used in the homogeneous system are used in the heterogeneous system. Two types of booklets should be prepared, one with answers and one without (the test booklet). The answer book can be used in subsequent years, while the test booklets must be replaced annually.

Pretesting   Students may start with different types of facts (addition, subtraction, multiplication, division) and at various sets within a type of fact. Pretesting to determine a starting set can be done in a group setting or individually. In a group setting, the teacher administers a written pretest that includes the basic facts with the easier facts listed at the top.

As mentioned previously, the teacher allows students 2 minutes to work as many problems as they can. We are not aware of any specific guidelines for placing students into math facts programs. In general, students who answer 30 or more facts in 2 minutes may start at Set G. Students who answer 45 or more might start at Set M. Students who answer 60 or more could start at Set R. Students who answer 85 or more facts in the 2-minute pretest probably do not need to be placed in a program for that type of fact.

Individual oral or written testing allows for a more accurate starting point for most students. To test individuals, the teacher uses the sequences in Figures 6.1 through 6.4. The teacher begins by testing the facts in Set A, then Set B, and so on, until reaching a set in which the student makes two or more errors. Any fact problem that a student cannot answer within several seconds should be counted as wrong. This set should be the student's starting point. This type of individual testing is more appropriate for tutoring individuals or small groups rather than whole-class settings.

Daily Practice   In this program, students work in pairs. As a general rule, teachers should pair students who are working near the same level. Each student has one booklet with answers and one booklet without answers. The student with the answer sheet acts as a tutor, while the other is the student.

The teacher has each student practice the top half of the worksheet twice. Each practice session is timed. The student practices by saying complete statements (4 + 2 = 6) rather than just answers. Saying the entire fact statement makes it easier for the tutor to follow along and helps the student remember the fact. If the student makes an error, the tutor corrects by saying the correct statement and having the student repeat the statement. The teacher allows students a minute and a half when practicing the top part and a minute when practicing the bottom part. After the allotted time, the teacher has the second student begin practicing. This procedure is repeated twice for the facts on the top half and twice for the facts on the bottom half of the worksheet.

After allowing each student to practice the top and bottom sections of her individual fact sheet twice, the teacher tells the students to get ready for a test. Students work in their individual test booklets. The teacher stops students at the end of a minute. The students are to stop answering immediately. The students trade test and answer booklets to correct each other's work. They count the number of facts answered correctly and record that number across from the letter for the respective set of facts on the student's record form (see **Figure 6.6** and the discussion under "Student Record Form").

The next day, the same procedure is followed. However, if a student answered all but two of the facts correctly on the previous day's testing, the student moves on to the next worksheet in the sequence. The teacher begins the lesson by having students inspect their record forms to determine the series they are to practice.

Cooperative student behavior is essential to make this system work. The teacher should encourage cooperative behavior among students. Rules for the activity might include (a) talking softly, (b) following teacher instructions, and (c) honestly recording scores. Students may be tempted to record inaccurate scores on the test. To guard against cheating, the teacher must monitor student performance carefully during practice. If a student performs quite poorly during practice yet turns in an excellent testing record, testing may be inaccurate. The teacher should follow-up individually with these students.

Student Record Form   A record form that can be used during this exercise appears in **Figure 6.6**. In the first column, the worksheet letters are listed. Across from each letter are seven columns used to record the number of facts answered correctly on a test. The first day the student

FIGURE 6.6 **Student record form**

page	TRY 1	TRY 2	TRY 3	TRY 4	TRY 5	TRY 6	TRY 7	
Z								Z
Y								Y
X								X
W								W
V								V
U								U
T								T
S								S
R								R
Q								Q
P								P
O								O
N								N
M								M
L								L
K								K
J								J
I								I
H								H
G								G
F								F
E								E
D								D
C								C
B								B
A								A

does a particular worksheet, the number of facts answered correctly is written in the first column across from that worksheet letter. The second day, the number is written in the second column across from the worksheet letter, and so on. On the right side of the chart is a progress rocket. Each time the student meets the criterion for a worksheet (28–30 correct), the student shades in the space for that worksheet on the rocket. On the next lesson, the student works on the next worksheet in the sequence. Many elementary-aged students find moving up levels on the rocket very motivating.

Summary The heterogeneous group program, while targeting individual student needs, requires extensive preparation by the teacher at the beginning of the school year because several booklets of worksheets must be made. Also, instruction is necessary to teach students the procedures. The advantage of this program, though, is that once worksheets are prepared and students know what to do, the program provides the individualization needed to allow each student to progress at her optimal rate.

This program also is easily adapted for use in tutoring programs. Whether same-age students work together in pairs (peer tutoring), older students work with younger students (cross-age tutoring), or adults work with individual students (volunteers or parents), the same materials and basic procedures can be used. That is, students practice orally with feedback from their tutors and then take a timed test and record their performance.

Parental Involvement

Parents who would like to help their children at home are often not sure what to do, how to do it, or whether they will interfere with what the teacher is doing at school. Math fact practice is a good way to involve parents. Teachers should try to secure a commitment from parents to work with their children on facts at home for about 10 minutes three or four days a week. This practice is easily coordinated with classroom activities. If possible, parents should be invited to an orientation during which the teacher explains the fact program she is using and reviews suggestions for working with children at home.

The teacher could prepare a tutoring guide for the parents, specifying exactly how to implement a home practice program. During the orientation, the teacher would demonstrate recommended procedures and talk about motivation. Teachers must encourage parents to interact with their children in positive ways so that home practice becomes an opportunity for students to experience success. A communication system should be set up to inform parents about which facts they should include in the exercises. A weekly letter including the facts to work on might be sent home along with progress reports.

Motivational Practice Activities

If students require additional practice for mastery, the teacher or tutor can make flash cards for particularly difficult facts and use the flash cards prior to the oral worksheet practice. The flash cards can be sent home for additional practice or turned into a fun game that might be played at recess. Flash cards also are an excellent way to provide cumulative review. Tutors might begin each session with a flash card review of the 15 previously introduced facts before introducing a new set.

One exercise that is motivating for most students is the math fact race. The teacher puts a scorecard on the board with one row for teacher points and one for student points:

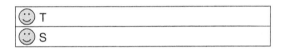

The teacher then presents a fact or shows a flash card, pauses a second or two, and calls out a student's name. The teacher then hesitates a second more and says the answer. If the student responds correctly before the teacher says the answer, the students get the point. Note that pausing before calling on a student (but after stating the fact) increases the probability that all students will attend to the question.

The race game also can be modified so that one group of students competes with another group. The teacher divides the class in half, placing an equal number of higher and lower performers in each group. The teacher conducts the game by saying a fact, pausing a second or two, and then calling on a student. The student earns a point for his team if he responds correctly.

Note that the games should be played in a way to avoid embarrassing individual students. Rules encouraging appropriate behavior should be discussed before playing the game and enforced during the game. Rules such as "Encourage others" or "Be respectful" are helpful in playing the game.

During free times, students can play board games in which the students pick a card from a deck of fact flash cards. If they say the fact correctly, they get to hit the spinner and move their marker on the board the number of spaces indicated by the spinner.

Motivation is an important factor in all fact mastery programs. If students practice at home or at other times during the school day, their learning rate will likely increase. Teachers can encourage students to study by establishing incentive programs based on their performance. The incentives need not be material rewards but might include time earned on a computer, extra minutes at recess, or other activities that are highly desirable.

Commercial Programs

In many programs, addition and subtraction facts are taught using pictures. While pictures aid students in using a counting strategy to solve computation problems, pictures are a deterrent to memorization. If pictures are available, some students invariably resort to counting the pictures instead of trying to remember the answer. For example, in one program we examined, a third of the exercises given to students for basic fact practice contained illustrations. For those problems, students needed only to count the pictures and write the answer rather than recall the answers from memory. The amount of actual fact practice provided was minimal. Some programs also use fact families to introduce math facts. Rarely, however, do these programs use relationship activities frequently enough to teach fact acquisition to mastery.

Teachers need to remember that if the objective of an exercise is to promote acquisition of facts, then no pictures or other prompts, such as the use of fingers, should be available to students during the activity. Many struggling students have learned to rely on their fingers to figure out facts. Teachers should not initially discourage students from using their fingers *during computation exercises only*, since memorizing basic facts may require months and months of practice. While working on memorization activities, however, the use of fingers should be avoided.

A critical aspect of any fact program is the provision of adequate practice to develop mastery. An important part of adequate practice is the cumulative review of previously introduced facts integrated with the presentation of new facts. This type of practice and review is not present in most commercial math programs. For example, in another program we examined, all basic addition facts were introduced in only three lessons (six student practice pages). Those same facts (sums to 18) were not reviewed until six lessons later, when the relationship between addition and subtraction was introduced. The program did not provide another opportunity for students to practice addition facts in that level.

One type of fact practice noticeably absent from the programs we examined was fluency practice (timed fact drills). Whereas programs traditionally address issues of accuracy (number right, number wrong), they have not included exercises whereby students must meet a specified rate criterion as well. For students to be able to recall facts quickly in more complex computation problems, students must know their math facts at an acceptable level of "automaticity." Therefore, teachers using these programs must be prepared to supplement by providing more practice and establishing rate criteria that students must achieve.

APPLY WHAT YOU LEARNED

 Click on the √ to answer the questions online.

1. Your principal asks you to describe the procedure you are using to facilitate learning basic facts. Write a description of the math facts program you have in place.

2. Assume you are constructing worksheets for subtraction facts. More specifically, you are now preparing a worksheet for Set U. (a) List the facts that would appear on the upper half of the worksheet. Next to each fact, write how often it would appear on the top half. (b) Describe the guidelines you would use in preparing the bottom half of the student worksheet.

3. You are presenting the relationship format to prepare students for the facts in Set M of the multiplication sequence. Write what you do.

4. Assume the students have learned the basic multiplication facts in sets A through M in the fact sequence of this text. Which computation problems would be appropriate to assign to students, and which would not be appropriate?

$$\begin{array}{ccc} 34 & 82 & 34 \\ \times 5 & \times 6 & \times 9 \\ \hline \end{array}$$

$$\begin{array}{ccc} 65 & 87 & 48 \\ \times 7 & \times 8 & \times 2 \\ \hline \end{array}$$

5. The parents of the children in your class want to know why you spend so much time on memorization activities. What would your reply be?

Format 6.1
PLUS-ONE FACTS

TEACHER	STUDENTS
Part A: Next Number	
1. When I put my hand down, you say the next number.	
2. *(Hold up hand.)* 1, 2, 3, 4, *ffiivve (drop hand).*	6
To correct: My turn: 1, 2, 3, 4, *ffiivve (drop hand),* 6.	
New problem. Tell me the next number: 3, 4, 5, 6, *ssevvenn (Drop hand. Repeat step 2 with 3, 4, ffiivve and 7, 8, nniinne.)*	8
3. When I put my hand down, you say the next number. *Sssiiixxx (drop hand).*	7
To correct: My turn: *sssiiixxx (drop hand),* 7.	
4. *(Repeat step 3 starting with 8, 4, 9, 2, 5. Give individual turns to several students.)*	
Part B: Plus-One Rule with Stretch Prompt	
1. Everyone listen to the rule. When you plus one, you say the next number. My turn: *ffoouurr* + 1 = 5. *Eeighht* + 1 = 9.	
2. Get ready to tell me the answers to some plus-one problems. Remember to say the next number: 5 + 1, *ffiivve* + 1 = *(signal).*	6
Yes, 5 + 1 = 6.	
To correct: Listen: 5. What number comes next? So 5 + 1 = 6.	
3. Listen: 3 + 1. *Thrreee* + 1 = how many? *(Signal.)*	4
Yes, 3 + 1 = 4.	
(Present step 3 with examples like the following until students answer all plus-one problems in a row correctly: 9 + 1, 7 + 1, 2 + 1, 8 + 1, 4 + 1.)	
Part C: Plus-One Rule without Prompt	
1. Remember, when you plus one, you say the next number.	
2. 8 + 1 = (pause, then signal).	9
Say the whole statement.	8 + 1 = 9
3. *(Repeat step 2 with the following examples: 4 + 1, 7 + 1, 5 + 1, 9 + 1.)*	

Format 6.2
SERIES SAYING
(See Video Parts A/B/C)

TEACHER	STUDENTS
▶	

Part A: Reading Statements

1. *(Write the following problems on the board.)*

   5 + 2 = 7
   6 + 2 = 8
   7 + 2 = 9
   8 + 2 = 10

<table>
<tr><td>Everybody, I'll touch them. You read. Get ready. (Point to numerals and symbols in each statement. Repeat step 1 until students can read statements at a rate of a statement each 3 seconds.)</td><td>5 + 2 = 7
6 + 2 = 8
7 + 2 = 9
8 + 2 = 10</td></tr>
</table>

Part B: Reading Statements with Answers Erased

<table>
<tr><td>1. Now I'm going to erase the answers. (Erase answers.)

Now read the statement and tell me the answer.</td><td>5 + 2 = 7
6 + 2 = 8
7 + 2 = 9
8 + 2 = 10</td></tr>
</table>

To correct: Respond with students until they appear able to respond without assistance.

Part C: Saying Statements

<table>
<tr><td>1. Now I'll make it even harder and erase everything. (Erase everything.) Get ready to say the statements starting with 5 + 2. (Either clap or snap fingers to set pace for students to respond.)</td><td>5 + 2 = 7
6 + 2 = 8
7 + 2 = 9
8 + 2 = 10</td></tr>
</table>

2. *(Repeat Part C until all students respond correctly and then present individual turns.)*

Part D: Random Fact Drill

1. *(Write facts in random order on board.)*

   7   5   6   8
   +2   +2   +2   +2
   ___ ___ ___ ___

   When I signal, say the whole statement with the answer.

2. *(Point to left of 7 + 2, pause 2 seconds, then touch board.)*	7 + 2 = 9

3. *(Repeat step 2 with remaining facts.)*

4. *(Repeat step 3 until students can respond to all facts with the 1-second pause.)*

Format 6.3
THREE-NUMBER FACT FAMILIES: ADDITION AND MULTIPLICATION FACTS
(See Video in Part A)

TEACHER	STUDENTS

▶

Part A: Structured Board Presentation

1. *(Write the following boxes and numerals on the board.)*

☐ 8
 2

_____ + _____ = _____
_____ + _____ = _____

I want to make addition statements using the numbers 8 and 2.

I'll write the big number in the box. What is 8 + 2? *(Write 10 in the big box.)*   **10**

(Write 8 + 2 = 10 on the first set of lines.)

2. We can make another addition statement. If 8 + 2 = 10, then 2 + 8 = 10. *(Write 2 + 8 = 10 on the second set of lines.)*

| Say the statement that begins with 8. | 8 + 2 = 10 |
| Say the statement that begins with 2. | 2 + 8 = 10 |

3. *(Erase statements.)* Let's say both statements we can make with the numbers 8, 2, and 10.

| Say the statement that begins with 8. | 8 + 2 = 10 |
| Say the statement that begins with 2. | 2 + 8 = 10 |

4. *(Write the following boxes and numbers on the board.)*

☐ 5
 2

| What's the big number that goes with 5 and 2? | 7 |

To correct: What does 5 + 2 equal? Yes, 7 is the big number.

| Say an addition statement using those numbers. Start with 5. *(Pause.)* | 5 + 2 = 7 |
| Say the other addition statement that starts with 2. *(Pause.)* | 2 + 5 = 7 |

(Repeat step 4 with 6 and 2, 9 and 2.)

Part B: Discrimination Practice

Now let's see if you can tell me the answers to some problems.

| What is 2 + 6? *(Pause.)* | 8 |

(Repeat with 2 + 8, 2 + 5, 2 + 7. Repeat Part B until students can respond to any fact with only a 1-second pause.)

continued

Format 6.3 (continued)
THREE-NUMBER FACT FAMILIES: ADDITION AND MULTIPLICATION FACTS

TEACHER	STUDENTS
Part C: Supervised Worksheet	

Fill in the big number and write the two addition statements that can be made from those numbers.

Format 6.4
THREE-NUMBER FACT FAMILIES: SUBTRACTION AND DIVISION FACTS   [See Video in Part A]

TEACHER	STUDENTS

Part A: Structured Board Presentation

1. (Write the following lines and symbols on the board.)

What big number goes with 5 and 3? (Pause.)	8
To correct: $5 + 3 =$ what number?	
(Write 8 in box.)	
2. We can use the numbers 5, 3, and 8 to figure out subtraction statements. When you subtract, you always start with the big number. What is the big number?	8
So, I'll write 8 at the start of these subtraction problems.	
3. Listen: $8 - 3$. What will I end up with?	5
Say the first statement.	$8 - 3 = 5$
(Write $8 - 3 = 5$.)	

TEACHER	STUDENTS
4. Listen: 8 − 5. What will I end up with?	3
Say the whole statement.	8 − 5 = 3
(Write 8 − 5 = 3.)	
5. Say both subtraction statements.	8 − 3 = 5
	8 − 5 = 3
(Repeat steps 1–5 with 3 and 4, 6 and 3.)	
Part B: Structured Worksheet	
1. *(Give students worksheets with problems similar to these.)*	
Touch box a. You have to use the three numbers to make up statements. First, say the addition statements.	
2. Say an addition statement that starts with 3. (Pause.)	3 + 4 = 7
Say the other addition statement.	4 + 3 = 7
Write the addition statements. *(Check students' work.)*	
3. Now we'll write the subtraction statements. Which number will go first in both subtraction statements?	7
Say the subtraction fact that begins 7 − 3.	7 − 3 = 4
Say the subtraction fact that begins 7 − 4.	7 − 4 = 3
Write the subtraction statements. *(Check students' work.)*	
(Repeat steps 1–3 with remaining examples.)	

Addition

LEARNING OUTCOMES

7.1 Discuss the two stages of teaching addition to young students and the sequence of problem types appropriate for each stage.

7.2 Explain the importance of the equality principle and outline procedures for teaching it.

7.3 Outline instructional strategies to teach beginning addition including addition the slow way, missing addend addition, and addition the fast way.

7.4 Discuss the differences in the instructional strategies for teaching the three types of multi-digit addition problems.

SKILL HIERARCHY

Our discussion of addition is divided into two stages. The beginning stage discusses strategies designed to establish a conceptual understanding of the process of addition. These strategies, usually taught with semi-concrete objects or representations, are introduced in kindergarten. The multi-digit stage requires mental computation rather than relying on representations of concrete objects. This typically begins during first grade and continues into the upper-elementary grades.

During the beginning stage, students are taught to solve simple addition problems with concrete or semi-concrete objects representing each addend. For example, when solving the problem 4 + 2, students are taught to draw four lines under the numeral 4 and two lines under the numeral 2. The students then determine the sum by counting all of the lines. Counting, numeral identification, and equality preskills must be mastered in order to work these problems. Missing addend problems in which an addend must be computed $(4 + \square = 7)$ are also presented during this stage. An understanding of equality is also essential to solving missing addend problems.

In the advanced stage, when multi-digit addition is taught, students work problems without making concrete representations for each addend. A preskill necessary for solving column addition problems is knowledge of basic addition facts. The ability to accurately and quickly respond to a fact problem allows students to focus their attention on the strategies for solving multi-digit problems. Too little attention is usually given to the process by which students learn to memorize basic addition facts. In order to aid the teacher in teaching this critical preskill, we have devoted an entire chapter to the process of teaching addition, subtraction, multiplication, and division facts (see Chapter 6).

INSTRUCTIONAL SEQUENCE AND ASSESSMENT CHART

Grade Level	Problem Type	Performance Indicator		
K	Begin fact memorization	See Chapter 6		
K	Adding two one-digit numbers within 5	4 +1	3 +2	2 +2
1	Determining an unknown whole number	8 + □ = 11	2 + □ = 7	3 + □ = 9
1	Adding a two-digit and a one- or two-digit number; no renaming	35 +21	64 +23	35 +2
1	Adding two two-digit numbers; renaming from ones to tens	37 +46	48 +14	57 +27
1	Adding three single-digit numbers	1 3 +2	4 4 +3	1 3 +5
1	Complex facts; adding a single-digit number to a teen number—sum below 20	Test students individually; teacher asks: 13 + 3 = 14 + 4 = 12 + 2 =		
2	Adding a three-digit and a one- or two-digit number; no renaming	326 +21	423 +5	570 +21
2	Adding one-, two-, and three-digit numbers; no renaming	4 21 +2	14 71 +10	21 14 +33
2	Adding a three-digit and a one-, two-, or three-digit number; renaming from ones to tens	247 +315	258 +13	276 +8
2	Adding two two- or three-digit numbers; renaming from tens to hundreds	374 +261	83 +43	187 + 81
2	Adding two three-digit numbers; renaming from ones to tens and tens to hundreds	376 +185	248 +164	437 +275
2	Adding three two-digit numbers; renaming— ones column totals less than 20	48 14 +12	39 16 +23	34 24 +12
	Adding three or four numbers; renaming from ones to tens and from tens to hundreds—sums of columns below 20	385 6 24 +120	157 23 245 + 3	8 156 280 +42
2	Adding three two-digit numbers—ones column totals 20 or more	28 17 +28	29 16 +35	38 18 +15
3	Adding three, four, or five multi-digit numbers; renaming in all or some columns totaling 20 or more	892 1486 38 286 +35	8 4086 85 193 +242	3856 2488 1932 +1583

The first type of column problem introduced in the advanced stage involves adding multi-digit numbers in which the sum in each column is less than 10; accordingly, **renaming** is not required (36 + 13). The next major type of problem involves adding two or more multi-digit numbers in which the sum of one or more columns is greater than 10 and requires renaming (36 + 15). The initial problem in this group involves adding two double-digit numerals such as 45 + 37. Problems with hundreds and thousands numbers are introduced after students have been taught to read and write those numerals.

The third major type of problem involves addition of three or more multi-digit numbers. The difficulty of these problems increases as the sum of each column becomes greater. For example, adding 23 + 14 + 32 is not difficult, since a sum never reaches 10. On the other hand, in a problem such as 39 + 16 + 27, the sum for the first two numbers in the one's column is more than 10 (9 + 6 = 15). The student must not only rename but also must be able to figure out facts in which a single-digit number is added to a two-digit number. The sum of the first two digits in the ones column, 9 and 6, is 15. The students must then add 7 to 15 to figure the sum of the ones column. We refer to problems in which a student must mentally add a single-digit number to a two-digit number as **complex addition facts**. A great deal of practice is necessary for students to master complex addition facts.

The Instructional Sequence and Assessment Chart shown on the previous page includes our recommended instruction and assessment sequence.

CONCEPTUAL UNDERSTANDING

The major objective of beginning addition instruction is to develop a conceptual understanding of addition as a union of disjoint sets. Most educators agree that, at this stage, demonstrations should involve concrete objects. Math educators recommend a variety of methods for introducing addition. Using the term *sets* and giving demonstrations of joining two sets are suggested in some commercial programs:

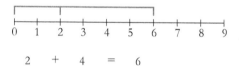

3   +   2   =   5

Demonstrations through number lines also are suggested:

0 1 2 3 4 5 6 7 8 9

2   +   4   =   6

The direct instruction strategies recommended in this text use lines as semi-concrete objects to represent the members of sets. While nothing is wrong with using concrete manipulatives, having students draw lines has several advantages. Drawing lines graphically demonstrates equality (the same number of lines are on both sides of the equal sign), and teachers can more readily monitor student performance on written work because the lines provide a written record of student performance, which makes diagnosis of errors easier.

A unique feature of the direct instruction strategies for introducing the addition process is the integration of the equality principle into the strategy. It is important that initial strategies demonstrate the application of the equality principle because a grasp of equality is necessary for success in more complicated exercises.

Equality can be taught by presenting a functional definition and a series of positive and negative examples. The definition is functional in that it describes a condition that must be met for the equality principle to apply. *We must end with the same number on this side and the other side of the equal sign.* **Format 7.1: Equality Introduction** is a format for introducing equality. This format should be presented during the beginning stage before addition is introduced. The format includes three parts. In Part A, the teacher introduces the equal sign and equality rule. In Part B, the teacher demonstrates examples in which the sides are equal and examples in which the sides are not equal. Diagrams like the one below in which lines are written inside two adjoining circles are written on the board.

▶ **Format 7.1A:**
Equality Introduction
Watch how Michaela demonstrates the equality rule.

   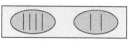

**Format 7.1B:
Equality Rule**

Watch how Michaela demonstrates when the equality rule.

The teacher leads the students in determining whether an equal sign would be drawn between the circles. Part C is a less structured worksheet exercise similar to Part B. Note that in Parts B and C, students are asked to say the rule. Saying the rule may be quite difficult for lower-performing students. To ease this difficulty, the teacher might first model, lead, and test, saying just the first half of the rule: *We must end with the same number.* Lower performers may need many repetitions. After several days, the teacher provides practice in saying the last half of the rule and then the entire rule.

Making lines for each addend and then counting the lines is called *addition the slow way.* Students draw the appropriate number of lines under each numeral:

$$4 + 2 = \square$$
$$\text{IIII} \quad \text{II}$$

Students count the lines and then draw the same number of lines on the other side of the equal sign and write the answer in the box:

$$4 + 2 = \boxed{6}$$
$$\text{IIII} \quad \text{II} \quad \text{IIIIII}$$

By counting the lines one by one and drawing the same number of lines on the other side, the concept of equality is reinforced. Note that in this strategy, *plus* is used as a verb; students are taught, "The plus sign says to count all the lines." Later the terms *addition* and *adding* are introduced. Separating the teaching of the concept of addition and the related terminology makes it easier for the students to master strategies for addition initially. Substituting the terms at a later date decreases the cognitive demands made on the students when learning a new strategy.

Problems with **missing addends** are introduced after students demonstrate mastery of beginning addition exercises. In solving problems with missing addends:

$$4 + \square = 7$$
$$\text{IIII} \quad \text{IIIIIII}$$

The teacher points out that the sides are not equal. The students must draw lines to make the sides equal and then write the numeral representing the number of lines drawn.

After the students can solve addition and missing addend problems, using a line-drawing strategy, a new strategy, called *addition the fast way,* is introduced. In addition the fast way, students make lines only under the second addend, count the lines beginning with the first numeral (*ffoourr,* 5, 6), and then write the answer in the box. Addition the fast way represents a transition from the semi-concrete stage in which objects are drawn to represent each member of the set to the stage in which no concrete representations are used. A similar fast-way strategy can be taught for missing addend problems.

INSTRUCTIONAL PROCEDURES: BEGINNING ADDITION

Addition the Slow Way

Addition the slow way is an important strategy because it is the first problem-solving strategy taught. The following preskills are those that students should have mastered before addition the slow way is introduced:

1. Identifying and writing the numerals 0–10 and the symbols $+$, $-$, $=$, and $\square$
2. Equality rule
3. Reading an equation
4. Drawing the appropriate number of lines to represent a numeral
5. Counting the lines in two groups
6. Writing the numeral that represents a set of objects

SUMMARY BOX 7.1

Beginning Addition Strategy

1. Students read equation: 5 + 2 = how many?
2. Students recite equality rule: "We must end up with the same number on this side AND the other side of the equal sign."
3. Students draw lines under the first addend and then under the second addend.
4. Students count all lines on that side of the equal sign.
5. Students apply the equality rule and make lines under the box on the other side of the equal sign.
6. Students write a numeral to represent the number of lines.

The format for teaching students to work addition problems the slow way appears in **Format 7.2: Teaching Addition the Slow Way.** In Part A, the teacher works the problem on the board. The steps in the strategy are summarized in **Summary Box 7.1**.

When presenting Part A, the teacher should repeat the example until students can correctly respond to all of the questions. If a student hesitates or responds incorrectly, the teacher would model the correct answer, then repeat the question, and ask the students to respond. Following the correction, all the steps in Part A of **Format 7.2** are repeated demonstrating how all the steps fit together.

Part B is a structured worksheet exercise, and Part C is a less structured worksheet exercise. Example selection for all worksheet exercises should include only numerals that students can identify and write. Sums should not exceed 10. On the worksheets, spaces should be left under the numerals for students to draw lines. Once they develop 80% to 90% accuracy in working the problems, students may work independently on this type of exercise. Eight to 10 problems should appear daily on student worksheets for several weeks. Note that on worksheets, spaces are drawn below each numeral to prompt drawing the lines.

Missing Addend Strategy

The strategy discussed in this section teaches students to find the missing addend in a problem such as 5 + □ = 8. The strategy is based on the equality rule *(We must end with the same number this side and the other side of the equal sign).* Students are presented this form of problem to enhance their understanding of the equality principle and to demonstrate that the equality principle may be used to solve a variety of problem types.

To solve this simple form of missing addend problems, the students first find the side of the equal sign that tells how many they end with. The teacher then points out that the sides are not equal until the students end with the same number on both sides. The teacher directs the students to draw lines on the side with the box so that the sides will be equal and to fill in the missing numeral.

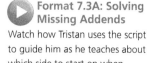

Format 7.3A: Solving Missing Addends

Watch how Tristan uses the script to guide him as he teaches about which side to start on when solving for missing addends.

Format 7.3: Solving Missing Addends presents the missing addend strategy. Part A teaches students the component skill of determining the side to start working on. The exercise points out that since a box doesn't tell how many lines to draw, it can't be the side to start on. Parts B and C are structured board and worksheet exercises, respectively. Note that in step 5 of Part B and step 7 of Part C, the teacher reminds the students that the lines under a box tell what numeral goes in the box.

$$5 + \square = 7$$
$$\|$$

This prompt prevents errors like 5 + 7 = 7 in which students write the number that they counted to instead of writing the numeral for the number of lines for the missing addend.

Part D is a less structured worksheet exercise that includes an equal mixture of missing addend and regular addition problems. In Part D, the teacher leads the students through steps designed to teach the students when to apply the missing addend strategy. The teacher then instructs the students to make both sides equal and finally to fill in the missing numeral. Lower-performing students may need a great deal of practice on this before they can discriminate when and how to apply the regular addition and missing addend strategies. Examples should be limited to problems in which the sum is 10 or less. This limitation is suggested to prevent the tasks from becoming too cumbersome.

When the missing addend is zero, as in $8 + \square = 8$, the teacher can use this wording to replace steps 6, 7, and 8 in Part C:

6. This is a special kind of problem. The sides are already equal. Eight on both sides. So you shouldn't make any lines. You plus zero lines. Write a zero in the box.
7. Eight plus how many equals 8?
8. Say the whole statement.

We recommend that teachers present several examples in which the missing addend is zero in Part C , for example, $8 + \square = 8$ and $2 + \square = 2$. Teachers should continue to present problems in which the missing addend is zero in Part D.

Addition the Fast Way

Addition the fast way (see Format 7.4: Teaching Addition the Fast Way) is taught as a transitional step between the strategy in which students draw lines for each member of the sets represented by each addend and later exercises in which students memorize addition facts. When time for math instruction is limited, teachers can skip addition the fast way and move directly into fact teaching (see Chapter 6). The addition the fast way strategy differs from addition the slow way in that the student draws lines only to represent the addend following the plus sign:

$$7 + 4 = \square$$
$$||||$$

When solving the problem, the student starts counting at the number represented by the numeral in the first addend position and then counts the lines (in the problem above, students count "*ssevvenn*, 8, 9, 10, 11"). Then the student writes the numeral representing the sum in the box on the other side of the equal sign. The student does not draw lines under the box. The only new preskill for this strategy is rote counting beginning at a number other than 1.

Addition the fast way is introduced when students are able to work a mixture of addition and missing addend problems with 80% to 90% accuracy. Teachers can expect some students to have difficulty coordinating counting from a number other than 1 and touching lines. For students who consistently have difficulty with this step, the teacher should present an exercise focusing solely on this component skill. The teacher might write a series of problems in which the lines are drawn:

$$5 + 3 \qquad 7 + 2$$
$$||| \qquad ||$$
$$3 + 4 \qquad 9 + 5$$
$$|||| \qquad |||||$$

The teacher models and tests counting until the students can consistently count correctly. For example, for $5 + 3$, the teacher says, "*Ffiivve,*" then touches each line and counts "6, 7, 8." The teacher then tests by presenting another example, $7 + 2$, touching 7 and saying, "Get it going," to indicate that students begin with 7 and then count each line.

Example selection criteria for addition the fast way problems are somewhat different from those for addition the slow way. Larger numerals can be written in the first addend position because the student no longer has to draw lines to represent that amount. The second addend, however, should remain a smaller number (1–8). Teachers must design the problems so that the sum is represented by a numeral the students have been taught to write.

After students work addition problems the fast way accurately, subtraction instruction can begin (see Chapter 8). After students work addition problems fluently, memorization of addition facts should begin (see Chapter 6).

Diagnosis and Remediation

Previously, we have stressed the importance of immediately correcting all student errors. At times, it may become apparent that a pattern of errors persists. This section presents basic procedures for diagnosing and remedying persistent errors in beginning addition. The basic steps below apply to diagnosing and remedying errors on any type of problem.

1. Diagnosis: The teacher analyzes worksheet errors and hypothesizes about the cause of each error.
2. Confirmation: The teacher interviews the student to determine the cause of the error if it is not obvious.
3. Reteaching: The teacher provides reteaching through board and/or worksheet presentations of a component skill or a strategy.
4. Assess: The teacher tests the student on a set of problems similar to the ones on which the original errors were made.

Once students begin working problems independently using a specific strategy, the errors they make on their worksheets fall into two main categories (fact errors are not possible at this stage because facts are not used nor have they been taught).

1. Component-skill errors: a difficulty on one or more of the component skills or preskills used in the strategy
2. Strategy errors: a fundamental lack of understanding of the strategy

The similarities in the suggested remediation for each type of error should be noted.

Component-Skill Errors   Component-skill errors may be made on symbol identification and writing, counting and/or drawing lines, and application of the equality rule. When errors are related to component-skills, error patterns are more readily apparent. Therefore, a teacher often can determine the cause of these errors by carefully analyzing worksheets. For example, on an addition the fast way worksheet, a student made the following errors:

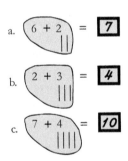

By analyzing the errors made by the student, the teacher can determine whether the student had trouble coordinating counting from a number or incorrectly identified the numeral representing the first addend while touching the first line under the second addend. For example, in problem a above, the student may have touched the first line under 2 while saying *sssiiixxx* and then would have said 7 when touching the second line.

To remedy a component-skill error, the teacher presents practice exercises on the component skill in isolation for several lessons before returning to the more advanced problems. For example, to remedy the errors made by the student above, the teacher would present an exercise on coordinating counting and touching lines. The teacher would focus on that one skill until the student reached a criterion of about 90% correct responses. Then the teacher would give the student addition problems similar to those in the original exercise. This would assess if mastery of the component skill allows students to successfully complete the strategy. If students do not demonstrate mastery of the strategy, additional structured practice on the strategy may be required or another component-skill error may be present.

Another possible component error involves symbol identification. If a student missed a problem because of numeral misidentification (identifying 6 as 9), the teacher would reteach identifying the numeral 6 for several lessons. During this time, the student would not be asked to solve problems including the numeral 6.

Strategy Errors A strategy error indicates a fundamental lack of understanding of how to sequence the steps in the problem-solving strategy. In the example below, a strategy error occurred when, after drawing lines under each numeral, the student wrote the next number in the counting sequence (10) in the box instead of the total number of lines counted (9). This error clearly indicates that the student is not employing the strategy.

$$3 + 6 = 10$$
$$|||\quad ||||||$$

To remedy a strategy error, the teacher reintroduces the format in which the strategy is taught to the student, beginning with the structured board presentation, and then progresses to the structured and less structured worksheet presentations. A common strategy error students make when solving problems with missing addends involves adding the addend and the sum: $6 + 15 = 9$. Such errors indicate students are not applying the equality principle. For these types of errors, the teacher begins with the structured board presentation, Part B of Format 7.3: Solving Missing Addends, then progresses to worksheets in Parts C and D.

INSTRUCTIONAL PROCEDURES: MULTI-DIGIT ADDITION

Column addition problems may be divided into three groups. Simplest are those that do not require renaming:

$$\begin{array}{r} 24 \\ +15 \\ \hline \end{array}$$

Next are problems with two multi-digit addends, where renaming is necessary:

$$\begin{array}{r} 424 \\ +317 \\ \hline \end{array}$$

Most difficult are problems with more than two multi-digit addends with renaming:

$$\begin{array}{r} 671 \\ 424 \\ +317 \\ \hline \end{array}$$

Students work column addition problems by using their knowledge of facts. Therefore, problems should be constructed from facts the students have been taught.

Problems Not Requiring Renaming

Column addition problems without renaming are usually introduced in first grade after students have learned to read and write numerals through 99 and are able to mentally determine answers to about 25 basic addition facts. Remember that basic addition facts include all possible pairings in which the addends are single-digit numbers. Students need many months of practice before they have memorized all basic facts. However, the introduction of multi-digit addition problems need not be delayed until students have memorized *all* basic addition facts. Initial examples, however, should be designed to include the easier addition facts. Exercises to help memorize basic addition facts are discussed in detail in Chapter 6.

The procedure for teaching students to work these problems is relatively simple. The teacher has the students read the problem and then points out the place value columns, telling students to first add the ones and then add the tens. Teaching students to always begin working in the ones column helps prevent errors on more difficult renaming problems. Although students can compute the correct answer if they begin in the tens column on problems that don't require renaming, they will eventually have difficulty when they start working problems that do require renaming. Therefore, students should be taught to always begin solving the problem in the ones column.

$$
\begin{array}{ccccccc}
24 & & 24 & \text{BUT} & 24 & & 24 \\
\underline{+12} & \text{then} & \underline{12} & \text{NOT} & \underline{+17} & \text{then} & \underline{+17} \\
6 & & 36 & & 3 & & 311
\end{array}
$$

After learning which column to begin with when solving a problem, students add the ones and then the tens, writing the sum for each column. The teacher asks about the number of tens rather than the quantity represented by the tens number; that is, for

$$
\begin{array}{c}
34 \\
\underline{+21}
\end{array}
$$

the students indicate they are adding 3 tens and 2 tens, not 30 and 20, to remind students they are working in the tens columns. We do not include a format in the book for this problem type because the teaching procedure is quite simple: A teacher first uses a structured board presentation and then structured and less structured worksheet exercises. The transition from structured board to independent worksheet can be made in about four lessons.

Problems Requiring Renaming

Problems requiring renaming are usually introduced during first grade. Preskills include working addition problems without renaming, reading and writing numerals, knowing basic addition facts, and using expanded notation with teen and tens numbers.

Preskill   A unique preskill for renaming involves adding three single-digit numbers. For example, when adding tens in

$$
\begin{array}{c}
1 \\
37 \\
\underline{+29} \\
6
\end{array}
$$

the student must add $1 + 3$ to get the sum of 4 and then add the sum to 2. Adding three numbers is significantly more difficult for low performers than adding two numbers. When adding three numbers, the student must add the first two numbers, remember the answer, and then add the third number to that sum.

Adding three single-digit numbers should be taught several weeks prior to the introduction of renaming problems. The format for teaching students a strategy to solve these problems appears in **Format 7.5: Adding Three Single-Digit Numbers.** The format contains only two parts: a structured board presentation and a structured worksheet presentation. Since relatively few steps are involved, a less-structured worksheet format is not needed.

The most common error made on this format occurs in step 6 of Part A and step 4 of Part B when students are asked to identify the next two numbers to be added. Students often respond with the second and third numbers instead of the sum of the first two numbers and the third number. For example, in the following problem

$$
\begin{array}{c}
2 \\
3 \\
\underline{+4}
\end{array}
$$

the students answer $3 + 4$ rather than $5 + 4$. In Part A, the teacher tries to prompt the correct response by referring to that question as the "hard part." If students do make the error, the teacher must model and test the answer and then repeat the entire sequence from the beginning. ("Now we're adding $5 + 4$. What are we adding now? What is $5 + 4$?. . . Let's do the whole problem again from the beginning.")

There are two example selection guidelines for this format. In about half of the examples, the top numeral should be 1 because in most renaming a 1 is placed in the tens column. Initially, the sum of the three single digits should be 10 or less so that students will be able to concentrate on adding the three numbers rather than figuring out more difficult basic facts.

Introducing the Problems   The first type of renaming problem involves adding a two-digit numeral to another one- or two-digit numeral. Renaming is explained to students by pointing out that a tens number may not appear in the ones column and must be placed on top of the tens column. For example, leading the students through the problem

$$\begin{array}{r} 37 \\ +25 \\ \hline \end{array}$$

the teacher asks the students what 7 + 5 equals. After the students say 12, the teacher says, "We have a problem. Twelve equals 1 ten and 2 ones. We can't have a ten in the ones column. So, we put the 1 ten at the top of the tens column" (teacher writes 1 over 3) "and the 2 ones under the ones column" (teacher writes 2 under 5). Format 7.6: Adding Two Numerals with Renaming can be used for introducing renaming.

While Part A focuses student attention on the fact that they cannot have a ten in the ones column, Part B sets up the sequence of steps the students will follow when working problems on their own. The vocabulary used in this format was selected to foster the students' understanding of the operation. For example, under step 6 in Part A, it is important to remind the students that they are adding tens ("How many tens do we end up with?") so that they remember the values of the numbers and do not just think of the numbers as individual numerals (3 in the tens column represents 30, not 3). Note that in Part B, step 3, the teacher prompts the students less on determining what 13 equals. Instead of just telling the students that 13 = 10 + 3, the teacher encourages the students to answer independently.

A common error made on renaming problems involves renaming the wrong numeral. For example, in working the problem 37 + 27, the student places the 4 above the tens column and writes 1 under the ones column. If the students write the numerals in the wrong places, the teacher should not merely model where to write the numerals but should ask students the critical questions (Part B, step 3) so that they can see why the numerals need to be in the appropriate places. After the students correctly answer the questions, the teacher can demonstrate how to put a ten on top of the tens column.

If a student hesitates in answering on a particular step, the teacher should say the answer, repeat the question, and have the student respond again. After using this correction procedure, the teacher should then present the entire problem to give students the opportunity to successfully work through all of the steps in the strategy.

As students learn to read and write larger numbers, renaming problems with these numbers are introduced. First, problems in which students rename to the hundreds column are introduced. The format for presenting problems in which the students must rename to the hundreds column would be very similar to the format for renaming to the tens column (Format 7.6: Adding Two Numerals with Renaming). For example, the students are working this problem:

$$\begin{array}{r} 283 \\ +185 \\ \hline \end{array}$$

After asking the students what 8 tens + 8 tens equals, the teacher would say, "We have a problem. Sixteen tens equals 1 hundred plus 6 tens. We can't have a hundred in the tens column, so we put it at the top of the hundreds column" (teacher writes 1 over the 2) "and put the 6 tens here" (teacher writes 6 under the tens column).

Problems in which students rename twice, to the tens column and then to the hundreds column, are introduced next. These problems and future problem types will require only a brief introduction, because once students understand the process of renaming, they usually have little difficulty generalizing. Lower-performing students, however, may need more supervised practice with worksheets containing a variety of problem types. **Summary Box 7.2:** Addition with Renaming outlines the steps in the renaming strategy.

When introducing the strategy using the structured board and worksheet parts of a format, the teacher should use only examples of the type being introduced. When presenting the less structured and supervised parts of the format, the teacher should give the students a cumulative review

FIGURE 7.1 Sample worksheet for adding with renaming

356	486	395	495	386
+277	+281	−243	+235	−241
489	37	523	924	924
+232	+28	+206	−201	+31
372	938	356	284	565
+472	−214	+217	+382	+265
87	87	299	468	98
+47	−47	+91	−354	+97

worksheet. Worksheets are designed to provide cumulative review so that previously taught types of problems receive systematic practice. We recommend that one-third to one-half of the problems on the worksheet be the most recently introduced type pf problems. The others should be addition problems of previously introduced types and subtraction problems. The problems should be written in random order. Several examples of the new problem type can appear at the beginning of the work-sheet. Otherwise, no more than two or three problems of the same type should appear consecutively.

Cumulative review is especially important when introducing renaming. A student has not mastered renaming until he can discriminate when renaming is appropriate. Addition problems that do not require renaming must be included so that students do not get into the habit of always putting a 1 at the top of the tens column. Likewise, subtraction problems must be included so that the students receive continued practice discriminating addition from subtraction.

An example of a worksheet for a lesson that takes place several days after introducing renaming to the tens and the hundreds columns appears in **Figure 7.1**. Note that more than one-third of the problems contain double renaming. Of the other addition problems, several involve just renaming from the tens to the hundreds columns, and several involve no renaming at all. About one-third of the problems are subtraction problems.

Three or More Addends

The last major problem type includes those problems with three or more multi-digit addends. Some of these problems are particularly difficult because the student is required to mentally add a number represented by a single-digit numeral to a number represented by a two-digit numeral. For example, note the problems below:

$$
\begin{array}{r}
36 \\
16 \\
+24
\end{array} \Big] 12 + 4 \qquad
\begin{array}{r}
47 \\
24 \\
+13
\end{array} \Big] 11 + 3
$$

$$
\begin{array}{r}
5839 \\
2467
\end{array} \Big] 16 + 9
$$

$$
\begin{array}{r}
3589 \\
+2849
\end{array} \Big] 25 + 9
$$

SUMMARY BOX 7.2

Addition with Renaming

1. Students read the problem.
2. Students begin adding in the ones column.
3. If the sum of the ones column is 10 or more, students determine that they must rename.
4. Students use expanded notation to determine the number of tens and ones in the sum of the ones column.
5. Students rename by putting the tens in the tens column and the ones in the ones column.
6. Students add the first two tens in the tens column and then add the next ten to that sum.
7. Students write the sum of tens in the tens column.

In each problem, the sum of the first two addends in the ones column is a teen number (12, 11, and 16). The next step in each problem involves adding a single-digit numeral to a teen numeral (12 + 4, 11 + 3, 16 + 9). As mentioned earlier, we call facts in which a single-digit number is added to a two-digit number *complex addition facts*. Learning complex addition facts is a critical preskill that takes many months of practice to master. Teachers should begin practice exercises on this preskill after students know about 50 basic addition facts.

Format 7.7A: Complex Addition Facts with a Total Less than 20
Watch how Tristan gives his students think time before asking them to respond.

Format 7.7: Complex Addition Facts with a Total Less Than 20 shows how to present adding a single-digit number to a teen number when the total does not exceed 19(14 + 3, 15 + 2). Students are typically introduced to these problems sometime in first grade. The students learn to transform a complex fact into two simple facts. For example, students transform 16 + 3 into 10 + 6 + 3, add 6 + 3, and then add 10 + 9. Note that extensive practice on this skill is required to develop fluency.

After students can solve this first type of complex addition fact mentally, they can begin column addition problems involving three or more numerals that require renaming. These problems can be introduced with a relatively simple format. The teacher has the students add all the numerals in the ones column. After the sum of the ones column is computed, the students rename to the tens column and write the ones under the ones column. A similar procedure is followed with the tens, hundreds, and thousands columns. Note that examples should be carefully selected so that students do not encounter complex addition facts that have not been previously taught.

Self-Checking After students become proficient in working renaming problems with three addends, they should be taught to check their answers. A checking procedure for addition is adding from the bottom digit in each column, assuming the students start with the top digit in each column when they originally work the problem. The teacher introduces checking using a worksheet exercise. Students complete the first problem, and the teacher says, "Here's how to check your work to make sure you have the right answer. Start with the bottom number and add up the column. What are the first two numbers?... What's the answer?... What's the answer for the next two numbers?... Is that what you wrote in the answer for the ones column and at the top of the tens column?... Let's start from the bottom again... What are the first two numbers you add in the tens column?... What's the answer for the next two numbers?... Is that what you wrote for the answer?"

Determining whether students check their work is difficult because checking doesn't require any additional writing. An exercise to encourage checking involves giving students already-worked problems, about half of which have incorrect answers, and instructing students to check the answers and correct mistakes.

Diagnosis and Remediation

As mentioned previously, the teacher must carefully analyze student work to provide remediation accordingly. In the multi-digit stage of addition instruction, students might make three types of errors persistently: facts, component, and strategy. In the area of addition, the most common errors involve facts, the component skill of renaming, and inattention to the sign in the problem.

Fact Errors Fact errors cause most column addition errors. Such errors are sometimes easy to identify, as in the problems below:

a.
$$\begin{array}{r} 11 \\ 357 \\ +248 \\ \hline 606 \end{array}$$

b.
$$\begin{array}{r} 1 \\ 228 \\ +744 \\ \hline 971 \end{array}$$

c.
$$\begin{array}{r} 1 \\ 648 \\ +281 \\ \hline 919 \end{array}$$

Note that in each example, the student missed the problem because of a fact error (in problem a, the student wrote 16 for 7 + 8). In some cases, however, teachers cannot easily determine if a fact error caused the incorrect answer. For example, in the following problems, the errors could have been caused by failing to rename or by a fact error. In problem d, the student might have incorrectly added $1 + 5 + 4$ in the tens column or failed to rename.

d.
$$
\begin{array}{r}
\textit{1} \\
357 \\
+248 \\
\hline
595
\end{array}
$$

e.
$$
\begin{array}{r}
\textit{1} \\
228 \\
+743 \\
\hline
961
\end{array}
$$

In order to determine the specific cause of the errors, the teacher should look for error patterns. For example, the teacher should check the errors to see if the same facts were consistently missed. Also, the teacher should utilize the information she has about the student's performance on recent fact worksheets. To confirm the diagnosis, the teacher should observe the student reworking some of the missed problems and have her explain her thinking.

The remediation procedure depends on the nature of the fact errors. If a student consistently misses the same facts, the teacher provides extra practice on those facts. On the other hand, some students are erratic in their performance, answering a fact correctly one time and missing it the next. For such students, the teacher may increase the incentives for accurate work.

A final note on facts concerns teachers who work with older students who rely on their fingers to figure out basic facts. Unfortunately, since lower-grade classrooms often do not provide adequate practice on fact mastery, many students may be using their fingers to figure out basic facts. Teachers should be careful not to forbid the students to use their fingers if that is their only strategy for deriving an answer. Rather, the teacher should ensure that students are using a finger strategy that is relatively efficient and that students use the strategy accurately. Mistakes in finger strategies may occur because a student makes errors in counting or does not coordinate putting up his fingers and counting (the student does not put up a finger for each number counted). The ultimate goal is to teach students to master their facts and to stop relying on finger counting altogether.

Component-Skill Errors   The first component-skill error involves renaming. Note the errors in the problems below:

$$
\begin{array}{r}
\textit{6} \\
48 \\
+28 \\
\hline
121
\end{array}
\qquad
\begin{array}{r}
\textit{5} \\
39 \\
27 \\
+19 \\
\hline
112
\end{array}
$$

The student work clearly presents a pattern of errors suggesting the diagnosis of incorrectly renaming. Because the pattern of errors is so clear, additional confirmation is not necessary before introducing remediation exercises. Errors in which students place the numbers incorrectly are quite serious because they indicate a fundamental misunderstanding of basic place value concepts. Remediation of the component skill involves a set of problems containing boxes in which the sum of the ones column and the numeral above the tens column are to be recorded. For each problem, the teacher tells the student the sum of the numerals in the ones column and then asks how many tens and ones make up that sum. The student answers and then fills in the numerals. The remediation set should contain approximately 10 examples that look similar to the following.

$$
\begin{array}{cccc}
\square & \square & \square & \square \\
68 & 45 & 24 & 86 \\
+19 & +29 & +18 & +27 \\
\hline
\square & \square & \square & \square
\end{array}
$$

After the student demonstrates mastery of the retaught component skill, the teacher leads the students through a set of four to six addition problems using Part C of **Format 7.6: Adding Two Numerals with Renaming.** The first three to four examples of the less structured worksheet should be problems in which renaming is required. Examples in the worksheet should also contain some discrimination problems in which renaming is not required so that students do not get into the habit of always writing a 1 above the tens column. Students have shown mastery when they complete at least 90% of all problems on the discrimination worksheet correctly.

Failure to attend to the sign is a common cause of errors in column addition problems:

$$
\begin{array}{r} 342 \\ +131 \\ \hline 211 \end{array}
\qquad
\begin{array}{r} 304 \\ -201 \\ \hline 505 \end{array}
$$

If such errors occur on more than 10% of the problems, students should be given a special worksheet with an equal mix of addition and subtraction problems in random order:

$$
\begin{array}{r} 37 \\ -15 \\ \hline \end{array}
\begin{array}{r} 28 \\ +13 \\ \hline \end{array}
\begin{array}{r} 47 \\ +24 \\ \hline \end{array}
\begin{array}{r} 38 \\ -16 \\ \hline \end{array}
\begin{array}{r} 47 \\ +25 \\ \hline \end{array}
\begin{array}{r} 86 \\ -23 \\ \hline \end{array}
\begin{array}{r} 48 \\ +20 \\ \hline \end{array}
$$

The teacher presents the less structured worksheet exercises, instructing students to circle and say the sign before working each problem.

Strategy Errors Strategy errors demonstrate a fundamental misunderstanding of the strategy. An example of one type of strategy error appears below:

$$
\begin{array}{r} 35 \\ +27 \\ \hline 512 \end{array}
\qquad
\begin{array}{r} 68 \\ +18 \\ \hline 716 \end{array}
$$

This is quite a serious error, indicating the student does not understand the concept of renaming. The remediation procedure for all strategy errors involves reteaching the format for that particular type of problem. The teacher presents several problems using a structured board presentation and then leads the students through several worksheet problems using the structured and then the less structured parts of the format.

A summary of the errors common to column addition and the diagnosis and remediation procedures appropriate for each appear in **Figure 7.2**. Unless otherwise noted, after each remediation procedure, the teacher needs to give students worksheets similar to the ones on which the original errors were made in order to test whether the remediation was effective.

FIGURE 7.2 Diagnosis and remediation of addition errors

Error Pattern	Diagnosis	Remediation Procedures	Remediation Examples
Fact Errors			
a. $\begin{array}{r}46\\+17\\\hline 64\end{array}$ $\begin{array}{r}263\\+174\\\hline 447\end{array}$	Basic fact errors. Student doesn't know the fact 6 + 7.	Emphasize 6 + 7 in fact memorization exercises. See Chapter 6.	
Component-Skill Errors			
b. $\begin{array}{r}{\scriptstyle 3}\\46\\+17\\\hline 81\end{array}$ $\begin{array}{r}{\scriptstyle 2}\\53\\+29\\\hline 91\end{array}$	Renaming errors. Student renames incorrectly, writing the tens digit in the ones column.	Steps from structured worksheet exercise that focus on renaming. (Format 7.6, Part B, steps 1–3)	10 problems in this form: $\begin{array}{r}\square\\69\\+36\\\hline\square\end{array}$ $\begin{array}{r}\square\\46\\+29\\\hline\square\end{array}$
c. $\begin{array}{r}49\\+17\\\hline 32\end{array}$ $\begin{array}{r}253\\-174\\\hline 427\end{array}$	Sign discrimination error. Student subtracts instead of adding, and vice versa.	Less structured worksheet exercise. Have students circle the sign before working each problem. (Format 7.6, Part C, steps 1–4)	Mix of addition and subtraction problems.

Note: After addressing any component-skill error, assess students using worksheets similar to the ones on which errors were originally made in order to determine if the remediation was successful.

Strategy Errors			
d. $\begin{array}{r}46\\+17\\\hline 513\end{array}$ $\begin{array}{r}253\\+174\\\hline 3127\end{array}$	Student does not carry; writes the entire number in the sum. Have student solve a problem while thinking out loud to determine student knowledge of preskills.	Present the format beginning with structured board exercise. (Format 7.6, Part A)	

APPLY WHAT YOU LEARNED

 Click on the √ to answer the questions online.

1. Identify the problem type for each of the following examples. List the problems in the order in which they appear on the Instructional Sequence.

   a. 462
      +371

   b. 35
      16
      +24

   c. 46
      87
      +19

   d. 84
      +13

   e. 348
      +135

   f. 368
      +259

2. The following is an excerpt from Format 7.3 for solving missing addends. Student responses are included. Specify how the teacher would use the equality principle to correct the error.

   Missing Addend Format

   PART B: STRUCTURED BOARD PRESENTATION

TEACHER	STUDENTS
(Write the following problem on the board.) $4 + \boxed{} = 6$ |||| ||||||	
4. We want to end with the same number on both sides. (Point to $4 + \boxed{}$.) "How many on this side now?"	4
"Think. How many do we have to end with on this side?"	4

3. Below is an excerpt from an independent worksheet to be given to students who have just demonstrated accuracy in solving problems requiring the addition of two two-digit numbers with renaming from the ones to tens columns. The teacher has made some errors in constructing the worksheet.

   a. Indicate the inappropriate examples.

   b. Identify any omitted problem types that should be included on the worksheet.

   Worksheet

   a. 462   b. 75   c. 141   d. 38   e. 582
      +183   +16   +324   +26   +15

   f. 1   g. 46   h. 617   i. 58
      3   +15   +124   +25
      +6

4. At the beginning of the unit, the teacher tested Leslie. Her work on the performance indicators appears below. Specify the type of problems with which instruction should begin for Leslie. Explain your answer.

   a. ¹37   ¹48   ¹57   b. ¹247   ¹258   ¹276
      +46   +14   +27   +315   +13   +8
      ──   ──   ──   ───   ───   ───
      83   61   84   562   272   284

   c. 13 + 3 = 16   d. 374   248   437
      14 + 4 = 18   +261   +364   +285
      12 + 2 = 14   ───   ───   ───
                            535   511   652

   e. ¹276   ¹248   ¹437
      +185   +365   +285
      ───   ───   ───
      461   512   622

5. Below are 11 problems that appeared on the worksheets to be done independently by the students in Mrs. Ash's math group. Next to each student's name are the problems missed by the student. For each student:

a. Diagnose: Specify the probable cause or causes of the student's errors

b. Confirm: Verify the diagnosis, if needed

c. Remediate: Indicate if a component skill or strategy should be retaught and the examples that could be used

d. Assess: Provide examples that could be used to determine student mastery of the strategy

37	364	57	36	48	72	58	57	48	34	514
+26	+212	−23	+22	+28	+26	−32	+34	−24	+26	+23

Errors:

Ian
$$\begin{array}{r} 3 \\ 37 \\ +26 \\ \hline 91 \end{array} \qquad \begin{array}{r} 6 \\ 48 \\ +28 \\ \hline 121 \end{array}$$

Moniqua
$$\begin{array}{r} 37 \\ +26 \\ \hline 513 \end{array} \qquad \begin{array}{r} 48 \\ +28 \\ \hline 616 \end{array} \qquad \begin{array}{r} 34 \\ +26 \\ \hline 510 \end{array}$$

Pablo
$$\begin{array}{r} 37 \\ +26 \\ \hline 11 \end{array} \qquad \begin{array}{r} 1 \\ 48 \\ -24 \\ \hline 72 \end{array}$$

6. Specify a diagnosis and remediation for each of the students listed below.

a. For each student, describe the probable cause or mistaken strategy responsible for the errors.

b. For each remediation, indicate the format and the part of that format you would begin remediation with. If no format appears in the book for that problem type, indicate the page in the text that discusses that problem type.

Student A

$3 + \boxed{7} = 7$
||||

$5 + \boxed{8} = 8$
|||

$4 + \boxed{9} = 9$
|||||

$2 + \boxed{6} = 6$
|||||

Student B

$6 + 3 = \boxed{8}$
|||

$7 + 2 = \boxed{8}$
||

$2 + 4 = \boxed{5}$
|||||

$3 + 5 = \boxed{7}$
|||||

7. Write the wording the teacher uses in the structured worksheet part in presenting the following problem:

$$\begin{array}{r} 162 \\ +283 \\ \hline \end{array}$$

8. Below are worksheets made by three teachers for the less structured part of the format for teaching students to work problems with renaming from the ones to tens columns. Two teachers constructed unacceptable lists. Identify these teachers and tell why each is unacceptable. For the unacceptable lists, specify what could be done to make the list acceptable.

a.
37	37	237	481	374	48	786
+25	−25	+86	+110	−213	+24	+346

b.
48	78	37	58	73	57
+26	+25	+8	+24	+28	+18

c.
47	47	385	68	28	74	92	75	342
+25	−25	+214	+48	+36	+23	−31	+38	+26

Format 7.1
EQUALITY INTRODUCTION   (See Videos in Parts A and B)

TEACHER	STUDENTS

Part A: Structured Board Presentation

1. *(Write the following problem on the board.)*

(Point to equal sign.) This is an equal sign. What is this? → Equal sign

2. Here's a rule: We must end with the same number on this side *(point to left side of equal)* and the other side of the equal sign.

3. *(Point to left side.)* Let's see if we end with the same number on this side and on the other side.

4. *(Point to left side.)* Count the lines on this side as I touch them. *(Point to each line as students count.)* → 1, 2, 3, 4, 5

5. How many did we end with on this side? → 5

6. So we must end with 5 on the other side. *(Point to right side.)*

7. Let's count the lines. *(Point as students count.)* → 1, 2, 3, 4, 5

Did we end with 5? → Yes

So the sides are equal. We ended with the same number on this side and the other side.

Part B: Less Structured Board Presentation

1. *(Write the following problem on the board.)*

Listen to the equal rule: We must end with the same number on this side and on the other side of the equal sign. Say the equal rule. *(Repeat rule with students until they can say it without assistance.)*

2. Let's see if the sides are equal.

3. *(Point to left side.)* How many do we end with on this side? *(Pause, signal.)* → 4

4. *(Point to right side.)* How many do we end with on this side? *(Pause, signal.)* → 2

5. Do we end with the same number on this side *(point to the right side)* and on the other side? → No

6. Are the sides equal? → No

7. The sides are not equal, so I don't write an equal sign.

(Repeat steps 1–7 with several examples, half equal and half unequal. Give individual turns to several students.)

TEACHER	STUDENTS
Part C: Less Structured Worksheet	
1. *(Give students worksheet with these problems.)*	
Touch problem a.	
2. Say the equal rule.	We must end with the same number on this side and on the other side of the equal sign.
3. Count and see if the sides are equal. *(Pause.)* Are the sides equal?	No
To correct: (Point to left side). Count these lines. Tell me how many you end with. *(Point to right side.)* Count these lines. Tell me how many you end with. Did you end with the same number on this side and the other side?	
4. Do you write in an equal?	No
5. *(If answer to 3 is yes, write the equal.)*	
(Repeat steps 1–5 with remaining problems.)	

Format 7.2
TEACHING ADDITION THE SLOW WAY

TEACHER	STUDENTS
Part A: Structured Board Presentation	
1. *(Write the following problem on the board.)*	
$5 + 3 = \square$	
Read the problem.	5 + 3 = how many?
(Point to the equal sign.) What is this?	Equal
2. Listen to the equal rule: We must end with the same number on this side *(circle 5 + 3)* and on the other side *(circle box)* of the equal sign.	
What is the equal rule?	We must end with the same number on this side and on the other side of the equal sign.
3. *(Point to 5.)* How many in the first group?	5
I'll draw five lines under the 5. Count as I draw the lines. *(Draw five lines on the horizontal line under the 5.)*	1, 2, 3, 4, 5

continued

Format 7.2 *(continued)*
TEACHING ADDITION THE SLOW WAY

TEACHER	STUDENTS
4. *(Point to + 3.)* This says "plus three." Plus tells us to draw more lines, so I draw three lines under the 3. Count as I draw the lines. *(Draw three lines on the horizontal line under the 3.)*	1, 2, 3
5. We've drawn all the lines on this side. Let's count and see what we end with. Count as I touch the lines. *(Touch lines.)*	1, 2, 3, 4, 5, 6, 7, 8
What number did we end with?	8
We must end with the same number on this side and on the other side of the equal sign.	
6. *(Point to 5 + 3.)* We ended with 8 on this side. So what number must we end with on the other side?	8
I'll draw the lines. You count and tell me when to stop. *(Draw lines on the horizontal line under the box.)*	1, 2, 3, 4, 5, 6, 7, 8, stop
5 + 3 = ☐ ||||| ||| ||||||	
To correct: If children don't say stop after 8, keep drawing lines, then say, We made a mistake. You have to tell me to stop. (Repeat from step 5.)	
7. The lines under a box tell what numeral goes in the box. How many lines are under the box?	8
So what numeral goes in the box?	8
(Write 8 in the box.) What does 5 + 3 equal?	8
8. Say the whole statement.	5 + 3 = 8
9. *(Repeat steps 1–8 until students can answer several problems with no errors.)*	

Part B: Structured Worksheet Presentation

(Here is a sample worksheet item.)

   a. 5 + 3 = ☐
   ___ ___ ___

1. Touch problem a.	
2. Read the problem as I clap. Get ready. *(Clap at 1-second intervals.)* 5 + 3 = how many?	
3. How many in the first group?	5
Make the lines.	Students draw five lines.
4. The next part of the problem says plus 3. What do you do when you plus 3?	Make three lines.
5. Make the lines under the 3.	Students draw three lines.
6. Let's count all the lines on this side. Put your finger over the first line. *(Check.)* Touch and count the lines as I clap. *(Clap one clap per second.)*	1, 2, 3, 4, 5, 6, 7, 8
5 + 3 = ☐ ||||| ||| ||||||	

TEACHER	STUDENTS
7. How many lines did we end with?	8
8. So how many must we end with on the other side of the equal?	8
9. Make the lines and write the numeral.	
10. What does 5 + 3 equal?	8
11. Say the statement. *(Repeat steps 1–11 with additional problems.)*	5 + 3 = 8
Part C: Less Structured Worksheet	
1. *(Give students worksheets with problems.)* Touch problem a. 6 + 3 = ☐	
2. Read the problem.	6 + 3 = how many?
3. First you make six lines, then you plus. How do you plus 3?	Make three lines.
4. Make the sides equal and fill in the missing numeral. *(Check.)*	
5. What does 6 + 3 equal?	9
6. Say the statement. *(Repeat steps 1–6 with additional problems.)*	6 + 3 = 9

Format 7.3
SOLVING MISSING ADDENDS   (See Video in Part A)

TEACHER	STUDENTS
▶	
Part A: Preskill—Side to Start On	
1. *(Write the following problems on the board.)*	
$\quad$ 4 + ☐ = 6	
$\quad$ 1 + ☐ = 3	
$\quad$ 3 + 2 = ☐	
$\quad$ 8 + ☐ = 9	
$\quad$ 5 + 3 = ☐	
$\quad$ Listen: I'm going to tell you something about the side you start with. You start with the side that tells how many lines to draw. Listen again: You start with the side that tells how many lines to draw.	
2. My turn. *(Point to 4 + ☐ in the first problem.)* Can I start on this side? No. How do I know? Because the box does not tell me how many lines to draw. *(Point to 6.)* Can I start on this side? Yes. How do I know? Because a 6 tells how many lines to draw.	
3. Now it is your turn. *(Point to 4 + ☐ in the first problem.)* Can I start on this side?	No
$\quad$ How do you know?	Because a box does not tell how many lines to draw.
4. *(Point to 6.)* Can I start on this side? *(Repeat steps 1–4 with remaining problems.)*	Yes

continued

Format 7.3 *(continued)*
SOLVING MISSING ADDENDS

TEACHER	STUDENTS
Part B: Structured Board Presentation	
1. *(Write the following problem on the board.)*	
$4 + \square = 6$	
—— —— ——	
Read this problem.	4 + how many = 6
2. This is a new kind of problem. It doesn't tell us how many to plus. We have to figure out how many to plus. What must we figure out?	How many to plus
3. We use the equal rule to help us. The equal rule says we must end with the same number on this side *(point to 4 + $\square$)* and on the other side *(point to 6)* of the equal sign. First we figure the side we start counting on.	
(Point to 4 + $\square$.) Do I start counting on this side?	No
Why not?	The box does not tell how many lines to make.
(Point to 6.) Do I start counting on this side?	Yes
The 6 tells me to make six lines. *(Draw six lines on the horizontal line under the 6.)*	
4. We want to end with the same number on both sides. *(Point to 4 + $\square$.)* How many on this side now?	4
I'll draw four lines. *(Draw four lines on the horizontal line under 4.)* Think. How many do we need to end with on this side?	6
To correct: (Repeat the equal rule.) What number did we end with on the other side? What number do we have to end up with on this side?	
We have 4. We want to end with 6. Count as I make the lines. Tell me when to stop. *(Point to 4.)* How many in this group?	4
Get it going. *(Draw lines on the horizontal line under box as students count.)*	ffoouurr, 5, 6, stop
To correct: If students do not say stop after saying 6, tell them, We ended with 6 on the other side. We must end with 6 on this side. *Then repeat from step 4.*	
5. What number did we end with?	6
We made the sides equal. Are we going to write 6 in the box?	No
To correct: If children say yes, Remember: the lines under the box tell what numeral goes in the box.	
The number of lines under the box tells us what numeral to write in the box. What numeral? *(Write 2 in box.)*	2
6. 4 + how many = 6?	2
Say the whole statement. *(Repeat steps 1–6 with additional problems.)*	4 + 2 = 6
Part C: Structured Worksheet Presentation	
(Below is a sample worksheet item.)	
$5 + \square = 8$	
—— —— ——	

TEACHER	STUDENTS
1. Touch problem a. Read the problem.	5 + how many + 8
2. Touch the side you start counting on.	Students touch side with 8.
3. Make the lines under the 8.	Students make eight lines.
4. Touch the side that says "5 + how many."	Students touch that side.
5. How many do you have on that side now? Make five lines under the 5.	5 Students make five lines.
6. Think: How many do you have to end up with on that side? *To correct:* You want to make the sides equal. You ended with 8 on the other side, so you must end with 8 on this side.	8
7. Touch the 5. You have five lines so far. Make more lines under the box so that you end with 8 on that side. How many did you end with on that side? Are you going to write 8 in the box? No, the lines under the box tell us what numeral to write in the box.	Students draw more lines. 8 No
8. Count the lines you made under the box and write the numeral.	Students write 3.
9. 5 + how many = 8? Say the whole statement. *When the missing addend is zero,* as in 8 + □ = 8:	3 5 + 3 = 8
10. This is a special kind of problem. The sides are already equal. Eight on both sides. So you shouldn't make any lines. You plus zero lines. Write a zero in the box. *(Check.)*	
11. Eight plus how many equals 8?	Zero
12. Say the whole statement.	8 + 0 = 8

Part D: Less Structured Worksheet

1. *(Give students a worksheet with an equal mix of addition and missing addend problems.)*

   a. 5 + 3 = □   d. 3 + 4 = □
   b. 4 + □ = 6   e. 6 + □ = 7
   c. 3 + □ = 8   f. 5 + 3 = □

   Touch problem a. Read the problem.   5 + 3 = how many?

2. Touch the side you start counting on.

3. Make the lines on that side and get ready to tell me how many you end with. *(Pause.)* What do you want to end with?   8

4. Touch the other side. *(Pause.)* What do you want to end with?   8

5. Make lines to make the sides equal.   Students make lines.

6. Count the lines under the empty box and write the numeral.   Students write 8 in box.

Format 7.4
TEACHING ADDITION THE FAST WAY

TEACHER	STUDENTS
Part A: Structured Board Presentation	
1. *(Write the following problem on the board.)*	
5 + 3 = ☐ ‾‾‾	
I'll touch and you read.	5 + 3 equals how many?
2. We're going to work this problem a fast way. We draw lines under the numeral after the plus. *(Point to + 3.)* What does this say?	Plus three
So how many lines are we going to draw?	3
I'll make the lines. *(Draw 3 lines under the 3.)*	
3. Watch me count the fast way. *(Touch 5 and then each line.)*	
Ffiivve, 6, 7, 8.	
Now it's your turn to count the fast way. How many are in the first group? Get it going . . . . count. *(Touch 5 for 2 seconds and then touch each line.)*	*ffiivve*, 6, 7, 8
4. How many did we end with on this side?	8
So how many must we end with on the other side?	8
I'll write an 8 in the box. *(Write 8 in the box.)*	
5. Read the whole statement. *(Repeat steps 1–5 with 7 + 4 and 9 + 5.)*	5 + 3 = 8
Part B: Structured Worksheet	
1. *(Write the following problem on the board.)*	
4 + 2 = ☐ ‾‾‾	
(Point to 4 + 2 = ☐.) Touch this problem on your worksheet. *(Pause.)* Read the problem out loud. Get ready. *(Clap for each symbol.)*	4 + 2 = how many?
2. Let's work this problem the fast way. Touch the numeral after the plus. *(Pause.)*	
How many lines are you going to plus?	2
Make the lines under the 2. *(Check.)*	
3. Touch the 4 and get ready to count the fast way. Four. Get it going. *(Clap as students touch and count.)* Count.	*ffoouurr*, 5, 6
To correct: *(Teacher models.)* My turn . . . .. *(If necessary, moves student's finger as he counts.)*	
4. How many did you end with on the side you started with?	6
How many must you end with on the side with the box?	6
Yes, 6 equals 6. What numeral will you write in the box?	6
Do it.	
5. Read the whole statement.	4 + 2 = 6

TEACHER	STUDENTS
Part C: Less Structured Worksheet	
(Make a worksheet with addition problems similar to the following.) $4 + 3 = \square$	
1. Everybody, read the first problem on your worksheet. Get ready. *(Clap for each symbol.)*	4 + 3 equals how many?
2. *(Work problem.)* Now you're ready to plus lines and count the fast way. What are you going to do? Do it. *(Check students as they work.)*	Plus the lines and count the fast way.
3. Read the whole statement.	4 + 3 = 7

Format 7.5
ADDING THREE SINGLE-DIGIT NUMBERS

TEACHER	STUDENTS
Part A: Structured Board Presentation	

1. *(Write the following problems on the board.)*
 	
  1   1   3
  3   2   1
+2 +4 +6
 	
You're going to learn how to work a special kind of problem today. Read this problem.
	
	1 + 3 + 2

2. Watch me work it. First I add 1 + 3. What do I add first? What is 1 + 3? *(Pause.)*	1 + 3 4
3. 1 + 3 = 4. Now I add 4 + 2. What do I add next? What is 4 + 2? *(Pause.)*	4 + 2 6
4. So I write the 6 below the line.	
5. Let's see if you remember. What are the first numbers I add?	1 + 3
6. What is 1 + 3? *(Pause.)* Here's the hard part. What are the next numbers I add? To correct: *(If student says 3 + 2, repeat steps 2–6.)* What is 4 + 2? *(Pause. Write 6.)*	4 4 + 2 6
7. Read the problem and the answer. *(Repeat with two more examples. Give individual turns to several students.)*	1 + 3 + 2 = 6
Part B: Structured Worksheet Presentation	

(Students have worksheets with 10 problems of the type below.)
 	
  2   1   5
  4   4   2
+3 +3 +2	

continued

Format 7.5 *(continued)*
ADDING THREE SINGLE-DIGIT NUMBERS

TEACHER	STUDENTS
1. Touch the first problem. Read it.	2 + 4 + 3
2. Touch the first numbers you add. *(Monitor responses.)* What are they?	2 + 4
3. What is 2 + 4? *(Pause.)*	6
4. Now tell me the next numbers you add. *(Pause.)* Yes, 6 + 3.	6 + 3
5. What is 6 + 3? *(Pause, signal.)* Write 9 below the line.	9
6. Read the problem now. *(Repeat Part B with two more examples. Have students finish the worksheet independently.)*	2 + 4 + 3 = 9

Format 7.6
ADDING TWO NUMERALS WITH RENAMING

TEACHER	STUDENTS
Part A: Structured Board Presentation	
1. *(Write the following problems on the board.)* 36 48 26 +27 +26 +16	
1. Read this problem as I point.	36 + 27 = how many?
2. What column do we start working in?	The ones column
3. What are the first two numbers we're going to add? *To correct: Point to 6 and 7. Repeat step 3.*	6 + 7
4. What is 6 + 7?	13
5. We have a problem. Thirteen equals 1 ten and 3 ones. We can't have a 10 in the ones column, so we put the 1 ten at the top of the tens column. Where do we put the 10?	At the top of the tens column
(Write 1 over 3.) We write three ones under the ones column. Where do we put the three ones? *(Write 3 under 7.)*	Under the ones column
6. What are the first two numbers to add in the tens column?	1 + 3
What does 1 + 3 equal? *(Pause.)*	4
Now what two numbers will we add?	4 + 2
What is 4 + 2?	6
How many tens do we end up with?	6 tens
We end up with 6 tens, so I'll write 6 under the tens column. *(Write 6 in the tens column.)*	

TEACHER	STUDENTS
7. We are finished. *(Point to 63.)* What does 36 + 27 equal?	63
Read the problem and say the answer.	36 + 27 = 63
(Repeat steps 2–7 with remaining problems.)	

Part B: Structured Worksheet Presentation

(Students have worksheets with the following problems.)

45	57	36	47
+38	+37	+16	+26

TEACHER	STUDENTS
1. Touch the first problem on your worksheet. Read the problem.	45 + 38 = how many?
2. What column do you start working in?	The ones
What are the first two numbers you're going to add?	5 + 8
What is 5 + 8? *(Pause.)*	13
3. There's a problem. What does 13 equal?	1 ten and 3 ones
Can we have a ten in the ones column?	No
So where do you put the ten?	At the top of the tens column
Write a 1 at the top of the tens column. *(Monitor student responses.)*	13 equals 1 ten and 3 ones
How many ones are left?	3
Write them under the ones column. *(Check.)*	
4. Look at the tens column. What are the first two numbers to add in the tens column?	1 + 4
What is 1 + 4? *(Pause.)*	5
Now what numbers will you add?	5 + 3
What is 5 + 3?	8
How many tens do you end up with?	8 tens
Write the tens under the tens column. *(Monitor student responses.)*	
5. You're finished. What does 45 + 38 equal?	83
Read the problem and say the answer.	45 + 38 = 83
(Repeat steps 1–5 with remaining examples.)	

Part C: Less Structured Worksheet

(Give students a worksheet containing some problems that involve renaming and some that do not.)

47	53	42	78
+25	+24	−31	+18

78	56	75	26
+21	+36	−23	+43

TEACHER	STUDENTS
1. Everyone, read problem one on your worksheet.	47 + 25
What type of problem is this: addition or subtraction?	Addition
2. What are the first two numbers you add?	7 + 5
What is 4 + 7? *(Pause.)*	12

continued

Format 7.6 *(continued)*
ADDING TWO NUMERALS WITH RENAMING

TEACHER	STUDENTS
3. Do you have to move a ten over to the tens column?	Yes
4. Now work the problem on your own. *(Pause.)*	
5. What does 47 + 25 equal? *(Repeat steps 1–5 with remaining problems.)*	72

Format 7.7
COMPLEX ADDITION FACTS WITH A TOTAL LESS THAN 20
(See Video in Part A)

TEACHER	STUDENTS
Part A: Structured Presentation	
1. I want to add 15 + 3 in my head.	
2. Fifteen equals 10 + 5, so when we add 15 + 3, we add 10 and *(pause)* 5 + 3. When we add 15 + 3, we add 10 and what numbers?	5 + 3
3. What is 5 + 3? *(Pause.)*	8
What is 10 + 8?	18
So what is 15 + 3?	18
4. Say the whole statement. *(Repeat steps 1–4 with 14 + 2, 11 + 4, 14 + 3, 15 + 3, 12 + 2. Give individual turns on steps 1–3.)*	15 + 3 = 18
Part B: Less Structured Presentation	
1. Listen: 14 + 3. What does 14 equal?	10 + 4
2. So when we add 14 + 3, we add 10 plus what numbers?	4 + 3
3. What is 4 + 3? *(Pause.)*	7
4. Say the whole statement.	14 + 3 = 17
5. What is 14 + 3? *(Repeat with 14 + 5, 12 + 3, 16 + 3, 13 + 4, 15 + 3. Give individual turns to several students.)*	17
Part C: Supervised Practice	
1. What does 11 + 4 equal? *(Pause.)* To correct: (Use step 1 from Part B.)	15
2. Say the whole statement. *(Repeat step with 17 + 2, 14 + 5, 12 + 6, 16 + 3, 11 + 6, 13 + 5. Give individual turns to several students.)*	11 + 4 = 15

CHAPTER

8

Subtraction

LEARNING OUTCOMES

8.1 Discuss the two stages of teaching subtraction to young students and the sequence of problem types appropriate for each stage.

8.2 Describe the procedures recommended to promote conceptual understanding of beginning subtraction.

8.3 Outline instructional procedures to teach beginning subtraction including the cross-out strategy and missing subtrahend strategy.

8.4 Discuss the differences in the instructional strategies for teaching subtraction without renaming and subtraction with renaming.

SKILL HIERARCHY

• • • • • • • •

Subtraction instruction, like addition instruction, may be divided into two stages. During the beginning stage, introducing the concept, the teacher presents strategies for solving simple subtraction problems with a single-digit minuend, such as $9 - 6 =$; the strategy at this stage involves semi-concrete objects that represent each member in the subtraction problem. The counting, numeral, and equality preskills for subtraction are the same as for addition. After subtraction has been initially taught, problems with a missing subtrahend can be presented. In these problems, all numerals should be below 10 to simplify computation ($7 - \square = 3$ and $5 - \square = 3$). Again, the strategy involves using semi-concrete objects to represent the numerals in a problem.

In the advanced stage, multi-digit subtraction, students compute basic facts mentally (without semi-concrete prompts). Basic subtraction facts are the 90 possible combinations in which a one-digit subtrahend is subtracted from a one- or two-digit minuend and the difference is a one-digit number. Procedures for teaching students to answer and eventually memorize basic subtraction facts are discussed in Chapter 6.

Three basic types of column subtraction problems are included in the multi-digit stage. The easiest is the problem in which the subtrahend is smaller than the minuend in each column; renaming is not required:

$$\begin{array}{r} 49 \\ -24 \\ \hline \end{array}$$

49

INSTRUCTIONAL SEQUENCE AND ASSESSMENT CHART

Grade Level	Problem Type	Performance Indicator		
K	Conceptual introduction			
1	Subtracting a one- or two-digit number from a two-digit number; no renaming	57 −20	45 −3	28 −4
1	Subtracting a one- or two-digit number from a two-digit number; renaming required	54 −18	46 −9	70 −38
2	Subtracting a one-, two-, or three-digit number from a three-digit number; renaming tens to ones	382 −37	393 −174	242 −6
2	Subtracting a two- or three-digit number from a three-digit number; renaming from hundreds to ten	423 −171	418 −83	
2	Subtracting a two- or three-digit number from a three-digit number; renaming from tens to ones and hundreds to tens	352 −187	724 −578	534 −87
2	Tens minus 1 facts	$70 - 1 = \square$ $40 - 1 = \square$ $80 - 1 = \square$		
2	Subtracting a two- or three-digit number from a three-digit number, zero in tens column; renaming from tens to ones and hundreds to tens	504 −21	905 −164	700 −86
3	Subtracting a three- or four-digit number from a four-digit number; renaming from thousands to hundreds	4689 −1832	5284 −4631	3481 −1681
3	Subtracting a one-, two-, three-, or four-digit number from a four-digit number; renaming required in several columns	5342 −68	6143 −217	5231 −1658
3	Subtracting a two-, three-, or four-digit number from a four-digit number; a zero in either the tens or hundreds column	4023 −184	5304 −1211	5304 −418
3	Hundreds minus 1 facts	$700 - 1 = \square$ $400 - 1 = \square$ $800 - 1 = \square$		
3	Subtracting a one-, two-, three-, or four-digit number from a four-digit number; a zero in the tens and hundreds column	4000 −1357	2001 −1453	8000 −4264
3	Subtracting a one-, two-, three-, or four-digit number from a four-digit number with zeros in the hundreds, tens, and ones columns	1000 −283	1000 −82	1000 −80
4	Subtracting involving five- and six-digit numbers; with renaming	342,523 −18,534		38,402 −15,381
4	Thousands minus 1 facts	$5000 - 1 = \square$ $3000 - 1 = \square$ $1000 - 1 = \square$		
4	Subtracting from a number with four zeros	80,000 −826		50,000 −8260

In the second type of problem, one or more columns have a subtrahend that is larger than the minuend:

$$\begin{array}{r} 374 \\ -28 \\ \hline \end{array} \qquad \begin{array}{r} 5437 \\ -2859 \\ \hline \end{array}$$

Such problems require renaming:

$$\begin{array}{r} 34 \\ -15 \\ \hline \end{array} \quad \text{becomes} \quad \begin{array}{r} {}^{2}\!\!\not{3}4 \\ -15 \\ \hline \end{array}$$

Students need not have memorized all basic subtraction facts before problems with renaming are introduced. They should, however, know enough facts to allow teachers to include a variety of renaming problems.

The third type of problem includes column subtraction problems that require renaming. Included are problems with zeros in the minuend:

$$\begin{array}{r} 306 \\ -216 \\ \hline \end{array} \quad \text{becomes} \quad \begin{array}{r} {}^{291}\!\not{3}\!\not{0}6 \\ -216 \\ \hline \end{array}$$

and

$$\begin{array}{r} 4000 \\ -258 \\ \hline \end{array} \quad \text{becomes} \quad \begin{array}{r} {}^{3991}\!\not{4}\!\not{0}\!\not{0}\!\not{0} \\ -258 \\ \hline \end{array}$$

and problems with renaming in consecutive columns:

$$\begin{array}{r} 421 \\ -247 \\ \hline \end{array} \quad \text{or} \quad \begin{array}{r} 6342 \\ -4971 \\ \hline \end{array}$$

A more complete list of problem types and a suggested sequence of introduction appear in the Instructional Sequence and Assessment Chart.

CONCEPTUAL UNDERSTANDING

A number of alternative demonstrations for introducing subtraction are suggested in elementary mathematics textbooks. Among these are diagrams using pictures of objects; for example, $5 - 3$ is represented as

Another approach is the use of number lines; for example, $8 - 3$ is represented as

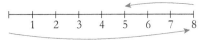

This text recommends a strategy that uses lines as semi-concrete objects. The strategy teaches subtraction as crossing out; for example, $7 - 4$ is represented as

╫╫╫│││

We recommend delaying the introduction of subtraction until students have demonstrated mastery of the regular addition strategy. However, subtraction may be introduced prior to or after addition problems with missing addends.

INSTRUCTIONAL PROCEDURES: BEGINNING SUBTRACTION

Cross-out Strategy

In the cross-out strategy recommended here, the student first draws the number of lines for the minuend and then subtracts by crossing out the number of lines indicated by the subtrahend:

$$6 - 4 = \blacksquare$$

││╫╫╫╫

Next, the student counts the remaining lines and draws an equal number of lines on the other side of the equal sign:

$$6 - 4 = \boxed{}$$

| | ┼┼┼┼ | |

Finally, the student writes the numeral representing that set of lines:

$$6 - 4 = \boxed{2}$$

| | ┼┼┼┼ | |

Format 8.1: Subtraction with Lines shows the format for introducing subtraction. Note that *minus* is used as a verb: "How many lines are you going to minus?" Since students have already learned to identify the minus sign, they learn that the minus sign tells them to cross out lines. Later, the term *subtraction* is introduced, and students learn that a minus tells them to subtract. This is done intentionally to allow students to understand the concept of subtraction without the additional demand of new vocabulary.

In Parts A and B of the format, the teacher presents structured board and worksheet exercises focusing solely on the preskill task of crossing out lines and counting the remaining lines. Because line drawing is a fine motor skill, many students in beginning mathematics instruction may require extensive practice before they become proficient in crossing out the appropriate number of lines. Part C is a structured worksheet exercise in which the teacher leads students as they work entire problems: drawing lines for the first group, crossing out lines for the amount to be subtracted, counting how many lines they end with, and then applying the equality rule. The minuend in subtraction problems should be 10 or less so that drawing lines does not become too cumbersome. Part D, the less structured worksheet exercise, is the critical part of the format. The worksheet includes a mix of addition and subtraction problems. Instructionally-naive students often have difficulty discriminating which of the two similar problem-solving strategies to use. The format provides systematic practice in helping students make this discrimination. Supervised practice is continued until students can work problems with 80% to 90% accuracy.

Missing Subtrahend Strategy

Missing subtrahend problems ($7 - \square = 3$, $8 - \square = 1$) can be introduced when the students can do a worksheet including a mix of addition, regular subtraction, and addition problems with missing addends with 80% to 90% accuracy. Since the strategy for working this type of problem is relatively difficult to teach (students must circle some lines and cross out the remaining lines), we recommend not presenting the strategy until the end of first grade when the students have had ample practice with the equality principle through missing addend problems.

The strategy for missing subtrahend problems includes the steps shown in **Summary Box 8.1**.

SUMMARY BOX 8.1

Subtraction: Missing Subtrahend Strategy

1. Students read problem.	Seven minus how many equals three?
2. Students draw lines under minuend.	$7 - \boxed{} = 3$
3. Students determine the number they must end with on both sides.	|||||||
4. Students circle three of the seven lines, since they must end with three to make sides equal.	$7 - \boxed{} = 3$ ⫲|||||
5. Students cross out uncircled lines.	$7 - \boxed{} = 3$ ⫲|┼┼┼
6. Students count crossed-out lines and write numeral in the box.	$7 - \boxed{4} = 3$ ⫲|┼┼┼

The format for teaching missing subtrahend problems is similar to that for the missing addend operation. The teacher has the students (a) draw lines under the numeral, (b) circle the number of lines representing the difference, (c) cross out the remaining lines, and (d) count crossed-out lines and write the appropriate numeral in the empty box.

The teacher introduces the entire strategy in structured board and worksheet exercises, stressing the equality principle. Finally, the teacher presents a less structured worksheet exercise that includes a mix of subtraction, missing subtrahend, addition, and missing addend problems.

Diagnosis and Remediation

Diagnosis and remediation procedures for beginning subtraction problems are very similar to those discussed for beginning addition problems. The basic steps below apply to diagnosing and remedying errors:

1. Diagnosis: The teacher analyzes worksheet errors and hypothesizes about the cause of each error.
2. Confirmation: The teacher interviews the student to determine the cause of the error if it is not obvious.
3. Reteaching: The teacher provides reteaching through board and/or worksheet presentations focused on a component skill or a strategy.
4. Assess: The teacher tests the student on a set of problems similar to the ones in which the original errors were made.

Once students begin working problems independently on their worksheets, their errors usually fall into two main categories:

1. Strategy errors: a fundamental lack of understanding of the strategy
2. Component-skill errors: a deficit in one or more of the component skills or preskills used in the strategy

Strategy errors are remedied by reintroducing the related format. Until the remedy is complete, problems of that type should not appear on independent worksheets.

Component-Skill Errors   Component-skill errors are often difficult to diagnose. Note that in the following problem, the student's error may have resulted from misidentifying 3 as 4 or simply not crossing out the correct number of lines: $9 - 3 = \boxed{5}$.

The teacher can determine the specific cause of the errors by looking for patterns. If a student works all of the problems correctly except those that include the numeral 3, the cause of the errors would be the misidentification of the numeral 3. In addition to looking for patterns, the teacher can ask the students to read each problem and describe what they are doing as they work to confirm the cause of the errors.

Once the teacher determines the specific component-skill deficit, he would reteach that specific skill for several lessons. If the skill is one that would cause students to miss many problems (a skill such as crossing out lines), the teacher would not present any subtraction problems until the students can perform the component skill independently. If the component skill is one that causes students to miss just some problems (numeral misidentification), the teacher excludes subtraction problems with that feature from independent worksheet assignments until the students demonstrate mastery of that component skill.

A common component-skill error is confusing signs and adding rather than subtracting. Teachers can expect most students to make this error occasionally. However, a remediation procedure is necessary when the error occurs frequently (in more than 10% of problems). The remediation procedure involves reintroducing the less structured worksheet from **Format 8.1**, Part D, and instructing students to circle the sign before solving the problem.

Fact Memorization

Students need an understanding of the subtraction operation, which the crossing-out strategy provides. However, students also must learn to memorize the subtraction facts to reduce difficulties in learning multi-digit operations. Fact memorization instruction should begin as soon as students reach the 80% to 90% accuracy criterion during supervised practice of one-digit minus one-digit subtraction problems.

INSTRUCTIONAL PROCEDURES: MULTI-DIGIT SUBTRACTION PROBLEMS

This section deals with subtraction problems with multi-digit numbers. A critical component skill of multi-digit problems is renaming. Two basic renaming strategies are suggested in mathematics texts. The first, the additive balancing or equal addends method, involves adding a tens unit to both the subtrahend and the minuend. In solving a problem with two-digit numbers, the tens unit is added to the ones column of the top numeral, while the tens unit is added to the tens column of the bottom numeral:

$$
73 \quad \text{becomes} \quad \overset{1}{73}
$$
$$
\frac{-48}{25} \qquad \qquad \frac{-5\!\!4 8}{25}
$$

This involves application of the compensation principle for subtraction: *The difference between two numbers is unaltered by the addition of the same amount to both terms.* In turn, the compensation principle includes the equality principle. Since few students know the compensation principle and many don't know the equality principle, the equal addends strategy tends not to be understood by most students.

The second method, sometimes called decomposition, involves renaming the minuend so that a unit from a higher-order column is written in a lower-order column:

$$
73 \quad \text{becomes} \quad \overset{6\,1}{73}
$$
$$
\frac{-48}{25} \qquad \qquad \frac{-48}{25}
$$

Note that the minuend 73 has been rewritten as 60 and 13.

The direct instruction procedures are based on the renaming method because this method is used by most teachers in North America. The procedures emphasize knowing when to rename and the mechanics of renaming. The conceptual understanding of renaming is also emphasized but in separate exercises from those for teaching the mechanics of working problems. This separation is done to simplify the formats for teaching the mechanics.

Three main groups of problems are discussed in this chapter: (a) problems that do not require renaming, (b) problems that require renaming from one column, and (c) problems requiring renaming in two consecutive columns, including problems with a zero in the column that must be renamed.

Column Subtraction—No Renaming

Column subtraction problems that do not require renaming are taught in basically the same way as addition problems that do not require renaming. As was the case for addition, we recommend not introducing column problems until students have memorized approximately 12 subtraction facts. In working subtraction problems, students subtract in the ones column and then in the tens column. Also, as in addition, students read the number of tens in the tens column rather than the numerals: They would say, "Three tens minus two tens" rather than "30 minus 20."

Subtraction with Renaming

Subtracting a one- or two-digit number from a two-digit number when renaming is required is the first type of subtraction problem on the Instructional Sequence and Assessment Chart involving renaming. It is usually introduced during late first grade. The three preskills for solving this

Format 8.2: Teaching Regrouping
Watch how Michaela introduces the concept of regrouping.

problem type are (a) the place value–related skills inherent in reading and writing numerals over 10, (b) knowledge of at least six facts that can be used for renaming (facts in which the first number is 10 or more), and (c) a conceptual understanding of renaming. **Format 8.2: Teaching Regrouping** includes a process to teach the concept of **regrouping** (with objects), which builds the foundation for renaming (with numerals).

Format 8.2 presents a diagram showing several packages, each of which contains 10 objects and several single objects. The teacher tells a story that involves giving away some of those objects: "A boy has 34 nails. He wants to give 8 nails to his sister." The teacher points out that to give 8 nails to his sister, the boy will have to open a package of 10. The teacher erases one pack of 10 nails and draws 10 single nails. The teacher then erases 8 nails and counts the remaining packages and single nails. This format, with similar examples, is presented for several days prior to introducing the renaming format.

The procedures for introducing renaming appear in **Format 8.3: Subtraction with Renaming**. In Part A, students discriminate when renaming is necessary. This discrimination is critical in preventing mistakes in which students subtract the smaller from the larger number regardless of which number is on top (74 − 38, students take 4 from 8). The teacher presents this rule: *When we take away more than we start with, we must rename.* This rule is not intended to be absolutely mathematically correct but serves as a functional rule to teach the concept. After presenting this rule, the teacher leads students in applying the rule. The teacher points to the top numeral in the ones column and asks the students how many they are starting with and then points to the numeral below it and asks whether they must rename if they take away that number. Example selection is critical in this format. The teacher must include an unpredictable mix of problems, some requiring renaming and some not.

Part A should be presented for several lessons. The teacher should then test each student individually on a set of about seven problems, asking of each, "Do we have to rename in this problem?" Student performance determines what the teacher does next. If students miss no more than one of the seven problems, the teacher can present Part B, in which the strategy for working problems is presented. If students miss more than one question, Part A is presented for several more lessons.

Part B introduces the component skill of renaming. The teacher explains to the students that they rename by taking a ten and putting it with the ones number. In 75 − 38, they take a ten from the seven tens and put it with the five ones. After modeling several problems, the teacher tests students, making sure they can follow the steps for renaming.

Parts C and D are structured board and worksheet exercises in which the entire strategy is presented, applying the rule for when to rename. The application of a rule requires a modified correction procedure for these parts of the format. When students incorrectly identify when to rename, the teacher stops the students and reminds them of the rule. The students then repeat the rule. The teacher then asks guiding questions to help the students apply the rule: "What are we starting with in the ones column? . . . What are we taking away? . . . Are we taking away more than we start with? . . . So do we rename? . . ." The teacher then returns to the beginning of instruction for that problem. After the students correctly solve the problem, additional examples are provided.

Part E is a less structured worksheet exercise that includes an equal mix of problems that do and do not require renaming. Worksheet exercises should be included in lessons until students can perform with 80% to 90% accuracy. After several days of worksheet exercises with only subtraction problems, the teacher would include some addition problems for discrimination practice.

Problems requiring renaming become more difficult as the number of digits in the minuend and subtrahend increases. The structured format for presenting each new problem type is quite similar to the structured format just discussed. For example, when problems involving renaming hundreds are introduced, the teacher would first ask the students to identify what they are starting with and taking away in the tens column and then ask if it is necessary to rename to work the problem. The teacher then leads students through solving the problem. In multi-digit problems that require renaming in several columns, the teacher leads the students through working each column, always asking, "What does the column tell us to do? . . . Must we rename?"

The examples for the practice worksheets should include a mix of the currently introduced and previously introduced problem types. When the first problems requiring renaming from tens are introduced, about three-quarters of the problems should involve subtraction and one-quarter addition. Of the subtraction problems, only about half should require renaming. When problems involving renaming from the hundreds are introduced, half of the subtraction problems should require renaming from the hundreds, a quarter from the tens, and a quarter should not require renaming. Some addition problems should also be included. **Figure 8.1** is an example of a worksheet that could be presented after problems requiring renaming from the hundreds are taught. Note the mixture of problem types: c, e, h, and j require renaming from hundreds; b and i from tens; a and g do not require renaming; and d and f are addition.

Self-Checking   After students become proficient in working renaming problems, they should be taught to check their answers. A checking procedure for subtraction is adding the subtrahend and the difference. The teacher introduces checking on a worksheet exercise. After the students complete the first problem, the teacher says,

> Here's how to check your answer to a subtraction problem. Add the bottom two numbers. What's the answer? . . . Is that the same as the top number in the problem? So your answer is correct.

To demonstrate why the checking procedure works, teachers should use simple problems like:

$$\begin{array}{r} 12 \\ -8 \\ \hline 4 \end{array}$$

The teacher uses the same questions: "Add the bottom two numbers . . . What's the answer? . . . Is that the same as the top number? . . ." With familiar facts, students more readily see that the procedure makes sense. The same type of exercise suggested for encouraging students to use the addition self-check can be used to encourage students to check their subtraction work. Teachers give students a worksheet with some problems worked correctly and some incorrectly. Students are asked to find the problems worked incorrectly by using the self-check strategy.

Complex Renaming Problems

This group includes problems in which several consecutive columns must be renamed. First, we discuss problems that do not include zeros in the minuend. Working such problems does not involve new skills, just applying the renaming skill in consecutive columns. Errors often occur because students become confused over the crossed-out digits. When the problem 327 − 149 is worked, the numeral in the hundreds column is 2 and the numeral in the tens column is 1, neither of which comes from the original problem:

$$\begin{array}{r} 21\,1 \\ \cancel{3}\cancel{2}7 \\ -149 \\ \hline 178 \end{array}$$

An important aspect of the teaching procedure is closely monitoring students as they write on their worksheets. Students who are not careful will make errors because of extensive crossing out and rewriting. Therefore, teachers should stress precisely where numerals are to be written. Having students write and solve problems on grid paper can assist students in correctly placing the digits.

Students encounter more difficulty with problems that require renaming zero. The Instructional Sequence and Assessment Chart provides examples of problems in which the minuend

FIGURE 8.1 Sample worksheet with renaming problems

a. 392	b. 346	c. 423	d. 728	e. 547
− 81	−118	−180	+324	− 83

f. 547	g. 285	h. 248	i. 347	j. 236
+38	−84	−58	−109	−46

includes one or more zeros and renaming is required. The basic strategy students are taught is to rename several digits at once. For example, in the problem

$$
\begin{array}{r}
304 \\
-87 \\
\hline
\end{array}
$$

students treat the 3 hundreds as 30 tens. When they do this (take 1 ten from the 30 tens), the 30 is crossed out and replaced with 29:

$$
\begin{array}{r}
29\,1 \\
3\cancel{0}4 \\
-87 \\
\hline
\end{array}
$$

Students would follow a similar procedure when working problems containing zeros in both the tens and hundreds columns:

$$
\begin{array}{r}
299\,1 \\
3\cancel{0}\cancel{0}2 \\
-89 \\
\hline
\end{array}
$$

The students would treat the 3000 as 300 tens, crossing out the 300, writing 299 in its place, and putting a ten in the ones column. This procedure was suggested by Cacha (1975) as a means of simplifying renaming that involves zeros.

A preskill for solving problem types that involve renaming numbers with zeros is learning the tens-numbers-minus-one facts, such as $60 - 1, 90 - 1, 40 - 1$. These facts are presented about a week prior to introducing problems such as

$$
\begin{array}{r}
407 \\
-129 \\
\hline
\end{array}
$$

The format for teaching tens-numbers-minus-one facts consists of two steps. First, the teacher says a tens number (a two-digit number ending in zero) and asks the students to indicate what number precedes it. "What number comes before 80?" Second, the teacher introduces the rule that when you minus 1, you say the number that comes just before the number given. Then the teacher has the students apply the rule to a series of examples. The entire procedure appears in **Format 8.4: Preskill: Tens Numbers Minus One.**

Once students have mastered the tens-minus-one preskill, they can be presented with the format for renaming numbers with a zero, which appears in **Format 8.5: Renaming Numbers with Zeros.**

The format has three parts. Part A includes a board demonstration by the teacher of how to work the problem. Part B includes steps in which the teacher guides students through solving problems on their worksheets. Part C is a less structured worksheet guide. During the structured board and worksheet exercises, each problem should require renaming. In Part C, the less structured worksheet exercise, students are presented with a mix of problem—half require renaming, and half do not. For example, a typical worksheet might look like **Figure 8.2.**

In about half of the problems, the numbers in the ones column require renaming; in the other half of the problems, renaming in the ones column is not required. The mix is very important to prevent students from developing the misrule of always renaming when they see a zero

Format 8.5A
Renaming Numbers
with Zeros

Watch how Tristan introduces renaming numbers with zeros.

FIGURE 8.2 Worksheet problems for renaming with zeros

1. 402
  − 69
	2. 503
	−161
		3. 305
		  − 65
			4. 302
			  − 86
				5. 504
				−128

6. 703
  − 42
	7. 500
	  − 36
		8. 300
		  − 40
			9. 700
			  − 4
				10. 206
				  − 36

11. 508
  − 32
	12. 500
	  − 26
		13. 300
		  − 20
			14. 501
			  − 61
				15. 302
				  − 48

in the tens column. The importance of mixing problems on the worksheets cannot be overemphasized. If the examples used are not carefully designed to provide discrimination practice, the students might develop a serious misrule of always crossing out the hundreds numeral and zero, as in the problem below:

$$\begin{array}{r} \overset{29}{3\cancel{0}2} \\ -41 \\ \hline 251 \end{array} \qquad \begin{array}{r} \overset{39}{4\cancel{0}2} \\ -52 \\ \hline 340 \end{array}$$

Problem types become more complex as the number of digits increases, particularly the number of zeros involved in renaming. The following example shows subtraction from a thousands number with zeros in the hundreds and tens columns.

$$\begin{array}{r} 3004 \\ -86 \\ \hline \end{array}$$

The preskill for this type of problem is hundreds-minus-one facts ($800 - 1$, $300 - 1$). The teaching procedure for hundreds-minus-one facts is basically the same as for tens-minus-one facts. The teacher presents the structured board and worksheet formats using wording similar to that found in in **Format 8.5**. The only difference is that the teacher points out that in a problem such as

$$\begin{array}{r} 3004 \\ -128 \\ \hline \end{array}$$

students rename from 300 tens. "What are you going to take one ten from? What is 300 minus 1? . . . So cross out 300 and write 299." Again, the less structured worksheet exercise is critical for providing discrimination practice.

The worksheet should include a mix of problems like that in **Figure 8.3**.

In some problems, students must rename in the ones column. In some problems, students rename in the tens column. In still others, students must rename in the hundreds column. Teachers can expect students to need a great deal of supervised practice on this before they reach an acceptable accuracy criterion.

Two additional problem types that may cause students difficulty require renaming from the numbers 10, 100, 1000, or 1100. Problems in which the student must rename from 10, 100, or 1000 may cause difficulty because the students do not replace each digit with another digit, as in

$$\begin{array}{c} \overset{799}{8\cancel{0}\cancel{0}4} \end{array}$$

Instead, they replace only two of the three digits, as in

$$\begin{array}{c} \overset{99}{\cancel{1}\cancel{0}0} \end{array}$$

$$\begin{array}{c} \overset{991}{\cancel{1}\cancel{0}\cancel{0}4} \end{array} \quad \text{with} \quad \begin{array}{c} \overset{7991}{8\cancel{0}\cancel{0}4} \end{array}$$

Without instruction, students may write the nines in the wrong columns:

$$\begin{array}{r} \overset{99}{\cancel{1}\cancel{0}\cancel{0}0} \\ -193 \\ \hline 9807 \end{array}$$

FIGURE 8.3   Sample worksheet: Renaming with two or more zeros

a. 3004	b. 3004	c. 3001	d. 7005	e. 7005
− 289	− 302	−1394	−2101	−2104

f. 7005	g. 6000	h. 6000	i. 4000
−1149	− 80	− 8	− 50

The teaching procedure for these problems need not be elaborate. The teacher models working several problems and then supervises students as they work the problems.

Diagnosis and Remediation

Fact Errors   Basic fact errors usually are obvious. For example, in problems a and b below, the student has made obvious errors involving the facts $13 - 6$ and $12 - 8$, respectively.

$$
\text{a.} \quad
\begin{array}{r}
3\!\!\!/1 \\
4\!\!\!/35 \\
-162 \\
\hline
283
\end{array}
\qquad
\text{b.} \quad
\begin{array}{r}
4\!\!\!/1 \\
5\!\!\!/28 \\
-186 \\
\hline
352
\end{array}
$$

In order to determine the specific cause of the errors, the teacher should look for error patterns. For example, the teacher should check the problems with errors to see if the same facts were consistently missed. Also, the teacher should utilize the information she has about the student's performance on recent fact worksheets. To confirm the diagnosis, the teacher should observe the student reworking some of the missed problems and have her explain her thinking.

The remediation procedure depends on the nature of the fact errors. If a student consistently misses the same facts, the teacher provides extra practice on those facts. On the other hand, some students are erratic in their performance, answering a fact correctly one time and missing it the next. For such students, the teacher may increase the incentives for accurate work.

Strategy Errors   Errors caused by failure to rename are illustrated below. In problem a, the error is in the ones column. In problem b, there are errors in the hundreds and ones columns.

$$
\text{a.} \quad
\begin{array}{r}
342 \\
-128 \\
\hline
226
\end{array}
\qquad
\text{b.} \quad
\begin{array}{r}
2584 \\
-1827 \\
\hline
1363
\end{array}
$$

Again, the frequency of the error must be considered before remediation is planned. An occasional error, occurring no more than in 1 out of 10 problems, needs no extensive remediation. The teacher simply has students rework the problem. More frequent errors of this type require in-depth remediation, beginning with reteaching Part A of Format 8.3. Part A focuses on when renaming is required. The teacher presents several problems similar to the ones missed by the student. The teacher points to each column in a problem and asks if renaming is required to work that column. This exercise is continued until students can respond correctly to four or five problems consecutively. Next the teacher leads the students through a structured worksheet exercise with several problems (Part D in Format 8.3), then through less structured worksheet problems (Part E). Finally, the teacher assesses by having the students work a group of problems as he closely monitors. This set of problems should include a mix of problem types so that the teacher can be sure students are discriminating when renaming is required. Students have mastered the strategy when they complete 80% to 90% of the problems accurately.

Component-Skill Errors   Errors involving the procedures of renaming are illustrated below:

$$
\text{a.} \quad
\begin{array}{r}
1 \\
35 \\
16 \\
\hline
29
\end{array}
\qquad
\text{b.} \quad
\begin{array}{r}
6\!\!\!/1 \\
5\!\!\!/4 \\
-28 \\
\hline
46
\end{array}
\qquad
\text{c.} \quad
\begin{array}{r}
20\!\!\!/1 \\
3\!\!\!/02 \\
-54 \\
\hline
158
\end{array}
$$

In problem a, the student forgot to subtract a ten from the three tens when renaming. This error is not uncommon when renaming is first introduced. For remediation, students are given practice rewriting two-digit numerals. Teachers might use the following wording:

> You're going to practice renaming. Touch the first numeral. (Check that students are touching the first numeral.) What do you do first to rename this number? Do it. Write a 1 to show one ten. Remember to cross out and write a new tens numeral.

The error in problem b indicates the student is adding rather than subtracting the ten when renaming. The remediation procedure begins with the teacher drawing attention to the fact that when you rename from the tens column, you must *take away* a ten. The teacher then follows the same procedure as described for problem a.

The error in problem c indicates that the student either is having difficulty with tens-numbers-minus-one facts or is confused regarding the strategy to use. The teacher should watch the student work several problems to confirm the cause of the error. If the problem relates to tens-minus-one facts, the teacher reteaches tens-minus-one facts (60 − 1, 30 − 1, 80 − 1, etc.) from Format 8.4. When students demonstrate mastery of tens-minus-one facts, they are presented with the less structured part of the format for that type of problem. If the error reflects a strategy error, then a more in-depth remediation is needed. The teacher would present all parts of Format 8.5.

FIGURE 8.4 **Diagnosis and remediation of subtraction errors**

Sample Patterns	Sample Diagnosis	Remediation Procedures	Remediation Examples
a. $\begin{array}{r}3\cancel{1}\\ \cancel{4}37\\ -180\\ \hline 247\end{array}$ $\begin{array}{r}63\\ -28\\ \hline 34\end{array}$	Fact error: 13 − 8	Emphasis on 13 − 8 in fact drill.	
b. $\begin{array}{r}1\\ 34\\ -18\\ \hline 26\end{array}$ $\begin{array}{r}1\\ 352\\ -\ 71\\ \hline 381\end{array}$	Component skill: Student did not rename column borrowed from.	You're going to practice rewriting. Touch the first numeral (check). What do you do first to rewrite this number? . . . Do it. Write a 1 to show one ten. Remember to cross out and write a new number for the first digit.	For examples, present a worksheet with these numerals: a. 27 b. 38 c. 71 d. 42
c. $\begin{array}{r}34\\ -18\\ \hline 24\end{array}$ $\begin{array}{r}72\\ -36\\ \hline 44\end{array}$	Strategy: Renaming not done.	Present renaming format starting with Part A, in Format 8.3.	Examples specified for Format 8.3.
d. $\begin{array}{r}291\\ 3\cancel{0}4\\ -\ 21\\ \hline 2713\end{array}$ $\begin{array}{r}51\\ \cancel{6}4\\ -24\\ \hline 310\end{array}$	Strategy: Renaming was done unnecessarily.	Same as c	Same as c
e. $\begin{array}{r}71\\ \cancel{8}3\\ -48\\ \hline 35\end{array}$ $\begin{array}{r}31\\ \cancel{5}1\\ -2\\ \hline 39\end{array}$	Fact error: Minus 1.	a. Present minus-1 facts b. Present less-structured worksheet for the particular problem type.	Mix: some problems require renaming, and some do not. Renaming problems sample all types introduced to date.
f. $\begin{array}{r}35\\ -14\\ \hline 49\end{array}$	Component skill: Sign discrimination; student added instead of subtracting.	a. Present less-structured part of Format 8.3 Have student circle sign, then work the problem.	Equal mix of addition and subtraction.
g. $\begin{array}{r}211\\ \cancel{3}04\\ -\ 26\\ \hline 288\end{array}$	Component skill: Problems with zero in tens column; inappropriate renaming.	a. Present tens-minus-1 preskill (if necessary). b. Present the format for renaming numbers with zeroes (Format 8.5)	6–8 problems Examples specified for Format 8.5
h. $\begin{array}{r}291\\ 3\cancel{0}2\\ -\ 41\\ \hline 2511\end{array}$ $\begin{array}{r}391\\ 4\cancel{0}2\\ -\ 52\\ \hline 3410\end{array}$	Strategy: Renaming unnecessarily.	Format 8.5, Part C	Example specified for Format 8.5

A special group of problems that may cause students difficulty are problems with a zero in the ones column of the minuend or subtrahend:

$$\begin{array}{cc} 70 & 74 \\ -34 & -30 \\ \hline \end{array}$$

Students often become confused when working problems with zero, answering 70 − 34 as 44 or 74 − 30 as 40. If a teacher notes errors with this problem type, a special exercise composed of problems like the ones below should be given. A teacher would first review minus-zero facts, pointing out that when you minus zero you end with the same number you started with, then lead students through working the problems. The exercise is continued until students can work the problems with 90% accuracy for several days in a row.

$$\begin{array}{cccc} 60 & 64 & 40 & 43 \\ -34 & -30 & -20 & -20 \\ \hline \end{array}$$

$$\begin{array}{ccc} 40 & 78 & 70 \\ -23 & -30 & -38 \\ \hline \end{array}$$

After reteaching the component skill, the teacher assesses the students on a set of problems similar to the ones on which the original errors were made to ensure mastery of the strategy.

A summary of the diagnosis and remediation procedures for subtraction appears in **Figure 8.4**.

APPLY WHAT YOU LEARNED

 Click on the √ to answer the questions online.

1. Below are Maria's and Alex's performances on a set of performance indicators. Specify the problem type with which instruction should begin for each student.

Maria

a.
$$\begin{array}{ccc} \overset{3}{4}23 & \overset{3}{4}18 & \overset{1}{2}28 \\ -171 & -83 & -137 \\ \hline 252 & 335 & 91 \end{array}$$
b.
$$\begin{array}{ccc} \overset{4}{3}\overset{1}{5}2 & \overset{1}{7}\overset{1}{2}4 & \overset{2}{5}\overset{1}{3}4 \\ -187 & -578 & -87 \\ \hline 245 & 266 & 567 \end{array}$$

c. 70 − 1 = 69
40 − 1 = 39
80 − 1 = 79

d.
$$\begin{array}{ccc} \overset{4}{5}03 & \overset{4}{5}\overset{1}{0}4 & 700 \\ -87 & -26 & -86 \\ \hline 486 & 428 & 786 \end{array}$$

e.
$$\begin{array}{ccc} 4689 & \overset{4}{5}\overset{1}{2}84 & 3481 \\ -1832 & -4631 & -1681 \\ \hline 3257 & 653 & 2201 \end{array}$$

Alex

a.
$$\begin{array}{ccc} \overset{3}{4}\overset{1}{2}3 & \overset{3}{4}\overset{1}{1}8 & \overset{1}{2}28 \\ -171 & -83 & -137 \\ \hline 252 & 335 & 91 \end{array}$$
b.
$$\begin{array}{ccc} \overset{4}{3}\overset{1}{5}2 & \overset{1}{7}\overset{1}{2}4 & \overset{2}{5}\overset{1}{3}4 \\ -187 & -578 & -87 \\ \hline 245 & 266 & 567 \end{array}$$

c. 70 − 1 = 69
40 − 1 = 39
80 − 1 = 79

d.
$$\begin{array}{ccc} \overset{49}{5}\overset{1}{0}3 & \overset{49}{5}\overset{}{0}4 & \overset{69}{7}00 \\ -87 & -26 & -86 \\ \hline 415 & 478 & 614 \end{array}$$

e.
$$\begin{array}{ccc} \overset{1}{4}689 & 5284 & 3481 \\ -1832 & -4631 & -1681 \\ \hline 3857 & 1453 & 2200 \end{array}$$

2. Below is an excerpt of the independent worksheet to be given to students who have just demonstrated accuracy in solving problems involving renaming from hundreds to tens. The teacher made some errors in constructing the worksheet.

   a. Indicate the inappropriate examples and specify the problem type.

   b. Identify any omitted problem types that should be included on the worksheet.

a.	524	b.	504	c.	324	d.	533
	−186		−328		−192		−261

e.	824	f.	602	g.	523	h.	65
	−161		−159		−186		−32

3. Describe the problem type that each example below represents. List the problems in the order they are introduced. Write the grade level when each problem type is typically introduced.

$$63 \quad 353 \quad 48 \quad 523 \quad 346 \quad 503$$
$$-18 \quad -182 \quad -23 \quad -486 \quad -128 \quad -87$$

4. These 12 problems that appeared on the worksheet to be done independently by the students in Mr. Kuboyama's math group. Next to each student's name are the problems missed by the student. For each student:

   a. Specify the probable cause or causes of the student's error.

   b. Describe the remediation procedure. Be specific (name format part).

4023	4702	8346	342	7304	430
−1857	−2563	−1895	−185	−1286	−82

2036	3248	3852	402	3826	8306
−518	−1026	−1624	−81	−63	−1243

James

39	29
4̸0̸2	8̸3̸0̸6
−81	−1243
311	7053

Isabella

391₁	69₁
4̸0̸2̸3	4̸7̸0̸2
−1857	−2563
2165	1138

Santiago

79
4̸7̸0̸2
−2563
2239

Caleb

342	3852
+185	+1624
157	228

5. Specify the wording the teacher would use in the structured worksheet presentation for the problem.

$$314$$
$$-182$$

6. In presenting **Format 8.3**, Part A, a board format for introducing renaming problems, the teacher asks for this problem, "Must we rename?" The student says, "No." Specify the wording the teacher uses in making the correction.

$$57$$
$$-28$$

7. These less structured worksheets were made by several teachers for the less structured part of the format for teaching students to work problems that require renaming from the hundreds column. Two

teachers constructed unacceptable lists. Identify these teachers and tell why each list is unacceptable. For each unacceptable list, specify what could be done to make the list acceptable.

a. $\begin{array}{r}342\\-181\end{array}$ $\begin{array}{r}623\\-182\end{array}$ $\begin{array}{r}483\\-193\end{array}$ $\begin{array}{r}362\\-181\end{array}$ $\begin{array}{r}534\\-184\end{array}$ $\begin{array}{r}235\\+132\end{array}$ $\begin{array}{r}427\\-193\end{array}$ $\begin{array}{r}329\\-152\end{array}$ $\begin{array}{r}427\\-121\end{array}$

b. $\begin{array}{r}383\\-195\end{array}$ $\begin{array}{r}432\\-150\end{array}$ $\begin{array}{r}342\\-186\end{array}$ $\begin{array}{r}282\\-195\end{array}$ $\begin{array}{r}346\\-138\end{array}$ $\begin{array}{r}425\\+132\end{array}$ $\begin{array}{r}524\\-187\end{array}$ $\begin{array}{r}473\\-197\end{array}$ $\begin{array}{r}392\\-161\end{array}$

c. $\begin{array}{r}428\\-368\end{array}$ $\begin{array}{r}328\\-209\end{array}$ $\begin{array}{r}526\\-385\end{array}$ $\begin{array}{r}48\\-29\end{array}$ $\begin{array}{r}362\\-182\end{array}$ $\begin{array}{r}364\\-148\end{array}$ $\begin{array}{r}325\\+132\end{array}$ $\begin{array}{r}436\\-214\end{array}$ $\begin{array}{r}329\\+142\end{array}$

Format 8.1
SUBTRACTION WITH LINES

TEACHER	STUDENTS
Part A: Structured Board Presentation—Preskill of Minusing Lines	
1. *(Write the Following Problem and lines on the board.)*	
6 − 2	
||||||	
Everyone, read this problem.	6 − 2
This is a minus problem. What kind of problem is this?	A minus problem
2. *(Point to minus 2.)* What does this say?	Minus 2
Minus 2 tells us to cross out two lines.	
What does minus 2 tell us to do?	Cross out two lines.
Watch me cross out two lines.	
(Draw two minuses through two lines and count each time.) Minus 1, minus 2.	
3. Let's see how many lines we have left. I'll touch, and you count.	1, 2, 3, 4
How many did we end up with?	4
(Repeat steps 1–3 with 7 − 4, 5 − 3.)	
Part B: Structured Worksheet—Preskill of Minusing Lines	
(Students have worksheets with four to six problems like the one below.)	
6 − 2	
||||||	
(Note that the lines under the first numeral in each problem are already drawn.)	
1. Touch problem a on your worksheet. *(Check.)* Read the problem.	6 − 2
What kind of problem is this?	A minus problem
2. Touch the first group. How many lines are in the first group?	6
How many lines are you going to minus?	2
Minus the lines. *(Check that students minus two lines.)*	
To correct: When you minus 2, you cross out two lines.	
3. Now count and see how many lines you have left. *(Pause.)*	
How many did you end with?	4
(Repeat steps 1–3 with remaining examples.)	

continued

Format 8.1 *(continued)*
SUBTRACTION WITH LINES

TEACHER	STUDENTS
Part C: Structured Worksheet—Entire Strategy	
(Give the students a worksheet with four to six problems like the ones below.)	
$\quad$ 5 − 3 = ▢	
$\quad$ 4 − 2 = ▢	
$\quad$ 2 − 0 = ▢	
$\quad$ 8 − 4 = ▢	
1. Touch the first problem on your worksheet. *(Check.)* Read the problem.	5 − 3 = how many?
2. What kind of problem is this?	A minus problem
$\quad$ Touch the first group. How many lines are you going to draw?	5
$\quad$ Draw five lines under the 5.	
3. How many lines are you going to minus?	3
$\quad$ Minus the lines. *(Monitor worksheet responses.)*	
4. Now count and see how many lines you end with. *(Pause.)* How Many?	2
5. So how many must you end with on the other side of the equal?	2
$\quad$ Draw two lines and write the numeral in the box.	
6. Now read the whole statement.	5 − 3 = 2
$\quad$ 5 − 3 = ▢ how many?	2
$\quad$ Say the statement again.	5 − 3 = 2
(Repeat steps 1–6 with the remaining problems.)	
Part D: Less Structured Worksheet	
1. *(Give the students a worksheet with an equal mix of addition and subtraction problems.)*	
$\quad$ a. 4 + 3 = ▢ $\qquad$ f. 7 − 0 = ▢	
$\quad$ b. 8 − 2 = ▢ $\qquad$ g. 6 − 4 = ▢	
$\quad$ c. 7 − 5 = ▢ $\qquad$ h. 2 + 4 = ▢	
$\quad$ d. 5 − 4 = ▢ $\qquad$ i. 5 + 3 = ▢	
$\quad$ e. 7 + 0 = ▢	
$\quad$ This worksheet is tricky. In some problems you plus, and in some problems you minus. When you plus, you make more lines. What do you do when you plus?	Make more lines
$\quad$ When you minus, you cross out lines. What do you do when you minus?	Cross out lines
2. Touch problem a. Read it.	4 + 3 = how many?
$\quad$ Is that a plus or minus problem?	Plus problem
$\quad$ What do you do when you plus?	Make more lines
3. Make the lines under the first group, then plus.	
4. Now make the sides equal and fill in the box.	
$\quad$ *(Repeat steps 2–4 with the remaining problems.)*	

Format 8.2
TEACHING REGROUPING   (See Video)

TEACHER	STUDENTS

1. *(Draw the following boxes on the board.)*

   [10] [10] [10]

   A boy has nails. He has three packages with 10 nails in each package and 4 nails not in a package. Let's figure out how many nails he has in all. *(Point as you count.)* 10, 20, 30, 31, 32, 33, 34.

2. The boy wants to give 8 nails to his sister. We have a problem. He can't give 8 nails to his sister the way the nails are now. He has 4 nails and packages of 10 nails. He has to regroup the nails. When we regroup, we put a group of 10 with the 4 nails. What do we do when we regroup in this problem?   **Put a group of 10 with 4.**

3. We open a pack of 10 nails *(erase a group of 10 nails)* and put the 10 nails over here.

   (Draw the following on the board.)

   [10] [10] ||||| |
              ||||| |

4. We still have 34 nails. They're just in different groups. We have two groups of 10 and a group of 14.

   Now let's give 8 away. *(Erase 8.)* Let's see how many we have left. *(Point to 6)* How many?   6

   (Point to remaining boxes of nails.) 2 tens equal how many?   20

   Yes. What is 20 plus 6?   26

   Right, 26. The boy starts with 34. He gives away 8 and ends with 26.   26

5. *(Present one or two more problems.)*

Format 8.3
SUBTRACTION WITH RENAMING

TEACHER	STUDENTS

Part A: When to Rename

1. *(Write the following problem on the board.)*

   $$\begin{array}{r} 75 \\ -49 \\ \hline \end{array}$$

   Here's a rule about renaming with subtraction problems: When we take away more than we start with, we must rename. My turn. When do we rename? When we take away more than we start with.

   Your turn. When do we rename?   **When we take away more than we start with.**

   (Repeat statement with students until they can say it by themselves.)

continued

Format 8.3 *(continued)*
SUBTRACTION WITH RENAMING

TEACHER	STUDENTS
2. *(Point to the 5.)* What number are we starting with in the ones column?	5
We're starting with 5 and taking away 9. Do we rename? *(Pause and signal.)*	Yes
Right, we have to rename because we're taking away more than we start with; 9 is more than 5.	
3. *(Write the following problem on the board.)*	
75 −43	
What number are we starting with in the ones column?	5
What are we taking away?	3
Do we rename if we take away 3? *(Pause, signal.)*	No
We don't rename. We're not taking away more than we start with.	
4. *(Write the next problem on the board.)*	
38 −27	
What are we starting out with now in the ones column?	8
What are we taking away?	7
Do we rename? *(Pause, signal.)*	No
Why?	We're not taking away more than we start with.
5. *(Repeat step 4 with these problems.)*	
38 42 42 42 −29 −37 −30 −33	
(Give individual turns to several children.)	
Part B: Steps in Renaming	
1. *(Write these problems on the board.)*	
53 75 92 −26 −28 −15	
(Point to first problem.) Read this problem.	53 − 26
The ones column tells us to start with 3 and take away 6. What does the ones column tell us to do?	Start with 3 and take away 6
Do we have to rename? *(Pause, signal.)*	Yes
Yes. We start with 3 and take away more than 3.	
2. Here's how we rename: First we take one ten from the 5 tens. What do we do first?	Take one ten from the 5 tens
Next we put that ten with the 3 ones. What do we do next?	Put the ten with the 3 ones
(Write 1 by 3 to show that 1 ten has been added to the 3 ones.)	
We just took 1 ten from the 5 tens. How many tens do we have left?	4

TEACHER	STUDENTS
We cross out the 5 in the tens column and write 4. *(Cross out the 5 in the tens column and write 4 above it.)*	
(Repeat steps 1 and 2 with additional problems.)	
Part C: Structured Board Presentation	
1. *(Write this problem on the board.)*	
43 −16	
Read the problem.	43 − 16
What does the ones column tell us to do?	Start with 3 and take away 6
Do we rename? *(Pause, signal.)*	Yes
To correct: Here's the rule: When we take away more than we start with, we must rename. What's the rule?	When we take away more than we start with, we must rename.
What are we starting with in the ones column?	3
Are we taking away more than 3?	Yes
So, do we rename?	Yes
2. *What do we do first to rename?*	Take one ten from the 4 tens
(Point to 4.) If we take one ten from the 4 tens, how many tens will be left?	3 tens
So I cross out the 4 and write 3 to show that 3 tens are left. *(Cross out 4 and write 3.)*	
3. *What do we do next?*	Put that ten with the 3 ones
Right, put the ten with the 3 ones. *(Write 1 in front of 3.)*	
Now we have 13 in the ones column.	
Figure out what 13 − 6 is. *(Pause.)* What's 13 − 6? *(Pause, signal.)*	7
We write 7 in the ones column. *(Write 7 under the line.)*	
4. The tens column says 3 tens minus 1 ten. How many is 3 tens minus 1 ten? *(Pause, signal.)*	2 tens
We write 2 in the tens column. *(Write 2 under the line.)*	
5. What is 43 minus 16?	27
(Repeat steps 1–5 with additional problems.)	
Part D: Structured Worksheet	
1. *(Give students worksheets with these problems.)*	
92 86 64 −35 −17 −49	
Read the first problem on your worksheet.	92 − 35
2. What does the ones column tell you to do?	Start with 2 and take away 5
Do you rename? *(Pause, signal.)*	Yes

continued

Format 8.3 *(continued)*
SUBTRACTION WITH RENAMING

TEACHER	STUDENTS
3. What do you do first to rename?	Take one ten from the 9 tens
If you take one ten from the 9 tens, how many will be left?	8 tens
So cross out the 9 and write 8 above it. *(Check student work.)*	
4. What do you do now?	Put that ten with the 2 ones
Do that. Put the ten with the 2 ones. *(Check student work.)*	
How many do you have in the ones column?	12
5. What is 12 − 5? *(Pause, signal.)*	7
Write 7 under the line in the ones column.	
6. Look at the tens column. What does the tens column tell us to do?	Start with 8 tens and take away 3 tens
What is 8 tens minus 3 tens?	5 tens
Write 5 under the line in the tens column.	
7. What is 92 minus 35?	57
(Repeat steps 2–7 with remaining problems.)	
Part E: Less Structured Worksheet	
1. *(Give students a worksheet like the following:)*	

a.   84   b.   32   c.   46   d.   56   e.   23
    −23   +29   −8   −32   +65

f.   42   g.   34   h.   58   i.   95   j.   78
    −26   −26   −52   −38   −32

k.   10   l.   88   m.   35   n.   63   o.   29
    +11   +12   −17   −7   −27

TEACHER	STUDENTS
Touch problem a.	
2. Read the problem.	
What kind of problem is this?	
(Ask the following questions for subtraction problems only.)	
3. Look at the ones column and get ready to tell me if you need to rename. *(Pause.)* Do you need to rename?	No
(If the answer is yes, present step 4. If the answer is no, go to step 5.)	
4. Where do you get the ten from?	
How many tens will you have left?	
5. Work the problem.	
(Repeat steps 2–5 with remaining problems.)	

Format 8.4
TENS NUMBERS MINUS ONE

TEACHER	STUDENTS
1. I'll say numbers, and you say the number that comes just before. Listen: 60. What comes just before? *(Pause 2 seconds. Signal.)* *To correct:* Model counting from 57 for the students, emphasizing 59. Repeat the question. *(Repeat step 1 with 30, 80, 40, 70.)*	59
2. Listen: When you minus one, you say the number that comes just before. I'll say a problem, and you tell me the answer. Listen: 60 − 1 is . . . *(Pause, signal.)* *To correct:* What number comes just before 60? *(Repeat step 3 with 30 − 1, 80 − 1, 40 − 1, 70 − 1.)*	59

Format 8.5
RENAMING NUMBERS WITH ZEROS   **(See Video in Part A)**

TEACHER	STUDENTS
▶	
Part A: Structured Board Presentation	

1. *(Write this problem on the board.)*
 	
   304
−186
 	
   Read the problem.
	304 − 186

2. What do we do in the ones column?	Start with 4 and take away 6
Do we have to rename? *(Pause, signal.)*	Yes
3. We have a problem. We can't take a ten from zero tens, so we have to take a ten from the 30 tens. We're going to take one ten from 30 tens. *(Circle 30 with finger.)*	
What are we going to take one ten from?	30 tens
What is 30 tens minus 1 ten?	29 tens
So I cross out 30 and write 29 above it. *(Cross out 30 and write 29 above.)*	
4. Now I'll put the 1 ten with the 4 ones. *(Write 1 ten by the 4 ones.)* What is 1 ten and 4 ones?	14
What is 14 − 6? *(Pause, signal.)*	8
So I write 8 in the ones column. *(Write 8 in the ones column.)*	
5. Now look at the tens column. How many tens are we starting with now?	9
What is 9 − 8?	1
So I write 1 under the tens column. *(Write 1 under the tens column.)*	
6. How many hundreds are we starting with now?	2
What is 2 − 1?	1
So I write 1 in the hundreds column. *(Write 1 in the hundreds column.)*	

continued

Format 8.5 *(continued)*
RENAMING NUMBERS WITH ZEROS

TEACHER	STUDENTS
7. What is the answer to this problem?	118
(Repeat steps 1–7 with these examples: 504 − 327, 602 − 148.)	

Part B: Structured Worksheet

$$406 \qquad 905 \qquad 403$$
$$-287 \quad\; -626 \quad\; -248$$

TEACHER	STUDENTS
1. Touch the first problem. Read it.	406 − 287
2. What does the ones column tell us to do?	Start with 6 and take away 7
Do you have to rename? *(Pause.)*	Yes
3. Can you take one ten from zero tens?	No
Where are you going to get the 1 ten?	From 40 tens
What is 40 tens minus 1 ten?	39 tens
Cross out the 40 and write 39 above it. *(Check work.)*	
Now put the 1 ten with the 6 ones. *(Check work.)*	
4. Now work the problem in the ones column.	
What is 1 ten and 6 ones?	16
What is 16 − 7?	9
Write it. *(Check work.)*	
5. How many tens are you starting with now?	9
What is 9 − 8?	1
Write it. *(Check work.)*	
6. How many hundreds are you starting with now?	3
What is 3 − 2?	1
Write it. *(Check work.)*	
Read the whole problem and say the answer.	406 − 287 = 119
(Repeat steps 1–6 with remaining examples.)	

Part C: Less Structured Worksheet

a.	804	b.	905	c.	609
	−619		−164		−426

d.	605	e.	302	f.	508
	−197		−42		−349

TEACHER	STUDENTS
1. Touch problem a.	
2. Read the problem.	804 − 619
3. Look at the ones column and get ready to tell me if you need to rename. *(Pause.)* Do you need to rename?	Yes
Where do you get the ten from?	From 80 tens
4. Work the problem. *(Monitor students.)*	
(Repeat steps 1–4 with remaining problems.)	

CHAPTER

9

Multiplication

LEARNING OUTCOMES

9.1 Discuss the two stages of teaching multiplication to young students and the sequence of problem types appropriate for each stage.

9.2 Describe the procedures recommended to promote conceptual understanding of beginning multiplication.

9.3 Outline instructional procedures to teach single-digit and missing factor multiplication strategies.

9.4 Explain the instructional procedures to teach multi-digit multiplication.

SKILL HIERARCHY
· · · · · · · ·

Our discussion of **multiplication** is divided into two stages. The beginning stage involves presenting strategies designed to establish a conceptual understanding of the process of multiplication. These strategies typically are taught to students in second grade. The advanced stage involves teaching students to work multi-digit problems in which students rely on mental computation rather than on representations of concrete objects. This stage typically begins during third grade and continues into the upper grades.

During the beginning stage, a procedure for solving simple multiplication problems with concrete or semi-concrete objects to represent the members in each group is presented. For example, when determining the total in an array such as the one below, students are shown that they can count by 3 four times and end with 12. When solving the problem 3×4, the students are taught to hold up four fingers for the second **factor** and then skip count by threes for each of the four extended fingers: 3, 6, 9, 12. (The teaching procedures for skip counting are discussed in Chapter 4.) Students should have mastered at least three skip-counting series before multiplication is introduced.

O O O O
O O O O
O O O O

Missing-factor problems, in which one factor and the **product** are given and a missing factor must be computed (e.g., 4 × □ = 12), also are presented during this stage. In the missing-factor strategy, students do not know the number of fingers to extend because a box or unknown represents the second factor. For these problems, students hold up a fist and extend a finger every time they skip count, stopping at the product. In 3 × □ = 15, students extend a fist, count 3 (extending one finger), count 6 (extending a second finger), count 9 (extending a third finger), count 12 (extending a fourth finger), and count 15 (extending a fifth finger). Since they extended five fingers, the unknown factor is 5: 3 × 5 = 15. The teacher then summarizes by asking students how many times they counted to end up with 15. Teachers working with upper-elementary-grade students who have limited knowledge of multiplication might consider beginning instruction with basic fact memorization exercises instead of presenting finger strategies that could result in an overreliance on using fingers.

In the advanced stage, when multi-digit numbers are multiplied, students work problems using knowledge of basic multiplication facts. Therefore, basic multiplication facts must be taught as a prerequisite skill. Exercises to facilitate memorization of basic facts can begin a month or so after students have learned to use the count-by strategy to work multiplication problems. (See Chapter 6 for a discussion of teaching basic facts.) In addition to basic multiplication facts, renaming and complex addition facts (adding a single digit to a multi-digit addend) also are necessary preskills. Knowledge of complex facts such as 72 + 4 is required in many problems with multi-digit factors. For example, in working 95 × 8, students first multiply 5 × 8 and then must add the 4 from the 40 to 72, the product of 9 × 8:

$$
\begin{array}{r}
4 \\
95 \\
\times\ 8 \\
\hline
760
\end{array}
$$

The need for teaching complex facts can be avoided by presenting a low-stress multiplication algorithm. In the low-stress multiplication algorithm, students write out the complete answer every time they multiply. This strategy requires no renaming:

$$
\begin{array}{r}
32 \\
\times\ 24 \\
\hline
8 \\
120 \\
40 \\
600 \\
\hline
768
\end{array}
$$

Students add the products, a process that seldom involves complex facts. The major disadvantage of the low-stress algorithm, which is discussed later in this chapter, is its limited acceptance in U.S. schools.

Another preskill for multi-digit operations is expanded notation. When students multiply 34 × 7, they need to understand that they are multiplying 4 × 7 and 30 × 7, which assumes knowledge of the expanded notation skill of translating 34 into 30 and 4 (see **Figure 9.1**).

There are two basic types of multi-digit multiplication problems. The first type involves a single-digit factor and a multi-digit factor. This type includes both problems that do not require renaming and those that do. In the easier group, the first product is less than 10, and renaming is not required; for example, 32 × 3 does not require renaming in the first product (2 × 3 = 6). Problems in the harder group, such as 32 × 7, require renaming; in 2 × 7 = 14, the 10 from 14 is moved to the tens column. The second major type of problem involves multiplying two multi-digit numbers (32 × 13, 189 × 43, 342 × 179). A more detailed description of the various multiplication problem types appears in the Instructional Sequence and Assessment Chart.

INSTRUCTIONAL SEQUENCE AND ASSESSMENT CHART			
Grade Level	**Problem Type**	**Performance Indicator**	
K	Count by tens to 100		
1	Count by twos to 20 Count by fives to 60		
2	Count by nines to 90 Count by fours to 40 Count by twenty-fives to 100 Count by sevens to 70 Count by threes to 30 Count by eights to 80 Count by sixes to 60		
3	One digit times one digit	$2 \times 7 =$ $9 \times 3 =$ $5 \times 6 =$	
3	Missing factor multiplication; both factors are one-digit numbers	$2 \times \square = 8$ $5 \times \square = 10$ $9 \times \square = 36$	
3	One-digit factor times two-digit factor; no renaming	$\begin{array}{r} 43 \\ \times\ 2 \\ \hline \end{array}$ $\qquad$ $\begin{array}{r} 31 \\ \times\ 5 \\ \hline \end{array}$ $\qquad$ $\begin{array}{r} 32 \\ \times\ 4 \\ \hline \end{array}$		
3	One-digit factor times two-digit factor; renaming	$\begin{array}{r} 35 \\ \times\ 5 \\ \hline \end{array}$ $\qquad$ $\begin{array}{r} 43 \\ \times\ 9 \\ \hline \end{array}$ $\qquad$ $\begin{array}{r} 17 \\ \times\ 2 \\ \hline \end{array}$		
4	One-digit factor times two- or three-digit factor; problem written horizontally	$5 \times 35 =$ $9 \times 34 =$ $7 \times 56 =$	
4	One-digit factor times three-digit factor	$\begin{array}{r} 758 \\ \times\ 2 \\ \hline \end{array}$ $\qquad$ $\begin{array}{r} 364 \\ \times\ 5 \\ \hline \end{array}$ $\qquad$ $\begin{array}{r} 534 \\ \times\ 9 \\ \hline \end{array}$		
4	One-digit factor times three-digit factor; zero in tens column	$\begin{array}{r} 405 \\ \times\ 3 \\ \hline \end{array}$ $\qquad$ $\begin{array}{r} 302 \\ \times\ 5 \\ \hline \end{array}$ $\qquad$ $\begin{array}{r} 105 \\ \times\ 9 \\ \hline \end{array}$		
4	One-digit factor times three-digit factor; horizontal alignment	$352 \times 9 =$ $7 \times 342 =$ $235 \times 5 =$	
4	Two-digit factor times two-digit factor	$\begin{array}{r} 37 \\ \times\ 25 \\ \hline \end{array}$ $\qquad$ $\begin{array}{r} 26 \\ \times\ 52 \\ \hline \end{array}$ $\qquad$ $\begin{array}{r} 34 \\ \times\ 25 \\ \hline \end{array}$		
4	Two-digit factor times three-digit factor	$\begin{array}{r} 324 \\ \times\ 29 \\ \hline \end{array}$ $\qquad$ $\begin{array}{r} 343 \\ \times\ 95 \\ \hline \end{array}$ $\qquad$ $\begin{array}{r} 423 \\ \times\ 29 \\ \hline \end{array}$		
5	Three-digit factor times three-digit factor	$\begin{array}{r} 284 \\ \times\ 346 \\ \hline \end{array}$ $\qquad$ $\begin{array}{r} 242 \\ \times\ 195 \\ \hline \end{array}$ $\qquad$ $\begin{array}{r} 624 \\ \times\ 283 \\ \hline \end{array}$		
5	Three-digit factor times three-digit factor; zero in tens column of multiplier	$\begin{array}{r} 382 \\ \times\ 506 \\ \hline \end{array}$ $\qquad$ $\begin{array}{r} 320 \\ \times\ 402 \\ \hline \end{array}$ $\qquad$ $\begin{array}{r} 523 \\ \times\ 703 \\ \hline \end{array}$		

FIGURE 9.1   **Using expanded notation to explain multi-digit multiplication**

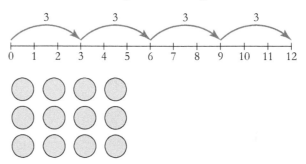

$$\begin{matrix} 27 \\ \underline{\times 4} \end{matrix} = \begin{matrix} 20 \\ \underline{\times 4} \\ 80 \end{matrix} + \begin{matrix} 7 \\ \underline{\times 4} \\ 28 \end{matrix} = 108$$

$$20 \times 4 \quad + \quad 7 \times 4$$
$$80 \quad + \quad 28 \quad = 108$$

CONCEPTUAL UNDERSTANDING

The meaning of multiplication can be conveyed in various ways. The most common ways of introducing the concept are repeated addition, equivalent sets, number lines, and arrays. For example, multiplication of 3 × 4 can be represented using a number line or an array. See below.

In this chapter, we recommend using an equivalent sets (array) demonstration to introduce the concept of multiplication. The discussion of Format 9.1 in the next section includes procedures for teaching the concept.

INSTRUCTIONAL PROCEDURES: BEGINNING MULTIPLICATION

Single-Digit Multiplication

Format 9.1A Single Digit Multiplication
Watch how Michaela introduces the concept of multiplication.

Multiplication with single-digit factors can be introduced when students have mastered three count-by series (twos, fives, nines) and can read and write all numerals between 1 and 99. Single-digit multiplication is typically taught in third grade. **Format 9.1: Single-Digit Multiplication** is divided into five parts. Since an equivalent-sets representation is easier for students to understand, we introduce the multiplication concept in Part A with illustrations of equivalent sets. The students are shown a group of equivalent sets and told they can figure the total a "fast way" when each set has the same number. After verifying that each set has the same number, the teacher demonstrates how to write the problem as a multiplication problem. Next, the teacher demonstrates how to use skip counting to determine the total. In the final step of Part A, students count the members of the sets one at a time to verify that the answer derived through multiplication is correct. Part A should be included only the first two or three days that the format is presented.

In Part B, students learn to translate a multiplication statement into terms that indicate how the problem is to be solved. For example, in initial problems, the multiplication sign ($\times$) is read as "count by." Students are taught to read the multiplication statement $5 \times 2 =$ as "count by 5 two times." By reading the statement this way, students know exactly what to do to derive an answer. "Count by 5 two times" tells them to extend two fingers for the number of times they skip count and then to skip count by fives. After several weeks, students learn to read problems in the conventional manner (e.g., 4×3 is read as "4 times 3").

When reading multiplication problems in Part B, students begin with the multiplication sign, saying "count by" and then the first numeral; 5×3 is read "count by 5 three times." Since translating multiplication problems differs from reading addition or subtraction problems, in which students read in a strict left-to-right order, multiplication problems require a slightly different signal. The teacher should point under both the numeral and the times sign when having students translate problems. For some students, the teacher may need to point under the sign first and then point to the first numeral to emphasize that the multiplication sign is read before the numeral.

In Part C, the teacher guides students in solving several multiplication examples in a structured board presentation. First, students read and translate a problem. They hold up the appropriate number of fingers, and the teacher models skip counting while touching each extended finger. Next, the students skip count each time they touch an extended finger. Finally, the students work three new problems without the benefit of teacher modeling.

Part D is the structured worksheet presentation. The teacher has the students extend the appropriate number of fingers, identify the skip-counting number, and then work the problem. Part E is the less structured worksheet part of the format. Students work a set of problems on their own with the teacher carefully monitoring their performance. After students demonstrate accuracy during group instruction, they are given 5 to 10 problems daily in independent worksheet exercises.

When having the students count and touch their fingers in step 3, Part C, the teacher must be sure that students coordinate saying the numbers while touching their extended fingers. Struggling students may say the first number in the skip-counting series before touching the first extended finger. In 2×5, for example, students may say 2 and then, when they touch their finger, count 4, continuing to count 6, 8, 10, 12. The correction for this error is to model, then lead by actually guiding the student's hand to coordinate touching and counting, and then test by watching while the student touches and counts alone. As a delayed test, the teacher should then present a series of examples for the students to practice only the touching and counting and not the entire sequence of steps in Part C. Instead of presenting all of the steps, the teacher tells the student the problem and how many fingers to hold up and then has the student touch and count. For example, the teacher would present a series of examples using this wording: "You're going to count by 5 three times. Hold up three fingers. Good. Now count by 5. Remember to touch each finger as you count by 5." With this correction, the teacher is providing intensive practice on an important component skill prior to reintroducing the entire strategy.

Two example-selection guidelines are recommended for this format. First, example selection should be coordinated with count-by instruction. The first digit in the multiplication problem should be taken from a skip-counting series the students previously have mastered. For example, a problem such as 6×7 would not be included until students have mastered counting by sixes. As a general rule, problems with a specific numeral as the first digit should be included in multiplication tasks after students have reviewed that count-by series for about 2 weeks. Second, there should be a mix of problems. As a general rule, no more than two or three problems in a row should have the same numeral as the **multiplicand** or **multiplier**. Following is an example of an acceptable set of examples:

$$
\begin{array}{ll}
5 \times 2 & 2 \times 2 \\
2 \times 4 & 5 \times 4 \\
9 \times 3 & 9 \times 1 \\
9 \times 5 & 5 \times 3
\end{array}
$$

The mix of problems helps to ensure that students develop the habit of carefully attending to both factors.

Missing-Factor Multiplication

Missing-factor multiplication, or algebra multiplication, is not only a useful skill in its own right but also is a critical preskill for the simple division strategies discussed in the next chapter. In order to solve a missing-factor multiplication problem, students must determine the number of times they count by a certain number. For example, in the problem $5 \times \square = 15$, students figure out how many times they have to count by 5 to get to 15. Students extend a finger every time they skip count; they extend one finger when they say 5, a second when they say 10, and a third when they say 15. The three extended fingers represent the missing factor.

Missing-factor multiplication problems can be introduced after students have mastered solving regular multiplication problems. A timeframe of at least 3 to 4 weeks between the introduction of regular multiplication and problems with missing factors is recommended to enable students to develop this mastery.

In Part A of Format 9.2: Missing-Factor Multiplication, students learn to translate the problem type. Next, the teacher models the strategy. The teacher holds up a closed fist to indicate that the number of times to count is unknown and then extends a finger every time she skip counts. Then the teacher tests the students by guiding them through several examples. In Part B, the structured worksheet, students apply the strategy as the teacher guides them to hold up a fist, identify the skip-counting number and the product, and extend a finger each time they count. Part C is the less structured worksheet in which students are taught to discriminate between regular problems and algebra problems (e.g., $2 \times 8 = \square, 2 \times \square = 8$).

Example-selection guidelines are identical to those for regular multiplication. The first factor in the problem should represent a count-by series the students have mastered. Different numerals should appear as the first factor. Independent practice worksheets should include an equal mix of regular multiplication and multiplication problems with missing factors.

Diagnosis and Remediation

Four errors, two component-skill and two strategy, are commonly seen in single-digit multiplication. The first type of error results from skip counting incorrectly. Students may either forget a number or switch from one series to another while counting. Although this count-by component skill error is usually obvious on worksheets, it can only be confirmed by asking students to work problems aloud. A worksheet illustrating this count-by component-skill error appears below. Note that of the eight problems on the worksheet, only two were missed. Both these missed problems had 9 as one factor and a numeral of 5 or more as the other factor.

$$5 \times 4 = 20 \qquad 9 \times 3 = 27$$
$$10 \times 3 = 30 \qquad 10 \times 6 = 60$$
$$2 \times 7 = 14 \qquad 9 \times 5 = 47$$
$$9 \times 6 = 50 \qquad 5 \times 2 = 10$$

The errors indicate that the student may have had difficulty remembering the higher numbers in the count-by-9 series. To remedy the count-by skill deficit, the teacher provides practice on counting by nines for several lessons. The student shouldn't be required to solve any multiplication problems involving with nines until he has mastered counting by nines.

The second error pattern is one in which answers are consistently off by one count-by number. For example, in regular multiplication problems, a student might answer a set of problems like this: $9 \times 6 = 63, 7 \times 6 = 49, 5 \times 6 = 35$. Quite often the cause of this error is that the student says the number for the first group and then begins counting as opposed to touching and counting simultaneously. For example, a student working 4×3 may say the number 4 before touching his fingers and then say 8, 12, and 16 as he touches the three raised fingers. This type of error can be confirmed by watching the student as he works the problems.

To remedy this type of error, the teacher presents Part C of Format 9.1: Single-Digit Multiplication, the structured board part of the multiplication format. The teacher continues

FIGURE 9.2 Diagnosis and remediation of single-digit multiplication errors

Error Pattern	Diagnosis	Remediation Procedures	Remediation Examples
Component-Skill Errors			

a. $9 \times 6 = 51$
   $8 \times 4 = 32$
   $6 \times 5 = 30$
   $9 \times 3 = 26$
	Student doesn't know count-by-nines series.	Present Part B of **Format 4.5**: Count-By.	Practice counting by nines

b. $9 \times 6 = 63$
   $8 \times 4 = 40$
   $6 \times 5 = 36$
	Student not coordinating touching and counting.	Present Part C of **Format 9.1**: Single-Digit Multiplication.	Regular multiplication problems

Note: After addressing any component-skill error, assess students using problems similar to the ones on which errors were originally made in order to determine if the remediation was successful.

Strategy Errors			

c. $9 \times 6 = 15$
   $8 + 4 = 12$
   $6 \times 5 = 11$
	Student is confusing addition with multiplication; not attending to the sign in the problems.	Present Part E of **Format 9.1**: Single-Digit Multiplication. Instruct students to circle the sign before working each problem on the less structured worksheet.	Mix of addition and multiplication problems

d. $2 \times \boxed{16} = 8$
   $6 \times \ 5 = \boxed{30}$
   $9 \times \ 6 = \boxed{54}$
   $4 \times \boxed{32} = 8$
	Student is confusing regular multiplication and missing factor multiplication.	Present Part C of **Format 9.2**: Missing Factor Multiplication.	Mix of regular multiplication problems and problems with a missing factor

to present this part until the students can respond correctly to approximately four consecutive problems. Several days of practice on this exercise should be provided before students are given problems to work independently.

The third type of error occurs when students confuse the multiplication and addition operations. This type of error can be confirmed by examining student work samples and interviewing students, if needed. The remediation procedure involves presenting the less structured format for regular multiplication, which includes a mix of multiplication and addition problems. For remediation purposes, the teacher would instruct students to circle the sign in the problems before working them.

The fourth type of error common to single-digit multiplication occurs when students confuse regular and missing-factor multiplication, writing $5 \times \boxed{50} = 10$ or $2 \times \boxed{8} = 4$. The remediation procedure involves reviewing the less structured part of Format 9.2: Missing-Factor Multiplication, which contains a mixture of regular and algebra multiplication problems. The teacher would present the less structured worksheet with about 10 problems, observing and correcting errors. This remediation continues daily until students correctly answer 9 of 10 problems without teacher assistance for several days in a row. The diagnosis and remediation information is summarized in **Figure 9.2**.

INSTRUCTIONAL PROCEDURES: MULTI-DIGIT MULTIPLICATION

Two algorithms for solving problems with multi-digit factors are commonly taught. One algorithm is called the long-form or low-stress algorithm. The other algorithm is called the short form. Both forms are illustrated in **Figure 9.3**.

Both algorithms are based on the distributive property of multiplication, which states that the product of a multiplier and a multiplicand will be the same as the sum of a series of products from multiplying individual number pairs. For example, $3 \times 24 = (3 \times 20) + (3 \times 4)$.

The advantages of the long-form algorithm are that it does not alternate between multiplication and addition and seldom requires renaming. Moreover, it clearly shows the distributive

FIGURE 9.3 Two algorithms for multi-digit multiplication

Long Form	Short Form
232	*21*
× 7	232
14	× 7
210	1624
1400	
1624	

property of multiplication. Its disadvantage, however, is that in problems involving multi-digit factors, many numerals must be written as partial products:

$$
\begin{array}{r}
245 \\
\times\ 37 \\
\hline
35 \\
280 \\
1400 \\
150 \\
1200 \\
6000 \\
\hline
9065
\end{array}
$$

The advantage of the short-form algorithm lies in its relative efficiency in solving problems with multi-digit factors and its widespread usage. Its disadvantages lie with the difficulty a student may have when alternating between addition and multiplication and with the inclusion of complex addition facts.

In this section, we discuss in detail the procedures for teaching the short-form algorithm, primarily because it is the one used in most classrooms. The section on the short-form algorithm is divided into two parts. The first addresses problems in which one of the factors is a single-digit number and the other factor a multi-digit number. The second part addresses problems in which each factor is a multi-digit number.

Single-Digit Factor and Multi-Digit Factor

Multiplication problems in which a single-digit factor and multi-digit factor are multiplied usually are introduced during mid-third grade.

Preskills   Three preskills necessary to work these problems are (a) multiplication facts; (b) place value skills, including expanded notation and placing a comma in the proper position when writing an answer in the thousands; and (c) complex addition facts in which a single-digit number is added to a two-digit number.

Basic multiplication facts include all of the possible combinations of single-digit factors. Memorizing basic facts is a very demanding and lengthy process. Most students will not have memorized all basic multiplication facts by mid-third grade. Therefore, initially, problems should be limited so that they include only basic facts the teacher is sure students have memorized. As students learn more basic facts, these should be integrated into multiplication problems.

When introducing multiplication facts to students, teachers may find multiplication maps useful (see **Table 9.1**). Each map is designed to facilitate learning multiplication facts for a particular series. Students who can visualize the maps in their minds learn and remember facts more easily.

Each map has a unique pattern. For nines, the second digit decreases by 1, while the first digit increases by 1. For fives, the last digit of the numerals in the first column is 5; the last digit of the numerals in the second column is zero. For fours, the second digits repeat after 20 (4, 8, 12, 16, 2_0_, 2_4_, 2_8_, 3_2_, 3_6_, 4_0_). The pattern for threes shows that all values below the top row have a second digit one less than the digit above it. For sevens, the second digit of each number is one more than the digit above it. Teachers need to provide lots of practice with number maps and count-bys. Practice activities may require students to write missing numerals or complete blank maps.

TABLE 9.1 Multiplication Maps for 9s, 5s, 3s, 7s, and 4s

9s:

A	B	C	D	E
9	9	9	9	9
18		_8	1_	
27	27	_7	2_	
36		_6	3_	
45	45	_5	4_	
54		_4	5_	
63	63	_3	6_	
72		_2	7_	
81	81	_1	8_	
90		_0	9_	90

5s:

A		B		C		D		E	
5	10	5		_	1_	5	_0	5	
15	20	15		1_	2_	_5	_0		30
25	30	25		2_	3_	_5	_0		
35	40	35		3_	4_	_5	_0		
45	50	45		4_	5_	_5	_0	45	

3s:

A			B			C			D		
3	6	9	_	_	_	3	6	9	3		
12	15	18	1_	1_	1_	_2	_5	_8		24	
21	24	27	2_	2_	2_	_1	_4	_7			
30			3_			_0					

7s:

A			B			C			D		
7	14	21	_	_	_	7	14	21	7		
28	35	42	2_	3_	4_	_8	_5	_2		56	
49	56	63	4_	5_	6_	_9	_6	_3			
70			7_			_0					

4s:

A					B					C				
4	8	12	16	20	_	_	1_	1_	2_	4	8	_2	_6	_0
24	28	32	36	40	2_	2_	3_	3_	4_	_4	_8	_2	_6	_0

The preskill of expanded notation is needed in order for the students to understand the renaming procedure in the short-form algorithm. Procedures for teaching expanded notation and other place value concepts appear in Chapter 5.

The preskill of correctly placing commas seems trivial but needs to be taught. After completing problems with larger numbers, students are expected to place a comma in the answer. The procedure is simple. The teacher presents the following rule: The comma is written between the hundreds and the thousands. Then the teacher models and tests application of the rule. The teacher writes a series of three-, four-, and five-digit numerals on the board and then demonstrates how to find where to place the comma. Starting at the ones column, the teacher points to each numeral, saying "ones, tens, hundreds, thousands," and then places the comma between the hundreds and the thousands columns. After modeling several examples, the teacher tests the students with a new set of examples.

Complex addition facts involve mentally adding a single-digit number to a two-digit number (35 + 7, 27 + 3, 42 + 5). Complex addition facts were discussed earlier in the addition chapter as a preskill for adding a series of multi-digit numbers. This type of addition fact is found in the short-form multiplication algorithm, when the student adds the renamed units to the product of a column. For example, in the problem 35 × 9, the student first multiplies 9 × 5 and gets 45. Because the student has learned expanded notation, she knows that 45 is the same as four tens and five ones and places the numerals in the appropriate columns.

$$\begin{array}{r} 4 \\ 35 \\ \times\ 9 \\ \hline 5 \end{array}$$

The student then multiplies 9 × 3 for a product of 27. Next, the student must mentally add the complex addition fact, 4 + 27:

$$\begin{array}{r} 4 \\ 35 \\ \times\ 9 \\ \hline 315 \end{array}$$

There are easier and more difficult types of complex addition facts. In the easier type, the sum has the same number of tens as the original two-digit addend: $\underline{6}4 + 3 = \underline{6}7$, $\underline{4}3 + 5 = \underline{4}8$, $\underline{7}5 + 4 = \underline{7}9$. In the more difficult type of complex addition facts, the sum has a tens number one higher than the original two-digit addend: $\underline{3}6 + 7 = \underline{4}3$, $\underline{5}8 + 8 = \underline{6}6$, $\underline{4}8 + 4 = \underline{5}2$, $\underline{4}9 + 9 = \underline{5}8$.

Instruction on complex addition facts begins in late first grade. First, students are taught to add a single-digit number to a teen number: 14 + 3, 16 + 2, then 17 + 6, 15 + 8, and so on. After several months of practice with teen numbers, students are introduced to complex facts with tens numbers, first with easier facts (24 + 3, 36 + 2). The more difficult facts are introduced in second grade (49 + 6, 45 + 8). Practice is continued for many months to develop fluency. Procedures for teaching complex addition facts appear in Chapter 7.

Strategy   Column multiplication is initially introduced with simple problems without renaming. That is, the product of the numbers in the ones column should be less than 10:

$$\begin{array}{cccc} 34 & 43 & 31 & 32 \\ \times\ 2 & \times\ 2 & \times\ 5 & \times\ 4 \end{array}$$

When presenting this type of problem, the teacher points out that the student first multiplies the ones and then the tens. The teaching procedure would be quite similar to the one that involves renaming (see **Format 9.3: One-Digit Factor Times Two-Digit Factor—Renaming**).

Problems with renaming are introduced several days after problems without renaming have been presented. In Part A of **Format 9.3**, the structured board presentation, the students break the problem into two parts. The two parts for 5 × 47 are 5 × 7 ones and 5 × 4 tens. After multiplying in the ones column, the teacher models how to rename, multiply the second part of the problem, add the renamed number, and write the answer. Parts B and C provide structured and less structured worksheet practice.

Note in the format the balance between explaining to students the concept and providing clear guidance in the procedures of working the problem. Also note the use of a place value grid or graph paper. The purpose of the grid is to prompt the students to place numerals from the product in the proper columns. Proper placement of numerals in the product, though not a critical component of these problem types, is critical in problems with two multi-digit factors. The place value grid would appear on students' worksheets for about a week and then could be dropped. The day the grid is dropped, the teacher leads the students through several problems, pointing out the need to write numerals in the proper positions. The teacher also examines students' worksheets carefully for column alignment errors.

Multi-digit problems written horizontally are introduced after students can correctly work vertically aligned problems. The teacher presents a strategy in which the students rewrite the problem vertically, writing the one-digit factor under the multi-digit factor. In later grades, the teacher presents a strategy in which students multiply horizontally, writing the product and renaming:

$$\overset{12}{5 \times 324} = 1620$$

This strategy is taught prior to introducing fraction multiplication and division problems with multi-digit divisors, both of which involve horizontal multiplication:

$$\frac{5}{4} \times 324 \qquad 324\overline{)1620}^{\,5}$$

Problems with a one-digit factor and a three-digit factor (243 × 5 and 342 × 9) are introduced in fourth grade. The format for presenting problems of this type is essentially the same as the format for introducing problems with a two-digit factor. The same basic explanation for renaming from the ones to the tens column is used in presenting renaming from the tens to the hundreds column. In 543 × 5, students multiply the 4 tens and add the renamed ten. Then the teacher explains that they can't have 21 tens in the tens column, so they write a 2 over the hundreds column to represent 20 tens (2 hundreds). The remaining ten is written under the tens column in the answer. Note that, at this point, the teacher need not require the students to say that 20 tens equal 200 but simply to write the 2 in the hundreds column.

A special problem type includes a zero in the tens column of the three-digit factor (403 × 5 and 306 × 2). Students may have trouble adding the renamed ten to zero. This type of problem is introduced shortly after problems with three-digit factors are introduced. Several problems of this type should be presented daily for about 2 weeks. The first several days the teacher models a few problems and then closely supervises students as they work the problems independently.

Example Selection   Two rules govern example selection. First, the basic facts included in problems should be those that the student has already mastered. Second, less structured, supervised practice, and independent worksheets should include a mixture of problems. About half of the worksheet should contain problems of the most currently introduced type while the other half should contain previously introduced multiplication problem types. About 10% of the worksheet should contain addition problems to keep students in the habit of carefully examining the sign in a problem before working it.

Self-Checking   In mid-fourth grade, or whenever students become proficient in multiplying by a one-digit factor and dividing by a one-digit divisor, students should be taught to check their answers. A checking procedure for multiplication is to divide the answer by the one-digit factor. If the quotient equals the other factor, the answer is correct. The teacher introduces self-checking with a worksheet exercise. After her students complete the first multiplication problem (7 × 35), the teacher says, "Here's how to check your work to make sure you have the right answer. We multiplied by 7, so we divide 7 into the answer. What's the answer to the multiplication problem? Divide 7 into 245. Write the problem and work it. Is the answer 35? So the answer for the multiplication problem must be correct."

Determining whether students have checked their work in multiplication is easy because checking requires writing a division problem. An exercise to encourage self-checking is to give students already-worked problems, half of which have incorrect answers. The teacher would instruct the students to check their answers and find the mistakes.

Two Multi-Digit Factors

Problems with two multi-digit factors are usually introduced during mid-fourth grade and include four types of problems. The simplest problems involve two two-digit factors. The next most difficult problems are those with a two-digit factor and a three-digit factor. This type is introduced during late fourth grade. The last type, which is presented during fifth grade, includes two three-digit factors.

The preskills for introducing problems with two multi-digit factors include the preskills for problems with a one-digit and multi-digit factor (basic multiplication facts, place value skills, complex addition facts) and a new preskill, column addition with renaming, which is required when the student must add the partial products.

Format 9.4: Two-Digit Factor Times Two-Digit Factor shows how to present problems in which both factors are two-digit numbers. We recommend using a place value grid or graph

FIGURE 9.4 **Using a place value grid in multi-digit multiplication**

```
      |3|4|2|
    × |  |2|5|
    ───────────
    |1|7|1|0|
  + |6|8|4|0|
    ───────────
    |8|5|5|0|
```

```
      |  |4|6|
    × |  |2|6|
    ───────────
    |  |2|7|6|
  + |  |9|2|0|
    ───────────
    |1|1|9|6|
```

paper for the first several weeks this problem type appears. Examples of problems worked in a grid appear in **Figure 9.4**.

In Part A, the teacher presents the numbers in the order in which they are multiplied. For example, in the problem

$$\begin{array}{r} 52 \\ \times\, 37 \\ \hline \end{array}$$

"We multiply 7 × 2, then 7 × 5, then 3 × 2, then 3 × 5." This part focuses simply on procedures. Part B is a structured board presentation in which the teacher models the steps in solving a problem. Note in steps 3 and 5 that the teacher summarizes what has been done to that point: "First we multiplied 52 by 7 ones, now we'll multiply 52 by 3 tens." Step 3 also points out that when multiplying by the tens number, a zero must first be placed in the ones column. This step is critical.

$$\begin{array}{r} 52 \\ \times\, 37 \\ \hline 175 \\ \hline 0 \\ \hline \end{array}$$

Part C is a structured worksheet presentation. Step 5 of Part C, during which the teacher leads students in multiplying by the tens number, is the step in which students are most likely to have difficulty. Note the wording is very specific regarding where numerals are placed. Part D is a less structured worksheet presentation. It includes problems with a two-digit factor and problems with a one-digit factor as the bottom factor as well as some addition problems with a one-digit addend.

Diagnosis and Remediation

The specific cause of errors is sometimes obvious, as in problem a below, and sometimes not obvious, as in problem b. In problem a, we can readily assume the student made a fact error, multiplying 7 × 6 and writing 58.

a.
$$\begin{array}{r} {}^{5} \\ 36 \\ \times\, 7 \\ \hline 268 \end{array}$$

b.
$$\begin{array}{r} {}^{4} \\ 36 \\ \times\, 7 \\ \hline 242 \end{array}$$

In problem b, we cannot be sure of the error. The student may have multiplied wrong or added wrong. If the cause of the error is not clear, the teacher should have the student rework the problem in front of her so that she can confirm the specific cause.

Fact Errors The remediation procedure for basic fact errors depends on the number of fact errors made by the student. If a student makes a few fact errors, the teacher simply records the facts the student missed and incorporates them into practice exercises for the next several lessons. If a student makes fact errors on more than 10% of the problems, the teacher should test the student individually to determine what action to take. The teacher tests the student verbally on the facts missed (What is 8 × 7? 9 × 4? 8 × 6?). If the student responds correctly to the missed facts, the teacher should tentatively conclude that rushing through the problems caused the errors. The remediation procedure would involve increasing motivation to perform accurately. If the student's performance indicates she does not know many basic facts, the teacher should devote more time to basic facts and, if possible, limit problems to include only basic facts the student knows or give students a fact table from which they can derive the answers.

Component-Skill Errors   Many of the component-skill errors in column multiplication are related to addition. Renaming errors may involve either (a) renaming the wrong number or moving a number to the wrong column:

$$\begin{array}{r} \overset{2}{58} \\ \times\ 9 \\ \hline 477 \end{array} \qquad \begin{array}{r} \overset{1}{312} \\ \times\ 7 \\ \hline 2274 \end{array}$$

or (b) forgetting to add the renamed number:

$$\begin{array}{r} \overset{7}{58} \\ \times\ 9 \\ \hline 452 \end{array} \qquad \begin{array}{r} \overset{1}{82} \\ \times\ 7 \\ \hline 564 \end{array}$$

If students make frequent errors in which they rename the ones number to the tens column, the error may be due to a lack of understanding of place value. The teacher would test the students on the tasks in the writing tens numerals format (see **Format 5.8: Writing Tens Numerals Using Place Value Concepts**). When the students consistently respond correctly to those tasks, such as how many tens in 57, the teacher would reintroduce the multiplication format, beginning with the structured worksheet exercise.

If students miss many problems because they fail to add the renamed number, the teacher would first present the structured worksheet part of **Format 9.3** again and then progress to the less structured worksheet exercise emphasizing the need to rename the added tens.

Addition mistakes account for a sizable proportion of student errors on multiplication problems. Below are several examples of addition errors:

$$\text{a.}\ \begin{array}{r} \overset{5}{88} \\ \times\ 7 \\ \hline 626 \end{array} \qquad \text{b.}\ \begin{array}{r} \overset{3}{34} \\ \times\ 9 \\ \hline 296 \end{array} \qquad \text{c.}\ \begin{array}{r} \overset{5}{28} \\ \times\ 7 \\ \hline 186 \end{array}$$

To confirm that addition is the cause of the error, the teacher may interview the student or ask him to think out loud while working. For example, in problem a, the student added 5 to 56 and obtained the incorrect sum of 62. If students make frequent addition errors, the teacher would place extra emphasis on teaching complex addition facts. Teachers working with older students who have little knowledge of basic addition facts should permit students to use their fingers in computing complex addition facts; however, they should insist on accuracy. Providing additional practice on worksheets that include only complex addition facts would be useful for these students.

Students often have difficulty with problems that have a zero in the tens column:

$$\begin{array}{r} 306 \\ \times\ 7 \\ \hline \end{array}$$

Students may multiply the renamed number:

$$\begin{array}{r} \overset{24}{306} \\ \times\ 7 \\ \hline 2382 \end{array}$$

or treat the zero as if it were a 1:

$$\begin{array}{r} \overset{14}{306} \\ \times\ 7 \\ \hline 2212 \end{array}$$

The remediation procedure for errors on this type of problem begins with testing and, if necessary, teaching times-zero facts: "When you multiply by zero, you end up with zero. What is 5×0? 8×0? 3×0?" The teacher would then give students a worksheet containing 10 to 20 partially completed problems. On that worksheet, the multiplication in the ones column would be complete and the renamed numeral written above the tens column, as follows:

$$\begin{array}{r} \overset{4}{306} \\ \times\ \ 7 \\ \hline 2 \end{array}$$

The problems on the worksheet should contain a random order of problems with zero in the tens column, 1 in the tens column, and other numerals in the tens column. About half of the problems should contain zero in the tens column. The teacher would lead the students through several problems beginning with the multiplication in the tens column. After the teacher leads the students through several problems, the students would complete the rest without assistance. Finally, the teacher would have the students independently complete a worksheet similar to the original.

Errors unique to problems with two multi-digit factors include not writing a zero in the ones column when multiplying by tens:

$$\begin{array}{r} 46 \\ \times\ 24 \\ \hline 184 \\ 92 \\ \hline \end{array}$$

and inappropriately recording the partial products so that numbers are added in the wrong columns:

$$\begin{array}{r} 425 \\ \times\ \ 37 \\ \hline 2975 \\ 12750 \\ \hline 42455 \end{array}$$

Both errors can be identified by closely examining student work.

To remedy the first error, caused by forgetting the zero, the teacher leads students through about three multiplication problems using Part C of **Format 9.4**, the structured worksheet presentation for a two-digit factor times a two-digit factor. In Part C, the teacher prompts students to write a zero when multiplying by tens. After students have correctly completed several problems during the structured worksheet presentation of the format, the students are ready to complete the less structured practice. The worksheet for the less structured practice should contain four or five multi-digit problems with a one-digit factor and about 10 to 15 multiplication problems with two-digit factors. Using some problems with single-digit factors provides necessary discrimination practice. Students must remember and apply the rule about zeros correctly rather than write a zero in every problem.

To remedy errors caused by students' inadvertently writing numerals in the wrong columns, the teacher should point out the errors to the students and remind them to carefully align the columns. Often, just providing feedback on why the students missed the problems is enough to encourage students to be more careful. However, if students continue to make column alignment errors, the teacher should reintroduce the use of the place value grid or graph paper. The teacher should lead students through working the first couple of problems using Part C in **Format 9.4**, the structured worksheet, and have the students complete the remaining problems independently.

Students also may answer problems incorrectly because of an error in adding the partial products. In problem a below, the student failed to rename from the hundreds digit to the thousands digit when adding the partial products. In problem b, the student made a basic addition error ($7 + 9 \neq 18$):

$$\begin{array}{ll}
\text{a.} \quad \begin{array}{r} 688 \\ \times\ 94 \\ \hline 2752 \\ 61920 \\ \hline 63672 \end{array}
&
\text{b.} \quad \begin{array}{r} 688 \\ \times\ 94 \\ \hline 2752 \\ 61920 \\ \hline 63872 \end{array}
\end{array}$$

Renaming errors often result from carelessness. Teachers should insist that students write neatly. The remediation for renaming errors might involve giving the students a worksheet with about 10 problems. In each problem, the multiplication should be done already. The student's task is to add the partial products. After the student can perform accurately on this worksheet, the teacher has the student complete the original worksheet independently.

Strategy Errors   Strategy errors indicate that the student simply has not learned the steps in the algorithm. Below are examples of student performance that indicate a strategy error:

$$\begin{array}{r} 428 \\ \times \quad 3 \\ \hline 12624 \end{array} \qquad \begin{array}{r} 32 \\ \times 57 \\ \hline 160224 \end{array}$$

The remediation for such errors involves presenting the entire format for the particular problem type, beginning with the structured board presentation. The diagnosis and remediation information is summarized in **Figure 9.5**.

FIGURE 9.5 **Diagnosis and remediation of multi-digit multiplication errors**

Error Pattern	Diagnosis	Remediation Procedures	Remediation Examples
Fact Errors			
a. $\begin{array}{r}^{34}\\156\\\times\ 7\\\hline 1090\end{array}$	Student makes an error in problems containing the fact 6×7.	Provide practice for the student with 6×7.	
b. $\begin{array}{r}^{1}\\406\\\times\ 3\\\hline 1248\end{array}$ $\begin{array}{r}^{4}\\106\\\times\ 7\\\hline 712\end{array}$	Student multiplies the zero as if it were a one.	Reteach times-zero facts.	1×0 2×0 3×0 4×0 5×0 6×0 7×0 8×0 9×0
Component-Skill Errors			
c. $\begin{array}{r}^{34}\\156\\\times\ 7\\\hline 1090\end{array}$ $\begin{array}{r}^{8}\\46\\\times\ 3\\\hline 201\end{array}$ $\begin{array}{r}156\\\times\ 7\\\hline 752\end{array}$	Student renames incorrectly.	Present **Parts C, D, and E of Format 5.8: Writing Tens Numerals Using Place Value Concepts. Then present** the structured worksheet from **Format 9.3: One-Digit Factor Times Two-Digit Factor—Renaming.**	$\begin{array}{r}64\\\times\ 9\\\hline\end{array}$ $\begin{array}{r}39\\\times\ 5\\\hline\end{array}$
d. $\begin{array}{r}^{1}\\46\\\times\ 3\\\hline 148\end{array}$ $\begin{array}{r}^{34}\\156\\\times\ 7\\\hline 982\end{array}$	Student does not add the renamed number correctly.	Teach complex addition facts and provide practice.	$12 + 1 =$ $15 + 4 =$ $32 + 9 =$ $21 + 5 =$
e. $\begin{array}{r}^{1}\\406\\\times\ 3\\\hline 1238\end{array}$ $\begin{array}{r}^{24}\\106\\\times\ 7\\\hline 982\end{array}$	Students multiples the renamed number.	Teach times-zero facts and provide practice. Then present the structured worksheet from **Format 9.3: One-Digit Factor Times Two-Digit Factor—Renaming.**	Times-zero facts; $\begin{array}{r}802\\\times\ 7\\\hline\end{array}$ $\begin{array}{r}103\\\times\ 5\\\hline\end{array}$

continued

FIGURE 9.5 *(continued)*

Error Pattern		*Diagnosis*	*Remediation Procedures*	*Remediation Examples*
f. 406 × 3 **1208**	106 × 7 **702**	Student does not rename when the problem includes a zero.	Modify **Format 9.3: One-Digit Factor Times Two-Digit Factor—Renaming** to include single-digit times three-digit factor problems with zero in the tens column.	103 × 5 802 × 7
g. *1* 46 × 23 **138** **92** **230**	*4* 56 × 17 **392** **56** **448**	Student does not write zero in the ones column when multiplying by tens.	Present the less structured practice from **Format 9.4: Two-Digit Factor Times Two-Digit Factor**.	Include a mix of problems with two-digit and one-digit factors as the second factor.
h. *1* 46 × 23 **138** **920** **9338**	*4* 56 × 17 **392** **560** **5992**	Student does not align numerals in columns appropriately, causing an addition error.	Present the structured worksheet from **Format 9.4: Two-Digit Factor Times Two-Digit Factor**. Provide grid or graph paper to the student to support proper alignment of columns.	35 × 18 92 × 37
i. 96 × 78 **768** **6720** **6488**		Students does not rename when addition partial products, resulting in an addition error.	Reteach adding partial products, and then provide a worksheet focused on adding partial products for practice.	35 × 18 92 × 37

Note: After addressing any component-skill error, assess students using problems similar to the ones on which errors were originally made in order to determine if the remediation was successful.

APPLY WHAT YOU LEARNED

 Click on the √ to answer the questions online.

1. Describe the problem type each example below represents. List the problems in the order they are introduced. Write the grade level when each type is typically introduced.

   a. 758
      × 2

   b. 9 × 4 = ☐

   c. 3 × 26

   d. 32
      × 2

   e. 37
      × 2

   f. 258
      × 37

   g. 37
      × 24

   h. 5 × ☐ = 20

2. Describe the strategy recommended in this text for introducing the concept of multiplication.

3. At the beginning of a unit, the teacher tested Paul. His performance on the performance indicators appears below. Specify the problem type with which instruction should begin. Explain your answer.

   Paul

   a. 43   31   32
      × 2   × 5   × 4
      86   **155** **128**

   b. 35   43   17
      × 5   × 9   × 2
      1525 **3627** **34**

   c. 5 × 35 = **175**
      9 × 34 = **296**
      7 × 56 = **392**

   d. 758   364   534
      × 2   × 5   × 9
      1516 **1820** **4806**

   e. 403   302   105
      × 5   × 5   × 9
      2105 **1600** **1305**

4. Below are 10 problems that appeared on a worksheet that was done independently by the students in Mr. Wilson's math group. Next to each student's name are the problems missed by the student. For each student, specify the probable cause or causes of the student's error. Describe how Mr. Wilson will confirm the cause(s), provide remediation, and assess for mastery.

$$\begin{array}{ccccccccccc} 24 & 342 & 61 & 23 & 203 & 60 & 21 & 28 & 432 & 48 \\ \times\,37 & \times\,7 & \times\,84 & \times\,53 & \times\,5 & \times\,9 & \times\,43 & \times\,73 & \times\,6 & \times\,37 \end{array}$$

Moniqua

$$\begin{array}{r} 203 \\ \times\;\;5 \\ \hline 1105 \end{array}$$

Jennifer

$$\begin{array}{r} 48 \\ \times\,37 \\ \hline 338 \\ 1440 \\ \hline 1778 \end{array} \qquad \begin{array}{r} 28 \\ \times\,73 \\ \hline 84 \\ 1980 \\ \hline 2064 \end{array}$$

Peter

$$\begin{array}{r} 203 \\ \times\;\;5 \\ \hline 1065 \end{array} \qquad \begin{array}{r} 60 \\ \times\;9 \\ \hline 549 \end{array}$$

Shelley

$$\begin{array}{r} 24 \\ \times\,37 \\ \hline 168 \\ 72 \\ \hline 240 \end{array}$$

Melissa

$$\begin{array}{r} 23 \\ \times\,53 \\ \hline 69 \\ 1150 \\ \hline 1119 \end{array} \qquad \begin{array}{r} 28 \\ \times\,75 \\ \hline 140 \\ 1960 \\ \hline 2000 \end{array}$$

5. A student makes the following component error on the less structured worksheet presentation:

$$\begin{array}{r} 7 \\ 43 \\ \times\;9 \\ \hline 2 \end{array}$$

Assume this type of error occurs frequently. How would the teacher remediate this error and assess for mastery?

6. Write the wording the teacher would use in the structured worksheet part of a format in presenting the following problem:

$$\begin{array}{r} 304 \\ \times\;\;7 \end{array}$$

7. A student's worksheet assignment contains the following worked problems:

$$3 \times \boxed{27} = 9 \qquad 2 \times \boxed{12} = 6$$

What error is the student making? Describe how the teacher would confirm the error, provide remediation, and assess for mastery.

Format 9.1
SINGLE DIGIT MULTIPLICATION   (See Video Part A)

TEACHER	STUDENTS
▶	

Part A: Pictorial Demonstration

1. *(Write the following boxes on the board.)*

continued

Format 9.1 *(continued)*
SINGLE DIGIT MULTIPLICATION

TEACHER	STUDENTS
2. We're going to learn a fast way to work problems that talk about the same number time and time again. *(Point to each column and ask the following question.)* How many in this group?	5
Are we talking about the same number time and time again?	Yes
3. When we talk about the same number time and time again, we make a times problem. What number are we talking about time and time again?	5
So we write 5. *(Write 5.)*	
How many groups of 5 do we have?	3
To correct: Count the groups of 5. *(Point to each group as students count.)*	
So I write times 3. *(Write × 3.)*	
4. Read the problem.	5 × 3
We can figure out 5 × 3 a fast way. We count by 5 three times: *(Point to each group of 5 as you count.)* 5, 10, 15. There are 15 in all.	
5. Let's count by ones and make sure 15 is right. *(Point to each individual member as students count.)*	1, 2, 3, 4 . . .15
Are there 15?	Yes
So we can count the fast way when we talk about the same number time and time again. *(Repeat steps 1–4 with the following boxes.)*	

▢ ▢ ▢ ▢
▢ ▢ ▢ ▢

Part B: Analyzing Problems—Reading Partial Problems

1. *(Write these partial problems on the board.)*
    5 ×
    10 ×
    2 ×
    9 ×

2. *(Point to ×.)* This sign tells you to count by. What does it tell you to do?	Count by
3. *(Point to 5 ×.)* So this tells you to count by 5. What does this tell you to do?	Count by 5
4. *(Point to 10 ×.)* What does this tell you to do?	Count by 10
5. *(Point to 2 ×.)* What does this tell you to do?	Count by 2
6. *(Point to 9 ×)* What does this tell you to do?	Count by 9

Analyzing Problems—Reading Entire Problems

7. *(Point to 5 ×.)* What does this tell you to do?	Count by 5
(Write 3 after 5 ×: 5 × 3.) Now this problem tells you to count by 5 three times. What does this problem tell you to do?	Count by 5 three times
8. *(Point to 10 ×.)* What does this problem tell you to do?	Count by 10
(Write 4 after 10: 4 × 10.) What does this problem tell you to do now?	Count by 10 four times
9. *(Point to 2 ×.)* What does this problem tell you to do?	Count by 2
(Write 5 after 2 ×: 2 × 5.) What does this problem tell you to do now?	Count by 2 five times
10. *(Point to 9 ×.)* What does this problem tell you to do?	Count by 9
(Write 4 after 9 ×: 9 × 4.) What does the problem tell you to do now?	Count by 9 four times

TEACHER	STUDENTS
11. Let's start over. *(Point to 5 × 3.)* What does this problem tell you to do? *(Repeat step 11 with each problem. Give individual turns to several students.)*	Count by 5 three times
Part C: Structured Board Presentation	
1. *(Write this problem on the board.)* 2 × 5 = □	
2. What does this problem tell us to do? *(Point to problem as students read.)*	Count by 2 five times
How many times are we going to count?	5
So I'll put up five fingers. Watch me count by 2 five times: *(Count and touch fingers.)* 2, 4, 6, 8, 10.	
3. Now it's your turn to count by 2 five times. How many times are you going to count?	5 times
Hold up five fingers.	
You're counting by 2 five times. What number are you going to count by?	2
Touch a finger every time you count. Counting by 2. Get ready, count. *(Clap at intervals of 2 seconds.)*	Students touch an extended finger every time they count: 2, 4, 6, 8, 10
What number did you end with?	10
So I'll write a 10 in the box. *(Write 10.)*	
4. *(Write the problem below on the board.)* 2 × 3 = □	
5. What does this problem tell us to do?	Count by 2 three times
How many times are you going to count?	3
Hold up your fingers. *(Monitor students' responses.)*	
What number are you going to count by?	2
Get ready to count. *(Clap at intervals of 2 seconds.)*	Students touch an extended finger every time they count: 2, 4, 6
How many did you end with?	6
So I'll write 6 in the box. *(Write 6.)* When we count by 2 three times, what do we end with?	6
6. *(Repeat steps 4 and 5 with 5 × 4 = □, 10 × 3 = □, 2 × 4 = □, and 9 × 3 = □).* *(Give individual turns to several students.)*	
Part D: Structured Worksheet	

1. *(Give students a worksheet with problems like the following.)*
   a. 5 × 3 = □
   b. 10 × 4 = □
   c. 2 × 6 = □	

continued

Format 9.1 *(continued)*
SINGLE DIGIT MULTIPLICATION

TEACHER	STUDENTS
2. *(Touch problem a.)* What does the problem tell you to do?	Count by 5 three times
How many times are you going to count?	3
Hold up your fingers. *(Monitor responses.)*	Students hold up three fingers.
What number are you counting by?	5
3. Get ready. Count. *(Clap at intervals of about 1 second.)*	Students count 5, 10, 15, touching each extended finger.
When you count by 5 three times, what do you end with?	15
Write 15 in the box. *(Check student work.)*	
(Repeat steps 2 and 3 with remaining problems.)	
Part E: Less Structured Worksheet	
1. *(Give students a worksheet with a variety of multiplication and addition problems like the following.)*	
a. $5 \times 4 = \square$	
b. $5 + 4 = \square$	
c. $10 \times 3 = \square$	
d. $10 \times 5 = \square$	
e. $10 + 5 = \square$	
2. Touch problem a. Put your finger under the sign. What does the problem tell you to do, plus or count by?	Count by
Say the problem.	Count by 5 four times
Work it and write how many you end with in the box. *(Monitor student responses.)*	
(Repeat step 2 with remaining problems.)	

Format 9.2
MISSING-FACTOR MULTIPLICATION

TEACHER	STUDENTS
Part A: Structured Board Presentation—Model and Test Translation	
1. *(Write the problem below on the board.)*	
$5 \times \square = 20$	
2. Here's a new kind of problem. Here's what it tells us to do. *(Point to each symbol as you read.)* Count by 5 how many times to end with 20?	
3. *(Point to $\square$.)*	
Does this problem tell how many times we count by 5?	No
Right, we have to figure out how many times we count by 5.	

TEACHER	STUDENTS
4. Your turn to read the problem. I'll touch, and you read.	
(*Touch ×, then 5, □ =, and 20. Repeat step 4 until students respond correctly.*)	Count by 5 how many times to end with 20?
5. Let's work this problem. What are we going to count by?	5
Do we know how many times we count?	No
I hold up a fist to show that I don't know how many times to count. How many are we going to end with?	20
6. My turn. I'm going to count by 5 and end with 20. (*Begin with a closed fist, then hold up a finger each time you count: 5, 10, 15, 20.*)	
I put up a finger each time I counted. Here's how many times I counted. How many?	4
So how many fives in 20?	4
7. Now it's your turn. Say what the problem tells us to do. (*Point to 5 × □ = 20.*)	Count by 5 how many times to end with 20
You have to figure out how many times we count. What do you have to figure out?	How many times we count
What are you counting by?	5
Do you know how many times to count?	No
So hold up a fist. What number are you going to end with?	20
8. Each time I clap, count by five and put up a finger. (*Students are to hold up a finger each time you clap. Clap at 2-second intervals.*)	Students count 5, 10, 15, 20, putting up a finger each time they count.
How many times did you count by 5?	4
I'll write a 4 in the box. (*Write 4 in box.*)	
(*Repeat steps 7 and 8 with 2 × □ = 14, 10 × □ = 30, 9 × □ = 36, 2 × □ = 6.*)	
Part B: Structured Worksheet	
1. (*Give the students a worksheet with the following problems.*)	
a. 5 × □ = 20	
b. 2 × □ = 10	
c. 10 × □ = 40	
d. 9 × □ = 18	
e. 5 × □ = 30	
2. Touch problem a. What does the problem tell you to do?	Count by 5 how many times to end with 20
3. What do you have to figure out?	How many times we count
Put up your fist. What are you counting by?	5
What are you going to end with?	20

continued

Format 9.2 (continued)
MISSING-FACTOR MULTIPLICATION

TEACHER	STUDENTS
4. Count and put up a finger each time you count. Get ready. Count. (Clap at 2-second intervals.)	Students count 5, 10, 15, 20, putting up a finger each time they count.
How many times did you count?	4
Write 4 in the box.	
(Repeat steps 2–4 with remaining problems.)	
Part C: Less Structured Worksheet	
1. (Give students a worksheet with an equal mix of regular and missing factor problems.)	
a. $5 \times \square = 10$	
b. $9 \times 3 = \square$	
c. $2 \times \square = 8$	
d. $2 \times 6 = \square$	
2. Touch problem a. (Monitor students' responses.)	
3. What does the problem tell you to do?	Count by 5 how many times to end with 10?
4. What are you counting by?	5
5. Does the problem tell you how many times to count?	No
6. Show me what you hold up.	Students hold up fist.
7. Work the problem and write the answer in the box.	
(Repeat steps 2–7 with remaining problems.)	

Format 9.3
ONE-DIGIT FACTOR TIMES TWO-DIGIT FACTOR—RENAMING

TEACHER	STUDENTS
Part A: Structured Board Presentation	
1. (Write the problem below on the board.)	
$$\begin{array}{r} 4\,7 \\ \times\ \ 5 \\ \hline \end{array}$$	
2. Read the problem.	5×47
3. To work this problem, first we multiply 5×7	
4. What do we do first?	Multiply 5×7
5. Next we multiply 5×4 tens. What do we do next?	Multiply 5×4 tens
(Repeat steps 2–5 until students respond correctly.)	
6. What is 5×7?	35
We can't write 35 in the ones column. We must rename. How many tens are in 35?	3 tens

TEACHER	STUDENTS
I put 3 above the tens column and put a plus sign in front of it to remind us to add those tens.	
Thirty-five has 3 tens and how many ones?	5
I write the 5 under the ones column.	

```
  +3
 |4|7|
×| |5|
 | |5|
```

7. Now we multiply 5 × 4 tens. How many tens is 5 × 4 tens?	20
8. Now we add the 3 tens we placed above the tens column. What is 20 + 3?	23
Yes, 23 tens. 23 tens is the same as 2 hundreds and 3 tens, so I write 2 hundreds and 3 tens in the answer.	

```
  +3
 |4|7|
×| |5|
|2|3|5|
```

| 9. What does 5 × 47 equal? | 235 |

(Repeat steps 1–9 with the problems below.)

```
 36      42      34
× 2     × 9     × 5
```

Part B: Structured Worksheet

1. *(Give students a worksheet with the following problems.)*

```
a. |2|5|    b. |1|4|    c. |4|8|    d. |7|6|    e. |3|7|
  ×| |9|      ×| |7|      ×| |2|      ×| |5|      ×| |2|
   | | |       | | |       | | |       | | |       | | |
```

2. Read problem a.	9 × 25
What numbers do we multiply first?	9 × 5
What is 9 × 5?	45
How many tens in 45?	4
Write plus 4 over the tens column. How many ones in 45?	5
Write the 5 under the ones column.	
3. What numbers do we multiply next?	9 × 2
What is 9 × 2?	18
What do we do now?	Add 4
What is 18 + 4?	22
Write 22 next to the 5 under the line. What is 9 × 25?	225
Read the whole problem.	9 × 25 = 225

(Repeat steps 2 and 3 with remaining examples.)

Part C: Less Structured Worksheet

1. *(Give students a worksheet with the following problems.)*

```
a.  35     b.  79     c.  35
   × 5        × 2        + 5

d.  64     e.  83     f.  83
   × 9        × 5        + 5
```

continued

Format 9.3 (continued)
ONE-DIGIT FACTOR TIMES TWO-DIGIT FACTOR—RENAMING

TEACHER	STUDENTS
2. Read problem a.	5 × 35
What type of problem is this?	Multiplication
(If the problem is addition, tell students to work the problem.)	
What will you do first?	Multiply 5 × 5
What is 5 × 5?	25
Rename the tens in 25 and write the ones.	
3. What numbers do we multiply next?	5 × 3
Then what do we do?	Add the 2
Work the rest of the problem. (Pause.)	
4. What is 5 × 35?	175
(Repeat steps 2–4 with remaining problems.)	

Format 9.4
TWO-DIGIT FACTOR TIMES TWO-DIGIT FACTOR

TEACHER	STUDENTS
Part A: Order of Multiplying	
1. (Write these problems on the board.)	
$$\begin{array}{r} 5\ 8 \\ \times\ 4\ 3 \\ \hline \end{array}$$ $$\begin{array}{r} 2\ 7 \\ \times\ 9\ 5 \\ \hline \end{array}$$ $$\begin{array}{r} 4\ 2 \\ \times\ 5\ 7 \\ \hline \end{array}$$	
2. (Point to 58 × 43.) Read the problem.	58 × 43
Here's how we work multiplication problems with two numbers on the bottom. First, we multiply all the numbers on the top by the ones. (Point to 3.) Then we multiply all the numbers on the top by the tens. (Point to 4.)	
3. My turn. (Point to the numerals as you say them.) First we multiply 3 × 8, then 3 × 5, then 4 × 8, then 4 × 5.	
4. (Point to 3.) What numbers do we multiply first?	3 × 8
(Point to 3.) What numbers do we multiply next?	3 × 5
(Point to 4.) What numbers do we multiply next?	4 × 8
(Point to 4.) What numbers do we multiply next?	4 × 5
(Repeat steps 2–4 with remaining problems. Give individual turns.)	

TEACHER	STUDENTS
Part B: Structured Board Presentation	
1. *(Point to the problem below.)*	
$$\begin{array}{r} 5\ 8 \\ \times\ 4\ 3 \\ \hline \end{array}$$	
Read the problem.	58×43
2. What numbers do we multiply first?	3×8
3. What is 3×8?	24
(Point above the tens column.) What number do I write here?	
(Write 2.)	2
(Point under the ones column.) What number do I write here?	
(Write 4.)	4
4. What numbers do we multiply next?	
5. What is 3×5?	3×5
6. What else do we do?	15
What is $15 + 2$?	Add 2
	17
There are no more numbers on top to multiply, so I write the 17 under the line next to the 4. *(Write 17.)*	
7. We multiplied 3×58. What is 3×58?	174
I cross out the 2 we wrote above the tens column and the 3 to show we're finished with those numbers.	
$$\begin{array}{r} \not{2} \\ 5\ 8 \\ \times\ 4\ \not{3} \\ \hline 1\ 7\ 4 \end{array}$$	
8. Now we multiply 4 tens $\times$ 58. Tens numbers have a zero, so we put a zero in the ones column to show we're multiplying by tens. How do we show we're multiplying by tens?	Put a zero in the ones column.
(Write 0 under 4.)	
Now we multiply 4×8, then 4×5. What is 4×8?	32
(Point above tens column.) What number do I write here?	3
(Write 3.)	
(Point next to zero.) What number do I write here?	2
(Write 2.)	
$$\begin{array}{r} 3 \\ \not{2} \\ 5\ 8 \\ \times\ 4\ \not{3} \\ \hline 1\ 7\ 4 \\ 2\ 3\ 2\ 0 \end{array}$$	
9. Now what numbers do we multiply?	4×5
What is 4×5?	20
What do we do now?	Add 3
What is 20×3?	23
Where do I write the 23?	Next to the 2
(Write 23.)	

continued

Format 9.4 *(continued)*
TWO-DIGIT FACTOR TIMES TWO-DIGIT FACTOR

TEACHER	STUDENTS
10. First we multiplied 3 × 58 and ended with 2330. Now let's add those numbers and figure out what 43 × 58 equals. What is 4 + 0?	4
(Write 4.)	
What is 7 + 2?	9
(Write 9.)	
What is 1 + 3?	4
(Write 4.)	
What is 0 and 2?	2
(Write 2.)	
11. We're finished adding. I'll put in the comma. Where does it go?	Between the 2 and 4
(Write the comma.)	
What does 43 × 58 equal?	2,494
(Repeat steps 1–11 with 22 × 87, 16 × 94, and 35 × 79.)	

Part C: Structured Worksheet

1. *(Give students worksheets with problems such as these.)*

   a. $\begin{array}{r} 2\,8 \\ \times\,3\,6 \\ \hline \end{array}$ b. $\begin{array}{r} 6\,4 \\ \times\,2\,8 \\ \hline \end{array}$ c. $\begin{array}{r} 8\,7 \\ \times\,4\,5 \\ \hline \end{array}$

2. Touch problem a on your worksheet. *(Pause.)* Read the problem.	36 × 28
What numbers are you going to multiply first?	6 × 8
What is 6 × 8?	48
Write it; don't forget to rename. *(Monitor responses.)*	
3. What do you multiply next?	6 × 2
What is 6 × 2?	12
What do you do now?	Add 4
What is 12 + 4?	16
Write 16 next to the 8. *(Monitor responses.)*	
4. Are you done multiplying by 6?	Yes
Cross out the 6 to show you're finished. *(Monitor responses.)*	
5. You multiplied 6 × 28. Now multiply 30 × 28. What do you write to show that you are multiplying by tens?	zero
Write it. *(Monitor responses.)* What numbers do you multiply now?	3 × 8
What is 3 × 8?	24
Write the 4 next to the zero. Write the 2 over the 2. *(Monitor responses.)*	
6. Now what are you going to multiply?	3 × 2
What is 3 × 2?	6
What do you do now?	Add 2
What is 6 + 2?	8
Write it. *(Monitor responses.)*	

TEACHER	STUDENTS
7. You multiplied 6 × 28 and 30 × 28. Add the sums to see what 36 × 28 equals, then put in the comma. *(Pause to allow students to add.)*	
8. What is 36 × 28?	1008
(Repeat steps 2–8 with several examples.)	
Part D: Less Structured Practice	
1. *(Give students worksheets with a mix of multiplication problems with two-digit and one-digit factors and some addition problems. Use the following prompts as students work through the problems.)*	
2. Touch problem _____. *(Pause.)* Read the problem.	
What kind of problem is this?	
(If the problem involves addition or multiplication with one-digit factors, have the students solve independently. If the problem involves multiplication with two-digit factors, use the prompts in steps 2–3.)	
3. What numbers do you multiply first?	
What numbers do you multiply next?	
What numbers do you multiply next?	
What numbers do you multiply next?	
4. What are you going to do just before you start to multiply by 5 tens?	Write a zero
Right, remember to write the zero. Work the problem.	
(Repeat with remaining problems.)	

Division

LEARNING OUTCOMES

10.1 Discuss the two stages of teaching division to young students and the sequence of problem types appropriate for each stage.

10.2 Describe the ways in which division can be introduced using concrete demonstrations.

10.3 Outline instructional strategies to teach single-digit division including problems without remainders, division facts, and problems with remainders.

10.4 Discuss the differences in the instructional strategies for teaching multi-digit division problems with one-digit divisors and two-digit divisors.

SKILL HIERARCHY
· · · · · · · ·

As with all major operations, **division** is introduced in two stages: the beginning stage and the multi-digit division stage. During the beginning stage, exercises providing concrete demonstrations of the division concept are presented. With concrete objects or pictures, the teacher illustrates how groups of objects can be divided into equal-sized small groups, first illustrating problems that have no remainder and, later, problems that have a remainder.

During the multi-digit stage, students are taught algorithms to solve division problems that have multi-digit **quotients**. A significant period of time is needed between the introduction of the beginning stage and presentation of division algorithms. During that time, the teacher should present exercises to facilitate memorization of basic division facts. Once students know their division facts, division problems with one-digit **divisors** (and multi-digit quotients) can be introduced. Division problems with two-digit divisors are substantially more difficult and therefore are introduced later. A list of the specific problem types and when they are typically introduced appears in the Instructional Sequence and Assessment Chart.

INSTRUCTIONAL SEQUENCE AND ASSESSMENT CHART

Grade Level	Problem Type	Performance Indicator		
3	One-digit divisor and one-digit quotient; no remainder.	$3\overline{)15}$	$2\overline{)12}$	$5\overline{)20}$
3	One-digit divisor and quotient with remainder.	$5\overline{)38}$ R	$2\overline{)9}$ R	$5\overline{)22}$ R
3	Division equation with ÷ sign; no remainder; single-digit divisor and quotient.	$8 \div 2 = \square$ $20 \div 5 = \square$ $36 \div 9 = \square$		
4	One-digit divisor; two- or three-digit dividend; two-digit quotient; no remainder.	$5\overline{)85}$	$2\overline{)172}$	$2\overline{)54}$
4	One-digit divisor; two- or three-digit dividend; two-digit quotient; remainder.	$5\overline{)87}$	$2\overline{)173}$	$2\overline{)55}$
4	One-digit divisor; two- or three-digit dividend; quotient has two digits, one of which is zero; remainder.	$5\overline{)53}$	$9\overline{)274}$	$9\overline{)366}$
4	One-digit divisor; two- or three-digit dividend; two-digit quotient; express remainder as fraction.	Write the remainders as fractions. $5\overline{)127}$	$2\overline{)91}$	$9\overline{)364}$
4	One-digit divisor; three- or four-digit dividend; three-digit quotient.	$5\overline{)635}$	$2\overline{)1343}$	$2\overline{)738}$
4	Same as 4 above; zero in quotient.	$5\overline{)2042}$	$2\overline{)1214}$	$5\overline{)520}$
4	Four-digit quotient; one-digit divisor, four- or five-digit dividend.	$5\overline{)8753}$	$2\overline{)11325}$	$9\overline{)36286}$
4	Rounding to the nearest 10.	76 rounds off to _____ tens 405 rounds off to _____ tens 297 rounds off to _____ tens		
5	Two-digit divisor; one- or two-digit quotient; all estimation yields correct quotient.	$23\overline{)94}$	$56\overline{)857}$	$47\overline{)1325}$
5	Same as above except estimation procedures yield quotient that is too large or small.	$24\overline{)82}$	$67\overline{)273}$	$35\overline{)714}$

CONCEPTUAL UNDERSTANDING

There are at least four basic ways to provide concrete demonstrations of division:

1. Removing equivalent disjoint subsets: A picture of 6 fish is shown. The teacher says, "Let's put these fish in little bowls. We'll put 2 in each bowl. Let's see how many bowls we'll need. We put 2 in the first bowl. That leaves 4, and then we put 2 in the second bowl. Then we put 2 in the third bowl. We need three bowls if we put 2 fish in each bowl."

2. Arrays: A group of objects aligned in equal columns is an array.

The teacher says, "Let's see how many sets of 6 there are in 30." The teacher counts each set of 6 as he circles them and then summarizes, "There are 5 sets of 6 in thirty."

3. Linear models: A linear model is usually characterized by use of a number line. In multiplication, students start at zero and jump to the right; 3×4 may be demonstrated as making 3 jumps of 4 units. Division problems are illustrated by saying, "If we start at 12, how many jumps of 4 do we make to get back to zero?"

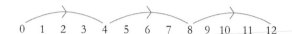

4. Repeated subtraction: This way of introducing division is similar to the removal of equivalent disjoint subsets. The teacher says, "We want to find out how many groups of 4 are in 12. Here's one way to find out. We keep subtracting 4 until we run out. We subtract 4 from 12. That equals 8. Then we subtract 4 from 8. That equals 4, and 4 from 4 equals zero." The teacher then has students count the number of times they subtracted to derive the answer.

Direct instruction procedures introduce the division concept through disjoint sets. Removing equivalent disjoint sets easily illustrates the relationship between multiplication and division as well as the concept of a remainder. Initial direct instruction exercises teach students to remove equivalent sets by circling groups of lines.

Students must have mastered two preskills prior to the introduction of division. The first preskill is knowledge of basic multiplication facts. Students need not have memorized all multiplication facts before division is introduced, but they should at least have memorized multiplication facts with 2 and 5 as factors. A second preskill is column subtraction with renaming, which often is required when students subtract to find a remainder.

Division is usually presented during mid-third grade. Exercises to teach division facts are introduced about a week or two after the concept of division is introduced. We recommend teachers present facts in related series as outlined in Chapter 6. Ample practice to enable students to develop fluency with a set of facts must be provided before a new set is introduced. Cumulative review of all previously introduced facts also must be provided. Practice exercises to teach basic division facts usually are provided daily for many months.

The concept of remainder is introduced after students have learned about 20 division facts. More specifically, we recommend that students know the division facts with divisors of 2 and 5 before the remainder concept is introduced. Similar to the introduction of division without remainders, the first exercises in which students are introduced to remainders require the students to circle groups of lines. After several days, exercises to teach students to compute quotients mentally in problems with remainders are presented. Practice on division facts with remainders continues for several months.

INSTRUCTIONAL PROCEDURES: BEGINNING DIVISION

Problems Without Remainders

Format 10.1: Introducing Division outlines the procedure for introducing division. The format contains four parts. Part A begins with the teacher modeling and testing the translation of a division problem. For example, the problem $5\overline{)20}$ is read as "5 goes into 20 how many times?" rather than "20 divided by 5." The purpose of this translation is to draw attention to the divisor, since it specifies the size of the equivalent groups, the critical feature in using lines to solve division problems. Also, the translation facilitates the use of multiplication facts. Note that the students are taught to translate problems so that they are read as a form of missing-factor multiplication.

Part B is a structured board exercise in which the teacher demonstrates with lines the process of taking a big group and making smaller, equal-sized groups. When working the problem, the teacher points out the function of the numbers in a problem. In 20 divided by 5, the 20 tells how many lines in all, the 5 tells how many in each group, and the 4 tells how many groups. One minor but important aspect of Part B addresses where the quotient is written. If the **dividend** is a two-digit numeral, the quotient is written over the last digit of the dividend. For example, in the problem 20 divided by 5, the quotient 4 is written over the zero. The purpose of having students write the quotient in the correct place is to prepare them for using the traditional algorithm to solve problems with multi-digit quotients. Improper placement of digits in the quotient can lead to errors:

$$
\begin{array}{r}
13 \\
5\overline{)607} \\
\underline{5} \\
17 \\
\underline{15} \\
2
\end{array}
$$

Parts C and D are structured and less structured worksheet exercises. In both exercises, students are given problems for which lines are already drawn. Note that a variety of divisors can be included in these exercises, since knowledge of facts is not required. Students make groups the size of which are defined by the divisor. Note also that students are assigned only two or three problems a day for practice. This exercise is designed to provide a conceptual basis for understanding division. Therefore, teachers need only develop accuracy in such exercises; fluency is not as important at this point.

Division Facts

A week or so after students have been introduced to division through the line-circling exercises described in Format 10.1, exercises to facilitate mastery of basic facts can begin. Exercises that demonstrate the relationship between multiplication and division facts using fact number families are presented prior to exercises that promote memorization. (See Format 6.4 in Chapter 6.)

$$
3 \times 4 = 12 \qquad 4 \times 3 = 12
$$

$$
\begin{array}{cc}
4 & 3 \\
3\overline{)12} & 4\overline{)12}
\end{array}
$$

After relationship exercises are presented for several days for a set of facts, those facts are incorporated into memorization exercises. We recommend that students continue saying the facts in the statement form "5 goes into 20 four times" rather than "20 divided by 5 equals 4" because the former uses the language presented when division problems with multi-digit quotients are introduced. Procedures to teach basic facts are discussed in more depth in Chapter 6.

Problems with Remainders

The concept of remainders is an important skill in and of itself and is also a preskill for the short-form division algorithm involving multi-digit quotients. Problems with remainders can be introduced when the students have learned division facts with divisors of 2 and 5.

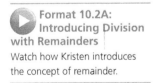
Format 10.2A: Introducing Division with Remainders
Watch how Kristen introduces the concept of remainder.

Format 10.2: Introducing Division with Remainders illustrates how to introduce the remainder concept. In Part A, the teacher writes a problem on the board and has the students read it. After students read the problem, the teacher draws lines. For 13 divided by 5, the teacher draws 13 lines, then asks the students for the number in each smaller group and begins drawing circles around groups of 5 lines. After drawing two groups, the teacher points out that he cannot draw a circle around the last lines because there are not 5 lines. The teacher tells the students that only two groups of 5 can be made and that the other lines are called the remainder. The teacher then states the answer to the problem: 5 goes into 13 two times with a remainder of 3.

In Parts B and C, the students are given a worksheet with several division problems with remainders. In Part B, next to each problem is a diagram illustrating the problem. For example, next to the problem

$$5\overline{)17}$$

17 lines would be drawn with circles around groups of 5 lines:

The diagram is drawn so that the teacher may concentrate on the mechanics of where to write the number of groups, how to figure out how many parts are used (multiply 5 × 3), where to write the number of parts used (under the 17), and how to compute the remainder (subtract 15 from 17). Note that practice on this exercise is typically continued for a week or two, since the exercise is designed primarily to teach conceptual understanding.

Remainder Facts

As mentioned earlier, students should have been taught at least 20 division facts before the remainder concept is introduced. About a week after the remainder concept is introduced, exercises to teach students to mentally compute division facts with remainders can be introduced using problems like those below:

$$5\overline{)27} \qquad 6\overline{)34}$$

This skill is a critical preskill for division problems with multi-digit quotients because most of these problems will have remainders. For example, in

$$3\overline{)147}$$

students must first determine that 3 goes into 14 four times with a remainder. After multiplying 3 × 4, they subtract to compute the exact remainder. **Format 10.3: Introducing Remainder Facts** shows how to teach students to mentally compute division facts with remainders.

Part A uses a diagram like the one below to introduce remainder facts. The teacher writes numerals rows, circling numerals that are all multiples of a particular divisor. In the example below, numerals with a divisor of 5 are circled.

1	2	3	4	⑤	6	7	8	9	⑩
11	12	13	14	⑮	16	17	18	19	⑳
21	22	23	24	㉕					

If the teacher is introducing the second part of a series, the teacher writes the higher numerals in the series. For example, if the second half of the 5 series is being introduced, the teacher writes in a single row:

㉕	26	27	28	29	㉚	31	32	33	34
㉟	36	37	38	39	㊵	41	42	43	44
㊺	46	47	48	49	㊿				

After writing the series on the board, the teacher points out that the circled numerals are the numbers that 5 goes into without a remainder. The teacher then models answering the question of how many times 5 goes into various numbers; for example, "5 goes into 23 four times with a remainder; 5 goes into 10 two times with no remainder; 5 goes into 9 one time with a remainder." Note that at this point, the quantity of the remainder is not stated. The teacher then tests the students on a set of similar examples.

In Part B, the teacher tests the students on various division facts with and without remainders, letting the students refer to the diagram. Part C is a structured worksheet exercise designed to provide practice that facilitates memorization of the facts. The students write the quotient and then multiply and subtract to figure out the remainder. The teacher leads the students through several problems and then has them complete the work independently.

Parts A and B need to be presented only when the first several sets of facts are introduced. Once students have learned to compute division facts mentally with twos and fives and nines, problems with other divisors can be introduced without using the diagram as a prompt.

The sequence in which new division facts with remainders are introduced parallels the sequence in which basic division facts without remainders are introduced. (See Chapter 6 on basic facts for the suggested sequence for introducing division facts.) About 2 weeks after a set of division facts with a particular divisor has been taught, division facts with remainders for the same divisors and quotients are presented. For example, after students master the division facts for fives:

$$\text{e.g., } 5\overline{)30} \qquad 5\overline{)35} \qquad 5\overline{)40} \qquad 5\overline{)45}$$

problems with the same divisor and quotient but with remainders are introduced:

$$\text{e.g., } 5\overline{)32} \qquad 5\overline{)41} \qquad 5\overline{)43} \qquad 5\overline{)48} \qquad 5\overline{)36} \qquad 5\overline{)38}$$

The daily worksheet exercise should include several problems. About half of the problems should represent the most recently introduced set of division facts, while the other half of the problems should consist of those previously introduced. Although most problems should have remainders, some of the problems should not so that students don't develop the misrule that all division problems must have remainders. Finally, several problems in which the quotient is zero should be included:

$$5\overline{)3} \qquad 9\overline{)6} \qquad 2\overline{)1}$$

Teaching students to mentally compute the answer to such problems prepares them for long division problems in which zero is in the quotient.

Figure 10.1 is a sample worksheet exercise based on the assumption that students have previously mastered problems with divisors of 2, 5, and 9 and are being introduced to the first half of the sevens series. Worksheet exercises like Figure 10.1 should be presented daily for several months. Students who develop fluency in computing division facts with remainders are less likely to have difficulty when more complex division problems are introduced.

Diagnosis and Remediation

Determining the cause of errors while introducing the division concept is fairly easy. The more common causes, in addition to not knowing basic facts, are component-skill errors:

1. Writing quotients that are either too small or too large
2. Subtracting incorrectly
3. Confusing the placement of the quotient and remainder

Fact Errors   Basic fact errors are illustrated below:

$$\text{a. } 7\overline{)33} \qquad \text{b. } 9\overline{)42} \qquad \text{c. } 7\overline{)32}$$
$$\phantom{\text{a. }}\underline{30} \qquad \phantom{\text{b. }}\underline{38} \qquad \phantom{\text{c. }}\underline{26}$$

(with quotients 5, 4, 4 respectively)

As usual, the remediation procedure for basic fact errors depends on the number of fact errors the student makes. If a student makes just occasional fact errors, the teacher simply records the facts the student misses and incorporates those facts into practice exercises for the next several lessons. If a student makes fact errors on more than 10% of the problems, he should be tested individually to determine what action to take next. If the teacher finds that the student responds correctly on the individual test to all the missed facts, the teacher should tentatively conclude that the errors resulted from hurrying through the problems. The remediation procedure is to increase the student's motivation to perform accurately. If the student's test performance indicates he does not know many previously introduced basic facts, he should

FIGURE 10.1   Sample worksheet exercise

$7\overline{)18}$	$9\overline{)46}$	$7\overline{)26}$	$7\overline{)31}$	$2\overline{)7}$	$5\overline{)32}$	$7\overline{)35}$	$9\overline{)27}$
$7\overline{)4}$	$7\overline{)17}$	$9\overline{)58}$	$9\overline{)65}$	$7\overline{)27}$	$5\overline{)3}$	$7\overline{)41}$	$9\overline{)53}$
$5\overline{)30}$	$7\overline{)11}$	$7\overline{)25}$	$7\overline{)32}$	$9\overline{)31}$	$5\overline{)18}$	$7\overline{)3}$	$7\overline{)25}$
$9\overline{)49}$	$9\overline{)26}$	$5\overline{)48}$	$2\overline{)17}$	$7\overline{)36}$	$7\overline{)28}$	$7\overline{)19}$	$7\overline{)36}$

be tested on all previously taught multiplication and division facts and provided systematic, intensive instruction on those facts. Also, for several weeks, the teacher should carefully control the assignments given to the student so that only facts the student knows appear on worksheet problems, if possible.

Component-Skill Errors   One component-skill error involves writing a quotient that is either too large or small. Examples of this error are illustrated below. Problems a and b are examples of computing too small a quotient; problems c and d are examples of computing too large a quotient.

$$
\begin{array}{llll}
\text{a.} \;\; 5)\overline{28} & \text{b.} \;\; 7)\overline{35} & \text{c.} \;\; 6)\overline{32} & \text{d.} \;\; 4)\overline{19} \\
\quad\;\; \underline{20} & \quad\;\; \underline{28} & \quad\;\; \underline{36} & \quad\;\; \underline{20}
\end{array}
$$

(with quotients 4, 4, 6, 5 respectively)

If either type of error occurs in more than 10% of the problems students work independently, the teacher should present an exercise that teaches students to compare the remainder and divisor to determine the accuracy of their answer.

The content of the exercise depends on the type of error made. If the student writes quotients that are too small:

$$
\begin{array}{c}
6 \\
5)\overline{37} \\
\underline{30} \\
7
\end{array}
$$

Format 10.4A: Remediation for Division with Remainders—Quotients Too Small
Watch how Kristen efficiently presents multiple practice examples.

the teacher presents an exercise like the one in **Format 10.4: Remediation for Division with Remainders—Quotient Too Small**.

This format contains an exercise in which students are given a worksheet composed of division problems with the quotients written. In half of the problems the quotient is correct, and in the other half the quotient is too small:

$$
\begin{array}{c}
3 \\
9)\overline{38} \\
\underline{27} \\
11
\end{array}
$$

Format 10.4B: Remediation for Division with Remainders—Quotients Too Small
Watch how Kristen has students apply a rule for remainders.

In Part A, the teacher tells students that they must compare the remainder and the divisor to see if they worked the problem correctly. Note that the term "divisor" is not used by the teacher. If students divide by 9, they are taught that the remainder must be smaller than 9; if they divide by 5, the remainder must be smaller than 5; if they divide by 3, the remainder must be smaller than 3; and so on. In Part B, the teacher leads students through determining if the quotient is correct by completing the problem and comparing the remainder to the divisor. In problems in which the remainder is bigger than the divisor, the teacher points out that another group can be made and instructs the student to cross out the answer and, in its place, write the next higher numeral. For example, in the problem

$$
\begin{array}{c}
2 \\
5)\overline{16} \\
\underline{10} \\
6
\end{array}
$$

the teacher has the students cross out 2 and write 3 as the answer. The student then erases 10, multiplies 3 × 5, and subtracts 15 from 16. The teacher guides students through several problems and then has them work additional problems on their own. This format is presented daily until students can successfully solve the problems for several consecutive days.

For errors such as

$$
\begin{array}{c}
7 \\
5)\overline{32}
\end{array}
$$

Format 10.5B: Remediation for Division with Remainders—Quotients Too Large
Watch how Kristen guides her students through correcting a quotient that is too large.

in which the answer is too large, the teacher should use the process illustrated in **Format 10.5: Remediation for Division with Remainders-Quotient Too Large**. In Part A, the teacher guides the students through a set of problems on the board, pointing out that if they can't subtract, the answer is too big, and the numeral in the answer must be made smaller. In Part B, the teacher has students work a set of examples in which half of the problems have a quotient that is too large and half have a quotient that is correct. As with the previous format, this should be presented for several lessons.

Column subtraction errors are easy to spot and usually result from a failure to rename. Problems a and b below illustrate subtraction errors.

$$
\text{a.}\quad 7\overline{)41} \atop {\underline{35} \atop 14} \text{ with } 5 \qquad\qquad \text{b.}\quad 9\overline{)71} \atop {\underline{63} \atop 12} \text{ with } 7
$$

The remediation procedure includes giving students a worksheet with several problems that require renaming. The teacher guides students through the first few problems and then has students work the remaining problems on their own. For example, in the problem

$$
\begin{array}{r} 5 \\ 7\overline{)41} \\ \underline{35} \end{array}
$$

the teacher would have the students identify the problem in the ones column, ask if they can subtract 5 from 1, and then prompt students to rename.

The final type of error involves confusing placement of the quotient and remainder. The remediation procedure is to present Part C of Format 10.3: Introducing Remainder Facts with several problems and then supervise the students as they work additional problems independently.

A summary of the diagnosis and remediation procedures for beginning division appears in **Figure 10.2**.

FIGURE 10.2 **Diagnosis and remediation of beginning division errors**

Error Pattern	*Diagnosis*	*Remediation Procedures*	*Remediation Examples*
Fact Errors			
a. $7\overline{)35}$ with 4, $\underline{32}$	Fact error: 35 ÷ 7	Provide systematic fact instruction for frequent fact errors.	÷ 7 facts
Component-Skill Errors			
b. $6\overline{)24}$ with 3, $\underline{18}$	Student computes a quotient that is too small.	Present **Format 10.4: Remediation for Division with Remainders— Quotient Too Small.**	Partially worked problems with the quotients provided. Half of the quotients should be too small, and half of them should be accurate. $9\overline{)42}$ with 3 $9\overline{)56}$ with 6
c. $7\overline{)26}$ with 4, $\underline{28}$	Student computes a quotient that is too large.	Present **Format 10.5: Remediation for Division with Remainders— Quotient Too Large.**	Partially worked problems with the quotients provided. Half of the quotients should be too large, and half of them should be accurate.
d. $8\overline{)62}$ with 7, $\underline{56}$, 14	Student subtracts incorrectly.	Present Parts C, D, and E of **Format 8.3: Subtraction with Renaming.**	Partially worked problems with accurate quotients in which the students must subtract
e. $7\overline{)29}$ with 1 R4, $\underline{28}$, 1	Student misplaces remainder and quotient.	Present Part C of **Format 10.3: Introducing Remainder Facts.**	Division with remainder problems

Note: After addressing any component-skill error, assess students using problems similar to the ones on which errors were originally made in order to determine if the remediation was successful.

INSTRUCTIONAL PROCEDURES: MULTI-DIGIT DIVISION

The second stage of instruction in division focuses on multi-digit problems, which become quite complex. Multi-digit quotients are grouped in this text according to the number of digits in the divisor. Problems with one-digit divisors are discussed first followed by a discussion of problems with two-digit divisors.

Two division algorithms are taught in most commercial programs. One is commonly called the long form; the other, the short form. The long-form and short-form algorithms are illustrated below:

LONG FORM	SHORT FORM

$$7\overline{)382}$$
$$\underline{350} \quad 50$$
$$32$$
$$\underline{28} \quad 4$$
$$4$$
$$\overline{}$$
$$54$$

$$54$$
$$7\overline{)382}$$
$$\underline{35}$$
$$32$$
$$\underline{28}$$
$$4$$

The advantage of the long-form algorithm is that it presents a clear interpretation of what is involved in division. The disadvantage is that most upper-elementary teachers expect students to use the short-form algorithm. The advantage of the short-form algorithm is the relatively easy set of preskills that must be mastered prior to introducing division problems. The disadvantage of the short-form algorithm is that students may not understand why it works.

In this section, we discuss in detail the procedures for teaching the short-form algorithm. We recommend this algorithm because it is the algorithm most teachers eventually encourage students to use. Lower-performing students typically will be less likely to be confused if only one algorithm is presented. The basic steps of the short-form algorithm are presented in **Summary Box 10.1**.

One-Digit Divisors

Problems with one-digit divisors and multi-digit quotients are usually introduced in early fourth grade. Students should know at least 30 to 40 basic division facts and the corresponding remainder facts prior to the introduction of this type of problem.

Two factors affect the difficulty level of single-digit divisor problems: the number of digits in the quotient and the presence of a zero in the quotient. The more digits in the quotient, the more difficult a problem is. For example, the first problem below is more difficult than the second problem

$$5\overline{)835} \qquad 5\overline{)125}$$

because the former will have a three-digit quotient while the latter will have a two-digit quotient. Each additional numeral in the quotient requires an extra set of computations. Similarly, a problem such as the first one below is more difficult than the second

$$5\overline{)52} \qquad 5\overline{)85}$$

SUMMARY BOX 10.1

Division: The Short-Form Algorithm

1. Students read the problem.
2. Students underline the part of the problem that they work first.
3. Students compute the underlined part and write the answer above the last underlined digit.
4. Students multiply, subtract, and bring down the next numeral.
5. Students read the "new" problem and compute a quotient.
6. Students write the answer above the digit they just brought down.
7. Students multiply and subtract to determine the remainder.
8. Students say the problem and answer.

because in the former problem, the quotient contains a zero. Without careful instruction, students are likely to leave out the zero.

$$\begin{array}{r} 1 \\ 5\overline{)52} \\ \underline{5} \end{array}$$

This section discusses procedures for teaching students to work all of these problem types.

Problems with Two-Digit Quotient   Format 10.6: Division with Two-Digit Quotients illustrates the procedures for introducing division problems with two-digit quotients. The format includes five parts. In Part A, the students are taught how to determine the part of the problem to work first. This important preskill is necessary because division problems are worked a part at a time. For example, when working the problem

$$5\overline{)375}$$

the student first works the problem

$$5\overline{)37}$$

and then, after multiplying and subtracting:

$$\begin{array}{r} 7 \\ 5\overline{)375} \\ \underline{35} \\ 25 \end{array}$$

the student divides 5 into 25. The strategy to determine which part to work first involves comparing the divisor with the first digit of the dividend. If the first digit of the dividend is at least as big as the divisor, only the first digit of the dividend is underlined. For example, in this problem, the 9 is underlined:

$$7\overline{)\underline{9}45}$$

because the part of the problem to work first is 7 goes into 9. If the first digit of the dividend is not at least as big as the divisor, students are taught to underline the first two digits of the dividend. For example, in this problem, 23 is underlined:

$$7\overline{)\underline{23}6}$$

because the part of the problem to be worked first is 7 goes into 23. Note that in presenting this important preskill, the teacher does not use the words divisor or dividend, but rather refers to "the number dividing by" and "dividing into."

Examples must be carefully selected for Part A. In half of the problems, the first digit of the dividend should be smaller than the divisor. In the other half, the first digit of the dividend should be the same or larger than the divisor. A variety of divisors can be included, since students are not actually working the problems at this point. Below is a sample set of problems appropriate to use when teaching this preskill.

a. $7\overline{)243}$ b. $5\overline{)85}$ c. $4\overline{)235}$

d. $7\overline{)461}$ e. $9\overline{)362}$ f. $8\overline{)89}$

Part B of this format is a worksheet exercise in which the students practice underlining the part of the problem they work first. The teacher guides the students through several problems and then has the students work the remaining problems on their own. The teacher repeats this part daily until students can perform accurately without teacher assistance. Part C is a structured board exercise in which the teacher demonstrates the entire short-form algorithm. Parts D and E in **Format 10.6** are structured and less structured worksheet exercises. Note that the teacher specifies where digits in the quotient are to be written. The first digit in the quotient is to be written over the last underlined digit:

$$\begin{array}{r} 3 \\ 7\overline{)2\underline{3}8} \end{array} \qquad \begin{array}{r} 1 \\ 8\overline{)\underline{8}2} \end{array}$$

Each succeeding numeral is to be written over the succeeding digit in the dividend:

$$\begin{array}{r} 613 \\ 7\overline{)\underline{4}291} \end{array}$$

As mentioned earlier, placing the digits of the quotient in the proper position helps students in solving problems with zeros in the quotient as well as with problems containing decimals.

The example-selection guidelines for all worksheet exercises remain the same as for Parts A and B. However, because the students work the problems, the divisors should be limited to familiar facts. Half of the problems should have two-digit dividends, and half should have three-digit dividends. All problems should have two-digit quotients. Below is a sample set of problems that might appear on a worksheet for this format. This worksheet assumes students have learned division facts with 2, 9, 5, and 7 as divisors.

a. $5\overline{)87}$ b. $9\overline{)324}$ c. $5\overline{)135}$

d. $7\overline{)86}$ e. $2\overline{)134}$ f. $7\overline{)94}$

g. $2\overline{)156}$ h. $7\overline{)79}$ i. $2\overline{)29}$

Zero in the Quotient Problems with zero as the last digit of a two-digit quotient require special attention. These problems should be introduced several weeks after division problems with two-digit quotients have been presented.

The critical part of the format occurs after students subtract and bring down the last digit. For example, in

$$\begin{array}{r} 3 \\ 7\overline{)214} \\ \underline{21} \\ 4 \end{array}$$

the teacher asks, "7 goes into 4 how many times?" Since the answer is zero, the teacher writes a zero above the 4. The teacher may have to model writing the answer for the first several problems. The teacher-led parts of the format are presented for several days. Thereafter, three or four problems with a quotient ending in zero should be included in daily worksheet exercises.

Quotients of Three or More Digits Problems with quotients of three or more digits are introduced only when students have mastered problems with two-digit quotients. No preskills or board exercises need be presented. The teacher merely presents the less structured part of Format 10.6 for several days, emphasizing the need to continue bringing down digits until an answer has been written above the last digit of the dividend.

Problems with a zero as one of the three digits in the quotient are introduced only after students can solve problems without zeros in the quotient. Problems with a zero as the last digit can be introduced a week or so after problems with three-digit quotients have been introduced. These problems should cause students relatively little difficulty, since two-digit quotients with a zero would have been taught earlier. On the other hand, problems with a zero as the second digit of a three-digit quotient, such as

$$\begin{array}{r} 103 \\ 5\overline{)515} \end{array} \qquad \begin{array}{r} 407 \\ 2\overline{)814} \end{array}$$

will be difficult for many students. A structured worksheet exercise (Part D of Format 10.6) should be presented to teach this type of problem. After bringing down the first numeral, the teacher would model by saying, "The next part says 5 goes into 1; 5 goes into 1 zero times, so I write 0 in the answer. What is zero times 5? So I write zero under the 1. Now we subtract and bring down the next numeral."

$$\begin{array}{r} 1\,0 \\ 5\overline{)517} \\ \underline{5} \\ 0\,1 \end{array}$$

The teacher presents the structured worksheet exercise for several days with three or four problems. Next, a less structured worksheet exercise containing about 10 problems, three or four of which have zero as the middle digit, is presented. Supervised practice is continued until students develop accuracy.

Problems with quotients of four or more digits are usually presented in fourth grade. For students who have mastered all types of problems with three-digit quotients, these longer problems should cause little difficulty.

Self-Checking   After students become proficient in working division problems with remainders, they should be taught to check their answers. A self-checking procedure for division involves having students multiply the divisor and quotient and add the remainder, if there is one. The teacher can introduce self-checking on a worksheet exercise in which the problems are already worked with about half of them having incorrect answers. The teacher instructs the students to check the answers using the self-checking strategy and to correct any mistakes they identify.

Two-Digit Divisors

Solving problems with two-digit divisors requires the integration of numerous component skills into a fairly lengthy strategy. The steps in the short-form algorithm for two-digit divisors are outlined in **Summary Box 10.2**.

The complexity of problems with two-digit divisors is affected mainly by whether the estimating, or rounding off, procedure produces a correct quotient. In some cases, the estimate may yield a quotient that is too large. For example, in the problem

$$53\overline{)203}$$

students round off 53 to 5 tens and 203 to 20 tens and then determine how many fives in 20. The estimated quotient, 4, when multiplied by 53, equals 212, which is too large to be subtracted from 203. Since the estimate yielded too large a quotient, the actual quotient must be 3, not 4.

In contrast, other estimates may yield a quotient that is too small. For example, in the problem

$$56\overline{)284}$$

when 56 is rounded off to 6 tens and 284 is rounded off to 28 tens, the estimate is a quotient of 4. However, 56×4 is 224, which when subtracted from 284 leaves a difference of 60, from which another group of 56 could be made. Because the estimated quotient yields too small a quotient, the actual quotient must be one larger than 4. Problems in which the estimated quotient is too large or too small are more difficult and should not be introduced until students can work problems in which the estimated quotients prove to be correct.

SUMMARY BOX 10.2

Division: Short-Form Algorithm—Two-Digit Divisors

1. Students read the problem.
2. Students underline the part to be worked first.
3. Students write the rounded-off problem.
4. Students compute the division problem using the estimate from the rounded-off problem.
5. Students multiply and determines if she can subtract.
6. Students adjust the quotient if the estimate is not correct (using the rules, if you can't subtract, make the answer smaller; if the remainder is too big, make the answer bigger).
7. Students compute the division problem and read the problem with the answer.

Preskills Students should have mastered all of the preskills needed to solve division problems with one-digit divisors before problems with two-digit divisors are introduced. Additional preskills that need to be taught include rounding off numbers to the nearest tens unit, which is discussed next, and multiplying multi-digit numbers, which was discussed in Chapter 9.

Rounding off numbers to the nearest tens unit is a critical skill for problems with two-digit divisors. The first part of the strategy teaches students to estimate how many groups the size of the divisor can be made from the dividend. For the problem

$$54\overline{)186}$$

the teacher asks, "How many times does 54 go into 186?" The estimate is derived by rounding off and expressing both the divisor and dividend as tens units: 54 is rounded to 5 tens and 186 is rounded to 19 tens. The students then figure out how many fives are in 19.

Format 10.7: Rounding to Nearest Tens Unit shows how to teach students to round off numbers to the nearest tens unit. In Part A, the teacher models and tests converting a tens number that ends in zero to a unit of tens: 340 equals 34 tens, 720 equals 72 tens, 40 equals 4 tens. The teacher repeats a set of six to eight examples until the students can respond correctly to all of the examples. In Part B, the teacher models and tests rounding numbers that end in any digit to the nearest tens unit. The teacher writes a numeral on the board and asks the students if the number is closer to the tens number preceding it or following it. For example, after writing 238 on the board, the teacher asks the students if 238 is closer to 230 or 240. After the students respond "240," the teacher asks, "So how many tens is 238 closest to, 23 tens or 24 tens?"

Part C is a worksheet exercise in which the student must write the tens unit closest to the number (342 = □ tens). Students may require several weeks of practice to master this skill. However, division problems with two-digit divisors should not be introduced until students master this preskill.

Several example-selection guidelines apply to this format: (a) half of the numbers to be rounded off should have a numeral less than 5 in the ones column, while the other half should have 5 or a numeral greater than 5; (b) about two-thirds of the examples should be three-digit numbers and one-third, two-digit numbers, so that practice is provided on the two types of numbers students will have to round off; and (c) numbers that may cause particular difficulty for students should not be included in initial exercises.

Two types of numbers may cause difficulty: (a) numbers in which the last two digits are 95 or greater (397, 295, 498), which require rounding off to the next hundreds grouping (397 rounds off to 40 tens, and 295 rounds off to 30 tens), and (b) numbers that have a zero in the tens column (408, 207, 305). Special emphasis should be given to these two types of examples about a week after the format is initially presented.

Problems with Correct Estimated Quotients Initially, division problems with two-digit divisors should be limited to problems in which the estimated quotients are correct. Also, the initial problems should involve a one-digit quotient. Problems containing a two-digit quotient can usually be introduced several days after problems with a one-digit quotient are presented.

The process for teaching correct estimated quotients with two-digit divisors appears in *Format 10.8: Correct Estimated Quotients with Two-Digit Divisors.* It includes four parts. Parts A and B teach preskills unique to the short-form algorithm: horizontal multiplication and estimating a quotient by rounding off the divisor and dividend.

Part A teaches students to multiply the estimated quotient and divisor, which are written horizontally, and to place the product below the dividend. In the problem

$$57\overline{)391}$$

the estimated quotient 6 and the divisor 57 are multiplied. The student first multiplies 6×7, which is 42. The 2 is placed under the 1 in the dividend, and the 4 is placed over the 5 in the divisor:

$$\overset{4\qquad 6}{57\overline{)391}}$$
$$\underline{2}$$

Format 10.8B:
Correct Estimated
Quotients with Two-Digit
Divisors
Watch how Kristen introduces
the box for rounding off.

The student then multiplies 6 × 5 and adds the 4. The total 34 is written under the 39 in the dividend:

$$
\begin{array}{r}
4\quad 6 \\
57\overline{)391} \\
342
\end{array}
$$

Part B presents the rounding-off strategy to determine the estimated quotient. The teacher writes a problem on the board and next to the problem writes a box with a division sign:

$$37\overline{)1582}\qquad \boxed{\overline{)}}$$

The rounded-off problem is written in the box. First, the teacher has students read the problem (37 goes into 1582) and underline the part to work first (37 goes into 158). The students then round off 37 to 4 tens and 158 to 16 tens and write the rounded-off problem in the box:

$$\boxed{4\overline{)16}}$$

After rounding off, the students figure out the answer to the rounded-off problem and write the answer above the last underlined digit in the original problem:

$$
\begin{array}{r}
4 \\
37\overline{)\underline{158}2}
\end{array}
\qquad \boxed{4\overline{)16}}
$$

Parts A and B can be introduced at the same time. Note that both parts contain two sections. In the first section of each part, the teacher presents several problems on the board. In the second section, the teacher leads the students through several worksheet problems and then has them work several problems on their own. When students can independently work most of the problems correctly, the teacher can introduce the entire strategy. Students must be able to perform the multiplication and estimation skills accurately before the entire strategy is presented in Part C.

Part C is a structured worksheet exercise in which students are guided through all of the steps in the strategy. For about the first two weeks, the boxes for rounding off should be included on students' worksheets. A sample problem on a worksheet would looks like this:

$$37\overline{)1582}$$

$$\boxed{\overline{)}}$$

$$\boxed{\overline{)}}$$

The upper box is for writing the rounded-off problem for the first part of the problem; the lower box is for writing the rounded-off problem for the second part of the problem.

Two example-selection guidelines are important to this format. First, all of the problems must yield estimated quotients that are correct. Second, in half of the problems, the first two digits in the dividend must be less than the divisor:

$$37\overline{)2431}\qquad 52\overline{)4681}$$

while in the other problems, the first two digits must be greater than the divisor:

$$37\overline{)441}\qquad 52\overline{)838}$$

Several problems with a one-digit quotient should be included in supervised and independent worksheets. The variety of problems requires students to use the steps of determining which part to work first.

Problems with Incorrect Estimated Quotients   In a minor, but still significant, proportion of problems with two-digit divisors, one or more estimated quotients will prove to be incorrect. For example, in the problem

$$39\overline{)155}$$

the estimated quotient would prove too large, since 4 × 39 equals 156. Problems in which the estimated quotient is incorrect should be introduced about a week after students have developed accuracy in working problems in which the estimates are correct. The initial problems presented should yield a one-digit quotient. The steps for presenting these problems appear in **Format 10.9: Incorrect Estimated Quotients.**

The format includes two parts. Part A focuses only on the skill of determining if the estimated quotient is correct and what to do if it is not correct. Separate sequences of steps are indicated for problems in which the estimated quotient is too large and for problems in which the estimated quotient is too small. The rules in the format are designed to minimize student confusion ("If you can't subtract, make the answer smaller. If the remainder is too big, make the answer bigger.").

In Part A, the students are given a worksheet on which the estimated quotient is written in each problem. The worksheet includes a variety of problems. One-third of the problems have a quotient that is too large:

$$5 \over 34\overline{)146}$$

One-third of the problems have a quotient that is too small:

$$4 \over 36\overline{)193}$$

The final third of the problems contain estimated quotients that are correct:

$$5 \over 28\overline{)153}$$

Students first multiply the quotient and divisor. If the product of these two numbers is greater than the dividend, the teacher points out that the answer must be less. In the problem

$$5 \over 34\overline{)146} \\ 170$$

the teacher says, "We can't subtract. We must make the answer smaller. Cross out the 5 and write 4." In problems in which the estimated quotient is too small, the teacher has the students compare their remainder to the divisor. If the remainder is as big as or bigger than the divisor, the quotient is to be made larger. For example, in the problem

$$4 \over 36\overline{)193} \\ 144 \over 49$$

the teacher points out that another group of 36 can be made from 49, so the answer is made bigger. The students erase the 4 in the answer and replace it with a 5.

A special type of problem yields an estimated quotient of 10 or above. For these problems, the teacher tells students that no matter how high the answer to the rounded-off problem, the highest number used in an answer is 9. For example, even though rounding off yields 11 as an estimated quotient, the student still uses 9 as the quotient. Several problems of this type should be included in the exercises.

$$24\overline{)228} \quad as \quad 2\overline{)23}$$

Practice on problems yielding an incorrect quotient is continued daily for several weeks. During this time, problems are limited to those that have one-digit quotients. Problems with multi-digit quotients are not introduced until students are successful at working problems with single-digit quotients. The teacher should prepare worksheets containing a variety of problems. **Figure 10.3** includes sets of problems that can be used in these exercises.

FIGURE 10.3   Examples of two-digit divisor problems with single-digit quotients

Estimate Yields Quotient That Is Correct

34)102	82)591	37)1723	72)3924	73)2308	53)230	27)94	52)2731
53)1752	29)2150	48)268	51)78	68)1528	27)941	51)2398	39)94
90)673	80)7485	19)813	86)5000	40)289	48)269	12)384	41)987
25)896	67)242	82)370	89)6703	58)1256	16)415	32)197	11)48
45)968	93)5780	42)534	75)183	28)154	36)2000	84)991	60)2486

Estimate Yields Quotient Too Large

73)289	84)246	91)632	64)3321	53)1524	16)60	23)170	13)68
93)2724	24)900	44)216	72)354	82)2401	52)1020	31)1500	31)180
54)102	71)3520	41)2450	72)2815				

Estimate Yields Quotient Too Small

26)185	35)175	38)193	35)1651	25)1852	46)283	86)260	75)300
37)2483	47)1898	57)342	29)114	48)3425	46)1823	85)6913	45)238
58)232	36)1892	16)861	17)698				

Problems in Which Estimated Quotient Is Greater Than 9

23)214	21)200	34)312	73)725	74)725	43)412	24)238	14)120
13)104	32)304						

Note that problems in which the estimated quotient is too small are particularly difficult for students. In order to prepare students for this format, the teacher should present an exercise for several days prior to introducing Format 10.9, focusing on when a remainder is too big. In this exercise, the teacher writes about six problems with two-digit divisors on the board and models how to determine if the remainder is too big.

Diagnosis and Remediation

Division problems may be worked incorrectly for numerous reasons. Fact errors may be common in the multi-digit stage of division however, the procedures for diagnosing and remediating fact errors remain the same as described earlier in this chapter.

Component-Skill Errors   Common component-skill errors are summarized in the diagnosis and remediation chart in **Figure 10.4**. The remediation procedures usually involve presenting a structured worksheet exercise focusing on the particular component-skill error made by the students. Types of errors may include incomplete quotients and quotients that are too small or too large.

Students may compute an incomplete quotient for a variety of reasons: (a) failure to bring down a digit, (b) failure to write a quotient above the last digit of the dividend, (c) confusion caused by zeros in the quotient, and (d) misalignment. To determine the cause of an incomplete quotient, the teacher may analyze student work and/or interview the student. When a type of error occurs frequently, remediation is necessary. Figure 10.4 outlines specific remediation procedures for each type of incomplete quotient error. As previously stated, the remediation includes a structured or less structured worksheet presentation by the teacher followed by additional practice. The original worksheets can be presented to the students after remediation to assess the students for mastery. Students should complete at least 90% of the original problems correctly.

FIGURE 10.4 Diagnosis and remediation of multi-digit division errors

Error Pattern	Diagnosis	Remediation Procedures	Remediation Examples

Component-Skill Errors

a.
```
      65
37)24319
    222
    211
    185
     26
```
Student computes an incomplete quotient: does not write a quotient for the last digit.

Present the students with partially worked problems on the graph or notebook paper turned sideways. First, ask the students if last digit in the dividend has an answer over it (grid paper will make this clearer). Ask the students to finish the partially completed problems.

```
       2 2
41)9 3 8 6
   8 2
   1 1 8
     8 2
     3 6
```

b.
```
     17
25)4319
   25
   189
   175
    14
```
Student computes an incomplete quotient: does not bring down a digit.

Present the structured worksheet of **Format 10.8: Correct Estimated Quotients with Two-Digit Divisors**. Be sure that students underline the part that they work first and emphasize step 6—"Is there a digit after the underlined part to bring down?"

79)24861

c.
```
      90
52)46815
   468
    15
```
Student computes an incomplete quotient in problems with zero in the quotient.

Present problems that are worked up to the point that students need to put a zero the quotient. Ask the students if the divisor can go into the number. In the example to the right, the teacher would ask, "Can 29 go into 15?" Model putting the 0 in the quotient, multiplying by zero, subtracting, and bringing down the next digit. After modeling several examples, provide the students with a less structured worksheet including problems that will have zero in the quotient and those that will not.

```
      1
29)3056
   29
   15
```

d.
```
     7
27)2248
  189
```
Student computes an incomplete quotient because of misalignment of products.

Present the structured worksheet of **Format 10.8: Correct Estimated Quotients with Two-Digit Divisors**. Present the problems on graph or grid paper. Emphasize where the students place the digits when multiplying.

27)2248

e.
```
      4
39)155
  156
    1
```
Student computes a quotient that is too large or too small.

Present **Format 10.9: Incorrect Estimated Quotients**.

84)246

```
     2
25)78
  50
  28
```

Note: After addressing any component-skill error, assess students using problems similar to the ones on which errors were originally made in order to determine if the remediation was successful.

The second type of error students commonly make is computing a quotient that is too large or too small. Although this type of error is usually obvious, the teacher may interview the student to confirm the diagnosis. Remediation for this type of error involves presenting Format 10.9: Incorrect Estimated Quotients. The teacher would begin with the structured worksheet, Part A, followed by the less structured worksheet in Part B. As with most types of errors, the original worksheet can be given to the students as an assessment. At least 90% of the original problems should be solved correctly to demonstrate mastery.

APPLY WHAT YOU LEARNED

 Click on the √ to answer the questions online.

1. Describe the problem type that each example below represents. List the problems in the order they are introduced.

    5)128   5)23   2)136   5)20   5)153

    27)122   5)736   27)136   5)526

2. What is the recommended procedure for introducing the concept of division in this text? Why is this procedure recommended?

3. Below is an excerpt from the independent worksheet to be given to students who have just demonstrated accuracy in solving problems with a one-digit divisor and a three-digit quotient. The teacher has made some errors in constructing the worksheet. Identify the errors the teacher has made.

    7)932   5)1432   3)1214   5)3752

    2)714   9)1436   5)823   6)1443

4. Below are eight problems that appeared on a worksheet to be done independently by the students in Ms. Adams's math group. Below each student's name are the problems missed by the student. For each student, specify the probable cause or causes of the student's errors. Describe the remediation procedure.

    6)8324   4)12385   7)493   8)7200   5)5214   7)9222   5)8253   9)72990

    Mia

    ```
        8332R2           925
    9)72990          8)7200
       70               70
       29               20
       27               16
       29               40
       27
       20
       18
        2
    ```

    Damitri

    ```
        396R1          142R4
    4)12385          5)524
       12               5
       38               21
       36               20
       25               14
       24               10
        1                4
    ```

    Julio

    ```
        131R5
    7)9222
       7
       22
       21
       12
        7
        5
    ```

5. Below is an error made by Charles on a worksheet assignment. Describe what the teacher says in making the correction.

$$4 R 40$$
$$36\overline{)184}$$
$$\underline{144}$$
$$40$$

6. Write the structured worksheet part of a format to present this problem:

$$7\overline{)213}$$

7. Specify the wording the teacher uses to correct the following errors:

a. $27\overline{)482}$ $\boxed{3\overline{)48}}$

b. $27\overline{)482}$ $\boxed{2\overline{)4}}$

8. Below is an excerpt from the independent worksheet to be given to students who have just demonstrated accuracy in solving problems with two-digit divisors and one- or two-digit quotients, in which estimating produces proper quotient. Indicate the inappropriate examples.

$23\overline{)989}$ $34\overline{)148}$ $76\overline{)793}$

$58\overline{)2938}$ $31\overline{)283}$ $49\overline{)1638}$

Format 10.1
INTRODUCING DIVISION

TEACHER	STUDENTS
Part A: Translating Division Problems	
1. *(Write these problems on the board.)*	
$5\overline{)15}^{\,3}$ $2\overline{)18}^{\,9}$ $6\overline{)30}^{\,5}$ $3\overline{)12}^{\,4}$	
$4\overline{)20}^{\,5}$ $7\overline{)28}^{\,4}$ $3\overline{)21}^{\,7}$	
This is a division problem. What kind of problem?	A division problem
It says *(Point to 5.)* 5 goes into *(Point to 15.)* 15 *(Point to 3.)* three times. What does the problem say? *(Point to 5, then 15, then 3 as students answer. Repeat step 1 with the problems below.)*	5 goes into 15 three times.
$2\overline{)18}^{\,9}$ $6\overline{)30}^{\,5}$	
2. *(Point to* $3\overline{)12}^{\,4}$ *.)* What does this problem say?	3 goes into 12 four times.
(Point to 3, then 12, then 4 as students answer. Repeat step 2 with the problems below.)	
$4\overline{)20}^{\,5}$ $7\overline{)28}^{\,4}$ $3\overline{)21}^{\,7}$	
(Give individual turns to several students.)	

TEACHER	STUDENTS
Part B: Structured Board Presentation	
1. *(Write on board: 5)15.)*	
What kind of problem is this?	A division problem
This problem says 5 goes into 15. What does this problem say? *(Point to 5, then 15.)*	5 goes into 15.
We have to find out how many times 5 goes into 15. When we divide, we start with a big group and make equal-sized smaller groups. *(Write 15 lines on board.)*	
2. This is a group of 15 lines. I want to divide this group of 15 lines into smaller groups. Each smaller group will have 5 lines in it. How many lines will be in each smaller group?	5
3. I'll touch the lines. You count. *(Touch five lines.)* This is a group of 5, so I'll put a circle around it. *(Circle five lines.)*	1, 2, 3, 4, 5
(Repeat step 3 with the remaining groups of five lines.)	
4. We divided 15 into groups of 5. Let's count the groups. *(Touch each group.)*	1, 2, 3
5. How many times does 5 go into 15? I write the 3 above the last digit in 15.	3
(Write $5{\overline{)15}}^{\,3}$.)	
Say what the problem tells us.	5 goes into 15 three times.
(Repeat steps 1–5 with 2)8.)	
Part C: Structured Worksheet	
1. *(Give students a worksheet like the following:)*	
a. 5)20 b. 2)8 c. 2)12	
2. Touch problem a. That problem says 5 goes into 20. What does the problem say?	5 goes into 20.
3. We have to find out how many groups of 5 we can make from 20. There are 20 lines under the problem. Make groups of 5 lines each. *(Check students' papers.)*	
4. How many groups did you make?	4
Write 4 above the last digit in 20. *(Monitor as students write 4.)*	
5. Now the problem says 5 goes into 20 four times. What does the problem say now?	5 goes into 20 four times.
(Repeat steps 2–5 with remaining problems.)	
Part D: Less Structured Worksheet	
1. *(Give students a worksheet with problems similar to the following:)*	
a. 2)10.	

continued

Format 10.1 *(continued)*
INTRODUCING DIVISION

TEACHER	STUDENTS
1. Touch problem a. *(Monitor as students touch $2\overline{)10}$.)*	
2. What does the problem say?	2 goes into 10.
3. How many in each group?	2
4. Make the groups and write how many groups over the last digit in 10. *(Monitor as students make circles around every two lines and write 5.)*	
5. Read the problem and the answer.	2 goes into 10 five times.

Format 10.2
INTRODUCING DIVISION WITH REMAINDERS   (See Video Part A)

TEACHER	STUDENTS
Part A: Introducing Remainders	
1. *(Write the following problem on the board.)* $5\overline{)13}$ *(Point to $5\overline{)13}$.)* What does the problem say?	5 goes into 13.
2. First let's solve the problem by making lines. The problem asks how many groups of 5 in 13, so I'll draw 13 lines. *(Make 13 lines on the board.)* The problem asks how many groups of 5 in 13, so I'll put a circle around each group of 5. *(Count out each group of 5 aloud; after circling each group, say,)* Here's a group of 5. *(After counting the last 3 lines, say,)* We only have 3 left so we can't make a group of 5. 	
3. Now let's see how many groups of 5 there are; count the groups as I touch them. *(Touch groups as students count.)*	1, 2
4. How many groups of 5 in 13?	2
Yes, there are two groups. *(Write $5\overline{)13}^{\,2}$.)*	
5. Are there lines left over?	Yes
We call those lines the remainder. How many lines are left over?	3
6. We say that 5 goes into 13 two times with a remainder of 3. How many times does 5 go into 13?	Two times with a remainder of 3.
(Repeat steps 1–6 with the problems below.) $2\overline{)9}$ $9\overline{)21}$	

TEACHER	STUDENTS

Part B: Structured Worksheet

1. *(Give students a worksheet like the following:)*

   a. $5\overline{)23}$ (IIIII) (IIIII) (IIIII) (IIIII)   III

   b. $2\overline{)7}$ (II) (II) (II)   I

   c. $9\overline{)25}$ (IIIIIIIII) (IIIIIIIII)   IIIIIII

   d. $5\overline{)14}$ (IIIII) (IIIII)   IIII

2. Read problem a.

                                      → *5 goes into 23.*

3. The problem asks how many groups of 5 we can make from 23. Next to the problem are 23 lines. A circle has been drawn around each group of 5 lines. How many groups of 5 are there?

    Write 4 on the line above the 3. *(Check students' work.)* → *4*

4. We want to figure out how many lines we used up, so we multiply 4 times 5. How do we figure how many lines we used up? → *Multiply 4 × 5.*

5. What is 4 × 5? → *20*

6. Write 20 under the 23. We started with 23 and used up 20, so write a minus sign in front of the 20. Read the subtraction problem we just wrote. → *23 − 20*

    Subtract and write the remainder. What is 23 minus 20? → *3*

7. We're all finished; 5 goes into 23 four times with a remainder of 3. How many times does 5 go into 23? → *Four times with a remainder of 3.*

    (Repeat steps 1–6 with problems b, c, and d.)

Part C: Less Structured Worksheet

1. *(Give students a worksheet with several problems similar to Part B. Use the following prompts as students work through the problems.)*

2. Read problem _____ . → _____ goes into _____

    How many times does _____ go into _____? → _____ times

    Write _____ above the _____ in _____ .

    How do we figure how many lines we used? → Multiply _____ by _____

2. What is _____ times _____?

continued

Format 10.2 (continued)
INTRODUCING DIVISION WITH REMAINDERS

TEACHER	STUDENTS
3. Write _____ under the _____ . Put in the minus sign.	
4. Subtract. (*Remind students to rename when applicable.*) What is the remainder?	
5. How many times does _____ go into _____?	_____ times with a remainder of _____

Format 10.3
INTRODUCING REMAINDER FACTS

TEACHER	STUDENTS
Part A: Structured Board Presentation	
1. (*Write these numerals on the board.*) 1 2 3 4 ⑤ 6 7 8 9 ⑩ 11 12 13 14 ⑮ 16 17 18 19 ⑳ 21 22 23 24 ㉕ Listen: 5 goes into the circled numerals without a remainder. Say the numbers that 5 goes into without a remainder.	0, 5, 10, 15, 20, 25
2. Five goes into the other numbers with a remainder. (*Point to 1, 2, 3, 4.*) These are numbers 5 goes into zero times with a remainder.	
3. My turn: How many times does 5 go into 2? Five goes into 2 zero times with a remainder.	
How many times does 5 go into 2?	Zero times with a remainder.
How many times does 5 go into 4?	Zero times with a remainder.
4. (*Point to 5.*) Five goes into 5 one time. (*Point to 6, 7, 8, 9.*) These are numbers 5 goes into one time with a remainder.	
How many times does 5 go into 8?	One time with a remainder.
How many times does 5 go into 6?	One time with a remainder.
5. (*Repeat step 4 using 5 goes into 15 and then 5 goes into 19 and 5 goes into 17.*)	
6. (*Repeat step 4 using 5 goes into 20, 5 goes into 24, 5 goes into 21. Tell the students that 5 goes into these numbers two times.*)	
Part B: Less Structured Board Presentation	
1. (*Write these numerals on the board.*) 1 2 3 4 ⑤ 6 7 8 9 ⑩ 11 12 13 14 ⑮ 16 17 18 19 ⑳ 21 22 23 24 ㉕ Say the numbers that 5 goes into without a remainder.	5, 10, 15, 20, 25

TEACHER	STUDENTS
2. *(Point to 13.)* **Think. 5 goes into 13 how many times?**	Two times with a remainder.
To correct: (Point to 10.) **Five goes into 10 two times.** *(Point to 11, 12, 13, 14.)* **These are the numbers 5 goes into two times with a remainder. Five goes into 13, two times with a remainder.** *(Repeat step 2.)*	
3. *(Repeat step 2 with 20, 24, 0, 3, 9, 16.)*	
Part C: Structured Worksheet	
1. *(Give students a worksheet with several problems similar to those below. Use the following prompts as students work through the problems.)* a. 5)$\overline{22}$ b. 5)$\overline{16}$ c. 5)$\overline{10}$ d. 5)$\overline{7}$	
2. **Read problem _____ .**	_____ goes into _____ .
3. **How many times does _____ go into _____ ?**	
To correct if a student says a number that is too low, as in $5\overline{)22}^{\,3}$ *, say:)* **We can make another group of five: 5 × 4 = 20.**	
To correct if a student says a number too high, as in $5\overline{)22}^{\,5}$ *, say:* **5 × 5 = 25. That's too big.**	
4. **Write _____ above the _____ in _____ .** **What do you multiply?**	_____ times _____
Multiply and subtract. *(Pause.)* **What is the remainder?** **How many times does _____ go into _____ ?**	_____ _____ times with a remainder of _____ .
(Repeat steps 2–4 with several more problems and then have students work the rest on their own.)	

Format 10.4
REMEDIATION FOR DIVISION WITH REMAINDERS— QUOTIENT TOO SMALL
(See Videos Parts A/B)

TEACHER	STUDENTS
▶	
Part A: Recognizing Quotients That Are Too Small	
1. *(Write this problem on the board.)* 5)$\overline{28}$ **This problem says 5 goes into 28. We're figuring 5 into a number, so the remainder must be smaller than 5.**	
2. **What does the problem say?**	5 goes into 28.
3. **So what do you know about the remainder?**	It must be smaller than 5.
4. *(Repeat steps 1–3 with* 7)$\overline{23}$ 2)$\overline{13}$ 6)$\overline{14}$ 5)$\overline{27}$ 3)$\overline{24}$ *.)*	

continued

Format 10.4 *(continued)*
REMEDIATION FOR DIVISION WITH REMAINDERS—QUOTIENT TOO SMALL

TEACHER	STUDENTS
▶	
Part B: Writing the Correct Answer	
1. *(Give the students a worksheet with the following problems.)*	
a. $5\overline{)28}$ with 4 b. $7\overline{)31}$ with 4 c. $9\overline{)24}$ with 2 d. $9\overline{)43}$ with 3	
e. $5\overline{)42}$ with 8 f. $2\overline{)13}$ with 5 g. $2\overline{)15}$ with 6 h. $5\overline{)28}$ with 5	
2. Problem a says 5 goes into 28 four times. We figure the remainder by multiplying 5×4 and then subtracting. Do that on your paper.	
3. What's the remainder?	8
4. Here's a rule: If the remainder is too big, we make the answer bigger. What do we do if the remainder is too big?	Make the answer bigger.
5. Is the remainder too big?	Yes
So what must we do?	Make the answer bigger.
The remainder is more than 5, so 5 can go into 28 another time. Cross out the 4 and write 5. *(Check.)* Now erase 20; multiply and subtract to figure the new remainder. What's the new remainder?	3
(Note: If the answer to step 4 is no, tell students,) So the answer is correct. Let's go to the next problem *(see step 5).*	
6. Is the remainder too big?	No
So the answer is correct. Read the problem.	5 goes into 28 five times with a remainder of 3.
7. *(Repeat steps 2–6 with additional problems, and then have students work remaining problems on their own.)*	

Format 10.5
REMEDIATION FOR DIVISION WITH REMAINDERS—QUOTIENT TOO LARGE   (See Video Part A)

TEACHER	STUDENTS
▶	
Part A: Recognizing Quotients That Are Too Large	
1. *(Write this problem on the board.)*	
$\begin{array}{r} 6 \\ 5\overline{)28} \\ \underline{30} \end{array}$	
What does this problem say?	5 goes into 28 six times.

TEACHER	STUDENTS
2. The problem is worked for you, but there is something wrong. Can you subtract 30 from 28?	No
3. Here's a rule: If you can't subtract, make the answer smaller. What do you do if you can't subtract?	Make the answer smaller.
4. We make the answer 1 smaller. What is 1 smaller than 6?	5
(Erase 6 and write 5.) What is 5 times 5?	25
5. (Erase 30 and write 25.) Can you subtract 25 from 28?	Yes
What is 28 − 25?	3
Read the problem.	5 goes into 28 five times with a remainder of 3.
6. (Repeat steps 1–5 with several examples.)	

Part B: Writing the Correct Answer

1. (Give the students a worksheet with the following problems.)

a. $6 \over 5\overline{)28}$ b. $4 \over 7\overline{)31}$ c. $2 \over 9\overline{)24}$

d. $5 \over 9\overline{)43}$ e. $8 \over 5\overline{)42}$ f. $7 \over 2\overline{)13}$

TEACHER	STUDENTS
2. Look at the problems on your worksheet. Some of the answers are too big. You'll have to fix them.	
3. Look at problem a. What is 6 × 5?	30
4. Can you subtract 30 from 28?	No
What must you do?	Make the answer 1 smaller
(Note: Do step 4 only if answer to step 3 is no.)	
5. Cross out the 6. What do you write?	5
Work the problem. (Check students' work.)	
(Repeat steps 1–5 with additional problems, and then have students work remaining problems on their own.)	

Format 10.6
DIVISION WITH TWO-DIGIT QUOTIENTS

TEACHER	STUDENTS
Part A: Determining Where to Begin	
1. When a division problem has lots of digits, we work the problem a part at a time. We always begin a problem by underlining the first part we work. Sometimes we underline just the first digit. Sometimes we underline the first two digits.	

continued

Format 10.6 *(continued)*
DIVISION WITH TWO-DIGIT QUOTIENTS

TEACHER	STUDENTS
2. *(Write the following problem on the board.)* $6\overline{)242}$	
Read the problem.	6 goes into 242.
We're dividing by 6. If the first digit in the number we're dividing is at least as big as 6, we underline the first digit in 242. If 6 can't go into the first digit, we underline the first two digits. Look at the numeral we're dividing into. The first digit we're dividing into is 2. Is 2 at least as big as 6?	No
So we underline the first two digits. *(Underline 24.)* $6\overline{)242}$	
The underlined problem says 6 goes into 24. What does the underlined problem say?	6 goes into 24.
(Repeat step 2 with these problems.) a. $5\overline{)87}$ b. $9\overline{)328}$ c. $4\overline{)38}$ d. $6\overline{)62}$ e. $3\overline{)245}$ f. $7\overline{)832}$	
Part B: Worksheet on Determining Where to Begin	
1. *(Give students a worksheet with the following problems.)* a. $7\overline{)248}$ b. $3\overline{)527}$ c. $7\overline{)486}$ d. $5\overline{)532}$ e. $5\overline{)234}$ f. $6\overline{)184}$ g. $6\overline{)932}$ h. $4\overline{)128}$ i. $4\overline{)436}$ j. $8\overline{)264}$	
2. Touch problem a. Read the problem.	7 goes into 248.
You're going to underline the part of the problem you work first. What are you dividing by?	7
Is the first digit you're dividing into at least as big as 7?	No
So what do you underline?	24
Underline 24. Say the underlined problem.	7 goes into 24.
(Repeat step 2 with five problems. Then have students underline the part they work first in remaining problems.)	
Part C: Structured Board Presentation	
1. *(Write the following problem on the board.)* $5\overline{)213}$	
Read this problem.	5 goes into 213.
Tell me the part to underline. *(Pause. Underline 21.)* $5\overline{)213}$	21
To correct: Look at the first digit. Is 2 at least as big as 5?	No
So what do you underline?	21
What does the underlined problem say?	5 goes into 21.
2. How many times does 5 go into 21? *(Pause.)*	4
3. I'll write the 4 over the last digit underlined. *(Write the following:)* $\begin{array}{r} 4 \\ 5\overline{)213} \end{array}$	

TEACHER	STUDENTS
4. Now multiply 4 × 5. What is 4 × 5?	20
(Write 20.)	
Now I subtract 20 from 21. What is 1 − 0?	1
(Write 1.)	
5. *(Point to 3.)* What's the next digit after the underlined part?	3
I bring it down and write it after the 1.	
(Write the steps in the problem so far.)	
$$\begin{array}{r} 4 \\ 5\overline{)213} \\ 20 \\ \hline 13 \end{array}$$	
What numeral is under the line now?	13
6. The next part of the problem says 5 goes into 13. What does the problem say now?	5 goes into 13.
How many times does 5 go into 13? *(Pause.)*	2
I write the 2 above the digit I brought down.	
(Write this step in the problem.)	
$$\begin{array}{r} 42 \\ 5\overline{)213} \\ 20 \\ \hline 13 \end{array}$$	
7. Now I multiply and subtract. What is 2 × 5? *(Pause.)*	10
I write 10 under the 13. *(Write 10.)* What is 13 minus 10? *(Pause.)*	3
8. The problem is finished. Every digit after the underlined part has a digit over it. 5 goes into 213, forty-two times with a remainder of 3. How many times does 5 go into 213?	42 times with a remainder of 3.
(Repeat steps 1–8 with 7)94 2)135 3)65.)	
Part D: Structured Worksheet	
1. *(Give students a worksheet with problems similar to the following.)* 3)137	
Touch the first problem. Read the problem.	3 goes into 137.
What do you underline? *(Pause.)*	13
2. Underline 13. What does the underlined problem say?	3 goes into 13.
3. How many times does 3 go into 13?	4
Write 4 above the last digit you underlined.	
4. What numbers do you multiply?	4 × 3
What is 4 × 3?	12
5. Write 12 under 13, then subtract. What is 13 − 12?	1

continued

Format 10.6 *(continued)*
DIVISION WITH TWO-DIGIT QUOTIENTS

TEACHER	STUDENTS
6. What is the next digit in the number you're dividing into? *(Pause.)*	7
Bring down the 7 and write it next to the 1. *(Check students' work.)*	$\begin{array}{r} 4 \\ 3\overline{)137} \\ 12 \\ \hline 17 \end{array}$
7. What numeral is under the line?	17
What does this part of the problem say?	3 goes into 17.
How many times does 3 go into 17? *(Pause.)*	5
8. Write the 5 above the digit you brought down. *(Monitor student responses.)*	
9. What numbers do you multiply?	5 × 3
What is 5 × 3?	15
Write 15 under 17 and subtract. What is 17 − 15?	2
Is there another numeral to bring down?	No
10. Every digit after the underlined part has a digit over it. So you finished the problem. What's the remainder?	2
How many times does 3 go into 137?	45 with a remainder of 2.
(Repeat steps 1–10 with additional problems.)	

Part E: Less Structured Worksheet

1. *(Give students a worksheet with problems similar to the following.)* 4)69	
Touch the problem. Read the problem.	4 goes into 69.
Underline the part you work first. *(Check students' work.)*	4)69̲
Say the underlined problem.	4 goes into 6.
How many times does 4 go into 6?	1
2. Write the 1, multiply, subtract, and then bring down the next digit. *(Pause.)*	
What numeral is under the line now?	29
3. Say the new problem.	4 goes into 29.
How many times does 4 go into 29?	7
Write 7 in the answer. Then multiply and subtract. *(Pause and monitor student responses.)* Is there another numeral to bring down?	No
Is the problem finished?	Yes
4. How many times does 4 go into 69?	17 with a remainder of 1.
(Repeat steps 1–4 with additional problems.)	

Format 10.7
ROUNDING TO NEAREST TENS UNIT

TEACHER	STUDENTS
Part A: Expressing Numerals As Tens Units	
1. *(Write the following numeral on the board: 190.)*	
What number?	190
Another way of saying 190 is 19 tens. What's another way of saying 190?	19 tens
2. *(Repeat step 1 with 80 and 230.)*	
3. What's another way of saying 140?	14 tens
4. *(Repeat step 3 with 280, 30, 580, 420, 60, 500, 280, 40, and 700.)*	
Part B: Structured Board Presentation	
1. *(Write the following numeral on the board: 186.)*	
What number?	186
2. Is 186 closer to 180 or 190?	190
To correct: If we have at least 5 in the ones column, we round off to the next higher tens unit. How many ones in 186? So we round off to 190.	
3. So is 186 closer to 18 tens or 19 tens? *(Pause.)*	19 tens
To correct: 186 is closer to 190. How many tens in 190?	
4. *(Repeat steps 2 and 3 with 142, 83, 47, 286, 432, 27, and 529)*	
Part C: Structured Worksheet	
1. *(Give the students a worksheet with the following problems.)*	
142 ___ tens 87 ___ tens 537 ___ tens 497 ___ tens	
287 ___ tens 426 ___ tens 248 ___ tens 321 ___ tens	
825 ___ tens 53 ___ tens 632 ___ tens 503 ___ tens	
546 ___ tens 182 ___ tens 428 ___ tens 278 ___ tens	
932 ___ tens 203 ___ tens 561 ___ tens 426 ___ tens	
2. Round off these numerals to the nearest ten. Write how many tens in the rounded off numeral.	
3. Touch the first numeral. *(Pause.)* Read the first numeral.	142
4. Think: 142 is closest to how many tens?	14 tens
To correct: Is 142 closer to 140 or 150? So, is 142 closer to 14 or 15 tens? *(Write the answer.)*	
5. Write 14 in the blank. *(Repeat steps 3–5 with several more problems and then have the students complete the rest independently.)*	

Format 10.8
CORRECT ESTIMATED QUOTIENTS WITH TWO-DIGIT DIVISORS

(See Video Part B)

TEACHER	STUDENTS
Part A: Preskill—Multiplying Quotient Times Divisor Structured Board Presentation	
1. (Write the following problem on the board.)	
$$\begin{array}{r} 4 \\ 54\overline{)231} \end{array}$$	
This problem says 54 goes into 231 four times. What does the problem say?	54 goes into 231 four times.
2. We have to figure out the remainder. We multiply 4 × 54. What do we multiply?	4 × 54
3. When I multiply 4 × 54, first I multiply 4 × 4, then I multiply 4 × 5. What is 4 × 4?	16
I write the 6 under the last underlined digit and write the 1 above the 5 in 54.	
(Write the 6 on the board.)	
$$\begin{array}{r} 4 \\ 54\overline{)231} \\ \hline 6 \end{array}$$	
4. Now I multiply 4 × 5 and add the 1 I renamed. What is 4 × 5?	20
And 1 more is?	21
I write the 21 in front of the 6. (Write this step of the problem on the board.)	
$$\begin{array}{r} 4 \\ 54\overline{)231} \\ \hline 216 \end{array}$$	
5. What is 4 × 54?	216
6. We subtract 216 from 231 to figure out the remainder. Can we start with 1 and subtract 6?	No
We must rename. (Write this step:)	
$$\begin{array}{r} 2 \quad 1 \\ 2 \; \cancel{3} \; 1 \end{array}$$	
What is 11 − 6?	5
What is 2 − 1?	1
7. 54 goes into 231 four times with a remainder of 15. Say that.	54 goes into 231 four times with a remainder of 15.
(Repeat steps 1–7 with the problems below.)	
$$\begin{array}{cc} 3 & 4 \\ 48\overline{)156} & 94\overline{)413} \end{array}$$	

TEACHER	STUDENTS
Part A: Preskill—Multiplying Quotient Times Divisor Structured Worksheet	
1. *(Give students a worksheet with problems like the following.)*	
a. $27\overline{)103}$ (quotient 3) b. $46\overline{)278}$ (quotient 6) c. $14\overline{)80}$ (quotient 5)	
2. Read problem a.	27 goes into 103 three times.
3. You need to multiply 3×27. When you multiply 3×27, what do you multiply first?	3×7
4. What is 3×7?	21
Write the 1 and the 2 tens. *(Monitor student responses.)*	
To correct: Write the 1 under the 3. *(Pause.)* Write the 2 tens above the 2 in 27.	
4. Now what do you multiply?	3×2
What is 3×2?	6
Add the 2 above the tens column. What's the answer?	8
Write the 8.	
5. Figure out the remainder. Be careful to rename.	
6. What is the remainder?	22
Yes, 27 goes into 103 three times with a remainder of 22.	
Say that.	27 goes into 103 three times with a remainder of 22.
(Repeat steps 2–6 with several problems, then have students work additional problems independently.)	
Part B: Preskill–Estimation Structured Board Presentation	
1. *(Write the following problem and the box on the board.)*	
$37\overline{)932}$ [$)$]	
What does the problem say?	37 goes into 932.
2. We have to underline the part we work first. Does 37 go into 9?	No
Does 37 go into 93?	Yes
So I underline the first two digits.	
3. I'll read the part we work first: 37 goes into 93. Say the part we work first.	37 goes into 93.
4. To find out how many times 37 goes into 93, we must round off. The box next to the problem is for rounding off.	

continued

Format 10.8 *(continued)*
CORRECT ESTIMATED QUOTIENTS WITH TWO-DIGIT DIVISORS

TEACHER	STUDENTS
5. First I round off 37; 37 is rounded off to how many tens?	4
(Pause and then write the four.)	
$4\overline{)}$	
93 is rounded off to how many tens?	9
(Pause and then write the 9.)	
$4\overline{)9}$	
Read the rounded-off problem.	4 goes into 9.
To correct: If we have at least 5 in the ones column, we round off to the next higher tens unit. How many ones in 93? So we round off to 9.	
6. Four goes into nine how many times?	2
So in the problem we started with, I write 2 over the last underlined digit. *(Write the 2.)*	
$\begin{array}{r} 2 \\ 37\overline{)932} \end{array}$	
(Repeat steps 1–6 with $24\overline{)136}$ $52\overline{)386}$ $34\overline{)942}$.*)*	
Part B: Preskill–Estimation Structured Worksheet	
1. *(Give students a worksheet with problems like the following.)*	
a. $79\overline{)246}$ $\boxed{)}$ b. $49\overline{)538}$ $\boxed{)}$	
c. $27\overline{)943}$ $\boxed{)}$ d. $36\overline{)193}$ $\boxed{)}$	
2. What does problem a say?	79 goes into 246.
3. What digits do you underline? *(Pause.)*	246
Underline the part you work first. Say the underlined problem.	79 goes into 246.
4. Let's write the rounded-off problem for 79 into 246 in the box. How many tens does 79 round off to? *(Pause.)*	8
Write 8 in the box. How many tens does 246 round off to? *(Pause.)*	25
Write 25 in the box. Read the rounded-off problem.	8 goes into 25.
Eight goes into 25 how many times?	3
5. Write the answer in the problem you started with. Write it above the last underlined digit.	
(Repeat steps 2–4 with the remaining problems, then have students work additional problems on their own.)	

TEACHER	STUDENTS
Part C: Structured Worksheet	
1. *(Give students a worksheet with problems like the following.)*	
38)1432	
[box with division symbol]	
[box with division symbol]	
Read the problem.	38 goes into 1432.
Underline the part you work first.	
What did you underline?	143
Read the underlined problem.	38 goes into 143.
2. Write the rounded-off problem in the box. How many tens does 38 round off to? *(Pause.)*	4
Write 4. How many tens does 143 round off to? *(Pause.)*	14
Write 14. Read the rounded-off problem.	4 goes into 14.
3. 4 goes into 14 how many times?	3
Write 3 above the last digit you underlined.	
4. Now we multiply 3 × 38. What is 3 × 8? *(Pause.)*	24
Write 4 below the last underlined digit. Write the 2 above the 3 in 38. *(Pause.)* Now multiply 3 × 3 and add 2. *(Pause.)*	
What's the answer? *(Pause.)*	11
Write 11 next to the 4.	
5. Now subtract 114 from 143. *(Pause.)*	
What is 143 − 114?	29
6. Let's see if there's a second part to work. Is there a digit after the underlined part to bring down?	Yes
(If the answer to step 6 is no, skip steps 7–10 and go directly to step 11.)	
7. Bring down that digit. What numeral is under the line now?	292
Say the new problem.	38 goes into 292.
8. Let's write the rounded-off problem in the second box. How many tens does 38 round off to?	4
Write 4. How many tens does 292 round off to?	29
Write 29. Read the rounded-off problem.	4 goes into 29.
9. How many times does 4 go into 29?	7
Write 7 in the problem you started with. Write it above the 2 you brought down.	

continued

Format 10.8 *(continued)*
CORRECT ESTIMATED QUOTIENTS WITH TWO-DIGIT DIVISORS

TEACHER	STUDENTS
10. Now we multiply 7 × 38. What do we multiply?	7 × 38
Multiply and write the answer below 292.	
(Pause.) What is 7 × 38?	266
Subtract 292 − 266 to find the remainder. *(Pause.)* What's 292 − 266?	26
Are there any more digits to bring down?	No
11. So you're done with the problem. How many times does 38 go into 1432?	37 times with a remainder of 26.
(Repeat steps 1–11 with several more problems.)	

Part D: Less Structured Worksheet

1. *(Give students a worksheet with problems like the following.)*

   18)‾604‾

Read the problem.	18 goes into 604.
Underline the part you work first. What did you underline?	60
Read the underlined problem.	18 goes into 60.
2. Write the rounded-off problem in the upper box. *(Pause.)*	
Say the rounded-off problem.	2 goes into 6.
3. Write the answer, then multiply. *(Pause.)* Say the subtraction problem.	60 − 54
Subtract 60 − 54. *(Pause.)* What is 60 − 54?	6
4. What do you do next?	Bring down the 4.
Do it.	
5. Say the new problem.	18 goes into 64.
6. Write the rounded-off problem in the second box. *(Pause.)* Say the rounded-off problem.	2 goes into 6.
7. Write the answer, then multiply and subtract. *(Pause.)*	
What is the remainder?	10
8. Are you finished? How many times does 18 go into 604?	33 times with a remainder of 10.

Format 10.9
INCORRECT ESTIMATED QUOTIENTS

TEACHER	STUDENTS
Part A: Structured Worksheet	
1. *(Give the students a worksheet with the following problems.)*	
a. $37\overline{)142}$ with 4 above; b. $48\overline{)299}$ with 5 above; c. $48\overline{)299}$ with 5 above; d. $79\overline{)315}$ with 4 above; e. $46\overline{)192}$ with 3 above; f. $52\overline{)148}$ with 3 above; g. $82\overline{)318}$ with 4 above; h. $34\overline{)178}$ with 5 above; i. $26\overline{)81}$ with 2 above	
2. The answers to some of these problems are wrong. To find out which ones are wrong, you figure out the remainder. If you can't subtract, you must make the answer *smaller*. If you find a remainder, but it is too big, you must make the answer *bigger*.	
3. Touch problem a. What does the problem say?	37 goes into 142 four times.
4. What are you going to multiply?	4×37.
Do the multiplication. Write the minus sign and stop.	
5. Say the subtraction problem.	$142 - 148$
6. Can you subtract 142 minus 148?	No
We can't subtract, so we must make the answer smaller.	
7. So you have to cross out the 4 and write a 3 above it. Do it, then erase the 148.	
8. Now multiply 3×37.	
9. Read the subtraction problem now.	$142 - 111$
10. Subtract and figure out the remainder. What is the remainder?	31
That's all we do for now.	
(Steps 4a–8a are for problems in which the estimated quotient is too small, as in the following problem.)	
$48\overline{)299}$ with 5 above	
5a. Say the subtraction problem.	$299 - 240$
Can you subtract 240 from 299?	Yes
Subtract. *(Pause.)*	
6a. What is the remainder?	59
Is the remainder too big?	Yes
To correct: What are we dividing by? Is the remainder at least as big as 48?	
You can make another group, so we make the answer bigger. Cross out the 5 and write 6. Erase 240.	
7a. Now multiply 6×48.	

continued

Format 10.9 (continued)
INCORRECT ESTIMATED QUOTIENTS

TEACHER	STUDENTS
8a. Read the subtraction problem now. Subtract.	299 − 288
9a. What's the answer? Can we make another group of 48? So we're all finished. *(Repeat steps 2–10 or 5a–9a with three of the remaining problems. Have students work the remaining problems on their own.)*	11 No

Part B: Less Structured Worksheet

1. *(Give students a worksheet with the following problems.)*

   a. 42)197   [ ]   b. 36)203   [ ]

   c. 58)232   [ ]

2. Touch problem a. Read the problem.	42 goes into 197.
3. Underline the part you work first. *(Monitor students' responses.)*	
4. Write the rounded-off problem. *(Pause.)* Say the rounded-off problem.	4 goes into 20.
5. What is the answer? Multiply 5 × 42. *(Pause.)* Can you subtract? *(Note: Present step 6 or 7.)*	5 No
6. *(If the answer to step 5 is no, say,)* So what must you do? Fix your answer then multiply and subtract.	
6. *(If the answer to step 5 is yes, say,)* Subtract _____ from _____. What is the remainder? Is the remainder too big? *(Continue if answer is yes.)* So what must we do? Erase _____ and write _____, then multiply and subtract. *(Pause.)* What is the remainder? Is that remainder too big? So we're finished. Say the whole answer. *(Repeat steps 2–6 with remaining problems.)*	

Problem Solving

LEARNING OUTCOMES

11.1 Discuss the recommended sequence for introducing word problems and the rationale for that sequence.

11.2 Describe the introductory strategy for teaching students to solve basic addition and subtractions problems.

11.3 Outline the number-family instructional strategies recommended to teach students to solve addition/subtraction word problems.

11.4 Discuss the differences in the instructional strategies for teaching addition/subtraction word problems and multiplication/division word problems.

11.5 Describe the common types of errors students make when solving word problems.

SKILL HIERARCHY

This chapter discusses procedures for teaching students to apply the four basic operations (addition, subtraction, multiplication, and division) to word problems that present situations requiring a mathematical solution. Procedures for teaching problem-solving strategies that include fractions, percent, decimals, time, money, and measurement are addressed in later chapters on those topics. In this chapter, addition and subtraction word problems are introduced together to provide discrimination practice. Multiplication and division word problems are taught together for the same reason. Multiplication and division word problems are introduced as soon as students have mastered previously introduced types of word problems (problems involving addition and subtraction) and have been taught to solve multiplication and division computation problems. It is important for students to work mixed sets of word problems involving all four operations once multiplication and division problems have been introduced to continue providing practice choosing the correct operation to solve the problem.

Addition and subtraction problems are usually introduced in late first grade. Analysis of addition and subtraction problems in commercial mathematics programs reveals three primary types of problem: temporal sequence problems, comparison problems, and classification problems. Simple versions of these three types of one-step problems are usually introduced by the end of second grade. Both initial and more sophisticated strategies for solving these problem types are introduced in this chapter.

Multiplication and division problems are usually introduced during third grade. Initially, the multiplication or division operation is signaled by the presence of the word "each" or "every." Later, the words "a" and "per" serve as signals for multiplication or division ("The crew works 7 hours a day," "There are 6 crayons per box"). Multiplication and division problems that do not contain key words are obviously more difficult. See the Instructional Sequence and Assessment Chart for a recommended sequence for introducing word problems.

Within the two basic groupings of word problems are problems with large numbers, multi-step problems, and problems with **distractors**. Problems with larger numbers are usually more difficult because the computation is more difficult and the operation required is often less obvious. Multi-step problems usually appear in third grade and require students to perform two or more steps, usually involving two or more different operations, to solve the problem. The simplest type of multi-step problem involves adding three numbers. Multi-step problems become more difficult as the number and type of computations required increase. The third type of these more difficult word problems contains irrelevant quantities or information that may distract students from the necessary steps to solve the problem. More information about these three problem types is presented later in the chapter.

INSTRUCTIONAL SEQUENCE AND ASSESSMENT CHART

Grade Level	Problem Type	Performance Indicator
1–2	Addition/subtraction simple action problems with key words	Deshawn had 7 apples. He got 3 more from the store. How many apples does he have in all?
		Lisa had some apples. She bought 3 more. She ended up with 12 apples. How many apples did she start with?
2	Addition/subtraction temporal sequence problems	Carlos had 7 apples. He gave 3 to his sister. How many does he have left?
2	Addition/subtraction comparison problems	Bill is 7 years old. Alice is 5 years old. How much older is Bill?
		Hole A is 5 feet deep. Hole B is 7 feet deeper than Hole A. How deep is Hole B?
		Hole A is 5 feet deep. Hole B is 7 feet deep. How much deeper is Hole B?
2	Addition/subtraction classification problems	Eight men are in the store. Three women are in the store. How many people are in the store?
		Ramona has 4 hats; 3 of the hats are blue. How many hats are not blue?
		Maria sold 5 hats in the morning. She sold 2 hats in the afternoon. How many hats did she sell?
2	Multi-step problems: add three numerals	LaToya ran 5 miles on Monday, 3 miles on Tuesday, and 4 miles on Wednesday. How many miles did he run altogether?
3	Multiplication/division problems with the word "each" or "every"	Marcus has 4 boxes. In each box there are 6 pencils. How many pencils does Marcus have?
		Tamara jogs 5 miles every day. How far will she jog in 3 days?
		There are 20 students. The teacher wants to divide them into 4 equal groups. How many students will be in each group?
3	Multiplication/division problems with the word "per" or a phrase using "a"	The ABC Company makes pens. They put 5 pens in a box. How many pens are in 3 boxes?
		Rosa runs 2 miles per day. How many days will it take her to run 8 miles?

3	Addition/subtraction problems with larger numerals	Travis ran 214 miles in January and 158 miles in February. How many more miles did he run in January?
		There are 153 students in the school. If there are 61 girls in the school, how many boys are there?
3	Multiplication/division problems with larger numerals	There are 35 students in every class. There are 5 classes in the school. How many students are in the school?
		Jean worked 2 days. If she makes $16 a day, how much did she make?
		Jill has 215 pencils. She wants to make bundles with 5 pencils in each bundle. How many bundles can she make?
3	Addition/subtraction problems with distractors	There are 20 blue pencils, 5 red pencils, and 16 yellow pens in a bag. How many pencils are in the bag?
		Bill weighed 120 pounds. He ran 5 miles. Now he weighs 117 pounds. How much did he lose?
		Bill had 12 hats; 5 hats were old. He gave away 3 old hats. How many hats does he have left?
4	Division and multiplication problems with larger numerals (two-digit divisor or multi-digit factors)	Sarah wants to save $385. If she puts $35 in the bank each month, how many months will it take her to save the $385?
		A factory produces 325 cars a day. How many cars will it produce in 25 days?
		A pound of apples costs 60¢. How much will 20 pounds of apples cost?
4	Multi-step problems: three numerals; the sum of two numerals is subtracted from the third numeral	Julie sold 12 pencils in the morning. Ann sold 15 in the afternoon. How many more must they sell before they've sold 50 altogether?
		Timmy weighed 84 pounds. He lost 4 pounds in May and 7 pounds in June. How much did he weigh at the end of June?
		Jean sold 10 pens in the morning. She began with 18. If she sells 2 more, how many will she have left?
4	Three numerals: two quantities are multiplied; the product is added or subtracted from a third numeral	Tom has 3 pens in each pocket. He has 5 pockets. Ann has 16 pens. Who has more pens? How many more?
		Ann has $7. If she works 4 hours and earns $3 each hour, how many dollars will she have at the end of the day?
4	Three numerals: two quantities are added; the sum is divided or multiplied	There are 10 boys and 20 girls in the class. Each row can sit 5 students. How many rows will there be?
		Jill earns $2 every morning and $4 every afternoon. How much will she earn in 6 days?
5	Four numerals: two sets of quantities are multiplied; the product of each is added	Pam ran 5 miles a day for 3 days and 6 miles a day for 2 days. How many miles did she run altogether?
		Tammy bought 3 cakes and 2 drinks. A cake cost 10¢. A drink cost 15¢. How much did Tammy spend?
5	Five numerals: two sets of quantities are multiplied; the product of each is added; the sum is subtracted or added to a given quantity	Bill needs $30. He worked 5 hours on Monday for $2 an hour. He worked 2 hours on Tuesday for $3 an hour. How much more money does he need?
		Bill weighed 135 pounds in May. He gained 3 pounds each month for the next 2 months. Then he gained 5 pounds each month for the next 3 months. How much does he weigh now?

Teachers also should be aware that word problems become more difficult as the problems include unfamiliar vocabulary and use more complex syntax. The two problems that follow illustrate the importance of vocabulary and syntax:

a. Antonio wrote 6 sentences. The teacher crossed out 2 of them. How many are left?

b. When the teacher read Ariana's paper, she deleted 15 sentences and 3 commas. She had initially written 52 sentences. How many sentences did she have at the end?

Both of these word problems are temporal sequence problems—problems that state the original amount and the amount of decrease. Problem b is more difficult for several reasons. First, problem b contains more difficult vocabulary. Students may not be familiar with the words "deleted" and "initially." If a student does not understand "deleted," she has no basis for solving the problem. Second, the amount that Antonio began with is stated first in problem a, but in problem b the amount Ariana began with is stated *after* the amount of the decrease. When the smaller numeral appears first, students are more likely to add. The third difficulty is the presence of the phrase "and 3 commas," a distractor that must be ignored. Finally, the numerals in problem b are larger, and the operation requires renaming. Understanding the features that make word problems more challenging helps teachers better prepare students for a variety of word problems.

CONCEPTUAL UNDERSTANDING

We support the use of activity-based strategies as an *introduction* to the concepts in word problems rather than the primary strategy for solving them, unlike many current approaches to mathematics instruction. For example, commercial programs often suggest that students solve word problems by using manipulatives or pictures to represent values or by working with their peers to act out the word problem. These activity-based approaches fail to demonstrate clear connections between the activities, the language of the word problems, and the procedures required to solve the problems. In addition, these activities are not an efficient use of instructional time. In this chapter, we present generalizable problem-solving strategies that are useful and efficient. Embedded in these strategies is instruction that addresses critical language concepts needed to express word problems numerically. As a result, the strategies included in this text demonstrate clear connections between the language of the problems and the mathematical procedures used to solve them.

INSTRUCTIONAL PROCEDURES: ADDITION AND SUBTRACTION PROBLEMS

The procedures for teaching addition and subtraction problems are divided into two parts. The first part introduces the concept of word problems to young students through the use of illustrations. The second part teaches a more generalizable problem-solving strategy that enables students to solve temporal sequence, comparison, and classification problems. The generalizable strategy addresses the difficulties caused by variations in word usage. The same verb (*gave away*) appears in examples a and b below. However, solving problem a requires addition while solving problem b requires subtraction.

a. Nicole gave away 7 stickers. Maria gave away 3 more stickers than Nicole. How many stickers did Maria give away?

b. Nicole had 15 stickers. Then she gave away 7 stickers. How many stickers does she have now?

Introducing the Concept

In first grade, word problems can be introduced when students can work a page of simple addition and subtraction problems, using a line-drawing strategy, with 80% to 90% accuracy. It is not necessary for students to know how to solve missing-addend problems or have any basic facts memorized in order to be introduced to word problems.

About 3 weeks prior to the introduction of word problems, the teacher would present a preskill format designed to teach students how to translate to symbols four key phrases: "get more," "get rid of," "end with," and "how many." The phrase "get more" translates to a plus sign, "get rid of" to a minus sign, "end with" to an equal sign, and "how many" to an empty box. The teacher would say each new phrase and tell students its translation. For example, the teacher might say, "Listen: When you get more, you write a plus sign. What do you write for get more?" Each second or third day, the teacher would introduce a new phrase and review the phrases introduced earlier.

After the students know these four terms, the teacher presents another preskill exercise in which she says a common verb and asks if the verb translates to a plus or a minus sign. Several common verbs should be presented, for example, "buys," "loses," "sells," "eats," "finds," "gives away," "breaks," and "makes." The teacher associates each verb with getting more or getting rid of before asking the students to translate the verb to a symbol. For example, the teacher asks, "When you buy something, do you get more or get rid of something? So when you buy something, do you plus or minus?"

Format 11.1: Introducing Problem Solving Concepts is presented when the students have mastered the preskills outlined above. The format includes two parts. In Part A, the teacher begins word problem instruction by demonstrating how a written or verbal word problem can be solved with semi-concrete objects (pictures or lines). For example, pictures could be used to illustrate the following problem: There were six children. Two children went home. How many were left? The teacher would draw 6 lines representing children and cross out 2 of the lines to represent the 2 children who went home. The remaining lines would be counted to determine the answer.

After demonstrating how a verbal or written word problem can be illustrated, the teacher demonstrates how a verbal or written word problem may be expressed numerically, translating it phrase by phrase into an equation.

There were six children.	6
Two children went home.	6 − 2
How many were left?	6 − 2 = □

In Part B, the structured worksheet exercise, the teacher gives students a worksheet with a set of problems. If the students do not have adequate decoding skills, the teacher should read the problems to them. The teacher has the students read the entire problem and then reread it phrase by phrase. After reading each phrase, students are directed to draw the appropriate picture. For example, after reading "Ann has seven apples," students draw pictures of seven apples. Then students read the problem again, phrase by phrase, and write the appropriate equation. After completing the equation, students figure out the answer by counting the pictures or lines.

Example selection for word problems is very important. The verbs in the problems should be fairly common terms such as "buy," "give away," "make," "break," "find," and "lose." Also, problems should contain words that the students are able to decode, and the problems initially should be relatively short. A random mix of addition and subtraction problems should be used so that students must discriminate between the two types of problems.

For the first several weeks, the last sentence in word problems should say, "ends with how many?" These words can be translated directly to the symbols = □. After several weeks, the questions can be phrased differently, such as, "How many does she have now?" and "How many does she have in all?" The teacher explains that these sentences mean the same as "ends with how many?" and can be translated into the symbols = □.

A Number-Family Problem-Solving Strategy

The introductory strategy of translating word problems phrase by phrase into an equation is used to demonstrate the relationship between words and equations representing everyday situations. Most word problems, however, cannot be translated phrase by phrase into an equation. Therefore, we recommend teaching a strategy that encourages students to integrate their knowledge of fact-number-family concepts (see Chapter 6) with basic language skills to solve temporal sequencing, comparison, and classification problems.

The number-family strategy is based on the concept that three numbers can be used to form four math statements. For example, the numbers 2, 5, and 7 yield $2 + 5 = 7$, $5 + 2 = 7$, $7 - 5 = 2$, and $7 - 2 = 5$. The numbers may be represented as the following number-family diagram:

$$\underrightarrow{2 \qquad 5 \quad {}^{7}}\ \square$$

A standard diagram is used to represent a number family. When using the number-family strategy to solve basic facts, students are taught that the big number (total) goes at the end of the arrow. If the big number is not known, a box goes at the end of the number-family arrow. In a typical problem, two of the numbers in the family are provided. Students place these numerals where they belong in the family and then determine whether the missing numeral is obtained by adding or subtracting. For example, the family

$$\underrightarrow{2 \qquad 5 \qquad}\ \square$$

does not give the total and yields the problem $2 + 5 = \square$.

$$\begin{array}{c}\square \\ \underrightarrow{2 \qquad\qquad} {}_{7}\end{array}$$

In the above diagram, the family does give the total, so it yields the problem $7 - 2 = \square$.

The key to applying the number-family analysis successfully to a range of problem types is the ability to analyze the language in the problem to determine the name for the total. For example, in a problem involving boys, girls, and children, the name for the total is children. If the problem gives a number for children, subtraction is required. If the total number of children is unknown, addition is required. Students first represent the analysis of the problem in a diagram and then use the diagram to determine the operation. Consider the following problem: There are 8 children at the party. Three are boys. How many girls are at the party? The number for children is given.

$$\begin{array}{c}\qquad\qquad\text{children} \\ \underrightarrow{3 \qquad \square \quad} {}_{8}\end{array}$$

and generates the subtraction problem $8 - 3 = \square$.

Conversely, when the following problem is presented: There are 8 girls and 3 boys at the party. How many children are at the party? The total number of children is not given; therefore, the number-family representation is

$$\begin{array}{c}\qquad\qquad\text{children} \\ \underrightarrow{8 \qquad 3 \qquad}\ \square\end{array}$$

The analysis generates an addition problem.

$$8 + 3 = \square.$$

The number-family analysis highlights the relationships between the concepts in the word problem and the values that are given. Very careful guided practice is required to teach students to use the language in a word problem to determine whether the total number is given. The analysis for each problem type is explained in detail later in this chapter.

Preskill for the Number-Family Strategy   An essential preskill for the number-family word problem strategy is figuring out the missing number when two of the three numbers in a fact family are given. Students are taught that if the total number is given,

$$\underrightarrow{4 \qquad \square \quad} {}_{9}$$

they subtract to find the missing number:

$$9 - 4 = \square$$

On the other hand, if the total number is not given,

$$\xrightarrow[\quad]{4 \qquad 9} \square$$

they add the two given numbers:

$$4 + 9 = \square$$

Note that prior to introducing this strategy, students should be able to compute some facts mentally rather than using lines and subsequent problems should include only the basic facts that students previously have mastered.

Format 11.2: Preskill: Fact Family—Finding the Missing Family Member introduces this preskill. This preskill should be taught approximately 2 or 3 weeks before temporal sequence problems are first introduced, typically sometime during second grade. Note that this format is similar to those used in Chapter 6 to teach basic facts. In that chapter, the phrases "big numbers" and "small numbers" were used. Those phrases can be replaced by the phrases "total number" and "parts of the total" when preparing students to solve word problems to prevent students from identifying the larger number as the "big" number.

When presenting the preskill diagrams, the teacher shows an arrow with two numerals and a box. Below are examples of the diagrams. In problem a, the total number is given, while in problem b, the total number is not given. The line below the diagram is for writing the equation to find the missing number.

$$a.\ \xrightarrow[\rule{2cm}{0.4pt}]{6 \quad \square \quad} 8 \qquad b.\ \xrightarrow[\rule{2cm}{0.4pt}]{6 \qquad 2} \square$$

Format 11.2 has four parts. Part A introduces the rule about what to do when the total number is given: When the total number is given, we subtract. After telling students the rule, the teacher demonstrates its application, writing on the board a diagram in which the total number is given:

$$\xrightarrow[\ 8 - 2 = 6\ ]{2 \quad \square \quad} 8$$

The teacher points out that because the total number is given, the students must subtract to figure out the missing number ($8 - 2 = 6$). And when they subtract, they must start with the total number.

Part B introduces the rule about what to do when the total number is not given: When the total number is not given, we add. After telling students the rule, the teacher demonstrates its application, writing on the board a diagram in which the total number is not given:

$$\xrightarrow[\ 3 + 7 = 10\ ]{3 \qquad 7} \square$$

The teacher points out that because the total number is not given, the two given numbers must be added to figure out the total number ($3 + 7 = 10$).

Part C is a structured worksheet with diagrams, half of which give the total number and half of which do not. The student's task is to write the appropriate equation on the line under each arrow and to figure out the missing number.

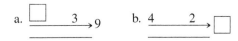

TABLE 11.1 Temporal Sequence Problems

- Verb indicates ending up with more.
  - *Addition*
    - a. James had 12 apples. He bought 17 more apples. How many apples did he end up with?
  - *Subtraction*
    - b. James had 12 apples. He bought more apples. Now he has 17 apples. How many apples did he buy?
- Verb indicates ending up with less
  - *Addition*
    - c. James had lots of apples. He sold 17 of the apples. He ended up with 12 apples. How many apples did he start with?
  - *Subtraction*
    - d. James had 17 apples. He sold 12 apples. How many apples did he end up with?

Part D is a less structured worksheet exercise in which the teacher asks students whether they add or subtract and then has them work the problem. In Parts C and D, the problems should not be written in a predictable order. Addition and subtraction problems should appear randomly.

Temporal Sequence Problems

In temporal sequence problems, a person starts out with a specified quantity, and then an action occurs (finds, loses, buys, sells) that results in the person ending up with more or less. The problems in **Table 11.1** illustrate why students cannot rely solely on the verb to determine the appropriate operation. Even though the presence of verbs such as "buys," "gets," and "finds" often indicates addition, some problem containing those words will require subtraction. Conversely, some word problems contain verbs that usually indicate subtraction but are solved with addition.

The strategy presented in the format for temporal sequence problems teaches the students to begin by looking at the overall structure of the word problem. Students then apply a two-step strategy for solving the problem. First, they determine whether the person in the problem starts or ends with the total. If the verb implies that the person ends with more, the person ends with the total. This is the case with the first two problems in Table 11.1: James buys more apples so he ends with the total. Students label the total accordingly:

Ends

Next, the students determine whether the total is given (Do we know how many James ends with?). In problem a, we do not know the total; we are asked how many James ends up with:

Ends

The two numbers given are recorded as parts:

12   17   Ends

Finally, students add to find the total. In problem b, the same diagram is used. Since James is buying apples, he ends with the total:

Ends

In problem b, however, the total is given. We know James ends up with 17 apples:

Ends
17

The total is given, so we must subtract to find how many he buys:

12 ☐ Ends
17

For problems c and d in Table 11.1, James sells apples. He ends up with fewer apples, so he starts with the total:

Starts

Next, we determine if the total is given (Do we know how many he starts with?). Problem c asks how many he starts with. The total is not given, so we add:

Starts
17   12 ☐

For problem d, we know James starts with 17:

Starts
17

The total is given so we subtract:

12 ☐ Starts
17

All temporal sequence problems are analyzed successfully using two questions: Do we start or end with the total? Is that total given? The steps to analyzing temporal sequence problems are outlined in **Summary Box 11.1**. Students must be familiar with the number-family rules presented in **Format 11.2: Preskill: Fact Family—Finding the Missing Family Member** to be successful in applying this strategy to problem solving.

Format 11.3: Temporal Sequence Word Problems outlines the procedure for teaching students to work this type of problem. Part A is a verbal exercise to establish the relationship between various verbs ("buys," "gives away," "loses") and a person starting or ending with more. Part B is a structured board presentation in which the teacher guides students through the

SUMMARY BOX 11.1

Temporal Sequence Word Problems

1. Students read the problem and determine whether the person starts or ends with more.

2. Students draw a number-family diagram and label starts or ends as the total.

3. Students fill in number-family diagram with labels and numbers that are given in the problem.

4. Students use number-family strategy to determine whether to add or subtract to find the unknown number.

Sam began with $25 in his savings account. He put another $4 into the account. How much money has he saved?

ENDS

25   4 ENDS
            ☐

25   4 ENDS
            29

problems. First, students determine whether the person in the problem starts or ends with more (the total). Next, they figure out whether the total is given. The teacher then places the values given in the problem on the number-family diagram. After the values are in place along the arrow, students apply their knowledge of the number-family rule: If the total, or big number, is missing, you add. If a small number is missing, you subtract.

Part C, introduced when students have mastered the steps in Part B, is a structured worksheet exercise. The teacher leads students through the same strategy, but the students construct the number-family diagrams that determine the correct operation. Part D is a less structured worksheet exercise in which the teacher asks the students to indicate if the person starts or ends with more (the total) and then has students complete the number-family diagram and figure out the answer.

When selecting examples for this format, the teacher constructs a minimum of two sets of four problems. Each set should contain two addition and two subtraction problems. In one addition problem, the person would start with more; in one addition problem, the person would end with more. Likewise, in one subtraction problem, the person would start with more, and in one subtraction problem, the person would end with more. The problems should be written in random order. Problems introduced initially should contain common verbs. Sentences should be relatively simple. All of the problems should result in equations that the students are able to work. For example, if students have not learned to regroup, subtraction problems should be limited to problems that do not require regrouping.

Comparison Problems

A comparison problem addresses two quantities and the difference between them. There are two basic types of comparison problems. In one type, a quantity is stated describing an attribute of an object or person, such as weight, length, height, or age. The difference between the objects or people is also stated. For example, "Brendan is 7 years old. Colleen is 3 years older." The student is asked to find the quantity of the other person or object: "How old is Colleen?"

In the second type of problem, the quantities of two objects or people are stated and the student is asked to find the difference between them: "Brendan is 7 years old. Colleen is 10 years old. How much older is Colleen?" Both types of comparison problems are introduced concurrently. All comparison problems can be solved using a number-family analysis. The larger of the quantities being compared represents the total. The smaller quantity and the difference are the parts of the total.

The two-step strategy for solving comparison problems is similar to that introduced for temporal sequence problems. It involves (a) determining which person or object represents the larger quantity and (b) determining whether the larger quantity is given or not given. For example, "Alicia got 10 problems correct. Asher got 2 fewer problems correct than Alicia. How many problems did Asher get correct?" In this problem, the number of problems Asher answered correctly is fewer, so the number of problems answered correctly by Alicia represents the total. Because the number of problems Alicia answered correctly is given, the problem requires subtraction. The steps to solving comparison problems are outlined in **Summary Box 11.2**.

SUMMARY BOX 11.2

Problem-Solving Strategy for Comparison Problems

1. Students read the problem and determine the bigger number.	Diane runs 3 miles each day. Mark runs 2 miles more each day. How many miles does Mark run each day?
2. Students fill in the number-family diagram with the label in the place for total	— ⟶ Mark
3. Students complete the diagram by filling in known values.	3　2　Mark ⟶ ☐
4. Students use number-family strategy to determine whether to add or subtract.	3　2　Mark ⟶ 5

Format 11.4: Comparison Problems shows how to present this type of problem. The format includes three parts. Part A is a preskill format designed to teach students how to determine the name for the bigger number. Note that this part assumes that students understand comparative words such as "deeper," "shallower," "thicker," "thinner," "bigger," "smaller," "heavier," and "lighter." Students who have difficulty with Part A may not understand the meaning of the comparatives. Teachers could test students' understanding of the language with diagrams or illustrations. For example, the teacher could present illustrations of two holes and ask, "Show me the hole that is deeper."

Another useful strategy for helping students determine which object is greater is to practice with sentences that compare two things without numerical values. For example,

a. The lake is closer than the city.
b. Brad worked longer than Rian did.
c. The bird stored fewer nuts than the raccoon.

Students would write partial number families for these sentences, writing the name for the larger quantity at the end of the number-family arrow. For example, in sentence a, the lake is closer than the city, so the city must be the larger value. Students would write the following number family:

City
————————→

After students master placing the name correctly in the number family, they can be taught to place the numerals in a comparison problem on the number-family arrow. Part B is a structured worksheet exercise with complete word problems. The teacher leads the students in applying the two-step strategy, first writing the name for the total and then writing a box or a quantity given for the total. For the problem "The lake is 23 miles closer than the city. The city is 59 miles away. How far away is the lake?" the students first write "city" for the total and then, since the quantity for city is given, write "59" under city. The students write the other quantity and a box for the small numbers on the number-family arrow.

Because the total is given in the number family, the number sentence is written:

$$59 - 23 = \square$$

The critical step in Part B occurs when the teacher asks if the problem gives a number for the total. If students do not read the problem carefully they may give a wrong answer. For example, if a problem states that Rachel is 12 years older than Sally, who is 7 years old, the total will tell how old Rachel is. When examining the problem, the students may misread the words "Rachel is 12 years older" as "Rachel is 12 years old" and write 12 as the total number.

If this type of error occurs frequently, the teacher would do a practice exercise that focuses only on this step. The teacher would present a series of problems verbally. For each problem, the teacher would tell the students what the total number tells about and would ask if the problem gives a numeral for the total. For example, "The total number tells how old Rachel is. Does a numeral in the problem tell how old Rachel is?" Six to eight problems would be presented in the exercise.

Part C is a less structured worksheet exercise in which the teacher leads students in applying the strategy. Each example set should include the following types of examples to provide discrimination practice.

1. Two addition problems in which one quantity is stated. The difference indicates the other quantity is greater:

Bill dug a hole 6 feet deep. Trey dug a hole 2 feet deeper than Bill's hole. How deep is the hole Trey dug?

Bill dug a hole 6 feet deep. Bill's hole is 2 feet shallower than the hole Trey dug. How deep is the hole Trey dug?

2. One subtraction problem in which one quantity is stated. The difference indicates the other quantity is smaller:

Bob dug a hole 6 feet deep. Jermaine dug a hole 2 feet shallower than Bob's hole. How deep is the hole Jermaine dug?

3. One subtraction problem in which both quantities are stated. Students must determine the difference.

Janet dug a hole 6 feet deep. Michael dug a hole 2 feet deep. How much deeper is Janet's hole?

Two addition problems would be included in each set to provide an equal mix of addition and subtraction problems.

Classification Problems

The steps for teaching students to work classification problems are outlined in **Summary Box 11.3** and Format 11.5: Classification Word Problems. Part A provides practice in the language preskill of identifying class names for groups of objects. The teacher says a superordinate class and two related subclasses and asks the students to tell which is the biggest class. This exercise assumes that students have already mastered the language related to classification. Teachers working with naive students may find that more extensive teaching in this skill is necessary.

In Part B, a structured worksheet exercise, the teacher introduces classification word problems. Students are given a worksheet with six to eight problems. Part B begins with the teacher reviewing with students that when the total number in a number family is given, they must subtract to find the answer; when the total number is not given, they must add. The teacher then states a problem and identifies the three groups mentioned in the problem: "There are eight children. Three are boys. How many are girls? This problem is about children, boys, and girls." After telling students the three groups, the teacher asks which word tells about the big class in this problem. Students are directed to write the word "children" at the end of the arrow to indicate the big class that the word problem is talking about.

Children

⟶

As with the comparison and temporal sequence word problems, students next determine whether the numeral for the total is given. In this example, the number family is completed as follows:

Children
3   ☐   8
⟶

SUMMARY BOX 11.3

Classification Problem-Solving Strategy

1. Students read the problem and underline the classes.

Jose has 3 <u>soccer balls</u> and 4 <u>baseballs</u>. How many <u>balls</u> does Jose have?

2. Students write the biggest class in the area for total number.

Balls
⟶

3. Students write the values for the two smaller classes, if known, in the number-family diagram.

3   4 Balls
⟶

4. Students use the number-family strategy to determine whether to add or subtract.

3   4 Balls
⟶ 7

Students apply the number-family rule, and since a small number is missing, they subtract to find the number of girls:

$$8 - 3 = 5 \text{ girls}$$

Part C is a less structured worksheet exercise. After reading a problem, the students write the name of the big class at the end of the number-family line above the place for the total. They reread the problem to figure out whether the total is given and then complete the number-family diagram. They are then able to apply the rules to solve the problem.

Several example selection guidelines need to be considered. First, practice examples should include an equal mix of addition and subtraction problems. Second, problems initially should be written in a relatively short form with few extraneous words. Third, relatively common classes should be used. A sample set of four problems appears below:

a. There were 75 cars in all. 15 were green cars. The rest were red cars. How many red cars were there?

b. Lauren had red marbles and blue marbles. She had 23 red marbles and 16 blue marbles. How many marbles did she have in all?

c. Tomas collected toy cars and airplanes. He had 43 toys in his collection. 14 were cars. How many were airplanes?

d. At Central Avenue School, there are 16 girls and 15 boys in first grade. How many children are in first grade?

During the first week that classification problems are introduced, the key words in the problem can be underlined to prompt the students to attend to the class names. For example, in problem a above, the words "cars," "red," and "green" would be underlined.

While students are learning to solve classification problems, they should continue to solve temporal sequence and comparison problems. After they have mastered classification problems, the teacher would give students worksheets that include a mix of classification, comparison, and temporal sequence problems. Worksheets would still include six to nine problems, with one-third representing each type of problem. When students first encounter a mix of problems, teachers would read the problems with the students and guide the students in setting up the number-family diagrams. Even though students have been successful at solving temporal sequence, comparison, and classification problems when presented independently, teachers should not assume students will be equally successful when two or three types of problems are combined on the same worksheet.

Format 11.6A/B: Using Tables to Solve Problems

Watch how Tristan maintains a brisk pace.

Format 11.6C: Using Tables to Solve Problems

Watch how Tristan uses think time.

Reading Tables Table problems are an efficient way to present sets of data and reinforce logic skills and number families. **Format 11.6: Using Tables to Solve Problems** introduces students to the idea that values in rows and columns are added to obtain totals. To find the total for a row or column, students use a running total. In a beginning table exercise, students learn that columns run vertically and rows horizontally. After students have sufficient practice adding both columns and rows of numerals in tables, headings are presented. These headings tell about the numerals in the columns and rows. For example,

Hours Worked				
	Mon.	Tues.	Weds.	Total
Josh	5	4	10	19
Jane	4	7	1	12
John	2	5	3	10
Total	11	16	14	

Students practice touching both headings and finding a particular cell. For example, students place one finger on "Tuesday" and move downward and another finger on "John" and move across until they meet at 5. After working with several examples, students should be ready to answer questions about a numeral in a particular cell, such as "How many hours did Jane work on Wednesday?" "Who worked the most hours on Tuesday?" "Who worked the most hours in all?"

After students are familiar with reading tables and adding numerals in rows and columns, the teacher can demonstrate how to apply the number-family strategy to solving problems in tables. Students first are introduced to the concept that tables with rows and columns can work like number families. Instead of just a line between the cells, the tables in the early problems should have arrows. The arrows remind the students that each row works like a number family. The first two numerals in the row represent small numbers. The total is the big number.

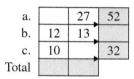

a.		27	52
b.	12	13	
c.	10		32
Total			

A small number is missing in row a. Students apply the number-family rule: If the small number is missing, you subtract. If the big number is missing, you add. Since a small number is missing in this example, students subtract to find the missing number in the row ($52 - 27 = 25$). In row b, a big number is missing, so students add to find the missing number in the family and write it in the table: $12 + 13 = 25$.

Teachers may want to separate the introduction of the number family in rows and the number family in columns, first working only with rows, then only with columns, and finally solving for unknown cells in both. The tables below show this progression.

	15	35
20	12	
14		26

10		9
	22	31
19	45	

35		50
10	18	

The final step involves teaching students how to transfer the information from a word problem to a table and answer questions. Using tables to work word problems that involve classification of data is a natural extension of what students learned when solving addition/subtraction classification word problems. The column and row headings show the names for the two subclasses (boys and girls) as well as the name for the big class (children). For example, the table might show the number of girls and boys attending soccer practice on two days, Tuesday and Thursday. The table for recording the data would look like this:

	Boys	*Girls*	*Children*
Tuesday			
Thursday			
Total			

Part D illustrates how teachers can teach students to record data, use the number-family strategy to complete the table, and then answer questions using the information from the table. Note that teaching all parts of **Format 11.6** will take a considerable amount of time and will occur over many days. Teaching students to use tables, however, is an efficient and logical approach to solving several types of problems.

▶ **Format 11.6D: Using Tables to Solve Problems**

Watch how Tristan monitors his students as they complete a worksheet using a table to solve a classification word problem.

Distractors

A distractor is information given in a word problem that is irrelevant to finding the solution to the problem. It is called a distractor because students have been accustomed to using all of the information that a problem provides, and the additional information may distract them from determining the correct equation. For example,

> Natasha had 4 stuffed dogs, 2 stuffed rabbits, 2 stuffed pigs, and 5 stuffed cats in her collection. Four of the stuffed animals are very old. How many stuffed animals does Natasha have in her collection?

Because the problem asks how many stuffed animals Natasha has in her collection, the irrelevant information is about the number of old animals and must be ignored in order to solve the problem correctly.

Students are most often introduced to problems with distractors in intermediate grades. Several practice problems would be given in which students state what they have been asked to solve and cross out the information that they don't need in order to solve the problem. Problems with distractors would be distributed throughout the math curriculum and practiced frequently until students can easily discern the relevant information when solving a problem.

Multi-step Word Problems

Frequently, students work temporal problems that require both addition and subtraction. These multi-step problems can be solved using number families. Here is an example of such a problem:

> Shane spends $12 on stamps. Then he spends $32 on a video game. If he ends up with $6, how much did he start out with?

Because this problem contains the word "spends," students may be likely to use only subtraction to solve the problem. Using a number-family analysis guards against this kind of mistake.

Format 11.7: Introducing Multi-step Word Problems is an adaptation of the addition/subtraction number-family strategy that can be used to solve this type of problem. In this adaptation, the values in the number family are labeled "in," "out," and "end up." "In" stands for how much the person started with and how much more of that item came in. "In" is always the big number; "out" and "end up" are the small numbers. "Out" stands for decreases in the items. The diagram below illustrates how the problem above can be represented.

$$\begin{array}{ccc} \textit{End up} & \textit{Out} & \textit{In} \\ & 12 & \\ & 32 & \\ 6 & \overline{44} & \boxed{50} \\ \hline & & \longrightarrow \end{array}$$

In applying the number-family strategy, students must add both "out" numbers to find the total for "out" before adding that to the "end up" number to arrive at the "in," or big number (the answer to the problem).

To prepare students to work multi-step problems, the teacher can have students practice the format with one-step subtraction and addition problems to teach the concepts of "in," "out," and "end up." If a sentence tells the amount that somebody has, that is an "in" number. The sentence "Caley had $15" gives a numeral for "in." If a sentence tells about increasing a value, it tells about a value for "in." "McKenzie collected 34 stamps" tells the increase in stamps: 34 is the numeral for "in." Values for "out" tell about reductions. "Howard gave away 3 apples" tells about "out"; "1500 gallons leaked out of the tanker" tells about "out." The value for "end up" is the amount that is left, or the difference between the amount "in" and the amount "out." In most problems, the amount for "end up" is the amount the person has after the final reduction or increase that the problem describes.

Using simple problems that contain only three values provides practice with the conventions before students are introduced to multi-step problems. Following are examples of simple problems that may be used in this type of practice exercise.

a. Maria starts a savings account with $567. Later, she takes some money out of her account, which leaves a balance of $329. How much money was taken out?

b. A florist starts out with no carnations. She buys 59 carnations and later sells 47 of them. How many carnations did she end up with?

c. Daniel had an empty fruit crate. He put some oranges in the crate. Then he gave away 23 of those oranges. The crate still has 19 oranges in it. How many oranges did he put in the crate?

After students have mastered these conventions, multi-step problems are introduced. These problems have more than one value for "in" or more than one value for "out." The values are shown stacked under the appropriate heading in the number family. Following is an example of a problem with values stacked under the "in" heading.

Carlos caught 12 salmon yesterday, 11 this morning, and 8 this afternoon. On his way home, he stopped at the marketplace and sold some of the salmon. He still has 15 salmon. How many did he sell at the marketplace?

End up	Out	In
		12
		11
		8
15	16	31

After students have mastered multi-step problems with more than one value for either the "in" or "out" headings, they are introduced to problems with multiple values for both headings. For example,

At the beginning of the workday, the elevator in the Federal Building is empty. Then 5 people get on the elevator. It stops at the fifth floor, and 2 more people get on. On the next floor, 4 people get off. On the seventh floor, 7 people get on, and 8 people get off. How many people are still on the elevator?

End up	Out	In
	4	5
	8	2
		7
2	12	14

INSTRUCTIONAL PROCEDURES: MULTIPLICATION AND DIVISION PROBLEMS

Multiplication and division operations are used to solve word problems that address equal-sized groups. These problems are stated in three basic forms. If a problem gives the number of groups and the number in each group, the problem is a multiplication problem; for example, "Malachi has 3 piles of toys. There are 2 toys in each pile. How many toys does Malachi have in all?" The equation representing that problem is $3 \times 2 = \square$. If the problem gives the total and asks either how many groups or how many in each group, the problem is solved with division; for example, (a) "Malachi has 6 toys. He puts 2 toys in each pile. How many piles does he end up with?" The equation is $6 \div 2 = 3$; (b) "Malachi has 6 toys. He wants to put the toys in 3 piles with the same number of toys in each pile. How many toys will he put in each pile?" The equation is $6 \div 3 = 2$. Once the students determine that the problem is addressing equal-sized objects or groups, they will know that it is either a multiplication or a division problem. Then the students can apply the same number-family strategy to determine whether the total number is given and, therefore, whether they must multiply or divide to solve the problem.

Multiplication and division problems almost always contain a word or phrase that indicates that the problem is referring to equal-sized groups. Most of the problems contain the word "each" or "every." Other indications of equal-sized groups include the word "per" and phrases like "in a box" or "in a dozen"; for example, (a) "Nick walked 4 miles per day. How many miles did Nick walk in 3 days?" (b) "There were 3 balls in a box. There were 6 boxes. How many balls in all?"

Multiplication and division word problems should not be introduced until students have mastered addition and subtraction word problems and have a working knowledge of basic multiplication and division facts.

Format 11.8: Introduction to Multiplication and Division Word Problems illustrates how word problems requiring multiplication and division may be introduced first using coins. Given that coins represent equal-sized groups, using coins as a representation for multiplication and division problems helps students understand the concepts involved in solving these types of word problems.

Initially, students focus on setting up the number families correctly and do not solve the problems. The number-family diagrams for this type of problem would consist of three parts: the value of the coin, the number of coins, and the total number (cents). The teacher would begin by showing students a picture of coins like the one below. Next to the picture would be a number-family diagram with a C representing the total number of cents, a D representing the number of dimes, and a box representing the missing value of one dime.

The students would write the value of a dime in the box.

The D would be crossed out and the number of dimes written above.

The students would then multiply the value of the dime by the number of dimes to determine the total number of cents.

The next step in the strategy is to introduce problems in which no coins are shown. For example:

a.   You have some nickels. You have 45 cents in all. How many nickels do you have?

To work problem a, students write the value of each nickel as the first small number and 45 as the big number for total cents, or cents in all. Since the big number is given, the answer is obtained by dividing: $45 \div 5 = 9$. There are nine nickels.

b.   You have quarters. You have 5 quarters. How many cents do you have in all?

For problem b, the value of a quarter is written as the first small number, and 5 is written for the second small number. The number of cents is the total amount (cents) in the number family and can be obtained by multiplying 25×5.

After students have mastered writing coin problems in number families, they are taught how to analyze the language in other multiplication/division problems and create the corresponding diagrams. As in addition/subtraction problems, the key to the number-family analysis lies in identifying the name for the total. Students are taught that one sentence in each problem tells how to draw the number-family diagram. That sentence is the one that tells about each part of the number family.

For example, "Each brick weighs 3 pounds." There are more pounds than bricks, so pounds is the name for the total. Brick is a small number. The weight of each brick is the other small number.

$$\xrightarrow[\hspace{3cm}]{\quad 3 \qquad\qquad B\quad} P$$

Initial instruction focuses on generating accurate number-family diagrams. After students master how to write the number family, they are asked to solve the problems.

In Part A of **Format 11.9: Setting Up Multiplication and Division Word Problems**, students practice analyzing statements and determining the total, while the teacher demonstrates how to draw the number-family diagram. In Part B, students generate number-family diagrams and solve written problems in a worksheet format.

Students often have difficulty determining the total number. For the sentence "Each box has 10 cookies," the total number is cookies because there are more cookies than boxes. If students confuse the total number with size, they will reverse the components. If students have difficulty determining the name for the total number, they can be taught that the word in the problem following "each" refers to a small number. If they use the information about "each" in the sentence above, they can identify one of the objects as the total number. "Each box has 10 cookies." The word following "each" is box. Box is the small number. The only other name in the sentence is cookies, so cookies must be the big number.

DIAGNOSIS AND REMEDIATION

Teachers need to monitor student performance on solving word problems daily. Efforts need to be made to determine the possible cause of errors in order to provide appropriate remediation. There are at least five possible causes of errors in solving word problems: (a) fact errors, (b) calculation errors, (c) decoding errors, (d) vocabulary errors, and (e) translation errors.

Fact Errors

A fact error occurs when the student chooses the correct operation and writes the problem correctly but fails to arrive at the correct answer because the student does not know her math facts. An example of a fact error follows:

There were 9 boys and 8 girls in the class. How many students were there?

$$9 + 8 = 16$$

The equation is written using the correct numerals and the correct operation, but the student failed to remember the fact. The remediation process would not require not repetition of word problem strategies but instead extra practice on memorization of basic facts.

Calculation Errors

A calculation error is one that a student makes when computing an answer. For example, failure to rename correctly would be a calculation error. Errors of this sort do not require reteaching of the word-problem strategies. Rather, remediation on the calculation procedure would be necessary.

Decoding Errors

Reading a word or words in a problem incorrectly is a decoding error. For example, if a student reads broke instead of bought in the following problem, he will use the wrong operation: "Taryn had 8 glasses. She bought 6. How many does she have now?" The decoding error would cause the student to subtract 6 from 8 rather than add 6 + 8. Having the student read the problem aloud helps determine whether the error is a decoding error.

Teachers can help students who have difficulty decoding by previewing difficult words before students encounter them in word problems. Teachers of students who are unable to decode written word problems easily should not require students to read the problems but should read the problems to the student.

Vocabulary Errors

Vocabulary errors occur when students do not know the meaning of key words in the word problems. For example, in the following problem, students must know that "receives" means "to get more."

> Curt has 18 pairs of socks. He receives 4 more pairs for his birthday. How many pairs of socks does he have now?

Teachers can easily determine if the error is related to vocabulary knowledge by simply asking the student what the word means. To prevent vocabulary errors, teachers would present the meaning of critical vocabulary words prior to presenting the word problems.

Translation Errors

If a student fails to translate a problem into the correct equation and uses the wrong operation, the student has made a translation error. For example,

> Naveah now has 7 video games. She started out with 2 video games that she received for her birthday. How many more video games has she gotten since then?

$$7 + 2 = 9$$

In this problem, the student added instead of subtracting. The teacher begins remediation by examining the student's work over a period of days to determine if the same type of problem is consistently missed. Remediation can be done through a worksheet exercise using the less structured format for that particular problem type. The worksheet should include at least 10 problems, half of which represent the type of problem that was missed with the other half including problems to provide discrimination practice.

APPLY WHAT YOU LEARNED

 Click on the √ to answer the questions online.

1. Tell what type of word problem each of the following examples represents using the types described in the Instructional Sequence and Assessment Chart.

   a. Terrell has 15 green apples and 17 red apples. He wants to split them equally among his four friends. How many apples should he give to each friend?

   b. Asia has been running for several months. She runs 5 miles each day. How many miles will she run in 10 days?

   c. There are 20 balls in the toy closet. Eight of the balls are baseballs. How many of the balls are not baseballs?

   d. Isabella has 2 pens in each pocket. She has 8 pens. How many pockets does she have?

   e. Emmy has 8 dollars. Then she earned 3 dollars. How many dollars does she have now?

   f. A girl is 15 years old. Her brother is 2 years younger. How old is her brother?

2. Word problems can be made easier or more difficult by changing one or more aspects. Outline several ways in which problems can be made more difficult. For each problem in the item above, change or add to the problem to increase its level of difficulty in some way.

3. Explain the possible cause of the following errors. When the cause of the error is unclear, tell what the teacher does to determine the specific cause. Specify the remediation procedure called for if errors of this type occur frequently.

   a. Valeria's team scored 54 points. The other team scored 19 points fewer. How many did the other team score? 36 points

   b. The ABC Company produced 1,534 pool tables last year. This year, production decreased by 112 pool tables. How many pool tables did the ABC Company produce this year? 1,646 pool tables

   c. Matias baked 6 cakes every week. He baked for 18 weeks. How many cakes did he bake? 3 cakes

   d. Tara took 20 shots in the basketball game. She made 15 shots. How many shots did she miss? 35 shots

   e. There are 10 boys and 20 girls in the class. Each row can seat 5 students. How many rows will there be? 35 rows

   f. There are 28 students. The teacher wants to divide them into 4 equal groups. How many students will be in each group? 6 students

   g. A factory produces 325 cars a day. How many cars will it produce in 25 days? 8,105 cars

4. Write a structured worksheet format using tables to guide students through solving this problem: Twenty-eight vehicles went past our house. Twelve of the vehicles were cars. How many vehicles were not cars?

5. Write a structured worksheet format to guide students through solving this problem: Ann runs 5 miles every day. So far she has run 20 miles. How many days has she run?

Format 11.1
INTRODUCING PROBLEM-SOLVING CONCEPTS

TEACHER	STUDENTS
Part A: Preskill: Visual Representation	
Addition Problem	
1. Listen: Ann has 7 apples. She gets 3 more apples. She ends with how many apples?	
2. Let's draw a picture of that problem. Ann has 7 apples. *(Draw the illustration below on the board.)*	

She gets 3 more apples, so I draw 3 more. *(Draw 3 more apples.)*

3. Let's write the equation. Here's the first sentence again. Ann has 7 apples. How many apples does Ann have?	7
I write 7 under the 7 apples. *(Write 7.)*	
Here's the next sentence. She gets 3 more apples. How many more apples did she get?	3

TEACHER	STUDENTS
Yes, Ann gets 3 more. What do I write for gets 3 more? *(Write + 3.)*	Plus 3
The problem says she ends up with how many apples? So I write equals and a box, like this: *(Write = □: 7 + 3 = □.)*	
4. Read the equation.	7 + 3 equals how many?
Let's count and see how many we end up with. *(Touch pictures of apples as students count.)*	1, 2, 3, 4, 5, 6, 7, 8, 9, 10
So Ann ends with 10 apples. *(Write 10 in the box.)*	

Subtraction Problem

TEACHER	STUDENTS
1. Listen: Ann has 7 apples. She gives away 3 apples. She ends with how many apples?	
2. Let's draw a picture of that problem. Ann has 7 apples, so I draw 7 apples. *(Draw apples.)*	

TEACHER	STUDENTS
She gives away 3 apples, so I'll cross out 3 apples. *(Cross out 3 apples.)*	

TEACHER	STUDENTS
3. Let's write the equation. Here's the first sentence again. Ann has 7 apples. How many apples did Ann have?	7
I'll write a 7 *(Write 7.)*	
Here's the next sentence. She gives away 3 apples. How many apples did she give away?	3
What do I write for gives away 3 apples?	Minus 3
Yes, she gives away 3, so we write −3. *(Write −3.)*	
The problem says she ends with how many apples? So I write equals and a box.	
(Write = □: 7 − 3 = □.)	
4. Read the equation.	7 − 3 equals how many?
Let's count the apples that are left and see how many she ends with. *(Touch the remaining apples.)*	1, 2, 3, 4
So, Ann ends with 4 apples. *(Write 4 in the box.)*	
(Repeat addition or subtraction steps 1–4 with several more problems.)	

Part B: Structured Worksheet

1. *(Give students a worksheet that contains a mix of addition and subtraction problems and includes a box and the word for the unit answer, like the following.)*

   a. Jim has 6 marbles. He finds 2 more marbles. He ends with how many marbles?

   □ marbles

continued

Format 11.1 *(continued)*
INTRODUCING PROBLEM-SOLVING CONCEPTS

TEACHER	STUDENTS
b. Jim has 6 marbles. He gives away 2 marbles. He ends with how many marbles?	

☐ marbles

TEACHER	STUDENTS
Touch problem a. Listen: Jim has 6 marbles. He finds 2 more marbles. He ends with how many marbles?	
2. Let's draw a picture of that problem. Jim has 6 marbles. Draw the marbles. *(Wait while the students draw on their papers, then draw the marbles on the board.)*	

TEACHER	STUDENTS
He finds 2 more marbles. Draw those. *(Wait, then draw the marbles on the board.)*	

TEACHER	STUDENTS
3. Let's write the equation.	
Read the first sentence again.	Jim has 6 marbles.
How many marbles did Jim have?	6
Write 6 under the 6 marbles. *(Wait, then write 6 on board.)*	
Read the next sentence.	He finds 2 more marbles.
How many more marbles did he get?	2
Yes, Jim finds 2 more. What do you write for finds 2 more?	Plus 2
Yes, write + 2. *(Wait, then write +2 on board.)*	
The problem says he ends with how many marbles? So, what do you write?	Equals box
Write equals how many. *(Wait, then write = ☐ on board: 6 + 2 = ☐.)*	
4. Read the equation.	6 + 2 equals how many?
Let's count and see how many we end with. *(Touch pictures of marbles as students count.)*	1, 2, 3, 4, 5, 6, 7, 8
Write 8 in the box after the equal sign.	
Now, write 8 in the answer box next to the word marbles. Jim ends with 8 marbles.	

Subtraction Problem

TEACHER	STUDENTS
1. Touch the next problem. Listen: Jim has 6 marbles. He gives away 2 marbles. He ends with how many marbles?	
2. Let's draw a picture of that problem. Jim has 6 marbles. Draw the marbles. *(Wait while students draw on their papers, then draw the marbles on board.)*	

TEACHER	STUDENTS
He gives away 2 marbles. Cross them out. *(Wait, then cross out two marbles.)*	

Ø Ø ◯ ◯ ◯ ◯   Ø Ø ◯ ◯ ◯ ◯

TEACHER	STUDENTS
3. Let's write the equation. Jim has 6 marbles. How many marbles does Jim have?	6
Write a 6. *(Write 6 on board.)*	
How many does he give away?	2
What do you write for gives away 2 marbles?	Minus 2
Yes, he gives away 2, so write −2. *(Write − 2 on board.)*	
The problem says he ends with how many marbles, so what do you write?	Equals box
Write it. *(Wait, then write = □ on board: 6 − 2 = □.)*	
4. Read the equation.	6 − 2 equals how many?
Let's count the marbles that are left and see how many he ends with. *(Touch the remaining marbles.)*	1, 2, 3, 4
Write 4 in the box after the equal sign. *(Wait, then write 4 in the box.)*	
Now write 4 in the answer box next to the word *marbles.* Jim ends with 4 marbles.	
(Repeat addition or subtraction steps 1–4 with several more problems.)	

Format 11.2
PRESKILL: FACT FAMILY—FINDING THE MISSING FAMILY MEMBER

TEACHER	STUDENTS

Part A: Subtraction Rule

1. *(Write this diagram on the board.)*

2   6
——→ 8

2. Three numbers go together to make a fact family. *(Point to 8.)*

The total number is always at the end of the arrow.

(Point to 2.) This number is part of the total.

(Point to 6.) Here's the other part of the total.

(Erase the 8.) Sometimes, we don't know the total and we have to figure it out.

2   6
——→ □

continued

Format 11.2 *(continued)*
PRESKILL: FACT FAMILY—FINDING THE MISSING FAMILY MEMBER

TEACHER	STUDENTS
(Write the 8 back in; erase the 6.) Sometimes, we don't know part of the total and we have to figure it out.	

3. *(Write the following diagram on the board.)*

Is the total number given in this problem?	Yes
Here's the rule: When the total number is given, we subtract. The total number is 10. So I start with 10 and subtract 3. *(Write 10 − 3 on the bottom line.)* What is 10 − 3?	7
So, I write equals 7. *(Write = 7 on the line.)*	
Now I write 7 in the empty box. *(Write 7 in box.)*	
The numbers 3 and 7 are the parts of the total. The number 10 is the total number.	

4. *(Write the following diagram on the board.)*

Is the total number given?	Yes
What do we do when the total number is given?	Subtract
Remember, when you subtract, you start with the total number. What problem do I write on the line?	12 − 5
(Write 12 − 5 on the line.) What is 12 − 5?	7
(Write = 7 on the line.) What number goes in the empty box? *(Write 7 in the box.)*	7
(Repeat step 4 with these problems.)	

Part B: Addition Rule

1. *(Write the following diagram on the board.)*

TEACHER	STUDENTS

2. In this problem, the total number is not given. When the total number is not given, we add.

    Is the total number given in this problem? — No

    Watch. The parts are 3 and 5, so I add 3 and 5. *(Write 3 + 5 on the line.)* What is 3 + 5? — 8

    So, I write equals 8. *(Write = 8 on the line.)*

    Now, I write 8 in the empty box. The numbers 3 and 5 are the parts of the total. The number 8 is the total.

3. *(Write the following diagram on the board.)*

    Is the total number given? — No

    What do we do when the total number is not given? — Add

    What problem do I write on the line? *(Write 7 + 2 on the line.)* — 7 + 2

    What is 7 + 2? *(Write = 9 on the line.)* — 9

    What number goes in the empty box? *(Write 9 in the box.)* — 9

    (Repeat step 3 with the problems below.)

Part C: Structured Worksheet

1. You must figure out the missing number in all these problems. It might be the total number or it might be part of the total.

    If the total number is given, what must you do? — Subtract

    If the total number is not given, what must you do? — Add

    (Repeat step 1 until students answer correctly.)

continued

Format 11.2 *(continued)*
PRESKILL: FACT FAMILY—FINDING THE MISSING FAMILY MEMBER

TEACHER	STUDENTS
2. Touch the first problem.	
Touch the box for the total.	
Is the total given?	No
So what must you do?	Add
What problem do you write on the line?	3 + 2
Write it.	
What is 3 + 2?	5
Write an equals sign and the answer.	
Fill in the empty box.	
(Repeat step 2 with remaining problems.)	
Part D: Less Structured Worksheet	
1. *(Give students a worksheet like that in Part C.)*	
2. Touch the first problem.	
3. Is the total number given or not given?	
4. Do you add or subtract?	
5. Write the equation on the line and write the answer.	
(Repeat steps 2–5 with all problems.)	

Format 11.3
TEMPORAL SEQUENCE WORD PROBLEMS

TEACHER	STUDENTS
Part A: Preskill—Determining if One Starts or Ends with More	
1. We're going to figure out if a person *starts* or *ends* with more.	
2. Jimmy *buys* books. Does he *start* or *end* with more?	Ends with more.
Jimmy *sells* books. Does he *start* or *end* with more?	Starts with more.
Mary *gives away* apples. Does she *start* or *end* with more?	Starts with more.
Mary *loses* money. Does she *start* or *end* with more?	Starts with more.
Mary *finds* money. Does she *start* or *end* with more?	Ends with more.
Sally *makes* some dolls. Does she *start* or *end* with more?	Ends with more.
Sally *throws away* her old shoes. Does she *start* or *end* with more?	Starts with more.
Mike *collects* some stamps. Does he *start* or *end* with more?	Ends with more.

TEACHER	STUDENTS
Part B: Structured Board Presentation	

1. *(Give students a worksheet with the following problems.)*

   a. Billy buys some ties. Then he buys 8 more ties. He ends up with 23 ties. How many did he buy at first?

   b. Sandra had 8 eggs in the fridge. She ate 2 eggs for breakfast. How many eggs does she have now?

   c. Walter had some apples in a basket. After he gave away 11 apples, he had 9 apples left. How many apples did he start with?

   d. Sam began with 14 bricks on his toy truck. He put another 12 bricks on the truck. How many bricks ended up on the truck?

2. We're going to make number families for these problems. First, we'll figure out if the person *starts* or *ends* with more. I'll read the first part of each problem.

3. Problem a. Billy buys some ties. Then he buys 8 more ties. Listen. Billy buys ties. So does he start or end with more?

                                                   Ends with more

   Yes, he ends with more, so *ends* is the name for the total.

   (Write the following diagram on the board.)

               Ends
   a. ——————→

4. Problem b. Sandra had 8 eggs in the fridge. She ate 2 eggs for breakfast. Listen. Sandra ate eggs. So does she start or end with more?

                                                   Starts with more

   Yes, she starts with more, so *starts* is the name for the total.

   (Write the following diagram on the board.)

               Starts
   b. ——————→

5. Problem c. Walter had some apples in a basket. After he gave away 11 apples, he had 9 apples left. Listen. Walter gave away apples. So does he start or end with more?

                                                   Starts with more

   He starts with more, so *starts* is the name for the total.

   (Write the following diagram on the board.)

               Starts
   c. ——————→

6. Problem d. Sam began with 14 bricks on his toy truck. He put another 12 bricks on the truck. Listen. Sam put more bricks on the truck. So does he start or end with more?

                                                   Ends with more

   He ends with more, so *ends* is the name for the total.

   (Write the following diagram on the board.)

               Ends
   d. ——————→

continued

Format 11.3 *(continued)*
TEMPORAL SEQUENCE WORD PROBLEMS

TEACHER	STUDENTS
7. Now let's go back and put in the numbers we know. Problem a. We know Billy ends with more. Let's see if we know how many he ends with. Billy buys some ties. Then he buys 8 more ties. He ends up with 23 ties. Do we know how many he ends with?	Yes
How many?	23
So I write 23 for *ends*.	
(Write 23 in the diagram.)	
a. $\xrightarrow{\text{Ends}}$ 23	
We don't know how many he buys at first, so I write a box.	
(Draw "how-many box" in the diagram.)	
a. □ $\xrightarrow{\text{Ends}}$ 23	
We know he buys 8 more.	
(Write 8 in the diagram.)	
a. □ 8 $\xrightarrow{\text{Ends}}$ 23	
8. Now we have our number family. The total is given. Do we add or subtract?	Subtract
Say the problem we work.	23 − 8
When we work that problem, we figure out he bought 15 ties at first.	
9. Problem b. We know Sandra starts with more. Let's see if we know how many she starts with. Sandra had 8 eggs in the fridge. She ate 2 eggs for breakfast. Do we know how many she starts with?	Yes
How many?	8
So write 8 for *starts*.	
(Write 8 in diagram.)	
b. $\xrightarrow{\text{Starts}}$ 8	
She ate 2 for breakfast, and we don't know how many she has now.	
(Write 2 and "how-many box" in diagram.)	
c. 2 □ $\xrightarrow{\text{Starts}}$ 8	
The total is given. Do we add or subtract?	Subtract
Say the problem we'll work.	8 − 2
What's 8 − 2?	6
So now she has 6 eggs left.	

TEACHER	STUDENTS

10. Problem c. We figured out Walter starts with more. Let's see if we know how many he starts with. Walter had some apples in a basket. He gave away 11 apples. Do we know how many he starts with?

    So I'll write a box for the total.

    (Write "how-many box" in diagram.)

               Starts
    c. ⟶ □

    We know he gives away 11 and has 9 left.

    (Write 11 and 9 in diagram.)

        11   9 Starts
    c. ⟶ □

No

11. We need to figure out the total. Do we add or subtract?

    Say the problem.

    11 + 9 = 20, so Walter started out with 20 apples.

Add
11 + 9

12. Problem d. We know Sam ends with more. Let's see if we know how many he ends with. Sam began with 14 bricks on his toy truck. He put another 12 bricks on the truck. How many bricks ended up on the truck?

    Do we know how many he ends with?

    So I'll write a box.

    (Write "how-many box" in the diagram.)

            Ends
    d. 14   12 □

No

13. He begins with 14 and puts on another 12.

    (Write 14 and 12 in the diagram.)

             Ends
    d. ⟶ □

    Do we add or subtract?

    Say the problem.

    When we add, we get 26.

    So 26 bricks ended up on the truck.

Add
14 + 12

Part C: Structured Worksheet

1. *(Give students a worksheet with the following problems.)*

    a. Tracy started out with $10 in her bank account. She put $8 in her account. How much money did she end up with in her account?

    b. Roger dropped and broke 4 glasses. If he started out with 9 glasses, how many glasses does he have now?

    c. After buying some toy cars at the swap meet, Tony had 17 cars in his collection. Before the swap meet, he had 12 cars in his collection. How many cars did he buy?

    d. Joe had too many kittens. He gave away 8 kittens and had 3 left. How many kittens did Joe start out with?

continued

Format 11.3 *(continued)*
TEMPORAL SEQUENCE WORD PROBLEMS

TEACHER	STUDENTS
2. You're going to make number families for these problems. Read problem a to yourself. Raise your hand when you know if Tracy *starts* or *ends* with more. *(Monitor students.)*	
3. Does Tracy *start* or *end* with more?	Ends with more
Make your number-family arrow. Write *ends* over the place for total. *(Check.)*	
Here's what you should have.	
(Write the following diagram on the board.)	

a.

```
          Ends
   ───────────▶
```

4. The problem asks how much she ends up with. Do we know how much she ends with?	No
So what do we write for *ends*?	A box
Write a box. Then put in the numbers the problem gives. *(Check.)*	
(Write to show: Draw the box first, then write 10 and 8 in the diagram.)	

a.

```
              Ends
    10      8 ☐
   ────────────▶
```

Here's the number family for problem a.	
5. Read problem b to yourself. Raise your hand when you know if Roger *starts* or *ends* with more. *(Monitor students.)*	
6. Does Roger *start* or *end* with more?	Starts with more
Make your number-family arrow. Write *starts* over the place for total. *(Check.)*	
7. Read the problem again. Raise your hand when you know what we write for *starts*. *(Monitor students.)*	
What did you write?	9
Yes, he starts with 9 glasses. Write 9 for the total, then complete the number family. *(Check.)*	
Here's the number family for problem b.	
8. *(Write the following diagram on the board.)*	

b.

```
            Starts
    4     ☐
   ──────────▶ 9
```

9. Read problem c to yourself. Raise your hand when you know if Tony *starts* or *ends* with more. *(Monitor students.)*	
10. Does Tony *start* or *end* with more?	Ends with more
Make your number-family arrow with the word *ends*. *(Check.)*	
11. Raise your hand when you know what to write for *ends*. *(Monitor students.)* What do you write?	17
Yes, he ends with 17. Complete the number family with two numbers and a box. *(Check.)*	
Here's the number family for problem c.	

TEACHER	STUDENTS
12. *(Write the following diagram on the board.)*	

c. $\xrightarrow[12 \quad \square]{}$ Ends 17

13. Read problem d to yourself. Raise your hand when you know if Joe *starts* or *ends* with more. *(Monitor students.)*	
14. Does Joe start or end with more?	Starts with more
Raise your hand when you know what to write for *starts. (Monitor students.)* What do you write?	A box
Yes, the problem asks how many kittens he starts out with, so you write a box.	
Complete the number family with two numbers and a box. *(Check.)*	
Here's the number family for problem d.	
15. *(Write the following diagram on the board.)*	

d. $\xrightarrow[8 \quad 3]{}$ Starts $\square$

16. Figure out the answer to each problem. Remember the unit names. *(Monitor while students work.)*	
17. Tell me the answer for each problem.	
Problem a. How much money did Milly end with?	18 dollars
Problem b. How many glasses does Roger have now?	5 glasses
Problem c. How many cars did Tony buy?	5 cars
Problem d. How many kittens did Joe start out with?	11 kittens

Part D: Less Structured Worksheet

1. *(Give students a worksheet with the following problems.)*

  a. J.R. found 9 shells on the beach. He already had 15 shells in his collection. How many shells does he have now?

  b. Luca went on a diet and lost 25 pounds. Before his diet, he weighed 195 pounds. How much does he weigh now?

  c. Mike started out with lots of fish. He threw back 8 fish and still had 9 left. How many fish did he start with?

  d. After Emily added 12 stories to her brick tower, the tower is 15 stories high. How high was her tower to start with?

2. For some of these problems, the person *starts* with more. For some, the person *ends* with more.

3. Problem a. Read the problem. Raise your hand when you know if the person starts or ends with more. *(Monitor students.)* Which is it?   Ends with more

4. Make the complete number family. Remember to label the total. *(Check.)* Here's what you should have.

5. *(Write the following diagram on the board.)*

a. $\xrightarrow[9 \quad 15]{}$ Ends $\square$

continued

Format 11.3 (continued)
TEMPORAL SEQUENCE WORD PROBLEMS

TEACHER	STUDENTS
6. Now figure out the answer. Remember the unit name. *(Check.)*	
7. How many shells does J.R. have now?	24 shells
(Repeat steps 3–7 with other items; each number family and step 7 is shown below.)	
b. $\xrightarrow[\quad 25 \quad \square \quad]{}$ Starts 195	
How much does Luca weigh now?	170 pounds
c. $\xrightarrow[\quad 8 \qquad 9 \quad]{}$ Starts □	
How many fish did Mike catch?	17 fish
d. $\xrightarrow[\quad 12 \quad \square \quad]{}$ Ends 15	
How high was Emily's tower to start with?	3 stories

Format 11.4
COMPARISON PROBLEMS

TEACHER	STUDENTS
Part A: Preskill: Determining the Total Number	
1. Comparison problems tell you about two persons or things. Here are some words you'll see in comparison problems: *bigger, older, smaller, taller, wider.* If the problem tells about two people and has a word that ends in *er*, you know it's a comparison problem.	
2. Let's practice figuring out which person or thing in a comparison problem tells about the big number.	
3. Listen: A dog weighs 7 pounds. A cat weighs 3 pounds more than the dog. Who does that problem tell about?	A dog and a cat
4. Listen to the problem again. *(Repeat problem.)* Who is heavier?	The cat
5. So the big number tells how many pounds the cat weighs.	
(Repeat steps 3–5 with the problems below.)	
Jill is 10 years old. Brian is 8 years younger. Who is older?	
Hole A is 6 feet deep. Hole B is 4 feet deep. Which hole is deeper?	
Jack ran 8 miles. Ann ran 2 miles more. Who ran farther?	
Jane weighs 60 pounds. Ann is 5 pounds lighter. Who is heavier?	
A yellow pencil is 5 inches long. A blue pencil is 3 inches longer. Which pencil is longer?	

TEACHER	STUDENTS
Part B: Structured Worksheet	
1. *(Give students worksheets with problems written in the form below.)*	

> a. Tom's stick is 2 feet long.
> Bill's stick is 5 feet longer.
> How long is Bill's stick?
>
> Answer:_____
>
> ─────────→
>
> b. Jack is 10 years old.
> May is 2 years younger.
> How old is May?
>
> Answer:_____
>
> ─────────→

TEACHER	STUDENTS
2. You're going to make number families for comparison problems. The name for the bigger number goes at the *end* of the arrow. The name for which number goes at the end of the arrow?	The bigger number
Yes, the bigger number tells about the total.	
3. Read problem a. *(Pause.)*	
4. Who does the problem tell about?	Tom and bill
Which is longer, Bill's stick or Tom's stick?	Bill's stick
Write Bill on the line above the end of the arrow. *(Check.)*	
5. Read the problem again. *(Pause.)*	
Does a number in the problem tell how long Bill's stick is?	No
Make a box below Bill. *(Check.)*	
6. The problem doesn't give a number for the total. The numbers in the problem tell about parts of the total. Write those numbers on the arrow. *(Check.)*	
7. Write the problem and figure out the answer. *(Check.)*	
What's the answer?	7 feet
8. So Bill's stick is 7 feet long.	
Write 7 feet on the answer line.	
9. Read problem b. *(Pause.)*	
10. Who does the problem tell about?	Jack and May
11. Who is older, Jack or May?	Jack
Write Jack on the line above the end of the arrow.	
12. Read the problem again. *(Pause.)*	
Does the problem tell how old Jack is?	Yes
How old?	10
Write 10 below Jack.	
13. The problem gives a number for the total.	
Complete the number family with a number and a box. *(Check.)*	

continued

Format 11.4 *(continued)*
COMPARISON PROBLEMS

TEACHER	STUDENTS
14. Write the problem and figure out the answer. *(Check.)*	
What's the answer?	8
15. So May is 8 years old.	
Write 8 years on the answer line.	
(Repeat steps 3–8 with remaining addition problems. Repeat steps 9–15 with remaining subtraction problems.)	

Part C: Less Structured Worksheet

TEACHER	STUDENTS
1. *(Give students a worksheet with a mix of addition and subtraction problems.)*	
a. Martha's cat weighs 2 pounds more than Sarah's cat. Martha's cat weighs 12 pounds. How much does Sarah's cat weigh?	
b. The trip to the library is 6 miles. The trip to the zoo is 3 miles further than the library. How far is it to the zoo?	
c. Greg has 12 cars in his collection. Will has 15 cars in his collection. How many more cars does Will have than Greg?	
d. There are 5 fewer children in Fay's family than in Joe's family. There are 3 children in Fay's family. How many children are in Joe's family?	
2. Read problem a. *(Pause.)*	
3. Make a number-family arrow. Write the word that tells about the total above the total place. *(Check.)*	
4. See if the number for the total is given in the problem. Then write two numbers and a box where they belong. *(Check.)*	$2 \quad \underrightarrow{\square} \quad$ Martha, 12
5. Write the problem and figure out the answer.	$\begin{array}{r} 12 \\ -2 \\ \hline 10 \end{array}$
Then write the whole answer. *(Check.)*	10 pounds
6. What's the answer?	10 pounds
(Repeat steps 2–6 with the remaining problems.)	

Format 11.5
CLASSIFICATION STORY PROBLEMS

TEACHER	STUDENTS
Part A: Preskill: Language	
1. I'll say some class names. You tell me the biggest class. Listen: *cats, animals, dogs*. What is the biggest class?	Animals
(Repeat step 1 with hammer, saw, tool; vehicle, car, truck; men, women, people; girls, boys, children.*)*	

TEACHER	STUDENTS

Part B: Structured Worksheet

1. *(Give students a worksheet with 6–8 problems written like those below.)*

> a. There are 8 *children*; 3 are *boys*. How many
>   are *girls*? _____
>
>   ───────────→
>
> b. Jill has 5 *hammers* and 4 *saws*. How many *tools* does
>   she have? _____
>
>   ───────────→

2. Let's review some rules you already know. If the total number is given, what do you do?

   If the total number is not given, what do you do?

   Students: Subtract / Add

3. In some problems, we don't see words like *find, lose, buy*, or *give away*, so we have to use a different way to do these problems.

4. Touch the first problem. I'll read it. There are 8 children; 3 are boys. How many are girls? The problem talks about children, boys, and girls. Which is the big class, *children, boys*, or *girls*?

   If *children* is the big class, then the number of children is the total number. So write *children* on the line above the total place.

   Students: Children

5. Listen. *(Repeat the problem.)* *Children* is the total number. Does the problem tell how many children?

   Make a box below children.

   So the total number is given. What is the total number?

   Write 8 in the box for the total number.

   (Note: If the first answer is no, tell the students), "The total is not given, so we don't write anything in the box for the total."

   Students: Yes / 8

6. Now we write the values for boys and girls on the arrow. How many boys?

   Write 3.

   We don't know how many girls, so we write a box above the arrow.

   Students: 3

7. Is the total number given?

   So what do you do to work out the problem?

   We start with 8 children and subtract 3 boys to find out how many girls.

   Write the equation and figure out the answer.

   If there are 8 children and 3 are boys, how many are girls?

   (Repeat steps 4–7 with remaining problems.)

   Students: Yes / Subtract / 5

continued

Format 11.5 *(continued)*
CLASSIFICATION STORY PROBLEMS

TEACHER	STUDENTS

Part C: Less Structured Worksheet

1. *(Give students a worksheet with problems in this form.)*

   Jerry has 7 pets; 4 are *dogs.*

   How many are *cats?*

Jerry has 7 pets; 4 are *dogs.*
How many are *cats?*
⟶

2. Touch the first problem.

3. Read the problem. Then write the name for the big class above the total place.

4. Write the two numbers and box where they belong.

5. Write the equation and figure out the answer.

6. Write the whole answer on the answer line.

   (Repeat steps 2–6 with remaining problems.)

Format 11.6
USING TABLES TO SOLVE PROBLEMS   (See Videos Parts A/BCD)

TEACHER	STUDENTS

Part A: Introducing Rows and Columns in a Table

1. *(Write the table below on the board.)*

6	6	1	
2	3	2	
1	1	2	

2. This is a table problem. To work this kind of problem, you have to add the numerals in each column and the numerals in each row. Remember that columns go up and down. Rows go side to side. Point to show me which way columns go. *(Check to make sure that students point up and down.)* Point and show me which way rows go. *(Check to make sure that students point side to side. Repeat to correct.)*

3. *(Touch the first column.)* I'll read the numerals in the first column: 6, 2, 1.

4. *(Touch the second column.)* Read the numerals in this column.

5. *(Touch the third column.)* Read the numerals in this column.

6. *(Touch the top row.)* I'll read the numerals in the top row: 6, 6, 1.

For steps 4 and 5, student responses in the STUDENTS column:

4. 6, 3, 1

5. 1, 2, 2

TEACHER	STUDENTS
7. *(Touch the middle row.)* Your turn. Read the numerals in the middle row.	2, 3, 2
8. *(Touch the bottom row.)* Read the numerals in the bottom row.	1, 1, 2

Part B: Finding Totals in Tables

TEACHER	STUDENTS
1. Go back to the first column. The numerals are 6, 2, 1. Here's how you work the problem. You add 6 and 2. What's the answer?	8
2. Then you add 8 and 1. What's the answer?	9
3. 9 is the *total* for the first column. *(Write 9 at the bottom of the first column.)*	
4. Your turn. Add the numerals in the next column and raise your hand when you know the answer. *(Wait for students to solve the problem.)* The numerals in this column are 6, 3, and 1. What is the answer, everyone?	10
5. *(Repeat procedure with last column.)*	
6. The numerals for the top row are 6, 6, and 1. What is 6 + 6?	12
What's 12 + 1? *(Write 13 at the end of the row.)*	13
7. Your turn. Add the numerals in the middle row and raise your hand when you have the answer. *(Wait for students to solve the problem.)* The numerals in this row are 2, 3, and 2. What is the answer, everyone?	7
8. *(Repeat procedure with last row.)*	

▶

Part C: Using the Number-Family Strategy to Solve for Missing Data

1. *(Write the following table on the board.)*

a		38	45
b	15	11	
c	12		31

TEACHER	STUDENTS
2. This is a table with arrows for the rows and columns. The arrows show you something interesting about the table. Each row and column works just like a number family. The first two numerals in the row are the small numbers. The total is the big number.	
3. *(Touch row a.)* A numeral is missing in that row. Is the missing numeral a big number or a small number?	A small number
(Write the following diagram on the board.)	

$$\xrightarrow{38} 45$$

TEACHER	STUDENTS
4. So do you add or subtract to find the missing numeral?	Subtract
5. Say the subtraction problem.	45 − 38
6. *(Touch row b. Write the diagram below on the board.)*	

$$\underline{1511}\rightarrow$$

TEACHER	STUDENTS
Here is the number family for that row. Is the missing numeral a small number or the big number?	The big number

continued

Format 11.6 (continued)
USING TABLES TO SOLVE PROBLEMS

TEACHER	STUDENTS
7. So do you add or subtract to find the missing numeral?	Add
8. Say the addition problem.	15 + 11
9. *(Touch row c.)* Is the missing numeral a small number or the big number?	A small number
10. So do you add or subtract?	Subtract
11. Say the subtraction problem.	31 − 12
12. Your turn. Write the problem and the answer for each row. Write the column problem for rows a, b, and c. *(Wait for students to finish the problems.)*	
13. Everyone, read the problems and the answers. Get ready: row a, row b, row c.	 45 − 38 = 7 15 + 11 = 26 31 − 12 = 19
14. What is the missing numeral in row a? *(Write 7 in row a.)* What is the missing numeral in row b? *(Write 26 in row b.)* What is the missing numeral in row c? *(Write 19 in row c.)*	7 26 19
15. Figure out the totals for each column. *(Wait for students to finish the column problems.)*	
16. Read the totals for the columns: first column, second column.	 34 68

Part D: Using Tables to Solve Word Problems

1. *(Students have worksheets with several problems similar to the one below.)*

   Facts: There are 23 red cars on Al's lot and Jim's lot has 12 green cars. The total number of red and green cars on Jim's lot is 43. The total number of green cars on both lots is 30.

	Red cars	Green cars	Total for both colors
Jim's lot			
Al's lot			
Total for both lots			

Questions

a. Are there fewer green cars or red cars on both lots?

b. How many green and red cars are on Al's lot?

c. There are 31 cars of some color on Jim's lot. What color?

d. Are there more green cars on Jim's lot or Al's lot?

TEACHER	STUDENTS
2. We're going to use a table to answer the questions listed above. First we need to fill in any missing information from the facts that are given. Read the first fact. Write the value from that fact in the correct place in the table. *(Repeat step 2 with the remaining facts.)*	There are 23 red cars on Al's lot.
3. Now you have enough information to complete the table using the number-family strategy. If one of the small numbers is missing, what do you do? If one of the totals is missing, what do you do? *(Monitor while students complete the table.)*	Subtract Add
4. Now that the table is complete, read question a and raise your hand when you know the answer. *(Call on an individual student to answer question a.)* Everyone, write the correct answer next to the question.	
5. *(Repeat step 4 for each question.)* *To correct: If students make a mistake locating the correct information, have them put their fingers on the cell that has the information to answer the question. Monitor where students place their fingers to determine if they are able to read the table. If they have problems locating the correct cells, then reteach Part C of this format, adding a question about the information represented in each row and column.*	

Format 11.7
INTRODUCING MULTI-STEP WORD PROBLEMS

TEACHER	STUDENTS
Part A: Introducing Ends-in-Out Format	
1. *(Write the following problems on the board.)* a. A wallet is empty. $432 goes into that wallet. Then some money goes out of that wallet. The wallet ends up with $85. How much went out? b. A florist starts without any roses. She picks up 87 roses. She sells 54 roses. How many roses does she end up with? c. Chandra had an empty basket. She put some eggs in the basket. Then she gave away 37 of those eggs. The basket still had 14 eggs in it. How many eggs did Chandra put in the basket? *End up Out In* $\longrightarrow$	
2. Listen while I read problem a. A wallet is empty. $432 goes into that wallet. Then some money goes out of that wallet. The wallet ends up with $85. How much went out?	
3. In this problem, some money goes into the wallet, and some money goes out of the wallet. How much money does the wallet end up with? So I will write $85 under "end up" in the number family. *(Write $85 on the board.)* *End up Out In* $85 $\longrightarrow$	$85

Format 11.7 *(continued)*
INTRODUCING MULTI-STEP WORD PROBLEMS

TEACHER	STUDENTS
4. Do we know how much money went out of the wallet?	No
So we do not know the other small number.	
5. Do we know how much money went into the wallet?	Yes
6. How much money went into the wallet?	$432
So we can write that for the big number. *(Write $432 under "in" on the board.)*	
End up *Out* *In* $85 ⟶ $432	
7. Now that we know two numbers for the number family, we can figure out the third number. What is missing, a big number or a small number?	A small number.
8. How do we find a missing small number?	Subtract
9. Say the subtraction problem.	$432 − $85
10. *(Repeat steps 2–9 for problems b and c.)*	
Part B: Structured Board Presentation—Multi-step Problems	
1. *(Write the following problems on the board.)*	
a. Josh had $17 in the bank. Later he put $12 in the bank. The next day he went to the bank and took out $11.50. How much money did Josh end up with in the bank?	
b. A water tank had some water in it. 250 gallons were taken from the tank. Then another 720 gallons were taken from the tank. The tank still had 1150 gallons in it. How many gallons were in the tank in the beginning?	
c. A farmer had 534 bales of hay. She fed 247 bales to her cattle. She sold 85 bales to a neighbor. She threw 4 bales away because they were moldy. How many bales did she end up with?	
2. Listen while I read problem a: Josh had $17 in the bank. Later he put $12 in the bank. The next day he went to the bank and took out $11.50. How much money did Josh end up with in the bank? The first part of the problem tells about the two values that went in the bank. Here is the number family:	
End up *Out* *In* ⟶	
3. What is the first value that went in the bank?	$17
(Write $17 in the number family.)	
End up *Out* *In* ⟶ $17	
4. What is the second value that went in the bank?	$12
(Write $12 on the board.)	

End up   *Out* *In*
            ⟶ $17
                 12	

TEACHER	STUDENTS
5. Do we know how much Josh took out of the bank?	Yes
How much?	$11.50
So we write $11.50 in the number family.	
(Write $11.50 on the board.)	
End up Out In $17 $11.50 12 ———————→	
6. Now we need to add the amounts that went into the bank. Say the problem.	$17 + $12
What is the total?	$29
(Write $29 on the board.)	
End up Out In $17 $11.50 12 ———————→ $29	
7. Now that we have two numerals in the number family, we can figure out the other number. What is missing, a big number or a small number?	A small number
8. How do we find a missing small number?	Subtract
9. Say the subtraction problem.	$29.00 − $11.50
10. Subtract to figure out how much money Josh ended up with in the bank. How much?	$17.50
11. *(Repeat for problems b and c.)*	

Format 11.8
INTRODUCTION TO MULTIPLICATION AND DIVISION WORD PROBLEMS

TEACHER	STUDENTS
1. *(Write the following diagrams on the board.)*	
Ⓓ Ⓓ Ⓓ ☐ D Ⓓ Ⓓ Ⓓ ————→ C	
2. We are going to use a multiplication number family to find out how many cents are in this picture. Remember, in multiplication number families, if the big number is not given, you must multiply. If the big number is given, then you must divide to find the answer.	
What must you do if the big number is not given?	Multiply
What must you do if the big number is given?	Divide
What coins are shown in this picture?	Dimes
3. The total number of cents is the big number. C is already written on the diagram for cents.	

continued

Format 11.8 *(continued)*
INTRODUCTION TO MULTIPLICATION AND DIVISION WORD PROBLEMS

TEACHER	STUDENTS
4. How many cents is *each* dime worth?	10 cents
So 10 is the first small number. *(Write 10 and D.)*	
10 D	
————————→ C	
5. How many dimes are there?	6
6. So I cross out the D for dimes and write 6. *(Cross out D and write 6.)*	
6	
10 D̶	
————————→ C	
7. Look at the diagram. Is the big number given?	No
8. If the big number is not given, what do you need to do?	Multiply
9. What is 10 times 6?	60
(Cross out C and write 60.)	
10. What is the total number of cents?	60 cents
11. *(Repeat steps 1–10 with similar problems using nickels, dimes, and quarters. Later problems do not need to show pictures of coins but can describe them as in the following problems.)*	
a. You have some nickels. You have 35 cents in all. How many nickels do you have?	
b. You have some dimes. You have 9 dimes. How many cents do you have in all?	
c. You have some nickels. You have 8 nickels. How many cents do you have in all?	
d. You have some quarters. You have 5 quarters. How many cents do you have in all?	
e. You have some dimes. You have 40 cents in all. How many dimes do you have?	

Format 11.9
SETTING UP MULTIPLICATION AND DIVISION WORD PROBLEMS

TEACHER	STUDENTS
Part A: Preskill: Writing Number Families	
1. *(Write the following problems on the board.)*	
a. Each box holds 7 cans. You have 35 cans. How many boxes do you have?	
b. Each room had 10 lights. There were 8 rooms. How many lights were there in all the rooms?	
c. Each dog had 9 bugs. There were 7 dogs. How many bugs were there on all the dogs?	
d. Each cat had 9 fleas. There were 36 fleas in all. How many cats were there?	
e. Each boy ate 2 hot dogs. There were 5 boys. How many hot dogs were eaten by all the boys?	

TEACHER	STUDENTS

2. These are word problems. To work them, you have to make multiplication number families. One sentence in each problem tells how to make the family. That sentence tells about each thing.

3. Listen while I read problem a. Each box holds 7 cans. You have 35 cans. How many boxes do you have? The first sentence gives you information for making the number family. Each box holds 7 cans. There are more cans than boxes. So cans is the big number.

4. What do we write to stand for box?   **B**

(Write the following diagram on the board.)

$$\xrightarrow{\hspace{3cm}}^{\textstyle B}$$

What do we write to show cans?   **C**

(Write the following diagram on the board.)

$$\xrightarrow{\hspace{3cm}}^{\textstyle B}\ C$$

If can is the big number and box is a small number, what is the other small number?   **7**

(Write the following diagram on the board.)

$$\xrightarrow{\hspace{3cm}}^{\textstyle 7\qquad B}\ C$$

5. Here is the number family. The next sentence tells you that you have 35 cans, so we cross out C and write 35.

(Write the following diagram on the board.)

$$\xrightarrow{\hspace{3cm}}^{\textstyle 7\quad B\qquad 35}\ \cancel{C}$$

6. Our number family shows a big number and a small number. You find the missing small number by finding out how many sevens are in 35.

7. How many boxes do you have?   **5**

(Write the final diagram on the board.)

$$\xrightarrow{\hspace{3cm}}^{\textstyle 7\quad \overset{5}{\cancel{B}}\qquad 35}\ \cancel{C}$$

8. *(Repeat steps 2–7 using problems b, c, d, and e.)*

Part B: Structured Worksheet

1. *(Give students a worksheet with 6 to 8 problems similar to those below.)*
   a. There are 6 chairs at each table. If there are 42 chairs, how many tables are there?
   b. Books are stacked on shelves with the same number of books on each shelf. There are 5 shelves and 40 books. How many books are on each shelf?

2. These are multiplication and division problems.

3. Read problem a to yourself. Raise your hand when you've found the sentence that tells how to make the number family. *(Pause. Call on a student to read.)*   There are 6 chairs at each table.

continued

Format 11.9 *(continued)*
SETTING UP MULTIPLICATION AND DIVISION WORD PROBLEMS

TEACHER	STUDENTS
4. There are 6 chairs at each table. Are there more chairs or more tables?	Chairs
So which name tells about the big number?	Chairs
5. Make the number family with two letters and a number. *(Check.)*	Students write 6 T ───────→ C
6. The problem gives a value for one of the names. Which name?	Chairs
7. Put that value in the number family. *(Check.)*	Students write 6 T 42 ───────→ C
8. Is the big number given?	Yes
So do you multiply or divide?	Divide
9. Work the problem and write the answer with a unit name. *(Check.)*	
10. What's the answer? *(Repeat steps 3–10 with other items.)*	7 tables

Measurement, Time, and Money

LEARNING OUTCOMES

12.1 Outline the recommended sequence for introducing measurement, time, and money and the rationale for that sequence.

12.2 Discuss how the basic concepts of measurement, time, and money are related.

12.3 Describe how the recommended teaching procedures for measurement are organized for both metric and customary measurement systems.

12.4 Outline the critical discriminations that students must make in order to tell time on an analog clock accurately.

12.5 Discuss the recommended sequence for teaching change-related money skills.

12.6 Outline procedures for diagnosing and remediating common error patterns in measurement, time, and money.

SKILL HIERARCHY

· · · · · · · ·

This chapter addresses three topics: measurement, time, and money. The measurement section includes a discussion of both customary and metric systems focused on length, weight, and capacity. The section on time provides guidance in teaching students to read both analog and digital clocks. The final section on money emphasizes instruction related to efficiently working with both coins and decimal notation.

INSTRUCTIONAL SEQUENCE AND ASSESSMENT CHART

Grade Level	Problem Type	Performance Indicator
	Measurement	
2	Customary units: length	_____ inches in a foot _____ feet in a yard About how long is a spoon? 6 inches 6 feet 6 yards About how tall is a person? 5 inches 5 feet 5 yards How long is the line? How long is the line?
2	Metric units: length	_____ centimeters in a meter About how long is a pen? 8 mm 8 cm 2 m 2 km About how long is a car? 2 mm 2 cm 2 m 2 km About how much does a cat weigh? 8 ounces 8 pounds 8 tons About how much does a car weigh? 2 ounces 2 pounds 2 tons
3	Customary units: liquid capacity	_____ cups in a pint _____ pints in a quart _____ quarts in a gallon
3	Metric units: weight	_____ grams in a kilogram About how much does a pencil weigh? 75 mg 75 g 75 kg 75 cg About how much does a newborn baby weigh? 4 mg 4 g 4 kg 4 cg
3	Metric units: capacity	_____ milliliters in a liter How much milk can we put in a baby bottle? 250 ml 250 dl 250 l 250 kl How much water would a basketball hold? 3 ml 3 dl 3 l 3 kl
3	Customary units: area and volume	What is the area of a room 8 feet long and 10 feet wide? _____

4	Customary units: length—using a ruler to the nearest eighth-inch	

Make an X over 2¼
Make an R over 1½
Make a T over 2⅜
Make a B over 2¼

4	Customary units: operations—regrouping required	

Circle the correct answer.

  4 feet 5 inches
+3 feet 8 inches

  8 feet 3 inches
  8 feet 1 inch
  7 feet 3 inches

4	Customary units: story problems—renaming	

Jasmine is 6 feet 2 inches. Her sister is 4 feet 10 inches. How much taller is Jill?

4	Conversions	

4 feet = _____ inches
2 yards = _____ feet
36 inches = _____ feet
20 meters = _____ centimeters
5000 centigrams = _____ grams
500 kilometers = _____ meters

5	Metric equivalencies—less common units	

Circle the answer.
A kilogram equals:
1 gm   10 gm   100 gm   1,000 gm
A milliliter equals:
a tenth of a liter
a hundredth of a liter
a thousandth of a liter

Time

2	Time expressed with hour stated first	

Put an X on the line under the clock that says 7:25.

continued

INSTRUCTIONAL SEQUENCE AND ASSESSMENT CHART *(continued)*

Grade Level	Problem Type	Performance Indicator
2	Expressing time as minutes after the hour	a. _____ minutes after _____ b. _____ minutes after _____ c. _____ minutes after _____ d. _____ minutes after _____

Money

Grade Level	Problem Type	Performance Indicator
1	Value of single coins	Show students a penny, nickel, dime, and quarter. Ask the students about the value of each coin: How much is a nickel? How much is a dime?
1	Determining value of groups of like coins	Ask students to count groups of pennies, nickels, dimes, or quarters.
2	Determining value of groups of different coins	Ask students to count groups of coins that include pennies, nickels, dimes, and quarters. Write the coins you would need to make 27¢. Write the coins you would need to make 79¢.
2	Adding dollars and cents	$1.32 $4.78 +$2.43 +$6.92
3	Determining change	You bought a soda for 27¢ and gave the clerk 35¢. How much change should you receive?
3	Decimal notation: reading and writing dollar and cents notations	Write four dollars and six cents _____ Write nine dollars and thirty cents _____ Write one dollar and five cents _____
4	Decimal notation: subtracting dollars and cents from whole dollar figures	$15.00 − $1.35 = $9.00 − $8.20 = $10.00 − $6.16 =
4	Adding and subtracting whole dollars and dollar and cents amounts	DeAndre had $6. He spent $3.25. How much does he have left? If you had $4 and you got $2.15 more, how much would you have?
4	Determining cost of purchase for two groups of items	You buy 3 pencils for 25¢ each and 5 pencils for 50¢ each. How much do you spend? You buy 5 pens for 75¢ each and 3 erasers for 48¢ each. How much do you spend?
4	Determining how much can be bought with specified amount	Yolanda wants to buy pencils that cost 27¢ each. She has 2 dollar bills and a dime. How many pencils can she buy?

CONCEPTUAL UNDERSTANDING

This chapter is devoted to three related but separate topics that are relevant to the type of practical math skills inherent in daily living. These topics are related in that each one uses numerical representations for concrete and abstract constructs required for general and workplace math literacy.

Measurement

Teachers working with beginning-level students should demonstrate with concrete objects how to use consistent units of measurement. Length is often introduced first. To develop a deeper conceptual understanding of measurement of length, the teacher may present an exercise in which students measure the lengths of various strips of paper using paper clips as the unit of measurement. The teacher demonstrates how to measure the paper strip by laying the clips along the edge of the paper and determining how long the paper is in paperclip units. For example, in the following illustration, the slip of paper is three clips long:

Following the demonstration, students are given the opportunity to independently determine the lengths of several strips of paper using paper clips.

This exercise serves two purposes. First, it introduces students to the concept of measuring a specific attribute, in this case, length. Second, it demonstrates how the units used for measurement are equivalent. The paper clips used in measuring length are always the same size.

Teachers can introduce weight measurement in the same way with a balance scale. First, the teacher demonstrates how the scale works, showing students that the weights on both sides of the scale are the same when the trays of the scale are the same height. Similarly, the teacher must show that when the weights are not the same, the side that is lower is heavier. Following the demonstration with a balance scale, the teacher introduces students to standard weights against which they can measure various objects. For example, blocks that weigh an ounce can be used as the measuring standard against which other objects can be measured.

For demonstrating the concept of capacity, the teacher can set out a number of empty cups, present a water-filled container, and pour the contents into the cups, one at a time, to determine the container's capacity. The teacher would then ask how many cups of water the container holds.

Time

Because the notion of time is not concrete, students have much more difficulty understanding the concepts underlying various measures of time. Before teaching specific time-telling skills, teachers may want to introduce the concept of duration of time by engaging students in a variety of activities. For example, one activity might involve having students close their eyes and raise their hands when they predict a minute has gone by. After students experience firsthand different lengths of time (seconds, minutes), they can be asked to predict how long various activities might take and then check their predictions.

Money

The need for instruction in money-related skills is derived from their importance in daily activities. Many students come to school having had some experience with money. Teachers often build upon this prior experience through developing classroom or school stores. Students can learn about the value of different currencies (tokens, school-based currency, or even coins) through exercises of exchanging those currencies for goods or activities.

MEASUREMENT: CUSTOMARY AND METRIC UNITS

There are two basic measurement systems: the customary system, which is used in the United States and a few other countries, and the metric system, which is used in the majority of countries in the world.

TABLE 12.1   Metric and Customary Units for Measuring Length, Weight, and Capacity

Customary Units

Length	Weight	Capacity
12 inches = 1 foot 3 feet = 1 yard 5,280 feet = 1 mile	16 ounces = 1 pound 2,000 pounds = 1 ton	2 cups = 1 pint 2 pints = 1 quart 4 quarts = 1 gallon

Metric Units

Meaning of Prefix	Length	Weight	Capacity
thousandth	millimeter (mm)	milligram (mg)	milliliter (ml)
hundredth	centimeter (cm)	centigram (cg)	centiliter (cl)
tenth	decimeter (dm)	decigram (dg)	deciliter (dl)
whole	meter (m)	gram (g)	liter (l)
10 wholes	dekameter (dkm)	dekagram (dkg)	dekaliter (dkl)
100 wholes	hectometer (hm)	hectogram (hg)	hectoliter (hl)
1,000 wholes	kilometer (km)	kilogram (kg)	kiloliter (kl)

The metric system has several advantages over the customary system. First, since the metric system uses the base-10 place value system, instruction in decimals directly relates to measurement skills. With customary units, different place value base systems are required for weight (16 ounces), length (12 inches, 3 feet), and so on. Second, in the customary system, there is no commonality among the units for various measurements, while there is commonality among the metric units. The prefixes in the metric system ("milli-," "centi-," "deci-," "deka-," "hecto-," "kilo-") are used in each area: length, weight, and capacity.

Table 12.1 includes the various customary and metric units for expressing length, weight, and capacity. Note the consistency of the metric system. The prefix in front of a unit tells the unit's relation to the base unit. At the same time, note how the various units in the customary system are different from one another.

A concern of many teachers is not whether to teach about the metric system but rather whether both systems should be taught simultaneously and, if not, which should be taught first. Unfortunately, there is no simple answer to this question. However, we have noticed that lower-performing students are likely to confuse facts from one system with facts from the other system when both are introduced concurrently. This information leads us to recommend that the two systems be taught independently of one another, preferably at different times during the year. Low-performing students should be familiar with common units from one system before the other system is introduced.

During the early grades, measurement instruction is relatively simple. Common units and equivalences are introduced, and students use tools to measure objects to the nearest whole unit. During the later elementary grades, measurement instruction becomes more complex as less commonly used units are introduced and more sophisticated uses of measuring tools are presented. Conversion problems in which students must convert a quantity expressed as one unit to a larger or smaller unit (5 meters = 500 centimeters) also are introduced.

Common Units and Equivalencies

During the early grades, students learn the more common units and their equivalencies. See **Figure 12.1** for a table of commonly taught measurement facts. The basic procedure for introducing new units to students includes five steps. The teacher does the following:

1. Tells the function of the specific unit; for example, "Inches tell how long something is. We use inches to measure objects that are not very long. Feet also tell how long something is. We use feet to measure objects that are pretty long."

2. Illustrates the unit; for example, the teacher draws lines on the board and shows students the length of an inch or a foot. For demonstrating weight, the teacher might give students blocks weighing an ounce or a pound.

3. Demonstrates how to use measuring tools, measuring to the nearest whole unit.

4. Presents application exercises in which the students determine the appropriate tool to use when measuring an object; for example, "What unit would we use to tell how long a piece of paper is? What unit would we use to tell how long the whiteboard is?"

5. Presents an equivalency fact, such as 12 inches equals one foot.

FIGURE 12.1   Measurement facts

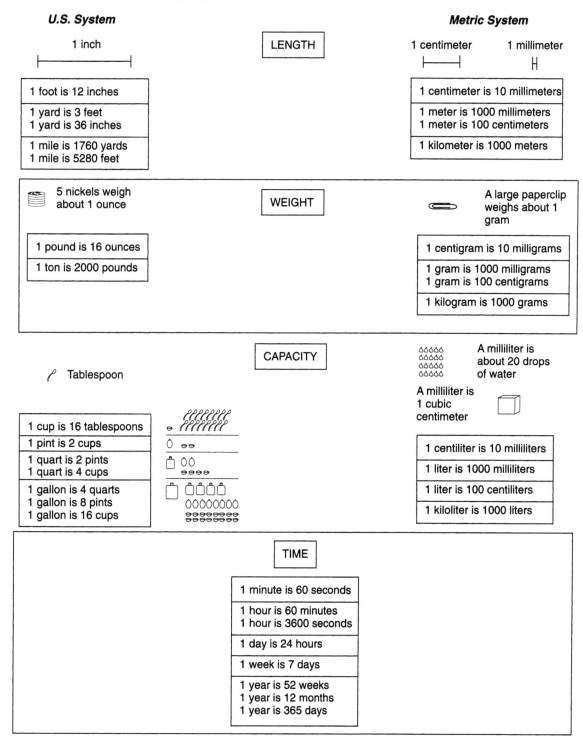

FIGURE 12.2   **Measurement review worksheet**

Circle or fill in the answer.

1. A pencil is about 6 _____ long.		feet	pounds	inches	pints
2. A cat weighs about 8 _____.		feet	pounds	inches	pints
3. A woman is about 5 _____ tall.		feet	pounds	inches	pints
4. He drinks a _____ of milk every day.		foot	pound	inch	pint
5. How many inches in a foot?		_____			
6. How many feet in a yard?		_____			
7. How many ounces in a pound?		_____			
8. How many pints in a quart?		_____			
9. About how many pounds does a dog weigh?		2	20	200	
10. About how many feet high is a door?		8	80	800	

Application exercises (step 4) and equivalencies (step 5) should incorporate review of previously introduced units from all areas. For example, if students have learned inch, foot, ounce, pound, and pint, a representative set of questions might include: "What unit would we use to tell how tall a person is? What unit would we use to tell how much a person weighs? What unit would we use to tell how much a letter weighs? What unit would we use to tell how long a pencil is?"

Equivalency review might include these questions: "How many ounces in a pound? How many inches in a foot? How many pints in a quart?" Review can be provided daily in worksheet exercises. A sample worksheet appears in **Figure 12.2**.

In addition to worksheet exercises, the teacher should incorporate measurement tasks into daily activities. Scales, thermometers, rulers, and liquid containers should be readily accessible. Teachers should provide opportunities for students to use measuring skills with concrete objects.

The sequence and rate of instruction for measurement facts and skills must be carefully controlled. New information is introduced cumulatively. That is, a new piece of information is not introduced until mastery of prior skills and information is demonstrated. Also, cumulative review of previously introduced information should be incorporated into daily exercises that introduce new skills.

In later elementary grades, after decimals have been taught, exercises designed to teach students about the structure of the metric system should be presented. **Format 12.1: Metric Prefixes** shows the steps for teaching students the prefixes for the metric system. In Parts A and B, the teacher presents the meaning of the prefixes. The prefixes for units less than 1 ("milli-," "centi-," and "deci-") are presented in Part A. Note that the teacher must emphasize the /th/ ending of the words "thousandth," "hundredth," and "tenth" so that students will note they are fractions and pronounce them correctly. In Part B, the teacher presents the prefixes indicating units greater than 1 ("deka-," "hecto-," and "kilo-"). Depending on the level of students, a week or more of practice may be required to teach the meanings of these prefixes. The teacher should not go on to Part C until the students demonstrate knowledge of all the metric prefixes that have been introduced.

Part C teaches students to use their knowledge of metric prefixes to tell the value of metric units. For example, the teacher models by saying, "Since *milli-* means "a thousandth," *milligram* refers to a thousandth of a gram." Part D is a structured worksheet exercise in which students must find and circle the numerical representation of a specific metric unit. For example, a worksheet problem may ask students to identify the amount that equals a centimeter from the following choices: 100 meters, .01 meter, .10 meter. Note that the ability to read decimal numerals is a prerequisite for this task. Daily worksheet exercises would continue for several weeks.

Abbreviations for metric units also should be introduced in a worksheet exercise. Note that students may have difficulty translating the abbreviation to its corresponding word. Prior to introducing a worksheet exercise, teachers should devote instructional time to teaching metric abbreviations.

Measuring Tools

Calibrated measurement instruments include rulers, scales, and thermometers. Every calibrated instrument is divided into segments representing specific quantities. The easiest type of instrument to read is one in which each line represents one unit. For example, on most rulers found in kindergarten classrooms, each line represents one inch; likewise, on many weather thermometers, each line represents one degree.

Often, instruments label only some of the lines that stand for quantities:

Those instruments require students to figure out what the unmarked lines represent before they are able to read them. Instruments like the ruler and scales found in grocery stores often contain lines that represent fractions of a unit (¼ inch, ⅛ pound). In the early grades, students learn to measure to the nearest whole unit, for example, length to the nearest inch (or centimeter) and weight to the nearest pound (or kilogram).

The ruler is often the first measuring tool introduced. The teacher would explain that the numerals on the ruler indicate how many inches from the end of the ruler to the line corresponding to that numeral. The teacher then models using the ruler to measure several lines or objects, pointing out the need to properly align the front end of the ruler and the beginning of the line or object being measured. Finally, the teacher has the students practice using the ruler.

For measuring weight using a calibrated scale, the students would put an object on the scale and read the numeral closest to the pointer. For measuring capacity, the students would fill a container with water, pour the water into a calibrated flask, and read the numeral closest to the water level. When teaching students to use measuring tools on which a line represents each unit but the relative value of each line is not shown:

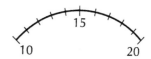

the teacher models how to count from the last given unit to the target unit. In the example below, the teacher models counting from 25, touching and counting each line—25, 26, 27, 28—to the quantity.

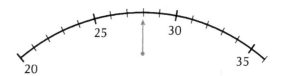

In later grades, students are taught to read fractional parts of units. For example, once students can read rulers to the nearest inch, they can be introduced to rulers that include fractional parts. Rulers in the customary system are usually calibrated to allow measurement to the closest sixteenth of an inch. Because the different marks on the rulers tend to confuse students, we recommend preparing a set of rulers that includes a progression of fractional parts. In the first ruler, each inch is divided into halves. In the second ruler, each inch is divided into fourths. In the third and fourth rulers, each inch is divided respectively into eighths and sixteenths of an inch. **Figure 12.3** illustrates a recommended set of rulers. Note that a preskill for using these tools is the ability to read and write mixed fractions.

A ruler in which an inch is divided into a greater number of parts is introduced only after students have demonstrated mastery in using the preceding ruler in the set.

A simple model-test procedure can be used to teach students to read units to the nearest half-inch. The teacher points out that since the line between the numerals divides the inch into two equal parts, each line represents a half-inch. The same procedure is used to introduce rulers divided into fourths. The teacher points out that since there are four parts between each inch, each inch is divided into fourths. The teacher then models and tests, reading the ruler starting at the ¼-inch mark: ¼, ²⁄₄, ¾, 1, 1¼, 1²⁄₄, 1¾, 2, and so on. Note that the teacher would not have the students read ²⁄₄ as ½ at this time to emphasize that ¼-inch is the unit of measurement.

FIGURE 12.3 Recommended set of rulers

a. Marked to the nearest half of an inch

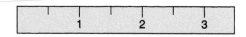

b. Marked to the nearest quarter of an inch

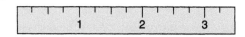

c. Marked to the nearest eighth of an inch

d. Marked to the nearest sixteenth of an inch (standard rulers)

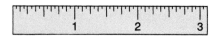

The teacher then presents an exercise in which she points to a line on the ruler and has students identify the measurement.

When students can identify the lengths represented by fourths on the ruler, the teacher can present an exercise to teach that the line that indicates $\frac{2}{4}$ of an inch also is the line that indicates $\frac{1}{2}$ of an inch. The teacher explains that the line is in the middle of the inch and so divides it into halves. The teacher explains further that when using a ruler, the length is always reported with the smallest numerical denominator. Therefore, instead of saying a line is $3\frac{2}{4}$ inches, the line is said to be $3\frac{1}{2}$ inches. A practice exercise in which the teacher has the students find the lines on the ruler that represent various distances would follow the explanation ("Find the line on the ruler that shows $4\frac{1}{2}$ inches. Find the line that shows $2\frac{1}{4}$ inches," etc.). Practice can be provided in worksheet exercises like the one in **Figure 12.4**.

Rulers in which each inch is divided into eighths are introduced when students (a) can use rulers in which each inch is divided into fourths and (b) have learned fraction equivalency skills. Students should have had enough practice rewriting $\frac{6}{8}$ as $\frac{3}{4}$, $\frac{4}{8}$ as $\frac{1}{2}$, and $\frac{2}{8}$ as $\frac{1}{4}$ so that they can make these conversions with ease. The teacher introduces the ruler containing eighths by pointing out that since each inch is divided into eight parts, the lines tell about eighths of an inch. The teacher then has students read the lines on the ruler representing eighths ($\frac{1}{8}$, $\frac{2}{8}$, $\frac{3}{8}$, $\frac{4}{8}$, $\frac{5}{8}$, $\frac{6}{8}$, $\frac{7}{8}$, $1\frac{1}{8}$).

After several days, the teacher presents exercises teaching students to express $\frac{2}{8}$, $\frac{4}{8}$, and $\frac{6}{8}$ as $\frac{1}{4}$, $\frac{1}{2}$, and $\frac{3}{4}$, respectively. The teacher reminds students that length is always reported with fractions expressed in their simplest, smallest possible terms, and then he models and tests the various equivalencies.

The same basic procedure is followed for introducing rulers in which each inch is divided into sixteenths. These rulers should not be introduced, however, until students are comfortable using the ruler divided into eighths. Daily practice over a long period is needed to develop student fluency in these skills.

FIGURE 12.4 Worksheet exercise for determining length

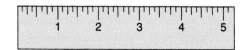

Make an X over the line that indicates $3\frac{3}{4}$ inches.
Make an R over the line that indicates $2\frac{1}{2}$ inches.
Make an S over the line that indicates $\frac{5}{8}$ of an inch.
Make a B over the line that indicates $2\frac{3}{8}$ inches.

Conversion Problems

This section addresses problems in which students must convert a quantity expressed as one unit into an equal quantity expressed in terms of a larger or smaller unit; for example, 3 feet can be converted to 36 inches, 2 meters to 200 centimeters. The preskill for conversion problems is knowledge of equivalencies. Students cannot convert 5 kilograms to grams unless they know the number of grams in 1 kilogram. Conversion problems should not be taught until students have mastered the necessary equivalencies.

There are four basic steps in any conversion problem: (a) determine whether the "new" unit is larger or smaller than the original unit, (b) determine the operation, (c) determine the equivalency fact, and (d) solve the problem. These steps are listed in **Summary Box 12.1**.

Converting Metric Units   Early elementary grade teachers should limit examples of conversions with small quantities of common units (5 meters = _____ centimeters). In later grades, teachers can present the conversion strategy with larger numbers. Below is a description of the procedure for teaching conversion with metric units. Before the metric conversion strategy is introduced, students should know the equivalencies of the metric units, be able to read and write mixed decimals and decimal numerals, and be able to multiply and divide by multiples of 10 by moving the decimal point to the right or the left. When dividing, the decimal point is moved to the left. For example, when dividing by 10, the decimal point is moved one place to the left ($75 \div 10 = 7.5$); by 100, two places ($75 \div 100 = .75$); by 1,000, three places to the left ($75 \div 1000 = .075$). When multiplying, the decimal point is moved to the right. Instructions for teaching multiplying decimals by multiples of 10 appears in Chapter 14, "Decimals," in **Format 14.9: Preskill: Multiplying Decimals by Multiples of 10**. A similar exercise would be used to teach students to divide by multiples of 10.

Before beginning conversion exercises, the teacher should give students worksheets like the one in **Figure 12.5**, designed to provide practice in dividing and multiplying by multiples of 10. The discussion in Chapter 14 on multiplying decimals by multiples of 10 specifies types of examples to include in these worksheet exercises. In some multiplication problems, students should have to add one or more zeros ($100 \times 3.5 = 350.0$). In some division problems, students should have to add a zero in front of the original digits ($3.5 \div 100 = .035$). Such examples are difficult and require initial modeling and extended practice over several weeks.

SUMMARY BOX 12.1

Steps in Basic Conversion Problems

	Problem a	Problem b	Problem c	Problem d
1. Determine whether the new quantity is a bigger or smaller unit.	48 inches = _____ feet Change inches to feet. Feet is a bigger unit.	3 pounds = _____ ounces Change pounds to ounces. Ounces is a smaller unit.	5 kilograms = _____ grams Change kilograms to grams. Grams is a smaller unit.	300 centimeters = _____ meters Change centimeters to meters. Meters is a bigger unit.
2. Determine the operation: Multiply if changing to a smaller unit; Divide if changing to a bigger unit.	Since change is to a bigger unit, division is required.	Since change is to a smaller unit, multiplication is required.	Since change is to a smaller unit, multiplication is required.	Since change is to a bigger unit, division is required.
3. Determine the equivalency fact.	12 inches in a foot	16 ounces in a pound	1,000 kilograms in a gram	100 centimeters in a meter
4. Solve the problem.	48 inches ÷ 12 = 4 feet	3 pounds × 16 = 48 ounces	5 kilograms × 1000 = 5,000 grams	300 centimeters ÷ 100 = 3 meters

FIGURE 12.5   Worksheet on multiplying and dividing by 10

a. $37 \times 100 =$ _____	b. $4 \div 1000 =$ _____	c. $53.2 \times 100 =$ _____	d. $7.04 \times 10 =$ _____
e. $4.8 \times 1000 =$ _____	f. $28.5 \div 10 =$ _____	g. $72 \times 1000 =$ _____	h. $.37 \times 100 =$ _____
i. $7 \div 100 =$ _____	j. $.37 \times 100 =$ _____	k. $5.43 \times 10 =$ _____	l. $.4 \times 1000 =$ _____
m. $37 \div 10 =$ _____	n. $4.2 \div 10 =$ _____	o. $72 \div 10 =$ _____	p. $38 \div 10 =$ _____
q. $52 \times 100 =$ _____	r. $4.8 \div 1000 =$ _____	s. $400 \div 1000 =$ _____	t. $52 \div 100 =$ _____

**Format 12.2B:
Metric Conversions**

Watch how Kristen introduces
the metric conversion rule.

**Format 12.2C: Metric
Conversions**

Watch how Kristen introduces
her students to all of the steps of
the conversion strategy.

A format for presenting the conversion strategy appears in **Format 12.2: Metric Conversions**. As mentioned earlier, this format assumes that students have mastered the metric equivalencies. If students have not learned the equivalency preskills, they will find the conversion exercises quite difficult and frustrating. The format contains four parts: Parts A and B teach important component skills. Part A teaches students to determine whether they are changing the original unit to a bigger or smaller unit. Part B presents the rules: When we change to a bigger unit, we divide; when we change to a smaller unit, we multiply. Part B concludes with an exercise in which the teacher writes sets of units on the board, such as centigram → gram, and leads the students in determining the appropriate operation.

Part C is a structured board presentation in which the teacher presents all the steps in the conversion strategy. After the students determine whether to multiply or divide, the teacher leads them through using the equivalency fact to determine the number by which to multiply or divide. "There are 100 centigrams in a gram, so we divide by 100." Finally, the teacher demonstrates moving the decimal as a quick way of multiplying or dividing by multiples of 10. Part D is a structured worksheet exercise. Because this exercise incorporates several difficult component skills, a great amount of practice is necessary to develop mastery.

Four example-selection guidelines are important in teaching conversion problems:

1. In all problems, one of the units should be a base unit. The base units are grams, meters, or liters.
2. In half of the problems, the students should convert a unit to a larger unit; in the other half, the students should convert to a smaller unit.
3. In half of the problems, the quantity of original units should be a whole number; in the other half, the quantity should be a decimal or mixed number.
4. The amount the student multiplies or divides should vary from problem to problem, for example, 10 in one problem, 1,000 in the next, 100 in the next.

An example of an appropriate set of problems, following the guidelines, appears below. The answers are in parentheses.

    142 centigrams = _____ grams (1.42)
    9.8 grams = _____ milligrams (9,800)
    35 decigrams = _____ grams (3.5)
    20 hectograms = _____ grams (2,000)
    4.35 grams = _____ milligrams (4,350)

Note that the examples shown in **Format 12.2: Metric Conversions** all refer to grams. The next day's unit of measurement might include liters or meters.

Converting Customary Units   Teaching students to convert quantities from one unit to another is more difficult in the customary system than in the metric system for three specific reasons. First, in metric conversions the students always multiply or divide by a multiple of 10, but in conversion problems with customary units, the number to multiply or divide by varies from problem to problem; converting inches to feet requires division by 12, and converting feet to yards requires division by 3.

A second reason for increased difficulty involves the procedures used when the converted unit is not a multiple of the original unit. In that case, the answer must be expressed in terms of a mixed number with two different units (7 feet = 2 yards, 1 foot).

A final reason why customary conversions are more difficult is that conversions are sometimes made to a unit two or more steps removed. In the metric system, the original unit is simply multiplied or divided by 10, 100, or 1,000. In the customary system, several conversions may be required. For example, to convert gallons to cups, the student must first convert gallons to quarts, quarts to pints, then pints to cups.

The sequence for introducing conversion problems with customary units should be carefully controlled, with easier problems introduced first. The three basic types of conversion problems in the customary system are illustrated below:

1. Converting a quantity of a specified unit into a quantity of the next larger or smaller unit (examples involve whole numerals only):

28 days equal _____ weeks
6 feet equal _____ yards
24 inches equal _____ feet
4 weeks equal _____ days
2 yards equal _____ feet
2 feet equal _____ inches

2. Converting a unit into a mixed numeral (and vice versa) containing the next larger or smaller quantity:

27 inches equal _____ feet _____ inches
19 ounces equal _____ pound(s) _____ ounces
13 days equal _____ weeks(s) _____ days
2 feet 3 inches equal _____ inches
1 pound 3 ounces equal _____ ounces

3. Converting a unit into a unit twice removed:

2 yards equal _____ inches
2 quarts equal _____ cups
72 inches equal _____ yards
16 cups equal _____ quarts

The preskills for teaching conversion problems with customary units are knowledge of equivalencies and knowledge of multiplication and division facts. Since measurement conversion tasks are usually introduced before students can divide by two-digit numbers, the teacher may choose to teach the students to count by twelves. Knowing this count-by series will help students in converting inches to feet and in determining dozens.

The format for introducing the first type of customary conversion problems (problems in which a unit is converted evenly into the next larger or smaller unit) is basically the same as that for converting metric units (see **Format 12.2: Metric Conversions**). The teacher has students (a) determine whether the "new" unit is larger or smaller than the original unit, (b) determine the operation, (c) determine the equivalency fact, and (d) solve the problem. "We want to find how many ounces in 6 pounds. We're changing to a smaller unit, so we multiply. There are 16 ounces in a pound, so we multiply by 16."

The procedure for problems in which the conversion results in a remainder (27 inches equal 2 feet 3 inches) is the same as for the previous type of problem except the teacher must explain what to do with the remainder. For example, in solving the problem 27 inches = _____ feet, after the students determine that 27 must be divided by 12, the teacher points out that since 12 goes into 27 with a remainder, the remainder tells the number of inches left.

A format for converting a mixed quantity to a lower unit appears in **Format 12.3: Converting from Mixed Numbers**. When converting 2 feet 11 inches to inches, the teacher has the students cross out the 2 and write 24, the number of inches, above it. Then they add that quantity, 24 inches, to the 11 inches to end up with 35 inches.

Problems in which students must convert to a unit twice removed are quite difficult (2 yards = _____ inches). The strategy we recommend involves having the students translate the quantity unit by unit. For example, in converting 2 yards to inches, the student would first convert 2 yards to 6 feet, then 6 feet to 72 inches.

Operations

This section addresses addition, subtraction, multiplication, and division operations with measurement units. As with most measurement-related skills, performing operations with customary units is more difficult than performing operations with metric units. The differences arise in problems that require renaming. Since the metric system uses a base-10 place value system, renaming presents no problems. Students merely apply the renaming skills they learned previously in decimal instruction. However, when working with customary units, there is not a consistent base to use when renaming. For example, the base for pounds is 16 (16 ounces in one pound); for feet, 12 (12 inches in one foot). Students must be taught to use these bases rather than base 10 for problems that require renaming.

Addition and subtraction problems with measurement units are usually introduced in fourth or fifth grade. The operations cause little difficulty in measurement problems that do not involve renaming:

$$
\begin{array}{l}
6\text{ lb }4\text{ oz} \\
\underline{+1\text{ lb }1\text{ oz}} \\
7\text{ lb }5\text{ oz}
\end{array}
\qquad
\begin{array}{l}
6\text{ lb }4\text{ oz} \\
\underline{-1\text{ lb }1\text{ oz}} \\
5\text{ lb }3\text{ oz}
\end{array}
\qquad
\begin{array}{l}
6\text{ lb }4\text{ oz} \\
\underline{\times2\phantom{\text{ lb oz}}} \\
12\text{ lb }8\text{ oz}
\end{array}
$$

$$
\begin{array}{l}
3\text{ lb }2\text{ oz} \\
2\overline{)6\text{ lb }4\text{ oz}}
\end{array}
\qquad
\begin{array}{l}
6.4\text{ kg} \\
\underline{+1.1\text{ kg}} \\
7.5\text{ kg}
\end{array}
\qquad
\begin{array}{l}
6.4\text{ kg} \\
\underline{+1.1\text{ kg}} \\
5.3\text{ kg}
\end{array}
$$

$$
\begin{array}{l}
6.4\text{ kg} \\
\underline{\times2\phantom{\text{ kg}}} \\
12.8\text{ kg}
\end{array}
\qquad
\begin{array}{l}
3.2\text{ kg} \\
2\overline{)6.4\text{ kg}}
\end{array}
$$

Problems that do require renaming, on the other hand, are quite difficult:

$$
\begin{array}{l}
\overset{4}{\cancel{5}}\text{ lb }\ \overset{18}{\cancel{2}}\text{ oz} \\
\underline{-3\text{ lb }4\text{ oz}} \\
1\text{ lb }14\text{ oz}
\end{array}
\qquad
\begin{array}{l}
\overset{1}{} \\
3\text{ weeks }4\text{ days} \\
\underline{+1\text{ weeks }5\text{ days}} \\
5\text{ weeks }\overset{\cancel{9}}{\underset{2}{}}\text{ days}
\end{array}
\qquad
\begin{array}{l}
\overset{4}{\cancel{5}}\text{ ft }\overset{14}{\cancel{2}}\text{ in} \\
\underline{-2\text{ ft }8\text{ in}} \\
\underline{-2\text{ ft }6\text{ in}}
\end{array}
$$

A preskill for renaming problems is converting units, which was discussed previously. When working an addition problem, the teacher instructs students to always start working with the smaller unit. The difficult part of addition problems occurs after students have derived a sum that includes enough of the smaller unit to form a larger unit. In the following problem,

$$
\begin{array}{l}
3\text{ ft }\ \ 8\text{ in} \\
\underline{+2\text{ ft }\ \ 6\text{ in}} \\
\phantom{+2\text{ ft }\ \ }14\text{ in}
\end{array}
$$

the students add 8 and 6 to equal 14 inches, which is more than 1 foot. Because 12 inches equals 1 foot, the student must add 1 unit to the feet column and subtract the 12 inches from the 14 inches, leaving the remaining 2 inches.

$$
\begin{array}{l}
\phantom{+3\text{ ft }\ \ }\overset{1}{} \\
3\text{ ft }\ \ 8\text{ in} \\
\underline{+2\text{ ft }\ \ 6\text{ in}} \\
\phantom{+2\text{ ft }\ \ }\overset{\cancel{14}}{\underset{2}{}}
\end{array}
$$

The teacher leads students through sets of problems, renaming when needed: "Remember, we're adding inches. How many inches in a foot? Yes, 12 inches in a foot. So if we have 12 or more inches in the inches column, we must rename 12 inches as one foot."

Format 12.4: Renaming Customary Units shows how to teach addition problems with renaming. Teaching students when to rename and what numerals to use is critical when teaching operations with customary units. Part A of the structured board presentation focuses on when renaming is appropriate. Part B is a structured worksheet that provides discrimination practice in renaming with the appropriate numerals. Note that discrimination practice should include problems that require renaming and problems that do not require renaming. The examples in the format involve weight units; similar exercises should be done with length and capacity units.

After students can rename a variety of units when adding, they are given problems with subtraction. The difficult aspect of subtraction problems lies in renaming the minuend. For example, to work the following problem,

$$8 \text{ lb } 4 \text{ oz}$$
$$-3 \text{ lb } 8 \text{ oz}$$

students must rename 8 pounds 4 ounces, by taking a pound from 8 pounds (leaving 7 pounds), and increasing the ounces by 16 ounces (a pound) so there are 20 ounces:

$$\begin{array}{c} 7 \quad 20 \\ 8 \text{ lb } 4 \text{ oz} \\ -3 \text{ lb } 8 \text{ oz} \end{array}$$

We recommend that teachers introduce this skill by first presenting problems in which a mixed unit is subtracted from a whole unit. Following are examples of such problems:

$$\begin{array}{cc} 3 \text{ ft} & 8 \text{ lb} \\ -1 \text{ ft } 4 \text{ in} & -2 \text{ lb } 5 \text{ oz} \end{array}$$

The teacher leads students through working these problems, pointing out the need to rename and how to rename: "We must take a foot from 3 feet. I'll cross out 3 feet and write 2. I took a foot from 3 feet. How many inches in a foot? So I write 12 in the inches column." After several days of practice, more difficult problems in which two mixed numbers are involved can be introduced. An example of a structured worksheet part of a format for subtraction problems with renaming appears in **Format 12.5: Subtraction with Renaming**.

Multiplication and division problems that require renaming with measurement units are quite difficult. A strategy for working multiplication problems involves teaching the students to first multiply each unit. For example, in the problem

$$\begin{array}{c} 5 \text{ ft } 7 \text{ in} \\ \times \quad 4 \end{array}$$

the students first multiply 4×7 inches, then 4×5 feet, writing the products for each:

$$\begin{array}{c} 5 \text{ ft } 7 \text{ in} \\ \times \quad 4 \\ \hline 20 \text{ ft } 28 \text{ in} \end{array}$$

After the products are written for each unit, the students rename, converting the smaller quantity and adding:

$$\begin{array}{c} 5 \text{ ft } 7 \text{ in} \\ \times \quad 4 \\ \hline 20 \text{ ft } 28 \text{ in} \\ 2 \text{ ft } \quad 4 \text{ in} \\ \hline 22 \text{ ft } \quad 4 \text{ in} \end{array}$$

Division problems, on the other hand, require a unique strategy. The students rewrite the quantity in terms of its lower units before working the problem. For example, in dividing 3 pounds 4 ounces by 2, we suggest converting 3 pounds 4 ounces to 52 ounces, dividing 52 by 2, which equals 26 ounces, then converting the 26 ounces to 1 pound 10 ounces.

Word Problems

Word problems involving measurement units can be introduced as soon as students have learned to work the respective operations. The strategies are the same as outlined in Chapter 11. Students may require explicit instruction when solving measurement word problems. Initial modeling and extensive practice are required with the introduction of each operation. Following are examples of measurement word problems for different operations:

Division:

> Marshawn has 2 feet of ribbon. He wants to make kites. Each kite needs 4 inches of ribbon. How many kites can Marshawn make?

Subtraction:

> Tania weighed 8 pounds, 4 ounces when she was born. Three months later, she weighed 11 pounds, 7 ounces. How much weight did she gain in those 3 months?

Multi-step:

> Rose's plant is 4 feet tall. If it grows 3 inches a year for 5 years, how tall will it be?

TIME

Telling time is not as easy for all students to learn as teachers sometimes assume. Its difficulty is due to the number of discriminations students must make. The following list outlines discriminations that, if not properly taught, tend to cause errors, especially for low-performing students:

1. Discriminating the direction the clock hands move (clockwise versus counter-clockwise);
2. Discriminating the minute hand from the hour hand;
3. Discriminating minutes (which are not represented by the numerals on the clock) from hours (which are represented by the numerals on the clock) and;
4. Discriminating time-related vocabulary; for example, when to use "after" and when to use "before."

Because of these potentially troublesome discriminations, telling time is divided into two stages. First, students are taught a strategy for figuring out the time and expressing it as minutes after the hour. Second, when students have mastered minutes after the hour, alternate ways of telling time are taught, such as reading a digital clock, using the terms "quarter past" and "half past," and expressing time as minutes before the hour. See the Instructional Sequence and Assessment Chart for details and examples.

Minutes After the Hour

Preskills   The four major preskills for telling time are (a) knowledge of the direction in which the hands of the clock move, (b) discrimination of the hour hand from the minute hand, (c) counting by fives, and (d) switching from counting by fives to counting by ones, which is needed to determine the number of minutes (5, 10, 15, 16, 17, 18, 19).

The preskill of knowing which direction the hands on a clock move is critical if students are to figure out the correct hour. A convenient way to teach students about direction on a clock is to have them fill in the missing numerals on several clocks containing boxes instead of numerals:

By doing this exercise, students can develop the pattern of moving in a clockwise direction around the clock face. In the first exercises, some of the numerals should be included as prompts on the clock (3, 6, 9, 12). After several lessons, however, these prompts should be removed, and the students should fill in all the numerals themselves. Teachers need to monitor students carefully while they work to make sure they fill in numerals in the proper direction. Teachers also can use a clock with movable hands and ask students to move the clock hands in the appropriate direction to assess student understanding of the concept.

Counting by fives is the initial way students are taught to determine the number of minutes. They are taught to start at the top of the clock, say, zero, and then count the numerals by fives until they reach the minute hand. Later, the procedure is modified to teach students to determine the number of minutes when the minute hand is not pointing to a multiple of 5. Procedures for teaching counting by fives can be found in Chapter 4.

Discrimination of the hour hand from the minute hand is taught by describing each hand (the short hand is the hour hand, and the long hand is the minute hand) and then by providing discrimination practice in which students identify the hands. The teacher should present pictures of clocks and ask about each hand: "Which hand is this? How do you know it's the minute hand? Yes, the long hand is the minute hand." Commercial instructional clocks are well-suited for this exercise because teachers can manipulate the hands of the clock. The hands on the clocks used for initial instruction should be easy to tell apart.

Units of 5 Minutes   The steps for teaching students to tell time by determining the number of minutes (in units of 5) after the hour is divided into five parts. (See **Format 12.6: Expressing Time as Minutes After the Hour**.) Part A teaches students to read the hour. The teacher reminds students that the hour hand is the short hand and demonstrates how to figure out the hour by starting at the top of the clock and saying the numerals on the clock until reaching the hour hand.

Part B teaches students to determine the number of minutes after the hour. The teacher instructs students that the long hand is the minute hand and that the minute hand says to count by fives. The teacher then models and tests figuring out the minutes. The students are taught to start at the 12, say zero, and then count by 5 for each numeral, stopping at the numeral to which the minute hand is pointing. All examples in this format would have the minute hand pointing directly to a numeral.

Part C includes a board demonstration of how the strategies for determining minutes and hours are combined into a complete strategy for figuring out the time. Parts D and E are structured and less structured worksheet exercises in which the students are shown clocks and asked to write the time. Daily practice with telling time should be continued for several weeks until students have mastered the concepts.

To help students discriminate the hour and minute hands, we recommend that for the first several days, teachers use illustrations like the one below, in which the minute hand is drawn longer than usual. Note that in the illustration, the minute hand extends outside the clock and is written as a thin line so that it does not block students' view of the numerals on the clock.

When constructing a set of practice examples, the teacher must be quite careful to include a wide range of problems. In half of the clocks, the hour hand should be pointing toward the right side of the clock; on the other clocks, the hour hand should be pointing toward the left side of the clock. The same recommendation holds true for the minute hand. Varying examples helps prevent students from developing misrules that the strategies apply only to certain positions on the clock.

Also, examples should be arranged so that in half of the examples, the minute hand is pointing to a numeral larger than the one to which the hour hand is pointing. If the minute hand were pointing to the smaller numeral in all the examples, students might inadvertently learn that the hand pointing to the smaller numeral is the minute hand.

For the first week or two, examples in which the minute hand is pointing to the 12 are expressed as zero minutes after the hour. When students have demonstrated the ability to use the minutes-after strategy, the teacher can present the convention for saying o'clock. "When it's zero minutes after 4, we say it is 4 o'clock."

As students learn multiplication facts, they should be encouraged to use their knowledge of facts in determining the minutes rather than always starting at the top and counting by fives. The teacher explains that in figuring out minutes, each numeral stands for a group of five. Therefore, when the minute hand points to 4, it is the same as four groups of five. Instead of counting, the minutes can be determined by solving 4×5.

Units of Single Minutes   After several weeks of practice expressing time with examples in which the minute hand points directly to a numeral, students can learn to express time when the minute hand is pointing between numerals. Note the following example:

No elaborate teaching format is required to introduce this skill. Students are told that when they count the spaces in between the numerals, they are counting by ones. The teacher then models the process of counting by fives and switching to ones: "5, 10, 15, 20, 21, 22, 23; the time is 23 minutes after 7."

Alternate Ways of Expressing Time

Digital Clocks   When students are able to express time as minutes after the hour, digital clocks may be introduced. The time on digital clocks is represented by the hour followed by the minutes. For example, 3:14 is read as three-fourteen, which means 14 minutes after 3. Prior to introducing digital clocks, students need to be taught to translate minutes after the hour to the hour followed by the minutes. The teacher would model and have students practice expressing time in both ways, such as:

"I'll say the time one way, and then say it another way. Listen: 8:24. I'll say the time the other way: 24 minutes after 8. Your turn: 8:24. Say the time the other way." Repeat with 4:15, 7:32, 9:28.

The purpose of this practice is to ensure that students understand the relationship between these two ways of expressing time before they are introduced to digital clocks. To teach students to read a digital clock, the teacher simply models and tests several examples of telling time on a digital clock.

After students have learned to read time from analog and digital clocks, students can be taught how to write time using a colon. A written task, like the one below, in which students are required to express the time as both minutes after the hour and as the hour and then minutes, should be introduced next. This activity not only strengthens the relationship between telling time as minutes after the hour and the hour followed by minutes but also provides practice in writing time using a colon.

_____ minutes after _____

_____ : _____

Times representing less than 10 minutes after the hour are particularly difficult to write, since a zero must be added when the time is expressed both verbally and in written form. For example, 8 minutes after 6 is written as 6:08 and stated as six oh eight. This type of example should not be introduced until students have mastered easier ones. Several of these more difficult examples should appear thereafter on worksheet exercises.

Quarter After and Half Past   The terms "quarter after" and "half past" are introduced when students master expressing time as minutes after the hour: A "quarter after" means 15 minutes after; "half past" means 30 minutes after. Teachers working with struggling students would not introduce both terms at the same time. The instructional procedure for teaching "quarter after" consists of modeling and testing on several examples:

1. Another way of saying 15 minutes after 2 is a quarter after two.
2. What's another way of saying 15 minutes after 2?
3. What's another way of saying 15 minutes after 8?

Next, an exercise in which the teacher states the time as a quarter after and the students restate it as minutes after is presented: "If it's a quarter after 2, how many minutes after 2 is it?" The same procedure is used to teach half past the hour. The final task consists of a discrimination exercise including times representing both quarter after and half past the hour:

1. What's another way of saying 15 minutes after 6?
2. What's another way of saying 30 minutes after 6?
3. If it's half past 4, how many minutes after 4 is it?
4. If it's a quarter after 4, how many minutes after 4 is it?

Minutes Before the Hour   Teachers should not introduce telling time as minutes before the hour until students can express time as minutes after the hour with accuracy and fluency. The procedure for teaching students to express time as minutes before the hour is somewhat similar to the one used for teaching students to express time as minutes after the hour. First, the teacher presents a strategy to figure out the hour, then a strategy to figure out the minutes, and then an exercise in which both strategies are applied to express the time. Format 12.7: Expressing Time as Minutes Before the Hour outlines the steps in this strategy.

In Part A, the teacher places the hour hand between two numerals and then models and tests identifying the hour after and the hour before. For example, if the hour hand were pointing between 5 and 6, the teacher would say the hour is after 5 and before 6. In Part B, the teacher shows students how to figure out the number of minutes before the hour. He points in a counterclockwise direction and explains that in determining minutes before the hour, students need to start at the 12 but count in "this" direction (pointing counterclockwise). He would model and test several examples before introducing Part C, a structured board exercise in which the teacher leads students through expressing time as minutes before the hour. Part D is a structured worksheet that provides practice expressing time as minutes before the hour.

During the first week that expressing time as minutes before the hour is presented, the minute hand should point directly to the numerals so that all minutes are multiples of five. Examples in which the minute hand points to a line between the numerals are introduced later. Examples should be limited to times that are 30 minutes or less before the hour because typically those are the only times expressed as minutes before the hour.

MONEY

· · · · · · · ·

The need for instruction in money-related skills is derived from their importance in daily activities. Included in this chapter are procedures for (a) determining the value of a group of coins, (b) consumer-related instruction, and (c) decimal notation for money. A more in-depth list of problem types appears in the Instructional Sequence and Assessment Chart.

Determining the Value of a Group of Coins

The preskills for determining the value of a group of coins include the ability to identify and tell the value of individual coins and knowledge of the 5, 10, and 25 count-by series. Students usually are taught to identify coins in the first grade. This is a fairly simple preskill to teach, given that many students already will be able to recognize coins. A format similar to that used in symbol identification is taught for coin identification. The teacher initially models and tests the name of the coin and then models and tests its value: "This is a nickel. What is this? . . . A nickel is worth 5¢. How much is a nickel worth? . . . " For this task, the teacher can use either real coins or pictures of coins.

The penny and nickel should be introduced first. After students can label and state their values, dimes can be introduced, followed by quarters. Note that the coins are introduced cumulatively, which implies that students must be able to discriminate the new coin from previously introduced coins before the teacher can present a new example.

The preskill required for counting groups of similar coins is knowledge of the respective count-by series. Once students have learned the count-by series, they have little trouble applying the skill to coin counting. In teaching students to count groups of similar coins for the first time, the teacher indicates the value of the coin and then models counting. For example, "Here is a group of nickels. Each nickel is worth 5¢. To find out how many cents this group of nickels equals, I count by fives. My turn." The teacher then counts by fives as she touches each coin. After modeling, the teacher tests students on counting several sets of identical coins. Worksheet exercises like the one in **Figure 12.6** should follow the teacher's presentation.

Problems in which students determine the value of a set of mixed coins are usually introduced in second grade and contain just two or three coins. In later grades, the number of coins counted can be increased. We recommend a two-step strategy: (a) grouping like coins together and (b) starting with the coin worth the most and counting all like coins before counting the lower valued coins. For example, in counting two quarters, three dimes, and two nickels, students would begin counting the two quarters (25, 50), switch to the dimes (60, 70, 80), and switch once more to the nickels (85, 90).

Beginning with higher-valued coins is recommended over beginning with lower-valued coins, since counting lower-valued coins first often results in a difficult counting sequence. For example, to count a quarter, dime, nickel, and two pennies starting with the lower valued coins, the student would count 1, 2, 7, 17, 42; as opposed to starting with higher-valued coins and counting 25, 35, 40, 41, 42, which is much easier.

A preskill for counting a group of unlike coins is knowledge of addition facts in which 10, 5, or 1 is added to a two-digit number ending in zero or 5 (70 and 10 more is. . . 70 and 5 more is. . .). This preskill is taught using a model-test procedure in which the teacher models then tests students on a set of problems (40 and 10 more, 45 and 5 more, 40 and 1 more).

Facts in which 10 is added to a two-digit number ending in 5 (35 + 10, 65 + 10) are particularly difficult because the sequence of counting by 10s that always yields a tens multiple

FIGURE 12.6 Coin counting worksheet

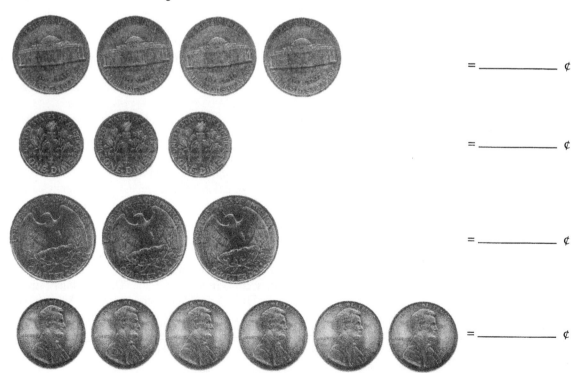

(10, 20, 30) cannot be applied. Therefore, these facts should not be introduced until the easier facts are mastered. If teachers use worksheets to provide this practice, they should write problems horizontally and indicate to students that they are to complete the problems mentally.

Determining equivalencies involving coins is a basic money skill that serves as a prerequisite for many consumer skills. Two kinds of equivalent change exercises are presented in Format 12.8: Coin Equivalencies. In Part A of the format, the teacher has students determine the number of smaller-valued coins equal to a larger-valued coin. In this exercise, students are always counting similar coins. In Part B of the format, the students must count a set of mixed coins to determine whether a given amount of change is equivalent to the amount stated. Initially, coin equivalency problems should include pennies, nickels, dimes, and quarters (a quarter equals two dimes and a nickel). Larger values, including dollar bills, are introduced later.

Worksheet exercises like **Figure 12.7** present a different application of the coin equivalency skill. In these exercises, students circle the appropriate more, less, or equal sign between two groups of coins. To introduce this exercise, the teacher leads the students in counting the coins in each group. After counting the coins, the students are instructed to write above each group its value. If the values are equal, the student is instructed to circle the equal sign. If the values of the groups are not equal, the students circle the appropriate more than or less than sign.

Consumer-Related Money Skills

Two consumer-related money skills are discussed in this section: (a) verifying the change received from a purchase and (b) counting change. These skills are generally taught in third grade. The primary preskill for counting change is the ability to count groups of coins.

Verifying Change Received   The easiest way to verify change received when making a purchase is to begin at the price of the item(s) and then count the coins received as change. **Format 12.9: Verifying Change** outlines the teaching procedures for this strategy. Students begin counting from the price of the item starting with the least valued coin, continuing with greater valued coins until the original amount given for the item is reached.

Initial examples should be relatively easy, including small numbers of coins. An example appropriate for the introduction of the skill might consist of paying 40¢ for an object costing 36¢. To verify the change in this example, students need to count only pennies: 37, 38, 39, 40. A later example might involve paying a dollar for an object costing 36¢, for which students would need to count pennies, dimes, and quarters.

Problems involving more than one dollar are introduced last. Note that the same strategy applies to counting change from dollars. The student counts the change to determine if the object's cost plus the change equals the payment price. For example, if an object costing 37¢ is paid for with a $10 bill, counting change would proceed as follows: 38, 39, 40, 50, 75, one dollar, 2, 3, 4, 5, 10 dollars. Again, practice is provided on worksheet exercises and through hands-on activities, such as a classroom store.

Counting Change   When purchasing an item in a store, the student should use a strategy that allows her to figure out the coins to give as quickly as possible. We recommend that students begin counting with the largest valued coins. For example, if a student has an assortment of coins and wants to buy something costing 28¢, the fastest way to count the exact amount is to use a quarter and three pennies. We recommend that the teacher introduce the rule "When

FIGURE 12.7   **Worksheet on equivalent change**

you count to reach an exact amount of money, you start with the coins that are worth the most." Next, the teacher models several examples and then gives students problems to solve. The steps for teaching this skill appear in Part A of Format 12.10: Counting Coins to Reach an Exact Amount. Because most cash registers display the exact amount of change to give, this procedure also can be used to teach students to count change as a store clerk would.

A mistake often made by students is inappropriately allocating only pennies for the value of the ones. For example, when counting out 38¢, students might count out 30¢ using a quarter and a nickel and then count out eight pennies instead of using a quarter (25), a dime (35), and 3 pennies. One way to prompt students to use larger coins when possible is to limit the number of pennies they are given during practice exercises, thereby forcing students to use nickels and dimes. Often, students will not have the appropriate coins to allow them to count an exact amount. For these situations, students must be taught to count an amount that exceeds the purchase price. Part B of Format 12.10 teaches students to make a purchase when they don't have the exact amount of change.

Decimal Notation in Money

Money problems expressed in decimal notation generally are introduced in third grade. A typical problem may state the following: A toy costs 39¢. You have a $5 bill. How much change should you receive? The solution is computed by subtracting 39¢ from $5 and is expressed as $4.61. Note that decimal notation for money is typically introduced before more comprehensive decimal instruction is taught so that students are able to solve real-world problems, like the one above. The students can be told that the two numerals to the right of the decimal tell about cents, while the numerals to the left of the decimal tell about dollars. A format for teaching students to read and write dollar figures expressed with decimal notation appears in Format 12.11: Decimal Notation for Money. Part A of the format involves teaching students to read decimal notation, while Part B teaches students to write decimal notation.

Practice should include examples without dollars ($.45, $.30) and examples without cents ($5.00, $13.00). Students can be expected to have difficulty writing amounts between 1 and 9 cents because of the need to place a zero after the decimal: $7.03, $14.08. These examples, therefore, should not be introduced in the initial exercises. Concentrated practice on this type of example should be provided in later lessons. At that time, the teacher explains that there must always be two digits after the decimal when writing dollar amounts. The teacher then models that when the number of cents is below 10, a zero and then the digit for the number of cents are written.

Word problems with money expressed in decimal notation should be introduced when students can read and write decimal notation for money. A common type of word problem that deserves special attention is illustrated below:

Scout bought a shirt for $13.62. She gave the clerk a $20 bill. How much change will Scout receive?

Atticus had $6. He was given $7.50 for working in his neighbor's yard. How much money does he have now?

In these problems, a dollar amount is expressed without cents after the decimal point. When working the problem, students must write the dollar amount with a decimal point and two zeros. The teacher should model the critical skill of aligning the numerals according to the decimal point before assigning students to work problems of this type independently.

DIAGNOSIS AND REMEDIATION

Measurement, time, and money errors fall into the same categories as the errors for other mathematics topics: fact errors, component-skill errors, and strategy errors. Note that the remediation usually involves reviewing critical parts of the relevant formats and providing students with additional practice. Examples of common errors for measurement, time, and money are outlined in **Figure 12.8**, along with suggested remediation procedures.

FIGURE 12.8 Diagnosis and remediation of measurement, time, and money errors

Error Pattern	Diagnosis	Remediation Procedures	Remediation Examples
Measurement			
12 yards = 4 feet 4)‾12‾	Student does not determine the appropriate operation when converting.	Present **Format 12.2**, Part B using customary units.	Provide a set of examples in which students determine the appropriate operation.
3 lbs. 15 oz. + 6 oz. ‾‾‾‾‾‾‾‾‾‾‾‾‾ 5 lbs. 1 oz.	Student does not rename customary units properly.	Present **Format 12.4**.	Provide a mix of addition problems that do and do not require renaming customary units.
Time			
 30 minutes after *1* *45* minutes after *8*	Students start counting by fives when touching the 12 instead of saying "zero."	Present **Format 12.6**. Review Part B to determine minutes after the hour.	Provide worksheets with pictures of analog clocks and a space labeled "minutes after."
 15 minutes after *7* *10* minutes after *4*	Students confuse the minute and hour hands.	Present **Format 12.6**. The teacher may initially elongate the minute hand to help students discriminate between the two hands.	Proved worksheets with pictures of analog clocks and a space labeled "minutes after."
Money			
Jaleel pays for a candy bar that costs 79 cents with the following coins: Q, Q, D, D, P, P, P, P, P, P, P, P, P	Student incorrectly applies the strategy of paying for something with coins of the highest value.	Present Part A of **Format 12.10**, emphasizing the strategy of starting with the highest valued coins and using the fewest coins.	Present examples of paying for items by starting with the highest valued coins.
Keisha has 7 dollars. She buys a piece of candy for 5 cents. How much money does she have left? $7.00 − .50 ‾‾‾‾‾‾‾‾ 6.50	Student does not write 5 cents correctly.	Present **Format 12.11**, Part B.	Present a set of examples that includes values that are less than 10 cents.

APPLY WHAT YOU LEARNED

 Click on the √ to answer the questions online.

1. Explain how measurement, time, and money are related.

2. Write a format for introducing the yard unit. Assume students have previously learned inches and feet, ounces and pounds. Include all five steps discussed in the text. For step 4, write six questions that you would ask your students.

3. Below are errors made by students on conversion tasks. For each error, tell the probable cause and specify a remediation procedure.

		1
Julio:	6 feet = _75_ inches	1 2 × 6 75
Jamika:	6 feet = _60_ inches	10 × 6 60
Joelle:	9 yards = _3_ feet	3⟌9

4. A student says the x is over the line that shows 1¾ inches. Specify the wording in the correction made by the teacher.

5. Specify the wording in the correction to be made by the teacher.

$$1 \text{ foot } 7 \text{ inches}$$
$$+ \quad\quad 8 \text{ inches}$$
$$\overline{2 \text{ feet } 5 \text{ inches}}$$

6. For each error, tell the probable cause and specify what the teacher says to correct.

Junior: 148 meters equal _____ km *148 ÷ 1000 = 1.48*

Flo: 148 meters equal _____ km *148 × 1000 = 148,000*

7. Write a structured-worksheet presentation to lead students through working this problem. 348 centimeters = how many meters?

8. Below are sets of examples prepared by teachers to use in initial exercises to teach telling time as minutes after the hour. Which sets are inappropriate and why?

Set A:	15 minutes after 8	10 minutes after 7
	10 minutes after 9	5 minutes after 7
Set B:	13 minutes after 2	25 minutes after 4
	37 minutes after 10	10 minutes after 9
Set C:	20 minutes after 7	35 minutes after 4
	15 minutes after 2	30 minutes after 8

9. Tell the probable cause of each student's error.

    a. Jayde

    30 minutes after 3   50 minutes after 8   10 minutes after 11

    b. Illya

    50 minutes after 12   20 minutes after 9   35 minutes after 5

    c. Xavi

    30 minutes after 2   15 minutes after 8   50 minutes after 6

10. Specify the wording the teacher uses in correcting the first error made by each student in problem 8. The wording will be different for each student.

11. When counting a quarter, a dime, and two nickels, students count as specified below. Tell the probable cause of the errors. Specify what the teacher says to correct each student. (Assume students know the value of each coin.)

    Justine—25, 30, 35, 40

    Royce—5, 10, 20, 35

12. Tell the probable cause for each error. Specify what the teacher says to correct each student. Sierra had 5 dollars. She buys a pencil for 4 cents. How much money does she have left?

    Austin:
    $$\begin{array}{r}\overset{4}{\$\cancel{5}.00}\\-.04\\\hline \$4.06\end{array}$$

    Lydia:
    $$\begin{array}{r}5\\-4\\\hline 1\end{array}$$

Format 12.1
METRIC PREFIXES

TEACHER	STUDENTS
Part A: Prefixes for Less Than 1	
1. *(Write the following prefixes on the board.)* milli- —thousandth of centi- —hundredth of deci- —tenth of one whole	
2. These are prefixes used in the metric system. They tell us how much of the base unit we have.	
3. *(Point to milli-, centi-, deci-.)* These prefixes say there is less than one whole. What do these prefixes tell?	There is less than one whole.
4. *(Point to milli-.)* This says *milli-*. What does it say? *Milli* means "a thousandth of." What does *milli-* mean? *(Repeat step 3 with centi-, and deci-.)*	Milli A thousandth of
5. Let's read all of these prefixes and what they mean. *(Point to milli-, centi-, deci-.)*	
6. *(Erase the words thousandth of, hundredth of, tenth of.)* *(Point to milli-.)* What is this prefix? What does *milli-* mean? *(Point to centi-.)* What is this prefix? What does *centi-* mean? *(Point to deci-.)* What is this prefix? What does *deci-* mean? *(Point to the three prefixes in random order until students identify all three correctly.)*	Milli A thousandth of Centi A hundredth of Deci A tenth of
Part B: Introducing Prefixes (More Than One Whole)	
1. *(Write the following prefixes on the board.)* milli- centi- deci- one whole deka- —ten wholes hecto- —one hundred wholes kilo- —one thousand wholes	
2. What does *milli-* mean? What does *centi-* mean? What does *deci-* mean?	A thousandth of A hundredth of A tenth of

TEACHER	STUDENTS
3. Let's read the prefixes that tell about more than a whole.	
(Point to deka-.) This says *deka-*. What does it say?	Deka
What does *deka-* mean?	10 wholes
(Point to hecto-.) This says *hecto-*. What does it say?	Hecto
What does *hecto-* mean?	100 wholes
(Point to kilo-.) This says *kilo-*. What does it say?	Kilo
What does *kilo-* mean?	1,000 wholes
(Erase the words: ten wholes, hundred wholes, thousand wholes.)	
4. *(Point to deka-.)* What does this say?	Deka
What does *deka-* mean?	10 wholes
(Repeat step 3 with hecto- and kilo-.)	
5. *(Point to the prefixes in random order until students can identify them all correctly.)*	
Part C: Structured Board Presentation	
1. What does *kilo-* mean?	1000 wholes
2. *Kilo-* means 1000 wholes. So *kilometer* means "1,000 meters." What does *kilometer* mean?	1000 meters
Yes, a kilometer equals 1000 meters. Say that.	A kilometer equals 1000 meters.
(Repeat steps 1 and 2 with millimeter, hectogram, centigram.)	
3. What does *deciliter* mean?	A tenth of a liter
To correct: What does *deci-* mean? *(Repeat step 3.)*	
(Repeat step 3 with the following examples.)	
dekaliter—10 liters	
centigram—a hundredth of a gram	
kiloliter—1000 liters	
dekagram—10 grams	
centiliter—hundredth of a liter	
Part D: Structured Worksheet	
1. *(Give students a worksheet with problems like the ones below.)*	
a. A kilogram equals 1,000 grams .001 gram 100 grams	
b. A millimeter equals 1,000 meters .001 meters .01 meters	
c. A centigram equals 100 grams .001 grams .01 grams	
d. A hectoliter equals .01 liters .1 liters 10 liters 100 liters	
2. Look at problem a. You have to circle what a kilogram equals. What does *kilo-* mean?	A thousand wholes
So what does a kilogram equal?	A thousand grams
3. Circle the answer.	
(Repeat steps 2 and 3 with several examples.)	

Format 12.2
METRIC CONVERSIONS   (See Videos Parts B & C)

TEACHER	STUDENTS
Part A: Relative Sizes of Units	

1. *(Write the following chart on the board.)*

milligram	centigram	decigram	gram	dekagram	hectogram	kilogram
$\frac{1}{1000}$ gm	$\frac{1}{100}$ gm	$\frac{1}{10}$ gm	1 gm	10 gm	100 gm	1000 gm

TEACHER	STUDENTS
2. These are the metric units for measuring weight. Milligram is a thousandth of a gram. It is the smallest unit. What is the smallest unit?	Milligram
Kilogram is a thousand whole grams. It is the biggest unit. What is the biggest unit?	Kilogram
3. *(Start at gram and point to the left.)* If we move this way, we're changing to a smaller unit.	
(Point to the right.) If we move this way, we're changing to a bigger unit.	
4. *(Point to the left.)* Which way am I changing?	To a smaller unit
(Point to the right.) Which way am I changing?	To a bigger unit
5. *(Point to centigram.)* If we have centigrams and we want to change to grams, which way are we changing?	To a bigger unit
(Repeat step 4 with grams to kilograms, grams to milligrams, hectograms to grams, kilograms to grams, grams to decigrams.)	
6. *(Erase the board.)* I want to change centigrams to grams. What does a centigram equal?	A hundredth of a gram
When I change centigrams to grams, which way are we changing?	To a bigger unit
(Repeat step 6 with same examples as in step 5.)	

Part B: Determining Appropriate Operations

TEACHER	STUDENTS
1. Here are two important rules: When we change to a bigger unit, we divide. Say that.	When we change to a bigger unit, we divide.
When we change to a smaller unit, we multiply. Say that.	When we change to a smaller unit, we multiply.
2. What do we do when we change to a bigger unit?	Divide
What do we do when we change to a smaller unit?	Multiply
3. *(Write on board: gram to centigram.)* When we change from grams to centigrams, are we changing to a bigger unit or a smaller unit?	To a small unit
Do we multiply or divide when we change from grams to centigrams?	Multiply
To correct: If we have grams and we change to centigrams, which way are we changing? If we change to a smaller unit, what do we do?	
(Repeat step 3 with these examples: g to kg, g to mg, hg to g, kg to g, g to dg.)	

TEACHER	STUDENTS
Part C: Structured Board Presentation	
1. *(Write the following problem on the board.)*	
350 centigrams = _____ grams	
2. This problem says, 350 centigrams equals how many grams? We're changing centigrams to grams. What are we doing?	Changing centigrams to grams
3. Are we changing to a bigger or smaller unit?	Bigger
4. We're changing to a bigger unit, so do we multiply or divide?	Divide
Yes, when we change to a bigger unit, we divide.	
5. How many centigrams in each gram?	100
So we divide by 100. Let's divide by moving the decimal. When we divide by 100, what do we do to the decimal?	Move it to the left 2 places
6. *(Write 350 next to grams.)* If I move the decimal point two places to the left, where will it be?	Between the 3 and 5
(Write on board: 350 centigrams = 350 grams)	
7. Read the problem now.	350 cg = 3.5 g
(Repeat steps 1–5 with the problems below.)	
314 grams = _____ milligrams	
(Move decimal point 3 places to right.)	
315 grams = _____ kilograms	
(Move decimal point 3 places to left.)	
7 centigrams = _____ grams	
(Move decimal point 2 places to left.)	
18 kilograms = _____ grams	
(Move decimal point 3 places to right.)	
30 meters = _____ decimeters	
(Move decimal point 1 place to right.)	
Part D: Structured Worksheet	
1. *(Give students a worksheet with problems like the one below.)*	
a. 232 centiliters equal _____ liters	
2. Read problem a. Are you changing to a bigger or smaller unit?	Bigger
3. So do you multiply or divide?	Divide
4. What do you divide by?	100
Which way do you move the decimal point?	To the left
How many places do you move it?	Two
5. Write the answer. *(Monitor responses.)*	
Read the problem.	232 centiliters = 2.32 liters
(Repeat steps 2–5 with remaining problems.)	

Format 12.3
CONVERTING FROM MIXED NUMBERS

TEACHER	STUDENTS
1. *(Write the following problems on the board.)*	
a. 3 feet 4 inches = _____ inches	
b. 2 weeks 3 days = _____ days	
c. 2 pounds 3 ounces = _____ ounces	
d. 3 gallons 1 quart = _____ quarts	
2. Read problem a. This problem asks us to change 3 feet 4 inches into inches in all. First we'll find how many inches in 3 feet. Then we'll add it to 4 inches.	
(Write in. + over first problem.)	
in.+	
3 feet 4 inches = _____ inches	
What do we do first?	Find how many inches are in 3 feet
Then what do we do?	Add 4 inches
3. Let's change 3 feet to inches. Are we changing to a bigger or smaller unit?	Smaller
So what do we do?	Multiply
4. How many inches in a foot?	12
So you'll multiply by 12. Everybody, how many inches in 3 feet?	36
Cross out 3 feet and write 36 above it.	
5. Now what do we do?	Add it to 4 inches
6. How many inches in all?	40
Write it in front of inches.	
7. Read the problem.	3 feet 4 inches = 40 inches
(Repeat with additional examples.)	

Format 12.4
RENAMING CUSTOMARY UNITS

TEACHER	STUDENTS
Part A: Structured Board Presentation	
1. *(Write the following problem on the board, with blanks for the ounces.)*	
3 lbs _____ oz	
+2 lbs _____ oz	
___ lbs _____ oz	
2. First, we add the ounces; then we add the pounds. How many ounces in a pound?	16
That means that if we end up with 16 or more ounces, we have to rename.	
3. I'll write numerals for ounces. Tell me if we have to rename.	

TEACHER	STUDENTS
4. (Write 7 and 5 in the blanks.)	
What's the answer for ounces?	12
Do we have to rename 12 ounces as pounds?	No
(Repeat steps 3 and 4 with 9 + 9, 9 + 5, 8 + 9, 8 + 8, 9 + 6.)	
Part B: Structured Worksheet	

1. (Give students a worksheet with 8–10 problems such as the ones below.)
 	
    a. 5 lb 9 oz   b. 4 lb 2 oz
      +3 lb 9 oz +3 lb 11 oz	

2. Touch problem a. Read The Problem.	5 pounds 9 ounces plus 3 pounds 9 ounces
3. We start by adding ounces.	
4. What is 9 + 9? Write 18 under the line.	18
5. How many ounces in a pound?	16
6. Do we rename 18 ounces as pounds?	Yes
7. Cross out 18 and write a 1 over the pounds column.	
8. We had 18 ounces. We put a pound in the pounds column. How many ounces did we take from 18 ounces when we renamed? *To correct:* A pound has 16 ounces.	16
9. We had 18 ounces; we moved 16 ounces. How many ounces are left? Write 2 under the ounces.	2 ounces
10. Now add the pounds. How many pounds?	9 pounds
11. Read the whole answer.	9 pounds 2 ounces
(Repeat steps 1–11 with additional problems.)	

Format 12.5
SUBTRACTION WITH RENAMING

TEACHER	STUDENTS

1. (Write the following problem on the board.)
 	
   5 lb 2 oz
  −2 lb 9 oz	

2. Read the problem.	5 lb 2 oz minus 2 lb 9 oz
3. Can you start with 2 ounces and subtract 9 ounces?	No
4. You must rename. Cross out 5 pounds and write 4.	
5. We took one pound from five pounds. How many ounces in a pound?	16

continued

Format 12.5 *(continued)*
SUBTRACTION WITH RENAMING

TEACHER	STUDENTS
6. Write 16 + in front of the 2 ounces.	
7. How many ounces do we start with now?	18
8. Cross out 16 + 2 and write 18 above it.	
9. And what does 18 − 9 equal?	9
So how many ounces do you end up with?	9 ounces
Write it.	
10. How many pounds do you end up with?	2 pounds
Write it.	
11. What's the answer?	2 lb 9 oz
(Repeat with additional examples.)	

Format 12.6
EXPRESSING TIME AS MINUTES AFTER THE HOUR (UNITS OF 5 MINUTES)

TEACHER	STUDENTS
Part A: Determining the Hour	
1. *(Draw the following clock on the board.)*	
2. One of the hands is missing on this clock. *(Point to the hour hand.)* This short hand is the hour hand. What is the short hand?	The hour hand
3. Let's figure out what hour the hand is after. We start at the top of the clock and say the numbers until we come to the hour hand. I'll touch; you say the numbers. Say stop when I come to the hour hand. *(Starting with 12, touch each numeral and then the hour hand as the children say the numbers.)*	12, 1, 2, 3, 4, 5, stop
4. What was the last numeral I touched?	5
5. The hour hand is after 5. So, the hour is after 5. Tell me about the hour.	After 5
(Repeat steps 1–5 with after 8.)	
6. *(Point the hour hand to after 5.)* Now let's figure out the hour a fast way, without counting. Look at the clock. What numeral is the hour hand after?	5
So tell me about the hour.	After 5
(Repeat step 6 with several more examples: after 9, after 2, after 6, after 3, after 10.)	

TEACHER	STUDENTS
Part B: Minutes After the Hour	
1. *(Draw the following clock on the board.)*	
2. This long hand is the minute hand. What is the long hand called? The minute hand is very funny. It tells you to count by 5. What does the minute hand tell you to do?	The minute hand Count by 5
3. Watch me figure out the minutes. *(Point to the minute hand.)* I touch the top of the clock and say zero. Then I count by 5 until I come to the minute hand. *(Touch the clock above 12.)* Zero. *(Starting with 1, touch each numeral as you count: 5, 10, 15, 20, 25.)*	
4. Tell me about the minutes.	25 minutes
5. Your turn. I'll touch the numerals; you count by 5. Remember to say zero when I touch the top of the clock. *(Touch the clock above 12 and then touch each numeral as the children count.)*	0, 5, 10, 15, 20, 25
6. Tell me about the minutes. Yes, 25 minutes. *(Repeat steps 4–6 with five more examples: hand points to 3, hand points to 7, hand points to 2, hand points to 10, hand points to 4.)*	25 minutes
Part C: Structured Board Presentation	
1. *(Draw the following clock on the board.)*	
2. We're going to figure out what time this clock shows. First we'll figure out the minutes. Then we'll figure out the hour.	
3. First the minutes. Which hand is the minute hand, the short hand or the long hand?	The long hand
4. What does the minute hand tell you to count by? Where do you start counting? What do you say? *(Repeat steps 3 and 4 until all questions are answered correctly.)*	Count by 5 At the top of the clock Zero
5. Count by 5 to the minute hand. *(Touch the top of the clock and then the numerals as the children count.)* How many minutes? I'll write the answer. *(Write 15 minutes under the clock.)*	0, 5, 10, 15 15

continued

Format 12.6 *(continued)*
EXPRESSING TIME AS MINUTES AFTER THE HOUR (UNITS OF 5 MINUTES)

TEACHER	STUDENTS
6. We know it's 15 minutes, but we don't know about the hour. Look at the hour hand. Tell me about the hour.	After 6
7. Yes, after 6. I'll write the answer. *(Write after 6.)* That's the time the clock shows, 15 minutes after 6. What time does the clock show? Say the time.	15 minutes after 6
(Repeat steps 1–7 with 5 minutes after 7, 45 minutes after 4, 20 minutes after 2, 25 minutes after 10.)	

Part D: Structured Worksheet

1. *(Give students a worksheet that includes about six to eight clocks like those above.)*

_____ minutes after _____　　_____ minutes after _____

2. Everyone touch the first clock on your worksheet. First you'll figure out the minutes, then you'll figure out the hour.	
3. Which is the minute hand?	The long hand
What does the minute hand tell you to count by?	Count by 5
Where do you start counting?	At the top of the clock
What do you say at the top of the clock?	zero
Let's figure out the minutes.	
4. Touch the 12. Count and touch as I clap. *(Clap once each second.)*	0, 5, 10, 15, 20, 25, 30, 35
How many minutes?	35 minutes
Write 35 in front of the word "minutes."	
5. Touch the hour hand. Tell me about the hour.	After 4
Yes, it says after 4. Write 4 in the next space.	
6. Now tell me what time that clock says.	35 minutes after 4
(Repeat steps 2–6 with each remaining clock.)	

Part E: Less Structured Worksheet

1. *(Give the students a worksheet with problems like the one below.)*

_____ minutes after _____

2. Touch clock a. You're going to figure out the time and write it under the clock.	
3. Figure out the minutes and write the minutes in the first blank. *(Monitor responses.)* How many minutes?	20
4. Now figure the hour and write it in the last blank.	
5. Read what time the clock says.	20 minutes after 6

Format 12.7
EXPRESSING TIME AS MINUTES BEFORE THE HOUR

TEACHER	STUDENTS
Part A: Determining the Hour	
1. *(Draw the following clock on the board.)*	
2. In telling time, you've learned to say how many minutes after the hour. Another way of telling time is to say the number of minutes before the hour.	
3. Look at this clock. What hour is it after?	4
4. The next bigger number tells you the hour it's before. Tell me the hour it's before.	5
Yes, it's before 5. What is the hour?	Before 5
5. *(Move the hour hand between 7 and 8.)* Tell me the hour by saying what hour it is before.	Before 8
(Repeat step 5 moving the hand to five more positions: between 2 and 3, between 10 and 11, between 6 and 7, between 11 and 12, between 12 and 1.)	
Part B: Minutes Before the Hour	
1. *(Draw the following clock on the board.)*	
2. Now we'll figure out the minutes before the next hour. When we figure the minutes before the hour, we start at the 12 but we count this way *(Point ⌢)* until we get to the minute hand. My turn: 0, 5, 10, 15, 20. It's 20 minutes before. How many minutes before?	20 minutes before
3. Show me which way you count to figure the minutes before the hour. Where do we start counting?	At the 12
What do we say first?	Zero
(Move minute hand to 10.) Tell me how many minutes before.	10 minutes before
To correct: We're figuring out minutes before, so we count this way *(⌢)*. I'll touch, you count.	
(Repeat step 3 with four more examples: hand pointing to 10, 8, 11, 7.)	

continued

Format 12.7 *(continued)*
EXPRESSING TIME AS MINUTES BEFORE THE HOUR

TEACHER	STUDENTS
Part C: Structured Board Presentation	
1. *(Draw the following clock on the board.)*	
_____ minutes before _____	
2. Let's tell what time this clock says by telling how many minutes before the hour.	
3. *(Point to the hour hand.)* Which hand is this?	The hour hand
What hour is it before?	4
4. *(Write 4. Point to minute hand.)* Which hand is this?	The minute hand
How many minutes before 4 is it?	20 minutes
(Write 20.)	
To correct: Show me which way we count when we figure out minutes before. Count as I point.	
5. What time does the clock say?	20 minutes before 4
(Repeat steps 1–5 with additional times: 5 before 2, 25 before 8, 15 before 11, 10 before 12, 20 before 5.)	
Part D: Structured Worksheet	
1. *(Give students a worksheet with six to eight clocks. Under each clock is written _____ minutes before _____.)*	
2. Let's find out what time these clocks say by finding out how many minutes before the hour.	
3. Find the hour hand on clock a. What hour is it before?	Before 8
4. Now let's find out how many minutes before 8. Start at the top of the clock—remember which way to count. How many minutes before 8?	20 minutes
5. What time does this clock say?	20 minutes before 8
Fill in the blanks.	
(Repeat with remaining examples.)	

Format 12.8
COIN EQUIVALENCIES

TEACHER	STUDENTS
Part A: Counting Similar Coins	
1. *(Show students real or pretend coins.)* I want to find out how many nickels equal one dime. How much is a dime worth?	10 cents
So I count nickels until I get to 10. What do I count by when I count nickels?	5
Stop me when I get to 10. 5, 10. . .	Stop
How many nickels did I count?	2
So how many nickels equal one dime?	2
(Repeat step 1 to provide additional practice in counting similar coins to demonstrate equivalencies.)	
2. *(Review previously taught equivalencies.)*	
How many pennies in a nickel?	
How many nickels in a dime?	
How many pennies in a dime?	
Part B: Counting Mixed Coins	
I gave a friend a quarter and he gave me two dimes and a nickel. Let's figure out if these coins are worth the same as a quarter. How much is a quarter worth?	25 cents
Let's count the coins and see if they're worth 25¢. I'll touch. You count. *(Touch each dime and then the nickel as the students count.)*	10, 20, 25
Are those coins worth 25¢?	Yes
(Repeat Part B with additional equivalency problems with mixed coins.)	

Format 12.9
VERIFYING CHANGE

TEACHER	STUDENTS
1. *(Write the following on the board.)*	
36¢ P P P P D Q Q	
2. *(Point to P.)* This stands for penny.	
(Point to D.) This stands for dime.	
(Point to Q.) This stands for quarter.	
(Point to each letter in random order and ask,) What does this stand for?	
3. *(Point to 36¢.)* John bought apples that cost 36¢. He gave the cashier a dollar. We're going to count the change John got and see if it's right. We'll count from 36 and see if we end with a dollar.	
(Point to P.) What do we count by for these?	1
(Point to D.) What do we count by for this?	10
(Point to Q.) What do we count by for these?	25
4. Let's count the change. Start with 36—count. *(Point to letters as students count.)*	37, 38, 39, 40, 50, 75, 100
Did we end with a dollar?	Yes
(Repeat steps 1–4 with several more examples.)	

Format 12.10
COUNTING COINS TO REACH AN EXACT AMOUNT

TEACHER	STUDENTS
Part A: Choosing the Correct Coins	
(Have coins ready for each student to use.)	
1. Today you're each going to count out money. I'll tell you how much something costs and you count out the money to buy it. When you count to reach an exact amount of money, you start with the coins that are worth the most so you can use the fewest number of coins. If I want to buy something for 25¢, would I use 25 pennies or 1 quarter?	1 quarter
Why?	A quarter is worth more than a penny.
Right, a quarter is worth more than a penny. If I want to buy something that costs 20¢, would I use nickels or dimes?	Dimes
Why?	A dime is worth more than a nickel.
2. My turn. I want to buy a balloon that costs 31¢. I start with a quarter: 25, 30, 31. *(Write Q N P on board.)*	
3. Your turn. *(Pass out coins.)* A toy car costs 28¢. Start with the coin that's worth the most and count out 28¢.	Students should put out a quarter and three pennies.
(Monitor student responses.)	
(Repeat step 3 with several more examples.)	
Part B: Counting Coins When You Don't Have the Exact Amount	
1. I'm going to use the coins I have to buy something that costs 56¢.	
(Write 56¢. Below, write Q Q Q D D D.)	
This is all the money I have to use. I start with the coin that has the greatest value. I get as close as I can. If I don't have the exact amount, I have to give more. I'll get the extra money back as change. Watch.	
(Circle a coin each time you count: Q, Q, and D.)	
25, 50, 60.	
I paid more than 56¢, so I'll get some change back.	
(Give the students a worksheet with problems like the following.)	
a. 36¢ Q D D N	
b. 72¢ Q D D D N N P	
c. 29¢ D D D N N P P	
2. Your turn. Point to problem a on your worksheet.	
Start with the coin worth the most. If you don't have exactly 36¢, count more than 36. Circle the coins you'll use. Raise your hand when you're done.	
(When most hands are raised) Tell me the coins you circled.	Q, D, N
3. *(Repeat step 2 with the remaining problems.)*	

Format 12.11
DECIMAL NOTATION FOR MONEY

TEACHER	STUDENTS
Part A: Reading Decimal Notation	
1. *(Write the following on the board.)*	
$4.32	
2. Here is the way to write dollars and cents. *(Point to the decimal point in $4.32.)* This dot is a decimal point. It divides dollars and cents. *(Point to 4.)* This tells us four dollars. *(Point to 32.)* These two numbers tell us about cents. I'll read the amount: Four dollars and thirty-two cents.	
3. *(Write the following on the board.)*	
$3.62	
How many dollars?	3 dollars
How many cents?	62 cents
Say the whole amount.	$3.62
(Repeat step 3 with $7.20, $.45*, $6.00, $.30*.)	
*For examples with no dollars, the teacher should model the response on the first day the format appears.	
Part B: Writing with Decimal Notation	
1. *(Give each student a sheet of lined paper.)* You're going to write money amounts using a dollar sign and a decimal point.	
2. Listen: Eight dollars and thirty-two cents. Say that.	$8.32
How many dollars?	8 dollars
Write a dollar sign, then an 8.	
3. Eight dollars and thirty-two cents. How many cents?	32 cents
Write a decimal point on the line. Then write 32.	
4. What amount did you write?	$8.32
(Repeat steps 2–4 with these examples: $6.42, $.32, $4.10, $7.00, $.57, and $9.00.)	

Fractions

LEARNING OUTCOMES

13.1 Explain how instruction in fractions is organized around three major areas to illustrate the interrelationships among various fraction skills.

13.2 Discuss the recommended procedures for teaching fraction analysis to promote conceptual understanding of fractions to young students.

13.3 Explain the importance of teaching students rewriting strategies as a prerequisite for fractions operations and the role equivalent fractions plays in the rewriting strategies.

13.4 Outline instructional strategies to teach addition and subtraction of fractions with like and unlike denominators.

13.5 Outline instructional strategies to teach multiplication and division of fractions, including word problems.

13.6 Describe diagnosis and remediation procedures for common fraction errors.

SKILL HIERARCHY

We have included a Skill Hierarchy Chart in this chapter because fractions comprise one of the most complex sets of skills covered in elementary mathematics. This complexity is understandable, since the entire range of operations discussed in other sections of the book is applicable to fractional numbers. Unfortunately, fractions do not represent a simple extension of familiar skills. While early instruction on whole numbers covers counting by groups of 1 or more than 1, that instruction does not help students generalize to groups of less than one. In addition and subtraction of whole numbers, members of a second group relate to the members of the first group based on one-to-one correspondences. For example, in the problem $4 + 3$, students increase the first set in units of 1 (5, 6, 7), producing the answer 7. To solve $4 - 3$, students decrease the first set in units of 1, producing the answer 1. In contrast, in multiplication and division of whole numbers, a second group is related to the first group based on a one-to-many correspondence. For example, in solving for 8×2, students count units of 8 for each member of the second group (8, 16), producing the answer 16. In $16 \div 2$, students determine the answer by counting 1 for each unit of 2 in 16 (1, 2, 3, 4, 5, 6, 7, 8), producing the answer 8.

In operations containing fractions, the one-to-one and one-to-many correspondences involve fractional numbers. For example, to solve $\frac{2}{3} \times 4$ students count units of $\frac{2}{3}$ for each member of the second group. While students can quickly learn to count 2, 4, 6, 8 for 2×4, counting $\frac{2}{3}$, $\frac{4}{3}$, $\frac{6}{3}$, $\frac{8}{3}$, for $\frac{2}{3} \times 4$ is not easy. The problem $\frac{2}{3} \times \frac{4}{7}$ is even less comprehensible because students have no experience counting $\frac{4}{7}$ths times. Therefore, learning fractional correspondences with both whole numbers and other fractions requires instruction in new strategies.

Another major difficulty with fractions is the incompatibility of different units. Addition and subtraction can be carried out only with equivalent units. Whole numbers represent a simple type of equivalent unit, so they can be added and subtracted in any combination. In contrast, fractional numbers do not represent one type of unit: all thirds represent equivalent units and all fourths represent equivalent units, but thirds are not the same as fourths. Consequently, thirds and fourths cannot be added or subtracted as such. Prior to adding or subtracting fractions, the fractional units must be transformed into a common unit:

$$\frac{1}{4} + \frac{2}{3} = \frac{3}{12} + \frac{8}{12} = \frac{11}{12}$$

The necessity to transform or rewrite fractional numerals is a major source of difficulty in teaching fractions. (This is one reason for the appeal of decimals; they have the uniform base of multiples of 10.)

Instruction in fractions can be organized around the three main fraction topics outlined in the Skill Hierarchy: fraction analysis, rewriting fractions, and operations (addition, subtraction, multiplication, and division).

Since application of fraction skills depends on an understanding of fractional numbers, initial instruction on fraction concepts and conventions is critical. Early instruction must address fraction analysis skills such as constructing diagrams or figures to represent fractions, writing the fraction represented by diagrams or figures, decoding fractions, and determining if a fraction is **proper** or **improper**.

The second area, rewriting fractions, includes the following skills:

1. Rewriting an improper fraction as a **mixed numeral**: $\frac{13}{2} = 6\frac{1}{2}$
2. Rewriting a proper fraction using the smallest possible **denominator** (reducing fractions): $\frac{6}{8} = \frac{3}{4}$
3. Rewriting a fraction as an equivalent fraction: $\frac{2}{5} = \frac{4}{\square}$
4. Rewriting a mixed numeral as an improper fraction: $2\frac{1}{2} = \frac{5}{2}$

The third area, fraction operations, often requires students to use the fraction rewriting skills described above. For example, to work the problem $\frac{3}{4} + \frac{5}{6}$, the student must rewrite $\frac{3}{4}$ and $\frac{5}{6}$ as equivalent fractions with the same denominator: $\frac{3}{4} = \frac{9}{12}$ and $\frac{5}{6} = \frac{10}{12}$. The equivalent fractions $\frac{10}{12}$ and $\frac{9}{12}$ are then added to produce a sum of $\frac{19}{12}$, which may be converted to the mixed numeral $1\frac{7}{12}$. When working the problem $\frac{4}{5} \times 1\frac{3}{4}$, the student first must convert the mixed numeral $1\frac{3}{4}$ to the improper fraction $\frac{7}{4}$. The student then multiplies $\frac{4}{5} \times \frac{7}{4}$, ending with a product of $\frac{28}{20}$, which may be converted to the mixed numeral $1\frac{8}{20}$. The fraction part of this mixed numeral may be reduced so that the final answer reads $1\frac{2}{5}$.

The Skill Hierarchy Chart illustrates the interrelationships among the three areas of fraction skills. Note that many of the fractions skills on the chart are preskills for other skills. A sequence for teaching fractions must be designed so that all preskills for advanced problems have been presented before that type of problem is introduced. Note also how the focus of instruction is cyclical. For example, simple addition and subtraction problems involving fractions with like denominators are introduced at a relatively early stage in the sequence of instruction. Problems involving adding and subtracting fractions with unlike denominators are not introduced until significantly later in the sequence because several rewriting skills must be taught first. The Instructional Sequence and Assessment Chart suggests one possible order for introducing the important types of fraction problems. Teachers working with intermediate students will find it productive to test for and teach, when necessary, the skills appearing at the beginning of the sequence chart, since these skills lay the foundation for a conceptual understanding of fractions.

Skill Hierarchy Chart

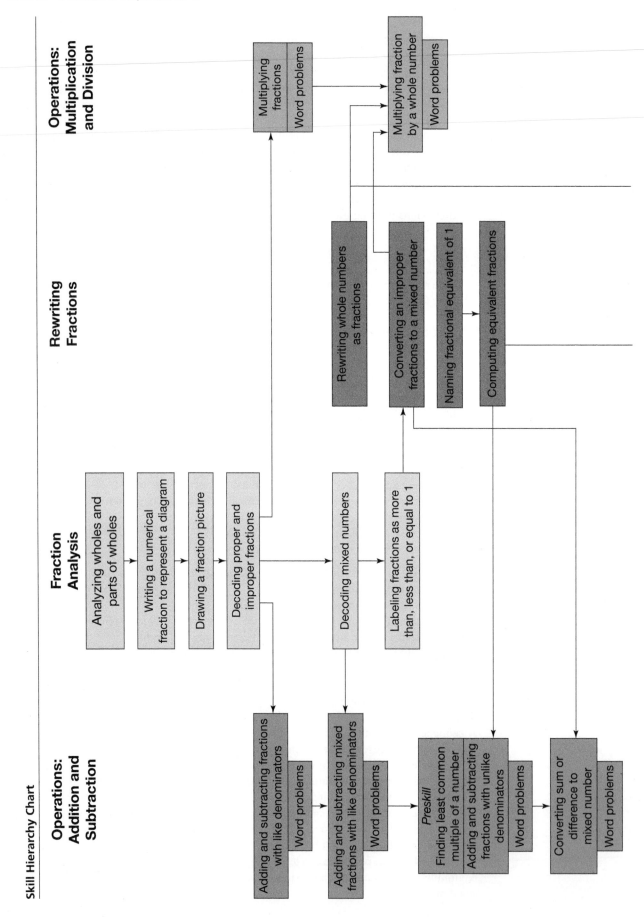

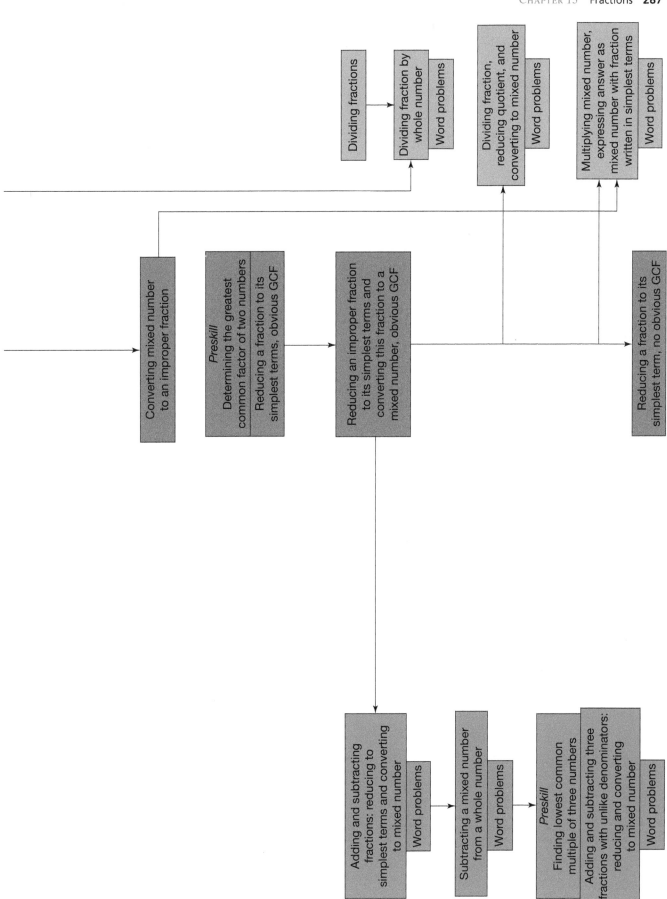

INSTRUCTIONAL SEQUENCE AND ASSESSMENT CHART

Grade Level	Problem Type	Performance Indicator
1	Identifying fractions that correspond to diagrams	a. Circle the picture that shows $^2/_4$.
		b. Circle the picture that shows $^4/_4$.
		c. Put X on the line below the picture that shows $^4/_3$.
		d. Put X on the line below the picture that shows $^3/_2$.
2	Drawing diagrams to correspond to fractions	$\frac{3}{4}$ =
		$\frac{2}{3}$ =
		$\frac{3}{2}$ =

Grade Level	Problem Type	Performance Indicator
2	Reading and writing fractions expressed as fractions	Write these fractions: a. two-thirds $= \dfrac{\square}{\square}$ b. five-halves $= \dfrac{\square}{\square}$ c. four-fifths $= \dfrac{\square}{\square}$ (Test students individually. "What does this say: $\dfrac{2}{3}, \dfrac{4}{5}, \dfrac{5}{2}$?")
2	Determining whether a fraction is more than, equal to, or less than 1	Write *more than, less than,* or *equal to* in each blank. $\dfrac{4}{3}$ is _____ 1 $\dfrac{7}{7}$ is _____ 1 $\dfrac{5}{6}$ is _____ 1
3	Adding and subtracting fractions with like denominators	$\dfrac{3}{5} - \dfrac{2}{5} =$ _____ $\dfrac{4}{7} - \dfrac{2}{7} =$ _____ $\dfrac{3}{5} + \dfrac{1}{5} =$ _____
3	Reading and writing mixed numerals	Write two and one-third _____ Write four and two-fifths _____ Write six and one-half _____ (Test students individually. "Read these numerals: $2\dfrac{1}{4}, 3\dfrac{2}{5}, 7\dfrac{3}{9}$.")
3	Writing a fraction as an equivalent to one whole group	$1 = \dfrac{\square}{4} \qquad 1 = \dfrac{\square}{7}$
4	Multiplying fractions	$\dfrac{3}{5} \times \dfrac{2}{3} =$ _____ $\dfrac{2}{5} \times \dfrac{3}{5} =$ _____ $\dfrac{2}{2} \times \dfrac{3}{5} =$ _____
4	Adding and subtracting mixed numbers: fractions with like denominators	$5\dfrac{4}{7} - \dfrac{2}{7} =$ _____ $3\dfrac{2}{5} - 1\dfrac{2}{5} =$ _____
4	Word problems: adding and subtracting mixed numbers and fractions with the same denominator	Bill ran $2^2/_4$ miles on Monday and $3^1/_4$ miles on Tuesday. How many miles did he run altogether? _____ miles Jack had $4^2/_8$ pounds of nails. Bill had $2^3/_8$ pounds of nails. How much more did Jack have? _____ pounds of nails Bob worked $2^1/_2$ hours on Monday and 3 hours on Tuesday. How many hours did he work altogether? _____ hours

continued

INSTRUCTIONAL SEQUENCE AND ASSESSMENT CHART *(continued)*

Grade Level	Problem Type	Performance Indicator
4	Rewriting fractions as mixed numerals	$\frac{12}{5}=$ _____ $\frac{8}{3}=$ _____ $\frac{21}{9}=$ _____
4	Rewriting whole numerals as fractions	$9=\frac{\square}{\square}$ $6=\frac{\square}{\square}$ $8=\frac{\square}{\square}$
4	Multiplying fractions by a whole number	$\frac{2}{3}\times 6$ $\frac{1}{3}\times 12$ $\frac{3}{5}\times 20$
4	Multiplying fractions by whole numerals and converting answers to mixed numerals	$\frac{2}{5}\times 14$ $\frac{3}{7}\times 8$ $\frac{2}{9}\times 15$
4	Word problems: multiplying fractions by whole numerals	There are 15 children in class. Two-thirds are boys. How many boys in the class? Jack has to study for 30 hours. He has done half of the studying. How many hours did he study? Ann's coach told her to run ¾ of a mile a day. How many miles will she run in 5 days?
4	Rewriting fractions as equivalent fractions with larger denominators	$\frac{2}{5}=\frac{\square}{10}$ $\frac{3}{4}=\frac{\square}{12}$ $\frac{2}{3}=\frac{\square}{9}$
4	Finding the least common multiple of two small numbers	Find the least common multiple of 6 and 4 _____ Find the least common multiple of 5 and 10 _____ Find the least common multiple of 5 and 2 _____
4	Adding and subtracting fractions with unlike denominators	$\frac{3}{4}-\frac{2}{3}=\frac{\square}{\square}$ $\frac{2}{5}+\frac{3}{10}=\frac{\square}{\square}$ $\frac{1}{2}-\frac{1}{3}=\frac{\square}{\square}$ $\frac{2}{6}+\frac{1}{2}=\frac{\square}{\square}$
4	Converting mixed numerals to improper fractions	$2\frac{1}{4}=\frac{\square}{4}$ $3\frac{1}{2}=\frac{\square}{2}$ $1\frac{3}{5}=\frac{\square}{5}$

Grade Level	Problem Type	Performance Indicator
4	Subtracting mixed numerals from whole numerals	$8 - 1\frac{2}{3} = $ _____ $9 - 2\frac{3}{5} = $ _____ $7 - 4\frac{1}{2} = $ _____
5	Comparing value of fractions	Which is greater: $\frac{2}{3}$ or $\frac{4}{5}$? $\frac{4}{5}$ or $\frac{2}{3}$? $\frac{2}{7}$ or $\frac{1}{2}$?
5	Word problems: adding and subtracting fractions with unlike denominators	Bill painted ½ of the wall. Jane painted ¼ of the wall. How much of the wall have they painted altogether? Tom ate ⅓ of the pie, and Jack ate ½ of the pie. How much of the pie did they eat?
5	Determining all factors of a given number	Write all the numerals for the factors of 12. Write all the numerals for the factors of 8.
5	Determining the greatest common factor	What is the greatest common factor of 8 and 12? What is the greatest common factor of 4 and 8? What is the greatest common factor of 12 and 15?
5	Reducing a fraction to its simplest terms	Reduce these fractions to their simplest terms: $\frac{12}{18} = \frac{\Box}{\Box}$ $\frac{16}{20} = \frac{\Box}{\Box}$ $\frac{6}{18} = \frac{\Box}{\Box}$
5	Adding fractions, reducing and converting to mixed numerals	Add these fractions; reduce the answers to simplest terms. Write answers as mixed numerals. $\frac{4}{6} + \frac{2}{5} = $ _____ $\frac{2}{4} + \frac{2}{3} = $ _____ $\frac{6}{10} + \frac{4}{5} = $ _____
5	Finding the lowest common multiple of three numbers	Find the lowest common multiple of 3, 6, and 4. Find the lowest common multiple of 2, 4, and 5. Find the lowest common multiple of 2, 5, and 10.
5	Adding and subtracting three fractions with different denominators	Add these fractions and write the answers with fractions written in simplest terms: $\frac{3}{5} + \frac{1}{2} + \frac{3}{6} = $ _____ $\frac{2}{3} + \frac{2}{4} + \frac{1}{6} = $ _____ $\frac{3}{4} + \frac{1}{2} + \frac{2}{5} = $ _____
5	Multiplying mixed numerals	$7\frac{3}{4} \times 3\frac{1}{2} = $ _____ $2\frac{3}{5} \times 4 = $ _____ $5 \times 2\frac{1}{2} = $ _____

continued

INSTRUCTIONAL SEQUENCE AND ASSESSMENT CHART *(continued)*		
Grade Level	**Problem Type**	**Performance Indicator**
5	Dividing fractions	$\dfrac{3}{4} \div \dfrac{2}{5} =$ _____ $\dfrac{5}{6} \div \dfrac{2}{3} =$ _____ $\dfrac{7}{9} \div \dfrac{1}{3} =$ _____
5	Dividing fractions by whole numerals	$\dfrac{2}{3} \div 4 =$ _____ $\dfrac{3}{5} \div 2 =$ _____ $\dfrac{2}{4} \div 7 =$ _____
5	Dividing mixed numerals by whole numerals	$3\dfrac{1}{2} \div 3 =$ _____ $2\dfrac{1}{5} \div 2 =$ _____ $7\dfrac{1}{2} \div 4 =$ _____
5	Word problems: division involving fractions	Two girls picked 5½ pounds of cherries. They want to split up the cherries equally. How much will each one get? Bill has 35 inches of ribbon. He wants to make shorter ribbons. If each ribbon is ½" long, how many ribbons can he make?

CONCEPTUAL UNDERSTANDING

Teaching fraction analysis skills is designed to provide students the necessary conceptual understanding of fractions. Concurrently with fraction analysis skills, we recommend teaching common conventions for reading and writing fractions. In this text, fraction analysis skills and common conventions are introduced in first grade. Most students, by first grade, have had some experience with fractions, like ½ and ¼. Beginning carefully designed fraction instruction early capitalizes on the students' prior knowledge and allows for a more efficient progression through all of the fraction-related skills. Our recommendation for beginning instruction in first grade takes into consideration the time necessary for students to achieve mastery of each of the preskills required for understanding more complex fraction operations. A solid understanding of fractions ensures that students are prepared for algebra. The skills included in this area are listed below in their order of introduction:

1. Learning part/whole discrimination: Students learn to discriminate between whole units, the number of parts each unit is divided into, and the number of parts used.
2. Writing a numerical representation for a diagram or figure of whole units divided into equal-sized parts, and vice versa:

3. Reading fractions: ¾ is read as "three-fourths."
4. Determining whether a fraction equals, exceeds, or is less than one whole.
5. Reading mixed fractional numerals: 3½ is "three and one-half."

Unlike the instruction typical of most commercial programs, the instructional strategies in the fraction analysis section are designed to introduce proper and improper fractions concurrently. This feature prevents students from learning the misrule that all fractions are proper fractions. Without adequate instruction, struggling students often learn this misrule as a result of only being introduced to proper fractions in the earlier grades. This misrule can be seen when students who can successfully draw a picture of ¾ cannot draw a picture of ⁵⁄₄. By introducing proper and improper fractions at the same time, teachers show students that the analysis applies to all fractions.

A second important feature of the analysis section is that students are taught initially to interpret what the denominator and **numerator** represent (in ¾ the 4 tells "four parts in each whole unit," and 3 tells "three parts are used") rather than to read the fraction in the traditional way (¾ as "three-fourths"). This unique way of reading fractions enables students to interpret fractions and facilitates conceptual understanding.

Part–Whole Discrimination

Format 13.1: Introducing Fractions shows how to introduce fractions to students. The goal of the format is to teach basic fraction (part–whole) concepts through the use of number lines. The reason for working with number lines from the onset is to ensure that students relate fractions to whole numbers. The specific objective is to teach students to discriminate between the number of parts in each whole unit and the number of whole units.

In Part A of **Format 13.1**, the teacher introduces students to number lines and how to identify the denominator ("bottom number") for fractions by counting the number of parts in each unit. Initially, each example set should include number lines with the same number of units divided into different numbers of parts. Each number line in the illustration below contains three units with each unit divided into a different number of parts. The first number line is divided into 4 parts per unit, the second number line is divided into 3 parts per unit, and the third number line is divided into 2 parts per unit.

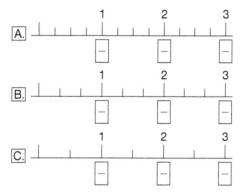

Next, in Part B, the students learn to write the numerator and the denominator of fractions for whole numbers on number lines. The bottom numeral is the number of parts in each whole unit. That number is the same for all whole units on a number line. The top numeral is the number of parts from the beginning of the number line. While this procedure illustrates the relationship between fractions and whole numbers, note that the concept of fractions equal to one is explicitly taught later in the instructional sequence.

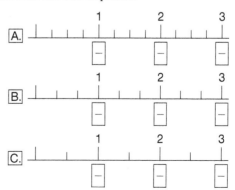

In Parts C and D, students are introduced to writing several fractions for each number line, including whole-number fractions. To figure out the fractions, students are taught to first count the number of parts in each unit and write the bottom numeral for all of the fractions on that number line. They then count the units from the beginning of each number line and write the top numeral for each of the fractions.

After students have worked with horizontal number lines for several days, teachers can introduce number lines that are vertically oriented. The procedure is the same. The number of parts in each unit is the bottom number of each fraction. The top number is the number of parts from the beginning of the number line.

After students have mastered identifying fractions using number lines, they work with figures, like circles or squares, that are divided into equal parts. **Format 13.2: Part–Whole Discrimination** teaches students to discriminate between the number of parts in each whole unit and the number of whole units using figures. In the format, the teacher writes a row of circles on the board and divides each into an equal number of parts. The teacher tells the students that each circle is called a whole unit and then leads the students through determining how many parts in each whole unit. Each example set should include a different number of circles. Also, the number of parts in each whole unit should vary from set to set. For example, the first set might include three circles, each divided into two parts. The next set might include five circles, each divided into four parts. This format should be presented for several consecutive days.

Some students may not see the relationship between the figures representing fractions and fractions on a number line. Therefore, using the same language when teaching the skills and correcting errors is critical. The teacher should stress the word *each* if students have problems with the figures, reminding them to count the parts in *each* whole unit.

Writing Numerical Fractions to Represent Figures

$$\oplus \oplus = \frac{\Box}{\Box}$$

Exercises in which the students write a numerical fraction to represent a figure (¾) are presented after the students have mastered the part–whole concepts presented in **Format 13.2: Part–Whole Discrimination**. The format for writing numerical fractions appears in **Format 13.3: Writing Numerical Fractions**. In Part A, the structured board presentation, students learn that the bottom number of a fraction tells how many parts in each whole unit, while the top number of a fraction represents how many parts are used (shaded). Parts B and C are structured and less structured worksheet exercises in which the students fill in the numerals to represent a diagram. Daily practice is provided for several weeks, followed by intermittent review.

Two guidelines are important for appropriate example selection for this skill. First, the number of parts in each whole unit, the number of whole units, and the number of parts used should vary among examples. Second, the examples should include a mixture of proper and improper fractions as well as some fractions that equal less than a whole unit:

$$\bigcirc = \frac{2}{3} \qquad \oplus = \frac{1}{4}$$

some examples that equal more than one unit:

$$\bigcirc \bigcirc \bigcirc \bigcirc = \frac{7}{2} \qquad \oplus \oplus = \frac{5}{4}$$

and just a few that equal one unit:

$$\oplus = \frac{4}{4} \qquad \bigcirc = \frac{2}{2}$$

During initial instruction, all examples should include circles divided into parts. After several weeks, other shapes (squares, rectangles, triangles) can be included in the exercises.

Special attention should be given to examples containing a series of units that are not divided:

$$\bigcirc \bigcirc \bigcirc = \frac{3}{1}$$

▶ Format 13.3A:
Writing Numerical Fractions
Watch how Lori uses think time effectively when eliciting responses from her students.

These figures need additional explanation. The teacher should point out that if a whole is not divided into parts, students should write a 1 on the bottom. The 1 tells that there is only one part in the whole unit. The next step is to have the students count the number of whole units and write that as the numerator. Examples that yield 1 as a denominator should not be introduced when fractions are initially presented but can be introduced about a week after initial instruction. Thereafter, about 1 in every 10 figures should be an example with 1 as a denominator. These examples are important, since they present a conceptual basis for exercises in which students will convert a whole numeral to a fraction ($8 = \frac{8}{1}$).

Drawing Figures to Represent Fractions

Prior to constructing figures, students should practice completing fractions and shading in the correct fractional parts on a number line. Translating numerical fractions into figures is a useful exercise for reinforcing conceptual understanding of the part–whole fraction relationship. Constructing figures can be introduced when students can accurately fill in the numerals to represent a figure. The procedure is relatively simple, so we haven't included a format. The teacher should begin instruction by modeling how to divide circles into equal-sized parts, emphasizing the need to divide the circles so that each part is the same size. Examples can be limited to fractions with 2, 3, or 4 as denominators. These examples allow for adequate discrimination without spending an inordinate amount of time teaching younger students to divide circles into more than four parts. After several days of practice dividing whole units into parts, the teacher would present a worksheet exercise, prompting the students as they draw figures. The teacher has the students say what each number tells, beginning with the bottom number. For ¾, the teacher would say the following: "Touch the bottom number. What does it tell you? . . . Draw four parts in each whole. . . . Touch the top number . . . What does it tell you?. . . Shade in three parts."

Figure 13.1 includes a sample worksheet. Note that each example has four circles. The purpose of keeping the number of circles constant is to prevent students from thinking that the number of whole units has something to do with the numerator and/or denominator.

Reading Fractions

When fractions are initially introduced, students are taught to decode the fraction by identifying what each numeral in the fraction represents. The fraction ¾ is read as "four parts in each whole; three parts are used." This translation is recommended because it accurately describes

FIGURE 13.1   Sample worksheet for drawing diagrams from numerical fractions

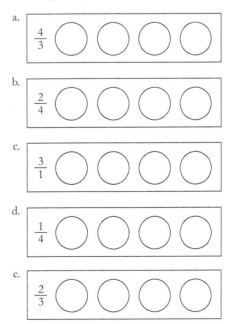

the fraction. Several weeks after fractions are introduced, reading fractions in the traditional way can be taught; for example, ¾ is read as "three-fourths." **Format 13.4: Reading Fractions** shows how to teach students to read fractions in the traditional way. The teacher writes several fractions on the board and models how to read the fractions, testing after each example. Then the teacher tests students on reading the fractions without first providing the model. To correct student errors, the teacher would model the correct response again, test the students, and then use the **alternating pattern** to provide practice on the missed example.

This format for reading fractions should be presented daily until students can accurately read fractions and then reviewed intermittently. Thereafter, students will receive practice in reading fractions at the same time new fraction skills are introduced. For example, in adding fractions, students will practice reading fractions when they are asked to read the problem aloud.

Two example-selection guidelines should be followed in teaching students to read fractions. First, the introduction of fractions with the numerals 2, 3, or 5 as denominators should be delayed several lessons because these denominators are not pronounced by adding the suffix "-ths" to the number as is the case for sixths, ninths, and fourths. When a 2 appears as the denominator, students will say "halves," not "twoths"; when a 3 appears, students will say "thirds," not "threeths"; when a 5 appears, students will say "fifths," not "fiveths." These denominators need to be introduced one at a time using a model-test procedure. Fractions with 2 as a denominator might be introduced first. When introducing 2 as a denominator, about half of the examples in the teaching set should contain 2 in the denominator, while the other half should represent a variety of previously introduced denominators:

$$\frac{1}{2} \quad \frac{1}{4} \quad \frac{3}{2} \quad \frac{3}{8} \quad \frac{5}{2} \quad \frac{5}{7} \quad \frac{1}{6} \quad \frac{4}{2}$$

When students have mastered denominators of 2, they are introduced in the same way to fractions with 5, then 3, as denominators.

A second example-selection guideline addresses the numerators. In about a fourth of the examples, the numeral 1 should be written as the numerator. These examples are included so that the students can see the difference between how a fraction is said when the numerator is 1 and when the numerator is more than 1: one-eighth versus four-*eighths*.

Determining Whether a Fraction Equals, Exceeds, or Is Less Than One Whole

Determining whether a fraction equals, exceeds, or is less than one whole is an important skill and also serves as a prerequisite for later exercises in which students are expected to convert an improper fraction like ¹⁶⁄₇ to a mixed numeral: 2²⁄₇. This skill can be introduced when students can accurately read fractions the traditional way. The teaching procedures appear in **Format 13.5: Determining Whether a Fraction Equals, Exceeds, or Is Less Than One Whole**. Part A is a pictorial demonstration in which the teacher draws pictures representing fractions of various values (more than 1, less than 1, equal to 1) and asks the students if the picture shows one whole, more than one whole, or less than one whole unit.

In Part B, the teacher presents rules to be used in determining whether a numerical fraction equals, exceeds, or is less than one whole unit. First, students are taught the rule that when the top and bottom number of a fraction are the same, the fraction equals one whole. After this rule is presented, the teacher tests the students' application of the rule, using a series of numerical fractions, about half of which equal one whole:

$$\frac{5}{5} \quad \frac{6}{4} \quad \frac{4}{4} \quad \frac{9}{2} \quad \frac{9}{9} \quad \frac{5}{5} \quad \frac{7}{3} \quad \frac{2}{7} \quad \frac{8}{8}$$

Next, the teacher instructs students that when the top number of a fraction is more than the bottom number, the fraction equals more than one whole, and when the top number is less than the bottom number, the fraction equals less than one whole. Finally, the students are shown fractions and asked to tell whether the fraction is equal to, more than, or less than 1. A structured worksheet exercise follows in which students must circle either *more*, *equal*, or *less* when given numerical fractions:

$$\frac{3}{4} \quad \text{more equal less}$$

$$\frac{8}{8} \quad \text{more equal less}$$

Note that in this format, the words "numerator" and "denominator" are not used. The purpose of excluding the terms is to avoid possible confusion between the terms. Similarly, use of the term improper fraction is not necessary for the students to understand the concept and, therefore, is not included in this format.

Examples for Parts B and C and independent practice should include a variety of problems. In about a third of the examples, the numerator and denominator of the fraction should be the same:

$$\frac{4}{4} \quad \frac{8}{8} \quad \frac{3}{3}$$

In another third, the numerator should be more than the denominator:

$$\frac{7}{5} \quad \frac{3}{2} \quad \frac{4}{2}$$

In another third, the numerator should be less than the denominator:

$$\frac{2}{3} \quad \frac{4}{7} \quad \frac{3}{4}$$

Reading and Writing Mixed Numerals

The above illustration may be expressed as the improper fraction ⁹⁄₄ or as the mixed fractional numeral 2¼. Reading and writing mixed numerals can be introduced relatively early in the fraction sequence, as soon as students can correctly determine when a fraction equals, exceeds, or is less than one whole. However, the teacher must keep in mind that exercises designed to teach students to convert mixed numbers to improper fractions and vice versa should not be introduced until much later in the fraction sequence because these conversions require students to know basic multiplication facts.

Part A of **Format 13.6: Reading and Writing Mixed Numerals** includes a pictorial demonstration that requires students to express the illustrations of improper fractions as mixed numeral by counting the number of whole units shaded and writing those numerals. Below is a sample exercise:

$$= \frac{\boxed{9}}{\boxed{4}} = \boxed{2}\frac{\boxed{1}}{\boxed{4}}$$

Part B is designed to teach students to read mixed numerals. The teacher uses a model-test procedure, having students first say the whole numeral, then the fraction, and then the mixed numeral. Note that the teacher emphasizes the word "and" when reading mixed numerals. The purpose of emphasizing "and" is to prevent errors in which the student either combines the whole numeral and the numerator, reading 4⅔ as "forty-two thirds," or leaves out the numerator, reading 5⅓ as "five thirds."

Part C is an exercise in which students are taught to write mixed numerals. The exercise begins with the teacher dictating a mixed number and having students first say the whole number and write the corresponding numeral. Then the students say the fraction part of the mixed number before writing the fraction. The teacher points out that when students write mixed numerals they are to make the whole numeral big and the numerals in the fraction small.

INSTRUCTIONAL PROCEDURES: REWRITING FRACTIONS

The procedures in this section all involve the process of changing a fraction from one form to another without changing its value—that is, maintaining equivalency. Three main types of conversion skills are discussed:

1. Determining the missing number in a pair of equivalent fractions:

$$\frac{3}{5} = \frac{\square}{10}$$

   This type of problem is a critical component skill for problems involving adding and subtracting fractions with unlike denominators.

2. Reducing fractions to their lowest terms. A fraction is said to be at its lowest term (or simplest form) when both the numerator and denominator have no common factor except 1:

$$\frac{20}{24} \text{ can be reduced to } \frac{5}{6}$$

3. Converting mixed numerals to improper fractions:

$$3\frac{1}{2} = \frac{7}{2}$$

   and improper fractions to mixed numerals:

$$\frac{17}{5} = 3\frac{2}{5}$$

A general preskill for all rewriting skills is knowledge of basic multiplication and division facts. To perform all three types of conversion problems, students must be able to multiply and divide. Therefore, we recommend introducing rewriting fractions in fourth grade.

The strategies presented here are designed so that students not only learn the necessary computation required to change fractions into equivalent forms but also understand the underlying concepts of equivalency. Without understanding equivalency, students will be able to apply very few of the skills they learn. For example, if students do not understand that when the numerator and denominator are the same, the fraction is equal to 1, they will not understand why $\frac{3}{4}$ can be multiplied by $\frac{5}{5}$ to create the equivalent fraction $\frac{15}{20}$. Although the equivalency concept is relatively sophisticated, the language of the strategies is simplified to make them accessible to all students.

Completing Equivalent Fractions

Instruction in equivalent fractions begins with problems in which the student must determine the missing numerator in an equivalent fraction:

$$\frac{3}{4} = \frac{\square}{12} \qquad \frac{1}{2} = \frac{\square}{10}$$

The basic strategy is to multiply the first fraction by a fraction that equals one. In working the first problem above, the student determines that to end up with an equivalent fraction that has 12 as a denominator, the fraction $\frac{3}{4}$ must be multiplied by $\frac{3}{3}$:

$$\frac{3}{4} \times \frac{(3)}{(3)} = \frac{9}{12}$$

Equivalency is maintained because, by definition, the **identity element** for multiplication is 1. When multiplying $\frac{3}{4}$ by $\frac{3}{3}$, we are multiplying $\frac{3}{4}$ by a fraction that equals 1. Therefore, we are not changing the value of $\frac{3}{4}$.

Preskills Several skills should be mastered before equivalency problems are introduced: (a) knowledge of the terms numerator and denominator, (b) the ability to multiply fractions, and (c) the ability to construct a fraction that equals one whole.

The terms "numerator" and "denominator" are usually introduced in second or third grade. The teaching procedure is simple. The teacher tells students the numerator is the top number in the fraction and the denominator is the bottom number in the fraction. The teacher then provides practice by writing several fractions on the board and having students identify the denominator and numerator of each fraction using examples presented in a random order. Daily practice is necessary so students won't forget or confuse the terms.

Multiplication of two fractions is usually taught in fourth grade. Procedures for teaching this skill are presented later in this chapter.

Constructing fractions equal to one whole is introduced about 2 weeks prior to introducing equivalent fraction problems. **Format 13.7: Preskill: Constructing Fractions Equal to 1** includes procedures for constructing fractions equal to 1. Part A is a structured board exercise in which a rule for constructing fractions equal to 1 is introduced: "When the top number is the same as the bottom number, the fraction equals 1." In Part B: Structured Worksheet, the teacher presents examples of applying the rule with problems such as:

$$1 = \frac{\square}{4}$$

in which the student must fill in the missing numerator of a fraction equal to one whole.

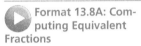 **Format 13.8A: Computing Equivalent Fractions**
Watch how Lori asks her students to apply the equivalent fractions rule.

Format The procedure for computing equivalent fractions is shown in **Format 13.8: Computing Equivalent Fractions**. Part A includes a pictorial demonstration introducing the concept of equivalent fractions. The teacher first defines the term "equivalent fractions," explaining that fractions are equal when they show that equal amounts of the whole units are used. The teacher then draws two circles on two clear plastic sheets, each divided into a different number of parts but each with equal portions shaded:

The teacher points out that these fractions are *equivalent*, since the same amount of each whole unit is shaded. The same demonstration is presented with a figure in which unequal proportions of the whole units are shaded:

The teacher points out that the fractions are not equivalent, since the shaded amounts of the whole units do not take up the same space.

Part B introduces a critical rule: When you multiply by a fraction that equals 1, the answer equals the number you start with. The teacher introduces this rule and then presents a set of problems demonstrating how this rule is applied. In some of the problems, the original fraction is multiplied by a fraction that equals 1, and in some, the original fraction is multiplied by a fraction not equal to 1. The students are to tell whether the answer will equal the original fraction.

Part C is a structured board exercise in which the teacher presents the strategy for working equivalency problems such as:

$$\frac{3}{4} = \frac{\square}{20}$$

The teacher explains that the equal sign tells that the fractions are equal. The student's task is to find the missing numerator in the second fraction.

The teacher writes parentheses after the first fraction

$$\frac{3}{4}\left(\ \ \right) = \frac{\square}{20}$$

explaining that the students must multiply the first fraction by a fraction that equals 1, which will be written inside the parentheses. The parentheses indicate multiplication. The teacher demonstrates how to figure out the denominator to be written inside the parentheses by using a missing-factor multiplication strategy. In the problem above, the teacher asks, "4 times what number equals 20?"

The answer, 5, is written as the denominator inside the parentheses:

$$\frac{3}{4}\left(\frac{}{5}\right) = \frac{\square}{20}$$

The teacher then points out that since the fraction inside the parentheses must equal one whole, the numerator must be the same as the denominator. The missing number in the equivalent fraction can be determined by multiplying the numerator in the first fraction and the numerator in the second fraction:

$$\frac{3}{4}\left(\frac{5}{5}\right) = \frac{15}{20}$$

Example Selection There are three example-selection guidelines for this format. First, the denominator of the first fraction must be a number that can be multiplied by a whole number to end with the denominator of the second fraction. Therefore, problems such as:

$$\frac{2}{3} = \frac{\square}{5} \qquad \frac{4}{5} = \frac{\square}{8} \qquad \frac{2}{3} = \frac{\square}{7}$$

are not appropriate to include, while problems such as:

$$\frac{2}{3} = \frac{\square}{6} \qquad \frac{4}{5} = \frac{\square}{10} \qquad \frac{2}{3} = \frac{\square}{9}$$

are appropriate. Second, the fraction equal to one in the parentheses should vary from problem to problem. For example, in one problem, the numerator and denominator in the second fraction could be four times bigger than the original:

$$\frac{3}{5} = \frac{\square}{20}$$

in the next problem, two times bigger:

$$\frac{5}{6} = \frac{\square}{12}$$

in the next, five times bigger:

$$\frac{2}{3} = \frac{\square}{15}$$

and so on. The third guideline is that all problems should require multiplication; that is, the numbers in the fraction to be completed should be greater than the numbers in the first fraction.

Reducing Fractions

We recommend that reducing fractions be introduced during fifth grade using a **greatest-common-factor** (GCF) strategy. In this strategy, students are taught to reduce a fraction to its simplest terms by identifying the greatest common factor of the numerator and denominator. For example, the fraction $\frac{9}{15}$ is reduced by identifying 3 as the greatest common factor of 9 and 15. When the factor 3 is pulled out, $\frac{9}{15}$ becomes $\frac{3}{5}$. The greatest-common-factor strategy is a viable strategy only for problems in which it is relatively easy to find the greatest common factor ($\frac{18}{27}$, $\frac{30}{35}$, $\frac{8}{16}$). Nearly all of the problems that require reducing that students encounter in fifth grade can be reduced to simplest terms using the greatest-common-factor strategy. Later, students will be taught to pull successive factors out of larger numbers.

Preskills Teaching students to find the greatest common factor of two numbers is the critical preskill for reducing fractions. The greatest common factor of two numbers is the largest number that can be multiplied by whole numbers to end with the two target numbers. For example, the greatest common factor of 12 and 18 is 6. Six can be multiplied by whole numbers to reach12 and 18.

The first step in teaching students to find the greatest common factor of two numbers is to teach them to determine all possible factors for a given number. For example, the numbers 1, 2, 3, 4, 6, and 12 are all factors of 12, since they can all be multiplied by another whole number to reach 12. **Table 13.1** includes a list of the factors for the numbers 1 through 50. Once the students can easily determine all factors for a number, finding the greatest common factor is relatively easy.

Format 13.9: Preskill: Determining Factors outlines the procedures for teaching students to determine factors. In Part A, the teacher introduces the term "factor," defining factors as any numbers that are multiplied together. In Part B, the teacher presents a strategy for figuring out all of the factors for a target number. The teacher writes the numeral for the target number on the board and beside it writes spaces for each factor. For example, if the target is 15, the teacher writes 15 on the board and puts four blanks beside it, since four numbers (1, 3, 5, 15) are factors of 15. The teacher then tells the students that they are going to find all of the numbers that are factors of 15 by asking if they can multiply a number by another number and end up with 15. The teacher always begins with one: "A number multiplied by 1 always equals itself. Is 1 a factor of 15?" The teacher then points out that they can find another factor by determining what number times that factor equals the target number. For example, after determining that 15 is a factor of 15, the teacher asks, "What number times 1 equals 15?" The answer, 15, is the factor of 15 that goes with 1. The teacher writes 1 in the first space and 15 in the last space.

The teacher then asks about other numbers, beginning with 2 and proceeding forward (3, 4, 5, 6, . . .): "Can we multiply 2 and end with 15? No, so 2 is not a factor of 15," and so on. The teacher instructs the students to stop her when she says a number that is a factor of the target number. When the students identify another factor of the target number, the teacher

TABLE 13.1 Factors for 1 to 50

Number Factors* (other than the number itself and 1)[†]	
4: 2, 2	28: 14, 2; 7, 4
6: 3, 2	30: 15, 2; 10, 3; 6, 5
8: 4, 2	32: 16, 2; 8, 4
9: 3, 3	33: 11, 3
10: 5, 2	34: 17, 2
12: 6, 2; 3, 4	35: 7, 5
14: 7, 2	36: 18, 2; 9, 4; 6, 6
15: 5, 3	38: 19, 2
16: 4, 4; 8, 2	39: 13, 3
18: 6, 3; 9, 2	40: 20, 2; 10, 4; 8, 5
20: 10, 2; 5, 4	42: 21, 2; 14, 3; 7, 6
21: 3, 7	44: 22, 2; 11, 4
22: 11, 2	45: 15, 3; 9, 5
24: 12, 2; 8, 3; 6, 4	46: 23, 2
25: 5, 5	48: 24, 2; 12, 4; 8, 6
26: 13, 2	49: 7, 7
27: 9, 3	50: 25, 2; 10, 5

*Factors are listed in pairs.
[†]Numerals not in list have only the number itself and 1 as factors.

once again leads them in finding the corresponding factor to produce the target number. If 15 is the target number, the students say stop after the teacher says 3. The teacher asks what number times 3 equals 15. The students answer 5. The teacher points out that 3 and 5 are both factors of 15. When target numbers over 20 are introduced, the teacher models the answer for the larger numbers. That is, the teacher tells the student any two-digit number that is a factor of the target number. For example, when introducing 28, the teacher says that 14 and 2 can be multiplied to equal 28.

Part C is a worksheet exercise. Numerals for target numbers are written on the worksheet. Students are to fill in the factors, beginning with the smallest factor. The objective of this format is to develop fluency in naming all possible factors of numbers. A systematic plan for introducing new target numbers and reviewing target numbers should be followed. One or two new target numbers can be introduced daily. (**Table 13.2** contains a suggested sequence for introducing target numbers.) Part A of the format is used only with the first pair of target numbers. New target numbers are introduced using the board presentation in Part B. The worksheet exercise described in Part C could be done independently after the first several lessons. A target number should appear on practice worksheet exercises daily for several weeks after it is introduced to develop fluency.

Determining the Greatest Common Factor Format 13.10: Determining the Greatest Common Factor (GCF) is introduced when the students are able to determine the factors of any target number below 20. The format is relatively simple. The teacher defines the phrase "greatest common factor" as the largest number that is a factor of both target numbers. The teacher then leads the students through finding the greatest common factor. First, the teacher asks students what the largest factor of the smaller target number is and if that factor is also a factor of the other target number. The teacher continues until the greatest common factor is identified. For example, when 8 and 20 are the target numbers, the teacher asks the following questions:

"8 is the largest factor of 8. Is 8 a factor of 20?" (No.)
"What is the next largest factor of 8?" (4.)
"Is 4 a factor of 20? (Yes.)
"So, 4 is the greatest common factor of 8 and 20."

TABLE 13.2 Sequence for Introducing Target Numbers and Their Factors

Day	Factors of These Numbers Are Introduced	Day	Factors of These Numbers Are Introduced
1	12, 7	16	27, 29
2	10, 3	17	28
3	16, 5	18	30, 31
4	8, 13	19	32, 33
5	4, 6, 9	20	34, 37
6	2, 17	21	35, 39
7	12, 19	22	36, 41
8	14, 23	23	38, 43
9	15	24	40, 47
10	18	25	42
11	20	26	44
12	21	27	45
13	22	28	46
14	24	29	48
15	25, 26	30	49
		31	50

After about 5 days of presenting the format, the teacher gives students daily worksheet exercises to work independently. The worksheet includes 8 to 12 problems in which students find the greatest common factor of two target numbers. A typical error in independent exercises involves writing a common factor that is not the *greatest* common factor of the two target numbers; for example, writing 3 as the greatest common factor of 12 and 18. The correction involves pointing out to students that they can find a larger common factor.

Example-selection guidelines are quite important. In about half of the problems, the greatest common factor should be the smaller of the two target numbers (6, 18; 4, 8; 2, 10; 5, 20). If examples such as these are not included, students might develop the misrule that the smaller number is never the greatest common factor. Examples should be limited to numbers for which students have been taught to find factors. Initially, both target numbers should be under 20. As students learn to determine factors for larger numbers, the larger numbers can be included. Several examples should be included in which 1 is the greatest common factor, as in 4 and 7 or 6 and 11. These prepare students for fractions that cannot be reduced ($\frac{4}{7}$, $\frac{6}{11}$).

Reducing Fractions   **Format 13.11: Reducing Fractions** is introduced when students are able to determine the greatest common factor of any two target numbers below 20. The format includes three parts. Part A is a board exercise in which the teacher presents the strategy for reducing fractions. The teacher writes a fraction on the board with an equal sign next to it. Next to the equal sign are parentheses and a fraction bar for the reduced fraction:

$$\frac{12}{16} = (\ ) \ \underline{\qquad}$$

The greatest common factor of the two target numbers (the numerator and denominator of the original fraction) determines the fraction equal to one inside the parentheses. For example, the greatest common factor of 12 and 16 is 4. Therefore, the fraction in the parentheses will be $\frac{4}{4}$, which equals 1. The teacher then asks, "12 equals 4 times what number?" The answer is 3, which is the numerator of the reduced fraction. The teacher then asks, "16 equals 4 times what number?" The answer is 4, which is the denominator of the reduced fraction. Since multiplying by 1 does not change the value of the fraction, $\frac{4}{4}$ can be crossed out. Crossing out the fraction equal to 1 leaves the reduced fraction:

$$\frac{12}{16} = \left(\frac{\cancel{4}}{\cancel{4}}\right) \frac{3}{4}$$

Part B is a structured worksheet exercise in which the teacher first asks for the greatest common factor of the numerator and denominator of a fraction. The teacher then instructs the students to write the corresponding fraction equal to 1 in parentheses. Finally, the teacher instructs students how to solve for the missing factors in the reduced fraction. Part C is a less-structured worksheet exercise that provides additional practice.

The steps for reducing fractions are outlined in **Summary Box 13.1**.

There are three example-selection guidelines for exercises on reducing fractions. First, the numerators and denominators should be ones for which students have been taught to find factors. At first, both the numerator and denominator should be below 25. As students learn to find factors for larger numbers, fractions with these larger numbers can be included.

Second, a third of the fractions should have the greatest common factor as the numerator. For example, in the fractions $\frac{4}{12}$, $\frac{8}{16}$, and $\frac{5}{20}$, the numerator is the greatest common factor. Finally, about a third of the fractions should already be expressed in their simplest terms ($\frac{4}{7}$, $\frac{3}{5}$, $\frac{6}{11}$) to show students that not all fractions can be reduced. An example set following these guidelines appears below:

a. $\dfrac{12}{15}$ b. $\dfrac{4}{8}$ c. $\dfrac{5}{7}$ d. $\dfrac{8}{12}$ e. $\dfrac{3}{5}$

f. $\dfrac{5}{15}$ g. $\dfrac{4}{12}$ h. $\dfrac{6}{9}$ i. $\dfrac{9}{11}$

SUMMARY BOX 13.1

Reducing Fractions

1. $\dfrac{10}{15}$ Students read the fraction.

2. $\dfrac{10}{15} = \left(-\right)\dfrac{\square}{\square}$ Students determine the greatest common factor for the numerator and denominator.

3. $\dfrac{10}{15} = \left(\dfrac{5}{5}\right)\dfrac{\square}{\square}$ Students construct a fraction equal to one using the greatest common factor.

4. $\dfrac{10}{15} = \left(\dfrac{5}{5}\right)\dfrac{\boxed{2}}{\boxed{3}}$ Students find the numerator for the fraction by solving $5 \times \square = 10$ and find the denominator by solving $5 \times \square = 15$.

5. $\dfrac{10}{15} = \left(\dfrac{\cancel{5}}{\cancel{5}}\right)\dfrac{2}{3}$ Students cross out the fraction equal to one and identify $\dfrac{2}{3}$ as the reduced fraction.

All items have numerators and denominators that are below 25. Items b, f, and g are fractions in which the smaller number is a factor of the larger number. Items c, e, and i are fractions that are already expressed in their simplest terms.

Reducing Fractions with Larger Numbers   After several weeks of practice reducing fractions using the greatest common factor strategy, students can be introduced to the concept of pulling out successive common factors. When the greatest common factor is difficult to find, students can reduce the fraction to its simplest terms by repeatedly pulling out factors. Note the examples below:

$$\text{a.} \quad \frac{45}{75} = \left(\frac{5}{5}\right)\frac{9}{15} = \left(\frac{3}{3}\right)\frac{3}{5} = \frac{3}{5}$$

$$\text{b.} \quad \frac{24}{72} = \left(\frac{2}{2}\right)\frac{12}{36} = \left(\frac{6}{6}\right)\frac{2}{6} = \left(\frac{2}{2}\right)\frac{1}{3} = \frac{1}{3}$$

The teacher guides students through sets of problems, pointing out clues students can use to determine if a fraction is reduced to its simplest term. For example, if both the numerator and the denominator are even numbers, the fraction can still be reduced. Or, if the numerator and denominator both end in either 5 or zero, the fraction can still be reduced.

The teacher then presents an exercise in which students check answers to determine if the answers are reduced to their simplest terms. During that exercise, the teacher gives students a worksheet with problems similar to those below, some of which have not been reduced to their simplest terms. The students are asked to find those fractions that can be further reduced and to reduce those fractions.

$$\text{a.} \quad \frac{64}{72} = \left(\frac{\cancel{4}}{\cancel{4}}\right)\frac{16}{18} = \qquad \text{d.} \quad \frac{65}{85} = \left(\frac{\cancel{5}}{\cancel{5}}\right)\frac{13}{15} =$$

$$\text{b.} \quad \frac{45}{75} = \left(\frac{\cancel{5}}{\cancel{5}}\right)\frac{9}{15} = \qquad \text{e.} \quad \frac{48}{64} = \left(\frac{2}{2}\right)\frac{24}{32} =$$

$$\text{c.} \quad \frac{21}{30} = \left(\frac{\cancel{3}}{\cancel{3}}\right)\frac{7}{10} = \qquad \text{f.} \quad \frac{56}{84} = \left(\frac{2}{2}\right)\frac{28}{42} =$$

Converting Mixed Numerals and Improper Fractions

An improper fraction, one whose numerator is greater than its denominator, is a fraction that equals more than one whole. An improper fraction may be converted to a mixed numeral by dividing its numerator by its denominator. For example, to convert the fraction $^{13}/_5$ to a mixed numeral, we divide 13 by 5, which equals 2 with a remainder of 3. The remainder is written as the fraction $^3/_5$; the improper fraction $^{13}/_5$ is converted to the mixed numeral $2^3/_5$.

Converting a mixed numeral to an improper fraction requires the reverse operation, multiplication rather than division. Students first change the whole number into a fraction by multiplying the whole number by the number of parts in each whole, indicated by the denominator. For example, in the mixed numeral 6¼, students convert the whole number 6 into a fraction by multiplying 6 by the denominator of ¼:

$$\text{for } 6 = \frac{\ }{4}, \text{ students write } \frac{24}{4}$$

After students convert the whole number to a fraction, they add the numerators of the fractions:

$$6\frac{1}{4} = \frac{24 + 1}{4} = \frac{25}{4}$$

On the Instructional Sequence and Assessment Chart, we recommend that converting improper fractions to mixed numerals be introduced in early fourth grade. Students apply this skill when they rewrite their answers after adding or multiplying fractions. Converting a mixed numeral to an improper fraction should not be introduced until several months later. We recommend separating the introduction of these conversion skills to decrease the probability of students confusing the two operations. Converting mixed numerals to and from improper fractions requires that students have a good understanding of the difference between a whole unit and parts of a unit. Therefore, students should have mastered all of the fraction analysis skills presented earlier.

Format 13.12AB: Converting Improper Fractions to Mixed Numbers
Watch how Lori uses voice emphasis to help students discriminate between whole and fractional numbers.

Converting Improper Fractions to Mixed Numerals   Part A of **Format 13.12: Converting Improper Fractions to Mixed Numerals** is a pictorial demonstration in which the teacher shows how to construct a figure to determine how many whole units an improper fraction equals.

Part B is a structured board presentation in which the teacher presents the strategy of dividing the numerator by the denominator. Note the special emphasis given to explaining how to write the remainder as a fraction. The teacher explains that the denominator of the new fraction in the mixed number must be the same denominator as in the original fraction.

Part C is a structured worksheet exercise. The division symbol, along with boxes for the whole number and the fraction remainder, are written as prompts on the students' worksheets:

$$\frac{11}{4} = \overline{)\ }\ \Box\frac{\Box}{\Box}$$

The teacher begins the exercise by instructing the students to look at the fraction and determine whether it is less than one whole, equal to one whole, or more than one whole. If the fraction is less than 1 or equal to 1, students are instructed to leave the fraction as it is. If the fraction equals more than 1, they are instructed to divide and write the answer as a mixed numeral.

Part D is a less structured worksheet exercise in which students convert improper fractions to mixed numbers with minimal teacher prompting. Teachers should insist that students write the whole numeral part of the answer and the fraction part of the answer neatly. Teachers should watch for students writing answers in which the numerator of the fraction could easily be mistaken for a whole numeral. In the following example, $3\frac{2}{5}$ is written as $\frac{32}{5}$:

$$5\overline{)17}\ ^{32/5}$$

Examples should be selected to provide appropriate discrimination practice. First, there should be a mixture of problems. About half of the fractions should translate to a mixed number; about a fourth should translate simply to a whole number (⁶⁄₃, ¹⁶⁄₄ ¹⁰⁄₅); finally, about a fourth should be proper fractions. Including proper fractions ensures that students do not attempt to inappropriately convert all fractions to mixed number $\left(\frac{3}{4} = 1\frac{1}{4}\right)$.

After students have had several weeks of practice converting improper fractions to mixed numbers and reducing fractions to their lowest terms, they can be given exercises in which they must first convert the fractions to mixed numbers and then reduce the fractions. No special format is required for such exercises. The teacher gives students a worksheet with directions similar to these: "Change any fraction that equals one or more whole units to a mixed number. Then reduce the fractions." A set of examples would include a mix of proper and improper fractions, some of which can be reduced and some of which are written in their simplest form. A sample set might include these fractions:

$$\frac{16}{12} \quad \frac{6}{8} \quad \frac{9}{7} \quad \frac{14}{6} \quad \frac{5}{7}$$

$$\frac{8}{24} \quad \frac{20}{8} \quad \frac{9}{12} \quad \frac{24}{10}$$

Exercises of this type should be continued for several months to develop fluency.

Converting Mixed Numbers to Improper Fractions

Converting Mixed Numbers to Improper Fractions   Format 13.13: **Converting Mixed Numbers to Improper Fractions** includes four parts. Parts A and B teach the component skill of translating any whole number into an improper fraction by multiplying the number of whole units by the number of parts in each whole:

$$\ln 6 = \frac{}{4}, \text{ students multiply } 6 \times 4$$

Because this component skill is very important, both a board and a worksheet exercise are presented.

Part C, a structured board presentation, teaches the strategy to convert a mixed number into an improper fraction. First, the students determine the fraction equivalent to the whole number; then they add the fraction portion of the mixed number. For example, with 6¾, students multiply 6×4 and then add 3 to determine the answer:

$$6\frac{3}{4} = \frac{24 + 3}{4} = \frac{27}{4}$$

Part D is a structured worksheet exercise that provides additional practice.

INSTRUCTIONAL PROCEDURES: ADDITION AND SUBTRACTION OF FRACTIONS

Addition and subtraction of fractions include three basic types of problems. The first type has like denominators:

$$\frac{3}{8} + \frac{1}{8} + \frac{2}{8} = \frac{\square}{\square} \qquad \frac{7}{9} - \frac{3}{9} = \frac{\square}{\square}$$

Problems of this type can be introduced during the primary grades, since relatively few preskills are required to work the problems. The students learn that to work such problems, they work only across the numerators; the denominators remain constant:

$$\frac{2}{5} + \frac{1}{5} = \frac{3}{5} \qquad \frac{7}{9} - \frac{3}{9} = \frac{4}{9}$$

The second type includes problems with unlike denominators. Problems in this group are limited initially to those in which the **lowest common denominator** (LCD) is relatively easy to figure out. Problems of this type are usually introduced during fifth grade. The strategy for solving these problems involves first figuring out the lowest common denominator, rewriting each fraction as an equivalent fraction with that denominator, and then working the problem:

$$\frac{5}{6} \text{ becomes } \frac{5}{6}\left(\frac{2}{2}\right) = \frac{10}{12}$$

$$\frac{3}{4} \text{ becomes } \frac{3}{4}\left(\frac{3}{3}\right) = \frac{9}{12}$$

$$\frac{10}{12} - \frac{9}{12} = \frac{1}{12}$$

The third type includes problems in which the lowest common denominator is difficult to determine because relatively large numbers are involved. We recommend using the equivalent fractions strategy for solving these types of problems. Initially, we recommend finding a common denominator of two large numbers by multiplying the denominators. For example, in the problem $^5\!/_{13} + {}^3\!/_{18}$, the common denominator is 234. This is determined by multiplying 13 by 18. Given these two factors, students can generate the fractions equal to one that produce fractions with like denominators and solve the problem.

$$\frac{5}{13}\left(\frac{}{18}\right) = \frac{}{234} \qquad \frac{3}{18}\left(\frac{}{13}\right) = \frac{}{234}$$

$$\frac{5}{13}\left(\frac{18}{18}\right) = \frac{90}{234} \qquad \frac{3}{18}\left(\frac{13}{13}\right) = \frac{39}{234}$$

$$\frac{90}{234} + \frac{39}{234} = \frac{129}{234}$$

Finally, the student would need to reduce the answer to the addition problem using **Format 13.11: Reducing Fractions**. Another strategy typically used with older students for reducing fractions with large numbers involves prime factorization to determine the least common denominator. Prime factorization is discussed in more detail in Chapter 18.

Fractions with Like Denominators

Adding and subtracting fractions with like denominators is a relatively simple operation that can be introduced after fraction analysis skills have been taught in third grade. Part A of **Format 13.14: Adding and Subtracting Fractions with Like Denominators** includes a pictorial demonstration in which the teacher illustrates adding fractions. In Part B, the teacher presents the rule that students can add and subtract only fractions in which each whole has the same number of parts.

Parts C and D are structured and less structured worksheet exercises in which the students are presented with a set of addition and subtraction problems. Half of the problems should have like denominators:

$$\frac{3}{4} - \frac{1}{4} \qquad \frac{4}{7} + \frac{2}{7}$$

and half different denominators:

$$\frac{3}{4} - \frac{1}{3} \qquad \frac{5}{7} + \frac{2}{3}$$

Students are instructed to identify and cross out the problems with unlike denominators and work the problems with like denominators. The problems with unlike denominators are included to encourage students to pay attention to the denominators when working problems.

During the first week or two of instruction, adding and subtracting fraction problems should be written horizontally. When students can work problems written horizontally, vertically aligned problems should be introduced:

$$\frac{3}{4} \qquad \frac{4}{8} \qquad \frac{5}{7}$$
$$-\frac{1}{4} \qquad +\frac{3}{8} \qquad +\frac{2}{3}$$

The teacher introduces vertically aligned problems using Parts C and D of Format 13.14. Teachers should not assume that because students can work horizontally aligned problems, they will be able to work vertically aligned problems.

Problems with Mixed Numbers

Adding and subtracting mixed numbers in which the fractions have like denominators:

$$3\frac{2}{5} - 1\frac{1}{5}$$

can be introduced when students can read and write mixed numerals and can add and subtract fractions with like denominators. The teaching procedure is relatively simple: The students first work the fraction part of the problem and then the whole number part of the problem. Both horizontally and vertically aligned problems should be presented.

Fractions with Unlike Denominators

Adding and subtracting fractions with unlike denominators is usually introduced during late fourth grade. A strategy for solving problems with unlike denominators is outlined in **Summary Box 13.2**. Note the integration of several component skills.

Preskills   Two preskills should be mastered before the format for adding and subtracting fractions with unlike denominators is introduced: (a) finding the least common multiple of two numbers and (b) rewriting a fraction as an equivalent fraction with a given denominator (see **Format 13.8: Computing Equivalent Fractions**).

The least common multiple (LCM) of two numbers is the smallest number that has both numbers as factors. For example, the least common multiple of the numbers 6 and 8 is 24, since 24 is the smallest number that has both 6 and 8 as factors. Likewise, the least common multiple of 6 and 9 is 18, since 18 is the smallest number that has 6 and 9 as factors.

Format 13.15: Preskill: Finding the Least Common Multiple shows how to teach students to figure out the least common multiple of two numbers. This format assumes that students are able to skip count by twos through nines. About 2 months prior to introducing the least common multiple, the teacher should begin reviewing the skip-counting series. Students who know their basic multiplication facts but have not learned skip counting should have little trouble learning to skip count. (See Chapter 4 for teaching skip counting.)

The strategy for finding the least common multiple requires students to say the skip-counting series for two numbers and to select the smallest number appearing in both series. This strategy

---

SUMMARY BOX 13.2

Steps for Problems with Unlike Denominators

1. $\frac{3}{4} + \frac{1}{6}$ Students read problem and say, "The problem can't be worked as it is because the denominators are not the same."

2. $\frac{3}{4} + \frac{1}{6}$ Students determine that the least common multiple of 4 and 6 is 12. Thus 12 is the least common denominator. Both fractions must be rewritten with denominator of 12.

3. $\frac{3}{4}\left(\frac{3}{3}\right) + \frac{1}{6}\left(\frac{2}{2}\right)$ Students determine the fraction equal to one by which each original fraction must be multiplied to equal 12.

4. $\frac{3}{4}\left(\frac{3}{3}\right) + \frac{1}{6}\left(\frac{2}{2}\right)$ Students rewrite each fraction so that it has a denominator of 12.

5. $\frac{3}{4}\left(\frac{3}{3}\right) + \frac{1}{6}\left(\frac{2}{2}\right) = \frac{11}{12}$ Students work the problem with equivalent fraction.

is viable for examples in which the numbers are small. A more sophisticated strategy must be taught to figure the least common multiple of larger numbers.

The format for teaching least common multiple includes two parts. In Part A, the teacher writes count-by series for two numbers on the board so that students can visually find the least common multiple. At that time, the teacher also introduces the term "multiple." Part B is a worksheet presentation in which the teacher leads students in finding the least common multiple for several pairs of numbers and then monitors as students complete a worksheet on their own. Daily practice on worksheet exercises involving finding the least common multiple of two numbers is continued until students demonstrate mastery.

There are two example-selection guidelines for the least-common-multiple format. First, in about half of the problems, the larger number should be a multiple of the smaller number. For the numbers 3 and 12, 12 is a multiple of 3. The least common multiple of 12 and 3 is 12. The second guideline pertains to the other half of the problems in which the larger number is not a multiple of the lower number. In these problems, both numbers should be below 10.

▶ Format 13.16A: Adding and Subtraction Fractions with Unlike Denominators

Watch how Lori uses the preskill from Format 13.15 to correct the error a student makes in finding the least common multiple.

Format   Format 13.16: Adding and Subtracting Fractions with Unlike Denominators has three parts. Part A is a structured board presentation, which begins with the teacher writing a problem on the board and asking the students if the fractions can be added (or subtracted) as they are written. After the students determine the fractions cannot be added (or subtracted) because the denominators are not the same, the teacher tells the students that they can work the problem by rewriting the fractions so that both have the same denominator. The teacher then demonstrates the problem-solving strategy outlined earlier: writing the least common multiple of both denominators; multiplying each fraction by a fraction equal to 1 (which enables them to be rewritten with their lowest common denominator) and then adding (or subtracting) the rewritten fraction.

In Parts B and C, the structured and less structured worksheet exercises, the teacher leads students through working problems. Note that Format 13.16 includes problems in which both fractions are rewritten. In many problems, only one fraction will need to be rewritten (in ¾ + ⅛, only ¾ needs to be rewritten as ⅝). When initially presenting this type of problem, the teacher has the students write the fraction $\frac{1}{1}$ next to the fraction that does not need to be rewritten:

$$\frac{3}{4}\left(\frac{2}{2}\right) + \frac{5}{8}\left(\frac{1}{1}\right)$$
$$_8 \qquad\qquad _8$$

After several weeks, the teacher can explain that if the denominator of the rewritten fraction does not need to be changed, multiplying by $\frac{1}{1}$ is not needed.

There are three example-selection guidelines for this format. The first addresses the manner in which problems are written. During the first 2 weeks, all problems should be written horizontally. When students can work horizontal problems, they can be introduced to vertically aligned problems.

The second guideline pertains to the variety of problems. Half of the problems should have denominators in which the larger denominator is a multiple of the smaller denominator. For example, in the problem

$$\frac{3}{5} + \frac{2}{10}$$

the larger denominator, 10, is a multiple of the smaller denominator, 5. In the other half of the problems, the denominators should be one-digit numerals that require finding a new common denominator:

$$\frac{3}{5} + \frac{2}{3} \qquad \frac{3}{4} + \frac{2}{5} \qquad \frac{5}{6} - \frac{1}{4}$$

Several problems involving adding and subtracting fractions with like denominators also should be included. A sample set of problems appears below. Note that problems c and f have like denominators. Problems b, e, and g have a lower denominator that is a factor of the larger denominator. In problems a, d, and h, both fractions must be rewritten.

a. $\frac{3}{4} + \frac{2}{5}$ b. $\frac{7}{9} - \frac{2}{3}$ c. $\frac{5}{6} - \frac{1}{6}$

d. $\frac{5}{6} - \frac{4}{9}$ e. $\frac{1}{5} + \frac{3}{10}$ f. $\frac{4}{9} + \frac{3}{9}$

g. $\frac{7}{10} - \frac{1}{2}$ h. $\frac{3}{4} - \frac{2}{3}$

Reducing and Rewriting Answers as Mixed Numerals

The skills of reducing fractions to their lowest common terms and converting an improper fraction to a mixed numeral can be integrated into problems after students have had several weeks of practice working problems with unlike denominators. Students should be given problems that require them to convert the answer to a mixed number (when necessary) and/or reduce. Teachers should lead students through determining the correct answers for several days. Daily practice with six to eight problems should continue for several weeks.

More Complex Problems with Mixed Numbers

A rather difficult problem type involving mixed numbers is illustrated below:

$$\begin{array}{r} 8 \\ -3\frac{2}{4} \\ \hline \end{array}$$

This is a subtraction problem involving renaming. The student must rewrite the 8 as 7 and $\frac{4}{4}$ to work the problem. Prior to introducing such a problem, the teacher would present an exercise like the one below in which the student must rewrite a whole number as a whole numeral and a fraction equivalent to 1 ($6 = 5 + \frac{4}{4}$).

$$6 = \boxed{5} + \frac{\square}{4} \qquad 9 = \boxed{8} + \frac{\square}{6}$$

$$6 = \boxed{5} + \frac{\square}{3}$$

In leading students through this preskill exercise, the teacher points out that they have to take one whole away from the original whole number and rewrite that one whole as a fraction. Once this preskill is taught, students should have little difficulty with problems that involve renaming.

Comparing Fractions

Students are often asked to compare the values of fractions. For example, which has the greater value, $\frac{1}{5}$ or $\frac{1}{3}$? Which has the lesser value, $\frac{2}{3}$ or $\frac{5}{9}$? During second and third grade, students usually are asked to compare fractions with numerators of 1 but with different denominators. The teacher can prepare students for these comparison questions by providing pictorial demonstrations illustrating that the more parts a unit is divided into, the smaller the size of each part. The rule is: The bigger the denominator, the smaller the value of each part. For example, $\frac{1}{10}$ is smaller than $\frac{1}{5}$. The demonstrations can be followed by a rule-application exercise in which the teacher presents pairs of fractions with numerators of 1 and asks which fraction has a greater value.

In later grades, students are asked to compare fractions that have numerators other than 1 ($\frac{3}{4}$ and $\frac{5}{9}$). The strategy for comparing the two fractions involves rewriting fractions so that they have common denominators ($\frac{3}{4}$ would be rewritten as $\frac{27}{36}$ and $\frac{5}{9}$ as $\frac{20}{36}$).

Once fractions have been rewritten so they have common denominators, their values are readily apparent. Procedures for teaching students to rewrite fractions with common denominators are the same as those discussed in the early steps of the format to add and subtract fractions with different denominators: determining the least common multiple of the denominators and multiplying each fraction by a fraction equal to 1.

Word Problems

The basic guideline for introducing fraction word problems is that a new type of fraction problem should be integrated into word problem exercises as soon as the students can accurately compute problems of that type. For example, word problems involving adding and subtracting fractions with like denominators should be introduced after students can compute these types of problems independently. Word problems with unlike denominators should be introduced only after students have mastered the strategy for adding and subtracting those types of fractions. All of the various types of addition and subtraction problems described in the problem-solving chapter (Chapter 11) should be included in the exercises. **Figure 13.2** is a sample of problems that could be included on a worksheet given to students shortly after they learn how to add/subtract mixed numbers with fractions that have like denominators. Note the variety of word problem types (classification, action, and comparison).

FIGURE 13.2   Sample word problem worksheet with mixed numbers and like denominators

1. Tina ran $3\frac{2}{5}$ miles in the morning and $2\frac{1}{5}$ miles in the afternoon. How many miles did she run altogether?
2. We had $\frac{3}{4}$ of an inch of rain on Monday and $\frac{1}{4}$ of an inch of rain on Tuesday. How much more rain did we have on Monday?
3. Ricardo's cat weighed $14\frac{2}{6}$ pounds. If the cat gains $3\frac{1}{6}$ pounds how much will it weigh?
4. Joan bought $6\frac{2}{4}$ pounds of meat. After she cooked the meat, it weighed $2\frac{1}{4}$ pounds. How much less does it weigh now?

INSTRUCTIONAL PROCEDURES: MULTIPLICATION AND DIVISION OF FRACTIONS

Multiplying Fractions

The first type of multiplication problem, which involves multiplying two proper fractions, is usually introduced in fourth grade:

$$\frac{3}{4} \times \frac{2}{5} \qquad \frac{4}{9} \times \frac{1}{3}$$

The second type, which also is usually introduced during fourth grade, involves multiplying a fraction and a whole numeral. This type of problem is important, since it occurs often in word problems:

$$\frac{3}{4} \times 8$$

The third type of problem, usually introduced in fifth grade, involves multiplying one or more mixed number:

$$5 \times 3\frac{2}{4} \qquad 4\frac{1}{2} \times 2\frac{3}{5} \qquad \frac{3}{4} \times 2\frac{1}{2}$$

Multiplying Proper Fractions

Multiplying proper fractions can be introduced several weeks after students have learned to add and subtract fractions with like denominators. The steps for multiplying fractions are presented in **Format 13.17: Multiplying Two Proper Fractions**. The reason multiplying proper fractions is taught first is that it is a prerequisite for finding equivalent fractions and for the second type of multiplication problem, a fraction multiplied by a whole number.

The format includes two parts. In Part A, the structured board presentation, the teacher presents a rule about multiplying fractions—Work top times the top and bottom times the bottom—and demonstrates how to apply the rule to several problems. Part B is a structured worksheet presentation. Note that the examples in this part include both multiplication problems and problems that involve addition and subtraction of fractions. This mixture is essential to provide students with practice in discriminating between the multiplication strategy (multiply across the top and bottom) and the addition/subtraction strategy (work only across the top). Part B begins with a verbal exercise in which the teacher asks students how they work a particular type of problem ("What do you do when you multiply fractions? What do you do when you add or subtract fractions?").

Multiplying Fractions and Whole Numbers

Problems that involve multiplying a fraction and a whole number are important because they have many real-life applications. For example, consider the following problem: "A boat engine called for $\frac{2}{3}$ of a quart of oil for every gallon of gasoline. John had 9 gallons of gas. How much oil did he need?"

Multiplying fractions and whole numbers in word problems can be introduced when students have mastered multiplying proper fractions and converting an improper fraction to a mixed number. The steps in the problem-solving strategy are outlined in **Summary Box 13.3**.

Using pictorial demonstrations that represent multiplying a whole number by a fraction should precede the introduction of the format to promote conceptual understanding. For example, for the problem $\frac{2}{3} \times 6$ the teacher would show six circles divided into thirds. In each of the circles, two of the thirds would be shaded.

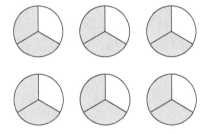

SUMMARY **BOX 13.3**

Multiplying Fractions and Whole Numbers

1. Student reads the problem.		$\frac{3}{4} \times 8$
2. Student changes the whole numeral into a fraction.		$\frac{3}{4} \times \frac{8}{1}$
3. Student multiplies numerators and denominators.		$\frac{3}{4} \times \frac{8}{1} = \frac{24}{4}$
4. Student converts product into a whole numeral or mixed numeral.		$\frac{3}{4} \times \frac{8}{1} = \frac{24}{4} = 6$

The teacher would point out that the picture shows $\frac{2}{3}$ six times. Then the teacher would have the students count the shaded parts in all of the circles (12 shaded parts). The teacher would then write the fraction $\frac{12}{3}$ to represent all of the shaded parts and three parts in each whole. This fraction would be reduced to show that $\frac{2}{3} \times 6$ equals 4 wholes.

Format 13.18: Multiplying a Fraction and a Whole Number

Watch how Lori uses pictures to show her students that a whole number can be converted to a fraction.

Format 13.18: Multiplying a Fraction and a Whole Number teaches students to multiply a fraction and a whole number. Part A introduces an essential component skill: converting a whole number to a fraction. Any whole number may be converted to a fraction by putting it over a denominator of 1. Part B is a structured board presentation during which the teacher models the strategy: converting a whole number to a fraction, multiplying fractions, and determining how many wholes the product of the fractions equals. Part C is a structured worksheet presentation. Note that the worksheet is set up with the prompt taught in Part B. After the fraction bar is a division sign and a box for the answer:

$$\frac{3}{4} \times 8 = \underline{\quad} = \overline{)\quad} = \square$$

Examples should be carefully designed. Some problems should have answers that are whole numbers:

$$\frac{3}{4} \times 8 = 6$$

and some should have answers that are mixed numbers:

$$\frac{2}{3} \times 7 = 4\frac{2}{3}$$

Initially, the whole number should represent a relatively small number (below 20). As students learn to multiply and divide larger numbers, the examples should include hundreds and then thousands numbers:

$$\frac{3}{4} \times 2000$$

Multiplying Mixed Numbers

Multiplying a mixed number and a whole number is an important component skill for advanced map-reading skills. For example, if 1 inch equals 50 miles, how many miles will $3\frac{1}{2}$ inches equal?

$$50 \times 3\frac{1}{2} = 175$$

Initially, we recommend teaching a strategy in which the students convert a mixed number into an improper fraction before working the problem. See **Summary Box 13.4** in which problems a and b illustrate the recommended steps.

Later, a more sophisticated strategy involving the distributive property may be introduced for problems in which a whole number and mixed number are multiplied. The students first multiply the whole-number factor by the whole number from the mixed-number factor, then multiply the whole-number factor by the fraction, and finally add the products. This process is shown below:

$$5 \times 3\frac{1}{2} = (5 \times 3) + \left(5 \times \frac{1}{2}\right)$$

$$= 15 + 2\frac{1}{2}$$

$$= 17\frac{1}{2}$$

SUMMARY BOX 13.4

Multiplying Mixed Numbers

Steps	Problems
	a. $5\frac{1}{2} \times 3\frac{2}{4} =$ $\qquad$ b. $5 \times 2\frac{3}{4} =$
1. Convert mixed number to improper fraction.	$\frac{11}{2} \times \frac{14}{4} =$ $\qquad$ $\frac{5}{1} \times \frac{11}{4} =$
2. Multiply.	$\frac{11}{2} \times \frac{14}{4} = \frac{154}{8}$ $\qquad$ $\frac{5}{1} \times \frac{11}{4} = \frac{55}{4}$
3. Convert answer to mixed numeral.	$19\frac{2}{8} = 19\frac{1}{4}$ $\qquad$ $13\frac{3}{4} = 13\frac{3}{4}$ $\frac{154}{8} = 8\overline{)154}$ $\qquad$ $\frac{55}{4} = 4\overline{)55}$

Dividing Fractions

To introduce students to division of fractions, we recommend highlighting the relationship between fractions and multiplication/division number families. The number family relationships clearly illustrate the relationship between whole numbers and fractions. Students should be presented this concept as an introduction to dividing fractions no later than fifth grade. Teachers should introduce the fraction bar as another way of saying "divided by." The fraction $\frac{1}{2}$ also can be read as "1 divided by 2." After students have practiced reading fractions both ways, they learn that multiplication number families can be turned.

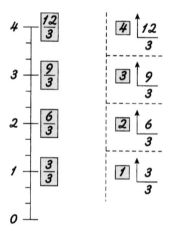

Students practice identifying the big number and the two small numbers. Later, students apply this knowledge to number lines.

Students then complete the fractions for the number lines. The fraction for 1 on the number line is $\frac{3}{3}$. The fraction for two is $\frac{6}{3}$. Next to the numerals on the number line, students complete the number families that are turned. The numeral that goes in the box is the whole number on the number line. The numerals for the fractions are the vertically oriented numbers in the family. After students master reading fractions as division problems, teachers can introduce writing fractions as division problems. The teacher would have the students read the fraction, read the fraction as a division problem, write the regular division problem, and solve.

Dividing fractions is usually introduced in fifth grade. Fraction division problems may be divided into three types. First are those in which a proper fraction is divided by a proper fraction:

$$\frac{2}{3} \div \frac{3}{4} \qquad \frac{4}{5} \div \frac{2}{7}$$

This type of problem, while used infrequently, is introduced first because it prepares students for the second type of problem in which a fraction is divided by a whole number:

$$\frac{3}{4} \div 2$$

Problems such as the one above are more common. For example, John has $\frac{3}{4}$ of a pound of candy. He wants to split the candy up equally among his two friends. How much candy should he give to each friend?

The third type of problem involves dividing a mixed number:

$$3\frac{1}{2} \div 4 \qquad 5\frac{1}{2} \div 2\frac{1}{3}$$

The strategy taught to solve division problems involves inverting the second fraction, changing the sign to a multiplication sign, and then multiplying. For example, $\frac{3}{4} \div \frac{2}{3}$ is worked by inverting $\frac{2}{3}$ so that the problem becomes $\frac{3}{4} \times \frac{3}{2} = \frac{9}{8}$. Because the procedure is simple, we have not included a separate format. The teacher explains that division of fractions can be difficult. In order to make division of fractions easier, we "invert and multiply." We recommend that the teacher demonstrate this procedure using several examples on the board before providing structured worksheets.

Although the strategy for dividing fractions is relatively simple, the rationale for using this strategy is more complex. **Figure 13.3** provides a rationale for teachers who wish to demonstrate why this procedure is appropriate.

Problems in which students divide by a whole number are solved by first converting the whole number to a fraction and then inverting that fraction:

$$\frac{3}{4} \div 2 = \frac{3}{4} \div \frac{2}{1} = \frac{3}{4} \times \frac{1}{2} = \frac{3}{8}$$

Problems that include a mixed number are solved by converting the mixed number to an improper fraction, inverting, and multiplying.

Word Problems—Multiplication and Division

Multiplication and division word problems can be introduced after students have mastered multiplying and dividing fractions. Multiplication word problems with fractions usually involve figuring out what a fractional part of a specified group equals. Here is a typical problem:

There are 20 children in our class; $\frac{3}{4}$ of the children are girls. How many girls are in the class?

This type of problem is introduced shortly after students can solve problems in which a fraction and a whole number are multiplied $\left(\frac{3}{4} \times 20 \right)$. As an intermediate step to prepare students for the word problems, the teacher can present problems with prompts like these:

$$\frac{3}{4} \text{ of } 12 = \frac{\square}{\square} = \square \qquad \frac{2}{3} \text{ of } 9 = \frac{\square}{\square} = \square$$

FIGURE 13.3 Rationale for fraction division strategy

To divide a fraction by another fraction, students are taught to invert the second fraction and multiply, which is essentially a shortcut. The strategy is based on two principles: the multiplicative identity element (any number multiplied [or divided] by 1 equals that number) and the inverse principle (any number multiplied by its inverse equals 1).

$$\frac{2}{3} \div \frac{4}{5} = \frac{2}{3} \times \frac{5}{4}$$

To explain the invert and multiply strategy, **we first rewrite the division problem with a fraction bar as a fraction over a fraction.** Remember, the fraction bar can be translated as "divide by." We still read the problem as $\frac{2}{3}$ divided by $\frac{4}{5}$.

$$\frac{\frac{2}{3}}{\frac{4}{5}}$$

Next we convert the denominator to 1. We want a 1 in the denominator because of the identity principle—a number divided by 1 equals that number. (Dividing by 1 is easier than dividing by any other number.) **To convert the denominator $\left(\frac{4}{5}\right)$ to 1, we must multiply it by its inverse $\left(\frac{5}{4}\right)$.** Any number multiplied by its inverse equals 1. In this example, $\frac{4}{5} \times \frac{5}{4} = \frac{20}{20} = 1$. In the original problem, this step looks like the following:

$$\frac{\frac{2}{3}}{\frac{4}{5}}\left(\frac{}{\frac{5}{4}}\right) = \frac{}{\frac{20}{20}} = \frac{}{1}$$

If we multiply the denominator by $\frac{5}{4}$, we also must multiply the numerator by $\frac{5}{4}$ because of the identify principle—$\frac{5}{4}$ over $\frac{5}{4}$ is the same as multiplying by 1. Multiplying by a fraction of one is the procedure introduced earlier to generate equivalent fractions.

$$\frac{\frac{2}{3}}{\frac{4}{5}}\left(\frac{\frac{5}{4}}{\frac{5}{4}}\right) = \frac{}{1}$$

When we multiply the numerator, we get our answer to the division problem.

$$\frac{\frac{2}{3}\left(\frac{5}{4}\right)}{1} = \frac{\frac{10}{12}}{1} = \frac{10}{12}$$

Inverting and multiplying is an easy and efficient way to divide fractions.

$$\frac{2}{3} \div \frac{4}{5} = \frac{2}{3} \times \frac{5}{4} = \frac{10}{12}$$

Students are taught that "of" in this problem can be translated to "multiply." The problem ¾ of 12 would be converted to ¾ × 12 and then solved:

$$\frac{3}{4} \times \frac{12}{1} = \frac{36}{4} = 9$$

As students are able to solve operations with larger numbers, the examples in the word problems should include larger numbers. Instead of $\frac{2}{3}$ of 12, a problem might ask for $\frac{2}{3}$ of 126.

The most common type of division word problem involves dividing a fraction by a whole number. Here is an example of this type of problem:

Mia has $\frac{2}{3}$ of an apple left. She wants to share it equally with her 2 friends. How much of the apple should she give to each friend?

This type of problem can be introduced when students can work problems in which a fraction can be divided by a whole number.

DIAGNOSIS AND REMEDIATION OF COMMON FRACTION ERRORS

Students may miss fraction problems for one or a combination of the following reasons:

1. Fact error (dividing 18 by 3 and ending with 5, multiplying 7×8 and ending with 54): If a student misses a problem solely because of a fact error, the teacher need not spend time working on the fraction skill but should reteach the facts.
2. Component-skill error: The student makes an error on a previously taught skill, which causes the student to miss the current type of problem. For example, when working the problem $\frac{2}{3} \times 12$ the student converts 12 to the fraction $\frac{1}{12}$ instead of $\frac{12}{1}$ writing $\frac{2}{3} \times \frac{1}{12} = \frac{2}{36}$. The remediation procedure involves reteaching the earlier-taught component skill. In the example given, the teacher first would reteach the student how to convert a whole number to a fraction. When the student's performance indicates mastery of the component skill, the teacher would lead the student through solving the original type of problem using the structured worksheet part of the appropriate format.
3. Strategy error: A strategy error occurs when the student does not correctly follow the steps to solve a problem. For example, when attempting to convert $\frac{12}{4}$ to a whole number, the student subtracts 4 from 12, ending with 8. The remediation procedure involves reteaching the entire strategy beginning with the structured board part of the format.

The following sections give examples of common errors made on the various types of fraction problems along with suggestions for remediation.

Errors in Reading and Writing Fractions and Mixed Numerals

Students should read the problem as the first step in any format. If the teacher notices the student reading a fraction or mixed numeral incorrectly, the teacher would reintroduce the appropriate format. For example, if a student misread $\frac{3}{2}$ as "two-thirds," then the teacher would present **Format 13.4: Reading Fractions**. Or if a student read $5\frac{1}{3}$ as $\frac{5}{3}$, the teacher would present **Format 13.6: Reading and Writing Mixed Numerals**.

Errors in Adding and Subtracting Fractions

When adding fractions with like denominators, students usually will make strategy errors or fact errors. Note the problems below:

a. $\frac{7}{9} - \frac{2}{9} = \frac{5}{0}$ b. $\frac{4}{8} + \frac{2}{8} = \frac{6}{16}$

c. $\frac{7}{9} - \frac{2}{9} = \frac{6}{9}$ d. $\frac{4}{8} + \frac{6}{8} = \frac{11}{8}$

Problems a and b illustrate strategy errors. The student does not know that the denominators are not added or subtracted. The remediation procedure involves reintroducing **Format 13.14: Adding and Subtracting Fractions with Like Denominators** beginning with Part A. Problems c and d,

FIGURE 13.4 Errors in addition with unlike denominators

Error Patterns	Diagnosis	Remediation Procedures	Remediation Examples
1. $\dfrac{4}{5} + \dfrac{2}{3} = \dfrac{4}{5}\left(\underset{15}{\times 3}\right) + \dfrac{2}{3}\left(\underset{15}{\times 3}\right) = \dfrac{6}{15}$	Component-skill error: student failed to multiply by a fraction equal to one in order to generate equivalent fractions with like denominators.	Present **Format 13.16** beginning with Part A, emphasizing step 5.	Addition problems with unlike denominators
2. $\dfrac{4}{8} + \dfrac{2}{4} = \dfrac{4\left(\underset{32}{\times 4}\right)^{16}}{8\left(\underset{}{\times 4}\right)} + \dfrac{2\left(\underset{32}{\times 8}\right)^{16}}{4\left(\underset{}{\times 8}\right)} = \dfrac{32}{32}$	Component-skill error: student did not find least common multiple. Note that the answer is correct.	Teacher points this out but emphasizes it's important to find the least common multiple. Present **Format 13.15.**	Find the LCM of 6 and 9, 8 and 6, 4 and 12, etc. Include examples when one of the denominators is the LCM.
3. $\dfrac{4}{5} + \dfrac{2}{3} = \dfrac{6}{8}$	Strategy error: student adds denominators.	Present entire format for fractions with unlike denominators (**13.16**) over, beginning with Part A.	Addition problems with unlike denominators
4. $\dfrac{5}{6} + \dfrac{2}{4} = \dfrac{5\times 2}{6\left(\underset{12}{\times 2}\right)}^{10} + \dfrac{2\times 3}{4\left(\underset{12}{\times 3}\right)}^{5} = \dfrac{15}{12}$	Fact error: student multiplied 2 × 3 incorrectly.	Teacher works on 2 × 3 fact.	

on the other hand, indicate fact errors. The remediation procedure depends on the number of problems missed. If a student misses less than 10% of the problems because of fact errors, the teacher works on the facts missed. If the student misses more than 10% of the problems because of fact errors, the teacher must work on improving fact accuracy through implementing a stronger motivational system and/or providing more practice on basic facts. (See Chapter 6.)

Problems involving adding or subtracting fractions with unlike denominators may be missed because of fact, component-skill, or strategy errors. Note the problems in **Figure 13.4**. The cause of each error and the suggested remediation procedures are provided for common mistakes.

APPLY WHAT YOU LEARNED

 Click on the √ to answer the questions online.

1. Below are various fraction-related problems. Describe the type each problem represents. List the types in their order of introduction.

   a. $\dfrac{2}{3} - \dfrac{1}{3}$

   b. Circle the picture that shows $\dfrac{2}{4}$

   c. Read this fraction: $\dfrac{3}{5}$

   d. $\dfrac{3}{4} + \dfrac{2}{5}$

   e. $5\dfrac{4}{7} - 3\dfrac{2}{7}$

   f. $\dfrac{12}{5} = \square$

   g. $\dfrac{3}{5} = \dfrac{\square}{10}$

   h. $5\dfrac{1}{2} \times 3$

   i. $3\dfrac{4}{5} = \dfrac{\square}{5}$

2. Write a structured worksheet presentation for teaching students how to solve the following type of problem:

   Draw a picture for this fraction: $\dfrac{3}{4} =$ ◯ ◯

3. A teacher is presenting the first lesson in which she is teaching students to decode fractions in the traditional manner (e.g., ⅔ is read as two-thirds). Below are four sets of examples. Which set is appropriate? Tell why the other three sets are not appropriate.

   a. $\dfrac{2}{3}$ $\dfrac{1}{2}$ $\dfrac{4}{5}$ $\dfrac{7}{3}$ $\dfrac{1}{4}$ $\dfrac{2}{9}$ $\dfrac{3}{2}$ $\dfrac{1}{5}$

   b. $\dfrac{1}{8}$ $\dfrac{1}{4}$ $\dfrac{1}{9}$ $\dfrac{1}{6}$ $\dfrac{1}{5}$ $\dfrac{1}{7}$

   c. $\dfrac{1}{8}$ $\dfrac{3}{4}$ $\dfrac{7}{6}$ $\dfrac{1}{6}$ $\dfrac{2}{8}$ $\dfrac{9}{4}$ $\dfrac{1}{4}$

   d. $\dfrac{3}{4}$ $\dfrac{7}{9}$ $\dfrac{8}{4}$ $\dfrac{2}{9}$ $\dfrac{4}{6}$ $\dfrac{8}{6}$ $\dfrac{5}{7}$

4. A student writes the mixed number five and one-third as ⅝. Specify the wording the teacher uses in making the correction.

5. Specify the wording the teacher uses in making the correction for the following error:

   $$\dfrac{3}{4} = \dfrac{\boxed{3}}{8}$$

6. Identify the examples below that would not be included in an early equivalent-fraction exercise.

   a. $\dfrac{2}{3} = \dfrac{\square}{9}$ b. $\dfrac{5}{7} = \dfrac{\square}{28}$ c. $\dfrac{3}{4} = \dfrac{\square}{6}$

   d. $\dfrac{4}{5} = \dfrac{\square}{20}$ e. $\dfrac{3}{5} = \dfrac{\square}{20}$ f. $\dfrac{4}{6} = \dfrac{\square}{10}$

7. Below are four sets of examples constructed by the teacher for an early reducing-fraction exercise. One set is appropriate. Three are not appropriate. Identify the inappropriate sets. Tell why they're inappropriate.

   a. $\dfrac{8}{12}$ $\dfrac{7}{9}$ $\dfrac{6}{18}$ $\dfrac{4}{6}$ $\dfrac{5}{20}$ $\dfrac{2}{3}$

   b. $\dfrac{8}{12}$ $\dfrac{6}{18}$ $\dfrac{4}{6}$ $\dfrac{5}{20}$ $\dfrac{3}{12}$ $\dfrac{6}{8}$

   c. $\dfrac{8}{12}$ $\dfrac{7}{9}$ $\dfrac{10}{15}$ $\dfrac{12}{20}$ $\dfrac{3}{5}$ $\dfrac{6}{8}$

   d. $\dfrac{4}{7}$ $\dfrac{5}{20}$ $\dfrac{22}{36}$ $\dfrac{8}{16}$ $\dfrac{18}{34}$ $\dfrac{5}{9}$

8. Write the structured worksheet presentation used in leading students through reducing the fraction ¹²⁄₁₈ to its lowest terms.

9. Below are sets of examples prepared by various teachers for an exercise in which students convert improper fractions to mixed numbers. Tell which sets are inappropriate.

   a. $\dfrac{9}{5}$ $\dfrac{11}{3}$ $\dfrac{9}{3}$ $\dfrac{12}{7}$ $\dfrac{14}{5}$ $\dfrac{12}{4}$

   b. $\dfrac{9}{4}$ $\dfrac{3}{7}$ $\dfrac{8}{2}$ $\dfrac{7}{5}$ $\dfrac{8}{3}$ $\dfrac{5}{9}$ $\dfrac{9}{3}$ $\dfrac{7}{3}$

   c. $\dfrac{9}{5}$ $\dfrac{3}{7}$ $\dfrac{5}{2}$ $\dfrac{4}{9}$ $\dfrac{7}{3}$ $\dfrac{9}{2}$

10. Below are sets of examples prepared by several teachers for an independent worksheet exercise focusing on adding and subtracting fractions with unlike denominators. Tell which sets are inappropriate. Explain why.

a. $\dfrac{6}{14} - \dfrac{3}{8}$ $\dfrac{5}{8} + \dfrac{1}{5}$ $\dfrac{4}{9} - \dfrac{5}{12}$ $\dfrac{3}{8} + \dfrac{2}{8}$

b. $\dfrac{3}{8} + \dfrac{1}{5}$ $\dfrac{5}{7} - \dfrac{1}{4}$ $\dfrac{3}{8} + \dfrac{2}{8}$ $\dfrac{3}{5} + \dfrac{2}{3}$ $\dfrac{2}{3} - \dfrac{1}{2}$ $\dfrac{4}{7} - \dfrac{2}{5}$

c. $\dfrac{3}{4} - \dfrac{2}{3}$ $\dfrac{4}{9} - \dfrac{2}{9}$ $\dfrac{2}{9} + \dfrac{2}{3}$ $\dfrac{5}{7} - \dfrac{1}{2}$ $\dfrac{3}{8} + \dfrac{1}{4}$ $\dfrac{3}{7} + \dfrac{2}{7}$

11. Below are examples of errors typically made by students. Specify the diagnosis and remediation for each student.

Xavier

$$\frac{7}{8} - \frac{1}{6} = \frac{6}{2}$$

Anna

$$\frac{5}{9} + \frac{2}{5} = \frac{5}{9}\left(\frac{5}{5}\right) + \frac{2}{5}\left(\frac{9}{9}\right) = \frac{5}{9}\overset{25}{\left(\frac{5}{5}\right)} + \frac{2}{5}\overset{18}{\left(\frac{9}{9}\right)} = \frac{42}{45}$$

Samuel

$$\frac{4}{5} + \frac{1}{2} = \frac{4}{5}\left(\frac{2}{2}\right) + \frac{1}{2}\left(\frac{5}{5}\right) = \frac{4}{5}\overset{8}{\left(\frac{2}{2}\right)} + \frac{1}{2}\overset{5}{\left(\frac{5}{5}\right)} = \frac{13}{10} = \frac{3}{10}$$

Destiny

$$\frac{3}{5} + \frac{2}{3} = \frac{3}{5}\left(\frac{5}{3}\right) + \frac{2}{3}\left(\frac{3}{5}\right) = \frac{3}{5}\overset{15}{\left(\frac{5}{3}\right)} + \frac{2}{3}\overset{6}{\left(\frac{3}{5}\right)} = \frac{21}{15}$$

12. Write a structured worksheet exercise to lead students through solving this problem:

$$8 - 3\frac{4}{5}$$

13. Specify the diagnosis and remediation procedures for each student.

Marquis

$$\frac{6}{7} \text{ of } 28 = \frac{162}{7} = 23\frac{1}{7}$$

Sara

$$\frac{6}{7} \text{ of } 28 = \frac{6}{196} = \frac{3}{98}$$

Diego

$$\frac{6}{7} \text{ of } 28 = \frac{168}{7}$$

Format 13.1
INTRODUCING FRACTIONS

TEACHER	STUDENTS
Part A: Number of Parts in Each Whole	

(Draw the following diagram on the board.)

A.   1   2   3

B.   1   2   3

C.   1   2   3

TEACHER	STUDENTS
1. *(Point to A.)* I've drawn whole units on a number line. The tall lines show the end of each whole unit.	
(Point to first tall line in A.) Here's a whole unit.	
(Point to second tall line in A.) Here's a whole unit.	
(Point to third tall line in A.) Here's a whole unit.	
(Draw a line under the first whole unit.)	
2. Look at the first whole unit. *(Point.)* The small lines show the parts in each whole unit. Count the parts inside the first whole unit.	1, 2, 3, 4
How many parts in the first whole unit? *(Write 4 for the denominator in the first box.)*	
(Underline the next whole unit.)	4
3. Look at the second whole unit. *(Point.)* Count the parts inside the second whole unit.	1, 2, 3, 4
How many parts in the second whole unit? *(Write 4 for the denominator in the second box.)*	
(Underline the third whole unit.)	4
Look at the third whole unit. *(Point.)* Count the parts inside the third whole unit. *(Write 4 for the denominator in the third box.)*	1, 2, 3, 4
How many parts in the third whole unit?	4
There are 4 parts in each whole unit. So the bottom number of the fraction is 4. *(Write 4 in the denominator of the fraction after line A.)*	
To correct:	
Note: This is an important preskill. If students do not understand the number of parts in each whole unit, they will not write the correct denominator for fractions.	
(First, point out to students the first whole unit on the number line.) This is where the first whole unit starts and where it stops. As I touch them, start at the beginning and count the parts in that whole unit. How many parts are in that unit? Now, let's count the parts in the next whole unit. How many parts are in that whole unit? There were 4 parts in the first whole unit and 4 parts in this whole unit. So how many parts are in *each* whole unit?	

continued

Format 13.1 *(continued)*
INTRODUCING FRACTIONS

TEACHER	STUDENTS
(Repeat the procedure until students who had problems have mastered this part. Note that some students may have serious problems because they don't understand that the second unit starts where the first unit ends.)	
4. *(Repeat steps 1–3 for examples B and C.)*	

Part B: Writing the Top Part

(Draw a diagram like the one below on the board.)

1. *(Point to number line A.)* Count the number of parts in each whole unit. *(Pause.)* How many parts in each whole unit?	4
Do I write that on the bottom or the top of the fraction? *(Write 4 as the denominator of all fractions on number line A.)*	Bottom
2. Now we are going to write the top numeral of the fraction right here. *(On number line A point to the top of box 1.)*	
To figure out the top numeral of the fraction we count from the beginning and stop here. Count the parts.	1, 2, 3, 4
Yes, when we counted from the beginning and stopped here. We have 4, so I write 4 on the top of the fraction.	
3. Now we are going to write the numeral for the top of the fraction right here. *(On number line A point to the top of box 2.)*	
Remember, to figure out the top numeral of the fraction we count from the beginning and stop here. Count the parts.	1, 2, 3, 4, 5, 6, 7, 8
Yes, when we counted from the beginning and stopped here. We have 8, so I write 8 on the top.	
4. Now we are going to write the top numeral of this fraction right here. *(On number line A point to the top of box 3.)*	
Remember, to figure out the top numeral of the fraction we count from the beginning and stop here. Count the parts.	1, 2, 3, 4, 5, 6, 7, 8, 9, 10, 11, 12
Yes, when we counted from the beginning and stopped here we have 12, so I write 12 on the top.	
(Repeat steps 1–4 for examples B and C.)	

TEACHER	STUDENTS

Part C: Writing Complete Fractions
 	
(Draw the following on the board.)
 	
1. Now we are going to write three fractions for each number line. Look at A. Count the number of parts in each whole unit. *(Pause.)* How many parts in each whole unit?
 	
  So do I write that on the top or the bottom of the fraction?
 	
  Yes, I write 8 on the bottom of each fraction.
 	
2. *(Touch the first fraction box.)* We are going to write a fraction right here. We figure out the top numeral of the fraction by counting from the beginning and stopping here. Count the parts.
 	
  Yes, there are 8 parts. So I write 8 on the top of this fraction.
 	
3. *(Touch the second fraction box.)* We are going to write a fraction right here. We figure out the top numeral of the fraction by counting from the beginning and stopping here. Count the parts.
 	
  Yes, there are 16 parts. So I write 16 on the top of this fraction.
 	
4. *(Touch the fraction box for the shaded part.)* Now, we are going to write a fraction for the shaded part. We figure out the top numeral of the fraction by counting from the beginning of the shaded part. Count the parts.
 	
  Yes, there are 21 shaded parts. So I write 21 on the top of the fraction.
 	
(Repeat steps 1–4 for B and C.)
 	
Part D: Structured Worksheet
 	
(Create a worksheet for students containing examples like the following.)
 	
	8
	
	Bottom
	
	1, 2, 3, 4, 5, 6, 7, 8
	
	1, 2, 3, 4, 5, 6, 7, 8,
	9, 10, 11, 12, 13,
	14, 15, 16
	
	1, 2, 3, 4, 5, 6, 7, 8, 9,
	10,11, 12, 13, 14, 15, 16,
	17, 18, 19, 20, 21

continued

Format 13.1 *(continued)*
INTRODUCING FRACTIONS

TEACHER	STUDENTS
1. You are going to write the fractions for the whole units and for the shaded parts. Touch A. Count the number of parts in each whole. How many parts in each whole unit?	4
Where do you write the 4?	On the bottom
Write 4 as the bottom numeral for each of the fractions.	
2. Now you are going to write the top numeral for this whole unit. *(Point to 1 on A.)* How do we figure out the top numeral of the fraction?	Count from the beginning and stop here
Raise your hand when you are done counting. What is the top number?	4
Write 4 as the top numeral in the first fraction.	
3. Now you are going to write the top numeral for the shaded part. How do we figure out the top numeral of the fraction?	Start counting at the beginning of the shaded part
Raise your hand when you are done counting. What is the top number?	6
Write 6 as the top numeral for the shaded part.	
4. *(Point to 2 on A.)* Now you are going to write the top numeral for this whole unit. How do we figure out the top numeral of this fraction?	Count from the beginning
Raise your hand when you are done counting. What is the top number?	8
Write 8 as the top numeral for that fraction.	
5. *(Point to 3 on A.)* Now you are going to write the top numeral for this whole unit. How do we figure out the top number?	Count from the beginning
Raise your hand when you are done counting. What is the top number?	12
Write 12 as the top numeral for that fraction.	
(Repeat steps 1–5 for B–D.)	

Format 13.2
PART–WHOLE DISCRIMINATION

TEACHER	STUDENTS
1. *(Draw the following circles on the board.)*	
2. *(Point to the first circle.)* This is a whole unit. What is this?	A whole unit
(Point to the second circle.) This is a whole unit. What is this?	A whole unit
How many units?	2
3. Each whole unit has parts. The parts are all the same size. Let's see how many parts are in each whole unit.	
4. *(Point to first unit.)* Count the parts as I touch them. *(Touch each part in the first circle.)*	1, 2, 3
How many parts in this whole unit?	3

TEACHER	STUDENTS
5. *(Point to the second circle.)* Now let's count the parts in this whole unit. *(Touch each part as students count.)*	1, 2, 3
6. How many parts in each whole unit?	3 parts
7. Yes, three parts in each whole unit. Say that.	3 parts in each whole unit
8. Now think: How many whole units? Yes, there are 2 whole units with 3 parts in each unit. *(Repeat steps 1–8 with other examples.)*	2

Format 13.3
WRITING NUMERICAL FRACTIONS (See Video in Part A)

TEACHER	STUDENTS
Part A: Structured Board Presentation	
1. *(Draw the following circles on the board.)*	
2. We're going to learn to write fractions. Fractions tell us how many parts in each whole unit and how many parts are used.	
3. The bottom number of a fraction tells how many parts in each whole. What does the bottom number tell?	How many parts in each whole
Look at this picture and think: how many parts in each whole?	4
To correct: Let's see how many parts are in each whole. *(Point to first circle.)* Count the parts as I touch them. *(Touch each part in the first circle. Repeat same procedures with next two circles.)* There are 4 parts in this whole and 4 parts in this whole. There are 4 parts in each whole.	
So what is the bottom number of the fraction?	4
I'll write 4 as the bottom number. That tells us 4 parts in each whole. What does the 4 tell us?	4 parts in each whole
4. The top number tells us how many parts are used. What does the top number tell us?	How many parts are used
We find how many parts are used by counting the shaded parts. *(Point to each shaded part.)* Count as I touch the parts. How many parts are shaded?	1, 2, 3, 4, 5 5
So I write 5 as the top number of the fraction. *(Write 5 on top.)* That tells us 5 parts are used. What does the 5 tell us?	5 parts are used
5. I'll say what the fraction tells us. *(Point to 4.)* 4 parts in each whole. *(Point to 5.)* 5 parts are used.	

continued

Format 13.3 *(continued)*
WRITING NUMERICAL FRACTIONS

TEACHER	STUDENTS
6. **You say what the fraction tells us.** *(Point to 4.)*	4 parts in each whole
(Point to 5.)	5 parts are used
(Repeat steps 5–6 until students respond without hesitation. Give individual turns to several students.)	
7. *(Repeat steps 1–4 with the problems below.)*	

Part B: Structured Worksheet

1. *(Give students a worksheet with problems like those that follow.)*

2. **Touch picture a. You're going to write the fraction for the picture.**	
3. **First we write how many parts in each whole. Where do you write the number of parts in each whole?**	In the bottom box
Look and see how many parts in each whole. *(Pause.)* **How many parts in each whole?**	3
Where do you write 3?	In the bottom box
Write the number.	
4. **Now we write the number of parts used. Where do you write the number of parts used?**	On the top
Count the shaded parts. *(Pause.)* **How many parts were used?**	4

TEACHER	STUDENTS
5. Touch the bottom number. *(Pause.)* What does that tell us?	3 parts in each whole
Touch the top number. What does that tell us?	4 parts are used
(Repeat steps 4–5 until students answer without hesitation. Give individual turns to several students on steps 4–5. Repeat steps 1–5 with remaining figures.)	
Part C: Less Structured Worksheet	
1. *(Give students a worksheet similar to the one in Part B.)*	
Touch problem a.	
2. Where do you write how many parts in each whole unit?	On the bottom
3. What do you write on the top?	How many parts are used
Write the numerals.	
4. Touch the bottom number. What does it tell us?	_____ parts in each whole
5. Touch the top number. What does the top number tell us?	_____ parts are used
(Repeat steps 1–5 with remaining examples.)	

Format 13.4
READING FRACTIONS

TEACHER	STUDENTS
1. *(Write the following fractions on the board.)* $$\frac{4}{9} \quad \frac{1}{9} \quad \frac{3}{4} \quad \frac{1}{4} \quad \frac{6}{7} \quad \frac{1}{7} \quad \frac{2}{4} \quad \frac{1}{4}$$ So far we've learned what fractions tell us to do. Today we're going to learn to read fractions a new way. My turn to read this fraction. *(Point to 4.)* Four *(point to 9)* ninths.	
2. Your turn. *(Point to 4, then 9.)*	Four-ninths
3. *(Repeat steps 1 and 2 with half the examples on the board.)*	
4. *(Repeat only step 2 with the remaining examples.)*	
To correct: Model and test correct answer; review series.	

Format 13.5
DETERMINING WHETHER A FRACTION EQUALS, EXCEEDS, OR IS LESS THAN ONE WHOLE

TEACHER	STUDENTS
Part A: Pictorial Demonstrations	
1. I'll draw a picture on the board. You tell me if we use up more than one whole, less than one whole, or just one whole. *(Draw the diagram below.)*	
2. Did I shade more than one whole, less than one whole, or just one whole?	Less than one whole unit
Yes, less than one whole unit. Each circle has 4 parts, but I only shaded 3 parts. *(Repeat step 2 with the examples below.)*	
Part B: Structured Board Presentation	
1. We're going to learn some rules so we can tell if a fraction equals one whole or equals more or less than one whole without drawing a picture.	
2. First rule: A fraction equals one whole when the top number and bottom number are the same. When does a fraction equal one whole?	When the top number and bottom number are the same
3. *(Write the following fraction on the board.)* $$\frac{4}{4}$$	
(Point to the fraction.) Does this fraction equal one whole?	Yes
How do you know?	The top number and bottom number are the same.
(Repeat step 3 with the problems below.) $$\frac{7}{4} \quad \frac{2}{3} \quad \frac{5}{5} \quad \frac{1}{4} \quad \frac{8}{8}$$	
4. Listen to these new rules: If the top number is *more* than the bottom number, the fraction equals *more* than one whole. When does a fraction equal more than one whole?	When the top number is more than the bottom number
If the top number is *less* than the bottom number, the fraction equals *less* than one whole. When does a fraction equal less than one whole?	When the top number is less than the bottom number

TEACHER	STUDENTS
5. *(Write the following fraction on board.)*	
$$\frac{3}{5}$$	
Is the top number the same as the bottom number?	No
So does the fraction equal one whole?	No
Is the top number more or less than the bottom number?	Less
So does the fraction equal more or less than one whole?	Less than one whole
How do you know?	The top number is less than the bottom number.
Yes, 5 parts in each whole and only 3 parts are used.	
(Repeat step 5 with the problems below.)	
$\dfrac{3}{4}$ $\dfrac{3}{3}$ $\dfrac{3}{2}$ $\dfrac{4}{5}$ $\dfrac{4}{4}$ $\dfrac{4}{2}$	
Part C: Structured Worksheet	
(Give students worksheets with problems like these.)	
a. $\dfrac{5}{4}$ more equal less b. $\dfrac{7}{7}$ more equal less c. $\dfrac{3}{7}$ more equal less	
1. In these problems you have to tell if a fraction is more than one whole, equals one whole, or is less than one whole.	
2. Read the fraction in problem a.	$\dfrac{5}{4}$
3. Does the fraction equal one whole?	No
4. Is the top number more or less than the bottom number?	More
So does the fraction equal more or less than one whole?	More than one whole
Put a circle around the word "more."	
(Repeat steps 1–4 with remaining problems.)	

Format 13.6
READING AND WRITING MIXED NUMERALS

TEACHER	STUDENTS
Part A: Pictorial Demonstrations	
(Draw the following diagrams on the board.)	
1. You're going to learn how to write the fraction in this picture a new way. First, let's write the fraction the old way. How many parts in each whole?	4

continued

Format 13.6 (continued)
READING AND WRITING MIXED NUMERALS

TEACHER	STUDENTS
2. Where do I write it? Write it.	On the bottom
3. How many parts are used?	14
4. Where do I write it? Write it.	On the top
5. Now we're going to write the fraction as a mixed number. A mixed number has a whole number and a fraction. What does a mixed number have?	A whole number and a fraction
6. First we count the number of wholes used up. Count as I point. How many wholes are used? So I write 3 in the box. *(Write 3 in the box.)*	3
7. Now we write the fraction to tell about the whole not used. *(Point to the last circle.)* What do I write as the bottom number in the fraction? *(Write 4.)* *To correct:* There are 4 parts in each whole. What do I write as the top number in the fraction? *(Write 2.)* *To correct:* There are 2 parts shaded. The fraction that tells about the whole not used says ²⁄₄.	4 2
8. The mixed number says three *and* two-fourths. hat does the mixed number say? There are 3 whole units used *and* ²⁄₄ of another whole unit used. *(Repeat steps 1–8 with these examples.)*	$3\frac{2}{4}$

a.

b.

c.

Part B: Structured Board Presentation

TEACHER	STUDENTS
1. *(Write the following on the board.)* $2\frac{1}{3}$	
2. A mixed number is a whole number and a fraction. What is a mixed number?	A whole number and a fraction
3. *(Point to: 2⅓.)* What's the whole number? What's the fraction?	 2 $\frac{1}{3}$

TEACHER	STUDENTS
4. My turn. We read this mixed number as two *and* one-third. How do we read this mixed number?	$2\frac{1}{3}$
5. *(Write the following on the board.)* $3\frac{2}{8}$	
What's the whole number?	3
What's the fraction?	$\frac{2}{8}$
Read the mixed number.	$3\frac{2}{8}$
(Repeat step 5 with these mixed numbers.) $5\frac{2}{7}$ $7\frac{1}{2}$ $3\frac{4}{5}$ $6\frac{1}{2}$	
Part C: Structured Worksheet	
1. Listen: 2¾. Say that.	$2\frac{3}{4}$
What is the whole number?	2
I write 2 so that it takes up the whole space.	
(Model writing on the board or document camera.)	
$\overline{\underline{2}}$	
2. Listen 2¾. What is the fraction?	$\frac{3}{4}$
I write the fraction line in the middle of the space next to the 2. Then I write the fraction numbers small. *(Model writing on the board or document camera.)* $\overline{\underline{2\ \frac{3}{4}}}$	
3. What is the mixed number?	$2\frac{3}{4}$
(Repeat steps 1–3 with the problems below.) $7\frac{1}{2}$ $4\frac{2}{5}$ *(Give students lined paper.)*	
4. Now it's your turn. You're going to write the mixed number 5⅔. What mixed number are you going to write?	$5\frac{2}{3}$
5. Listen: 5⅔. What is the whole number?	5
Write it. Make it big so that it touches both lines. *(Monitor responses.)*	
6. Listen: 5⅔. What is the fraction?	$\frac{2}{3}$
Put the fraction line right in the middle of the space next to the 5. Then write ⅔. Write the numbers small.	

continued

Format 13.6 *(continued)*
READING AND WRITING MIXED NUMERALS

TEACHER	STUDENTS
(Repeat steps 4–6 with these numbers.) $7\frac{2}{4}$ $9\frac{1}{3}$ $7\frac{1}{2}$ $5\frac{3}{8}$	
7. Listen: $3\frac{4}{6}$. Say it. Write it. *(Monitor responses. Repeat step 7 with the following mixed numbers.)* $7\frac{2}{4}$ $9\frac{1}{3}$ $7\frac{1}{2}$ $5\frac{3}{8}$	$3\frac{4}{6}$

Format 13.7
PRESKILL: CONSTRUCTING FRACTIONS EQUAL TO 1

TEACHER	STUDENTS
Part A: Structured Board Presentation	
1. Here's a rule: When the top number is the same as the bottom, the fraction equals one whole. When does a fraction equal one whole?	When the top number is the same as the bottom number
2. *(Write the following on the board.)* $\frac{\square}{5}$ What number is on the bottom of this fraction? What fraction with a 5 as the bottom number equals one whole?	5 $\frac{5}{5}$
To correct: A fraction equals 1 when the top number is the same as the bottom number. What's the bottom number? What must the top number be? *(Repeat step 2.)* Yes, $\frac{5}{5}$ equals one whole. *(Repeat step 2 with these problems.)* $\frac{\square}{8}$ $\frac{\square}{3}$ $\frac{\square}{6}$ $\frac{\square}{9}$	
Part B: Structured Worksheet	
(Give students worksheets with examples like these.) a. $1 = \frac{\square}{4}$ b. $1 = \frac{\square}{7}$ c. $1 = \frac{\square}{4}$ d. $1 = \frac{\square}{7}$	
1. When does a fraction equal one whole?	When the top number is the same as the bottom number
2. Touch problem a. It says 1 equals how many fourths? Read the problem.	1 equals how many fourths?

TEACHER	STUDENTS
3. Tell me the fraction with 4 as a denominator that equals one whole. Yes, ⁴⁄₄ equals one whole.	$\dfrac{4}{4}$
4. Fill in the missing number. *(Repeat steps 1–4 with remaining problems.)*	Students write 4 in box.

Format 13.8

COMPUTING EQUIVALENT FRACTIONS   (See Video in Part A)

TEACHER	STUDENTS

Part A: Pictorial Demonstrations

1. Fractions are equivalent when they show the same amounts. *(Draw these figures on clear plastic sheets. The circles should be the same size. Use a different color for each figure as in the video.)*

2. This is a picture of ⁵⁄₁₀. *(Point to first figure.)* This is picture of ¹⁄₂. *(Point to second figure.)*

3. Would a person who had ⁵⁄₁₀ of a pie have the same amount as a person who had ¹⁄₂ a pie?   **Yes**

   To correct: (Place one figure on top of the other. Outline the shaded part.) See, the shaded portion is the same size in both pies.

4. So are ⁵⁄₁₀ and ¹⁄₂ equivalent fractions?   **Yes**

5. Yes, ⁵⁄₁₀ and ¹⁄₂ both use the same amount of a whole.

   (Repeat steps 1–5 with these pairs.)

a. 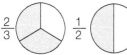   b.   c.

Part B: Multiplying by 1

1. When you multiply by 1, the answer equals the number you start with.

2. *(Write the following problem on the board.)*

   $$\dfrac{3}{8} \times 1$$

   What number do we start with? $\dfrac{3}{8}$

   Will our answer equal 1?   **Yes**

   How do you know?   **We are multiplying by 1**

   (Repeat step 2 with the following problems.)

   $\dfrac{1}{2} \times 1$ $\dfrac{1}{4} \times 5$

continued

Format 13.8 *(continued)*
COMPUTING EQUIVALENT FRACTIONS

TEACHER	STUDENTS
3. Here's a rule about fractions: When you multiply by a fraction that equals 1, your answer equals the number you start with. Listen, again. *(Repeat rule.)*	
4. *(Write the following problem on the board.)* $$\frac{4}{8} \times \frac{2}{2}$$	
What fraction do we start with?	$\frac{4}{8}$
What are we multiplying $^4/_8$ by?	$\frac{2}{2}$
5. Does $^2/_2$ equal 1?	Yes
So will our answer equal $^4/_8$?	Yes
How do you know?	We are multiplying by a fraction that equals 1.
(Repeat steps 4 and 5 with the problems below.) $$\frac{4}{8} \times \frac{4}{4} \quad \frac{5}{6} \times \frac{3}{6}$$ $$\frac{5}{6} \times \frac{2}{3} \quad \frac{3}{9} \times \frac{8}{8}$$ $$\frac{7}{2} \times \frac{9}{9} \quad \frac{2}{4} \times \frac{4}{4}$$	
Part C: Structured Board Problems	
1. *(Write the following problem on the board.)* $$\frac{2}{3}\left(\;\right) = \frac{\square}{12}$$	
2. We don't change the value of a fraction when we multiply it by a fraction that equals 1.	
3. These parentheses indicate multiplication. We're going to multiply $^2/_3$ by a fraction that equals 1. We have to figure out the fraction that equals 1.	
4. We are going to end with a fraction that has the same value as $^2/_3$. *(Point to 12.)*	
What's the denominator of the fraction we end with?	12
Three times what number equals 12?	4
So we multiply by a fraction that has a denominator of 4.	
5. *(Write 4 inside parentheses.)* $$\frac{2}{3}\left(\frac{}{4}\right) = \frac{\square}{12}$$	

TEACHER	STUDENTS

6. The fraction inside the parentheses must equal 1. If the bottom number is 4, what must the numerator be? `4`

 (Write a four in the numerator inside parentheses.)

$$\frac{2}{3}\left(\frac{4}{4}\right) = \frac{\square}{12}$$

 Yes, we multiply ⅔ by ⁴⁄₄. What do we multiply ⅔ by? $\frac{4}{4}$

7. We figured out the fraction equal to 1 that we're multiplying by. Let's multiply and figure out how many twelfths ⅔ equals. $2 \times 4 =$ how many? `8`

 (Write the problem on the board.)

$$\frac{2}{3}\left(\frac{4}{4}\right) = \frac{8}{12}$$

8. We multiplied ⅔ by a fraction that equals 1 and ended with ⁸⁄₁₂; ⅔ equals ⁸⁄₁₂.

 (Repeat steps 1–8 with these problems.)

$$\frac{3}{5} = \frac{\square}{10} \qquad \frac{2}{3} = \frac{\square}{15} \qquad \frac{2}{7} = \frac{\square}{21}$$

Part D: Structured Worksheet

(Give students a worksheet with problems similar to these.)

a. $\frac{3}{4}\left(\frac{}{}\right) = \frac{\square}{8}$ b. $\frac{5}{9}\left(\frac{}{}\right) = \frac{\square}{27}$ c. $\frac{1}{4}\left(\frac{}{}\right) = \frac{\square}{20}$

d. $\frac{2}{5}\left(\frac{}{}\right) = \frac{\square}{20}$ e. $\frac{3}{5}\left(\frac{}{}\right) = \frac{\square}{35}$ f. $\frac{2}{3}\left(\frac{}{}\right) = \frac{\square}{12}$

1. Touch problem a. It says ¾ Equals how many eighths? What does the problem say? $\frac{3}{4}$ equals how many eighths?

2. We have to multiply ¾ by a fraction that equals 1. What is the denominator of the fraction we start with? `4`

 What is the denominator of the fraction we end with? `8`

 Four times what number equals 8? `2`

 Write 2 as the denominator in the parentheses.

3. We're multiplying ¾ by a fraction that equals 1. What fraction with a denominator of 2 equals one whole? $\frac{2}{2}$

 Write 2 as a numerator in the parentheses.

4. We figured out the fraction equal to 1. Now what do we multiply to figure out the missing numerator? 3×2

 What is 3×2? `6`

 Write 6 in the box.

5. What fraction equals ¾? $\frac{6}{8}$

6. How do you know that ¾ equals ⁶⁄₈? We multiplied by a fraction that equals 1.

 (Repeat steps 1–6 with remaining problems.)

continued

Format 13.8 *(continued)*
COMPUTING EQUIVALENT FRACTIONS

TEACHER	STUDENTS
Part E: Less Structured Worksheet	
1. *(Give students a worksheet with problems like the one below. Note that parentheses aren't written in.)*	
a. $\frac{5}{6} = \frac{\square}{12}$ b. $\frac{3}{4} = \frac{\square}{20}$ c. $\frac{1}{3} = \frac{\square}{12}$ d. $\frac{1}{5} = \frac{\square}{20}$ e. $\frac{2}{5} = \frac{\square}{15}$ f. $\frac{3}{7} = \frac{\square}{14}$	
2. Touch problem a. Read the problem.	$\frac{5}{6}$ equals how many twelfths?
3. We must multiply $\frac{5}{6}$ by a fraction that equals 1. To keep the fractions equal, put parentheses next to $\frac{5}{6}$.	
4. Look at the numbers and get ready to tell me what we must multiply $\frac{5}{6}$ by.	$\frac{2}{2}$
To correct: What is the denominator of the fraction we start with? What is the bottom number of the fraction we end with? Six times what number equals 12? That's the denominator. The fraction we're multiplying equals 1. What fraction goes in the parentheses?	
Write $\frac{2}{2}$ in the parentheses.	
5. Multiply and write in the missing numerator.	
6. What fraction does $\frac{5}{6}$ Equal?	$\frac{10}{12}$
(Repeat steps 2–6 with remaining problems.)	

Format 13.9
PRESKILL: DETERMINING FACTORS

TEACHER	STUDENTS
Part A: Introducing the Concept	
1. *(Write the following problems on board.)* $5 \times 3 = 15$ $9 \times 2 = 18$ $7 \times 6 = 42$ Factors are numbers that are multiplied together.	
2. Read the first problem.	$5 \times 3 = 15$
What numbers are being multiplied?	5 and 3
So 5 and 3 are factors of 15. What are two factors of 15?	5 and 3
3. Look at the board and tell me two factors of 18.	9 and 2
4. Look at the board and tell me two factors of 42.	7 and 6

TEACHER	STUDENTS
Part B: Structured Board Presentation	
1. *(Write 12 on board.)*	
We want to list all of the factors for 12, beginning with the smallest factor.	
Listen: A number multiplied by 1 always equals itself. So is 1 a factor of 12?	Yes
Yes, 1 is a factor of 12. What number times 1 equals 12?	12
12 and 1 are factors of 12; 12 is the largest factor of 12; 1 is the smallest factor of 12.	
We're going to make a list of the factors of 12.	
Let's start with 1 $\times$ 12.	
(Write 1 $\times$ 12.)	
2. 1 is the smallest factor of 12.	
Let's find the next larger number we can multiply and end with 12. I'll say some numbers. You say stop when I come to a number that is a factor of 12.	
Listen, 2	Stop
To correct: (If students don't say stop at 2, say,) We can multiply 2 and end with 12, so 2 is a factor of 12.	
Yes, 2 is the next largest factor of 12. 2 times what number equals 12?	6
So 6 is the other factor of 12 that goes with 2.	
Let's add 2 $\times$ 6 to our list of factors of 12. *(Write 2 $\times$ 6.)*	
1 $\times$ 12.	
2 $\times$ 6	
3. Let's find the next largest factor of 12. I'll say some numbers. You say stop when I come to a factor of 12. We already have 1 and 2. Listen, 3.	Stop
To correct: (If students don't say stop at 3, say,) We can multiply 3 and end with 12, so 2 is a factor of 12.	
Yes, 3 is a factor of 12.	
3 times what other number equals 12?	4
So 4 is the other factor of 12 that goes with 3.	
Let's add 3 $\times$ 4 to our list of factors of 12. *(Write 3 $\times$ 4.)*	
1 $\times$ 12	
2 $\times$ 6	
3 $\times$ 4	
4. Listen, my turn. I know there are no more factors of 12. How do I know? Because the next number after 3 is 4, and we already have that number. We have all the factors of 12.	
Your turn. Do we have all the factors of 12?	Yes
How do you know?	Because the next number after 3 is 4, and we already have that number.

continued

Format 13.9 *(continued)*
PRESKILL: DETERMINING FACTORS

TEACHER	STUDENTS
5. When we say the factors of a number, we read the numbers in order, and we don't have to say *times*.	
My turn to say all the factors of 12: 1, 2, 3, 4, 6, 12. *(Point to the numerals as you say them.)*	
Your turn. Say all the factors of 12.	1, 2, 3, 4, 6, 12
6. *(Write 10 on board.)*	
We want to list all of the factors for 10, beginning with the smallest factor. Listen: A number multiplied by 1 always equals itself. So is 1 a factor of 10?	Yes
Yes, 1 is a factor of 10. What number times 1 equals 10?	
10 and 1 are factors of 10; 10 is the largest factor of 10; 1 is the smallest factor of 10.	10
Let's begin our list of factors of 10 with 1 × 10 *(Write 1 × 10.)*	
1 × 10	
7. Let's find the next largest number we can multiply and end with 10. I'll say some numbers. You say stop when I come to a number that is a factor of 10. 1 is the smallest factor of 10. What number comes next?	2
Is 2 a factor of 10?	
To correct: (If students say no, say,) We can multiply 2 and end with 10, so 2 is a factor of 10.	Yes
Yes, so 2 is the next largest factor of 10.	
2 times what number equals 10?	
So 5 is the other factor of 10 that goes with 2.	5
Let's add 2 × 5 to our list of factors of 10. *(Write 2 × 5.)*	
1 × 10	
2 × 5	
8. Let's find the next largest factor of 10. I'll say some numbers. You say stop when I come to a factor of 10. We already have 1 and 2. Listen: 3 *(pause)*, 4 *(pause)*, 5 *(pause)*.	Stop
To correct: (If students say stop at 3 or 4) We can't multiply that number and end with 10.	
Yes, 5 is a factor of 10. Do we already have 5?	Yes
9. So, do we have all the factors of 10?	Yes
How do you know?	Because the next number was 5, and we already have that number.
10. When we say the factors of a number, we read the numbers in order, and we don't have to say times.	
Your turn. Say all the factors of 10.	1, 2, 5, 10
(Repeat Part B with additional examples.)	

TEACHER	STUDENTS
Part C: Structured Worksheet	
(Give students worksheets with problems like those below and instructions to list all the factors for each number.)	
a. 16	
b. 12	
c. 7	
1. *(Touch a.)* What is the smallest factor of 16?	1
What is the other factor that goes with 1 to equal 16? Write 1 times 16 on the first line. *(Write 1 × 16.)*	16
2. 1 is the smallest factor of 16.	
What is the next largest factor of 16?	2
What is the other factor that goes with 2 to equal 16?	8
Write 2 × 8 below 1 × 16. *(Write 2 × 8.)*	
1 × 16 2 × 8	
What is the next largest factor of 16?	4
What is the other factor that goes with 4 to equal 16?	4
Write 4 × 4 below 2 × 8. *(Write 4 × 4.)*	
1 × 16 2 × 8 4 × 4	
3. Are there any more factors of 16?	No
How do you know?	Because the next number was 8, and we already have that number.
4. Say all the factors of 16.	1, 2, 4, 8, 16
(Repeat steps 1–4 with new target numbers. Have students do remaining problems on their own.)	

Format 13.10
DETERMINING THE GREATEST COMMON FACTOR (GCF)

TEACHER	STUDENTS
1. *(Present students with a worksheet with the following problems.)*	
a. What is the greatest common factor of 12 and 16?	
b. What is the greatest common factor of 10 and 5?	
c. What is the greatest common factor of 4 and 7?	
d. What is the greatest common factor of 10 and 15?	
e. What is the greatest common factor of 18 and 9?	
f. What is the greatest common factor of 12 and 9?	

continued

Format 13.10 *(continued)*
DETERMINING THE GREATEST COMMON FACTOR (GCF)

TEACHER	STUDENTS
2. Find problem a on your worksheet. Read the directions.	What is the greatest common factor of 12 and 16?
Let's find the greatest common factor of 12 and 16. The greatest common factor is the largest number that is a factor of 12 and 16. What is the largest number that is a factor of 12?	12
Is 12 a factor of 16?	No
12 cannot be the greatest common factor of 12 and 16. Why?	Because 12 is not a factor of 16
3. What is the next largest factor of 12?	6
Is 6 a factor of 16?	No
6 is not a factor of 12 and 16. Why?	Because 6 is not a factor of 16
4. What is the next largest factor of 12?	4
Is 4 also a factor of 16?	Yes
So what number is the greatest common factor of 12 and 16?	4
5. Write 4. *(Check students' responses.)*	
(Repeat steps 2–5 with remaining problems.)	

Format 13.11
REDUCING FRACTIONS

TEACHER	STUDENTS
Part A: Structured Board Presentation	
1. *(Write the following problem on the board.)* $$\frac{8}{12} = \left(\ \ \right)\underline{\quad\quad}$$	
2. We're going to reduce this fraction. First, we determine the greatest common factor of the numerator and denominator. What do we do first when we reduce a fraction?	Determine the greatest common factor of the numerator and denominator
3. We want to reduce $8/12$. What is the greatest common factor of 8 and 12? *(Pause.)*	4
To correct: Tell the correct answer. Explain why student's answer is incorrect.	

TEACHER	STUDENTS
4. So we write a fraction equal to 1 inside the parentheses using the greatest common factor. What's the fraction equal to 1 using the greatest common factor? *(Write the new fraction on the board.)* $$\frac{8}{12} = \left(\frac{4}{4}\right) \underline{\quad\quad}$$	$\frac{4}{4}$
5. Let's figure out the numerator of the reduced fraction. *(Point to symbols as you read.)* $8 = 4 \times$ what number? *(Pause.)* *(Write the 2.)* $$\frac{8}{12} = \left(\frac{4}{4}\right)\frac{2}{}$$	2
6. Let's figure out the denominator of the reduced fraction. *(Point to symbols as you read.)* $12 = 4 \times$ what number? *(Pause.)* *(Write the 3.)* $$\frac{8}{12} = \left(\frac{4}{4}\right)\frac{2}{3}$$	3
7. The fraction in parentheses equals 1. We don't change the value of a fraction when we multiply by 1, so we can cross out ⁴⁄₄. *(Cross out.)* The reduced fraction is ²⁄₃. What is the reduced fraction?	$\frac{2}{3}$
8. Read the statement. *(Repeat steps 1–8 with these problems.)* $\frac{15}{20} = \big(\big)\underline{\quad}$ $\frac{9}{36} = \big(\big)\underline{\quad}$ $\frac{16}{24} = \big(\big)\underline{\quad}$	$\dfrac{8}{12} = \dfrac{2}{3}$

Part B: Structured Worksheet

TEACHER	STUDENTS
1. *(Give students a worksheet with problems like those below.)* a. $\dfrac{10}{15} = \big(\big)$ b. $\dfrac{12}{16} = \big(\big)$ c. $\dfrac{8}{24} = \big(\big)$	
2. We're going to reduce these fractions. How do you reduce fractions?	Pull out the greatest common factor of the numerator and the denominator
3. Touch problem a. Read the fraction.	$\dfrac{10}{15}$
4. What is the greatest common factor of 10 and 15?	5
5. So what fraction do you write in the parentheses? Write it. *(Pause.)*	$\dfrac{5}{5}$

continued

Format 13.11 (continued)
REDUCING FRACTIONS

TEACHER	STUDENTS
6. The numbers across the top of the fraction say $10 = 5 \times$ what number? What do the numbers across the top say?	$10 = 5 \times$ what number?
7. What do the numbers across the bottom say?	$15 = 5 \times$ what number?
8. Fill in the numerator and denominator in the reduced fraction. (Monitor students as they write 2 and 3.) Cross out the fraction of 1 in the parentheses. (Pause.)	
9. What is the reduced fraction?	$\dfrac{2}{3}$
10. Read the statement.	$\dfrac{10}{15} = \dfrac{2}{3}$

(Repeat steps 2–10 with remaining problems.)

Part C: Less Structured Worksheet

1. (Present a worksheet like the following. Note that parentheses are not written.)

   Reduce these fractions:

   a. $\dfrac{15}{20}$ b. $\dfrac{8}{12}$ c. $\dfrac{6}{18}$

   d. $\dfrac{4}{7}$ e. $\dfrac{8}{16}$ f. $\dfrac{5}{8}$

TEACHER	STUDENTS
2. How do you reduce a fraction?	Pull out the greatest common factor of the numerator and the denominator
3. Read fraction a.	$\dfrac{15}{20}$
4. Make an equal sign. Then write parentheses on the other side of the equal.	Students write $\dfrac{15}{20} = \left(\ \ \right)$
5. What fraction are you going to write in the parentheses? (Pause.) To correct: What is the greatest common factor of _____ and _____? (Repeat steps 4 and 5.)	$\dfrac{5}{5}$
6. Write ⅝ in the parentheses. Then figure out the reduced fraction. (Pause.)	
7. Cross out the fraction of 1. (Check.)	
8. What is the reduced fraction?	$\dfrac{3}{4}$
9. Read the statement.	$\dfrac{15}{20} = \dfrac{3}{4}$

(Repeat steps 2–9 with remaining problems.)

Format 13.12
CONVERTING IMPROPER FRACTIONS
TO MIXED NUMBERS

(See Video in Part A)

TEACHER	STUDENTS

▶

Part A: Pictorial Demonstration

1. *(Write the following diagram on the board.)*

   $\frac{13}{5}$ ◯ ◯ ◯

2. *(Point to $^{13}/_5$)* Read this fraction.

3. Does $^{13}/_5$ equal more than one whole unit?

4. Let's make a picture and see how many whole units $^{13}/_5$ makes.

5. *(Draw the following circles on the board.)*

   ⊛ ⊛ ⊛

   How many parts in each whole?

6. *(Shade in 13 parts.)* How many parts do we use up?

7. Let's see how many whole units are used. *(Point to first circle.)* Is this whole unit used?

   (Point to second circle.) Is this whole unit used?

   (Point to third circle.) Is this whole unit used?

   How many whole units are used?

   Two whole units are used. Let's look at the last unit and count. How many parts are used?

   And how many parts in each whole?

   So, we can say $^3/_5$ of a unit. We have 2 whole units and $^3/_5$ of another unit. *(Write $2^3/_5$.)*

Part B: Structured Board Presentation

1. We're going to learn a fast way to figure out how many whole units in a fraction. We divide by the number of parts in each whole unit. What do we do to figure out how many whole units?

   (Write the following on the board.)

   $\frac{13}{5}$

   Read this fraction.

   Is this fraction equal to, more than, or less than one unit?

STUDENTS column:

2. $\frac{13}{5}$

3. Yes

5. 5

6. 13

7. Yes

   Yes

   No

   2

   3

   5

Part B:

1. Divide by the number of parts in each whole unit

   $\frac{13}{5}$

   More than one unit

continued

Format 13.12 *(continued)*
CONVERTING IMPROPER FRACTIONS TO MIXED NUMBERS

TEACHER	STUDENTS
2. I want to figure out how many whole units are in this fraction. How many parts in each whole?	5
So I divide by 5. *(Write the problem.)*	

$$\square\,\frac{\square}{\square}$$
$$5\overline{)13}$$

3. Let's divide. *(Point to box.)* How many fives in 13?	2
(Write 2.) We have 2 whole units. *(Point under 13.)* What number do I write here?	10
(Write –10 under 13.)	

$$\boxed{2}\,\frac{\square}{\square}$$
$$5\overline{)13}$$
$$\underline{-10}$$

4. We used 10 parts in 2 wholes. Now let's subtract and see how many parts we have left. What is 13 – 10?	3
5. Since we started with a fraction, we write the remainder as a fraction. Remember, there are 5 parts in each whole. *(Point to 5 in 5$\overline{)13}$.)*	
So we write 5 as the denominator of the fraction. *(Write 5.)* How many parts are remaining?	3
So I write 3 as the numerator of the fraction. *(Write the 3.)*	

$$\boxed{2}\,\frac{\boxed{3}}{\boxed{5}}$$
$$5\overline{)13}$$
$$\underline{10}$$
$$3$$

6. Tell me the mixed number for the fraction ¹³⁄₅.	$2\frac{3}{5}$
Yes, 2³⁄₅ is the same as ¹³⁄₅.	
7. *(Write 2³⁄₅ next to ¹³⁄₅.)* Read the statement.	$\frac{13}{5} = 2\frac{3}{5}$
(Repeat steps 1–7 with ¹²⁄₇ and ⁹⁄₄.)	

Part C: Structured Worksheet

1. *(Give students a worksheet with problems like the following.)*

a. $\dfrac{11}{4} = \,\overline{)}\;\square\,\dfrac{\square}{\square}$ b. $\dfrac{8}{5} = \,\overline{)}\;\square\,\dfrac{\square}{\square}$ c. $\dfrac{7}{3} = \,\overline{)}\;\square\,\dfrac{\square}{\square}$

TEACHER	STUDENTS
2. Touch problem a. Read the fraction.	$\dfrac{11}{4}$
Is $11\frac{1}{4}$ less than 1, equal to 1, or more than 1?	More than 1
So you have to change $11\frac{1}{4}$ to a mixed number. How many parts in each whole?	4
So you divide 4 into 11.	
3. Write the division problem.	Students write $4\overline{)11}$
How many 4s in 11?	2
We can make two whole units. Write the 2 in the big box. Multiply and subtract to find how many parts are left. *(Pause.)* How many parts are left?	3
4. Now let's figure out the fraction remainder. The denominator of the fraction tells how many parts in each whole. How many parts in each whole?	4
So write 4 as the denominator of the fraction.	Students write 4 in the bottom box of the fraction.
What do you write for the numerator?	3
Write it.	
5. What mixed number does $11\frac{1}{4}$ equal?	$2\dfrac{3}{4}$
Say the whole statement.	$\dfrac{11}{4} = 2\dfrac{3}{4}$

(Repeat steps 2–5 with remaining problems.)

Part D: Less Structured Worksheet

1. *(Present a worksheet like the following.)*

Rewrite the fractions that equal more than 1 as mixed numbers.

a. $\dfrac{12}{5}$ b. $\dfrac{3}{4}$

c. $\dfrac{15}{4}$ d. $\dfrac{5}{5}$

2. Some of these fractions equal more than one whole unit. If a fraction equals more than one whole unit, change it to a mixed number. What are you going to do if a fraction equals more than one unit?	Change it to a mixed number
If the fraction does not equal more than one whole unit, don't do anything.	
3. Touch problem a. *(Pause.)* Read the fraction.	$\dfrac{12}{5}$
Does the fraction equal more or less than one unit?	More than one unit
The fraction equals more than one unit, so what must you do?	Change it to a mixed number
What do you divide by?	5
Say the division problem.	5 goes into 12

continued

Format 13.12 (*continued*)
CONVERTING IMPROPER FRACTIONS TO MIXED NUMBERS

TEACHER	STUDENTS
Write the problem and work it. (*Pause.*)	
Remember to write the whole number as a big number and the numerator and denominator small.	
4. $^{12}\!/_5$ equals what mixed number?	$2\frac{2}{5}$
(*Repeat steps 2–4 with remaining problems.*)	

Format 13.13
CONVERTING MIXED NUMBERS TO IMPROPER FRACTIONS

TEACHER	STUDENTS
Part A: Structured Board Presentation - Converting Whole Numbers	
1. (*Write the following problem on the board.*)	
$6 = \dfrac{\square}{4}$	
2. This problem says 6 wholes equal how many fourths. What does the problem say?	6 wholes equal how many fourths
3. We want to figure out how many parts are used when we have 6 wholes. How many parts in each whole?	4
4. We're talking about the same number again and again, so we multiply 6 × 4. What numbers do we multiply?	6 × 4
5. What is 6 × 4?	24
6. Yes, 6 whole units equal 24 fourths. If we use 6 whole units and there are 4 parts in each unit, we use 24 parts.	
(*Repeat steps 1–6 with the problems below.*)	
$5 = \dfrac{\square}{3}$ $2 = \dfrac{\square}{6}$ $4 = \dfrac{\square}{5}$ $6 = \dfrac{\square}{3}$	
Part B: Structured Worksheet - Converting Whole Numbers	
1. (*Give students worksheets with problems such as the ones below.*)	
a. $5 = \dfrac{\square}{3}$ b. $2 = \dfrac{\square}{4}$	
c. $7 = \dfrac{\square}{2}$ d. $5 = \dfrac{\square}{9}$	
2. Touch problem a. (*Pause.*) Read the problem.	5 equals how many thirds
3. How many parts in each whole unit?	3
How many whole units?	5
4. What do we do to figure out how many parts are used?	Multiply
Yes, we multiply 5 × 3. Multiply and write your answer in the box.	

TEACHER	STUDENTS
5. Five equals how many thirds? Say the whole statement. *(Repeat steps 1–5 with several problems, and then have the students complete the rest independently.)*	$\dfrac{15}{3}$ $5 = \dfrac{15}{3}$
Part C: Structured Board Presentation – Converting Mixed Numbers	
1. *(Write the following problem on the board.)* $6\dfrac{1}{4} = \dfrac{}{4}$	
2. This problem says 6¼ equals how many fourths. What does this problem say?	$6\dfrac{1}{4}$ equals how many fourths
3. First we figure out how many fourths in 6 whole units. Then we add on ¼. *(Write + between 6 and ¼)* What do we do first?	Figure out how many fourths in six whole units
4. There are 6 wholes with 4 parts in each whole. What do I do to figure how many parts are used?	Multiply 6×4
5. What is 6×4 *(Pause.)* *(Write the 24.)* $6 + \dfrac{1}{4} = \dfrac{24 + 1}{4}$	24
6. How many parts are used in the last whole?	1
7. I add one part. *(Write + 1 in the numerator.)* $6 + \dfrac{1}{4} = \dfrac{24 + 1}{4} =$	
8. What is $24 + 1$? *(Write the following on the board.)* $\dfrac{25}{4}$	25
9. So $6\dfrac{1}{4} = \dfrac{25}{4}$. Say that. *(Repeat steps 1–9 with these fractions.)* $3\dfrac{2}{5} \quad 7\dfrac{3}{4} \quad 2\dfrac{3}{7} \quad 5\dfrac{1}{4}$	$6\dfrac{1}{4} = \dfrac{25}{4}$
Part D: Structured Worksheet – Converting Mixed Numbers	
1. *(Present a worksheet like the one below.)* Convert these mixed numbers to improper fractions. a. $3\dfrac{1}{2} = $ _____ $ = $ _____ b. $7\dfrac{3}{5} = $ _____ $ = $ _____	

continued

Format 13.13 *(continued)*
CONVERTING MIXED NUMBERS TO IMPROPER FRACTIONS

TEACHER	STUDENTS
c. $4\dfrac{2}{5}$ = _____ = _____	
d. $2\dfrac{3}{4}$ = _____ = _____	
2. Read the mixed number in problem a.	$3\dfrac{1}{2}$
3. How many parts in each whole unit?	2
Write 2 as the denominator in the new fraction.	Students write 2.
4. First we see how many halves in 3 whole units. Then we add ½. How do we figure out how many halves in 3 wholes?	Multiply 3 × 2
How many halves in 3 wholes?	6
Write 6.	
5. How many parts in the last whole?	1
Write + 1.	Students write $\dfrac{6+1}{2}$.
6. What is ⁶⁄₂ + ½?	$\dfrac{7}{2}$
Write equals ⁷⁄₂.	
7. What fraction does 3½ equal?	$\dfrac{7}{2}$
(Repeat steps 2–7 with remaining problems.)	

Format 13.14
ADDING AND SUBTRACTING FRACTIONS WITH LIKE DENOMINATORS

TEACHER	STUDENTS
Part A: Pictorial Demonstration	
1. *(Draw the following circles and lines on the board.)*	
⊗ ⊕	
____ + ____ = ____	
2. Let's write a problem that will tell us how many parts are used in these wholes.	
3. How many parts in each whole?	4
(Write the denominators.)	
$\dfrac{}{4} + \dfrac{}{4} = \dfrac{}{4}$	
We're talking about wholes with 4 parts in each whole.	

TEACHER	STUDENTS
4. *(Point to first circle.)* How many parts are used in this whole?	3
(Write the following on the board.)	
$\dfrac{3}{4}$	
(Point to second circle.) How many parts are used in this whole?	2
(Write the following on the board.)	
$\dfrac{3}{4} + \dfrac{2}{4} =$	
5. How many parts are used altogether?	5
(Write the following on the board.)	
$\dfrac{5}{4}$	
6. What does $\dfrac{3}{4} + \dfrac{2}{4}$ equal?	$\dfrac{5}{4}$
(Repeat steps 1–6 with the problem below.)	

$$\rule{2cm}{0.4pt} \;+\; \rule{2cm}{0.4pt} \;=\; \rule{2cm}{0.4pt}$$

Part B: Structured Board Presentation

1. We can only add and subtract fractions with the same number of parts in each whole. Listen again. We can only add and subtract fractions with the same number of parts in each whole. *(Write the problem on the board.)*	
$\dfrac{3}{4} + \dfrac{2}{5} =$	
2. Read this problem.	$\dfrac{3}{4} + \dfrac{2}{5} =$
3. *(Point to ¾.)* How many parts in each whole?	4
(Point to ⅖.) How many parts in each whole?	5
4. Can we add these fractions?	No
5. Right. We can only add fractions that have the same bottom number.	

(Repeat steps 2–5 with the problems below.)

$$\dfrac{3}{5} + \dfrac{2}{5} \qquad \dfrac{5}{7} - \dfrac{3}{9} \qquad \dfrac{3}{9} + \dfrac{3}{5}$$

$$\dfrac{4}{7} + \dfrac{2}{7} \qquad \dfrac{5}{7} - \dfrac{5}{9} \qquad \dfrac{4}{9} - \dfrac{3}{9}$$

(Give individual turns.)

continued

Format 13.14 *(continued)*

ADDING AND SUBTRACTING FRACTIONS WITH LIKE DENOMINATORS

TEACHER	STUDENTS
Part C: Structured Worksheet	
1. *(Give the students a worksheet with the following problems.)*	
a. $\dfrac{3}{5} + \dfrac{1}{5} =$ _____ f. $\dfrac{3}{4} - \dfrac{1}{4} =$ _____ b. $\dfrac{3}{5} + \dfrac{2}{7} =$ _____ g. $\dfrac{2}{3} + \dfrac{1}{4} =$ _____ c. $\dfrac{4}{7} - \dfrac{2}{7} =$ _____ h. $\dfrac{6}{9} + \dfrac{2}{9} =$ _____ d. $\dfrac{5}{9} - \dfrac{2}{3} =$ _____ i. $\dfrac{5}{7} + \dfrac{3}{5} =$ _____ e. $\dfrac{7}{9} + \dfrac{1}{9} =$ _____	
2. Remember, you can only add and subtract fractions that tell about the same number of parts in each whole.	
3. Touch problem a. Read the problem.	$\dfrac{3}{5} + \dfrac{1}{5}$
4. Can we add these fractions the way they are now?	Yes
(If the answer to step 3 is no, say to students,) You can't work the problem, so cross it out. *If the answer to step 3 is yes, do steps 4–6.)*	
5. We're talking about fractions with 5 parts in each whole, so the answer will have 5 parts in each group. Write 5 as the bottom number in the answer. *(Check students' work.)*	
6. Look at the top numbers. They tell the number of parts used. What is 3 + 1?	4
So what do you write for the top number in the answer?	4
Write it. *(Check students' work.)*	
7. Read the whole problem.	$\dfrac{3}{5} + \dfrac{1}{5} = \dfrac{4}{5}$
(Repeat steps 2–7 for the remaining problems.)	
Part D: Less Structured Worksheet	
1. *(Give students a worksheet with a mix of four addition and four subtraction problems. About half of the problems should have like denominators.)*	
2. Read the first problem. If you can work it, write the answer. If you can't work the problem, cross it out. *(Monitor student performance as they complete the worksheet.)*	

Format 13.15
PRESKILL: FINDING THE LEAST COMMON MULTIPLE

TEACHER	STUDENTS
Part A: Structured Board Presentation	
1. *(Write the following numbers on the board.)*	
3 6 9 12 15 18	
5 10 15 20 25	
2. *(Point to 3.)* These numbers are multiples of 3. Say them.	3, 6, 9, 12, 15, 18
(Point to 5.) These numbers are multiples of 5. Say them.	5, 10, 15, 20, 25
3. What is the smallest number that is a multiple of 3 and 5?	15
Yes, 15 is the least common multiple of 3 and 5.	
(Repeat steps 1–3 with these examples: 2 and 8, 6 and 8, 3 and 9.)	
Part B: Worksheet Presentation	
1. *(Give the students a worksheet with the following problems.)*	
Write the number which is the least common multiple for each pair of numbers.	
a. The LCM of 6 and 9 is _____.	
b. The LCM of 8 and 6 is _____.	
c. The LCM of 5 and 2 is _____.	
d. The LCM of 5 and 4 is _____.	
e. The LCM of 6 and 12 is _____.	
f. The LCM of 4 and 3 is _____.	
g. The LCM of 6 and 2 is _____.	
h. The LCM of 4 and 12 is _____.	
i. The LCM of 5 and 3 is _____.	
j. The LCM of 3 and 9 is _____.	
2. The instructions tell us to find the least common multiple of the numbers. *LCM* means "least common multiple." In problem a you must find the least common multiple of 6 and 9. The least common multiple is the lowest number that is in both count-by series.	
3. Touch problem a. Say the numbers that are multiples of 6. *(Stop students at 30.)*	6, 12, 18, 24, 30
4. Say the numbers that are multiples of 9. *(Stop students at 45.)*	9, 18, 27, 36, 45
5. What is the least common multiple of 9 and 6?	18
Write it in the space.	
(Repeat steps 3–5 with about half of the problems, then have the students complete the rest independently.)	

Format 13.16
ADDING AND SUBTRACTING FRACTIONS WITH UNLIKE DENOMINATORS

(See Video in Part A)

TEACHER	STUDENTS
▶	

Part A: Structured Board Presentation

1. *(Write the following problem on the board.)*

$$\frac{2}{3} + \frac{1}{4} = \underline{\hspace{2cm}}$$

2. Read this problem.

$$\frac{2}{3} + \frac{1}{4}$$

No

   Can we add these fractions the way they are written?

3. To work this problem, we must rewrite the fractions so they both have the same denominator. First, we figure out the least common multiple of the denominators. What is the denominator of the first fraction?

   3

   What is the denominator of the second fraction?

   4

4. What is the least common multiple of 4 and 3?

   12

   To correct: Say the numbers that are multiples of 3. Say the numbers that are multiples of 4. What is the least common multiple?

5. We must rewrite each fraction as equivalent fractions with denominators of 12. *(Write 12 under each denominator.)*

$$\frac{2}{3} + \frac{1}{4}$$
$$12 \quad \quad 12$$

   I want to rewrite ⅔ as a fraction that has 12 as a denominator. Remember, I don't want to change the value of ⅔. What fraction do I multiply ⅔ by to end with a fraction that has a denominator of 12?

$$\frac{4}{4}$$

   To correct: What is the denominator of ⅔? What must I multiply 3 by to end with 12? So I must multiply ⅔ times ¼. What do I multiply ⅔ by?

   (Write ¼ in parentheses.)

$$\frac{2}{3}\left(\frac{4}{4}\right) + \frac{1}{4}$$
$$12 \quad \quad \quad 12$$

   What is 2 × 4?

   8

   (Write 8.) What is 3 × 4?

   12

   (Cross out ⅔ Write the 12.)

$$\frac{2}{3}\left(\frac{\overset{8}{\cancel{4}}}{4}\right) + \frac{1}{4}$$
$$12 \quad \quad \quad 12$$

   We rewrote ⅔ as ⁸⁄₁₂? What did we rewrite ⅔ as?

$$\frac{8}{12}$$

TEACHER	STUDENTS
6. Now let's rewrite ¼ as a fraction that has 12 as a denominator. Remember, I don't want to change the value of ¼. What fraction must I multiply ¼ by?	$\frac{3}{3}$
To correct: What is the denominator of ¼? What do I multiply 4 by to end with 12? So I must multiply ¼ by ³⁄₃. What do I multiply ¼ by?	
(Write ³⁄₃.) $\underset{12}{\overset{8}{\frac{2}{3}\left(\frac{4}{4}\right)}} + \underset{12}{\frac{1}{4}\left(\frac{3}{3}\right)}$	
What is 1 × 3?	3
(Cross out ¼. Write 3 next to the 1.) What is 4 × 3?	12
(Write ³⁄₁₂.) $\underset{12}{\overset{8}{\frac{2}{3}\left(\frac{4}{4}\right)}} + \underset{12}{\overset{3}{\frac{\cancel{1}}{\cancel{4}}\left(\frac{3}{3}\right)}}$	
We rewrote ¼ as ³⁄₁₂. What did we rewrite ¼ as?	$\frac{3}{12}$
7. Now the denominators are the same and we can add. The problem now says ⁸⁄₁₂ + ³⁄₁₂. What does the problem say?	$\frac{8}{12} + \frac{3}{12}$
8. What is ⁸⁄₁₂ + ³⁄₁₂?	$\frac{11}{12}$
(Repeat steps 1–8 with the problems below.) $\frac{4}{5} - \frac{7}{10}$ $\quad \frac{3}{6} - \frac{1}{4}$ $\quad \frac{1}{9} + \frac{2}{3}$	
Part B: Structured Worksheet	
1. *(Give students worksheets with problems like the ones below.)* a. $\frac{5}{6} - \frac{2}{4} =$ d. $\frac{5}{10} - \frac{2}{5} =$ b. $\frac{2}{9} + \frac{2}{3} =$ e. $\frac{7}{9} - \frac{2}{3} =$ c. $\frac{2}{3} - \frac{3}{5} =$ f. $\frac{2}{5} - \frac{1}{3} =$	
2. Read problem a.	$\frac{5}{6} - \frac{2}{4}$
Can we work the problem the way it is?	No
(If the answer is yes, tell the students to work the problem. If the answer is no, continue the format.)	
Why not?	The denominators aren't the same
3. What are the denominators?	6 and 4
What is the least common multiple of 6 and 4?	12
Write 12 under each fraction.	

continued

Format 13.16 *(continued)*
ADDING AND SUBTRACTING FRACTIONS WITH UNLIKE DENOMINATORS

TEACHER	STUDENTS
4. The first fraction says $\frac{5}{6}$. Write parentheses next to it. *(Pause.)* What fraction do you multiply $\frac{5}{6}$ by so that you'll end with a denominator of 12?	$\dfrac{2}{2}$
Write $\frac{2}{2}$ in the parentheses. *(Check.)*	
To correct: The denominator is 6; 6 times what number equals 12? So we must multiply a fraction that has 2 as a denominator. We don't want to change the value of $\frac{5}{6}$, so we multiply it by $\frac{2}{2}$.	
Let's multiply $\frac{5}{6}$ by $\frac{2}{2}$ and write the new fraction. What is 5 × 2?	10
Write 10 over the fraction. Five-sixths equals how many twelfths?	$\dfrac{10}{12}$
(Cross out 5/6.)	
5. The second fraction says $\frac{2}{4}$. Write parentheses next to it. What fraction do you multiply $\frac{2}{4}$ by so that you'll end with a denominator of 12?	$\dfrac{3}{3}$
To correct: Use the same correction described in step 4.	
Multiply $\frac{2}{4}$ by $\frac{3}{3}$ and write the new fraction. *(Pause.)* Two-fourths equals how many twelfths?	$\dfrac{6}{12}$
(Check students' papers.) Cross out $\frac{2}{4}$.	
6. Read the problem saying the rewritten fractions.	$\dfrac{10}{12} - \dfrac{6}{12}$
Can you work the problem now?	Yes
How do you know?	The denominators are the same
7. Work the problem and write the answer. *(Pause.)*	
8. What is the answer?	$\dfrac{4}{12}$

Part C: Less Structured Worksheet

1. *(Give students a worksheet like the one for the structured worksheet exercise. Use the following prompts to guide the students through the worksheet.)*

2. Read problem a. Can we work the problem the way it is? *(If the answer is yes, tell students to work the problem. If the answer is no, continue the format.)*

   Why not?

3. What is the least common multiple of the denominators?

   Write it under the fraction. *(Pause.)*

4. What fraction will you multiply the first fraction by so that it will have a denominator of _____?

5. What fraction will you multiply the second fraction by so that it has a denominator of _____?

TEACHER	STUDENTS
6. Rewrite the fractions and work the problem. *(Monitor students' responses.)*	
7. What is your answer?	
(Repeat Steps 2–7 with about half of the problems, then have the students complete the rest independently.)	

Format 13.17
MULTIPLYING TWO PROPER FRACTIONS

TEACHER	STUDENTS
Part A: Structured Board Presentation	
1. *(Write the following problem on the board.)* $\frac{3}{4} \times \frac{2}{5} =$	
2. Read this problem.	$\frac{3}{4} \times \frac{2}{5}$
3. We work multiplication problems with fractions by multiplying top times the top and bottom times the bottom. How do we work multiplication problems with fractions?	Top times the top and bottom times the bottom
4. First we multiply top times the top. What is 3×2? *(Write the 6.)* $\frac{3}{4} \times \frac{2}{5} = \frac{6}{}$	6
5. Now we multiply bottom times the bottom. What is 4×5? *(Write the 20.)* $\frac{3}{4} \times \frac{2}{5} = \frac{6}{20}$	20
6. What does $\frac{3}{4} \times \frac{2}{5}$ equal?	$\frac{6}{20}$
(Repeat steps 1–6 with several more problems.)	
Part B: Structured Worksheet	
1. *(Give Students a worksheet with a mix of multiplication, addition, and subtraction problems like the following.)* a. $\frac{3}{4} + \frac{2}{4} = \frac{\square}{\square}$ b. $\frac{3}{2} \times \frac{4}{2} = \frac{\square}{\square}$ c. $\frac{6}{3} - \frac{1}{3} = \frac{\square}{\square}$ d. $\frac{6}{3} \times \frac{1}{3} = \frac{\square}{\square}$	
2. When you multiply fractions, you work top times top and bottom times bottom. When you multiply fractions, what do you do?	Top times top and bottom times bottom
3. But when you add or subtract fractions, you work only across the top. When you add or subtract fractions, what do you do?	Work only across the top

continued

Format 13.17 (continued)
MULTIPLYING TWO PROPER FRACTIONS

TEACHER	STUDENTS
4. What do you do when you add or subtract fractions?	Work across the top
What do you do when you multiply fractions?	Top times top and bottom times bottom
(Repeat steps 2–4 until firm.)	
5. Touch problem a. Read the problem.	$\dfrac{3}{4} + \dfrac{2}{4}$
What type of problem is this?	Addition
What do you do when you add fractions?	Work across the top
Work the problem. (Pause.) What's the answer?	$\dfrac{5}{4}$
(Repeat step 5 with remaining problems.)	

Format 13.18
MULTIPLYING A FRACTION AND
A WHOLE NUMBER   (See Video in Part A)

TEACHER	STUDENTS
▶	
Part A: Converting a Whole Number to a Fraction	
1. Listen to this rule: We can change a whole number into a fraction by giving it a denominator of 1. How do we change a whole number into a fraction?	Give it a denominator of 1
2. (Write 3 on board.) What number is this?	3
How do I change it into a fraction?	Give it a denominator of 1
Watch me change 3 into a fraction. (Write 1 under 3.)	
$\dfrac{3}{1}$	
3 over 1 is the same as 3. I'll draw a picture to show you that $\frac{3}{1}$ equals 3.	
(Draw the following circles.)	
$\frac{3}{1} = \bigcirc \; \bigcirc \; \bigcirc$	
We have three wholes used up.	
3. (Write 5 on board.) How do I change 5 into a fraction?	Give it a denominator of 1
Yes, 5 over 1 equals 5 wholes. (Write the fraction.)	
$\dfrac{5}{1}$	
(Repeat step 3 with 2, 9, 4, 8.)	

TEACHER	STUDENTS
Part B: Structured Board Presentation	
1. *(Write the following problem on the board.)*	
$\dfrac{3}{4} \times 8 = \underline{\hspace{1.5cm}} = \overline{)\hspace{1cm}} = \square$	
2. Listen to this rule about multiplying fractions: A fraction can only be multiplied by another fraction. Listen again. A fraction can only be multiplied by another fraction.	
3. Read this problem.	$\dfrac{3}{4} \times 8$
(Point to ¾.) Is this fraction multiplied by another fraction?	No
So before we can work the problem we have to change 8 into a fraction. How do I change 8 into a fraction?	Give it a denominator of 1
(Write the problem.)	
$\dfrac{3}{4} \times \dfrac{8}{1} =$	
4. Now we're ready to multiply across the top and bottom. What is 3×8?	24
(Write 24.)	
What is 4×1?	4
(Write ²⁴⁄₄.)	
5. Does ²⁴⁄₄ equal more or less than one whole?	More
How do we figure out how many whole groups ²⁴⁄₄ equals?	Divide 4 into 24
Four goes into 24 how many times?	6
(Write 6 in box.)	
6. What does ¾ × 8 equal?	6
(Repeat steps 1–6 with the problems below.)	
$\dfrac{2}{3} \times 9 \qquad \dfrac{3}{5} \times 10 \qquad \dfrac{1}{4} \times 8$	
Part C: Structured Worksheet	
1. *(Give students worksheets with problems similar to the following problem:)*	
$\dfrac{2}{3} \times 7 = \underline{\hspace{1cm}} = \overline{)\hspace{1cm}} = \square$	
2. Touch problem a. Read it.	$\dfrac{2}{3} \times 7$
(Point to ⅔.) Is ⅔ multiplied by another fraction?	No
So what do you have to do?	Change 7 into a fraction
Do it. *(Monitor responses.)*	
3. Now multiply the fractions. *(Monitor responses.)* What fraction did you end up with?	$\dfrac{14}{3}$

continued

Format 13.18 *(continued)*
MULTIPLYING A FRACTION AND
A WHOLE NUMBER

TEACHER	STUDENTS
4. Is $^{14}/_3$ more or less than one whole group?	More
How do you figure out how many whole groups?	Divide 3 into 14
Divide—remember to write the remainder as a fraction. *(Monitor Responses.)*	
5. What does $^2/_3 \times 7$ equal?	$4\frac{2}{3}$
(Repeat steps 2–5 with remaining problems.)	

CHAPTER
14

Decimals

LEARNING OUTCOMES

14.1 Discuss the seven main areas of decimal instruction and the sequence of the component skills for each area.

14.2 Discuss the relationship between fractions and decimals.

14.3 Explain the importance of introducing reading and writing decimals prior to teaching decimal operations.

14.4 Outline the general teaching procedures for teaching students to add, subtract, multiply and divide decimals.

14.5 Describe types of errors students may make when working problems with decimals.

SKILL HIERARCHY

Prior to beginning instruction in decimals, students need to have a strong background in place value concepts, rounding skills, and fraction analysis. Having a strong understanding of place value with whole numbers allows students to extend place value concepts to numbers less than one. The strategy recommended in this text for division with two-digit divisors includes rounding to the nearest ten. This strategy prepares students for rounding with decimals. Previous instruction with fraction skills provides students with the background needed to work with numbers that are less than one.

Initial instruction on decimals begins with teaching students to read and write decimals. After students demonstrate mastery of these skills, instruction in addition, subtraction, multiplication, and division of decimals can be introduced. The Instructional Sequence and Assessment Chart illustrates the seven main areas covered in decimal instruction:

1. Reading and writing decimals and mixed decimal numerals
2. Converting decimals to equivalent decimals
3. Adding and subtracting decimals
4. Rounding off decimals
5. Multiplying decimals
6. Dividing decimals
7. Converting values between the decimal notation system and fraction notation system

INSTRUCTIONAL SEQUENCE AND ASSESSMENT CHART

Grade Level	Problem Type	Performance Indicator
4	Reading tenths and hundredths	Circle the correct decimal: Five tenths 5 .05 .5 Four hundredths 4 .04 .4 Seven hundredths 70 .70 .07
4	Writing tenths and hundredths	Write these fractions as decimal numerals: $\dfrac{5}{100} =$ $\dfrac{5}{10} =$ $\dfrac{19}{100} =$

4	Reading mixed decimals: tenths and hundredths	Circle the correct mixed decimal:
		five and three-tenths
		  .53 5.03 5.3
		ten and four hundredths
		  1.04 10.04 10.4
		eighteen and six hundredths
		  18.6 1.86 18.06

4	Writing mixed decimals: tenths and hundredths	Write the mixed decimal for each mixed numeral: $10\dfrac{14}{100}$ _____ $16\dfrac{3}{10}$ _____ $40\dfrac{18}{100}$ _____
4	Column alignment: adding tenths, hundredths, and whole numerals	Write these problems in columns and work them: 8.23 + 12.1 + 6 = 7 + .3 + 45 = .08 + 4 + .6 =
4	Subtracting tenths and hundredths from whole numbers	5 − 3.2 = 8 − .34 = 7 − .3 =
4	Ordering mixed decimals	Rewrite these numerals in order beginning with the smallest: 18.8 10.10 10.3 10.03 ____ ____ ____ ____
5	Reading thousandths	Circle the correct decimal: five-thousands .05 .5 .005 .500 ninety-thousandths. .90 .900 .090 .009
5	Writing thousandths	Write these fractions as decimals: $\dfrac{342}{1000} =$ $\dfrac{60}{1000} =$ $\dfrac{5}{1000} =$

Grade Level	Problem Type	Performance Indicator
5	Multiplying decimals: one-digit or two-digit factor times three-digit factor	7.14 214 $\times$ .5 $\times$ .7
5	Multiplying decimals: zero to be placed after decimal point	.1 .02 $\times$ .7 $\times$ .8
5	Rounding off decimals	Round off these numbers to the nearest whole number: 8.342 _____ 7.812 _____ Round off these numbers to the nearest tenth: 8.34 _____ 9.782 _____ Round off these numbers to the nearest hundredth: 8.346 _____ 9.782 _____
5	Dividing: whole number divisor, no remainder	5)32.45 7)215.6 2).856
5	Dividing by whole number: quotient begins with zero	9).036 9).36 9).0036
5	Rounding off where there is a 9 or 99 after the decimal	Round off these numbers to the nearest tenth: 9.961 _____ 19.942 _____ 29.981 _____ Round off these numbers to the nearest hundredth: 14.993 _____ 14.996 _____ 29.9982 _____
5	Dividing: whole number divisor, zeros must be added to dividend after decimal point	Divide and write answer as mixed decimal: 2)3 5)3.1 4)21
5	Dividing: whole number divisor, rounding off	Divide: write answer to mixed decimal; round off to the nearest hundredth: 7)3.1 9)7 3)2
5	Converting proper fraction to decimal; no rounding off required	Rewrite these fractions as decimals: $\frac{2}{5} = \frac{3}{4} =$ $\frac{3}{10} =$
5	Converting proper fraction to decimal: rounding off required	Rewrite these fractions as decimals; round off to nearest hundredth: $\frac{3}{7} =$ $\frac{4}{6} =$ $\frac{2}{9} =$
5	Multiplying mixed decimal by 10 or 100: no zeros added	10 $\times$ 34.2 = 100 $\times$ 34.52 = 10 $\times$ 34.52 =

continued

INSTRUCTIONAL SEQUENCE AND ASSESSMENT CHART *(continued)*		
Grade Level	**Problem Type**	**Performance Indicator**
5	Multiplying mixed decimal by 10 or 100: zeros added	$100 \times 34.2 =$ $100 \times 3.42 =$ $100 \times 342 =$ $10 \times 342 =$
5	Dividing: divisor is decimal, no adding zeros in dividend necessary	$.2\overline{)23.74}$ $.2\overline{)14.26}$ $.05\overline{).345}$
5	Same as above: adding zero in dividend required	$.5\overline{)13}$ $.50\overline{)275}$ $.02\overline{)3.1}$ $.05\overline{)2}$
5	Converting decimal to fractions	Circle the correct answer: .75 equals $\frac{1}{4}$ $\frac{5}{7}$ $\frac{2}{3}$ $\frac{3}{4}$ .8 equals $\frac{4}{5}$ $\frac{8}{8}$ $\frac{1}{8}$ $\frac{2}{5}$ .67 equals $\frac{1}{4}$ $\frac{2}{3}$ $\frac{6}{7}$ $\frac{1}{6}$
5	Converting mixed numbers to mixed decimals	Rewrite these mixed fractions as mixed decimals: $2\frac{3}{5} =$ $7\frac{1}{4} =$

CONCEPTUAL UNDERSTANDING

Understanding the concepts underlying decimal skills relies on understanding the relationship between decimals and fractions. Fraction analysis is a preskill for decimals. Students must understand what the numerator and denominator in a fraction represent: the denominator signifying the parts in each whole; the numerator, the parts that are used. They also must understand the concept of whole units versus parts of a whole. Understanding fractions is critical because decimals are explained as an alternative representation of fractions that have 10 or a multiple of 10 (100, 1,000, etc.) as a denominator.

Conceptual understanding of decimals skills is promoted when reading and writing decimals are addressed prior to teaching the other decimal operations. Too frequently, an insufficient amount of instructional time is allotted to teaching students to accurately read and write decimals. Without adequate practice on these basic decimal reading and writing skills, students will encounter unnecessary difficulty when more advanced decimal skills are introduced.

INSTRUCTIONAL PROCEDURES: READING AND WRITING DECIMALS

Reading and Writing Decimals and Mixed Decimals

This section includes procedures for teaching students to read and write decimals and mixed decimals expressed as tenths, hundredths, and thousandths. Initial Direct Instruction procedures for teaching students how to read and write decimals focus student attention on the number of digits after the decimal point (one digit after the decimal point indicates tenths; two digits after the decimal point indicate hundredths; three digits after the decimal point indicate thousandths).

Decimals and mixed decimals representing tenths and hundredths are usually introduced in fourth grade, while decimals and mixed decimals representing thousandths are introduced in fifth grade. The sequence for introducing these skills follows:

1. Reading decimals representing tenths or hundredths
2. Writing decimals representing tenths or hundredths
3. Reading and writing mixed decimals; decimals represent tenths or hundredths
4. Reading decimals representing thousandths
5. Writing decimals representing thousandths
6. Reading and writing mixed decimals; decimals represent thousandths
7. Writing equivalent decimals

Note that students are taught to write decimal numerals immediately after they can read them.

Reading Decimals Representing Tenths and Hundredths   Format 14.1: Reading Decimals introduces students to decimals as an alternative system for writing fractions of tenths and hundredths. The teacher begins by writing two fractions on the board, one with 10 as a denominator and one with 100 as a denominator $\left(\frac{4}{10}, \frac{24}{100}\right)$ and has students read the fractions. Next, the teacher explains that there is another way to express fractions that have 10 or 100 as a denominator. The teacher explains that if one digit is written after the decimal point, the decimal tells how many tenths, but if two digits are written after the decimal point, the decimal tells how many hundredths. (If students are unfamiliar with the term "digit," they should be told that a digit is any written numeral from 0 to 9.)

After telling students the rule regarding the number of digits after the decimal, the teacher has the students read a list of numerals composed of an equal mixture of tenths and hundredths decimals. Several minimally different sets (.07, .70, .7 or .4, .04, .40) are included among the examples. The minimally different sets include three decimal numerals: a decimal representing tenths (.8) and two decimals representing hundredths. In one of these hundredth decimals, a zero would precede the numeral (.08), while in the other hundredth decimal, the zero would follow the numeral (.80). The purpose of these minimally different sets is to focus student attention on the number of digits following the decimal.

The correction for errors in reading decimals is to have students identify the number of places after the decimal point first, identify the place value, and then read the numeral. For example, if a student misreads .04 as "four-tenths," the teacher says, "How many digits after the decimal? So what does the 4 tell about? What is this numeral?"

A critical teacher behavior for this format is monitoring student responses. To prevent student problems with confusing whole numbers and decimal numbers, teachers should be sure that students are adding the "-ths" endings to tens, hundreds, and thousands. For example, teachers should be sure .40 is pronounced as "forty-hundredths," not "forty hundreds." Individual turns should be given frequently during the first several lessons. Practice on reading decimal numerals would be presented daily for 2 or 3 weeks. After the first several lessons, the teacher need not present all of the steps in Part A but would just write decimals on the board and have students read them (step 6).

Part B includes a worksheet exercise designed both to provide practice in reading decimals and to reinforce the relationship between decimal fractions and decimals. Students are given worksheets with two types of items. In the first type, a decimal numeral is written to the left of three fractions:

$$8 = \frac{8}{10} \quad \frac{8}{100} \quad \frac{1}{8}$$

The students read the decimal and then circle the fraction equivalent of the decimal numeral. In the second type, a fraction is written, and students must find the corresponding decimal among several similar-looking decimals:

$$\frac{4}{100} = .4 \quad .40 \quad .04$$

Writing Decimals Representing Tenths and Hundredths   Writing decimals representing tenths and hundredths is introduced after students can read those decimals accurately. **Format 14.2: Writing Decimals** includes two parts. Part A is a structured board format in which the teacher demonstrates how to write a decimal fraction as a decimal. The teacher writes a fraction on the board and has the students read it. The teacher then asks how many digits there must be after the decimal point and models writing the fraction as a decimal numeral. Special attention must be given to fractions with a hundred as the denominator and with a numerator of less than 10 $\left(\frac{7}{100}, \frac{4}{100}, \frac{1}{100}\right)$. When presenting these examples, the teacher demonstrates that in order to make two digits after the decimal, a zero must be written immediately after the decimal point. For example, in writing $\frac{7}{100}$, the teacher would write .07 and point out the zero immediately following the decimal point.

Practice on writing decimal numerals should be provided daily for several weeks. This practice can be provided on worksheets containing fractions with 10 or 100 as the denominator for which the students would be required to write the decimal equivalents.

The critical example-selection guideline for this format is basically the same as that for the reading decimals format. Several minimally different sets $\left(\frac{8}{10}, \frac{8}{100}, \frac{80}{100}\right)$ would be included to provide students with the practice to determine when a zero is needed immediately after the decimal point. Several extra examples of hundredths fractions with a numerator below 10 also would be included to provide extra practice on this difficult type of decimal.

Reading and Writing Mixed Decimals: Tenths and Hundredths   When the students are able to read and write tenths and hundredths decimals without prompting from the teacher, mixed decimals, numerals formed by a whole numeral and a decimal (9.3, 16.4, 27.02), can be introduced. Students are taught first to read mixed decimals and then to write them in **Format 14.3: Reading and Writing Mixed Decimals**. In Part A, the structured board presentation, the teacher introduces reading mixed decimals by explaining that the numerals before the decimal point represent whole numbers while the numerals after the decimal point tell about the decimal number. The teacher then models and tests students on reading several numerals, having the students read the whole numeral, the decimal, and then the mixed decimal. Note that in reading mixed decimals, the teacher should heavily emphasize the word "and" (15.03 should be read "fifteen *and* three hundredths"). This voice emphasis is designed to help students discriminate between the whole numeral and the decimal parts of the mixed decimal in preparation for writing mixed decimals. Reading mixed decimals is practiced daily for several weeks. No prompting is recommended after the first several days.

Part B, a structured worksheet exercise, includes two types of items. In the first type, the words representing a mixed decimal are written and the student must write the mixed decimal; for example, twenty-eight and four-hundredths is written as 28.04. This type of item is appropriate, of course, only for students able to decode well.

In the second type, a mixed fraction is written, and the student rewrites it as a mixed decimal:

$$12\frac{3}{100} \text{ is written as } 12.03$$

Reading and Writing Decimals Representing Thousandths   Decimals representing thousandths are introduced after students have mastered reading and writing decimals and mixed decimals representing tenths and hundredths. Thousandths decimals can be taught with **Formats 14.1** and **14.2** with the added explanation that if there are three digits after the decimal point, the decimal tells about thousandths.

During the first several lessons, examples should concentrate entirely on thousandths numerals. We recommend presenting minimally different groupings such as:

.800   .080   .008

.004   .040   .400

.070   .007   .700

In these sets, two of the three digits in each decimal are zeros and one digit is a numeral other than zero. In each decimal, the nonzero digit is placed in another position:

.003   .030   .300

After several lessons comprised of thousandths decimals, the teacher presents examples including tenths, hundredths, and thousandths. In these example sets, minimally different groupings should be included to focus student attention on the number of digits after the decimal point:

.4   .04   .004

.70   .070   .700

Writing decimals representing thousandths is particularly difficult because students must discriminate when to write two zeros after the decimal point (.001, .009) from when to write one zero after the decimal point (.010, .090). Therefore, the teacher should be prepared to provide extensive practice on minimally different thousandths examples.

Equivalent Decimals   Equivalent decimals are decimals that have the same value. The mixed decimals 8.30 and 8.3 are equivalent since they both represent the same quantity. Converting a decimal, mixed decimal, or whole number to an equivalent mixed decimal is an important preskill for addition, subtraction, and division with decimal numbers. For example, when subtracting .39 from 5, students will need to be able to convert 5 into 5.00. Students should be introduced to equivalent decimal conversions shortly after they can read and write decimals and mixed decimal numerals.

Format 14.4: Converting Decimals into Equivalent Decimals shows how to teach students to convert decimals into equivalent decimals. Although the rewriting skill is simple, because the students simply add or take away zeros, students should understand why those changes are permissible. Part A illustrates the rationale for adding zeros through the use of equivalent fractions. The teacher demonstrates that changing $\frac{3}{10}$ to $\frac{30}{100}$, for example, involves multiplying by a fraction equal to 1 $\left(\frac{10}{10}\right)$ and, therefore, does not change the value of the original fraction. Because $\frac{3}{10} = \frac{30}{100}$, then .3 = .30.

Part B is a structured board presentation demonstrating how to rewrite decimals. Part C is a worksheet exercise in which the students are given a chart containing columns for whole numerals, tenths, hundredths, and thousandths. The student's task is to write equivalent mixed decimals in spaces across the row. For example, 9.1 is written in the tenths column. The student would add a zero, writing 9.10 in the hundredths column; and add two zeros, writing 9.100 in the thousandths column. For whole numerals, the teacher explains that a whole numeral is converted into a mixed decimal by writing a decimal point after the numeral and writing zero(s) after the decimal point.

INSTRUCTIONAL PROCEDURES: DECIMAL OPERATIONS

Adding and Subtracting Decimals and Mixed Decimals

Addition and subtraction problems with decimals and/or mixed decimals can be divided into two groups for instructional purposes. The first group contains those problems in which each numeral in the problem has the same number of decimal places; for example, in the problems below, all numerals have decimals representing hundredths:

$$435.42 \qquad 24.35$$
$$+17.82 \qquad -1.48$$

The second group is composed of those problems in which the addends (in an addition problem) or the minuend and subtrahend (in a subtraction problem) have different numbers of digits after the decimal point:

$$9.1 \qquad 4 \qquad 4.23$$
$$-3.87 \qquad +3.64 \qquad -3.645$$

Decimals Having the Same Number of Places   Problems in which each numeral has the same number of digits after the decimal point can be introduced when students can read and write decimals and mixed decimals. Problems of this type are relatively easy. The only new step involves placing the decimal point in the answer. Because the teaching procedure is simple, no format has been included.

The first problems should be vertically aligned so students can be taught to bring the decimal point straight down without first having to determine if the columns are properly aligned. For these problems, the teacher just instructs students to write the decimal in the answer below the other decimal points.

Problems written horizontally (7.24 + 19.36) can be introduced shortly after the introduction of vertically aligned problems. For horizontal problems, we recommend teaching students to rewrite the problem so that the decimal points are in a column. When horizontal problems are introduced, teachers should monitor student worksheets daily to see that students align the numerals correctly. Teachers often provide grid paper for students to use to assist them in rewriting the problems accurately.

Decimals Having Different Numbers of Places   Problems in which each mixed decimal has a different number of digits after the decimal point are typically introduced 2 weeks after students can rewrite decimal numerals as equivalent decimal numerals by adding zeros after the decimal. The strategy for solving these more complex problems involves rewriting one or more of the mixed decimal numerals so that each mixed decimal in the problem has the same number of digits after the decimal point. Once the problem has been rewritten, students are instructed to bring the decimal point straight down and then solve the problem. For example,

$$
\begin{array}{ccc}
8.1 & \text{becomes} & 8.10 \\
-3.42 & & -3.42 \\
\hline
\end{array}
$$

Horizontally written problems should be introduced after students can solve the vertically aligned problems. The key to accurately solving horizontal problems is correctly realigning the numerals vertically. Without explicit instruction, students are likely to misalign the numerals, as illustrated below:

$$
\begin{array}{ccc}
3.72 + 18.4 & \text{becomes} & 3.72 \\
 & & +18.4 \\
\hline
\end{array}
$$

The strategy for rewriting the decimal numerals so that each has the same number of digits after the decimal point can be found in **Format 14.5: Addition/Subtraction of Unlike Decimals**.

Problems in which a decimal or mixed decimal is added to or subtracted from a whole number should receive special emphasis (7 − 3.8). Problems of this type are introduced several days after problems with mixed decimals expressing various decimal fractions are introduced. The teacher reminds students that a whole number is converted to a mixed decimal by placing a decimal point after it and adding zeros. The teacher models how to align and solve several problems of this type and then provides worksheets to students on which about half of the problems include problems with a whole number.

Rounding Off Decimals

Rounding off not only is a useful skill in and of itself but is also a necessary component skill for decimal division and **percent**. An example of rounding off in percentage problems occurs when converting $\frac{3}{7}$ to a percent: The 3 is divided by 7, which yields a decimal:

$$
7\overline{)3.000}^{\,.428}
$$

The decimal then is rounded off to hundredths to determine the approximate percent, 43%. Although rounding off decimals involves steps similar to those used in rounding off whole numbers, these two skills should not be introduced at the same time because of potential confusion. Rounding off whole numbers would have been presented many months before rounding off decimals is introduced (see **Format 10.7: Rounding to the Nearest Tens Unit**).

Format 14.6: Rounding Off Decimals shows how to present rounding off decimal numbers to the nearest whole number, tenth, hundredth, or thousandth. The rounding-off strategy taught in this format is composed of three steps:

1. The students determine how many digits will appear after the decimal point when the number is rounded off; for example, when rounding off to the nearest tenth, one digit will be left after the decimal.
2. The students count that number of digits and then draw a line. If 3.4825 is to be rounded to the nearest tenth, the students place a line after the digit in the tenth place, which is the 4 in this example: 3.4│825. The line serves as a prompt.
3. The students look at the numeral after the line. If it is a 5 or more, they add another unit to the digit before the line. For example, .53│7 rounded to the nearest hundredth is .54 because 7 appears after the line. If a numeral less than 5 appears after the line, no extra unit is added. For example, .54│2 is rounded to .54 because a numeral less than 5 follows the line.

There are three important example-selection guidelines for this format:

1. Half of the decimals should require the addition of another unit; that is, the numeral after the place to be rounded off should be 5 through 9. In the other half of the decimals, the numeral after the place to be rounded off should be less than 5.
2. The numerals should have two or three places after the place to be rounded off to provide practice in identifying which digit determines if another unit needs to be added.
3. Examples should include a mix of problems that require students to round off to the nearest tenth or to the nearest hundredth. The sample worksheet in Part B of the format shows an application of these guidelines.

A particularly difficult type of rounding-off problem arises when a unit is added to a 9, because the sum is 10. For example, rounding off .498 to the nearest hundredth requires students to add a whole unit to the nine-hundredths, which changes .498 to .50. Likewise, when rounding off 39.98 to the nearest tenth, the answer is 40.0. Problems of this type should be introduced after students have mastered easier rounding-off problems. When introducing the more difficult type, the teacher should model working several problems before having students work them independently.

Most errors in rounding off occur because students do not attend to the appropriate digit. A student is likely to round off .328 to .4 if she focuses on the 8 rather than the 2. The basic correction is to emphasize the steps in the strategy by asking the student:

1. How many digits will there be after the decimal when we round off to the nearest whole (or tenth or hundredth)?
2. Where do you draw the line?
3. What numeral comes just after the line?
4. So do you add another whole (or tenth or hundredth)?

Multiplying Decimals

Although the concept of multiplying decimals is difficult to illustrate, teaching students to solve a multiplication problem with decimals is relatively simple. One way of illustrating the rationale for the strategy of multiplying decimals is to use decimal fractions like these:

$$\frac{32}{100} \times \frac{4}{10}$$

The answer $\left(\frac{128}{1000}\right)$ would be written as the decimal .128. The teacher then would write the original problem in a decimal form: .32 × .4, point out the three decimal places in the two factors and make three decimal places in the answer. "The total number of decimal places in the factors is the same as the number of decimal places in the answer: .32 has two places; .4 has one place. That's three decimal places. The answer has three decimal places as well."

Format 14.7: Multiplying Decimals outlines a strategy for multiplying decimals or mixed decimal numbers. In the structured board presentation, the teacher introduces the strategy for figuring out where the decimal point goes in the answer. In the structured worksheet presentation, the teacher gives the student a worksheet with 10 to 15 multiplication problems that have answers included and leads students in determining where to place the decimal point. Note that in the problems on the worksheet, the decimal point in the factors appears in several different positions.

The less structured worksheet exercise includes a mix of multiplication and addition problems. The purpose of combining multiplication with addition is to ensure that students do not overgeneralize (to addition) the procedure of counting the places to determine where to put the decimal. Before the students work the problems, the teacher would remind them about placing the decimal point in different types of problems. "In addition problems, remember to bring the decimal point straight down. In multiplication problems, remember to count the digits after the decimal points in the numerals you multiply." The teacher would then carefully monitor the students as they work the first several problems. A worksheet might include these examples:

9.4	9.4	3.2
× .5	+ .5	× .57
.32	40	18
+ .57	× 3	× .32
.18	31.4	3.14
+ 32	× .05	+ .05

A potentially confusing type of multiplication problem is one in which the students must place a zero in front of the digits in the answer. For example, when multiplying .4 × .2, the student must add a zero before the 8: .4 × .2 = .08. Likewise, in .5 × .01, the student must place two zeros after the decimal: .5 × .01 = .005. This type of problem is introduced after the easier types of problems have been mastered. The teacher models solving several problems of this type and then includes about three such problems in daily worksheet assignments.

A common error found on independent work occurs when students simply forget to put the decimal point in the answer. The correction is to inform the students that they forgot to put in the decimal point. However, if the error occurs frequently, the teacher should prepare worksheets with about 10 to 15 problems, two-thirds of which contain decimals. In presenting the worksheet, the teacher tells students that the worksheet was designed as a challenge—some of the problems require decimal points in the answer, and some don't. The teacher then monitors closely as students complete the worksheet so that immediate corrections can be made if students make errors.

Dividing Decimals

Dividing decimal numbers is the most difficult decimal operation. Division with decimal numbers can be introduced when students can read and write decimals and perform long division. When long division with whole numbers was taught, the teacher stressed placing the digits in the quotient over the proper places in the dividend. For example, when working the problem 186 ÷ 2, the quotient would be written as in example a, not example b:

a. $2\overline{)186}$ with 93   b. $2\overline{)186}$ with 93

If students have not learned to write numerals in the quotient in the proper position, errors of misplacing the decimal in the quotient are likely to occur. In the example below, the first quotient is properly aligned.

$2\overline{)1.86}$ with .93   rather than $2\overline{)1.86}$ with 9.3

Procedures for teaching proper placement of the digits in the quotients of long division problems are discussed in Chapter 10.

Division problems with decimals can be categorized into four types of difficulty. The first three types have whole numbers as divisors.

1. Problems in which the quotient does not have a remainder and that require no conversion of the dividend:

$$
\begin{array}{r}
.69 \\
5\overline{)3.45}
\end{array}
\quad \text{or} \quad
\begin{array}{r}
.03 \\
7\overline{).21}
\end{array}
$$

2. Problems in which the dividend must be converted to an equivalent decimal so that no remainder will be present:

$$
\begin{array}{r}
.7 \\
5\overline{)3.7} \\
\underline{3\ 5} \\
2
\end{array}
\quad \text{becomes} \quad
\begin{array}{r}
.74 \\
5\overline{)3.70} \\
\underline{3\ 5} \\
20 \\
\underline{20}
\end{array}
$$

3. Problems with a remainder that requires rounding off:

$$
\begin{array}{r}
.34\ |\ 2 = .34 \\
7\overline{)2.40\ |\ 0} \\
\underline{2\ 1} \\
30 \\
\underline{28} \\
20 \\
\underline{14} \\
6
\end{array}
$$

4. Problems in which the divisor is a decimal or mixed decimal number and must be converted to a whole number

$$
.4\overline{)61.32} \quad \text{becomes} \quad .4\overline{)61.32}
$$

Decimal or Mixed Decimal Divided by a Whole Number   Division problems in which the dividend is a mixed decimal or decimal number and the divisor a whole number are usually introduced in late fourth or early to mid-fifth grade. An elaborate format is not required to introduce the problem type in which the dividend can be divided by the divisor without a remainder. Both of the following problems are examples of this type of problem.

$$
5\overline{)2.35} \qquad 7\overline{)84.7}
$$

The teacher presents the rule that the decimal point must be written on the line directly above where it appears in the numeral being divided. For example, when dividing 69.26 by 6, the student writes the problem:

$$
6\overline{)69.26}
$$

and then places the decimal point on the quotient line directly above the decimal in the dividend:

$$
\begin{array}{r}
. \\
6\overline{)69.26}
\end{array}
$$

The teacher then leads students through working several sets of problems, emphasizing the need to place the digits in the quotient in their proper places.

There are two example-selection guidelines for problems without remainders. First, the decimal point should appear in different positions in various problems:

$$
\text{a. } 5\overline{)3.725} \qquad \text{b. } 2\overline{)184.6} \qquad \text{c. } 9\overline{)1.836}
$$

$$
\text{d. } 7\overline{).364} \qquad \text{e. } 5\overline{)23.5} \qquad \text{f. } 5\overline{).215}
$$

Second, one or two problems in which a zero must be placed immediately after the decimal point should be included. In problems d and f above, the quotients are .052 and .043. The teacher may have to provide extra prompting on problems of that type by explaining that a digit must be written in every place after the decimal point. Therefore, in problem d, the teacher might say, "7 doesn't go into 3, so write a zero above the 3." Daily practice would include about 6 to 10 problems of this type.

The second type of decimal division problem requires the student to eliminate a remainder by rewriting the dividend as an equivalent decimal. For example, zeros need to be added to the dividend in each of the following problems:

$$
\begin{array}{ll}
\text{a. } 5\overline{)3.1} = 5\overline{)3.10}^{\,.62} & \text{c. } 4\overline{)3} = 4\overline{)3.00}^{\,.75} \\[2ex]
\text{b. } 2\overline{)3.45} = 2\overline{)3.450}^{\,1.725} & \text{d. } 5\overline{)2} = 5\overline{)2.0}^{\,.4}
\end{array}
$$

This type of problem is introduced after decimal division problems without remainders have been mastered.

The preskill of converting a decimal to an equivalent decimal should be taught prior to the introduction of this problem type. These problems are not very difficult and, like the previous type, do not require a lengthy teaching procedure. The teacher would explain that students should continue working until there are no remainders. He then would model working problems that require the addition of zeros. For example, after bringing down the final digit, 9, of the dividend in this problem:

$$
\begin{array}{r}
5.6 \\
6\overline{)33.9} \\
\underline{30} \\
3\,9 \\
\underline{3\,6} \\
3
\end{array}
$$

the teacher explains that he must keep dividing because he doesn't want a remainder: "I'll add a zero after the last digit in the decimal and divide again. Remember: Adding zeros after a decimal does not change the value of the numeral."

$$
\begin{array}{r}
5.65 \\
6\overline{)33.90} \\
\underline{30} \\
3\,9 \\
\underline{3\,6} \\
30 \\
\underline{30}
\end{array}
$$

Examples in these exercises should be designed so that the addition of one or two zeros to the dividend eliminates a remainder. Several examples such as

$$4\overline{)3} \quad \text{or} \quad 5\overline{)8}$$

in which a whole number is the dividend should be included. These problems would require the teacher to remind students to write the decimal point first and then add zeros after the whole number:

$$4\overline{)3} \quad \text{becomes} \quad 4\overline{)3.0}$$

The third type of decimal division problem requires rounding off. Students are usually instructed to work these problems to the nearest tenth, hundredth, or thousandth. The preskill required prior to teaching this type of problem is rounding off decimal numbers. The format for this skill appears in **Format 14.8: Dividing with Decimals—Rounding Off**. In Part A, the teacher demonstrates how to work the problem. Students first read the directions specifying to what decimal place (tenths, hundredths, thousandths) the answer is to be rounded. The teacher asks how many digits must be written after the decimal point in the answer, then instructs students to work the problem until they have written that many digits. Students are instructed to draw a line after that last digit in the answer and divide once more so they can decide how to round off the answer. The answer is then rounded off. If the numeral after the line is 5 or greater, another unit is added; if the numeral after the line is less than 5, no additional unit is added.

Special consideration should be given to those problems in which a whole number is divided by a larger whole number. These problems are very important because they prepare students to compute percentages; for example, "Daniella made 4 out of 7 basketball shots. What is her percentage for making shots?" We recommend that students round off answers in this type of problem to the nearest hundredth because percent is based on hundredths.

Dividing by a Decimal or Mixed Decimal The fourth type of division problem has a decimal or mixed decimal divisor. Problems of this type are relatively difficult because students must multiply the divisor and dividend by 10 or a multiple of 10 to convert the divisor into a whole number. Both the dividend and divisor must be multiplied by the same number so that the numerical value represented by the problem is not altered. For example, to work the problem $8.7 \div .35$, students must multiply the dividend and divisor by 100, converting .35 to 35 and 8.7 to 870.

The preskill of moving the decimal to the right when multiplying by a multiple of 10 should be taught and practiced for several weeks before introducing division problems with decimal divisors. **Format 14.9: Preskill: Multiplying Decimals by Multiples of 10** teaches this preskill. Students are taught that when a decimal number is multiplied by 10, the decimal point moves one place to the right; and when it is multiplied by 100, the decimal moves two places to the right.

Particularly difficult problems are those in which a zero must be added. For example, to multiply 8.7×100, the students must add a zero to the 8.7 so they can move the decimal point two places to the right: $8.7 \times 100 = 870$. The teacher would model several of these problems, explaining the need to add zeros. "You are multiplying by 100 so you will have to move the decimal point two places to the right, but you've only got one decimal place to the right. Add a zero so you can move the decimal point two places."

The examples in this preskill exercise should include a mix of problem types. The decimal point should not be placed in the same position from problem to problem. In half of the problems, 10 should be a factor, and in the other half, 100 should be a factor. Several problems should require that students add zeros to a mixed decimal (100×34.2; 100×14.2).

Also, several problems should include a whole number that must be multiplied by a multiple of 10 (10×34, 25×100). As the decimal point is moved over, zeros are added. For example, with 15×100, the student writes 15 and then adds two zeros (1500). The teacher would model working several of these problems.

Teachers should demonstrate that moving the decimal and adding a zero when multiplying by a multiple of 10 is acceptable by beginning with a problem like this:

$$\begin{array}{r} 3.4 \\ \times\ 10 \\ \hline 00 \\ 340 \\ \hline 34.0 \end{array}$$

The teacher points out that when she multiplies by 10, the answer is 34, with the decimal point moved one place to the right and a zero added. Next, the teacher writes this problem:

$$\begin{array}{r} 3.4 \\ \times\ 100 \\ \hline 00 \\ 000 \\ 3400 \\ \hline 340.0 \end{array}$$

and points out that when she multiplies by 100, the answer is also 340, with the decimal point moved two places to the right.

Division problems with decimal or mixed decimal divisors are introduced when students have mastered multiplying by multiples of 10 and can work all types of problems in which the divisor is a whole number and the dividend a decimal or mixed decimal. **Format 14.10: Dividing by Decimals** shows how to teach students to work problems with a decimal or mixed decimal divisor.

In Part A, the teacher presents a rule, "We cannot divide by a decimal," and demonstrates how the divisor and dividend must be revalued. Both the divisor and dividend are multiplied by whatever multiple of 10 is needed to change the divisor into a whole number. The teacher revalues the divisor first by moving the decimal point to the right. The dividend is revalued by moving the decimal point the same number of spaces to the right. Note that, in the format, the demonstration of how to revalue a problem is kept relatively simple to avoid confusing students with lengthy explanations.

Two example-selection guidelines are important to remember when teaching division with a decimal or mixed decimal divisor. First, the number of places in the divisor and dividend should vary from problem to problem. Interchanging the decimal divisor forces students to attend carefully to moving the decimal. For example, a worksheet might include the following problems with different types of decimal divisors:

a. $.5\overline{)3.75}$ b. $.05\overline{)37.5}$ c. $2.5\overline{)75}$

d. $.2\overline{)1368}$ e. $.03\overline{)24}$ f. $.5\overline{)21.85}$

A second guideline involves including some examples in which zeros must be added to the dividend (problems b, c, and e above). After a week or two, some problems in which a decimal or mixed decimal is divided by a whole number should be included so that students eventually receive adequate practice applying the strategies to the various types of problems.

If the teacher wishes to demonstrate the validity of moving the decimal point, she begins with a division problem:

$$.5\overline{)2.4} = \frac{2.4}{.5}$$

Let's work this division problem as a fraction. We don't divide by a decimal, so I have to change .5 into a whole number. I do that by multiplying by 10. If I multiply the denominator by 10, what do I have to do to the numerator? . . . Right, ten-tenths equal 1, and when we multiply by 1, we don't change the value of the fraction.

The teacher writes the following and says, "Now we can divide by a whole number."

$$\frac{2.4}{.5} \times \frac{10}{10} = \frac{24}{5} = 5\overline{)24}$$

Converting Fractions and Decimals

Decimals and fractions are both numerical systems for representing part(s) of a whole. Converting a fraction to a decimal is an important skill in and of itself as well as a component skill for percent problems. Converting a decimal to a fraction is less important because it has fewer practical applications.

Converting a Fraction to a Decimal   The strategy for converting a fraction to a decimal involves dividing the numerator by the denominator. For example, $\frac{3}{8}$ is converted to a decimal by dividing 8 into 3:

$$\frac{375}{8\overline{)3.000}}$$

This procedure initially was introduced in Chapter 12 in the section titled "Operations: Multiplying and Dividing Fractions."

The preskills for converting fractions to decimals were discussed earlier in this chapter. They are (a) decimal division problems in which a whole number is divided by a larger whole number ($3 \div 7$, $3 \div 5$) and (b) rounding off decimals. Because students who have mastered these preskills should have no difficulty converting a fraction to a decimal, an elaborate teaching procedure is not required. The teacher presents the rule: To change a fraction into a decimal, divide the numerator by the denominator. The teacher then models application of the rule with several problems and monitors students as they independently solve problems on a worksheet. Proper and improper fractions should be included in the exercise.

Initial examples of this strategy should be limited to fractions that can be divided evenly to the nearest tenth, hundredth, or thousandth:

$$\frac{4}{8} = 8\overline{)4.0} \quad \begin{array}{r} .5 \\ \hline 4\,0 \end{array}$$

Fractions that result in repeating decimals should not be introduced until several days later because they require rounding off. When these problems are presented, instructions should specify the place to which the decimal should be rounded off.

$$\frac{2}{3} = 3\overline{)2.0000} \quad .6666$$

Mixed numbers can be converted to a mixed decimal by first converting the mixed fraction to an improper fraction then dividing:

$$3\frac{2}{5} = \frac{17}{5} = 5\overline{)17.0} \quad 3.4$$

$$5\frac{3}{4} = \frac{23}{4} = 4\overline{)23.00} \quad 5.75$$

Conversion of a mixed number is introduced about a week after the introduction of repeating decimal problems.

In a final type of problem, the denominator is a two-digit numeral $\left(\frac{8}{12}, \frac{15}{18}\right)$. Students should be taught to first reduce the fraction to its lowest common terms before converting the fraction to a decimal:

$$\frac{6}{9} = \frac{2}{3} = 3\overline{)2.000} \quad .666$$

$$\frac{15}{18} = \frac{5}{6} = 6\overline{)5.000} \quad .833$$

Reducing is helpful because dividing by a one-digit divisor is easier than dividing by a two-digit divisor. If the fraction cannot be reduced, students must be able to work problems with a two-digit divisor. Daily practice should be provided over a period of several weeks on these types of problems.

Converting a Decimal to a Fraction   Converting a decimal to a fraction can be presented when students have learned to read and write fractions and can reduce fractions to their lowest terms. The strategy for converting a decimal to a fraction involves first rewriting the decimal as a decimal fraction and then reducing this decimal fraction to its lowest terms. For example, the decimal .75 would first be converted to the fraction $\frac{75}{100}$, which in turn would be reduced to $\frac{3}{4}$.

Initially, students would be given a worksheet like the one below, and the teacher would lead students through completing several items.

Decimal	Decimal Fraction	Reduced Fraction
.8	$\frac{8}{10}$	$\frac{4}{5}$
.80		
.35		

After several lessons, the teacher would introduce a worksheet exercise like the following. Circle the fraction that is equivalent to the decimal numeral.

.60	$\frac{6}{9}$	$\frac{3}{6}$	$\frac{3}{5}$	$\frac{6}{6}$
.75	$\frac{2}{3}$	$\frac{3}{4}$	$\frac{5}{7}$	$\frac{7}{5}$
.8	$\frac{8}{5}$	$\frac{1}{8}$	$\frac{4}{5}$	$\frac{3}{5}$

The teacher would guide students in converting the decimal to a decimal fraction and then in reducing this fraction to its lowest terms.

DIAGNOSIS AND REMEDIATION

Students may miss decimal problems for one or more of the following reasons:

1. Fact error: For example, when working the problem $9.63 \div 9$, the student writes 1.08 as the answer. The student's only mistake was dividing 9 into 63 incorrectly.

    If a student misses a problem because of a fact error, the teacher need not spend time working on the decimal skill but should reteach the specific fact.

2. Component-skill error: The student makes an error on a previously taught skill, which causes the student to miss the current type of problem. For example, when converting $\frac{3}{7}$ to a decimal, the student divides 3 by 7 correctly to .428 but then rounds off the answer to .42. The remediation involves reteaching the earlier-taught component skill. In the example given, the teacher would first reteach students how to round off. When the students demonstrate mastery of the component skill, the teacher would lead the students through solving the original type of problem using the structured worksheet part of the appropriate format.

3. Strategy error: A strategy error occurs when the student does not correctly follow the steps to solve a problem. For example, when attempting to convert $\frac{3}{4}$ to a decimal, the student divides 4 by 3. The remediation procedure involves reteaching the strategy, beginning with the structured board part of the format.

Figure 14.1, which describes diagnosis and remediation procedures for common errors made on the various types of decimal problems, appears below.

FIGURE 14.1 Diagnosis and remediation of decimal errors

Error Patterns	Diagnosis	Remediation Procedures	Remediation Examples
Adding or subtracting $3.5 + 2 = 3.7$ $5 - .3 = 2$	Component-skill error: failure to convert whole number to mixed decimal	Teach students to rewrite the numeral as mixed decimal, see **Format 14.4**. Present structured worksheet on addition and subtraction problems. See **Format 14.5**.	(1) Rewrite the following as mixed decimals to the hundredths place: 2, 5, 9, 7 (2) $14.7 - 2 =$ $11 - 4.3 =$
	Strategy error: placing decimal point in wrong position in answer	Present Parts B and C of **Format 14.7**. Be sure to include mix of addition and multiplication problems in the less structured worksheet exercise.	1) $\begin{array}{r}32.1\\ \times\ .9\\ \hline 2889\end{array}$ 2) $\begin{array}{r}.321\\ \times\ .9\\ \hline\end{array}$

Error Patterns	Diagnosis	Remediation Procedures	Remediation Examples
Dividing $\overset{46.1}{7)\overline{32.27}}$	Component-skill error: misalignment of digits in quotient	Review the procedure recommended in the section on "Decimal or Mixed Decimal Divided By a Whole Number." Be sure to emphasize the rule that the decimal point must be written on the line directly above the numeral being divided.	$2)\overline{28.46}$ $\dfrac{10.356}{4}$ $\dfrac{1.02}{4}$
$\overset{.63}{.05)\overline{3.15}}$	Strategy error: failure to rewrite divisor and dividend	Present **Format 14.10**.	$0.2)\overline{24.8}$ $\dfrac{.368}{.4}$ $\dfrac{1.55}{2.5}$
Rounding off 3.729 to 3.8 8.473 to 8.4	Strategy error: failure to use rounding off rules	Present **Format 14.6**.	Round .462 to the nearest tenth. Round .3814 to the nearest hundredth. Round 1.5659 to the nearest tenth.

APPLY WHAT YOU LEARNED

 Click on the √ to answer the questions online.

1. Describe the problem type that each example below represents. List the problems in the order they are introduced.

   a. $14.3 + 8.5$
   b. 7×34.8
   c. $9 - 3.28$
   d. Covert $\frac{4}{7}$ to a decimal
   e. Covert $\frac{2}{5}$ to a decimal
   f. $.9)\overline{28}$
   g. Read this number 8.04
   h. $9)\overline{2.7}$
   i. $9)\overline{2.8}$
   j. Round off 3.4785 to the nearest hundredth.

2. Construct a structured board presentation to teach students to read decimals expressed as thousandths.

3. Below are examples various teachers used in presenting reading decimals (tenths and hundredths). Tell which teacher used an appropriate set of examples. Tell why the other sets are inappropriate.

   Teacher A: .04, .09, .08, .05, .01, .07
   Teacher B: .7, .37, .48, .5, .28
   Teacher C: .7, .40, .07, .04, .70, .4

4. Specify the wording the teacher uses to present the following problem:

   $8 - .34 =$

5. Below is a set of examples constructed by a teacher for a rounding-off exercise. It is inappropriate. Tell why.

   Round off 3.482 to the nearest tenth
   Round off 7.469 to the nearest hundredth
   Round off 4.892 to the nearest tenth
   Round off 6.942 to the nearest whole

6. When asked to round off 3.738 to the nearest hundredth, a student writes 3.73. Specify the wording the teacher uses in making the correction.

7. Which problems below would not be included in the initial exercises for teaching students to divide a whole number into a decimal or mixed decimal number? Tell why.

   a. $.7\overline{)37.8}$ b. $4\overline{)23.5}$ c. $9\overline{)84.86}$

   d. $7\overline{)34.3}$ e. $9\overline{)3.87}$ f. $2\overline{)1.46}$

8. Tell the probable cause of each student's error below. Specify the remediation procedure for the error.

   Write this fraction as a decimal rounded off to the nearest hundredth: $\frac{5}{7}$

   Darnell

   $$\frac{5}{7} = 7\overline{)5.00} = 7\overline{)5.00}^{.614} = .61$$

   Deja

   $$\frac{5}{7} = 5\overline{)7.0}^{1.4}$$

   Nguyen

   $$\frac{5}{7} = 7\overline{)5.00|0}^{.71|4} = .72$$
   $$\underline{4\,9}$$
   $$10$$
   $$\underline{7}$$
   $$30$$
   $$\underline{28}$$
   $$2$$

Format 14.1
READING DECIMALS

TEACHER	STUDENTS
Part A: Structured Board Presentation	
1. *(Write the following fractions on the board.)* $\frac{3}{10}$ and $\frac{3}{100}$	
2. Read these fractions.	3 tenths, 3 hundredths
3. We're going to learn another way to write tenths and hundredths. *(Write a decimal point on the board.)* This is a decimal point. What is this?	A decimal point
One digit after the decimal point tells about tenths. What does one digit after the decimal tell about?	Tenths
Two digits after the decimal point tell about hundredths. What do two digits after the decimal point tell about?	Hundredths
Remember: If there is one digit after the decimal point, the numeral tells about tenths. If there are two digits after the decimal point, the numeral tells about hundredths.	
4. *(Write .9 on board.)*	
Listen: There's one digit after the decimal point. The 9 tells about tenths. This says "nine-tenths."	

TEACHER	STUDENTS
(Write .09 on board.) Listen: There are two digits after the decimal point. The 9 tells about hundredths. This says "nine-hundredths." Your turn.	
5. *(Write .3 on the board.)*	
How many digits after the decimal point?	1
What does the 3 tell about?	Tenths
Say the decimal numeral.	3 tenths
To correct: How many digits after the decimal point? There is/are _____ digit(s) after the decimal so the _____ tells about _____. The decimal says _____.	
(Repeat step 5 with .03, .30, .6, .60, .06, .58.)	
6. *(Write .7 on board.)*	
Say this decimal numeral.	
(Repeat step 6 with .70, .07, .9, .09, .90, .05, .4, .32.)	

Part B: Structured Worksheet

1. *(Present a worksheet like the following.)*

a. $.4 = \dfrac{4}{100} \quad \dfrac{4}{10} \quad \dfrac{40}{1000}$ g. $\dfrac{38}{100} = .3 \; .38 \; 38.$

b. $.40 = \dfrac{40}{100} \quad \dfrac{40}{10} \quad \dfrac{4}{10}$ h. $\dfrac{4}{100} = .40 \; .04 \; .4$

c. $.04 = \dfrac{40}{100} \quad \dfrac{40}{10} \quad \dfrac{4}{100}$ i. $\dfrac{40}{100} = .40 \; .4 \; .04$

d. $.61 = \dfrac{61}{100} \quad \dfrac{61}{10} \quad \dfrac{61}{1000}$ j. $\dfrac{8}{100} = .80 \; .08 \; .080$

e. $.06 = \dfrac{60}{100} \quad \dfrac{6}{100} \quad \dfrac{6}{10}$ k. $\dfrac{80}{100} = .80 \; .08 \; .8$

f. $.6 = \dfrac{6}{100} \quad \dfrac{6}{1000} \quad \dfrac{6}{10}$ l. $\dfrac{7}{10} = .70 \; .07 \; .7$

TEACHER	STUDENTS
2. Read the decimal numeral next to a.	4 tenths
We have to find the fraction that says .4.	
3. Read the first fraction.	4 hundredths
Read the next fraction.	4 tenths
Read the next fraction.	40 thousandths
4. The decimal says four-tenths. Draw a circle around the fraction that says four-tenths. *(Monitor student responses.)*	
5. Work problems b–f on your own. Remember to circle the fraction that says the same thing as the decimal.	
6. Read the fraction next to letter g.	38 hundredths
We have to find the decimal that says 38 hundredths.	
7. Read the first decimal.	3 tenths
Read the next decimal.	38 hundredths
8. It says the same thing as the fraction, so draw a circle around it. *(Monitor student responses.)*	
9. Work the rest of the problems on your own.	

Format 14.2
WRITING DECIMALS

TEACHER	STUDENTS
Part A: Structured Board Presentation	
1. *(Write $\frac{73}{100}$ on board.)*	
2. Read this fraction.	73 hundredths
3. I want to write 73 hundredths as a decimal.	
4. How many digits are there after the decimal point when a decimal tells about hundredths?	2
5. So I write a decimal point, then 73. What do I write after the decimal point to write 73 hundredths?	73
6. *(Write .73.)* Read the decimal.	73 hundredths

(Repeat steps 1–6 with: $\frac{7}{10}$, $\frac{7}{100}$, $\frac{70}{100}$, $\frac{4}{100}$, $\frac{48}{100}$, $\frac{6}{10}$, $\frac{6}{100}$, $\frac{6}{10}$, $\frac{60}{100}$, $\frac{3}{100}$.)

(Note: When presenting fractions like $\frac{7}{100}$, the teacher says in step 4, "So I write a decimal point, then zero seven.")

Part B: Less Structured Worksheet

1. *(Write these fractions as decimals.)*

a. $\frac{4}{100}$ = _____		g. $\frac{32}{100}$ = _____	
b. $\frac{4}{10}$ = _____		h. $\frac{28}{100}$ = _____	
c. $\frac{40}{100}$ = _____		i. $\frac{9}{10}$ = _____	
d. $\frac{7}{100}$ = _____		j. $\frac{92}{100}$ = _____	
e. $\frac{7}{10}$ = _____		k. $\frac{9}{100}$ = _____	
f. $\frac{70}{100}$ = _____		l. $\frac{5}{10}$ = _____	

TEACHER	STUDENTS
2. Read the directions.	Write these fractions as decimals.
3. Read the fraction next to a.	4 hundredths
4. How many digits must there be after the decimal point for hundredths?	2
5. What do you write after the decimal point to say four-hundredths?	04
6. Now write the decimal point and the numeral(s) to say seven-hundredths.	

(Repeat steps 2–6 with remaining examples.)

Format 14.3
READING AND WRITING MIXED DECIMALS

TEACHER	STUDENTS
Part A: Structured Board Presentation	
1. *(Write a decimal point on the board.)* The numerals on this side of the decimal point *(motion to the left)* tell about whole numbers. What do the numerals on this side of the decimal point *(motion to the left)* tell about?	Whole numbers
The numerals after the decimal point *(motion to the right)* tell about the decimal number.	
2. *(Write 2.4 on the board.)* This is a mixed decimal. It has a whole numeral and a decimal numeral. It says two and four-tenths. What is this mixed decimal?	2 and 4 tenths
What's the whole numeral in the mixed decimal?	2
What's the decimal?	4 tenths
Say the mixed decimal.	2 and 4 tenths
(Repeat step 2 with 9.03, 14.2, 16.23, 7.4, and 9.03.)	
3. *(Write 8.4 on board.)* Say the mixed decimal.	8 and 4 tenths
(Repeat step 3 with 8.04, 7.41, 19.2, 8.50, and 19.02.)	
Part B: Structured Worksheet	
1. *(Write the mixed decimal.)*	
a. eight and four tenths = _____	
b. sixteen and two-hundredths = _____	
c. five and sixteen-hundredths = _____	
d. eleven and four-tenths = _____	
e. eleven and four-hundredths = _____	
f. eleven and forty-hundredths = _____	
g. $17\frac{9}{10}$ = _____	
h. $8\frac{45}{100}$ = _____	
i. $16\frac{1}{100}$ = _____	
j. $16\frac{5}{100}$ = _____	
k. $16\frac{10}{100}$ = _____	
2. Read the words in a.	8 and 4 tenths
3. What's the whole numeral?	8
Write it.	
4. What's the decimal numeral?	4 tenths
Write it. Remember the decimal point. *(Monitor responses.)*	
5. What mixed decimal did you write?	8 and 4 tenths
(Repeat steps 2–5 with problems b–f.)	
6. Read problem g.	17 and 9 tenths
(Repeat steps 2–5 with the remaining items.)	

Format 14.4
CONVERTING DECIMALS INTO EQUIVALENT DECIMALS

TEACHER	STUDENTS
Part A: Demonstration	
1. Listen to this rule: When we write zeros after a decimal numeral, we don't change the value of the numeral. Say that.	When we write zeros after a decimal numeral, we don't change the value of the numeral.
2. *(Write on board: .3.)*	
Read this decimal.	3 tenths
I'll write a zero after the decimal. *(Add a zero: .30.)* Now read the decimal.	30 hundredths
I changed 3 tenths to 30 hundredths by adding a zero after a decimal numeral.	
3. I'm going to use fractions to show that 3 tenths equals 30 hundredths.	
(Write on board: $\frac{3}{10}$.)	
Read this.	3 tenths
We start with 3 tenths and we end with 30 hundredths.	
(Write on board: $\frac{30}{100}$.)	
What do I multiply 10 by to make it 100?	10
What do I multiply 3 by to make it 30?	10
(Write on board: $\frac{3}{10}\left(\frac{10}{10}\right) = \frac{30}{100}$.)	
I multiplied 3 tenths by 10 tenths: 10 tenths equal 1. Remember, when we multiply by 1, we don't change the value of a number. So 3 tenths equals 30 hundredths. *(Write .3 = .30.)*	
4. *(Repeat steps 2 and 3, changing .5 to .500.)*	
5. Here's another rule about zeros: If we cross out zeros at the end of a decimal numeral, we don't change the value of the decimal. *(Write .50.)* Read this decimal numeral.	50 hundredths
I'll cross out the zero at the end of the decimal. *(Cross out zero: .50.)* Now what does this decimal say?	5 tenths
6. Let's use fractions to show that 50 hundredths equal 5 tenths.	
(Write the problem on the board.)	
$\frac{50}{100} = \frac{5}{10}$	
50 = 5 times what number?	10
100 = 10 times what number?	10
(Write the rest of the problem.)	
$\frac{50}{100} = \frac{5}{10}\left(\frac{10}{10}\right)$	

TEACHER	STUDENTS
To make 5 tenths into 50 hundredths, we multiplied it by 10 tenths. 10 tenths equals 1. When we multiply by 1, we don't change the value of a number, so 50 hundredths equals 5 tenths.	
(Repeat steps 5 and 6 with $^{300}/_{1000} = {}^{3}/_{10}$*.)*	

Part B: Structured Board Presentation

1. *(Write 8.4 on the board.)*

   Read this numeral. — 8 and 4 tenths

   I want to rewrite this mixed decimal so that the decimal tells about thousandths.

2. When we write a decimal that tells about thousandths, how many digits must there be after the decimal point? — 3

3. I already have one digit after the decimal point, so how many zeros must I add? *(Write 8.400.)* — 2

4. Read the decimal numeral now. — 8 and 4 hundred thousandths

   Did we change the value of 8.4? — No

   No, 8.400 is the same as 8.4. When we add zeros at the end of the decimal, we don't change its value.

   (Repeat steps 1–4, changing 5.1 to 5.10; 9.300 to 9.3, 7 to 7.00, 9 to 9.0.)

Part C: Less Structured Worksheet

1. *(Give students a worksheet like this one.)*

   Mixed Decimals

	Ones	Tenths	Hundredths	Thousandths
a.	_____	3.7	_____	_____
b.	_____	_____	4.20	_____
c.	_____	9.2	_____	_____
d	_____	_____	_____	7.300
e.	6	_____	_____	_____

2. *(Point across row a.)* You have to fill in the missing mixed decimal numerals. Every mixed decimal in a row must have the same value. Read the numeral closest to a. — 3 and 7 tenths

3. Touch the space in the next column. The heading says hundredths. We must rewrite 3.7 so that the decimal expresses hundredths. How many digits must be after the decimal point for hundredths? — 2

   The mixed decimal 3.7 has one digit after the decimal. What must you do? — Add one zero

   Write the mixed decimal in the hundredths column. What mixed numeral did you write in the hundredths column? — 3.70

4. *(Repeat step 2 with the thousandths column.)*

   (Repeat steps 2 and 3 with remaining examples.)

   (Note: When converting whole numbers to mixed decimals, the teacher explains that a decimal point is written after the whole numeral. After the decimal point, zeros are added: one zero if the decimal expresses tenths, two zeros if it expresses hundredths, and three zeros if it expresses thousandths.)

Format 14.5
ADDITION/SUBTRACTION OF UNLIKE DECIMALS

TEACHER	STUDENTS
Part A: Structured Board Presentation	
1. When we add or subtract numerals containing decimals, we first rewrite them so they all have the same number of places after the decimal point. *(Write 13.7 − 2.14 on board.)*	
2. Read this problem.	13 and 7 tenths minus 2 and 14 hundredths
3. Which numeral has more places after the decimal point?	2.14
So we have to rewrite the problem so that each numeral is talking about hundredths.	
4. *(Point to 13.7.)* What can I do to 7 tenths to make it into a numeral with two places behind the decimal?	Add 0 after the 7
Yes, I write a zero after the 7. *(Write 0 after 7: 13.70.)* Now we have 70 hundredths. Read the problem now.	13 and 70 hundredths minus 2 and 14 hundredths
5. To work the problem, I'll write the problem in a column, making sure the decimal points are lined up. *(Write and solve the problem.)* 13.70 −2.14 11.56	
6. I'll write the decimal point in the answer. Remember, when we subtract numerals with decimals, we bring the decimal point straight down. *(Write the decimal point.)* 13.70 −2.14 11.56	
Read the answer.	11.56
(Repeat steps 1–6 with this problem: 18.9 − 3.425.)	
Part B: Structured Worksheet	
1. *(Give students a worksheet like this one.)* a. 7.1 − 3.45 e. 19.1 − 8.34 b. 16.345 + 8.3 f. 96.4 + 86.4 c. 51.43 + 6.85 g. 4.5 + 6.35 d. 13.6 − .346 h. 271. − 71.42	
2. Read item a on your worksheet.	7.1 − 3.45
3. Do the numerals have the same number of places after the decimal point?	No
4. Right. One numeral has tenths, and the other has hundredths. Which numeral has more places after the decimal?	3.45
So which numeral do you have to change?	7.1
What do you do to 7.1?	Add 0 after the 1

TEACHER	STUDENTS
Add the zero. *(Monitor responses.)* Now rewrite the problem in a column and work it.	
What is the answer?	1.65
(Repeat steps 1–4 with several more problems.)	

Format 14.6
ROUNDING OFF DECIMALS   (See Video Part A)

TEACHER	STUDENTS

Part A: Structured Board Presentation

1. *(Write .376 on board.)*

2. I want to round off this decimal to the nearest hundredth. When we talk about hundredths, how many digits will we have after the decimal? — 2

   I will count off two digits after the decimal point and then draw a line after that digit. *(Write. 37|6.)*

3. When we round off a decimal, we must look at the numeral that comes after the line. If the numeral is 5 or more, we must add another unit. What numeral comes after the line? — 6

   So must we add another hundredth? — Yes

   If we have 37 hundredths and we add another hundredth, how many hundredths do we have? — 38

   So .376 rounded to the nearest hundredth is . . . — .38

   (Write .38.)

4. *(Repeat steps 1–3 with the following problems.)*

   .372 rounded to the nearest tenth

   .1482 rounded to the nearest hundredth

   .382 rounded to the nearest whole

   .924 rounded to the nearest hundredth

Part B: Structured Worksheet

1. *(Give students a worksheet like this one.)*

   a. Round .462 to the nearest tenth _____
   b. Round .428 to the nearest tenth _____
   c. Round .8562 to the nearest hundredth _____
   d. Round .8548 to the nearest hundredth _____
   e. Round .3467 to the nearest hundredth _____
   f. Round .3437 to the nearest hundredth _____
   g. Round .417 to the nearest tenth _____
   h. Round .482 to the nearest tenth _____
   i. Round .3819 to the nearest hundredth _____
   j. Round .3814 to the nearest hundredth _____

continued

Format 14.6 *(continued)*
ROUNDING OFF DECIMALS

TEACHER	STUDENTS
2. Touch item a. What do we round off that decimal to?	To the nearest tenth
3. How many digits will be after the decimal point when you round off to the nearest tenth? Count one digit after the decimal point and draw a line.	1
4. Let's see if you add another tenth. What numeral comes just after the line?	6
So do you add another tenth?	Yes
You had four tenths. If you add a tenth, how many tenths do you have?	5
If you round off .462 to the nearest tenth, what do you have?	5 tenths
Write the answer on the line.	Students write .5.
(Repeat steps 2–4 with remaining problems.)	
Part C: Less Structured Worksheet	
(Give students a worksheet like the one in Part B.)	
1. Read item a.	
2. Draw a line to show where you round off.	
3. Round off and write your answer on the line.	
4. Read your answer.	
(Repeat steps 1–4 with remaining problems.)	

Format 14.7
MULTIPLYING DECIMALS

TEACHER	STUDENTS
Part A: Structured Board Presentation	
1. *(Write the following problem on the board.)* $\begin{array}{r} 34.2 \\ \times\ .59 \\ \hline 3078 \\ 17100 \\ \hline 20178 \end{array}$	
2. We're multiplying mixed decimals, so we have to put a decimal point in our answer. Here's a fast way to figure out where to write the decimal point in the answer. We count the places after the decimal points in both numerals we're multiplying.	
3. I'll touch the numerals after the decimal points and count them: *(touch 2)* one, *(touch 9)* two, *(touch 5)* three. How many decimal places in both numerals?	3
4. So I write the decimal point in the answer so that there are three places after it. *(Point between 7 and 8.)* One place. *(Point between 1 and 7.)* Two places. *(Point between 0 and 1.)* Three places. I put the decimal point here. *(Point between 0 and 1.)*	

TEACHER	STUDENTS
5. How many places after the decimal point?	3
Read the answer.	20.178

(Repeat steps 1–5 with the problems below.)

```
  34.2      34.2      351
×    5    ×  .7    × .05
```

Part B: Structured Worksheet

1. (Give students a worksheet like the following one.)

```
a.  32.1      b.  .321      c.  3.21      d.  321       e.  3.421
  × .9          × .9          × .9          × .9           × .7
  2889          2889          2889          2889          23947
```

```
f.   492      g.   4.92     h.  .492      i.   49.2
  × .53         × .53        × 5.3         ×  53
  1476          1476         1476          1476
 24600         24600        24600         24600
 26076         26076        26076         26076
```

```
j.   429      k.   .32      l.   3.2      m.   3.2
  ×  53         × .05        ×  5          × .05
  1476          160          160           160
 24600          000                        000
 26076          160                        160
```

2. These problems are worked already. All you have to do is put in the decimal points.

3. Touch problem a.

4. How many places are after the decimal points in both numerals being multiplied?	2
5. Where does the decimal point go in the answer?	Between the first 8 and the second 8
6. Write it.	
7. Read the answer.	28.89

(Repeat steps 2–7 with remaining problems.)

Part C: Less Structured Worksheet

1. (Give students a worksheet with a mix of multiplication and addition problems containing decimals and mixed decimals.) Remember: When you multiply, you count the places after the decimal point. When you add, you bring the decimal point straight down.

2. Work problem a.

3. Where does the decimal point go?

(Repeat steps 1–3 with remaining problems.)

Format 14.8
DIVISION WITH DECIMALS—ROUNDING OFF

TEACHER	STUDENTS
Part A: Structured Board Presentation	
1. *(Write the following instructions on the board.)*	
Work the problem, and express your answer to the nearest hundredth:	
$7\overline{)3.24}$	
2. Read the problem.	7 goes into 3 and 24 hundredths
The instructions tell us to work the problem to the nearest hundredth. How many digits after the decimal point when we have hundredths?	2
So we work the problem until we have two digits after the decimal point.	
(Solve the problem.)	

$$
\begin{array}{r}
.46 \\
7\overline{)3.24} \\
\underline{2\ 8} \\
44 \\
\underline{42} \\
2
\end{array}
$$

TEACHER	STUDENTS
3. We have hundredths in the answer, but we're not done because we have a remainder. We have to work the problem to thousandths and then round to hundredths. So I draw a line after the 6. *(Draw a line after the 6.)*	
4. We have to divide one more time so we know how to round off. Here's what we do. We add a zero after the 4 in the numeral we're dividing. Remember, when you add a zero after the last digit in a decimal numeral, you don't change the value of the numeral.	
(Add a zero.)	

$$
\begin{array}{r}
.46\,| \\
7\overline{)3.24\,|0} \\
\underline{2\ 8} \\
44 \\
\underline{42} \\
2
\end{array}
$$

TEACHER	STUDENTS
Now we can divide again. We bring down the zero. *(Write 0 next to 2.)* How many sevens in 20?	2
(Write 2 and 14.)	

$$
\begin{array}{r}
.46\,|2 \\
7\overline{)3.24\,|0} \\
\underline{2\ 8} \\
44 \\
\underline{42} \\
20 \\
\underline{14} \\
6
\end{array}
$$

TEACHER	STUDENTS
5. Do I round off to 46 hundredths or 47 hundredths?	46 hundredths
To correct: What numeral is after the rounding off line?	
That is less than 5, so we don't add another unit.	
(Repeat steps 1–5 with the problems below.)	
$9\overline{)4}$ Round off to nearest tenth.	
$7\overline{)26.3}$ Round off to nearest hundredth.	
$3\overline{)2}$ Round off to nearest hundredth.	
Part B: Structured Worksheet	
1. *(Give students a worksheet like the following one.)*	
a. Work these problems and round off to the nearest hundredth.	
1. $3\overline{)7.4}$ = 2. $6\overline{)5}$ =	
b. Work these problems and round off to the nearest tenth.	
3. $4\overline{)2.31}$ = 4. $7\overline{)3}$ =	
Read the instructions for a.	Work these problems and round off to the nearest hundredth.
Read problem one.	3 into 7.4.
2. You have to round the problem to the nearest hundredth. How many digits will there be after the decimal point in your answer?	2
Work the problem. Stop when there are two digits after the decimal point. *(Monitor students' work.)*	$$\begin{array}{r} 2.46 \\ 3\overline{)7.40} \\ \underline{6} \\ 1\,4 \\ \underline{1\,2} \\ 20 \\ \underline{18} \\ 2 \end{array}$$
3. You're not finished because you still have a remainder. Draw a line after the last digit in your answer. *(Pause.)* Now add a zero to 7.40 and divide again.	
4. What numeral did you write after the line in the answer?	6
So do you add another hundredth?	Yes
Write your rounded-off answer. *(Pause.)* What's your answer?	2.47
Part C: Less Structured Worksheet	
1. *(Give students a worksheet like the one given in Part B.)*	
2. Read the instructions for a.	
3. Read problem one.	
4. Where are you going to draw the line for rounding off: after the first, second, or third digit behind the decimal point?	Second digit
5. Work the problems and write your rounded-off answer.	

Format 14.9
PRESKILL: MULTIPLYING DECIMALS BY MULTIPLES OF 10

TEACHER	STUDENTS
Part A: Structured Board Presentation	
1. Here are some rules about multiplying decimals by 10 or 100: When you multiply by 10, you move the decimal one place to the right. What do you do to the decimal point when you multiply by 10?	Move it one place to the right
When you multiply by 100, you move the decimal point two places to the right. What do you do with the decimal point when you multiply by 100?	Move it two places to the right
2. *(Write on the board: 37.48 × 10.)*	
Read the problem.	37.48 × 10
We're multiplying by 10. What do you do to the decimal point when you multiply by 10?	Move it one place to the right
3. *(Write on the board: 37.48 × 10 = 3748.)*	
The decimal point was between the 7 and the 4. If I move it one place to the right, where will the decimal be?	Between the 4 and 8
(Write on board: 37.48 × 10 = 374.8.)	
Read the answer.	374.8
4. *(Repeat steps 2 and 3 with the problems below.)*	
37 × 100	
8.532 × 10	
7.2 × 100	
25 × 100	
Part B: Structured Worksheet	
1. *(Give the students a worksheet like the following one.)*	
a. 3.74 × 10 = e. 16 × 100 =	
b. .894 × 100 = f. 15 × 10 =	
c. 42.8 × 100 = g. .0382 × 10 =	
d. 3.517 × 10 = h. 49.2 × 100 =	
2. When you multiply by 10, what must you do?	Move the decimal one place to the right
When you multiply by 100, what must you do?	Move the decimal two places to the right
3. Read problem a.	3.74 × 10
4. You're multiplying by 10, so what must you do to the decimal point?	Move the decimal one place to the right
5. Where will the decimal point be in the answer?	Between the 7 and the 4
6. Write the answer.	
7. Read your answer.	37.4
(Repeat steps 2–7 with remaining problems.)	

Format 14.10
DIVIDING BY DECIMALS

TEACHER	STUDENTS
Part A: Structured Board Presentation	
1. *(Write the following on the board.)*	
$.5\overline{)51.75}$	
2. Here's a rule about decimal division: We don't divide by a decimal numeral. *(Point to .5.)* We must change the divisor to a whole numeral.	
3. *(Point to* $.5\overline{)51.75}$*)* What is the divisor in this problem?	.5
Can we work the problem the way it is?	No
What must we do?	Change the divisor to a whole numeral
4. We make five-tenths a whole numeral by moving the decimal point. A numeral is a whole numeral when there are no digits after the decimal point. How many places must I move the decimal point over to the right to make .5 into a whole numeral?	One
(Draw arrow: $.5\overline{)51.75}$*)*	
I moved the decimal one place to the right. We have to move the decimal point the same number of places in the dividend. How many places to the right must we move the decimal point in the dividend?	One
(Write on board: $.5\overline{)51.7.5}$*)*	
Now we can work the problem. I write the decimal point on the answer line, and then divide.	
(Write on board: $_x5.\overline{)51_x7.5}$*)*	
5. I'll divide.	
$$\begin{array}{r} 10.35 \\ 5.\overline{)51.7.5} \\ \underline{5} \\ 017 \\ \underline{15} \\ 25 \\ \underline{25} \end{array}$$	
6. What's the answer?	103.5
(Repeat steps 1–6 with the problems below.)	
$.05\overline{)5.125}$ $.7\overline{)28}$	
$.0\overline{)21.9}$ $.07\overline{)28}$	
Part B: Structured Worksheet	
1. *(Give students a worksheet like the following one.)*	
$.05\overline{)3.25}$ $.5\overline{)32}$ $.04\overline{)92}$	
$.3\overline{)9.6}$ $.03\overline{)9.6}$	
2. Read the first problem.	.05 into 3.25
3. What is the divisor?	.05

continued

Format 14.10 *(continued)*
DIVIDING BY DECIMALS

TEACHER	STUDENTS
4. Cross out the decimal point and move it to the right to make a whole numeral.	Students write $_\times 05.\overline{)3.25.}$
5. How many places did you move the decimal point to the right?	2
That's what you must do in the dividend. Cross out the decimal point and write it where it belongs. *(Monitor students' work.)*	Students write $_\times 05.\overline{)3_\times 25.}$
6. Now write the decimal point where it will be in the answer.	Students write $_\times 05.\overline{)3_\times 25.}$
7. Work the problem.	
8. What's the answer?	65
(Repeat steps 2–8 with remaining problems.)	

CHAPTER

15

Percent, Ratio, and Probability

LEARNING OUTCOMES

15.1 Explain how instruction in the areas of percent, ratio, and probability are organized to increase efficiency.

15.2 Discuss how the interrelationships among percent, ratio, and probability support the context for teaching these concepts together.

15.3 Discuss the recommended procedures for teaching percentage problems.

15.4 Describe how fraction skills are integrated into solving ratio problems.

15.5 Discuss how to introduce the concept of probability to students.

15.6 Describe the two most common types of errors involving percent, ratio, and probability and the recommended remediation procedures.

SKILL HIERARCHY

The introduction of percent, ratio, and probability follows instruction on most of the basic fraction and decimal skills discussed in the earlier chapters. Fraction and decimal skills serve as the preskills for percent, ratio, and probability problems. To solve a percentage problem, the student must be able to multiply mixed decimals; to solve a ratio problem, the student must be able to convert a fraction to a decimal or mixed decimal and round off the decimal or mixed decimal numeral; to solve a probability problem with different numbers of trials, the student must be able to find equivalent fractions.

As seen in the Instructional Sequence and Assessment Chart, we recommend beginning instruction in percent, ratio, and probability in fifth grade because these skills reinforce and support fraction instruction. Note on the chart that we recommend introducing percentage-related skills before ratio and probability skills.

INSTRUCTIONAL SEQUENCE AND ASSESSMENT CHART

Grade Level	Problem Type	Performance Indicator
5	Converting percentages to decimal figures	Write these percentages as decimals: 45% = 15% = 6% = 1% =
5	Determining a percent of a given number	What is 8% of 20? What is 25% of 12? What is 130% of 50?
5	Simple percentage word problems	Jane took 20 basketball shots. She made 60% of her shots. How many shots did she make? Tara scored 5% of her team's points. Her team scored 60 points. How many points did Tara score? In May a store sold 300 shirts. In June the store sold 130% of what it sold in May. How many shirts did it sell in June?
5	Converting a decimal to a percent	.32 = % .6 = % 3.4 = %
5	Converting a fraction to a percent: percentage comes out even	Convert these fractions to percentages: $\frac{3}{5} =$ % $\frac{7}{10} =$ % $\frac{5}{4} =$ %
5	Converting a fraction to a percent: rounding off required	$\frac{3}{7} =$ % $\frac{4}{9} =$ % $\frac{5}{3} =$ %
5	Simple ratio word problems: total is given	Bill took 20 basketball shots. He made 12. What is his shooting percentage? Ann has 15 friends; 9 of her friends are from Texas. What percentage of her friends are from Texas?
5	Single-event probability problems	Given a picture of a container with objects of two colors, what is the probability fraction for pulling out an object of one color?
6	Complex percentage problems	Jill earned $80 in May. In June she earned 30% more than she did in May. How much did Jill earn in June? Tim borrowed $200. He must pay 9% interest. How much must he pay back altogether?
6	Complex ratio problems; total not given	I got A's on 5 tests and B's on 4 tests. What percent of the tests did I get A's on? There are 4 boys and 6 girls. What percent of the class is boys?
6	Probability of two independent events	Bill has 5 blue pens and 15 red pens. What percent of the pens are blue? Given pictures of two or more containers, what is the probability of pulling a specified object from both containers?
6	Probability Word Problems	If a person has a pair of dice each with 2 red sides and 4 green sides, what it the probability of rolling both and getting 2 red sides?

CONCEPTUAL UNDERSTANDING

Percentage problems require the student to determine the quantity that represents a given percent of another quantity; for example, what is 30% of 60? Percentage skills are frequently used in daily life:

> You need to get 70% of the questions on the test correct to pass. If there are 20 problems on the test, how many must you get correct to pass?

Ratio problems require students to convert a numerical relationship (ratio) between two quantities into a percent. The fraction $\frac{3}{4}$ is converted to 75%. An example of using ratios in real-world situations is:

> Anna made 3 of 7 shots. What percent of her shots did she make?

Probability also has numerous practical applications, as in understanding weather predictions, political reports, and chances of winning the lottery. The probability of an event happening can be expressed in fractions ranging from 0 to 1 (0 = no chance; ½ = 50% chance; 1 = 100% chance). Depending on the context, the probability is reported in percent (20% chance of rain), ratios (the chance of winning the lottery is 1 in 14 million), or decimals (the probability of the result from a study being random is .001, therefore the results of this study are significant). We recommend introducing probability using fractions to reinforce and extend previously taught fractions and equivalent fractions concepts.

PERCENTAGE PROBLEMS

Two types of percentage problems are common to elementary mathematics instruction. The easier type of problem states a percent and quantity and asks students to find the percentage:

> The teacher said that 70% was a passing grade. There are 50 problems on the test. How many problems must I get to pass? (70% of 50 is .70 × 50 = 35)

The more difficult problem type requires students to calculate the percentage of an original quantity and then either add or subtract that amount from the original quantity:

> Bill borrowed $80 from the bank. He must pay 8% interest on the loan. How much must he pay back to the bank? (.08 × 80 = 6.40, $80.00 + $6.40 = $86.40)

Converting Percent to Decimal

Prior to introducing percentage problems, teachers would ensure that students have mastered multiplying decimal and mixed decimal numerals and converting a percent to a decimal.

Format 15.1: Converting Percent to Decimal introduces the concept of percent. The format contains three parts. In Part A, the teacher presents the percent sign and teaches students to read percent numerals. In Part B, a structured board presentation, the teacher demonstrates how a percent number can be converted to a decimal number by deleting the percent sign, and placing a decimal point so that there are two decimal places. Part C is a structured worksheet exercise. Daily worksheet practice should continue for several weeks.

Example selection is important when teaching this format. One-third of the percent figures should be below 10%, one-third between 10% and 100%, and one-third over 100%. For example, a conversion exercise might include the following percentages: 5%, 28%, 1%, 235%, 30%, 300%. Exposure to these types of problems provides students with the practice needed to generalize the strategy to a wide range of examples. Percentage below 10% are included to teach students that when converting a percent below 10%, they must write a zero in front of the decimal numeral (6% = .06, 1% = .01). Percentages of 100% and above are included to show that a whole number is present (354% = 3.54, 200% = 2).

Initially, examples that require converting a percent including a decimal, such as 87.5%, to a decimal are not included. This type of problem requires the students to add two more decimal places (87.5% = .875). Format 15.1 could be adapted to teach this procedure.

Simple Percentage Problems

Simple percentage problems involve multiplying a quantity by a given percent ($40 \times 30\% = 12$). This type of problem can be introduced after students can translate percentage to decimals and can accurately multiply decimal numerals. **Format 15.2: Solving Simple Percentage Problems** shows how to teach students to solve these types of problems.

Part A of this format is designed to teach students rules that will help them determine if their answers to subsequent problems are correct. The students are taught that if the problem asks for 100%, then the answer is the same as the number being multiplied ($100\% \times 20 = 20$). Likewise, if the percent is more than 100%, the answer is more than the number being multiplied; if less than 100%, the answer is less than the number being multiplied. Students then use the rules to predict the answers to numerical problems. Although these rules appear to be extremely simple, we have found through examining student errors that many students find it challenging to figure out these relationships on their own.

Part B is a structured board presentation in which the strategy for solving percentage problems is presented: Convert the percent to a decimal and then multiply that decimal and the amount given. Students apply the rules learned in Part A to check their answers.

Part C is a structured worksheet exercise. To simplify the multiplication, students may be instructed to write the two-digit numeral on the bottom when given a problem with a two-digit and a three-digit number. For example, in solving $125\% \times 60$, the student writes:

$$\begin{array}{r} 1.25 \\ \times\ 60 \\ \hline \end{array}$$

Examples for the worksheet should include sets of three problems in which the same numeral is multiplied. In one problem, the percent would be below 10%; in another problem, between 10% and 100%; and in another problem, more than 100%. For example, a sample set for an exercise might include these problems:

$$\begin{array}{ll} 30\ \% \times 60 & 25\ \% \times 36 \\ 3\ \% \times 60 & 2\ \% \times 36 \\ 130\ \% \times 60 & 125\ \% \times 36 \end{array}$$

These example-selection guidelines are designed to provide practice with a range of problems that reinforce the rule they learned in Part A.

Simple Percentage Word Problems

Simple percentage word problems state an amount and ask the student to determine a percentage (the number obtained by finding the percent of another number). A distinguishing characteristic of these problems is the inclusion of the word "of." Below are two typical simple percentage problems:

There are 60 children in our school; 75% of the children are girls. How many girls are there in our school?

Trina made 60% of her shots. She took 20 shots. How many shots did she make?

These word problems are introduced when students can calculate percentage problems such as $40\% \times 20$ accurately. As preparation for these word problems, teachers would give students computation problems in which the word "of" is substituted for the multiplication sign (75% of 48). After several lessons, the teacher would introduce word problems by modeling them and providing practice. After students have mastered solving this type of word problem, the teacher would remind the students to apply the rule for checking their answers found in Part A of **Format 15.2**.

The problem said she got 60% of her shots in. She took 20 shots. Is the answer going to be more than 20, equal to 20, or less than 20?

An independent worksheet would include problems with percentages below 10%, problems with percentages between 10% and 100%, and problems with percentages above 100%.

Complex Percentage Problems

Complex percentage problems usually give the percent that an original amount has either increased (or decreased) and asks the students to figure out the amount of the increase (or

FIGURE 15.1 **Sample interest exercise**

Amount of Loan	Interest Rate for 1 Year	Amount of Interest for 1 Year	Amount to Be Paid Back at End of 1 Year
a. $500	5%	_____	_____
b. $500	8%	_____	_____
c. $1000	4%	_____	_____
d. $1000	7%	_____	_____

decrease) and the new total. These complex percentage problems should be introduced after students have practiced simple percentage problems for several weeks. An example of a complex percentage problem is illustrated below:

> The bike store sold 50 bikes in May. In June the sales went up 20%. How many more bikes did the store sell in June than in May? How many bikes did the store sell in June?

The teacher models how to solve the problem: first computing the percentage increased or decreased by converting the percent to a decimal and then multiplying. This amount is then added to or subtracted from the original amount to determine the new total. For example, in the problem above, the student converts 20% to .20 and multiplies .20 $\times$ 50, resulting in 10. Therefore, the store sold 10 more bikes in June than in May. The additional 10 bikes are added to the 50 bikes sold in May to determine that 60 bikes were sold in June.

A special type of problem involves computing simple interest. The teacher can explain the term "interest" to students by using an explanation similar to the one below.

> When you borrow money from a bank, you must pay back the bank extra money. The extra money is interest. If the bank charges 10% interest, you must pay back the money you borrowed plus 10% of the amount you borrowed.

Figure 15.1 is a sample interest exercise. Students fill in missing amounts in a table to determine interest for various loans. More complex interest problems are introduced in later grades.

RATIO PROBLEMS

In ratio problems, students must convert a fraction to a percent. There are three basic types of ratio problems:

1. Numerical problems for converting a fraction to a percent.

$$\frac{2}{5} = 40\,\%$$

$$\frac{5}{4} = 125\,\%$$

2. Simple ratio word problems in which the total and one partial quantity are given and students calculate the percent.

Sara made 10 out of 20 shots. What percent of her shots did she make?

$$\frac{10}{20} = 50\,\%$$

3. Complex word problems in which students are required to add specific amounts prior to determining a percent.

Shilah made 10 shots and missed 10 shots. What percent of her shots did she make?

$$10 + 10 = 20 \qquad \frac{10}{20} = 50\,\%$$

Converting a Fraction to a Percent

Converting a fraction to a percent can be introduced several weeks after students have mastered simple percentage problems. **Format 15.3: Converting Decimals and Fractions to Percentages** teaches this conversion skill. Prior to this instruction, students need to have mastered converting fractions to decimals (dividing the numerator by the denominator in a fraction and rounding off the resulting decimal number).

The format includes five parts. In Part A, the teacher presents a strategy for converting decimal numerals to percentages: Write a percent sign and move the decimal point two places toward the percent sign. The wording for this procedure is designed to assist students in determining the direction to move the decimal point. After presenting the rule, the teacher applies the rule to a range of examples including mixed decimals and decimal numbers with tenth, hundredth, and thousandth decimal places.

Part B is a worksheet exercise in which students practice converting decimals to a percent. Initially, the teacher would guide the students through several conversions and then have the students work the remaining problems independently. As in Part A, the examples selected for Part B should include decimals expressed as tenths, hundredths, and thousandths in addition to one or two whole numbers and several mixed decimals. When converting a tenths decimal or whole number, the teacher tells the students the number of zeros to add:

$$.1 = .10 = .10\% = 10\%$$

A sample set for a worksheet exercise might include these numerals: 3.2, .475, 6, .08, .4, .37, 2, 6.1, 35, .875, and .1.

Prior to introducing Part C, the teacher would provide several days of practice on Part B. In Part C, a structured board exercise, the teacher presents the two-step strategy for converting fractions to a percent: First convert the fraction to a decimal, and then convert that decimal to a percent. The teacher would then demonstrate the application of the strategy with several fractions. **Summary Box 15.1** outlines the strategy introduced in Part C.

Part D is a structured worksheet exercise in which students are given a worksheet with prompts to help make the conversion. A prompted problem looks like this:

$$\frac{3}{4} = \overline{)} = .\underline{\hspace{2cm}} = \underline{\hspace{2cm}}\%$$

The teacher asks students how to change a fraction to a decimal, reminding students to put the decimal point in the answer. Then the teacher asks students how to covert the decimal to a percent and has the students calculate the answer. Part E is a less structured worksheet exercise in which the prompts are removed.

Two example-selection guidelines are critical for Parts C, D, and E. First, proper and improper fractions should be included so that students can see that the strategy also applies to percentages greater than $100\% \left(\frac{5}{4} = 125\%\right)$. The second example selection guideline relates to the need to round answers. Initially, problems should be limited to fractions that do not require rounding off to compute the percent. Problems that must be rounded off require an extra step and should not be introduced for several weeks. The fractions $\frac{3}{4}, \frac{1}{2}, \frac{7}{10}, \frac{6}{8}$, and $\frac{6}{4}$ are examples of fractions that do not require rounding off. Later, fractions such as $\frac{5}{7}, \frac{2}{9}, \frac{4}{3}, \frac{3}{11}$, and $\frac{5}{6}$ that do require rounding off may be included.

When problems requiring rounding off are introduced, the teacher tells the students to divide until the answer has three digits after the decimal and then round off to the nearest hundredth. For example, when converting $\frac{5}{7}$ to a percent, the student divides to the thousandths place, then writes a line after the 1 (the hundredths numeral), and then rounds off the answer to .71:

$$
\begin{array}{r}
.71\,|4 \\
7)\overline{5.00\,|0} \\
\underline{4\,9} \\
10 \\
\underline{7} \\
30 \\
\underline{28} \\
2
\end{array}
$$

After students have had several weeks of practice in converting fractions to decimals, the teacher can introduce the new steps of reducing the fraction before dividing when possible. For example, $\frac{9}{12}$ can be reduced to $\frac{3}{4}$, so students would divide 3 by 4 instead of 9 by 12. Reducing fractions prior to dividing is especially helpful when working with two-digit denominators. If the denominator can be reduced to one digit, the division problem will be much easier.

A final consideration in teaching students to convert fractions to decimals involves providing students with adequate practice so that they can memorize the percentages that more common fractions represent. The percentages for these fractions should be taught: $\frac{1}{4} = 25\%, \frac{3}{4} = 75\%, \frac{1}{2} = 50\%, \frac{1}{3} = 33\%, \frac{2}{3} = 67\%, \frac{1}{5} = 20\%$, and $\frac{1}{10} = 10\%$. To facilitate memorization of these percentages, the teacher may provide flash card practice or another type of memorization exercise. However, this memorization practice would not begin until after several weeks of instruction on converting fractions to percentages.

SUMMARY BOX 15.1

Converting Decimals and Fractions to Percentages

1. Students change a fraction to a decimal by dividing the numerator by the denominator.

$$\frac{3}{4} = 4\overline{)3.00} \quad \begin{array}{r} .75 \\ \hline \end{array}$$
$$\begin{array}{r} 28 \\ \hline 20 \\ 20 \end{array}$$

2. Students change the decimal to a percent by writing % sign and moving the decimal two places toward the percent sign.

$.75 = 75\%$

Simple Ratio Word Problems

In contrast to simple percentage problems in which a quantity and a percent are given, simple ratio word problems contain two related quantities, and students are asked to express the relationship between them as a percent. Problems a and b are examples of this type of problem:

a. There were 20 problems on the test. Jack got 14 correct. What percent of the problems did Jack get correct?

b. There are 12 children in our class; 8 are girls. What percent of our class is girls?

Most simple ratio problems are related to classification problems(see Chapter 11). They involve a subset of a total set, as in problems correct (subset) out of problems on the test (total set) or girls (subset) out of children (total set).

Format 15.4A:
Simple Ratio Word Problems

Watch how Joe teaches his students to solve simple ratio word problems.

Simple percentage problems can be introduced when students have mastered converting fractions to a percent figure. **Format 15.4: Simple Ratio Word Problems** contains three parts. In Part A, the structured board presentation, students are taught the component skill of converting the relationship expressed in the word problem to a fraction. The teacher presents the rule that the number that tells how many altogether is written as the denominator of the fraction; she then models and tests with several examples. For example, "Sheila took 12 shots; she made 10" translates to $\frac{10}{12}$.

Part B provides structured worksheet practice on converting ratio word problems to fractions. Part C is a less structured worksheet in which the teacher guides students in rewriting the relationship in the word problem as a fraction and then changing the fraction to a percent. Practice would include as many real-life situations as possible. (What percent of the children are girls? What percent of the days has it rained?)

Complex Ratio Word Problems

In complex ratio word problems, the students must add two quantities to derive a sum that will be the denominator of the fraction used to compute percent. For example, a problem may state that there are 4 boys and 6 girls and ask for the percent of the children that are girls. For that problem, the quantities 4 and 6 must be added to determine the denominator, since the fraction is

$$\frac{\text{girls}}{\text{boys and girls}}$$

Complex ratio word problems are not introduced until students have had several weeks of practice with simple ratio problems.

In **Format 15.5: Complex Ratio Problems**, the teacher guides students in identifying the denominator representing the total. For example:

> This problem asks what fraction of the children are girls, so the fraction will be girls over children. How many children? So what do I write for the denominator?

After providing guided practice, the teacher would give students worksheets with both simple and complex ratio problems, such as a and b below:

a. There are 6 children in the club, and 4 are girls. What percent of the children are girls?
b. There are 4 boys and 6 girls in the club. What percent of the children in the club are girls?

Note that the total in both problems is the number of children. In problem a, a simple ratio problem, the number of children is given. Problem b does not give the total, so 4 boys and 6 girls must be added to determine the total number of children, making it a complex ratio problem. Presenting related simple and complex problems is necessary to provide students with practice in determining the total (denominator of the fraction). When guiding students through the problems on the worksheet, the teacher would ask the students if the problem provides the quantity for the total. If the problem does not provide the total, the teacher would prompt the students to identify and add the subsets in order to obtain the quantity for the total before having students complete the problem.

Additional instruction on more difficult ratio word problems is presented in Chapter 18, "Pre-algebra." In that chapter we discuss how to teach students to set up ratio tables to solve typical word problems.

PROBABILITY PROBLEMS

Until relatively recently, probability was not introduced until high school. It is now commonly included in middle school commercial mathematics programs. We recommend introducing probability in fifth grade so students have opportunities to appreciate the connections between fractions and probability.

Probability is often introduced through activities such as flipping a coin, rolling a die, or selecting a specific shape from a group of shapes. This type of activity involving observing and recording data is referred to as **experimental probability**. Experimental probability activities involve identifying what a trial is (one flip, one roll, or one selection), conducting many trials, recording the data from these trials, and reporting the probability of a specified outcome. For example, a teacher may give students a coin and instruct the students to flip the coin and record when the coin lands in the heads position. The teacher would inform the students that one flip of the coin is called a "trial." Once the students have recorded the number of times the coin landed heads up (the outcome), the teacher would teach the students how to write a probability fraction that represents the outcome compared to the total number of trials. For example, if the coin landed heads up 12 out 20 trials, the probability fraction would be $\frac{12}{20}$, with the numerator representing the 12 times the coin landed heads up and the denominator representing the total number of trials.

When introducing experimental probability using activities that involve selecting objects from a group of objects (such as pulling colored pencils from a box), teachers must make certain that students follow several guidelines. These include (a) objects are selected from the container without looking, (b) only one object is selected at a time, (c) a record is kept of the object selected, and (d) the object is returned to the container before selecting another.

Experimental probability activities are designed to provide students with a conceptual understanding of probability. These types of activities also incorporate data analysis skills when students record the results of their experimental trials. Therefore, we recommended using these types of activities as an introduction to the concept of probability.

In contrast to experimental probability, where the focus is on observing events, theoretical probability focuses on predicting the likelihood of an event happening using mathematics. In this chapter we include instructional procedures for calculating the theoretical probability of single events, for different numbers of trials, and for two independent events or compound probability. Word problem instruction is also included as an application of probability skills to daily life.

Single-Event Probability

Format 15.6 Writing Probability Fractions contains three parts. Part A introduces students to probability fractions used to indicate the likelihood that an event will happen. Pictures are used to represent the problem. The picture might represent a box of pencils with 12 yellow pencils and 8 green pencils. The probability fraction for yellow pencils (the chances of choosing a yellow pencil out of all of the pencils) is $\frac{12}{20}$.

In Part B students write probability fractions for pictures. They learn that the denominator represents the total number of objects and the numerator indicates the likelihood of the specified object being pulled from the container in the picture. In Part C, a less structured worksheet, the teacher guides students through writing probability fractions for several pictures.

Format 15.7: Probability for Different Numbers of Trials requires understanding the concept of a trial and mastery of equivalent fractions. Part A teaches that any fraction that is equivalent to the probability fraction will provide information regarding the probability of an event with different numbers of trials. For example, if the probability fraction for pulling red marbles from a bag is $\frac{3}{5}$, indicating that in five trials one would expect to pull a red marble three times, then in ten trials one would expect to pull a red marble 6 times because $\frac{3}{5}$ is equivalent to $\frac{6}{10}$. Part B, the less structured worksheet, provides guided practice in writing probability fractions and equivalent fractions for pictures.

Compound Probability

Compound probability is less intuitive than single-event probability. Compound probability is the likelihood of two or more events happening together. The calculation for compound probability involves finding the probability fraction for each single event and multiplying them.

To provide justification for this procedure the teacher may describe a compound probability situation and show all of the possible outcomes. For example, the teacher may use the first picture in **Format 15.8: Introducing Compound Probability** in which there are 2 cans each with one star, one cube, and one circle. The question for this example asks the probability of pulling a star from both cans. The calculation to find the probability is $\frac{1}{3} \times \frac{1}{3} = \frac{1}{9}$. A table similar to the one below showing all of the possible combinations of shapes from the two containers can be used to justify this answer. The table shows the nine possible results of pulling one shape from each can. Only one of the nine trials $\left(\frac{1}{9}\right)$ results in pulling a star from each can.

Trials	#1	#2	#3	#4	#5	#6	#7	#8	#9
Can 1	Star	Star	Star	Cube	Cube	Cube	Circle	Circle	Circle
Can 2	Star	Cube	Circle	Star	Cube	Circle	Star	Cube	Circle

Format 15.8: Introducing Compound Probability has two parts. Part A, the structured board presentation, introduces the procedure for calculating compound probability first with two events and then with three. If students have mastered the preskill of multiplying fractions, this

calculation is relatively simple. In Part A, the teacher models finding compound probability using pictures of containers with shapes as described above. The second example in Part A illustrates the efficiency of this calculation. This example includes 10 shapes in each of three containers, resulting in 1,000 possible combinations, making drawing pictures unrealistic. Part B provides worksheet practice in calculating compound probability.

Probability Word Problems

When students have mastered single-event probability, they can apply their skills to word problems. **Format 15.9: Probability Word Problems** provides instructional procedures for applying probability skills to word problems. Initially these word problems should include only single-event probability, but as soon as students have learned to calculate compound probability, these problems can be included. Problems like the following can be used to provide opportunities for discrimination practice between single event and compound probability:

> There 4 blue marbles, 5 red marbles, 1 green marble, and 2 black marbles. You select one marble without looking. What is the probability of selecting a blue marble? Red? Green? Black? (single-event probability)

> You have two standard decks of cards (with 52 cards). You randomly draw one card from each deck. What is the probability of getting the queen of hearts from each deck? (compound probability)

DIAGNOSIS AND REMEDIATION

• • • • • • • •

Common percent, ratio, and probability errors fall into one of the two following categories:

1. Component-skill error: The student makes an error on a previously taught skill, which causes the student to complete the problem incorrectly. For example, when working the problem 5% of 75, the student multiplies .5 by 75 rather than .05 by 75. In this example, the student made an error converting the percent to a decimal. The remediation procedure involves reteaching the earlier-taught component skill of converting a percent to a decimal, being sure to include examples less than 10%. When the student's performance indicated mastery of the component skill, the teacher would assess the student the result of this remedy by providing a worksheet with problems similar to the original.

2. Strategy error: A strategy error is evident when the student shows no indication of following the steps in the strategy. For example, when attempting to calculate the compound probability of rolling a 5 on two dice at the same time, the student calculates $\frac{1}{6}$ rather than calculating $\frac{1}{6} \times \frac{1}{6} = \frac{1}{36}$. The remediation procedure involves reteaching the entire strategy beginning with the structured board part of the format.

APPLY WHAT YOU LEARNED

 Click on the √ to answer the questions online.

1. Below are errors made by students. Specify the probable cause of each error and describe a remediation procedure.

   a. What is 38% of 90?

   Jamel

   $$\begin{array}{r} 90 \\ \times\ .38 \\ \hline 720\ =\ 3420 \\ 2700 \\ \hline 3420 \end{array}$$

Hoang

$$90.00$$
$$\underline{+\ .38} = 90.38$$
$$90.38$$

Sara

$$90$$
$$\underline{\times .38}$$
$$720 = 9.9$$
$$\underline{270}$$
$$9.90$$

b. What is 5% of 60?

Grace

$$60$$
$$\underline{\times .5} = 30$$
$$30.0$$

c. Bill took 15 shots; he made 12 of his shots. What percent of his shots did he make?

Ewan

$$\frac{15}{12} = 12\overline{)15.0}^{\,1.25} = 125\%$$
$$\underline{12}$$
$$30$$
$$\underline{24}$$
$$60$$

Jet

$$\frac{12}{15} = 15\overline{)12.0}^{\,.69} = 69\%$$
$$\underline{90}$$
$$300$$
$$135$$

Tai

$$\frac{12}{15} = 15\overline{)12.0}^{\,.8} = 8\%$$
$$12.0$$

2. Specify the wording the teacher uses in a structured worksheet presentation for converting $\frac{3}{7}$ to a percent.

3. Below are sets of examples teachers constructed for an exercise to teach students to convert percent figures to decimals. Tell which sets are inadequate and why.

Set A:	85%	94%	30%	62%	53%	6%
Set B:	40%	5%	135%	240%	7%	82%
Set C:	130%	20%	72%	145%	80%	360%

4. Write word problems for a single-event probability situation and compound probability situation.

Format 15.1
CONVERTING PERCENT TO DECIMAL

TEACHER	STUDENTS
Part A: Reading and Writing the Percent Sign	
1. *(Write % on board.)* This is a percent sign. What is this?	A percent sign
2. *(Write 42% on board.)* This says 42%. What does this say?	42%
3. *(Write 30% on board.)* What does this say?	30%
(Repeat step 4 with 8%, 142%, 20%, 96%, and 300%.)	
Part B: Structured Board Presentation	
1. Percent means hundredths. What does percent mean?	Hundredths
2. 87% means 87 hundredths. What does 87% mean?	87 hundredths
(Repeat step 2 with 50%, 214%.)	
3. What does 30% mean?	30 hundredths
(Repeat step 3 with 248%, 8%.)	
4. How many decimal places in a hundredths number?	Two
5. Here's a rule for changing a percent number to a decimal number: Get rid of the percent sign and put in a decimal point so that there are two decimal places. How many decimal places must we have when we change a percent number to a decimal number?	Two
6. *(Write 236% on board.)* Read this.	236%
I want to change this numeral to a decimal. What does 236% mean?	236 hundredths
How many decimal places in a hundredths number?	Two
So I get rid of the percent sign and put in two decimal places. *(Write 2.36.)* Read this.	2 and 36 hundredths
Yes, 236% = 2.36.	
7. *(Write 8% on board.)* Read this.	8%
I want to change this numeral to a decimal. What does 8% mean?	8 hundredths
How many decimal places in a hundredths number?	Two
So I get rid of the percent sign and put in two decimal places. *(Write .08.)* Read this.	8 hundredths
Yes, 8% = .08.	
(Repeat steps 6 and 7 with 34%, 126%, 5%, 82%.)	
Part C: Structured Worksheet	
(Give students a worksheet with instructions and problems similar to those below.)	
1. Change these percent to decimals:	

1. Change these percent to decimals:

a. 35% = _____   e.   1% = _____

b. 200% = _____   f. 192% = _____

c.   6% = _____   g. 374% = _____

d. 72% = _____   h.   2% = _____

TEACHER	STUDENTS
2. Read the directions.	Change these percents to decimals.
3. Read the percent numeral in problem a.	35%
4. What does 35% mean?	35 hundredths
5. How many decimal places in a hundredths number?	Two
6. Where will we write the decimal point?	In front of the 3
7. Write the decimal numeral.	
8. What decimal did you write?	35 hundredths
Yes, 35% equals 35 hundredths.	
(Repeat steps 3–8 with remaining problems.)	

Format 15.2
SOLVING SIMPLE PERCENTAGE PROBLEMS (See Video in Part A)

TEACHER	STUDENTS
Part A: More/Less Than 100%	
1. *(Write 100% on board.)* I want to change 100% to a decimal, so I get rid of the percent sign and put in two decimal places. *(Write 1.00 on board.)* 100% equals what whole number?	1
Yes, 100% equals one whole. So when we multiply by 100%, we don't change the value of the number we're multiplying. The answer is the same as the number we're multiplying.	
2. Here are some rules about other percents: If we multiply by more than 100%, our answer is bigger than the number we're multiplying. If we multiply by less than 100%, our answer is less than the number we're multiplying.	
3. If you multiply by 100%, what do you know about the answer?	The answer is the same as the number we're multiplying.
4. If you multiply by less than 100%, what do you know about the answer?	The answer is less than the number we're multiplying
Right, when the percent is less than 100, you multiply by a number less than 1. So the answer must be less than the number we're multiplying.	
5. If you multiply by more than 100%, what do you know about the answer?	The answer is more than the number we're multiplying
(Repeat steps 1–5 until students respond correctly.)	
6. Here's a problem: 60% × 20. Say the problem.	60% × 20
What's the percent?	60
Is the answer more than 20, less than 20, or equal to 20?	Less than 20

continued

Format 15.2 *(continued)*
SOLVING SIMPLE PERCENTAGE PROBLEMS

TEACHER	STUDENTS
To correct: Remember: If the percent is less than 100, the answer is less than the amount we're multiplying. Is the percent less than 100? So, tell me about the answer.	
How do you know?	The percent is less than 100.
7. *(Repeat step 6 with 140% of 20, 100% of 20, 24% of 150, 100% of 150, and 60% of 150.)*	
Part B: Structured Board Presentation	
1. *(Write 75% × 20 on board.)* Read this problem.	75% × 20
What is the percent?	75
What is the amount?	20
Will the answer be more or less than 20?	Less than 20
2. Here's how we find the exact answer. We change the percent to a decimal, then multiply. How do we find the exact answer?	Change the percent to a decimal and multiply
3. First we write 75% as a decimal; 75% equals how many hundredths?	75
Yes, 75% can be written as 75 hundredths. *(Write .75.)*	
4. Now we multiply. *(Write the problem on the board.)*	
$$\begin{array}{r} 20 \\ \times\,.75 \\ \hline 100 \\ 1400 \\ \hline 1500 \end{array}$$	
We multiplied by a decimal numeral, so I must put a decimal point in the answer. Where do I put the decimal point?	After the 5
So what whole number do we end with?	15
5. What is 75% × 20?	15
Write 75% × 20 = 15. Say the statement.	75% × 20 = 15.
6. Let's see if that follows the rules. The amount we began with was 20. We were finding less than 100%. Our answer must be less than 20. Is 15 less than 20?	Yes
So our answer makes sense.	
(Repeat steps 1–6 with these problems: 125% × 20, 5% × 20, 120% × 65, 12% × 65, 20% × 65.)	
Part C: Structured Worksheet	
a. 30% × 50 = ☐	
b. 130% × 50 = ☐	
c. 3% × 50 = ☐	
d. 25% × 72 = ☐	
1. Read problem a.	30% × 50 =
What is the percent?	30
What is the amount?	50
Will the answer be more or less than 50?	Less than 50

TEACHER	STUDENTS
2. Remember, we find the exact answer by changing the percent to a decimal and then multiplying. How do we find the exact answer?	Change the percent to a decimal and then multiply
3. First you need to write 30% as decimal; 30% equals how many hundredths?	
4. Write 30% as 30 hundredths.	30
5. What do you do next?	Multiply by 50
6. Multiply. *(Pause.)* What is 30% × 50. *(Repeat steps 1–6 for problems b–d.)*	15

Format 15.3
CONVERTING DECIMALS AND FRACTIONS TO PERCENTAGES

TEACHER	STUDENTS
Part A: Converting Decimals to Percent	
1. We change a decimal to a percent by adding a percent sign after the numeral and moving the decimal point two places toward the percent sign. Listen again. *(Repeat rule.)* *(Write .486 on board.)*	
2. Read this decimal. I want to change this decimal to a percent. First I write the percent sign after the numeral. *(Write .486% on board.)*	486 thousandths
3. Now I move the decimal point two places, toward the percent sign. What do I do? *(Erase decimal point. Move the decimal point two places to right: 48.6%.)*	Move the decimal point two places toward the percent sign
4. What percent do we end with? *(Repeat steps 2–4 with 1.4, 2, .73, .04.)*	48.6%
Part B: Converting Decimal to Percent Worksheet	
1. *(Give students a worksheet with instructions and problems like the following one.)* Convert these decimals and mixed decimals to percentages:	

a. .38 = _____   e.   3 = _____   I. 7.3 = _____

b. 4.1 = _____   f. .542 = _____   j. .485 = _____.

c. .7 = _____   g. .04 = _____   k. .8 = _____

d. .07 = _____   h.   .4 = _____   l. .02 = _____

continued

Format 15.3 *(continued)*
CONVERTING DECIMALS AND FRACTIONS TO PERCENTAGES

TEACHER	STUDENTS
2. Read the instructions.	Convert these decimals and mixed decimals to percents.
3. Where do we write the percent sign?	After the numeral
4. What do we do to the decimal point?	Move it two places toward the percent sign
5. Touch a. Read the numeral.	.38
6. Write the digits 3 and 8 in the space next to the decimal. Write in the percent sign.	
7. What must you do to the decimal point?	Move it two places toward the percent sign
Put in the decimal. What percent does 38 hundredths equal?	38%
(Repeat steps 5–7 with several more problems; then have students work the rest on their own.)	
Part C: Structured Board Presentation	
1. *(Write ⁵/₄ on the board.)*	
I want to write this fraction as a percent. Here's how we change a fraction to a percent. First we change the fraction to a decimal and then change that decimal to a percent. Listen again. *(Repeat procedure.)* Read this fraction.	Five-fourths
2. I want to change this fraction to a percent. First I change the fraction to a decimal. What do I do first?	Change the fraction to a decimal.
How do I change ⁵/₄ to a decimal?	Divide 4 into 5
I'll work the problem. I divide until there is no remainder. *(Solve the problem.)*	
$$\frac{5}{4} = 4\overline{)5.00}^{\;1.25} = 1.25$$ $$\phantom{\frac{5}{4} = 4)}\underline{4}$$ $$\phantom{\frac{5}{4} = 4)}1\,00$$ $$\phantom{\frac{5}{4} = 4)}\underline{80}$$ $$\phantom{\frac{5}{4} = 4)}20$$	
What mixed decimal does ⁵/₄ equal?	1 and 25 hundredths
3. First I changed the fraction to a decimal. Now I change the decimal to a percent. What do I do next?	Change the decimal to a percent
I write the percent sign and move the decimal two places toward the percent sign. *(Write 125% on board.)*	
What percent does ⁵/₄ equal?	125 percent
(Repeat steps 1–3 with ³/₅, ¹/₂, and ⁷/₅.)	

TEACHER	STUDENTS
Part D: Structured Worksheet	
1. *(Give students a worksheet with instructions and problems like the following.)*	
Change these fractions to percentages:	
a. $\dfrac{3}{4} = \overline{)} = .\underline{} = \underline{}\%$	
b. $\dfrac{2}{5} = \overline{)} = .\underline{} = \underline{}\%$	
c. $\dfrac{8}{4} = \overline{)} = .\underline{} = \underline{}\%$	
2. In these problems, you must figure out the percent a fraction equals. First you change the fraction to a decimal. What do you do first?	Change the fraction to a decimal
How do you change $\frac{3}{4}$ to a decimal?	Divide 4 into 3
Divide 4 into 3. Don't forget to put the decimal point in the answer. *(Pause.)* What decimal does $\frac{3}{4}$ equal?	75 hundredths
Write 75 hundredths in the space next to the division problem. Now you change the decimal to a percent.	
3. What do you do?	Change the decimal to a percent
Do it and write your answer in the last space.	
4. What percent does $\frac{3}{4}$ equal?	75%
(Repeat steps 2–4 with remaining problems.)	
Part E: Less Structured Worksheet	
1. *(Give students a worksheet with instructions and problems like the following one.)*	
Change each fraction to a percent:	
a. $\dfrac{3}{4} =$ b. $\dfrac{5}{2} =$	
c. $\dfrac{3}{5} =$ d. $\dfrac{5}{4} =$	
2. Read the directions.	Change each fraction to a percent
3. Touch a.	
4. What is the first fraction?	Three-fourths
What do you do first to $\frac{3}{4}$?	Make it a decimal
Do it. Make $\frac{3}{4}$ into a decimal.	
What decimal does $\frac{3}{4}$ equal?	75 hundredths
5. Now write 75 hundredths as a percent. *(Pause.)*	75%
What percent does 75 hundredths equal?	
(Repeat steps 3–5 with remaining problems.)	

Format 15.4
SIMPLE RATIO WORD PROBLEMS
(See Video in Part A)

TEACHER	STUDENTS

Part A: Structured Board Presentation: Translating to Fractions

TEACHER	STUDENTS
1. Listen to this problem: Jill took 8 basketball shots; she made 4 of the shots. What fraction of the shots did she make? Listen again: Jill took 8 shots. She made 4 of the shots. What fraction of the shots did she make?	
2. The problem asks what fraction of her shots she made. The fraction will be how many she actually made over how many she took altogether. The denominator tells how many altogether. What does the denominator tell?	How many altogether
How many shots did she take altogether?	8
So I write 8 on the bottom.	
(Write the following on the board.)	
$\overline{8}$	
3. The numerator tells how many shots she made. How many shots did she make?	4
I write 4 on the top.	
(Write the fraction on the board.)	
$\dfrac{4}{8}$	
4. Jill took 8 shots. She made 4 shots. What fraction of her shots did she make?	Four-eighths
(Repeat steps 1–4 with the examples below.)	
a. Jill has 8 pencils; 5 are blue. What fraction of her pencils are blue?	
b. The class has 8 students; 5 are girls. What fraction of the students are girls?	
c. There are 10 apples in a bag; 6 of the apples are red. What fraction of the apples are red?	
d. Bill saved $5 so far. He needs $8 altogether. What fraction of the money he needs does he have?	

Part B: Structured Worksheet

TEACHER	STUDENTS
1. *(Give students a worksheet with instructions and problems like the ones below.)*	
Write the fractions for these problems:	
a. Jane made 12 out of the 16 shots she took during the game.	☐ / ☐
b. Alex has 15 friends; 10 of his friends live in California.	☐ / ☐

TEACHER	STUDENTS
c. Sarah won 8 out of the 12 races she ran in last year. d. Tim picked 30 flowers; 18 are roses.	☐ ☐ ☐ ☐
2. Read the directions.	Write the fractions for these problems.
3. Read problem a. What should the denominator of the fraction tell? What numeral tells about altogether? Say the fraction. Write it. *(Repeat step 2 with several problems and then have students do rest on their own.)*	How many altogether 16 Twelve-sixteenths
Part C: Less Structured Worksheet	

1. *(Give students a worksheet with problems like the ones below.)*
 	
  a. Jean ran in 8 races. She won 2 of the races. What percent of the races did she win?
  b. Ann's team won 6 out of 8 games. What percent of the games did Ann's team win?
  c. Dina got 12 out of 15 problems correct on her test. What percent of the problems did she get correct?
  d. Jill has 8 pencils; 4 of her pencils are red. What percent of her pencils are red?	

2. Read problem a. The problem asks for a percent. To find the percent, first you write a fraction. *(Repeat the problem.)* What fraction do you write? Write it.	Two-eighths
3. Now you change the fraction to a percent.	
4. What percent of the races did she win? *(Monitor while students work the rest of the problems independently.)*	25%

Format 15.5
COMPLEX RATIO PROBLEMS

TEACHER	STUDENTS
Part A: Determining the Fraction	
1. Listen to this problem: I'm going to tell you about the cars that a salesman sold in September. He sold 10 blue cars *(write 10 blue cars on board)* and 14 red cars *(write 14 red cars on board)* in September. What fraction of the cars he sold were red?	
2. The problem asks for the fraction of the cars that were red, so the fraction will be the number of red cars sold over the total number of cars sold. What should the denominator tell?	The total number of cars sold

continued

Format 15.5 *(continued)*
COMPLEX RATIO PROBLEMS

TEACHER	STUDENTS
How many cars were sold altogether? *(Pause.)*	24
(Write the following on the board.)	
‾‾ 24	
To correct: Remember: The dealer sold 10 blue cars and 14 red cars. To find the total number of cars sold, what must you do? What is 10 and 14?	24
3. What does the numerator tell?	The number of red cars sold
How many red cars were sold?	14
(Write the following on the board.)	
$\frac{14}{24}$	
4. What fraction of the cars sold in September were red?	$\frac{14}{24}$
(Repeat steps 1–4 with several examples of both simple and complex ratio problems.)	

Format 15.6
WRITING PROBABILITY FRACTIONS

TEACHER	STUDENTS
Part A: Structured Board Presentation: Introduction	
1. *(Draw the picture below on the board.)*	
We can write fractions to tell what we can expect to happen. The fraction doesn't tell us what will happen but what will probably happen. What does the fraction tell us?	What will probably happen
2. We will write a fraction that tells about the chances of pulling a triangle from this can. The denominator tells about the total number of things in the can. The numerator tells about the number of triangles. Again, the denominator tells about the total number of things in the can and the numerator tells about the number of triangles.	
What does the denominator tell?	The total number of things in the can
What does the numerator tell?	The number of triangles in the can

TEACHER	STUDENTS
3. We can do this for any container. If the can had 12 things in it, what would the denominator be?	12
If the can had 4 things in it, what would the denominator be?	4
If the can had 100 things in it, what would the denominator be?	100
4. The can on the board has 8 things in it. What would the denominator be for this can? *(Write the denominator for triangles.)*	8
5. There are 3 triangles in the can. What would be the numerator? *(Write the numerator for triangles.)*	3
The probability fraction for the chances of pulling a triangle from the can is ⅜. What is the probability fraction for the chance of pulling a triangle from the can?	$\frac{3}{8}$
6. Tell me again, how many things in the can?	8
Think about how many circles. What is the fraction for the chances of pulling out a circle?	$\frac{5}{8}$
(Write ⅝ in the circles fraction.)	
Which probability fraction is closer to one, ⅜ or ⅝?	$\frac{5}{8}$
So pulling a circle is more probable than pulling a triangle.	

7. *(Change the number of circles and triangles in the can.)*

Circles	Triangles
2	8
5	1
8	6

(For each, ask:)

What is the probability fraction for circles?

What is the probability fraction for triangles?

Which probability fraction is closer to 1?

So is it more probable that a circle or a triangle will be pulled?

Part B: Probability Fractions

1. *(Draw the picture below on the board.)*

Triangles

How many times you expect to pull a triangle

How many trials you could take

The probability fraction tells about the chances of pulling a triangle from the can. What does it tell about?	The chances of pulling a triangle from the can

continued

Format 15.6 *(continued)*
WRITING PROBABILITY FRACTIONS

TEACHER	STUDENTS
2. The denominator tells how many trials. What does the denominator tell about?	How many trials
The numerator tells how many times you would expect to pull out a triangle. What does the numerator tell?	How many times you would expect to pull a triangle
(Repeat until firm.)	
3. *(Write the following fractions on the board:* $5/9$, $10/14$, $2/3$, $3/10$, $4/5$. *For each probability fraction, ask:)*	
How many trials could you take?	
How many times would you expect to pull a triangle?	

Part C: Less Structured Worksheet

(Give students a worksheet like the following one.)
Write the probability fractions.

Touch the first box. *(Pause.)* What is the probability fraction for circles?	$\dfrac{3}{5}$
What is the probability fraction for stars?	$\dfrac{2}{5}$
Which fraction is closer to 1?	$\dfrac{3}{5}$
So is it more probable that a circle or a star will be pulled?	Circle
Write the probability fractions for each of the remaining boxes. *(Monitor students' responses as they work.)*	

Format 15.7
PROBABILITY FOR DIFFERENT NUMBERS OF TRIALS

TEACHER	STUDENTS
Part A: Structured Board Presentation	
1. *(Draw the picture below on the board.)*	

$$\frac{3}{8}=\frac{6}{16}$$
$$\frac{3}{8}=\frac{15}{40}$$
$$\frac{3}{8}=\frac{30}{80}$$

TEACHER	STUDENTS
2. You know that we can make predictions based on our probability fractions. If there are 8 things in the can and 3 of them are triangles, you can expect that if a person took 8 trials they would probably pull a triangle from the can 3 times.	
If the probability fraction $\frac{3}{8}$ is the fraction for 8 trials, then any fraction that is equivalent to $\frac{3}{8}$ will tell about a different number of trials.	
This is the equivalent fraction for a different number of trials. *(Point to $\frac{6}{16}$.)* We multiplied $\frac{3}{8}$ by $\frac{2}{2}$ to get the equivalent fraction. What is the new fraction?	$\frac{6}{16}$
This fraction tells us that if we took 16 trials, then we would expect to pull out 6 triangles.	
3. For the new fraction *(point to $\frac{6}{16}$)*, how many trials would you take?	16
How many times would you expect to pull out a triangle?	6
Yes, if you took 16 trials you would expect to pull 6 triangles.	
4. *(Point to $\frac{15}{40}$.)* This is an equivalent fraction. This fraction equals $\frac{3}{8}$. What is the equivalent fraction?	$\frac{15}{40}$
What fraction equal to one was $\frac{3}{8}$ multiplied by to get $\frac{15}{40}$?	$\frac{5}{5}$
For the new fraction *(point to $\frac{15}{40}$)*, how many trials would you take?	40
How many times would you expect to pull out a triangle?	15
So if you took 40 trials you would expect to pull 15 triangles. *(Repeat step 3 for $\frac{30}{80}$.)*	
5. *(Write on the board: $\frac{3}{5} = \frac{}{25}$.)*	
This probability fraction is $\frac{3}{5}$. The denominator for the new fraction is 25. Does 25 tell about trials or the number of times someone pulled out a triangle?	Number of trials
Remember how we made equivalent fractions. What do you multiply 5 by to get 25?	5
So what is the fraction equal to one that we multiply $\frac{3}{5}$ by?	$\frac{5}{5}$
So what is the numerator for our new fraction?	15
(Write 15 in the numerator of the new fraction.)	
6. *(Write on the board: $\frac{2}{3} = \frac{8}{}$.)*	
What number will be the denominator of the new fraction?	12
How do you know? *(Call on an individual.)*	We multiply 2 × 4 to get 8, so to get an equivalent fraction, we multiply by $\frac{4}{4}$.
That means that if you took 12 trials you would expect to pull 8 triangles.	
7. *(Write on the board: $\frac{3}{4} = \frac{}{24}$.)*	
Everyone, think about the fraction equal to one needed to complete the equivalent fraction. *(Pause.)* Use that fraction equal to one to find the numerator of the equivalent fraction. What is the numerator of the new fraction?	18
That means that if you took 24 trials, you would expect to pull 18 triangles.	

continued

Format 15.7 *(continued)*
PROBABILITY FOR DIFFERENT NUMBERS OF TRIALS

TEACHER	STUDENTS
Part B: Less Structured Worksheet	
1. *(Give the students a worksheet similar to the following.)*	

	Box 1:		Box 2:		Box 3:		
	Circles	Stars	Circles	Stars	Circles	Stars	Squares
	$\frac{3}{5}=\frac{}{25}$	$\frac{2}{5}=\frac{}{25}$	$\frac{6}{8}=\frac{}{16}$	$\frac{2}{8}=\frac{}{16}$	$\frac{2}{8}=\frac{}{32}$	$\frac{3}{8}=\frac{}{32}$	$\frac{3}{8}=\frac{}{32}$

TEACHER	STUDENTS
The probability fractions are written for each box. Find the equivalent fraction for the different number of trials.	
2. Touch the first box. What is the probability fraction for circles?	$\frac{3}{5}$
3. What is the denominator in the new fraction?	25
So this fraction will be for 25 trials. Think about the numerator for the new fraction. *(Pause.)* What is the new numerator?	15
So, if you took 25 trials how many times would you expect to pull a circle from the box?	15 times
(Repeat steps 2 and 3 for all examples.)	

Format 15.8
INTRODUCING COMPOUND PROBABILITY

TEACHER	STUDENTS
Part A: Structured Board Presentation	
1. Listen, a can had 12 things in it and 1 was a star. What is the probability of pulling a star from the can?	$\frac{1}{12}$
2. Listen, a can has 5 things and 3 are stars. What is the probability of pulling a star?	$\frac{3}{5}$
3. Listen, a can has 6 things in it and 6 are stars. What is the probability of pulling a star?	$\frac{6}{6}$
Yes, you would pull a star from the can on any trial you took.	

TEACHER	**STUDENTS**
4. For these problems we just did, you had only one can for each trial. Sometimes you have more than one can for each trial. The next problem shows 2 cans with shapes in them. In each can there are 3 shapes: 1 star, 1 circle, and 1 cube. *(Draw the following on the board.)* We want to find the probability of pulling a star from *both* cans.	
5. For this problem you pull from the first can and then from the second can. What is the fraction for stars in the first can? What is the fraction for stars in the second can?	$\frac{1}{3}$ $\frac{1}{3}$
6. To determine the probability of pulling a star from *both* cans, you multiply the fractions. What do you do to determine the probability of drawing a star from *both* cans? What is $\frac{1}{3} \times \frac{1}{3}$? So the probability of pulling a star from both cans is $\frac{1}{9}$.	Multiply the fractions $\frac{1}{9}$
7. What if there were a third can just like the first two? Say the fraction for pulling a star from the first can. Say the fraction for pulling a star from the second can. Say the fraction for pulling a star from the third can.	$\frac{1}{3}$ $\frac{1}{3}$ $\frac{1}{3}$
8. Say the multiplication problem for pulling a star from the 3 cans.	$\frac{1}{3} \times \frac{1}{3} \times \frac{1}{3}$
9. Raise your hand when you know what $\frac{1}{3} \times \frac{1}{3} \times \frac{1}{3}$ is. *(Wait.)* What does it equal? So the probability of someone pulling a star from all 3 cans is $\frac{1}{27}$. It would only happen about 1 out of every 27 trials.	$\frac{1}{27}$
10. Let's try another one. *(Draw the following on the board.)*  This example has 3 cans with shapes. All the cans have 10 shapes. The first can *(point)* has 1 star. Say the probability fraction for pulling a star from that can. *(Write $\frac{1}{10}$ under the can.)*	$\frac{1}{10}$

continued

Format 15.8 *(continued)*
INTRODUCING COMPOUND PROBABILITY

TEACHER	STUDENTS
11. The next can has 3 stars *(point)*. Say the probability fraction for pulling a star from that can. *(Write $\frac{3}{10}$ under the can.)*	$\dfrac{3}{10}$
12. The last can (point) has 7 stars. Say the probability fraction for pulling a star from that can. *(Write $\frac{7}{10}$ under the can.)*	$\dfrac{7}{10}$
13. Raise your hand when you can say the multiplication problem for pulling a star out of all 3 cans. *(Wait.)* Say the multiplication for the 3 cans. That equals $\dfrac{21}{1000}$ *(write on board)*. If you took a thousand trials of pulling objects from the 3 cans, you'd only pull out 3 stars about 21 times.	$\dfrac{1}{10} \times \dfrac{3}{10} \times \dfrac{7}{10}$

Format 15.9
PROBABILITY WORD PROBLEMS

TEACHER	STUDENTS
Part A: Structured Board Presentation	
(Students will need a piece of paper or whiteboard to write on. Write this problem on the board: A die has 6 sides; 2 sides are yellow, and 4 sides are green. If a person rolled the die 18 times, how many times would you expect a yellow side to come up?)	
1. What color parts are we interested in?	Yellow
2. So the probability fraction will tell about yellow sides and total sides. What is the probability fraction?	$\dfrac{2}{6}$
3. So if you rolled the die 6 times, how many times would you expect a yellow side to come up?	2 times
4. But the problem asks how many times we would expect yellow to come up if we rolled the die 18 times. That is 18 trials. *(Write $\frac{2}{6} = \frac{}{}$.)*	
5. We can make a new fraction that will tell about 18 trials. Listen: Each time the die is rolled is a trial. So there are 18 trials. Is 18 the numerator or the denominator for our new fraction? Yes, 18 is about trails, so it goes in the denominator. *(Write 18 in the new denominator: $\frac{2}{6} = \frac{}{18}$.)*	Denominator
6. We will use *y* to stand for yellow in the numerator. *(Write y in the numerator: $\frac{2}{6} = \frac{y}{18}$.)*	
7. On your paper or white board solve for *y*. *(Wait.)* What does *y* equal? So you would expect the yellow side to come up for 6 of the 18 trials. The answer to the question is 6. You would expect the yellow side to come up if you rolled the die 18 times.	6

TEACHER	STUDENTS
8. Let's try another word problem. *(Write the following on the board:*	
There are 52 cards in the deck: 13 have red fronts, 13 have green fronts, 13 have yellow fronts, and 13 have blue fronts. If you took 104 trials of taking a card from the deck, on how many trials would you take a card with a green front?)	
What color are we interested in?	Green
9. The problem tells about green cards and total cards. Raise your hand when you know the probability fraction for green cards. *(Pause.)* What is the probability fraction?	$\dfrac{13}{52}$
10. *(Write* $\dfrac{13}{52}$ *on the board.)* Yes, the fraction is $\dfrac{13}{52}$. So if you take	
52 cards, how many would you expect to be green cards?	13
Look at the problem; how many trials does the problem ask about?	104
Yes. Is 104 the numerator or denominator of the new fraction?	The denominator
Yes, 104 goes in the denominator. *(Write* $\dfrac{13}{52} = \dfrac{}{104}$*.)*	
11. We will use *g* to stand for green cards in the numerator.	
(Write $\dfrac{13}{52} = \dfrac{g}{104}$*.)*	
12. On your paper or white board, solve for *g*. *(Pause.)* What does *g* equal?	26
The answer to the question is 26. You would expect to take 26 green cards in 104 trials.	

16

Data Analysis

LEARNING OUTCOMES

16.1 Outline the recommended sequence for teaching tables and different types of graphs.

16.2 Discuss activities that may be used to promote conceptual understanding of graphs and statistics.

16.3 Outline the teaching procedures for reading and interpreting different types of graphs.

16.4 Explain the general teaching procedures recommended for teaching descriptive statistics.

16.5 Describe the diagnosis and remediation procedures for addressing common errors in data analysis.

SKILL HIERARCHY

An understanding of mathematics is often required to comprehend material from content areas such as science, social studies, or health. Mathematics in content-area material often appears in the form of **tables**, **graphs**, and **descriptive statistics**. For example, a health text might contain a graph illustrating the relationship between changes in the occurrence of lung cancer and changes in the percentage of people who smoke. Or a table in a science text might provide information about the size of, distance from the sun, and mass for the planets in our solar system. Descriptive statistics are central to the world of sports. For example, football statistics include the average number of yards gained per play. Baseball statistics including batting averages and earned run averages can be found on the websites of professional baseball teams. Students need specific skills to allow them to interpret information from a variety of sources.

The mathematics skills discussed in this chapter include reading and interpreting tables, graphs, and interpreting and calculating descriptive statistics. The Instructional Sequence and Assessment Chart lists the specific topics discussed in the chapter in their recommended order of introduction.

INSTRUCTIONAL SEQUENCE AND ASSESSMENT CHART

Grade Level	Problem Type	Performance Indicator
K	Classify and sort	a. Sort objects like blocks, crayons, or candy by color b. Group pictures of vehicles by truck, car, or van
K	Count the objects in a group and order multiple groups by size	Count the number of crayons in each group and order the groups from fewest to most
K	Read and use a table for up to three categories of data	(table below)

Candies	
Color of Candy	**Number of Candies**
Red	
Blue	
Orange	

Grade Level	Problem Type	Performance Indicator
1	Represent data for three categories	Graph the number of objects in three categories using a bar graph
1	Interpret data for three categories using a bar graph	a. How many red candies were in the bag? b. Are there more orange candies or blue candies? c. How many more trucks are there than cars?
2	Represent data on a line plot—*x*-axis uses single unit scale	Measure three different pencils and plot the measurements
2	Construct picture and bar graphs using single unit scale for up to four categories	Graph the number of objects in four categories using picture and bar graphs
2	Solve simple problems using information presented in a bar graph	a. How many total vehicles are represented on the graph? b. How many motorcycles and trucks are there? c. How many more cars are there than vans?
3	Represent a data set with several categories using scaled picture and bar graphs	Graph the number of students in the school who choose red, yellow, blue, green, black, pink, or orange as their favorite color. Each unit represents 5 students.
3	Solve one- and two-step problems using information presented in scaled picture and bar graphs	a. How many students choose blue or orange as their favorite color? Is this more or less than the number of students who choose green as their favorite color? b. Which group is greater: the number of students who chose orange or pink as their favorite color or the number of students who chose black or green?
3	Represent data on a line plot using a scale of less than 1	Measure three different pencils and create a line plot showing the measurements to the nearest ¼ inch. Measure four different books and create a line plot showing the measurements to the nearest ½ inch.
4	Solve problems involving addition and subtraction of fractions using information from line plots	Given a line plot showing different measurement of pencils using a scale of less than 1, ask students questions like the following: a. How much longer is pencil A than pencil B? b. What is the total length of pencil B and pencil C?
5	Solve problems involving fractions using information from line plots	Given a line plot showing different measurements of candy bars using a scale of less than 1, ask students questions like the following: a. How long would each candy bar be if they were laid end to end and then redistributed evenly?

continued

INSTRUCTIONAL SEQUENCE AND ASSESSMENT CHART *(continued)*		
Grade Level	**Problem Type**	**Performance Indicator**
6	Display data in dot plots, histograms, and box plots	
6	Measures of center and variability	Ms. Valerio gave a test to the 9 students in her class. The marks are written below:

Marcy	23	Diane	41
Kristen	18	Doug	35
Jerry	41	Kaitlin	41
Tim	23	Kathy	42
		Donna	38

a. What is the range?

b. What is the median?

c. What is the mode?

CONCEPTUAL UNDERSTANDING

Graphs and statistics summarize information visually and numerically. Graphs are easier to understand because they are visual representations of data and so are taught first. To introduce graphs, the teacher might give each student in the class a choice of four colors of square sticky notes and ask the students to choose their favorite color. On a white board, the teacher can draw the *x*-axis (number of students) and *y*-axis (favorite color). Students create a graph by placing their favorite color of sticky note on the corresponding column. After all of the students have placed their sticky notes on the graph, the teacher and the students can discuss the information represented on the graph. The initial questions would focus on the number of sticky notes in each column. Then the teacher could ask the students to compare columns.

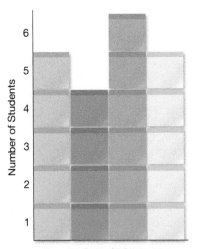

Favorite Color of Sticky Note

Statistical concepts are more difficult but also can be introduced with a visual representation. The concept of average may be represented as "fair share" or as a "balance point." Showing average using the fair share method can be illustrated with very simple picture graphs. The simple graph on next page shows the distribution of cookies among six students. The illustration shows how the cookies could be shared so that each student has the same number of cookies, a fair share. Fair share also may be demonstrated using concrete objects.

Distribution of Cookies

Student	Cookies
Maria	● ● ● ● ●
Andre	● ● ●
Luis	● ●
Eddie	● ● ● ● ● ●
Katie	● ●
Simone	● ● ●

Fair Share of Cookies

Student	Cookies
Maria	● ● ● ◖
Andre	● ● ● ◖
Luis	● ● ● ◖
Eddie	● ● ● ◖
Katie	● ● ● ◖
Simone	● ● ● ◖

The statistical concept of **mean** can be shown as the point on a balance bar. In the representation that follows, the sum of the distances from the mean of all the data points lower than the mean is equal to the sum of the distances of all the data points higher than the mean. We recommend using a balance bar representation as a method for verifying the calculation of the mean. The balance bar representation allows students to clearly see how the distances from the center are equal. In this example, the x's above the 1 are three units from the mean (3 + 3). The x above the 2 is two units from the mean. The sum of the distances from the mean for all of the x's below the mean is calculated by adding 3 + 3 + 2. A similar calculation is applied to determine the sum of the distances of the x's above the mean.

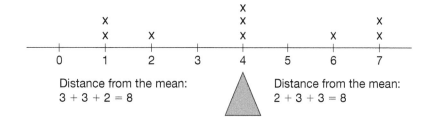

GRAPHS

A graph is a drawing or visual representation of a relationship between two or more sets of numbers. **Figure 16.1** includes examples of the various types of graphs students will encounter in the elementary grades. This chapter provides instructional recommendation for three types of graphs: bar graphs, line plots, and picture graphs. Graphs are typically introduced during first grade.

The sequence for introducing various types of graphs should be carefully coordinated with numeral reading and fraction skills so that students have mastered all of the related component skills before being asked to read graphs. Simple graphs are introduced first.

FIGURE 16.1 Types of graphs

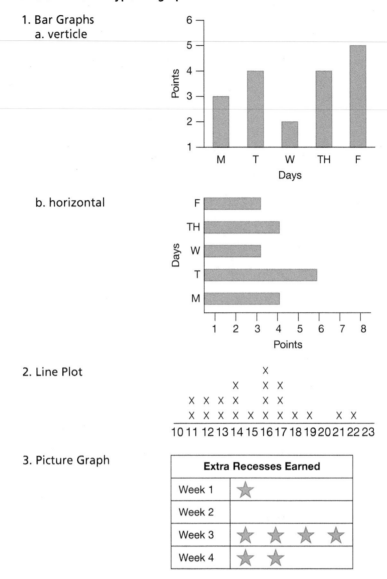

1. Bar Graphs
   a. verticle

b. horizontal

2. Line Plot

3. Picture Graph

Teaching students to interpret graphs involves modeling how to find information on the graph to answer a specific question. For example, students may be given a bar graph that shows the number of points Sarah scored in basketball games for each month of the school year. The teacher would first introduce the features of the graph and model how to answer a question using the graph.

A variety of literal questions should be included in initial examples. Literal questions ask for the amount at a particular time ("How many points did Sarah score in September?") or the particular time on which a specified quantity was given ("In which month did Sarah score 80 points?"). Questions calling for comparisons should be introduced gradually and eventually represent a greater proportion of the total questions ("How many more points did Sarah score in January than in September?"). Finally, questions requiring students to make inferences based on data from graphs, the most difficult type of question, should be included after students have mastered answering literal and comparison questions ("Why do you think Sarah scored more points in May than in September?"). More detailed information about teaching students how to read graphs can be found in Chapter 21, "Direct Instruction in Content-Area Reading," in *Direct Instruction Reading* (2016).

Classifying, Representing, and Interpreting Data

A table specifies the relationship among sets of numbers. Tables are introduced in kindergarten but remain a part of data analysis throughout elementary and middle school. Beginning in

FIGURE 16.2   Table for collecting data in early grades

Candies

Color	Number of Candies
Red candy	6
Blue candy	4
Orange candy	1

kindergarten, students are taught to gather and classify data. Format 16.1: Classifying Objects into Categories outlines the teaching procedure for introducing students to classifying objects from one broader category into three subcategories. In Part A, the teacher presents a set of triangles, circles, and squares to the students and leads them through determining how many of each shape is present. The data obtained by sorting the shapes are written by the teacher as three equations (e.g. $\triangle = 2$). In Part B, the students are given a structured worksheet with a set of shapes. The teacher leads the students in determining how many of each shape there are and completing the equations. Part C is a less structured worksheet in which the students independently count different shapes and complete the equations.

After students are able to accurately classify items of one broader category into at least three subcategories, they may be taught to record the data in a table. Initially, the table would include the name of the category of the objects as the title, the names of the subcategories, and a place for the students to record data related to each of the subcategories. The teacher would instruct the students to classify a set of objects into the appropriate subcategories and then record the number of items in each subcategory in the relevant box. **Figure 16.2** is an example of a table that may be used for this purpose.

In addition to teaching students how to record data in a table, teachers need to explicitly teach students how to read data from a table. A preskill for working with tables is knowledge of the terms "row" and "column." Teachers can explain the terms by showing students that rows in a table go across the page and columns go up and down the page.

The procedure for teaching students to read tables follows a model-test sequence using a table like the one below. The teacher first points out the title of the table to identify the topic. The teacher then points out the heading in each column and discusses the type of information found under each heading. After leading students through identifying the headings, the teacher points out how the students read across each row. Finally, the teacher models the strategy for locating information by looking for the intersection of rows and columns.

Trees in Our Parks

	Lincoln Park	Grant Park	Washington Park
Oak	16	8	2
Maple	3	17	14
Fir	5	19	11

After teaching students about the features of a table, the teacher must present carefully designed questions that require the students to use the table. Initially, these questions should be literal. A literal question can be answered by simply referring to the chart ("How many oak trees are in Washington Park?"). Comparative questions requiring students to tell the difference between two pieces of information ("How many more fir trees than maple trees are in Grant Park?") would be presented after students have mastered using a table to answer literal questions.

Picture Graphs

A picture graph is a type of graph that uses pictures to represent the relationships between two or more sets of numbers. We recommend introducing picture graphs in first grade, following instruction in reading and creating tables. **Format 16.2: Creating Picture Graphs** describes the teaching procedures for introducing pictures graphs in the early elementary grades. This format clearly illustrates the conceptual relationship between tables and graphs.

Picture graphs are more difficult when each picture stands for a quantity other than one. For example, a picture graph in which each symbol represents 100 units is more difficult than a picture graph in which each symbol represents one unit. In the illustration below, each smiley face represents 100 people. Interpreting picture graphs is even more difficult when fractional parts of a symbol are used. For example, in the illustration below, half of a smiley face represents 50 people (one-half of 100).

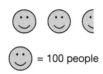

☺ = 100 people

Bar Graphs

This text includes two introductory formats for reading and creating bar graphs. **Format 16.3: Reading Bar Graphs** outlines the procedures for teaching students to read and interpret bar graphs. Part A is a structured board presentation in which the teacher explains the features of a bar graph and models reading the graph to obtain information. In Parts B and C, the teacher provides practice on reading and interpreting bar graphs on worksheets.

Format 16.4: Creating Bar Graphs describes the procedures for teaching students to construct bar graphs from data provided in a table. The format follows a model-lead-test procedure in which the teacher models using data from a table to create a bar graph and then leads students through the steps of constructing their own bar graphs. The procedures in these formats may be adapted for use with students in the upper grades. Adaptations would address extending these procedures to include more complex data, comparative questions, and horizontal presentations.

Two major factors determine the difficulty of interpreting bar graphs: (a) the amount of information on the graph and (b) the need for estimating amounts. Bar graphs become more complex as they show more than one set of relationships. For example, a simple bar graph may show the performance of one group of students on a series of tasks. A more complex bar graph would show the performance of several groups of students all on the same graph with separate bars representing each group. In reading a graph with more than one set of data, the student must be able to use the graph's key to determine which bar refers to which group. A bar graph with three sets of data is illustrated in **Figure 16.3**.

Bar graphs also become more complex when the top of the bar does not correspond exactly with a numeral on the y-axis and students must estimate the value shown by the bar, as shown in **Figure 16.3**. For example, when examining the relationship between 1 hour of watching TV and the average grade for third-period students, the top of the bar is between 90% and 100%. The students must estimate the average grade as 93%.

Line Plots, Stem and Leaf Plots

These two graphing procedures, included in most math curricula, may be new to some teachers. Line plots can be introduced in early elementary grades. A line plot illustrates the frequency of every data point on a number line. For example, the following are the results of a quiz taken by 21 students: 16, 14, 17, 14, 19, 11, 17, 12, 22, 18, 11, 16, 14, 12, 13, 16, 17, 15, 13, 16, and 21. When developing a line plot, these data are placed on a number line. In this example each score is represented by an "x."

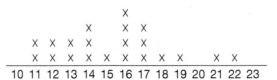

FIGURE 16.3 **Bar graph with three sets of data**

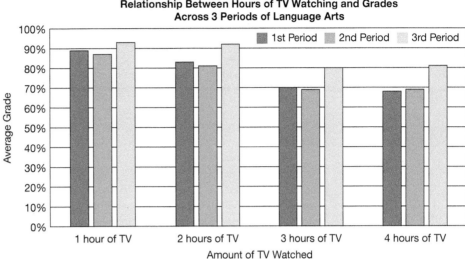

Stem and leaf plots typically introduced in middle school also illustrate the frequency of every data point in a set. The stem contains the tens digits. The leaf shows the ones digit for each of the data points. The illustration below shows the frequency of the test scores used in the example above:

Stem	Leaf
1	1 1 2 2 3 3 4 4 4 5 6 6 6 6 7 7 7 8 9
2	2

In the example above, the first score, 11, is represented by a stem of 1 and a leaf of 1. The second score of 11 is represented by the same stem of 1 and the second leaf of 1. The third score of 12 is represented by the stem of 1 and the leaf of 2. Likewise, the score of 22 is represented by the stem of 2 and the leaf of 2. Both line plots and stem and leaf plots can be used to illustrate the shape of distributions prior to introducing the concept of the normal curve. The procedures outlined in **Format 16.4: Creating Bar Graphs** may be adapted to teach students how to read and create line plots and stem and leaf plots.

DESCRIPTIVE STATISTICS

Descriptive statistics are numbers used to describe sets of data. The most common descriptive statistics are measures of central tendency (mean, **median**, and **mode**) and measures of variability (**range**, **mean absolute deviation**, and **interquartile range**). Although students begin working with data and graphs in first grade, descriptive statistics are not commonly introduced until middle school. Because some of these statistical calculations may be unfamiliar, we provide a brief review of each prior to discussing the recommended teaching procedures.

Measures of Central Tendency

The mean, the most commonly used descriptive statistic, is calculated by adding a group of numbers and dividing the sum by the number of numbers that were added. For example, the mean of the numbers 24, 26, 20, and 30 is calculated by adding these numbers and then dividing the sum, 100, by 4; the mean $(100 \div 4)$ is 25.

The median is the middle number of a set of numbers that has been arranged in order of magnitude. An example that might be used involves test scores for a class of nine students. First, the scores are listed in order:

64, 70, 70, 70, (78), 92, 94, 94, 98

The median is the middle score, 78. Four students scored less than 78, and four scored more than 78. The median is relatively easy to determine when working with an odd number of scores as in the example in previous page. If there are 17 scores, the median is the ninth number: eight numbers are smaller and eight are larger. The median is more difficult to determine for an even number of scores because there is no middle score. When there is an even number of scores the middle two numbers must be averaged. For example, if eight students score 13, 17, 19, 20, |24, 28, 31, 37, the median falls between 20 and 24 and is computed by calculating the average of these numbers. In the example below, the median equals 22.

$$\frac{20 + 24}{2} = \frac{44}{2} = 22$$

The mode denotes the most frequently occurring value in a collection of numbers. For example, when examining the following scores—64, 70, 70, 70, 78, 92, 94, 94, 98—we note that one student scored 84, three scored 70, one scored 78, one scored 92, two scored 94, and one scored 98. The score that occurred most often, 70, is the mode.

Statistical concepts should be introduced cumulatively, beginning with the mean. When students have mastered computing the mean, the median can be introduced. Similar teaching procedures can be used to teach each statistical concept. The teacher defines the term, models how to calculate the statistic, and then leads the students through application problems.

Sets of problems should reflect cumulative review. After each new statistical concept is introduced, the teacher should present exercises in which the students apply all the statistical concepts previously introduced. For example, if mean and median had been taught previously and mode had just been introduced, the teacher should present an exercise in which the students must compute all three statistics (mean, median, and mode).

We have included a format for teaching how to calculate a mean. **Format 16.5: Calculating the Mean** contains two parts. In Part A, the structured board presentation, the teacher presents two steps: (a) add the numbers (the sum) and (b) divide the sum by how many numbers were added. When initially presenting the format, examples should be prepared so that the mean is a whole number; that is, the sum of the quantities must be a multiple of the divisor. A problem in which the sum is 24 and the divisor is 5 would be inappropriate because 24 is not a multiple of 5.

Part B is a structured worksheet that requires students to calculate means for real-world problems. Note that the teacher asks students to read the problem and identify the first step in calculating the mean. After students add all the values, the teacher asks the students to complete the calculation. Finally, students write the answer with the appropriate label. We recommend constructing sets of four to five problems for each daily worksheet. As previously noted, after students have mastered calculating the mean, a demonstration illustrating the concept of mean with a balance bar may be presented to confirm the calculation.

The procedures for teaching median are similar to those for teaching mean. The teacher would present a structured board presentation in which he first defines median and then demonstrates finding the middle score (median) with both an odd number and an even number of scores in data sets that have been organized by magnitude. A less structured board presentation would lead students through the two steps to find the median: (a) arranging the numerals in order and (b) using the procedure previously presented in the structured board presentation. Having students first arrange numerals in order is an important step needed for determining median in everyday situations where data rarely appear in order of magnitude.

Note that examples need to include sets of data that have the same numeral more than once so that students practice including each numeral when arranging the numerals by magnitude. For example, when given the data set 100, 98, 75, 100, 69, 98, 85, students would need to order the set as 100, 100, 98, 98, 85, 75, 69, resulting in a median of 98. If each numeral were listed once (100, 98, 85, 75, 69), students would incorrectly identify 85 as the median.

Students need to learn when to use median rather than mean as a measure of central tendency. Teachers can introduce the concept of outliers by teaching the rule "We use median as a measure of central tendency when the data include outliers." The teacher then would have students apply the rule to sets of examples that require the students to discriminate when to use mean and when to use median.

Measures of Variability

Measures of variability describe the dispersion of a set of data. In this chapter, we include recommendations for teaching range, mean absolute deviation (MAD), and interquartile range. Range, the easiest measure of variability to determine, refers to the difference between the smallest and largest number in a set. For example, the distances that girls in Mr. Adams's class can throw the shotput are 32 ft., 29 ft., 41 ft., 18 ft., 27 ft., and 42 ft. The range is computed by subtracting 18 ft., the lowest score, from 42 ft., the highest score: $42 - 18 = 24$. The range is 24 ft.

Mean Absolute Deviation (MAD) is the distance of each data point from the mean of the set. Prior to teaching the calculation for MAD, students must be taught the concept of absolute value. Absolute value, the distance of a number from 0, is always positive. The absolute value of both 7 and -7 is 7. We recommend teaching absolute value by initially using the phrase "distance from 0" instead of the term "absolute value" to avoid teaching a new concept and new vocabulary simultaneously. The term "absolute value" easily can be introduced after students demonstrate understanding of the concept. With knowledge of absolute value, calculating MAD is not difficult but still requires several steps.

Summary Box 16.1 outlines the steps for calculating MAD. The first step is to calculate the mean for the set of numbers. The second step is to determine the deviation (difference) of each number from the mean. The next step is to find the absolute value for each deviation. The final

---

SUMMARY BOX 16.1

Calculating Mean Absolute Deviation

Data Set: 48, 52, 54, 55, 58, 59, 60, 62

Find the MAD for this data set.

Step 1. Find the mean.

$48 + 52 + 54 + 55 + 58 + 59 + 60 + 62 = 448$.
$448 \div 8 = 56$.
The mean is 56.

Step 2. Find the deviation of each number from the mean.

Number − Mean	Deviation from Mean
48 − 56	−8
52 − 56	−4
54 − 56	−2
55 − 56	−1
58 − 56	2
59 − 56	3
60 − 56	4
64 − 56	8

Step 3. Find the absolute value of the deviation from the mean.

Deviation from Mean	Absolute Deviation
−8	8
−4	4
−2	2
−1	1
2	2
3	3
4	4
8	8

Step 4. Find the mean of the absolute deviations (MAD).

$8 + 4 + 2 + 1 + 2 + 3 + 3 + 8 = 32$
$32 \div 8 = 4$
$MAD = 4$

step is to calculate the mean of the deviations by adding the absolute values of all of the deviations and dividing that sum by the number of absolute values that were added.

Interquartile range also requires several steps. **Summary Box 16.2** outlines the steps in determining the interquartile range. The first step is to determine the median of the data set. Next, the median of the first half of the set and the median of the second half are identified, resulting in four parts or quartiles. Finally, to find the interquartile range, the median of the first half is subtracted from the median of the second half of data.

The example in **Summary Box 16.2** has 10 numbers in the set, an even number of items. Because finding the median of an odd number of items is different, the procedure for finding the interquartile range varies when there is an odd number of values. For example, the following set includes an odd number of values: 5, 5, 7, 8, ⑪, 12, 15, 15, 16. The median, 11, is circled in blue. There are four numbers in the first half of the data and four in the second. In the case of having an odd number of values, the median is not part of either half. Therefore, in the example, 11 is not used in finding the medians of the first or second half. As illustrated below, the median of the first half is 6 and the median of the second half is 15. The interquartile range, the median of the second half minus the median of the first half, is 9 (15 − 6).

First Half	Second Half
5, 5, ⎮7, 8, ⑪, 12, 15, ⎮15, 16	
Median: 6	Median: 15

We recommend teaching MAD and interquartile range using the steps outlined in **Summary Boxes 16.1** and **16.2**. Teachers would first present the steps in the calculations, modeling several examples. Next, teachers would guide students through the calculations. As when teaching other statistics, we recommend following initial instruction with worksheets providing independent practice in using descriptive statistics.

SUMMARY BOX 16.2

Calculating Interquartile Range

Data Set: 8, 10, 10, 11, 11, 11, 12, 13, 13, 14

Step 1. Find the median.
8, 10, 10, 11, 11, ⎮11, 12, 13, 13, 14
The median is 11.

Step 2. Find the medians of the first and second half of the data set.

	First Half	Second Half
	8, 10, ⑩, 11, 11,	11, 12, ⑬, 13, 14

Step 3. Subtract the median of the first half from the median of the second half to find the interquartile range.

13 − 10 = 3

DIAGNOSIS AND REMEDIATION

Data analysis errors can be organized into the same categories that have been used throughout this text: fact errors (missing a math fact), component-skill errors (calculation or confusion errors), and strategy errors. The diagnosis and remediation procedures for the skills and concepts taught in both the Graphs and Descriptive Statistics sections should begin with determining the cause of the error. Both of those sections include discussions of critical discriminations and concepts, such as constructing and reading graphs that represent fractional values or understanding the need to include all of the values in order of magnitude when finding medians. Those discussions are designed to alert teachers to possible confusions that could be the cause of student errors. As always, teachers need to confirm their diagnosis by interviewing the students or by carefully examining written work. Once the diagnosis has been confirmed, the remediation usually involves reviewing critical parts of the relevant formats and providing students with additional practice.

Examples of common errors for graphs and descriptive statistics are outlined in **Figure 16.4** along with suggested remediation procedures.

FIGURE 16.4   **Data analysis diagnosis and remediation**

Error Pattern	*Diagnosis*	*Remediation Procedures*	*Remediation Examples*
Miles Run Each Day How many miles did Manuel run on Monday? Answer: 1 mile	Not estimating the value from a bar graph	The teacher would point out that the bar is halfway between 1 and 2 miles and ask the students, "What fraction is halfway between 1 and 2?"	Provide additional questions that require students to estimate the value of a bar. Include questions that do not require estimation.
Find the median: 9, 11, 15, 11, 12 Student's Work: 9, 11, 12, 15 Median is 11.5	Students do not include repeated occurrences of a single number when determining median	Remind students that every value must be included when determining the median.	Provide additional examples of data sets, some with repeated values and some without.
Find the mean: 12, 6, 4, 7, 9, 6 Student's Work: 12 + 6 + 4 + 6 + 7 + 9 = 44 44 ÷ 5 = 8.8	Student did not divide by the total number of values in the data set	Remind students to divide the sum of all of the values in the data set by the number of values in the data set, even when two values are repeated.	Provide additional examples of data sets, some including repeated values.

APPLY WHAT YOU LEARNED

Click on the √ to answer the questions online.

1. Explain how visual and numerical representations of data sets are related and sequential.

2. Why does the text recommend that teachers use the balance bar representation after teaching students to calculate the mean of a set of numbers?

3. For each pair of questions below, tell which is more difficult and how the difficulty is addressed by the instructional recommendations.

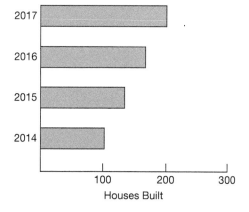

Pair one
a. How many houses were built in 2014?
b. How many houses were built in 2016?

Pair two
a. How many more houses were built in 2017 than 2014?
b. How many more houses were built in 2016 than 2015?

4. How are students taught when to use the median rather than the mean for calculating measures of central tendency?

5. Below are errors made by several students while solving the following word problem. Tell the cause of each error. Specify the remediation procedure.

Ashley played in 5 basketball games. She scored 25 points in the first game, 15 points in the second game, 17 points in the third game, 21 points in the fourth game, and 22 points in her last game. What was her average?

Royce	Jill		Ramon	
25	25	19.8	25	200
15	15	5)99	15	5)100
17	17	5	17	
21	21	49	21	
22	+22	45	+22	
100	99	40	100	

Format 16.1
SORTING

TEACHER	STUDENTS

Part A: Structured Board Presentation

1. *(Display the following for the students.)*

△ ○ □ ○ △ ○ □ ○ □

△ = _____   ○ = _____   □ = _____

2. *(Point to the shapes.)* Here's a row of shapes. Tell me each shape when I touch under it. *(Touch first shape.)*

   (Repeat with each of the following shapes.)

   Triangle

3. *(Point to △ = .)* We're going to complete the equations that show the total of each shape. I'm going to cross out each triangle as you count it. Count as I touch each triangle. *(Cross out each triangle as it is counted.)*

   How many triangles are there?

   (Write 2 after △ = .)

   1, 2

   2

4. *(Point to ○ = .)* Now we're going to find out how many circles there are. Count as I touch each circle. *(Cross out each circle as it is counted.)*

   How many circles are there?

   (Write 4 after ○ = .)

   1, 2, 3, 4

   4

5. *(Point to □ = .)* Now we're going to find out how many squares there are. Count as I touch each square. *(Cross out each square as it is counted.)*

   How many squares are there?

   (Write 3 after □ = .)

   1, 2, 3

   3

6. *(Point to △ = 2.)* How many triangles are there?

   2

7. *(Point to ○ = 4.)* How many circles are there?

   4

TEACHER	STUDENTS
8. *(Point to* ☐ *= 3.)* How many squares are there?	3

Part B: Structured Worksheet

1. *(Present a worksheet like the following to the students.)*

2. *(Point to the circles.)* These are shapes. Tell me the name of each shape when i touch it. *(Touch a circle.)*

   (Repeat with cubes and stars.) → Circle

3. You're going to complete the equations that show the total for each shape. Look at the circles. Count and cross out each circle. *(Pause while students count.)* How many circles are there? → 4

   Write 4 on the line next to the circle. *(Check students' work.)*

4. Look at the cubes. Count and cross out each cube. *(Pause while students count.)* How many cubes are there? → 4

   Write 4 on the line next to the cube. *(Check students' work.)*

5. Look at the stars. Count and cross out each star. *(Pause while students count.)* How many stars are there? → 1

   Write 1 on the line next to the star. *(Check students' work.)*

6. How many circles are there? → 4

7. How many cubes are there? → 4

8. How many stars are there? → 1

   (Repeat with additional examples.)

Part C: Less Structured Worksheet

1. *(Present a worksheet like the following to the students.)*

2. These are shapes. You're going to complete the equations that show the total for each shape. Count and cross out the smiley faces first. Then write the total number of smiley faces on the line next to the smiley face. Do the same thing for the stars and the hearts.

   (Repeat with additional examples.)

Format 16.2
CREATING PICTURE GRAPHS

TEACHER	STUDENTS

Part A: Structured Board Presentation

1. I'm going to show you how to use data from a table to make a picture graph. Here is what I know about some of my friends:

   (Display the following for the students.)

Favorite Ice Cream Flavor	
Flavor	**Number of Friends**
Chocolate	5
Strawberry	2
Vanilla	1

   (Point to "Chocolate.") Five of my friends like chocolate ice cream best.
   (Point to "Strawberry.") Two of my friends like strawberry ice cream best.
   (Point to "Vanilla.") Only one of my friends likes vanilla best.

2. *(Display the following for the students.)*

   This is the chart I'm going to use to create a picture graph. A picture graph uses pictures to show how many. What does a picture graph do? — **It uses pictures to show how many.**

   Yes, a picture graph uses pictures to show how many. The first thing I need to do is label my picture graph. This picture graph is going to show how many of my friends chose chocolate, strawberry, or vanilla as their favorite ice cream, so I'm going to label this picture graph "Favorite Ice Cream Flavor." *(Write "Favorite Ice Cream Flavor" at the top of the picture graph.)*

3. Now, I need to label each of my rows. This picture graph is going to show my friends' favorite ice cream flavors. What's the first flavor on my table? — **Chocolate**

   Yes, chocolate. *(Write "Chocolate" in the top cell of the first column.)*

4. *(Repeat step 3 for labeling the second and third rows as "Strawberry" and "Vanilla.")*

5. Now that my picture graph and all of the rows have labels, I can use pictures to show how many friends chose each flavor. The picture I'm going to use for this picture graph is a smiley face. Look at the table. How many of my friends chose chocolate as their favorite flavor? — **5**

6. Yes, 5. So I'm going to draw five smiley faces in the row for chocolate to show that five of my friends chose chocolate. *(Draw 5 smiley faces in the chocolate row.)*

7. Look at the table. How many of my friends chose strawberry as their favorite flavor? — **2**

8. Yes, 2. So I'm going to draw two smiley faces in the strawberry row to show that two of my friends chose strawberry. *(Draw 2 smiley faces in the strawberry row.)*

TEACHER	STUDENTS
9. *(Repeat steps 7 and 8 with "Vanilla." The finished picture graph should look like the following.)*	

Favorite Ice Cream Flavor

Chocolate	☺ ☺ ☺ ☺ ☺
Strawberry	☺ ☺
Vanilla	☺

(Repeat steps 1–9 with additional examples.)

Part B: Structured Worksheet

1. *(Give the students a worksheet like the following.)*

   Table:

Favorite Pizza Toppings	
Cheese	2 people
Pepperoni	4 people
Olives	2 people
Peppers	3 people

   Picture Graph:

TEACHER	STUDENTS
2. You're going to use the information in the table to make a picture graph. What does this table tell us about?	Favorite pizza toppings
3. Yes, this table tells us about favorite pizza toppings. What's the first topping the table tells us about?	Cheese
Yes, cheese. How many people chose cheese as their favorite topping?	2
4. What's the next topping the table tells us about?	Pepperoni
Yes, pepperoni. How many people chose pepperoni as their favorite topping?	4
5. *(Repeat step 4 for "Olives" and "Peppers.")*	
6. The first thing we need to do when making a picture graph is label the picture graph. What will this picture graph tell us about?	Favorite pizza toppings
Yes, write "Favorite Pizza Toppings" in the space at the top of the picture graph. *(Check students' labels.)*	
7. The next thing you need to do is label each of the rows. What's the first topping in the table?	Cheese
Yes, write "Cheese" in the box for the first row. *(Check students' labels.)*	
8. What's the next topping in the table?	Pepperoni
Yes, write "Pepperoni" in the box for the second row. *(Check students' labels.)*	

continued

Format 16.2 *(continued)*
CREATING PICTURE GRAPHS

TEACHER	STUDENTS
9. *(Repeat step 8 for "Olives" and "Peppers.")*	
10. Now that your picture graph and all of the rows have labels, you can use pictures to show how many people chose each topping. Use a triangle to show 1 person. Look at the table. How many people chose cheese as their favorite topping?	2
Yes, 2. Draw two triangles in the row next to "Cheese" to show that two people chose cheese as their favorite topping. *(Check students' work.)*	
11. Look at the table. How many people chose pepperoni as their favorite topping?	4
Yes, 4. Draw four triangles in the row next to "Pepperoni" to show that four people chose pepperoni as their favorite flavor. *(Check students' work.)*	
12. *(Repeat step 11 for "Olives" and "Peppers." The finished picture graph should look like the following:)*	

Favorite Pizza Toppings	
Cheese	△ △
Pepperoni	△ △ △ △
Olives	△ △
Peppers	△ △ △

(Repeat steps 1–12 with similar worksheets.)

Part C: Less Structured Worksheet

1. *(Present students with a worksheet like the following.)*
   Table:

Rainy Days	
August	0 days
September	3 days
October	8 days
November	10 days

Picture Graph:

2. Look at the table. What does this table tell about?	Rainy days

TEACHER	STUDENTS
3. That's right, rainy days. You're going to make a picture graph that tells how many rainy days there were in each month. Remember to label your picture graph first, then label each of the rows, and then draw the pictures to show how many rainy days there were in each month. If you don't know how to draw a cloud or a raindrop, you can draw a circle to show each rainy day. *(Monitor students as they create their picture graphs.)* *(Repeat steps 1–3 with similar worksheets.)*	

Format 16.3
READING BAR GRAPHS

TEACHER	STUDENTS
Part A: Structured Board Presentation	
1. *(Display the following for the students.)*	

Favorite Fruit

TEACHER	STUDENTS
2. This is a bar graph. A bar graph uses a bar to show how many. What does a bar graph do?	It uses a bar to show how many.
3. This bar graph tells about people and their favorite fruits. *(Point to the labels along the x-axis.)* These words tell the types of fruit. What do these words tell?	The types of fruit
4. *(Point to the numerals along the y-axis.)* These numerals tell how many people said each type of fruit was their favorite. What do these numerals tell?	How many people said each type of fruit was their favorite
5. *(Point to "Apple.")* I want to know how many people said apples were their favorite. To find out, I'm going to touch the line for zero just above the word apple. *(Touch "Apple.")* Then I'm going to slide my finger up the bar until I reach the top of the bar. *(Slide finger to the top of the bar and keep finger there.)* Now, I can slide my finger over to find the numeral for the line that I'm touching. *(Slide finger to the left and touch 15.)* I'm touching "15." That means that 15 people said apples were their favorite. How many people thought apples were best?	15

continued

Format 16.3 *(continued)*
READING BAR GRAPHS

TEACHER	STUDENTS
6. *(Repeat step 5 for "Banana" and "Strawberry.")*	

7. I want to know which fruit the most people said was their favorite. I can look at the bars and find the tallest bar. The bar for apples is the tallest bar. *(Point to the bar for apples.)* That tells me that the most people said that apples are their favorite fruit.

8. *(Repeat steps 1–7 with additional examples.)*

Part B: Structured Worksheet

1. *(Give the students a worksheet like the following.)*

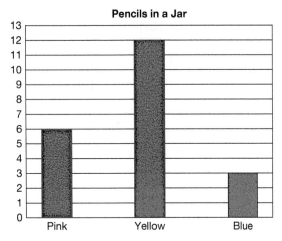

Pencils in a Jar

1. How many pink pencils were in the jar? _____
2. How many yellow pencils were in the jar? _____
3. How many blue pencils were in the jar? _____
4. What color were most of the pencils in the jar? _____

2. This bar graph shows how many pink, yellow, and blue pencils were in a jar.

3. Read number one.

   Look at the bar graph and figure out how many pink pencils were in the jar. *(Pause.)* How many pink pencils were in the jar?

   Write 6 in the space by number 1. *(Monitor students' responses.)*

4. *(Repeat step 3 for numbers 2–4.)*

STUDENTS
How many pink pencils were in the jar?
6

TEACHER	STUDENTS
Part C: Less Structured Worksheet	

1. *(Present students with a worksheet like the following.)*

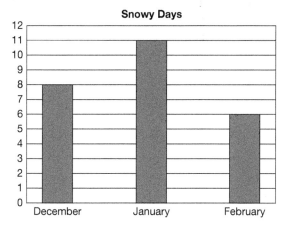

1. How many snowy days were in December? _____
2. How many snowy days were in January? _____
3. How many snowy days were in February? _____
4. Which month had the most snowy days? _____

2. This bar graph shows how many snowy days there were in December, January, and February. The bar shows how many snowy days there were in each month. Use the information in the bar graph to answer the questions on the worksheet. *(Monitor students' responses.)*

(Repeat steps 1 and 2 with additional examples.)

Format 16.4
CREATING BAR GRAPHS

TEACHER	STUDENTS
Part A: Structured Board Presentation	

1. I'm going to show you how to use data from a table to make a bar graph. Here is what I know about the pets in my neighborhood:

(Display the following for the students.)

Pets in My Neighborhood	
Pet	**Number of Pets**
Dogs	4
Cats	3
Fish	6

(Point to "Dogs.") There are four dogs in my neighborhood. *(Point to "Cats.")* There are three cats in my neighborhood. *(Point to "Fish.")* There are six fish in my neighborhood.

continued

Format 16.4 *(continued)*
CREATING BAR GRAPHS

TEACHER	STUDENTS
2. *(Display the following for the students.)*	

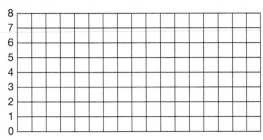

I'm going to create a bar graph. A bar graph uses a bar to show how many. What does a bar graph do?

It uses a bar to show how many.

Yes, a bar graph uses a bar to show how many. The first thing I need to do is label my bar graph. This bar graph is going to show how many dogs, cats, or fish are in my neighborhood, so I'm going to label this bar graph "Pets in My Neighborhood." *(Write "Pets in My Neighborhood" at the top of the bar graph.)*

3. Now, I need to label the parts of my bar graph. *(Point to the x-axis.)* This part is going to show each type of pet, so I'll write dog, cat, and fish under this line. *(Write dog, cat, and fish under the x-axis. The graph should now look like the following:)*

5. Now that my bar graph has labels, I can show how many of each pet are in my neighborhood. Look at the table. How many dogs are in my neighborhood?

4

6. Yes, 4. So I'm going to color above where it says "Dogs" until I come to the line for four. This will show how many dogs are in my neighborhood. *(Color in the column above "Dogs" beginning at zero and coloring up until the line for four is reached. Model counting out loud for the students while coloring.)*

7. Look at the table. How many cats are in my neighborhood?

3

8. Yes, 3. So I'm going to color above where it says "Cats" until I come to the line for three. This will show how many cats there are. *(Color in the column above "Cats" beginning at zero and coloring up until the line for three is reached. Model counting out loud for the students while coloring.)*

TEACHER	STUDENTS

9. *(Repeat steps 7 and 8 with "Fish." The finished bar graph should look like the following:)*

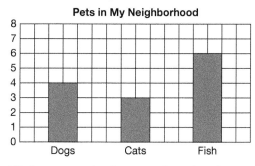

10. We've created a bar graph! What is our bar graph about?

(Repeat steps 1–10 with additional examples.)

Pets in my neighborhood

Part B: Structured Worksheet

1. *(Give the students a worksheet like the following.)*

   Table:

Favorite Sports	
Soccer	7 students
Football	8 students
Baseball	5 students

   Bar Graph:

   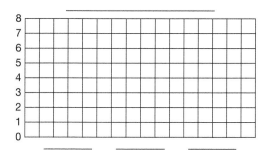

2. You're going to use the information in the data table to make a bar graph. What does this table tell us about?

   Favorite sports

3. Yes, this table tells us about favorite sports. What's the first sport the table tells us about?

   Soccer

   Yes, soccer. How many students chose soccer as their favorite sport?

   7

4. What's the next sport the table tells us about?

   Football

   Yes, football. How many students chose football as their favorite sport?

   8

5. *(Repeat step 4 for "Baseball.")*

6. The first thing we need to do when making a bar graph is label the parts of the bar graph. What will this bar graph tell us about?

   Favorite sports

   Yes, write "Favorite Sports" in the space at the top of the bar graph. *(Check students' labels.)*

continued

Format 16.4 *(continued)*
CREATING BAR GRAPHS

TEACHER	STUDENTS
7. The next thing you need to do is label the other parts of the bar graph. What's the first sport in the table?	Soccer
Yes, write "Soccer" in the first space at the bottom of the bar graph. *(Check students' labels.)*	
8. What's the next sport in the table?	Football
Yes, write "Football" in the second space at the bottom of the bar graph. *(Check students' labels.)*	
9. *(Repeat step 8 for "Baseball.")*	
10. Now that your bar graph has all of its labels, you can make a bar for each sport. Look at the table. How many students chose soccer as their favorite sport?	7
Yes, 7. Touch "soccer." Color above the word "soccer." Start coloring at the line for zero and continue coloring up until you get to the line for 7. This bar will show that seven students chose soccer. *(Check students' work.)*	
11. Look at the table. How many students chose football as their favorite sport?	8
Yes, 8. Touch "football." Color above the word "football." Start coloring at the line for zero and continue coloring up until you get to the line for 8. This bar will show that eight students chose football. *(Check students' work.)*	
12. *(Repeat step 11 for "Baseball." The finished bar graph should look like the following:)*	

Favorite Sports

| 13. We just made a bar graph about our favorite sports! | |
| *(Repeat steps 1–13 with similar worksheets.)* | |

TEACHER	STUDENTS

Part C: Less Structured Worksheet

1. *(Present students with a worksheet like the following.)*

   Table:

Number of Cupcakes	
Chocolate	9
Banana	10
Vanilla	6

   Bar Graph:

   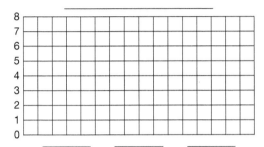

2. Look at the table. What does this table tell about? | Cupcakes

3. That's right, cupcakes. You're going to make a bar graph that tells how many chocolate, banana, and vanilla cupcakes there were. Remember to label your bar graph first, then write the labels that go below the bar graph, and then make the bar for each kind of cupcake. *(Monitor students as they create their bar graphs.)*

   (Repeat steps 1–3 with similar worksheets.)

Format 16.5
CALCULATING THE MEAN

TEACHER	STUDENTS

Part A: Structured Board Presentation

1. Listen: In basketball practice, Ben scored 4 points on Monday, 7 points on Tuesday, 3 points on Wednesday, and 6 points on Thursday. *(Write 4, 7, 3, 6.)* We want to figure the average number of points Ben scored each day. What do we want to figure out? | The average number of points Ben scored each day of practice

2. Here's how we figure out Ben's average. First we add; then we divide the sum by how many numbers we added. First we add; then what do we do? | Divide the sum by how many numbers we added

3. First we add. *(Write the problem on the board.)*

   $$\begin{array}{r} 4 \\ 7 \\ 3 \\ +6 \\ \hline \end{array}$$

   What is the sum of 4, 7, 3, and 6? | 20

continued

Format 16.5 *(continued)*
CALCULATING THE MEAN

TEACHER	STUDENTS
4. The sum is 20. We added. Now we divide by how many numbers we added. *(Point to 4, 7, 3, and 6 as you say,)* We added 1, 2, 3, 4, numbers.	
5. We added 4 numbers, so we divide 4 into 20. What do we divide?	4 into 20
How many times does 4 go into 20?	5
Yes, Ben's average is 5 points each day. What is Ben's average?	5 points each day
Did Ben score exactly 5 points every day?	No
5 points a day is his average.	
(Repeat steps 1–5 with the examples below.)	
Jill scored the following points in each game: 6, 8, 9, 5, 0, 10, 4.	
Tom ran these numbers of miles each day: 3, 1, 1, 7, 0, 0.	
Part B: Structured Worksheet	
1. *(Give students worksheets with several problems like the one below.)*	
Jack ran 5 miles on Monday, 2 miles on Tuesday, 4 miles on Wednesday, 0 miles on Thursday, and 9 miles on Friday. What is the average number of miles he ran each day?	
☐ _____ _____ _____	
2. Read the problem. What does the problem ask for?	The average number of miles he ran each day
3. What do we do first to figure the average?	Add the miles
Add all the miles. How many miles did he run altogether?	20
4. What do we do after we find the sum?	Divide by how many numbers we added
5. How many numbers did we add?	5
Say the division problem.	5 goes into 20
How many times does 5 go into 20?	4
Write 4 in the box.	
6. Now we have to label our answer. Read the last sentence.	What is the average number of miles he ran each day?
So the label is miles each day.	
What is the label for the answer?	Miles each day
Write the words. *(Pause.)*	
Say the whole answer.	4 miles each day
(Repeat steps 2–6 with additional problems.)	

Geometry

With Don Crawford

LEARNING OUTCOMES

17.1 Describe the scope of concepts that should be included in teaching geometry.

17.2 Describe the role language plays in the development of conceptual understanding of geometry.

17.3 Explain how nonexamples are used to teach students to identify and define geometric shapes.

17.4 Discuss the rationale for the formulas used to teach students to calculate area and volume.

17.5 Discuss the importance of modeling when teaching students to measure or construct figures using tools.

17.6 Outline the facts about angles and lines that are prerequisites for more advanced geometry.

17.7 Describe the general diagnosis and remediation procedures for addressing errors in geometry.

SKILL HIERARCHY

The geometry objectives discussed in this chapter fall into four major categories:

1. Identifying and defining various figures and concepts.

2. Calculating the measurements of a figure, such as determining perimeter, area, and circumference.

3. Using tools, such as a compass or protractor, to construct figures.

4. Using logic in working with angles and lines.

An outline of the specific geometry skills discussed in this chapter can be found in the Instructional Sequence and Assessment Chart. Next to most of the geometry objectives in this chart are asterisks. These asterisks correspond to the four categories above. One asterisk indicates that the objective falls under the category "Identifying and Defining Geometric Figures and Concepts." Two asterisks next to an objective indicate that the objective falls under "Calculating Measurements of Geometric Figures." Three asterisks next to an objective indicate that the objective falls under "Measuring and Constructing Geometric Figures Using Tools." Four asterisks next to an objective indicate that the objective fall under "Using Logic in Working with Angles and Lines."

INSTRUCTIONAL SEQUENCE AND ASSESSMENT CHART

Grade Level	Problem Type	Performance Indicator
K	Identify circle*	Mark each circle with X.
K	Identify rectangle*	Mark each rectangle with X.
K	Identify triangle*	Mark each triangle with X.
K	Identify square*	Mark each square with X.
K	Identify interior of closed figure*	Tell me when I touch the interior of this figure.
K	Identify exterior of closed figure*	Tell me when I touch the exterior of this figure.
1	Identify cube*	Mark each cube with X.
1	Identify sphere*	Mark each sphere with X.
1	Identify cone*	Mark each cone with X.
2	Identify the diameter of a circle*	What is a diameter? Put X on each line that is the diameter of a circle.

Grade Level	Problem Type	Performance Indicator
2	Identify the following polygons:*	
	Pentagon	Draw a P over the pentagon.
	Hexagon	Draw an H over the hexagon.
	Octagon	Draw an O over the octagon.
3	Find the perimeter**	Find the perimeter of this square. 4″ 4″
3	Find the area of rectangle or square**	Find the area of this rectangle. 3″ 6″
3	Identify pyramid*	Mark each pyramid with X.
3	Identify cylinder*	Mark each cylinder with X.
3	Identify parallel lines*	Circle each group of parallel lines.
3	Identify perpendicular lines*	Circle each group of perpendicular lines.
3	Identify a parallelogram	Circle each parallelogram.
4	Draw a line segment***	Draw the line segment CD. C A B D

continued

INSTRUCTIONAL SEQUENCE AND ASSESSMENT CHART *(continued)*

Grade Level	Problem Type	Performance Indicator
4	Define/identify radius*	What is the radius of a circle? Mark each line that is a radius with X.
4	Using a compass, construct a circle when given a radius***	Draw a circle that has a radius of 2 inches. Use a compass.
4	Label angles*	For each example, write the name of the angle.
4	Define degree/measure angles using a protractor**	Measure each of the following angles.
4	Construct angles using a protractor***	Construct the following angles. 90° _____ 45° _____
4	Define/identify right angle*	What is a right angle? Circle each right angle.
4	Define/identify acute angle*	What is an acute angle? Circle each acute angle.
4	Define/identify obtuse angle*	What is an obtuse angle? Circle each obtuse angle.
4	Define/identify right triangle*	What is a right triangle? Circle each right triangle.

Grade Level	Problem Type	Performance Indicator
4	Define/identify equilateral triangle*	What is an equilateral triangle? Circle each equilateral triangle.
4	Define/identify isosceles triangle*	What is an isosceles triangle? Circle each isosceles triangle.
4	Define/identify scalene triangle*	What is a scalene triangle? Circle each scalene triangle.
4	Find the perimeter of various polygons**	Find the perimeter of this figure. 5 m, 1 m, 3 m, 4 m, 4 m, 6 m
4	State the degrees in an angle, given examples of a right angle, a straight angle, or a full circle*	How many degrees in ∠A, ∠B, and ∠C?
5	Find the volume of a box (rectangular prism) using the formula**: Volume = Area of base × height	Find the volume of a box whose base is 5 inches long and 7 inches wide and whose height is 4 inches. 4″, 5″, 7″
6	Find the area of a triangle using the equation** $A = \dfrac{\text{base} \times \text{height}}{2}$	Find the area of this triangle. 5″, 4″, 5″, 7″

continued

INSTRUCTIONAL SEQUENCE AND ASSESSMENT CHART (continued)

Grade Level	Problem Type	Performance Indicator
6	Find the area of a parallelogram using the equation** $A = base \cdot height$	Find the area of this parallelogram. 5 cm 4 cm 6 cm
7	Find value of unknown component angles using facts about angles****	Find the value of $\angle B$ if $\angle A$ is one-third of a full circle. A B
7	Identify corresponding angles and that they are equal*	Identify which angle is equal to $\angle A$ in this diagram. A B C D E
7	Identify opposite angles and that they are equal*	Identify which angle is equal to $\angle A$ in this diagram. A B C E F
7	Use knowledge of facts about angles to compute values of angles in a complex diagram****	If $\angle A$ is equal to one-fifth of a circle, compute the value of angles B, C, and D in this diagram. A B C D
7	Use equation $\pi(pi) \cdot D = C$ to find $\pi(pi)$, D, or C**	Find the circumference of circle A and the diameter of circle B. 13 m 50"

Grade Level	Problem Type	Performance Indicator
7	Use the equation $A = \pi \cdot r \cdot r$ to find area of a circle given the radius or the diameter**	Find the area of the circle. 14 cm
7	Find the surface area of boxes (rectangular prisms)**	Find the surface area of this box. 18″ 5″ 6″
7	Find the surface area of rectangular pyramid**	Find the surface area of this pyramid. 15 inches 14 in 10 in 12 in
7	Find the surface area of a triangular pyramid**	Find the surface area of this pyramid with a triangular base. 25 cm 25 cm 20 cm 20 cm 18 cm 20 cm

continued

	INSTRUCTIONAL SEQUENCE AND ASSESSMENT CHART *(continued)*	
Grade Level	**Problem Type**	**Performance Indicator**

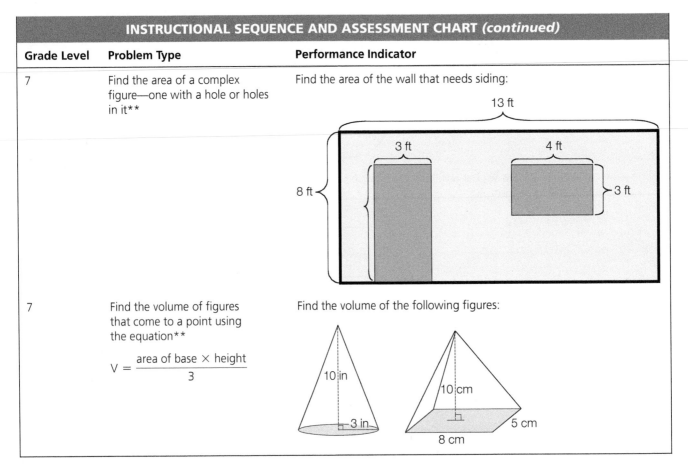

7	Find the area of a complex figure—one with a hole or holes in it**	Find the area of the wall that needs siding:
7	Find the volume of figures that come to a point using the equation** $V = \dfrac{\text{area of base} \times \text{height}}{3}$	Find the volume of the following figures:

CONCEPTUAL UNDERSTANDING

Geometric shapes such as circle, triangle, and square, often are introduced in kindergarten as vocabulary concepts during early language instruction. These language concepts are extended as students learn more geometry-related content. Eventually, students work with precise definitions of these geometric concepts that involve more complex mathematical language (a right triangle is a closed figure with three sides and a 90-degree angle).

Promoting conceptual understanding requires teachers to highlight the relationships among geometric concepts. Rather than only teaching students to memorize that **pi** equals 3.14, the concept of pi is taught by teaching students the relationship between the **diameter** and the **circumference** of a circle. By providing students with several examples of different-sized circles, each with their diameter and circumference identified, teachers can have students use calculators to find that the circumference divided by the diameter always yields pi, or 3.14. Additionally, visual representations are critical to providing conceptual understanding in geometry. The formats in this text for finding the area of rectangles, triangles, complex figures, and **volume** all include visual representations that promote conceptual understanding.

IDENTIFYING AND DEFINING GEOMETRIC FIGURES AND CONCEPTS

Table 17.1 lists many of the figures and relationships taught in elementary and middle school geometry units. The table shows the relationships among various figures and concepts. However, it is not intended to imply an order for introducing skills. A suggested order for introducing skills appears in the Instructional Sequence and Assessment Chart.

As mentioned earlier, teaching students to identify new figures and concepts is a form of vocabulary teaching. Three basic methods of vocabulary instruction are typically used to teach concepts: (a) examples only, (b) synonyms, and (c) definitions. A more detailed discussion of these methods of teaching vocabulary can be found in *Direct Instruction Reading* (2016). The examples-only method is used to present vocabulary terms and concepts that cannot be readily explained by using a synonym or definition. In teaching vocabulary through examples, the teacher constructs a set of examples, half of which are of the concept (positive examples) and half of which are of a similar but different concept (nonexamples). The example set must be carefully designed to show the range of positive examples and rule out possible misinterpretations.

TABLE 17.1   Figures and Relationships Taught in Elementary and Middle School Geometry Units

Figure/Relationship	Description	Example
Open Figures		
Line segment	The shortest distance between two points (*Note:* A line extends infinitely in space in two directions.)	
Ray	A line beginning at a point and extending infinitely into space	
Angle	Formed by two rays both of which have the same end point, which is called the vertex	
Right angle	Measures 90°	
Obtuse angle	Measures more than 90° and less than 180°	
Acute angle	Measures more than 0° and less than 90°	
Straight angle	Measures 180°	
Closed Figures		
Polygons	Simple (no crossed lines) closed figures bound by line segments	
Triangles	Three-sided figures	
Equilateral	All sides measure the same length	
Right	Contains one right angle	
Isosceles	Two sides of equal length	
Scalene	No two sides are of the same length	
Quadrilaterals	Four-sided figures	
Rectangle	Four right angles, two pairs of sides with equal lengths	
Square	Four equal sides, four right angles	
Parallelogram	Two pairs of parallel lines	
Rhombus	Parallelogram having two adjacent sides congruent	
Trapezoid	No right angles, one pair of nonparallel lines	
Additional polygons		
Pentagon	Five-sided figure	
Hexagon	Six-sided figure	
Octagon	Eight-sided figure	

continued

TABLE 17.1 (*continued*)

Figure/Relationship	Description	Example
Curved Figures		
Ovals		
Circles		
Center	Midpoint of circle	
Radius	Line segment extending from midpoint to edge	
Diameter	Line that divides the circle in half	
Three-Dimensional Shapes		
Cube		
Pyramid		
Cone		
Cylinder		
Sphere		
Line Relationships		
Perpendicular lines	Lines that intersect to form a 90° angle	
Parallel lines	Lines that exist beside each other without intersecting	
Figure Relationships		
Similarity	Having the same shape	
Congruence	Having the same shape and size	
Symmetry	A figure can be folded along a line and the two parts coincide	

For example, when ovals are introduced, a variety of ovals should be presented to demonstrate the range of figures called ovals:

The nonexamples used when teaching ovals should include circles so that the students will not misidentify circles as ovals. As the examples are presented, the teacher points to each example, saying, "This is an oval" or "This is not an oval," and then she tests the students by asking, "Is this an oval?"

Teaching vocabulary through synonyms involves explaining a new term by using a word or phrase already known to the students. For example, the word "interior" may be explained as "inside." Teaching vocabulary through definitions, on the other hand, involves a longer explanation with more detailed vocabulary. For example, a pentagon may be defined as "a closed figure having five straight sides." Following the presentation of either a synonym or a definition, the teacher presents a set of positive and negative examples (i.e., nonexamples), asking, "Is this a _____?"

The synonym or definition selected need not meet all the requirements of a formal definition of the concept but should be worded in student-friendly language. In fact, a teacher initially may choose a simplified definition that may not be technically correct but will help the students master the concept (a rectangle has four sides and four square corners). More sophisticated definitions then can be introduced in later grades.

Format 17.1: Identification/Definition—Triangle illustrates the procedure for teaching basic definitions. In Part A, the teacher models the definition. The teacher then tests students on applying the definition to a set of examples and nonexamples. Note that students not only are asked to identify which pictures are triangles but also are asked to explain how they know that the figure is a triangle using the definition they were taught. Part B is a less structured worksheet exercise in which students must apply the information they have learned by discriminating triangles from other geometric shapes.

Worksheets used for independent practice should contain two distinct sections. One section should test the application of the new definition, and the other should review concepts taught previously. The cumulative review represented by the second section serves two important functions. First, it helps prevent students from forgetting previously taught concepts. Second, it helps provide the discrimination practice needed when similar figures are presented. Student performance on the review sections of these worksheets can inform teachers when a new definition or concept can be introduced. Generally, new information should not be introduced until students demonstrate mastery on previously introduced information. In addition to worksheet review, extra practice can be incorporated into the classroom routines in the form of games and independent activities at classroom learning centers.

Prior to discussing the second major category in this chapter, geometric calculations, it is important to reaffirm the critical role that language concepts play in geometry instruction. For example, calculating the circumference of a circle is relatively simple if students understand the concepts: **radius**, **diameter**, **circumference**, and π **(pi)**. Once students develop conceptual understanding for the concepts, they can more easily be taught to apply the equation "diameter times π(pi) equals circumference."

CALCULATING PERIMETER, AREA, AND VOLUME

Students in elementary and middle school typically learn how to find (a) the **perimeter** of polygons; (b) the **area** of squares, triangles, rectangles, parallelograms, circles, and complex figures; (c) the **surface area** of rectangular prisms (boxes), rectangular pyramids, triangular pyramids; and (d) the **volume** of rectangular prisms, triangular pyramids, and rectangular pyramids. Recommendations regarding when to introduce each measurement skill can be found in the Instructional Sequence and Assessment Chart.

Perimeter and Area

In teaching the students to find the perimeter of a closed figure, the teacher defines perimeter and models adding the lengths of each side. After introducing the concept of perimeter, the teacher would present a structured worksheet exercise followed by independent practice.

Format 17.2: Finding the Area of Rectangles outlines how a teacher would most effectively teach the procedure for calculating the area of a rectangle. In Part A, the teacher illustrates the concept of area by showing how a rectangle may be divided into square units with horizontal and vertical lines drawn at the unit intervals. This visual representation is critical to establish the connection between what students know about multiplication (that one multiplies to determine the number of objects in groups of equal size) with the new skill of finding area. Note that the format uses a variety of common units such as inches, feet, yards, centimeters, and meters. Using different units enables students to generalize across problems.

FIGURE 17.1   Sample measuring worksheet

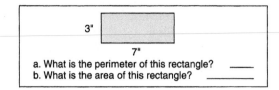

a. What is the perimeter of this rectangle?   _____
b. What is the area of this rectangle?   _____

The teacher conveys the meaning of the term "square unit" by referring to the illustrated squares. After presenting the illustration, the teacher gives a rule for determining the area (multiply the base times the height) and demonstrates its application, computing the area of several rectangles and squares. The teacher emphasizes the need to express the answer in terms of square units (square inches, square feet, etc.).

Part B, the less structured board presentation, is used after students have been introduced to the concept of area. In the less structured board presentation, the teacher reviews the equation for finding the area of a rectangle. Students identify the measurement of the height and base of the rectangles and calculate the area. The less structured board presentation is followed by structured worksheet and less structured worksheet exercises.

A sample worksheet exercise that promotes the discrimination between perimeter and area appears in **Figure 17.1**. Exercises like these are important to help prevent students from confusing perimeter and area.

A variety of equations can be used to teach area. In the format for finding area of a rectangle, we recommend using "base times height." This equation is better than "length times width" because it is more closely related to the equations for finding the areas of other figures. For example, the equation for finding the area of triangles is "base times height divided by two" (see Format 17.3). If the area of rectangles has been taught as "base times height," the relationship between the area of rectangles and triangles is easier for students to conceptualize.

Format 17.3: Finding the Area of Triangles includes a structured board presentation that explicitly demonstrates how the area of a rectangle (base times height) is related to the area of a triangle (bases times height divided by 2). This demonstration provides a sophisticated visual representation of the concept and is similar to the kinds of proofs students will have to construct in high school geometry.

The structured board presentation is followed by a less structured board presentation in which the teacher reviews with the students the formula for finding the area of a triangle. Students identify the base and height of triangles drawn on the board and calculate the area. The structured worksheet presentation includes both triangles and rectangles. The teacher asks questions prompting the students to identify the figure and the formula for finding the area of each figure. The structured worksheet is followed by a less structured worksheet with minimal prompts.

Once students can calculate the area of both rectangles and triangles, they more easily can be taught how to find the area of complex figures—ones that have figures inside of them. This skill is needed to find the area of a wall that has a window or a door in it when painting a room. Students learn to find the area of the whole figure, find the area of the interior figure, and then subtract the area of the interior figure from the area of the whole figure. Format 17.4: Calculating the Area of Complex Figures provides the steps for the recommended strategy. Students should be very comfortable with finding the area of both rectangles and triangles prior to being introduced to finding the area of complex figures.

In Part A, the structured board presentation, the teacher introduces the steps in the strategy and then leads the students through calculating the area of the figures. Part B is a structured worksheet exercise that provides practice on a variety of examples to promote generalization of the strategy. Part C is a less structured worksheet similar to the one used in Part B, with fewer teacher prompts.

As previously noted, we recommend teaching the area of a rectangle as "base times height" because this equation allows for generalization to other shapes. Because of the unique properties of parallelograms, for example, length times width will not yield the correct area.

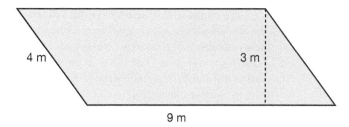

The structured board presentation in Format 17.5: Calculating the Area of Parallelograms includes a demonstration of why the equation works and how it is related to the equation for finding the area of rectangles. As in the previous formats, the structured board presentation is followed by a less structured board presentation that focuses on the application of the equation. The board presentations are followed by worksheet exercises in which the teacher guidance gradually fades.

Volume

Volume refers to the number of cubic units of space inside a three-dimensional shape. When teaching volume, we recommend using equations similar to the one used for calculating area. The equation "the area of the base times the height" can easily be applied to calculating volume for several other three-dimensional shapes. **Figure 17.2** illustrates the relationship between seven traditional formulas for calculating volume and the more generalizable equations recommended in this text. For example, once students know the equation for finding the area of a rectangle, they can calculate the volume of a rectangular prism. They calculate the area of the rectangular base and then multiply by the height of the prism. The same formula applies to calculating the volume of triangular prisms and cylinders. Finally, students learn that they can find the volume of a solid object that comes to a point (cone or pyramid) by calculating the area of the base times the height divided by 3.

FIGURE 17.2   A comparison of seven formulas for calculating volume

	Rectangular Prism	Triangular Prism	Cylinder
Generalizable Strategy	$B \times h$	$B \times h$	$B \times h$
Conventional	$l \times w \times h$	$\frac{1}{2} \times l \times w \times h$	$\pi \times r^2 \times h$

	Pyramids		Cone	Sphere
	Triangular Pyramid	**Rectangular Pyramid**		
Generalizable Strategy	$B \times \frac{1}{3}h$	$B \times \frac{1}{3}h$	$B \times \frac{1}{3}h$	$B \times \frac{2}{3}h$
Conventional	$\frac{1}{6} \times l \times w \times h$	$\frac{1}{3} \times l \times w \times h$	$\frac{1}{3} \times \pi \times r^2 \times h$	$\frac{4}{3} \times \pi \times r^3$

v = volume, l = length, r = radius, w = width, B = area of the base

In **Format 17.6: Calculating the Volume of Boxes**, a procedure similar to that for teaching the area of a rectangle, is used to teach students to determine the volume of a box. Introducing new concepts using familiar terms, such as box, is intended to reduce confusion. An important preskill for computing volume is multiplying three numbers. Students are taught to first multiply two of the numbers to find the area of the base and then multiply the product of those two numbers by the third, the height.

In Part A of the format, the teacher promotes understanding of the concept by using a visual representation illustrating how a box may be divided into cubic units. The teacher then demonstrates how multiplying the area of the base by the height gives the number of cubic units in the figure. In Part B, the teacher applies the equation (area of the base times the height) to figures without first including the illustrations of the individual cubic units. Finally, the teacher must emphasize that answers are expressed in terms of cubic units.

MEASURING AND CONSTRUCTING FIGURES USING TOOLS

Measuring and constructing figures requires the use of tools such as a ruler, compass, and protractor. In order to teach students to use these tools, teachers must provide a clear model of using the tool correctly as well as sufficient, structured practice with the tools. For example, in modeling the use of a compass, the teacher would emphasize the need to keep the compass upright when drawing a circle and not letting it slant.

Teaching students to measure the number of degrees in an angle requires teaching them to use a protractor. The teacher first models how to align (a) the base of the protractor and the base of the angle and (b) the vertex (point of the angle) with the center of the protractor base. The next step requires determining which row of numerals to read. As illustrated in **Figure 17.3**, protractors have two rows of numerals. If the baseline of the angle points to the right:

the lower numerals are read. If the baseline of the angle points to the left, the top numerals are read:

The final step involves determining the number of degrees by noting the places at which the **ray** and the protractor intersect. In Figure 17.3, the intersection is at 70. Therefore, the angle is 70°.

FIGURE 17.3   Using a protractor

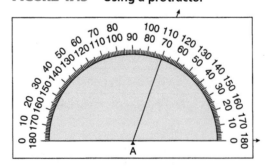

USING LOGIC IN WORKING WITH ANGLES AND LINES

Students can use a number of facts about angles and lines to work a variety of problems. These geometry facts serve as prerequisite skills for more advanced problem solving in geometry. These facts include: angles can be measured in degrees; there are 90 degrees in a "corner" or right angle; there are 360 degrees in a full circle; and there are 180 degrees in a half-circle or a straight angle.

FIGURE 17.4 Component angles of a straight line

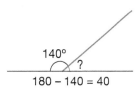

140°
?
180 − 140 = 40

Students also need to know that the degrees in an angle that is divided into two parts can be shown as the big number in a number family and the two parts (or component angles) are the small numbers in that family. (See Chapter 6 for a discussion of number families.) To find the value of unknown component angles like those illustrated in **Figure 17.4**, students learn to construct a number family equation with the big number (total degrees) and the two smaller numbers (degrees of each component angle). Using number family logic, given any two values, students can compute the third.

Because students have learned that a straight angle is 180 degrees, they only need to know the measurement of one of the two component angles of the straight angle to be able to figure out the measurement of the other component angle. They construct a number family starting with 180 degrees (the big number) and the measurement of the known component angle (one of the small numbers). Using the number family rules ("When you have a big number, you subtract to find the missing number") allows the students to generate an equation to solve for the value of the unknown component angle. They subtract the measurement of the known angle from 180 degrees to obtain the measurement of the unknown component angle.

After they can solve one-step problems of this type, students can learn how to solve more complex problems like the following.

Find the value of angle B:

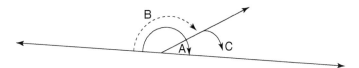

First, they find the value of one of the smaller angles by working from the information given. For the example above, if students are given information that Angle C is $\frac{1}{9}$ of a circle, students compute $\frac{1}{9}$ of 360 degrees (40 degrees) to find the value of that angle. In the second step, students find the value of the unknown second component angle (Angle B). Procedures for solving this type of two-step problem can be found in **Format 17.7: Finding the Value of Unknown Component Angles**. Note that the same procedure can be used to find unknown component angles of right angles or of a complete circle.

The more sophisticated skill of teaching students to find unknown angles in complex diagrams is introduced in **Format 17.8: Finding the Values of Unknown Angles in Complex Diagrams**. Prior to teaching this format, students need to be taught the concept of corresponding angles. This is best accomplished by using a series of examples and nonexamples.

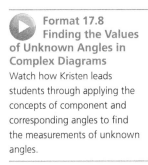

Format 17.8
Finding the Values of Unknown Angles in Complex Diagrams
Watch how Kristen leads students through applying the concepts of component and corresponding angles to find the measurements of unknown angles.

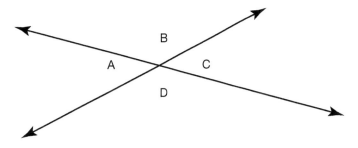

The teacher would present a diagram like the one above and point out that angles A and C are corresponding angles and, by definition, of equal size. Angles B and D also are corresponding angles. The teacher would then remind the students that Angles A and B are component angles and equal 180 degrees when added together. In the format, the measurement of one of the angles is always given. The concepts of component and corresponding angles can then be used to calculate the measurements of the remaining three angles. Students can build on the logic in this type of problem when they are presented with more complex problems, for example, problems where a line intersects two parallel lines, creating eight angles of only two sizes. These more complex problems are valuable preparation for later work on geometric proofs.

DIAGNOSIS AND REMEDIATION

Students may demonstrate a variety of problems related to concepts in geometry. For example, they may confuse geometric shapes or the formulas for calculating measurements of various geometric shapes. Also, they may forget the facts associated with angles and lines causing them to miscalculate the values of related angles. Regardless of the specific error, the procedures for diagnosing and remediating errors remain consistent—teachers would identify the confusion causing the student error (diagnose), confirm by examining the student's work or interviewing the student, review the critical content that addresses the student's confusion, then provide additional practice examples until the student has demonstrated mastery. **Figure 17.5** outlines recommended diagnosis and remediation procedures for three common geometry errors.

FIGURE 17.5 Diagnosis and remediation for common geometry errors

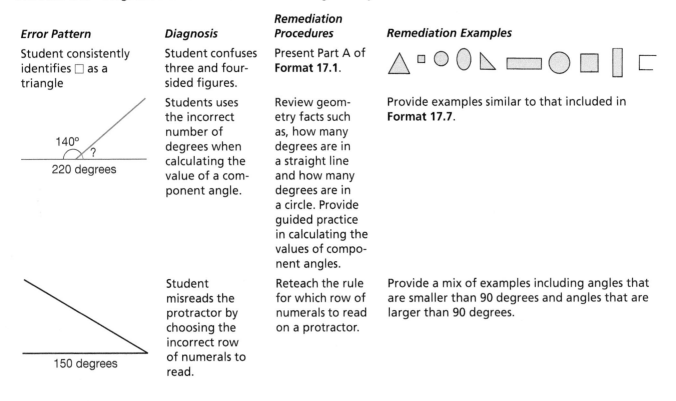

Error Pattern	Diagnosis	Remediation Procedures	Remediation Examples
Student consistently identifies □ as a triangle	Student confuses three and four-sided figures.	Present Part A of **Format 17.1**.	
(140° / ? / 220 degrees angle diagram)	Students uses the incorrect number of degrees when calculating the value of a component angle.	Review geometry facts such as, how many degrees are in a straight line and how many degrees are in a circle. Provide guided practice in calculating the values of component angles.	Provide examples similar to that included in **Format 17.7**.
(150 degrees triangle diagram)	Student misreads the protractor by choosing the incorrect row of numerals to read.	Reteach the rule for which row of numerals to read on a protractor.	Provide a mix of examples including angles that are smaller than 90 degrees and angles that are larger than 90 degrees.

APPLY WHAT YOU LEARNED

 Click on the √ to answer the questions online.

1. Describe how key concepts in geometry are sequenced.

2. Discuss how instructional language (e.g. vocabulary) for geometry concepts changes across grade levels.

3. Explain why students initially should be taught to determine the volume of a "box" rather than the more correct term "rectangular prism."

4. Using **Format 17.1** as a model, write a teaching format for introducing the concept of parallelogram.

5. Explain the rationale for teaching students a variation of base × height to calculate the area of rectangles, triangles, and parallelograms. Describe the teaching procedures that highlight how the three calculations are related.

6. Outline the three steps for finding the area of a complex figure such as a wall with a window in it.

7. Explain the rationale for teaching students to find the volume of boxes, cylinders, and rectangular or triangular prisms by using a variation of area of base × height of the figure. Outline the teaching procedures that highlight how the calculations are related.

8. How would teachers use visual representations to help students conceptualize and calculate the volume of a rectangular prism?

9. Write a teaching format for teaching students to measure:
   a. the perimeter of a rectangle,
   b. the area of a square, and
   c. the radius of a circle.

10. Outline the steps in teaching students to use a protractor. What examples and nonexamples should teachers be sure to include in their demonstration?

11. Construct a set of examples and nonexamples to use in teaching the concept of right angle.

12. A student consistently identifies squares as triangles. What would the teacher do?

Format 17.1
IDENTIFICATION/DEFINITION—TRIANGLE

TEACHER	STUDENTS
Part A: Structured Board Presentation	
(Present the following figures to the students.)	
1. Listen to this definition: A triangle is a closed figure that has three straight sides. How many sides does a triangle have?	3
2. I'm going to point to some figures, and you tell me if they are triangles. *(Point to △)*	
Is this a triangle?	Yes
How do you know?	It has three sides.
(Point to the remaining figures in the sequence.)	
Part B: Less Structured Worksheet	
1. *(Give students a worksheet with problems like the ones below.)* Draw a circle around each triangle.	

continued

Format 17.1 *(continued)*
IDENTIFICATION/DEFINITION—TRIANGLE

TEACHER	STUDENTS
Write the letter R over each rectangle.	
Write the letter S over each square.	
Write the letter T over each triangle.	
Write the letter C over each circle.	
Look at problem a on your worksheet. Read the directions.	Draw a circle around each triangle.
2. Touch the first figure. Is that a triangle?	Yes
So what are you going to do?	Draw a circle around it.
Do it.	
3. Touch the next figure. Is that a triangle?	No
So what are you going to do?	Nothing
4. *(Have students complete the worksheet independently.)*	

Format 17.2
FINDING THE AREA OF RECTANGLES

TEACHER	STUDENTS
Part A: Structured Board Presentation	
1. The area of a figure such as a rectangle is the number of squares (such as square inches or square feet) it takes to cover the rectangle. Listen again. The area of a figure is the number of squares it takes to cover the figure.	
2. What is the area of a figure?	The number of squares it takes to cover the figure
3. You can find the number of squares by multiplying the number of squares in each row by the number of rows. The number of squares in each row tells us the base. How many squares across the base of this rectangle?	13 squares
4. The number of rows tells us the height. How many rows high is this rectangle?	4 rows
5. To find the area of this rectangle, we multiply the base by the height. What do we multiply to find the area?	Base × height

TEACHER	STUDENTS
6. So the equation for finding the area of a rectangle is base × height. What is the equation for finding the area of a rectangle?	Base × height
7. We say the answer as square units. The rectangle above has a base of 13 feet and a height of 4 feet. To find the area of this rectangle, what two numbers do we multiply?	13 × 4
8. Our answer will be in square units, in this case square feet. What kind of units will we label our answer?	Square feet
9. So what is the area of this rectangle?	52 square feet

10. (Draw the following rectangle on the board:)

3							
2							
1	2	3	4	5	6	7	8

TEACHER	STUDENTS
11. The base of this rectangle is along the bottom. It is measured in feet. How many feet long is the base?	8 feet
12. What is the height of the rectangle?	3 feet
13. How many square feet in the area of this rectangle?	24 Square feet

(Put this rectangle on the board:)

2									
1	2	3	4	5	6	7	8	9	10

TEACHER	STUDENTS
14. This rectangle is measured in centimeters. What is the base of this rectangle?	10 centimeters
15. What is the height of the rectangle?	2 centimeters
16. What is the area of this rectangle?	20 Square centimeters

Teaching the equation

TEACHER	STUDENTS
1. The equation for the area of a rectangle can be written as "Area of a rectangle = base × height." (Write the following on the board:) Area of a rectangle = base × height. Read this equation.	Area of a rectangle = base × height
2. Now let's see if you can remember this equation. (Erase board.) What is the equation for the area of a rectangle?	Area of a rectangle = base × height

Part B: Less Structured Board Presentation

TEACHER	STUDENTS
1. Let's find the area of some rectangles. What is the equation for the area of a rectangle? (Write on the board as students say the equation.)	Area of rectangle = base × height
2. Here is a rectangle.	

continued

Format 17.2 *(continued)*
FINDING THE AREA OF RECTANGLES

TEACHER	STUDENTS
(Draw this figure and label the following dimensions for base and height.)	

3 m.

5 m.

3. What is the base of this rectangle?	5 meters
4. What is the height of this rectangle?	3 meters
5. What is the area of the rectangle?	15 square meters

6. *(Repeat steps 3–5 by changing the dimensions on the board of the figure to the following:)*

height: 4 cm	base: 9 cm
height: 8 feet	base: 10 feet
height: 3 inches	base: 4 inches
height: 1 yard	base: 2 yards

Part C: Structured Worksheet

(Give students a worksheet with the following figures:)

A.
2 m
5 m.

B.
4″
8″

C.
12 ft
8 ft

D.
11 cm
4 cm

1. State the equation for finding the area of a rectangle.	Area of rectangle = base times height
2. Write the equation for finding the area of a rectangle. *(Monitor student responses.)*	

TEACHER	STUDENTS
3. Look at figure A. What is the base? What is the height?	5 meters 2 meters
4. What is the area of figure A?	10 square meters
5. Look at figure B. What kind of figure is that?	Rectangle
6. So how do you find the area of figure B?	Multiply base × height
7. Find the area of each of these rectangles.	
8. *(Check student work.)*	
Part D: Less Structured Worksheets	
(Give students a worksheet with the following rectangles.)	

A.
4 m
5 m.

B.
16″
10″

C.
7 m.
9 m.

D.
12 ft
9 ft.

E.
12 in.
3 in.

F.
7 cm.
6 cm.

1. Write the equation for finding the area of a rectangle.

2. Find the area of the rectangles on this worksheet.

3. *(Monitor students as they work.)*

Format 17.3
FINDING THE AREA OF TRIANGLES

TEACHER	STUDENTS
Part A: Structured Board Presentation	
1. *(Draw this rectangle on the board.)* What is the equation for the area of a rectangle? 3 ft 8 ft	Base × height

continued

Format 17.3 *(continued)*
FINDING THE AREA OF TRIANGLES

TEACHER	STUDENTS
2. What would you multiply to find the area of this rectangle? What is the area?	8 times 3 24 square feet

3 ft

8 ft

3. If I draw a line from one corner of the rectangle to the opposite corner, then I have divided the rectangle into how many parts?	2
4. I have made two triangles. The area of each triangle is one part out of two parts in the whole rectangle. How do we say that fraction?	One half
5. If the area of each triangle is half of the rectangle, we can show the area of each triangle as the area of the rectangle divided by what number?	2
6. What is the equation for the area of a rectangle?	Area of a rectangle = base × height
7. So we can find the area of the triangle the same way we find the area of the rectangle, just divided by two. *(Write this on the board:)*	

$$\text{Area of the } \Delta = \frac{\text{base} \times \text{height}}{2}$$

Read this equation for finding the area of a triangle.	The area of a triangle equals base times height divided by two.
(Draw another rectangle.)	

8. Look at this rectangle. How would you find the area?	Multiply base × height
9. Watch how anywhere I draw a vertical line, I divided this rectangle into how many rectangles? *(Draw a vertical line inside the rectangle:)*	Two

TEACHER	STUDENTS
I'll shade the left hand rectangle.	

(Draw a diagonal line in each rectangle going from the outside bottom corner to the top of the vertical dividing line. Then put the letters A, B, C, D inside the resulting triangles:)

10. If I divide each of those rectangles with a line from corner to corner I have divided each rectangle into 2 triangles. The shaded left hand rectangle is divided into triangles A and B. The area of triangle A is what part of the area of the shaded left hand rectangle? — One-half

11. The area of triangle B is what part of the area of the shaded left hand rectangle? — One-half

12. The area of triangle C is what part of the area of the right hand rectangle? — One-half

13. The area of triangle D is what part of the area of the right hand rectangle? — One-half

(Draw heavier lines around triangles B and D.)

14. If I combine triangles B and D into one bigger triangle, the area of that combined triangle is what part of the area of the whole rectangle with which we started? — One-half

Yes, the area of this larger triangle is one half the area of the larger rectangle. So we can find the area of any triangle by multiplying the base times the height and then dividing that result by what number? — Two

15. So what is the equation for finding the area of a triangle? — Area of a triangle = base times height divided by 2

(Write on board as students state the equation:)

$$\text{Area of the } \Delta = \frac{\text{base} \times \text{height}}{2}$$

Part B: Less Structured Board Presentation

1. Let's find the area of some triangles. What is the equation for area of a triangle? — Area of a triangle = base times height divided by 2

(Write on board as students say:)

$$\text{Area of the } \Delta = \frac{\text{base} \times \text{height}}{2}$$

continued

Format 17.3 *(continued)*
FINDING THE AREA OF TRIANGLES

TEACHER	STUDENTS
2. **Here is a rectangle with a triangle inside.** *(Draw this figure and label the following dimensions for base and height.)*	

5 m.

8 m.

TEACHER	STUDENTS
3. **What is the base of this rectangle and triangle?**	8 meters
4. **What is the height of this rectangle and triangle?**	5 meters
5. **What is the area of the whole rectangle?**	40 square meters
6. **How are you going to find the area of the triangle inside?**	Divided by two
7. **What is the area of the triangle inside?**	20 square meters

8. *(Repeat steps 3–7 by changing the dimensions on the board of the figure to the following:)*

height: 3 inches   base: 4 inches
height: 10 feet   base: 12 feet
height: 4 cm   base: 9 cm
height: 8 yards   base: 10 yards

Part C: Structured Worksheet

Students have a worksheet with the following figures.

A. 7 m. 8 m.

B. 4 mi. 8 ft

C. 4" 8"

D. 11 cm 4 cm.

E. 4 mi. 2 mi.

TEACHER	STUDENTS
1. State the equation for finding the area of a triangle.	Area of a triangle = base times height divided by 2.
2. Write the equation for finding the area of a triangle.	Area of the Δ = $\dfrac{\text{base} \times \text{height}}{2}$
3. Look at figure A. What is the base?	8 meters
What is the height?	7 meters
4. Find the area of that figure. *(Pause.)*	
What is the area of figure A?	28 square meters
5. Look at figure B. What kind of figure is that?	Rectangle
6. So how do you find the area of figure B?	Base × height.
7. Look at figure C. What kind of figure is that?	Triangle
8. So how do find the area of figure C?	Base × height divided by 2.
9. Find the area of each of these figures. Remember to use the appropriate equation for each figure.	
10. *(Check student work.)*	

Part D: Less structured worksheet

(Give students a worksheet like the following:)

A.

4 m.
5 m.

B.

16"
10"

C.
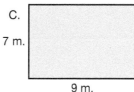
7 m.
9 m.

D.
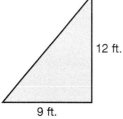
12 ft.
9 ft.

E.
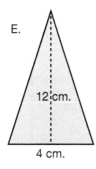
12 cm.
4 cm.

F.
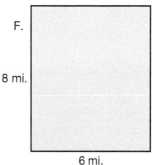
8 mi.
6 mi.

1. Write the equation for finding the area of a rectangle.	Area □ = base × height.
2. Write the equation for finding the area of a triangle.	Area of the Δ = $\dfrac{\text{base} \times \text{height}}{2}$
3. Find the area of the figures on this worksheet. Be careful to use the appropriate equation for each figure.	
4. *(Check student work.)*	

Format 17.4
CALCULATING THE AREA OF COMPLEX FIGURES

TEACHER	STUDENTS
Part A: Structured Board Presentation	
1. *(Draw the following figure on the board.)*	

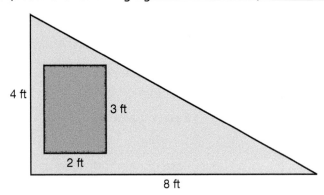

TEACHER	STUDENTS
The simplest way to find the area of a figure like this, with a missing part, is to calculate the area of the total figure, calculate the area of the missing part, then subtract the area of the missing part from the area of the total figure. What is first step to find the area of a figure with a hole in it?	Calculate the area of the total figure.
2. What is the second step?	Calculate the area of the missing part.
3. What is the third step?	Subtract the area of the missing part from the area of the total figure.
4. To find the area of this figure with a missing part in it, what will we calculate first?	The area of the triangle
5. What is the equation for finding the area of a triangle? *(Write this on the board as students say it.)* $$\text{Area of a } \Delta = \frac{b \times h}{2}$$	Base times height divided by two.
6. What is the base times the height for this triangle?	32
7. What is the area for the total triangle?	16 square feet
8. What is the second step to finding the area of this figure with a missing part?	Calculate the area of the missing part
9. The missing part in this figure is a rectangle with a base of 2 feet and a height of how many feet?	3 feet
10. What is the area of the missing part in this figure?	6 square feet
11. What is the third step in finding the area of a figure with a missing part?	Subtract the area of the missing part from the area of the total figure.
12. So we subtract the 6 square feet from what?	16 square feet
13. What's the area of this figure with a missing part?	10 square feet

TEACHER	STUDENTS

Part B: Structured Worksheet

1. *(Give students worksheets with problems like the following.)*

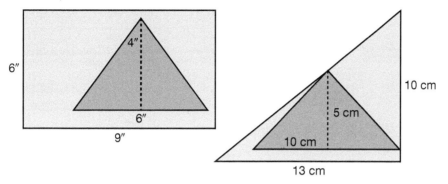

When we calculate the area of figures like these, with missing parts, what is the first step?	Calculate the area of the total figure
2. What is the second step?	Calculate the area of the missing part
3. What is the third step?	Subtract the area of the missing part from the area of the total figure
4. So what do we calculate first?	The area of the total figure
5. Calculate that for the first figure. *(Monitor student responses.)*	
6. What's the area of the total figure?	54 square feet
7. What do we calculate next?	The area of the missing part
8. Calculate that in the first figure.	
9. What's the area of the missing part in the first figure?	12 square feet
10. What is the third step in finding the area of the first figure with a missing part?	Subtract the area of the missing part from the total area
11. Calculate that for the first figure.	
12. What's the area of the first figure with the missing part?	42 square feet
13. *(Do steps 4–12 with the second figure.)*	

Part C: Less Structured Worksheet

1. *(Give students worksheets with problems like the following.)*

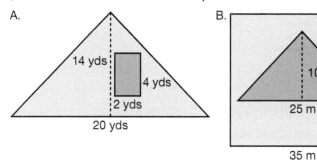

continued

Format 17.4 *(continued)*
CALCULATING THE AREA OF COMPLEX FIGURES

TEACHER	STUDENTS
When we calculate the area of figures with a missing part, what is the first step?	Calculate the area of the total figure.
2. What is the second step?	Calculate the area of the missing part.
3. What is the third step?	Subtract the area of the missing part from the area of the total figure.
4. Find the area of Figure A. *(Pause.)* What is the area of Figure A?	272 square yards
5. Find the area of Figure B. *(Pause.)* What is the area of Figure B?	800 square meters

Format 17.5
CALCULATING THE AREA OF PARALLELOGRAMS

TEACHER	STUDENTS
Part A: Structured Board Presentation	
1. *(Draw this rectangle on the board.)*	

TEACHER	STUDENTS
What is the equation for the area of a rectangle?	Base × height
2. What do you multiply to find the area of this rectangle?	9 × 5
What is the area?	45 square centimeters
3. Watch as I make this rectangle into a parallelogram with the same area. I take a triangle off of the left side and move it over to the right side. Have I changed the area of the figure or have I just moved it? *(Draw the following figure:)*	You just moved it.

TEACHER	STUDENTS
4. What two numbers did you multiply to find the area of the rectangle?	9 × 5
5. To end up with the same area for the parallelogram, do I multiply the base of the parallelogram, 9 centimeters, by the height of 5 centimeters or by the length of 7 centimeters?	You multiply by the height of 5 cm.

TEACHER	STUDENTS
6. Yes, the equation for the area of a parallelogram is base × height. What is the equation for the area of a parallelogram? *(Write as the students say it: Area of a parallelogram = base × height.)* *(Draw another parallelogram.)*	Area of a parallelogram = the base × the height

height = 10 inches   side = 13 inches   base = 25 inches

| 7. Look at this parallelogram. To find the area, you multiply the base of 25 inches times what? | The height of 10 inches |
| 8. What is the equation for finding the area of a parallelogram? | The base times the height |

Part B: Less Structured Board Presentation

| 1. Let's find the area of some parallelograms. What is the equation for the area of a parallelogram? *(Write on board as students say: A ▱ = base × height)* | The area of a parallelogram is the base times height. |
| 2. Here is a parallelogram. *(Draw this figure and label the following dimensions for base and height.)* | |

4 m   3 m   9 m

3. What is the base of this parallelogram?	9 meters
4. What is the height of this parallelogram?	3 meters
5. What is the area of this parallelogram?	27 square meters

6. *(Repeat steps 3–5 by changing the dimensions on the board of the figure to the following.)*

height: 5 inches	side: 6 inches	base: 8 inches
height: 10 feet	side: 12 feet	base: 20 feet
height: 8 cm	side: 9 cm	base: 10 cm
height: 2 yards	side: 3 yards	base: 4 yards

continued

Format 17.5 *(continued)*
CALCULATING THE AREA OF PARALLELOGRAMS

TEACHER	STUDENTS
Part C: Structured Worksheet	

(Give students a worksheet with the following figures.)

a.
8 m / 7 m
10 m

b.
5″ 4″
9″

c.
8 ft
4 ft

d.
11 cm / 10 cm
5 cm

TEACHER	STUDENTS
1. State the equation for finding the area of a parallelogram.	The area of a parallelogram is base times height.
2. Write the equation for finding the area of a parallelogram.	Area = base × height
3. Look at figure A. What is the base?	10 meters
What is the height?	7 meters
4. Find the area of that figure.	
What is the area of figure A?	70 square meters
5. Look at figure B. What kind of figure is that?	Parallelogram
6. How do you find the area of figure B?	Multiply the base × height.
7. Look at figure C. What kind of figure is that?	Rectangle
8. So how do find the area of figure C?	Multiply the base × height.
9. Find the area of each of these figures.	
10. *(Check student work.)*	

TEACHER	STUDENTS

Part D: Less Structured Worksheet

(Give students a worksheet like the following.)

a.
9 m / 8 m
5 m

b.
7"
3"

c.
8 m / 7 m
6 m

d.
7 ft
10 ft

e.
8 mi
6 mi
9 mi

1. Write the equation for finding the area of a rectangle or a parallelogram.

2. Find the area of the figures on this worksheet.

3. *(Check student work.)*

Area = base × height

Format 17.6
CALCULATING THE VOLUME OF BOXES

TEACHER	STUDENTS

Part A: Structured Board Presentation

1. *(Draw the following cube on board.)*

2. This is a cube. Each side of a cube is a square. Cubes are in the shape of dice. When you find how many cubes a box can hold, you are finding the volume of the box. When you find how many cubes a box can hold, what are you finding?

   (Draw this box on the board.)

   3 cm
   2 cm
   4 cm

Volume

Format 17.6 *(continued)*
CALCULATING THE VOLUME OF BOXES

TEACHER	STUDENTS
3. The equation for the volume of a box is volume = area of the base × height of the box. What is the equation for the volume of a box?	Volume = area of base × height of the box
4. The base is the shaded area on the bottom. On this box, the base measures 2 cm by 4 cm. What is the area of the base of this box?	8 square centimeters
5. Yes, the area of the base is 8 square centimeters. Next we multiply by the height. What is the height of this box?	3 centimeters
6. So what two numbers do we multiply to find the volume?	8 × 3
7. What is the volume of this box? Remember, the answer must be in cubic centimeters.	24 cubic centimeters

(Draw the following box on the board.)

3 ft

2 ft

8 ft

Here is another box.

8. What is the equation for finding the volume of a box?	Volume = area of the base × the height of the box
9. What two numbers do we multiply to find the area of the base of this box?	8 × 2
10. So what is the area of the base of this box, in square feet?	16 square feet
11. Once we have the area of the base, why do we multiply that by 3?	Because we have to multiply base × height of the box
12. What is the volume in cubic feet of this box?	48 cubic feet

Part B: Less Structured Board Presentation

1. Let's find the volume of some boxes. What is the equation for the volume of a box? *(Write the equation on the board as students say it.)*	Volume = area of the base times the height of the box

TEACHER	STUDENTS
2. Here is a box. *(Draw this figure and label the following dimensions for base and height.)*	

3. What is the area of the base of this box in square units?	9 square meters
4. What is the height of this box?	3 meters
5. What is the volume of this box?	27 cubic meters
6. *(Repeat steps 3–5 by changing the dimensions of the figure to the following.)*	

height: 5 inches   side: 6 inches   base: 7 inches
height: 10 feet   side: 12 feet   base: 11 feet
height: 4 cm   side: 5 cm   base: 6 cm
height: 2 yards   side: 3 yards   base: 4 yards

Format 17.7
FINDING THE VALUE OF UNKNOWN COMPONENT ANGLES

TEACHER	STUDENTS
1. *(Draw the following figure on the board.)*	

2. Angle A is the angle on one side of the straight line. Angle A is a half circle. How many degrees in a half circle?	180 degrees
3. Angle B and Angle C are parts, or components, of Angle A. So Angle B and Angle C added together would equal how many degrees?	180 degrees
4. So we can write a number sentence to show this. *(Write the following number sentence on the board.)* Angle B + Angle C = 180 degrees	

continued

Format 17.7 *(continued)*
FINDING THE VALUE OF UNKNOWN COMPONENT ANGLES

TEACHER	STUDENTS
5. If we know that Angle C is one-ninth of a circle, we can figure out how many degrees Angle C is, and we can figure out how many degrees Angle B is. How many degrees in a circle?	360 degrees
6. Angle C is one-ninth of a circle, so to find Angle C, we multiply 360 degrees by one-ninth. That looks like this: *(Write on the board.)* $$\frac{1}{9} \times \frac{360}{1} = \frac{360}{9}$$	
7. Divide 9 into 360. *(Pause.)* What is 9 into 360, everybody?	40
8. So we know that Angle C is 40 degrees. Now our equation says: *(Write the following number sentence on the board.)* Angle B + 40 = 180	
9. How do we find Angle B? Do we add or subtract?	Subtract
10. Raise your hand when you have found the answer. *(Wait for students to calculate the answer.)* How many degrees is Angle B?	140 degrees

Format 17.8
FINDING THE VALUES OF UNKNOWN ANGLES IN COMPLEX DIAGRAMS
(See Video)

TEACHER	STUDENTS
▶ 1. *(Draw the following on the board.)*	
2. These four angles are made by two intersecting lines. If we know the degrees for any one of the angles, we can figure out the degrees for any of the other angles. Angle A and Angle B are the two component parts of a straight line, or half a circle. So Angle A and B added together would be how many degrees?	180 degrees

TEACHER	STUDENTS
3. We can write a number sentence to show this. *(Write the following number sentence on the board.)* Angle A + Angle B = 180 degrees	
4. If we know that Angle B is one-third of a circle, we can figure out how many degrees Angle B is and we can figure out how many degrees Angle A is. How many degrees in a circle?	360 degrees
5. Angle B is one-third of a circle, so to find Angle B, we multiply 360 degrees by one-third. *(Write the following on the board.)* $\frac{1}{3} \times \frac{360}{1} = \frac{360}{3}$	
6. Divide 3 into 360. *(Pause.)* What is 3 into 360?	120
7. Now we know that Angle B is 120 degrees. Now the equation is Angle A + 120 = 180. *(Write the equation on the board.)*	
8. Do we add or subtract to find Angle A?	Subtract
9. How many degrees is Angle A?	60 degrees
10. What do we know about Angles A and C?	They are equal.
11. So if Angle A is 60 degrees, what do we know about Angle C?	It is 60 degrees.
12. And what do we know about Angles B and D?	They are equal.
13. So how many degrees is Angle D?	120 degrees

Pre-algebra

With Don Crawford

LEARNING OUTCOMES

18.1 Identify the recommended sequences for teaching skills in each of the following topics: introducing the coordinate system and algebraic functions, other types of numbers, expressions and equations, and ratio and proportions.

18.2 Outline two ways in which teachers can integrate conceptual understanding activities into instruction on specific instructional strategies.

18.3 Discuss how the strategy in this text for teaching students about the coordinate system differs from traditional algebra instruction on the coordinate system and how the differences reduce student confusion.

18.4 Discuss how understanding "other numbers," such as integers, serves as a prerequisite for algebraic reasoning.

18.5 Describe how the equality principle taught in earlier grades is related to the initial instruction in solving equations.

18.6 Outline how the earlier work on equivalent fractions (Chapter 13) and problem solving using tables (Chapter 11) is incorporated into the strategies for solving ratio and proportion problems.

18.7 Summarize the diagnosis and remediation procedures for addressing common errors in early algebraic reasoning.

Algebra is considered to be a "gatekeeper" subject because it is the first in a series of higher-level math courses that prepare students for success in college and the workforce. Consequently, pre-algebra instruction has been included in most commercial middle school curricula as a means for preparing students for their high school math courses. This chapter on pre-algebra addresses four major topics common to middle school courses that are designed to prepare students for algebra: (a) the coordinate system and simple algebraic **functions**; (b) other types of numbers such as **prime numbers**, **factors**, **positive** and **negative integers**, and **exponents**; (c) **expressions** and **equations**; and (d) ratios and proportions. Content also commonly found in pre-algebra courses includes many of the more complex skills found in the previous chapters on fractions, percent and ratios, data analysis, probability, geometry, and problem solving.

SKILL HIERARCHY

· · · · · · · · ·

The specific skills for each of the four topics listed above are outlined in the Instructional Sequence and Assessment Chart. The number associated with each skill indicates the grade level at which it is commonly introduced. All of the pre-algebra skills listed may be taught by sixth grade; however, in most commercial programs, pre-algebra skills are taught in seventh or eighth grade.

Note that the skills under each heading are listed in order for that specific topic. The topics may be taught in any order and simultaneously, with the exception of other types of numbers (OT). Teaching positive and negative integers (found in "other types of numbers") is a prerequisite for mastering algebraic equations.

INSTRUCTIONAL SEQUENCE AND ASSESSMENT CHART		
Grade Level	**Problem Type**	**Performance Indicator**
Coordinate System and Functions (CSF)		
5	Plot points on coordinate system given x and y values and reverse	 What letter is $(x = 7, y = 5)$? Write the coordinates for point A.
5	Students complete a function table, plot the points found, and connect the points in a line	 Complete the function table, plot the points, and connect them with a straight line.

continued

INSTRUCTIONAL SEQUENCE AND ASSESSMENT CHART *(continued)*

Grade Level	Problem Type	Performance Indicator
6	Given two pairs of *x* and *y* values, students determine the function, complete the function table, and graph the points	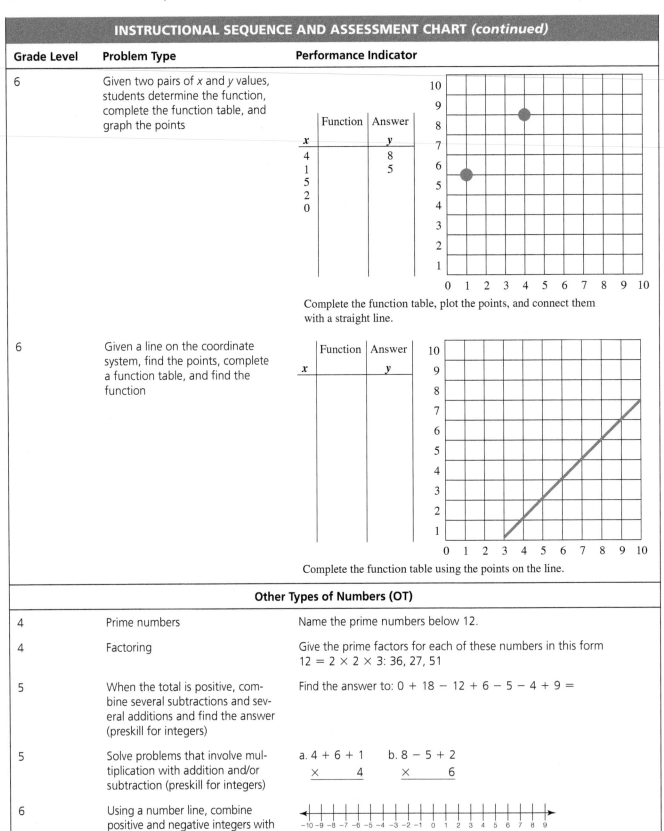
6	Given a line on the coordinate system, find the points, complete a function table, and find the function	

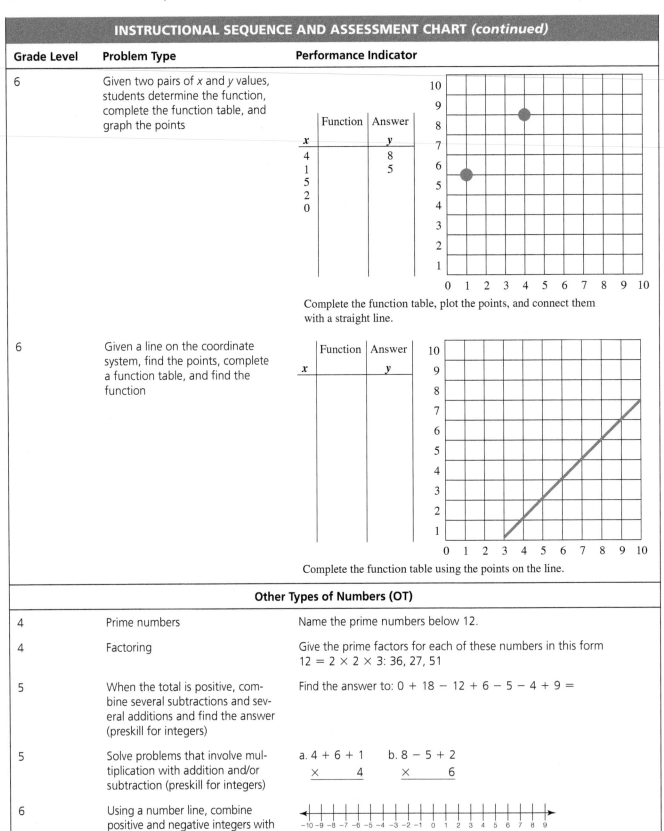

Complete the function table, plot the points, and connect them with a straight line.

Complete the function table using the points on the line.

Other Types of Numbers (OT)

Grade Level	Problem Type	Performance Indicator
4	Prime numbers	Name the prime numbers below 12.
4	Factoring	Give the prime factors for each of these numbers in this form 12 = 2 × 2 × 3: 36, 27, 51
5	When the total is positive, combine several subtractions and several additions and find the answer (preskill for integers)	Find the answer to: 0 + 18 − 12 + 6 − 5 − 4 + 9 =
5	Solve problems that involve multiplication with addition and/or subtraction (preskill for integers)	a. 4 + 6 + 1 b. 8 − 5 + 2 × 4 × 6
6	Using a number line, combine positive and negative integers with either negative or positive totals	a. −6 + 5 = b. −4 − 2 = c. 8 − 10 =
6	Absolute value	In each pair of numerals, write the one that is farther from zero: a. −8, +5 b. +7, −4 c. −2, +9

7	Combine positive and negative integers without a number line	a. +2 b. −3 c. −8 −9 −4 +3
7	Multiply by a positive or negative integer	a. $2 + 4 - 1$ b. 6 c. $9 - 8 + 4$ $\times$ -3 $\times -4$ $\times$ -7
7	Add and subtract positive and negative integers	a. $-4 + -3 =$ b. $-7 - -2 =$
8	Name the base and the exponent from expanded notation examples and the reverse	Name the base and the exponent for each of the following: a. $4 \times 4 \times 4 =$ b. $M \times M \times M \times M \times M =$ Write out the expanded notation problem expressed by each of the following: c. 1^4 d. D^3 e. 71^5
8	Combining exponents	Break the group of multiplied values into two groups, the part underlined and the rest. $6 \times 6 \times 6 \times 6 \times 6 \times 6 \times 6$ $6^7 = \underline{\quad} \times \underline{\quad}$ Combine these two terms into one: $4^5 \times 4^3 = \underline{\quad}$
8	Simplifying exponents	Reduce the following terms: (a) $\dfrac{3 \times 3 \times 3 \times 3 \times 3 \times 3 \times 3}{3 \times 3 \times 3 \times 3} =$ (b) $\dfrac{7 \times 7 \times 7}{7 \times 7 \times 7 \times 7 \times 7 \times 7} =$

Expressions and Equations

6	Write and evaluate expressions with letters for numbers in one-step problems	a. Find the value of j when $5j = 25$. b. Find the value of e when $24 = e + 10$. c. Find the value of r when $\dfrac{r}{2} = 9$.
6	Write and evaluate expressions with letters for numbers in two-step problems	a. Find the value of m when $2m + 5 = 17$. b. Find the value of y when $\dfrac{4}{5}y + 1\dfrac{1}{5} = 2$. c. Find the value of f when $43 = 5f - 7$.

Ratio and Proportion (R/P)

6	Ratio tables	The ratio of sand to gravel in a mixture is 4 parts sand to 9 parts gravel. If there are 260 pounds in the total mixture, how many pounds of sand are there? How many pounds of gravel are there?
7	Ratio tables problems using fractions for classes	In a factory, $\dfrac{3}{5}$ of the employees were women. The rest were men. There were 890 employees. How many employees were men? How many employees were women?
7	Ratio tables problems using fractions that compare	Abbey Hill is $\dfrac{3}{8}$ as high as Howard Hill. Abbey Hill is 240 feet high. How high is Howard Hill? How much higher is Howard Hill than Abbey Hill?
7	Ratio tables problems using percentages for classes	55% of the bagels are cheese. The rest of the bagels are plain. There are 9 plain bagels. How many cheese bagels are there? How many bagels are there altogether?
7	Ratio tables problems using percentages that compare	Train A is 40% longer than train B. If train B is 400 meters long, how long is train A? How much longer is train A than train B?

CONCEPTUAL UNDERSTANDING

Understanding algebra requires a conceptual understanding of the relationships and functions of numbers. We recommend integrating activities that develop conceptual understanding in two ways—either as an introduction to a topic or as a proof to show the reasoning behind a specific procedure. As with the other topics covered in this text, conceptual understanding may be developed using concrete objects (manipulatives), semi-concrete objects (drawings), and/or real-world examples. Throughout this chapter, specific examples of exercises related to conceptual understanding are embedded in the discussion of each of the four major topics.

COORDINATE SYSTEM AND FUNCTIONS (CSF)

The coordinate system and functions can be introduced to students as early as the fourth grade. At the beginning levels, students use only positive integers. Building on their knowledge of graphs and number lines (see Chapter 16), students learn that an x value is the distance of a point to the right of zero. A y value is the distance of a point up from zero. Students begin by finding the x value and the y value for given points on a coordinate system. After several lessons on finding values, students plot points on the coordinate system given the values.

Traditional algebra instruction identifies points, or ordered pairs, on the coordinate system as (5, 6), requiring students to remember that the first numeral is the x value and the second numeral is the y value. However, students learn the coordinate system more easily if they initially receive the points written as $(x = 5, y = 6)$. Over time, students will memorize the order of x and y.

Next, students learn to complete a function table such as the following.

x	Function x + 2	y
0	0 + 2	2
1	1 + 2	3
2	2 + 2	4
3		
4		
5		

The teacher models how to apply the function to determine the y value when the x value is given. In the preceding example, the teacher would model substituting 0 for x in the function $x + 2$ to derive y (0 + 2 = 2; y = 2). After completing the table, the students would plot the points on the coordinate system and connect the points with a straight line.

After several lessons on completing function tables, students are ready to derive the function when given two pairs of values. Initially, they are asked to choose between two possible functions that fit the first pair of values, eliminating the function that does not fit the second pair of values. Once students can choose the correct function, students are ready to derive the function given at least two pairs of values. Students are then taught to plot points from the function table on the coordinate system and draw a line. Format 18.1: Using and Plotting a Function outlines procedures for teaching students how to derive a function, plot the points, and draw a line representing the function. Later, the teacher would teach students how to derive the function when given points on the coordinate system connected bylines.

Coordinate systems allow for the visual representation of the relationship between two sets of data (the function). A function may be thought of as a rule that describes the relationship between two sets of numbers and can be used to solve for an unknown quantity. For example, the function $x + 2$ could be used to solve the following real-world problem:

Pearl is 2 years older than Paul. Paul will be 8 when they visit Disneyland again. Pearl wants to know how old she will be. Paul is currently 4. Create a function table to determine how old Pearl will be when she visits Disneyland again.

Known Quantity	Function	Answer
Paul's Age	*x + 2*	*Pearl's Age*
4	4 + 2	6
5	5 + 2	7
6	6 + 2	8
7	7 + 2	9
8	8 + 2	?

OTHER TYPES OF NUMBERS: PRIMES, FACTORS, INTEGERS, AND EXPONENTS

Using "other types of numbers" including prime numbers, factors, positive and negative integers, and exponents is a necessary prerequisite for algebraic reasoning using unknown variables. For example, finding prime numbers allows students to use an algebraic method and canceling to reduce fractions. Many of the skills introduced in this section may be introduced as early as fourth grade.

Primes and Factors

As mentioned above, finding prime factors enables students to use the algebraic method of reducing fractions and "canceling." Students learn that canceling is possible because they are canceling fractions that equal one and therefore do not change the value of the original fraction. For example, to reduce the fraction $\frac{24}{36}$, students find the prime factors of both 24 and 36 and then cancel the prime factors that appear in the numerator and the denominator (fractions that equal one).

$$\frac{24}{36} = \frac{2 \times 2 \times 2 \times 3}{2 \times 2 \times 3 \times 3} = \frac{\cancel{2} \times \cancel{2} \times 2 \times \cancel{3}}{\cancel{2} \times \cancel{2} \times 3 \times \cancel{3}} = \frac{2}{3}$$

Successfully teaching students to understand prime numbers and factors depends greatly on their facility with multiplication facts. Students who are not fluent with their multiplication facts cannot readily determine prime numbers or the factors of a nonprime number, nor can they use the test recommended in the following paragraph to determine if a number is a prime number.

Students are taught to test for a prime number by asking themselves, "Can this number be divided by something other than 1 and itself?" If the number in question can be divided by something other than 1 and itself, it is not a prime number. Teachers can have students apply this test to a list of numerals. The list should consist of half prime numbers and half nonprime numbers.

When adding and subtracting unlike fractions, students learn to find all of the factors of the two numerators. (See Chapter 13.) However, in pre-algebra, students are taught to find the **prime factors** of numbers and to represent the number as only prime factors multiplied together. The prime factors of 15 are 3 and 5 because both factors are prime numbers and $3 \times 5 = 15$. The prime factors of 12 are 2, 2, and 3; all factors are prime numbers, and $2 \times 2 \times 3 = 12$. The factors 2 and 6 are not prime factors because even though $2 \times 6 = 12$, 6 is not a prime number. The prime factors of 6 are 2 and 3; therefore, the prime factors of 12 are 2, 2, and 3.

Finding prime factors involves attempting to divide a number by each prime number, in order, as many times as possible. To find the prime factors of 35, students first attempt to divide 35 by 2 and 3 (the first prime numbers). However, neither 2 nor 3 divide into 35 evenly. Next, students would divide 35 by 5 (the next prime number). Since 35 divides by 7 evenly, and both 5 and 7 are prime numbers, they are the prime factors of 35.

For 36, students can divide by 2 evenly 18 times. Since 18 is not a prime number, students must continue the process of dividing until each factor is a prime number. The prime factors for 36 are 2, 2, 3, and 3 (see division below).

$$36 \div 2 = 18$$
$$18 \div 2 = 9$$
$$9 \div 3 = 3$$
$$2 \times 2 \times 3 \times 3 = 36$$

Teachers may instruct students to use a calculator to determine if each of the numerals on the list can be divided evenly by prime numbers less than 20 as a modification for students who are not fluent with their multiplication facts.

Integers

Integers include both positive and negative numbers. Many students have difficulty working with negative numbers. To to assist students' understanding of the concept of negative numbers, we recommend that teachers use a number line. Although students may be familiar with a number line, teachers must be sure that students understand the rule that when adding, you move to the right on a number line, and when subtracting, you move to the left. Students can use the number line to solve problems with positive and negative integers, for example, $-6 + 5 = \square$ or $-1 - 3 = \square$. Initially, students should be given only addition combinations so that they are not confused by the appearance of both operational signs (plus/minus) and signed values (positive/negative). Limiting initial examples ensures that only one new concept is introduced at a time.

As mentioned in Chapter 16, the concept of absolute value is introduced to students as "the distance from zero." Once students understand the concept of absolute value, teachers can use the concept when they teach students to solve problems with positive and negative integers. See **Format 18.2: Combining Integers** for this strategy. The first step of the structured board presentation involves teaching students the following rules:

1. If the signs of the numbers are the same, you add.
2. If the signs of the numbers are different, you subtract.
3. When you subtract, you start with the number that is farther from zero on the number line and subtract the other number.
4. The sign in the answer is always the sign of the number that was farther from zero.

The remaining part of the structured board presentation focuses on the application of these rules. Students will need considerable practice in using the rules to solve computation problems with positive and negative integers. The less structured board presentation provides abbreviated rules to help students master the rules prior to providing worksheet practice.

Next, students are taught to multiply integers. For a problem such as $5 \times (7 - 2 - 3)$, students copy the sign of each term and, using the **distributive property**, multiply the positive integer and each of the values $(35 - 10 - 15)$. After students have mastered such problems, they are taught a rule for multiplying by a negative integer: If you multiply by a negative value, you write the opposite of the sign. Using that rule, $-5 \times (7 - 2 - 3)$ would become $(-35 + 10 + 15)$. The rule is simple and efficient in that students need to learn only one rule rather than the traditional four rules:

positive $\times$ positive = positive
negative $\times$ positive = negative
negative $\times$ negative = positive
positive $\times$ negative = negative

Next, students can be introduced to conventional notation for combining positive and negative integers in addition and subtraction problems $(-8 + -3 = \square)$. Initially, to facilitate learning this notation, teachers may want to use exaggerated signs representing the operations (addition or subtraction). For example, the problem above could be written $-8 + -3$.

Next, students are taught to apply two rules. First, they are taught that the big minus sign indicates that you combine (add) the first number with the opposite of the second number. So $-4 - -5$ becomes $-4 + 5$ and $-4 - +5$ becomes $-4 + -5$.

The second rule students learn is: The big plus sign means you combine the two terms as they are. So $-4 + -5$ remains $-4 + -5$. After students master the application of the rules with exaggerated signs, we recommend that they practice rewriting problems using typical notation before solving the problems.

Exponents

Writing and combining exponents are skills commonly needed in complex problems. We suggest initially using expanded notation to assist students in understanding the concept of exponents. Expanded notation illustrates the relationship between repeated multiplication and exponents. Teachers provide students with several examples of repeated multiplication, such as $4 \times 4 \times 4$ or $D \times D \times D \times D$, and explain that the number that is repeated is called the **base number**. The **exponent** is the number of times the base number is repeated and is written as a little numeral above the base numeral. Therefore, in $4 \times 4 \times 4$, 4 is the base number, and the exponent is 3. This is written as 4^3.

Teachers need to provide many examples of repeated multiplication in which students are asked to identify the base number and the exponent. Students should practice writing base numbers and exponents as well. Finally, students should practice writing the expanded notation when given a base number and exponent.

Combining exponents can be illustrated by presenting examples of expanded notation divided into groups. For example, $(6 \times 6 \times 6) \times (6 \times 6)$. The teacher would point out that the examples fall into two groups and then use the examples to show that $6^3 \times 6^2 = 6^5$.

Similarly, expanded notation can be used to show how to simplify exponents. Simplifying exponents is just like simplifying prime factors in that the same numbers in the numerator and denominator are canceled (because they are fractions equal to 1).

EXPRESSIONS AND EQUATIONS

Typically, students learn to write and evaluate expressions $(3b + 4)$ with a letter representing a numerical value early in middle school as a preskill for solving algebraic equations. All of the instruction related to algebraic equations in this text is grounded in the equality principle: "We must end with the same number on this side and the other side of the equal sign." That principle was initially introduced in Chapter 7 as a preskill for the beginning addition strategy. This chapter introduces an extension of that rule: "Whatever you do to one side of an equation you must do to the other." A double-pan balance may be used to promote conceptual understanding of this rule.

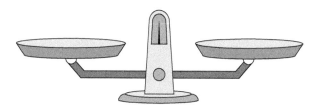

For example, a teacher may place 3 one-ounce weights on one pan (side) and demonstrate that 3 one-ounce weights must be added to the other pan (side) to establish equality between the two sides. The teacher could then add 2 additional one-ounce weights to one side to show inequality between the two sides. In order to balance the two sides, the teacher would add 2 one-ounce weights to the other pan. After the initial demonstration by the teacher, the students may be given the opportunity to manipulate the double-pan balance themselves to solve equations. Electronic versions of balance beams also are available for student practice.

Initial instruction for solving equations focuses on finding the value of one unknown variable in single-step problems, such as $3 + x = 8$. After students have mastered that skill, students are taught to find the value of a variable in problems requiring more than one step (4 + 5d = 12). Students who successfully isolate and solve problems involving a single variable are ready to learn to solve problems with multiple variables, combine like terms, and translate word problems into algebraic equations.

Solving for a Single Variable

In Part A of **Format 18.3: Solving One-Step Problems with Variables—Addition and Subtraction** the teacher introduces the students to the rule "Whatever you do to one side of an equation, you must do to the other." The teacher then models how to isolate the variable and solve to find the value of that variable. A preskill for isolating a variable is finding the inverse of positive and negative integers. A less structured board presentation and independent work follow to provide additional practice.

Two example-selection guides are relevant to this format. First, problems should include a variety of addition and subtraction equations. Second, the variables in the equations must appear on the right and left sides of the equal signs in a random order. Note that the range of examples provided in the less structured board presentation includes a variety of addition and subtraction problems as well as the appearance of variables on both sides of the equations.

After students have mastered finding the value of a variable in one-step problems involving addition and subtraction and simplifying fractions, **Format 18.4: Solving One-Step Problems with Variables—Multiplication and Division** may be presented. In Part A, Preskill: Finding the Reciprocal, students are taught the procedure for finding the reciprocals of fractions and whole numbers. Part B is a structured board presentation in which the teacher models solving for a variable in equations involving multiplication or division. Part C is a less structured board presentation that provides guided practice. Finally, Part D provides independent practice.

Students who have mastered finding the value of a variable in one-step problems using all four of the operations are ready to learn to find the value of a variable in two-step problems like the following:

$$16 + 4r = 28$$

The procedures for finding the value of a variable in two-step problems are similar to the procedures outlined in **Formats 18.3** and **18.4**. The teacher first would model isolating the **term** with the variable (4r) by adding the inverse of 16 (-16) to both sides of the equation. Then the teacher would model isolating the variable r by multiplying both sides of the equation by the reciprocal of 4 $\left(\dfrac{1}{4}\right)$. The equation would then be solved to determine the value of r. The teacher would follow modeling the procedure with guided and independent practice. Note that prior to introducing two-step problems, the teacher would need to teach the vocabulary word "term" to the students.

Substitutions

Students who have mastered finding the value of a single variable in one- and two-step problems can be introduced to equations with more than one variable. Students would be taught that the values of the variables in an equation cannot be determined if there is more than one variable. The values can be determined, however, if the value of one of the variables is known. The teacher would begin by writing a problem like the following on the board:

$$8p - 3j = 24 \qquad j = 8$$

The teacher first would model substituting 8 for j in the equation:

$$8p - 3(8) = 24$$

Then the teacher would ask the students for the product of 3(8) and update the equation again.

$$8p - 24 = 24$$

Because only one variable remains, the students are able to isolate the term $8p$ and solve to determine the value of p. After modeling a few examples, the teacher would provide guided and independent practice to the students including a variety of problems.

Like Terms

After teaching students to work with multiple variables, the teacher would build on the students' knowledge of combining integers to teach combining like terms to solve more complex problems. The teacher would introduce the concept by presenting an example and explaining that the terms can be combined when they all have the same variable. For example, $2q + 5q - 3q$ can be combined as $4q$ because $2 + 5 - 3 = 4$. The teacher would provide additional practice examples until the students demonstrate mastery of combining terms when all of the variables are the same. Then the teacher would introduce combining terms when more than one variable is present $(4r + 2f - 3f + 5r)$, stressing the importance of only combining terms with like variables $(9r - 1f)$.

Word Problems

Chapter 11 describes instructional procedures for teaching several types of word problems including classification and comparison problems. Once students understand how to solve basic algebraic equations, they can translate word problems into algebraic equations using variables and apply their algebraic knowledge to solving these problems.

Table 18.1 illustrates the similarities and differences in solving word problems using the fact family strategy introduced in Chapter 11 and algebraic strategies introduced previously in this chapter. If students have learned how to solve problems by applying the fact family rules for finding missing values, then the transition to using algebraic strategies is fairly straightforward. Table 18.1 illustrates the application of both strategies for comparison and classification problems.

The examples provided in Table 18.1 represent the simplest types of word problems that can be solved using algebraic strategies. Algebraic strategies are applicable to more complex problems as well. Word problems become more complex when they include more abstract variations in wording and/or more complex calculations that require knowledge of fractions, decimals, and percent, for example. Teachers need to be aware of how these variations in wording and how more complex calculations may cause difficulties for students. Table 18.2 illustrates how simple word problems become more complex with both wording changes and more difficult calculation demands. The next section on ratios and proportions also provides teachers instructional strategies to help students solve complex word problems.

RATIOS AND PROPORTIONS (R/P)

Successfully solving ratio problems first requires that students set up the problem accurately. We recommend teaching students to write the labels in the problem as numerators and denominators on both sides of the equal sign. In the problem below, students write the labels "TVs" as the numerator and "Radios" as the denominator. The students then repeat the fraction of TVs over Radios on the other side of the equal sign.

> The store has 3 TVs for every 7 radios. If there are 28 radios in the store, how many TVs are there?

$$\frac{TVs}{Radios} = \frac{TVs}{Radios}$$

The labels provide a prompt for students to successfully identify the numerals that are associated with TVs and those that are associated with Radios.

$$\frac{3\ TVs}{7\ Radios} = \frac{\Box\ TVs}{28\ Radios}$$

TABLE 18.1   Solving Simple Word Problems Using the Fact Family Strategy

Word Problem	Example	Fact Family Strategy—Using Fact Family Rules	Algebraic Strategy

Comparison	Joaquin saved $92 from his after-school job. His twin brother Julio saved $79. How much more did Joaquin save?	**SET-UP**
		
		JU Difference
		79
		            ☐ JO
		
		───────────▶ 92
		
		STRATEGY
		Fact family rule: When the big number is given, subtract to find the other small number. The big number, 92, is given; therefore, you need to subtract.
		
		SOLUTION
		92 − 79 = 13
			SET-UP
			
			79 + D = 92
			
			STRATEGY
			Isolate the variable by adding the inverse to both sides. To isolate *D*, add the inverse, −79, to both sides.
			
			SOLUTION
			79 + D = 92
			−79 −79
			      D = 13

Classification	There are 17 girls in the chemistry class, which has 24 students. How many of the students are boys?	**SET-UP**
		G Difference
		17
		            ☐ B
		
		───────────▶ 24
		
		STRATEGY
		Fact family rule: When the big number is given, subtract to find the other small number. The big number, 24, is given; therefore, you need to subtract.
		
		SOLUTION
		24 − 17 = 7
			SET-UP
			17 + D = 24
			
			STRATEGY
			Isolate the variable by adding the inverse to both sides. To isolate *D*, add the inverse, −17, to both sides.
			
			SOLUTION
			17 + D = 24
			−17 −17
			               7

TABLE 18.2   Instructional Recommendations for Solving Complex Word Problems

Simple Word Problem	Complex Word Problem—Variation in Wording	Instructional Recommendation
The school is 30 miles farther than the park. If it is 60 miles to the park, how far is it to the school? $s = 30 + p$	**It is 30 miles farther to the school than to the park.** If it is 60 miles to the park, how far is it to the school? Determining the equation is more difficult because the wording does not directly translate to the equation. Possible error: $30 + s = p$	Prior to introducing word problems with more complex wording, model translating the complex wording into simple sentences that translate directly to the equation and have students practice with similar translations before solving problems. **"It is 30 miles farther to the school than the park"** translates to "The school is 30 miles farther than the park."
The school is three times as far as the park. The distance to the school is 25 miles. How far is the park?	**The school is $\frac{1}{5}$ as far as the park.** The distance to the school is 25 miles. How far is it to the park? This problem is more difficult in that it requires knowledge of fractions.	Teachers must identify the calculation preskills required to solve the problems they encounter (fractions, percent, decimals).

Once the numerals are written alongside their appropriate labels, the problem can be solved using equivalent fractions. The next step in solving the problem involves identifying the fraction equal to one $\left(\dfrac{4}{4}\right)$ that will yield the equivalent fraction $\left(\dfrac{12}{28}\right)$ and the answer to the question: If there are 28 radios in the store, how many TVs are there? 12.

$$\frac{3\ TVs}{7\ Radios}\left(\frac{4}{4}\right)=\frac{12\ TVs}{28\ Radios}$$

Using Ratio Tables to Solve Classification Problems

Ratio tables are especially useful for solving word problems in that they allow students to see the relationships among the values in a problem. Following is an example of how to use a ratio table to solve a classification word problem.

A factory makes SUVs and cars. It makes 5 SUVs for every 3 cars made. If the factory made 1600 vehicles last year, how many cars and how many SUVs did it make?

Classification	Ratio	
Cars	3	600
SUVs	5	1,000
Vehicles	8	**1,600**

The bold information in the table is provided to the students in the text of the problem. Students are to figure out the missing numbers in order to answer the question. Students can apply their previous knowledge of classification word problems to solving ratio problems using tables. (See Chapter 11 for a discussion of classification word problems and table problems.) Since students have already been introduced to classification word problems, they are familiar with the fact that "Cars" and "SUVs" are the subclasses and that "Vehicles" is the superordinate class. They know that if the two small numbers are given (cars and SUVs), they must add to find the big number ($3 + 5 = 8$ vehicles).

Once completed, the numerals in the ratio column can be used to state the ratio between any two rows. It is already stated that the ratio of cars to SUVs was 3 to 5. After determining the number of vehicles, the ratio table shows that the ratio of SUVs to vehicles made is 5 to 8 and the ratio of cars to vehicles made is 3 to 8. This information enables the students to set up a simple ratio to find the missing information that is requested in the question. The setup to find the number of cars made looks like this:

$$\frac{3\ Cars}{8\ Vehicles}\times\frac{(\ \ )}{(\ \ )}=\frac{\Box\ Cars}{1,600\ Vehicles}$$

$$\frac{3\ Cars}{8\ Vehicles}\times\frac{200}{200}=\frac{600}{1,600}$$

A similar setup can be used to determine the number of SUVs made.

Because students are familiar with classification problems, they also know that if the superordinate class were known, they could find the other subclass by subtracting. For example, if a similar problem indicated that the ratio of SUVs to vehicles was 4 to 10, students could subtract 4 SUVs from 10 vehicles to determine the value for the other subclass, 6 cars. Setting up a ratio problem between the quantity given and the quantity requested in the problem will become routine for students with practice.

Using Ratio Tables with Fractions

Once students have mastered using simple ratio tables, teachers can introduce more sophisticated ratio tables that include fractions representing classes. Teachers first introduce problems

---

SUMMARY BOX 18.1

Rationale for Using Numerators of Fractions in Ratio Equations

1. When working with ratios, it's useful to use whole numbers instead of fractions in the ratio.

Understanding why the shortcut of using only the numerators works requires demonstrating how to convert the fractions in both the numerator and the denominator into whole numbers.

$$\frac{Shorter = \frac{3}{5}}{All = \frac{5}{5}}$$

2. Converting the numerator $\left(\frac{3}{5}\right)$ for "Shorter" into a whole number requires multiplying by 5 $\left(\frac{5}{1}\right)$ to get $\frac{15}{5}$ or 3. 5 was chosen because it is the denominator in the fraction that represents "All."

$$\frac{3}{5}\left(\frac{5}{1}\right) = \frac{15}{5} = 3$$

3. Because we need to multiply both the numerator and the denominator by the same fraction, we need to multiply $\frac{5}{5}$ by $\frac{15}{1}$ as well.

Multiplying the fraction by a fraction equal to one creates an equivalent fraction.

$$\frac{5}{5}\left(\frac{5}{1}\right) = \frac{25}{5} = 5$$

$$\frac{\frac{3}{5}\left(\frac{5}{1}\right) = \frac{15}{5} = 3}{\frac{5}{5}\left(\frac{5}{1}\right) = \frac{25}{5} = 5}$$

4. Students reduce the fractions in both the numerator and denominator to obtain whole numbers.

$$\frac{\frac{15}{5}}{\frac{25}{5}} = \frac{3}{5} = \frac{Shorter}{All}$$

5. The result is whole numbers for the ratio of shorter children to all children. The whole numbers in the ratio are the numerators of each of the fractions in the original problem.

$$Shorter = 3$$
$$All = 5$$

SUMMARY BOX 18.2

Ratio Tables Using Fractions for Classes

1. Students read the problem and figure out the fraction number family.

Two-thirds of the people at the coffee shop are drinking coffee. The rest are drinking tea. If 15 people are drinking tea, how many people are drinking coffee? How many people are in the coffee shop?

	Fraction family	Ratio	Quantity
Coffee			
Tea			
People			

2. Students complete the fraction family column.

	Fraction family	Ratio	Quantity
Coffee	$\frac{2}{3}$		
Tea	$\frac{1}{3}$		
People	$\frac{3}{3}$		

3. Students use numerator of fraction to complete ratio column.

	Fraction family	Ratio	Quantity
Coffee	$\frac{2}{3}$	2	
Tea	$\frac{1}{3}$	1	
People	$\frac{3}{3}$	3	

4. Students fill in known quantities.

	Fraction family	Ratio	Quantity
Coffee	$\frac{2}{3}$	2	
Tea	$\frac{1}{3}$	1	15
People	$\frac{3}{3}$	3	

5. Students write ratio equation.

$$\frac{2 \text{ Coffee}}{1 \text{ Tea}} = \frac{\square \text{ Coffee}}{15 \text{ Tea}}$$

6. Students solve ratio problem to answer question about coffee drinkers.

	Fraction family	Ratio	Quantity
Coffee	$\frac{2}{3}$	2	30
Tea	$\frac{1}{3}$	1	15
People	$\frac{3}{3}$	3	

7. Students use the number-family strategy to determine how many people are in the shop and complete the table.

	Fraction family	Ratio	Quantity
Coffee	$\frac{2}{3}$	2	30
Tea	$\frac{1}{3}$	1	15
People	$\frac{3}{3}$	3	45

in which one class is a fraction: For example, $\frac{1}{3}$ of the plants were trees. Since students know that all of the plants are represented as $\frac{3}{3}$, they can easily determine that $\frac{2}{3}$ of the plants are not trees. The superordinate class is always a fraction equal to one, and the two subclasses combine to equal one. Given a set of classifications represented as fractions, students can create a ratio table using the numerators of the fractions as the ratio. The problem below illustrates this type of problem along with a completed ratio table.

Three-fifths of the children in the school are shorter than the principal. If 128 children are taller than the principal, how many are shorter? How many children are there in the school?

Classification	Fraction Family	Ratio	Answer
Shorter	$\frac{3}{5}$	3	192
Taller	$\frac{2}{5}$	2	**128**
All	$\frac{5}{5}$	5	320

Students have been taught that if $\frac{3}{5}$ of the children are shorter, then the fraction that represents all the children is $\frac{5}{5}$. They subtract to find out that $\frac{2}{5}$ of the children are taller. The numerators express the ratio of each of those terms. In Part B of **Format 18.5: Ratio Tables Using Fractions for Classes** students are taught to put the numerators of the fraction family into the ratio column. To promote conceptual understanding, the teacher may choose to demonstrate to students why the numerators only can express the ratio. This explanation can be found in **Summary Box 18.1**.

Format 18.5B: Ratio Tables Using Fractions for Classes
Watch how Kristen leads her students through setting up a ratio table using fractions.

The numerators express the ratio of each of those classes, so that the ratio of shorter children to all the children is 3 to 5, and the ratio of the taller children to all children is 2 to 5. Once the ratios are determined, the students can find the unknown quantities by constructing a ratio between the known quantity (128 children who are taller) and the unknown quantity ("How many children are shorter?"). This is solved in the same manner as other ratio equations.

$$\frac{Taller}{Shorter}\frac{2}{3} \times \frac{(\ )}{(\ )} = \frac{128}{\square}$$

$$\frac{Taller}{Shorter}\frac{2}{3} \times \frac{64}{64} = \frac{128}{192}$$

See **Summary Box 18.2** for an illustration of the recommended steps in solving a ratio problem using fractions.

Using Ratio Tables to Solve Comparison Problems

Ratio tables also can be used to solve comparison problems. These problems contain a sentence that indicates the basis for the comparison. For example:

Louise was paid $\frac{5}{6}$ of what her boss was paid. If Louise is paid $1,800 a month, how much more does her boss get paid, and what does her boss get paid?

Louise was paid $\frac{5}{6}$ of what her boss was paid. Louise is being compared to her boss. Therefore, her boss is equal to one whole, $\frac{6}{6}$. To determine the difference, students are taught to generate the equation below. Note that teachers may want to call attention to the use of the word "difference" in labeling the parts of the family.

Difference		Louise		Boss
$\frac{1}{6}$	+	$\frac{5}{6}$	=	$\frac{6}{6}$

Once the number family is completed, students can put the numerators into a ratio table. Given any of the three values (Louise's pay, the difference, or her boss's pay), the students can construct ratio equations to determine the other two values. Here is a completed ratio table for the problem in which Louise is paid $1,800 a month. The solution to the word problem is that her boss was paid $2,160.

Comparison	Ratio	Pay
Difference	*1*	*360*
Louise	**5**	**1,800**
Boss	6	*2,160*

Using Ratio Tables with Percent Problems

Another type of ratio table students may be introduced to is a classification ratio table using percentages. Students are given one class as a percentage of the whole and the second class as the rest. For example:

> A store got 40% of its oranges from California. The store got the rest of its oranges from Florida. If the store had 170 total oranges, how many were from California and how many from Florida?

In the problem above, students learn that the superordinate class (all of the oranges) is always equal to 100%. Since the big number is known (100%), this is a subtraction problem. The percentage that came from Florida is determined by subtracting ($100\% - 40\% = 60\%$). Below is the completed number family that represents this problem.

California   Florida   All

40%   +   60%   =   100%

Students then put the information from the number family into a ratio table. Given the quantity of any of the three variables (total oranges, oranges from California, oranges from Florida), students can solve for the other two quantities. A completed ratio table for this problem appears below.

California	**40%**	*68*
Florida	*60%*	*102*
All	*100%*	**170**

The ratio equation to figure out the number of California oranges is

$$\frac{California}{All}\ \frac{4\ \times\ (\ )}{10\ \times\ (\ )} = \frac{\square}{170}$$

$$\frac{California}{All}\ \frac{4\ \times\ 17}{10\ \times\ 17} = \frac{68}{170}$$

Finally, students can learn to solve comparison problems using percentages. These are perhaps the most counterintuitive and difficult type of word problems. Determining the appropriate number sentence is critical to solving this type of problem. Students must understand that one of the variables that is being compared will be the variable equal to 100%. For example, in the problem below, students must compare the number of women's bicycles sold to the number of men's bicycles sold. The problem indicates that fewer women's bicycles are sold compared to the number of men's bicycles sold; therefore, the number of men's bicycles sold is the variable equal to 100% in this problem.

> A bike store sold 25% fewer women's bicycles than men's bicycles. *(Hint: Women's bicycles are being compared to men's, so which variable is equal to 100%?)* If the store sold 175 fewer women's bicycles, how many men's and women's bicycles did it sell?

Difference   Women's Bicycles   Men's Bicycles

25%   +   75%   =   100%

Difference	25%	175
Women's	75%	525
Men's	100%	700

$$\frac{\text{Difference}}{\text{Men's}} \quad \frac{25 \times ()}{100 \times ()} = \frac{175}{\square}$$

$$\frac{\text{Difference}}{\text{Men's}} \quad \frac{25 \times (7)}{100 \times (7)} = \frac{175}{700}$$

$$\frac{\text{Difference}}{\text{Women's}} \quad \frac{25 \times ()}{75 \times ()} = \frac{175}{\square}$$

$$\frac{\text{Difference}}{\text{Women's}} \quad \frac{25 \times (7)}{75 \times (7)} = \frac{175}{\mathbf{525}}$$

Students use the information given in the word problem to complete the ratio table and generate equations like the ones above to solve for the unknown values. Using that information, students can generate the answers to the questions in the problem. (The shop sold 700 men's bicycles and 525 women's bicycles.)

DIAGNOSIS AND REMEDIATION

Common errors related to pre-algebra skills outlined in this chapter fall into the basic error categories that have been used throughout this text: fact errors (missing a math fact), component-skill errors (calculation or confusion errors), and strategy errors. The diagnosis and remediation procedures for the skills and concepts taught in all of the algebraic reasoning sections in this chapter should begin with determining the cause of the error. Each of the pre-algebra sections includes a discussion of critical discriminations and concepts students must master prior to the introduction of the pre-algebra strategy. Those discussions were included to highlight common misunderstandings that could cause student errors. As always, teachers need to confirm their diagnosis by analyzing the error and interviewing the student, if necessary. Once the diagnosis has been confirmed, the remediation usually involves reviewing critical parts of the relevant formats and providing students with additional practice.

Examples of common errors for each of the pre-algebra sections discussed in this chapter are outlined in **Figure 18.1** along with suggested remediation procedures.

FIGURE 18.1 Pre-algebra diagnosis and remediation

Error Pattern	Diagnosis	Remediation Procedures	Remediation Examples
Plot the point for the coordinates (6, 2). 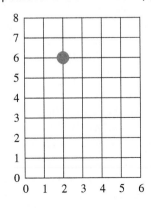	Students confuse the x and y axes when plotting two coordinates on a graph.	The teacher would reintroduce the coordinate system to students using points written as $(x = 6, y = 2)$. Once students have mastered finding and plotting coordinates using equations, the shortcut (6, 2) can be introduced.	Provide worksheet practice on plotting coordinates on a graph using the equations. One students have mastered that skill, introduce the shortcut during a guided practice exercise.

Error Pattern	*Diagnosis*	*Remediation Procedures*	*Remediation Examples*

Find the function for this table:

x	Function	Answer y
1		2
2		4

Student answer: Function is $x + 1$.

Student does not test the function with both pairs of values.	Present the structured worksheet from **Format 18.1**. Focus on the procedure for determining if the proposed function rule will work with all pairs of values.	Provide examples similar to the one on which the student made the error. Include examples in which more than one function rule may work for the first pair but not for all pairs.

$$\begin{array}{r} -16 \\ \underline{-15} \\ \mathbf{31} \end{array}$$

Student uses the wrong sign in the answer.

Reteach the less structured board presentation of the format for combining integers focusing on the fourth rule.

$$\begin{array}{r} -13 \\ \underline{-8} \end{array} \qquad \begin{array}{r} -9 \\ \underline{+20} \end{array}$$

$$\begin{array}{r} -5 \\ \underline{+7} \end{array} \qquad \begin{array}{r} -7 \\ \underline{-8} \end{array}$$

Solve for x:

$3x + 23 = 41$

Student's work

$3x + 23 = 41$

$\ -23\ \ -23$

$3x = 23$

$x = 7.7$

This is a calculation error. The student incorrectly subtracted 23 from 41 on the right side of the equation.

Assess the student's work to determine if subtraction errors are cause by regrouping errors.

If so, reteach using the structured worksheet part of **Format 8.3: Subtraction with Renaming**.

Problems that do and do not require renaming

$$\begin{array}{r} 53 \\ \underline{-26} \end{array}$$

$$\begin{array}{r} 42 \\ \underline{-30} \end{array}$$

Show the solution process to the following comparison problem with percentages using the ratio table shown.

Deshawn is 10% taller than his little brother. If Deshawn is 5 inches taller than his little brother, how tall is Deshawn, and how tall is his brother? (*Hint:* The little brother is being compared to Deshawn, so who is equal to one or 100%?)

Student's work:

	%	Inches
Deshawn	90	
Brother	*100*	
Difference	10	5

$$\frac{10 \times (.5)}{90} \quad \frac{5}{(.5)}$$

$90 \times .5 = 45$ *inches for Deshawn.*

His brother is 5 inches shorter or
$45 - 5 = 40$ *inches.*

The student didn't set up the ratio table correctly. Deshawn is 100%.

This is a strategy error. The teacher would model setting up the ratio table with several word problems. This can be followed with a structured worksheet like the one found in **Format 18.5**.

The Lakers scored 10% fewer points than the Bulls. (*Hint:* Lakers are being compared to the Bulls, so who is 100%?) If the Lakers scored 12 fewer points than the Bulls, how many points did the Lakers and the Bulls score?

APPLY WHAT YOU LEARNED

 Click on the √ to answer the questions online.

1. Describe how a teacher might sequence the skills listed in the four topics in this chapter.

2. How can teachers promote conceptual understanding for solving one-variable algebraic equations?

3. Describe the procedure for teaching students to complete the following function table.

x	Function	Answer y
0		0
1		4
2		8
3		
4		
5		

4. Construct a set of problems for use in **Format 18.2** for combining integers.

5. Construct a set of examples and nonexamples for students to use in determining if a number is a prime number.

6. Write a classification problem with fractions to be solved with a ratio table and show the solution.

7. Show the solution process to the following comparison problem with percentages using the ratio table shown.

> Sondra's new phone costs 20% more than Ruth's new phone. If Sondra's phone costs $200.00 more than Ruth's phone, how much is Sondra's phone, and how much is Ruth's? (*Hint:* Sondra is being compared to Ruth, so who is equal to one or 100%?)

Difference	20%	$200.00
Sondra's phone		
Ruth's phone		

8. Outline the steps for remediation in teaching students to solve the following problem:
   $4t = 16$
   $t = 12$

Format 18.1
USING AND PLOTTING A FUNCTION

TEACHER	STUDENTS

Part A: Structured Board Presentation

x	Function	Answer y
1		2
4		8
3		
0		
5		

1. You have made points on the coordinate system by using a table that shows the *x* values and the *y* values. When you connect the points, you get a straight line. The reason you get a straight line is that all of the points follow the same function rule. If you're following the same rule about adding, subtracting, multiplying, or dividing the *x* value to get the *y* value, you will get a straight line on the coordinate system. Let's find the function for this table, complete the table, plot the values, and see if we get a straight line.

   The first *x* value is 1. What is the *y* value? | 2

2. What would it take to get from 1 to 2? What would you add? | Add 1

3. Let's see if adding 1 will solve everything in this table. What is the second *x* value? | 4

   What is the *y* value? | 8

   Can you add 1 to the *x* value of 4 to get the *y* value? | No

   If adding didn't work, let's try multiplication. 4 × what number = 8? | 2

   Go back and check the first values. The *x* value is 1. Can you multiply it by 2 to get the *y* value of 2? | Yes

4. So how do we know that the function is *x* × 2? | Because the first *x* value of 1 × 2 = the first *y* value of 2 and the second *x* value of 4 × 2 = the second *y* value of 8

5. So we fill in the function part of this table as *x* × 2. What is the third *x* value? | 3

   So what is 3 × 2? | 6

   And where do we write that 6? | As the *y* value

6. What is the fourth *x* value? | 0

   So what is 0 × 2? | 0

   So what is the fourth *y* value? | 0

continued

Format 18.1 *(continued)*
USING AND PLOTTING A FUNCTION

TEACHER	STUDENTS
7. Figure out the fifth *y* value and fill it in. What did you fill in for the fifth *y* value?	10
8. Now we need to plot these points. The first two points are already plotted. What is the *x* value for the third point?	3
So the *x* value moves to the right how many spaces?	3 spaces
The *y* value moves up how many spaces?	6 spaces
Now plot that point and the two other points.	
9. Connect those dots with a ruler. Raise your hand if you got a straight line.	

Part B: Structured Worksheet

Function	Answer
x	*y*
1	4
4	7
3	
0	
5	

TEACHER	STUDENTS
1. Let's find the function for this table, complete the table, plot the values, and see if we get a straight line.	
The first *x* value is 1. What is the *y* value?	4
2. What would you add to get from 1 to 4?	3
3. Look at the second pair of values. Can you add 3 to the second *x* value and get the *y* value?	Yes
What is the number sentence for those values?	$4 + 3 = 7$
4. So what is the function?	$x + 3$
5. Find the rest of the values. Raise your hand when you're done.	
What is the fourth pair of values?	$x = 0, y = 3$
What is the fifth pair of values?	$x = 5, y = 8$
6. Plot those values then connect those dots with a ruler. Raise your hand if you got a straight line.	
7. *(Do steps 1–7 using different functions.)*	

Format 18.2
COMBINING INTEGERS

TEACHER	STUDENTS
Part A: Structured Board Presentation	
1. You've worked with positive and negative numbers on the number line. Here are some rules you can use to solve problems without using a number line. *(Write the following on a board or on a poster.)*	
1. If the signs of the numbers are the same, you add.	
2. If the signs of the numbers are different, you subtract.	
3. When you subtract, you start with the number that is farther from zero on the number line and subtract the other number.	
4. The sign in the answer is always the sign of the number that is farther from zero.	
2. *(Write this problem on the board.)* $$\begin{array}{r} -9 \\ +20 \\ \hline \end{array}$$	
3. Are the signs the same or different?	Different
4. If the signs are different, do we add or subtract?	Subtract
5. We start with the number that is farther from zero. Which number is farther from zero, 9 or 20?	20
6. Start with 20 and subtract 9. What is the answer?	11
7. The last rule tells us how to determine the correct sign. Read the rule.	The sign in the answer is always the sign of the number that is farther from zero.
8. So is the answer positive 11 or negative 11? How do you know?	Positive 11 Because 20 is the number farther from zero and it is positive
9. *(Write this problem on the board.)* $$\begin{array}{r} -7 \\ -9 \\ \hline \end{array}$$	
10. Are the signs the same or different?	The same
11. Do we add or subtract?	Add
12. Add 7 and 9. What is the answer?	16
13. The last rule tells us how to determine the correct sign. Read the rule.	The sign in the answer is always the number that is farther sign of the from zero.
14. So is the answer positive 16 or negative 16?	Negative 16
15. How do you know?	Because 9 is the number farther from zero and it is negative

continued

Format 18.2 *(continued)*
COMBINING INTEGERS

TEACHER	STUDENTS
16. *(Write this problem on the board.)* 12 −7	
17. Are the signs the same or different?	Different
18. If the signs are different, do we add or subtract?	Subtract
19. We start with the number that is farther from zero. Which number is farther from zero, 12 or 7?	12
20. Start with 12 and subtract 7. What's the answer?	5
21. The last rule tells us what?	The sign in the answer is always the sign of the number that is farther from zero.
22. So is the answer positive 5 or negative 5?	Positive 5
23. How do you know?	Because 12 is the number farther from zero and it is positive

Part B: Less Structured Board Presentation

1. *(Write the following abbreviations for the four rules.)* Same: Add Different: Subtract Start with number farther from zero Use sign of number farther from zero	
2. Here is a short reminder of the four rules for combining positive and negative numbers. Who can tell me the first rule?	If the signs of the same, you add.
3. Who can tell me the second rule?	If the signs of the numbers shown are different, you subtract.
4. Who can tell me the third rule?	When you subtract, you start with the number that is farther from zero on the number line and subtract the other number.
5. And who can tell me the last rule?	The sign in the answer is always the sign of the number that is farther from zero.
6. *(Write this problem on the board.)* −5 +7	

TEACHER	STUDENTS
7. Let's just talk about what we are going to do. Do we add or subtract?	Subtract
8. How do you know?	Because the signs are different
9. What number do we start with?	7
10. How do you know?	Because it is farther from zero
11. Will the answer be positive or negative?	Positive
12. How do you know?	Because the 7 is positive
13. Do the problem now. *(Pause.)* What's the answer?	2
14. *(Write this problem on the board.)* $$\begin{array}{r} -3 \\ \underline{-9} \end{array}$$	
15. Do we add or subtract?	Add
16. How do you know?	Because the signs are the same
17. Will the answer be positive or negative?	Negative
18. How do you know?	Because the 9 is negative
19. Work the problem. *(Pause.)* What's the answer.	Negative 12
20. *(Write this problem on the board.)* $$\begin{array}{r} -13 \\ \underline{+7} \end{array}$$	
21. Do we add or subtract?	Subtract
22. How do you know?	Because the signs are different
23. What number do we start with?	13
24. How do you know?	Because it is farther from zero
25. Will the answer be positive or negative?	Negative
26. How do you know?	Because the 13 is negative
27. Work the problem. What's the answer?	Negative 6

Part C: Structured Worksheet

1. *(Students have worksheets with problems such as these.)*

   a. $\begin{array}{r} -7 \\ \underline{-8} \end{array}$ b. $\begin{array}{r} +4 \\ \underline{-2} \end{array}$ c. $\begin{array}{r} +9 \\ \underline{-13} \end{array}$ d. $\begin{array}{r} -3 \\ \underline{+6} \end{array}$

TEACHER	STUDENTS
2. Before you do these problems, let's review the rules. What do you do if the signs are the same?	Add
3. And if you add, what sign will the answer be?	The sign of the number farther from zero

continued

Format 18.2 *(continued)*
COMBINING INTEGERS

TEACHER	STUDENTS
4. When do we subtract?	When the signs of the numbers are different
5. When we subtract, which number do we start with?	With the number that is farther from zero
6. What sign will the answer be?	The sign of the number that is farther from zero
7. Work the problems.	

Format 18.3
SOLVING ONE-STEP PROBLEMS WITH VARIABLES—ADDITION AND SUBTRACTION

TEACHER	STUDENTS
Part A: Structured Board Presentation	
1. *(Write the following equation on the board.)* $$p - 4 = 6$$	
2. You're going to learn how to find the value of a letter in an equation. First, you need to know that everything to the left of the equal sign is called the "left side." *(Point to the left side of the equation.)* What is everything to the left of the equal sign called?	The left side
Everything to the right of the equal sign is called the "right side." *(Point to the right side of the equation.)* What is everything to the right of the equal sign called?	The right side
3. We want to find the value for the letter p in this equation. To do that, we need to get p all by itself on one side of the equation. We're going to get p all by itself by adding the inverse of negative 4. What is the inverse of negative 4?	4
Negative 4 plus 4 equals 0, leaving p all by itself. *(Add to the equation so it looks like the following:)* $$p - 4 = 6$$ $$\quad + 4$$	
4. Here's an important rule about changing an equation: Whatever you do to one side of an equation, you must do to the other. Say the rule.	Whatever you do to one side of an equation, you must do to the other.
We added 4 to the left side of the equation. That means we also must add 4 to the right side of the equation. What do we need to do to the right side of the equation?	Add 4

TEACHER	STUDENTS
Yes, we added 4 to the left side of the equation, so we also need to add 4 to the right side of the equation. *(Add to the equation so it looks like the following:)* $p - 4 = 6 + 4$ $\quad\ + 4$	
5. Now that we have added 4 to both sides of the equation, we can work the equation. What is -4 plus 4? Yes, so we can cross out -4 and $+4$ on the left side of the equation. *(Add to the equation so it looks like the following:)* $p - \cancel{4} = 6 + 4$ $\quad\ \cancel{+\ 4}$	Zero
6. Now we work the right side of the equation. What is $6 + 4$? Right! Now our equation looks like this: *(Write the following next to the original equation on the board.)* $p = 10$	Ten
7. We changed both sides of the equation to find out that $p = 10$. What does p equal?	10
8. We can check our work by rewriting the equation with 10 in the place of p. *(Write the following on the board.)* $10 - 4 = 6$ Does $10 - 4 = 6$? Yes, it does. So we know that $p = 10$ because $10 - 4 = 6$.	Yes
9. *(Repeat steps 1–8 with additional examples.)*	
Part B: Less Structured Board Presentation	
1. *(Write problems like the following on the board. Give students paper and pencils for solving the equations.)* a. $r + 2 = 18$ b. $23 + a = 30$ c. $15 = e - 5$ d. $12 - p = 7$ e. $45 = u + 25$	
2. Read problem a. We want to find the value for r. To do that, you need to get r by itself by adding the inverse. What do you need to do to get r by itself? What's the inverse of 2? Do that. Add -2 to the side of the equation with r. *(Monitor students' work.)*	$r + 2 = 18$ Add the inverse -2
3. Now that you have added -2 to the left side of the equation, what must you do to the right side of the equation? Yes, whatever you do to one side of an equation you must do to another. Add -2 to the right side of the equation. *(Monitor students' work.)*	Add -2

continued

Format 18.3 *(continued)*
SOLVING ONE-STEP PROBLEMS WITH VARIABLES—ADDITION AND SUBTRACTION

TEACHER	STUDENTS
4. Now you can finish working the equation to find the value of *r*. Do that now. *(Monitor students as they solve for r.)*	
5. What does *r* equal?	*r* equals 16
6. You can check your work by rewriting the equation with 16 in the place of *r*. Do that now. *(Monitor students.)*	
You put 16 in the place of *r*. Read the new equation.	$16 + 2 = 18$
Does that make sense?	Yes
Yes, it does. So your answer is correct.	
7. *(Repeat steps 2–6 with the remaining problems. Instruct the students to follow the same steps to find the value of the letter regardless of which side the letter is on.)*	
Part C: Independent Practice	
1. *(Write problems like the following on the board. Give students paper and pencils for solving the equations.)*	
a. $m + 17 = 20$	
b. $50 - d = 25$	
c. $80 = 90 - z$	
d. $13 = j + 5$	
e. $9 + k = 9$	
2. Find the value of the variable in each of the equations. Remember to check your work by rewriting the equation with the value of the variable. *(Monitor students as they work.)*	

Format 18.4
SOLVING ONE-STEP PROBLEMS WITH VARIABLES—MULTIPLICATION AND DIVISION

TEACHER	STUDENTS
Part A: Preskill: Finding the Reciprocal	
1. You've learned how to find the value of a variable in addition and subtraction problems. Now you're going to learn how to find the value of a variable in multiplication and division problems. To do that, you need to know how to find the reciprocal of a number. The reciprocal of any number is the number you multiply by to equal one.	
2. The reciprocal of a whole number is 1 over that number. Let's say I wanted to find the reciprocal of 15. *(Write 15 on the board.)* To find the reciprocal of 15, I write a fraction with 1 as the numerator and 15 as the denominator. *(Write $\frac{1}{15}$ on the board.)* The reciprocal of 15 is $\frac{1}{15}$. What is the reciprocal of 15?	$\frac{1}{15}$

TEACHER	STUDENTS

3. Let's see if that works. *(Write* $15 \times \dfrac{1}{15} =$ *.)* We need to convert the whole number to a fraction. *(Write* $\dfrac{15}{1} \times \dfrac{1}{15} =$ *.)* We multiply across when multiplying fractions. *(Point to the numerators.)* What is 15×1?

(Write 15 in the place for the numerator after $\dfrac{15}{1} \times \dfrac{1}{15} =$ *. Point to the denominators.)* What is 1×15?

(Write 15 in the place for the denominator after $\dfrac{15}{1} \times \dfrac{1}{15} =$ *.)* $\dfrac{15}{1} \times \dfrac{1}{15}$ equals $\dfrac{15}{15}$. What does $\dfrac{15}{15}$ equal?

(Repeat steps 2 and 3 with 3, 4, 29, and 100.)

4. To get the reciprocal of a fraction, turn the fraction upside down. *(Write* $\dfrac{4}{5}$ *on the board.)* I need to find the reciprocal of $\dfrac{4}{5}$. I'm going to turn the fraction upside down to get the reciprocal of $\dfrac{4}{5}$. *(Write* $\dfrac{5}{4}$ *on the board.)* The reciprocal of $\dfrac{4}{5}$ is $\dfrac{5}{4}$. What is the reciprocal of $\dfrac{4}{5}$?

5. Let's see if that works. *(Write* $\dfrac{4}{5} \times \dfrac{5}{4} =$ *. Point to the numerators.)* What is 4×5?

(Write 20 in the place for the numerator. Point to the denominators.) What is 5×4?

(Write 20 in the place for the denominator.) $\dfrac{4}{5} \times \dfrac{5}{4} = \dfrac{20}{20}$. What does $\dfrac{20}{20}$ equal?

(Repeat steps 4 and 5 with $\dfrac{2}{3}, \dfrac{7}{5}, \dfrac{1}{2},$ *and* $\dfrac{7}{8}$.*)*

Part B: Structured Board Presentation

1. *(Write the following equation on the board.)*

$5e = 15$

2. We want to find the value for the variable *e* in this equation. To do that, we need to get *e* all by itself on one side of the equation. We're going to get *e* all by itself by multiplying by the reciprocal of 5, so that we end up with 1e. What is the reciprocal of 5?

5 multiplied by $\dfrac{1}{5}$ equals 1, leaving 1e or e. *(Add to the equation so it looks like the following:)*

$\left(\dfrac{1}{5}\right)5e = 15$

Students column: 15 · 15 · One · $\dfrac{5}{4}$ · 20 · 20 · One · $\dfrac{1}{5}$

continued

Format 18.4 *(continued)*

SOLVING ONE-STEP PROBLEMS WITH VARIABLES—MULTIPLICATION AND DIVISION

TEACHER	STUDENTS
3. Remember the rule about changing an equation: Whatever you do to one side of an equation, you must do to the other. Say the rule.	Whatever you do to one side of an equation, you must do to the other.
We multiplied the left side of the equation by $\frac{1}{5}$. That means we must multiply the right side of the equation by $\frac{1}{5}$. What do we need to do to the right side of the equation?	Multiply by $\frac{1}{5}$
Yes, we multiplied the left side of the equation by $\frac{1}{5}$, so we need to multiply the right side of the equation by $\frac{1}{5}$. *(Add to the equation so it looks like the following:)* $$\left(\frac{1}{5}\right)5e = 15\left(\frac{1}{5}\right)$$	
4. Now that we have multiplied both sides of the equation by $\frac{1}{5}$, we can work the equation. What is $\frac{1}{5}$ multiplied by 5?	1
Yes, so we can cross out $\frac{1}{5}$ and 5 on the left side of the equation. *(Add to the equation so it looks like the following:)* $$\left(\frac{1}{\cancel{5}}\right)\cancel{5}e = 15\left(\frac{1}{5}\right)$$	
5. Now we work the right side of the equation. What is 15 times $\frac{1}{5}$? *(Pause while students work.)*	3
Right! Now our equation looks like this: *(Write the following next to the original equation on the board.)* $$e = 3$$	
6. We changed both sides of the equation to find out that $e = 3$. What does e equal?	3
7. We can check our work by rewriting the equation with 3 in the place of e. *(Write the following on the board.)* $$5(3) = 15$$ Does $5 \times 3 = 15$?	Yes
Yes, it does. So we know that $e = 3$ because $5 \times 3 = 15$.	
8. Let's try another one. *(Write the following equation on the board.)* $$\frac{b}{2} = 9$$	

TEACHER	STUDENTS
9. We want to find the value for the variable b in this equation. To do that, we need to get b all by itself on one side of the equation. You need to know that $\frac{b}{2}$ is the same as $\left(\frac{1}{2}\right)b$. *(Erase $\frac{b}{2}$ and write $\left(\frac{1}{2}\right)b$ in its place.)* We're going to get b all by itself by multiplying by the reciprocal of $\frac{1}{2}$, so that we end up with 1b. What is the reciprocal of $\frac{1}{2}$? $\frac{1}{2}$ multiplied by $\frac{2}{1}$ equals 1, leaving 1b or b. *(Add to the equation so it looks like the following:)* $\left(\frac{2}{1}\right)\left(\frac{1}{2}\right)b = 9$	$\frac{2}{1}$
10. Remember the rule about changing an equation: Whatever you do to one side of an equation, you must do to the other. We multiplied the left side of the equation by $\frac{2}{1}$. What must we do to the right side of the equation? Yes, we multiplied the left side of the equation by $\frac{2}{1}$, so we need to multiply the right side of the equation by $\frac{2}{1}$. *(Add to the equation so it looks like the following:)* $\left(\frac{2}{1}\right)\left(\frac{1}{2}\right)b = 9\left(\frac{2}{1}\right)$	Multiply by $\frac{2}{1}$
11. Now that we have multiplied both sides of the equation by $\frac{2}{1}$, we can work the equation. What is $\frac{2}{1}$ multiplied by $\frac{1}{2}$? Yes, so we can cross out $\frac{2}{1}$ and $\frac{1}{2}$ on the left side of the equation. *(Add to the equation so it looks like the following:)* $\left(\frac{\cancel{2}}{\cancel{1}}\right)\left(\frac{\cancel{1}}{\cancel{2}}\right)b = 9\left(\frac{2}{1}\right)$	1
12. Now we work the right side of the equation. What is 9 times $\frac{2}{1}$? *(Pause while students work.)* Now our equation looks like this: *(Write the following next to the original equation on the board.)* $b = 18$	18
13. We changed both sides of the equation to find out that $b = 18$. What does b equal?	18

continued

Format 18.4 *(continued)*
SOLVING ONE-STEP PROBLEMS WITH VARIABLES—MULTIPLICATION AND DIVISION

TEACHER	STUDENTS
14. We can check our work by rewriting the equation with 18 in the place of *b*. *(Write the following on the board.)*	
$$\frac{18}{2} = 9$$	
Does 18 divided by 2 equal 9?	Yes
Yes, it does. So we know that *b* = 18 because 18 divided by 2 equals 9.	
15. *(Repeat with the following examples.)* $14 = 2s$, $5f = 25$, $4 = \dfrac{t}{4}$	
Part C: Less Structured Board Presentation	
1. *(Write problems like the following on the board. Give students paper and pencils for solving the equations.)*	
a. $5y = 30$	
b. $18 = 6e$	
c. $\dfrac{21}{x} = 7$	
d. $45 = 5n$	
2. Read problem a.	$5y = 30$
3. We want to find the value for *y*. What do you need to do to get *y* by itself?	Multiply by the reciprocal of 5
What's the reciprocal of 5?	$\dfrac{1}{5}$
After you multiply the side of the equation with *y* by $\dfrac{1}{5}$, what will you do?	Multiply the other side of the equation by $\dfrac{1}{5}$
Yes, whatever you do to one side of an equation you must do to the other.	
4. Work the equation now to find the value of *y*. *(Monitor students as they solve for x.)*	
5. What does *y* equal?	y equals 6
6. You can check your work by rewriting the equation with 6 in the place of *y*. Do that now. *(Monitor students.)*	
You put 6 in the place of *y*. Read the new equation.	5 times 6 equals 30
Does that make sense?	Yes
Yes, it does. So your answer is correct.	
7. *(Repeat steps 2–6 with the remaining problems. Instruct the students to follow the same steps to find the value of the variable regardless of which side the variable is on.)*	

TEACHER	STUDENTS
Part D: Independent Practice	
1. *(Write problems like the following on the board. Give students paper and pencils for solving the equations.)*	
a. $2t = 20$	
b. $\dfrac{100}{x} = 25$	
c. $80 = 20f$	
d. $13 = \dfrac{r}{2}$	
e. $9k = 9$	
2. Find the value of the variable in each of the equations. Remember to check your work by rewriting the equation with the value of the variable. *(Monitor students as they work.)*	

Format 18.5
RATIO TABLES USING FRACTIONS FOR CLASSES   (See Video in Part B)

TEACHER	STUDENTS
Part A: Structured Board Presentation: Figuring Out Fraction Number Families	
1. *(Put this problem on the board.)*	
Three-fifths of the bottles of glue in the store are white glue and the rest are super glue. If there are 26 bottles of super glue, how many bottles of white glue are in the store? How many total bottles of glue are in the store?	
Read the problem with students.	
2. This is a classification word problem. What words tell us about the classes in this problem?	Glue, white glue, super glue
3. What is the first class named in the problem? Underline that class.	Glue
4. What is the next class named in the problem? Underline that class.	White glue
5. What is the next class named in the problem? Underline that class.	Super glue
(Write this on board.) ____ + ____ = ____	
6. Write a number sentence like the one on the board. *(Pause.)*	
What is the big class?	Glue
Write that under the last blank. *(Pause.)*	
7. So what are the two smaller classes?	White glue and super glue
8. Where do we write those?	Under the first two blanks
9. Do that now. *(Pause.)*	
10. Let's look at the classes one at a time. Let's start with white glue. What fraction of the bottles of glue are white glue?	$\dfrac{3}{5}$

continued

Format 18.5 *(continued)*
RATIO TABLES USING FRACTIONS FOR CLASSES

TEACHER	STUDENTS
11. Where do we write $\frac{3}{5}$?	Over the blank labeled white glue.
12. Do that now. Does the problem tell us what fraction of the bottles of glue is super glue?	No
13. What do we write over super glue?	A box
14. Do that now. *(Pause.)* What do we write over the big class, glue?	$\frac{5}{5}$
15. Yes, $\frac{5}{5}$. The problem doesn't say $\frac{5}{5}$. So who remembers how we know that the big class is equal to $\frac{5}{5}$?	Because the big class is all of the glue, so it is equal to one whole, or $\frac{5}{5}$
16. The big number is given, so do we add or subtract?	Subtract
17. So what is the answer?	$\frac{2}{5}$

⏵

Part B: Structured Board Presentation: Ratio Tables

1. Now we are ready to draw and use a ratio table to solve problems. *(Draw this table on the board and ask students to copy it.)*

	Fraction family	Ratio	Quantity
White glue			
Super glue			
Glue			

TEACHER	STUDENTS
2. We have just figured out the fraction number family. What fraction of the bottles is white glue?	$\frac{3}{5}$
3. Write $\frac{3}{5}$ in the fraction family column next to white glue.	
4. What fraction is super glue?	$\frac{2}{5}$
5. Write that next to super glue. *(Pause.)*	
6. What fraction do we write for the big class of glue?	$\frac{5}{5}$
7. Write $\frac{5}{5}$ in the fraction family column. *(Pause.)*	
8. Now we are ready to complete the ratio column. We write the numerators of our fractions in the ratio column.	
What is the fraction for white glue?	$\frac{3}{5}$
What is the numerator?	3
Write the numerator in the ratio column. *(Pause.)*	

TEACHER	STUDENTS

9. **What is the fraction for super glue?** — $\frac{2}{5}$

 What is the numerator? — 2

 Write the numerator in the ratio column. *(Pause.)*

10. **What is the fraction for glue?** — $\frac{5}{5}$

 What is the numerator? — 5

 Write the numerator in the ratio column. *(Pause.)*

 (The completed table should look like the one below.)

	Fraction family	Ratio	Quantity
White glue	3/5	3	
Super glue	2/5	2	
Glue	5/5	5	

11. Now we are ready to solve the problem. We are going to do that by using ratio equations. We begin by writing into the table the quantity we know. Read the problem. *(Pause.)* **What quantity of glue bottles is stated in the problem?** — 26 bottles of super glue

 Write that quantity in the column across from super glue. *(Pause.)* Since we know the quantity of super glue, we call super glue the *known quantity.*

12. **What does the problem ask us to find out first?** — How many bottles of white glue were in the store

13. To find the answer, we are going to make a ratio equation of our known quantity, super glue, to our unknown quantity, white glue. First, we'll set up the ratio equation with the appropriate labels, then we'll fill in the known quantities

 Here's how we write the ratio equation. We start by labeling the numerator and denominator in the first fraction like this. *(Write the following equation on the board.)*

 $\frac{\text{super glue}}{\text{white glue}}$

 Then we write an equal sign and write the labels for the fraction on the other side.

 (Write the following on the board.)

 $\frac{\text{super glue}}{\text{white glue}} = \frac{\text{super glue}}{\text{white glue}}$

 Now we fill in the correct ratio for the first fraction. Look at the ratio column. What is the ratio of super glue to white glue? — $\frac{2}{3}$

 Complete the ratio for the first fraction.

 (Write the following on the board.)

 $\frac{\textbf{2}\ \text{super glue}}{\textbf{3}\ \text{white glue}} = \frac{\text{super glue}}{\text{white glue}}$

continued

Format 18.5 *(continued)*
RATIO TABLES USING FRACTIONS FOR CLASSES

TEACHER	STUDENTS
Now we fill in the known quantity for the second fraction. Look at the quantity column and find the known quantity. *(Pause.)* What is the known quantity?	26 bottles of super glue
Write the known quantity in the appropriate fraction on the other side of the equation. *(Write the quantity on the board.)* $$\frac{2 \text{ super glue}}{3 \text{ white glue}} = \frac{26 \text{ super glue}}{\text{white glue}}$$	
14. Now we're ready to solve for the quantity of white glue. Write a box by the label for white glue in the equation. $$\frac{2 \text{ super glue}}{3 \text{ white glue}} = \frac{26 \text{ super glue}}{\square \text{ white glue}}$$ We solve this by using equivalent fractions.	
We are looking for a fraction equal to one. What number times two equals 26?	13
So we write in 13 over 13. $$\frac{2 \text{ super glue}}{3 \text{ white glue}} \times \left(\frac{13}{13}\right) = \frac{26 \text{ super glue}}{\square \text{ white glue}}$$ Here's what you should have. What do we multiply to find out how many bottles of white glue were in the store?	3×13
What's the answer?	39 bottles of white glue
15. Now we can fill in the quantity for white glue in the table. Where are we going to write 39?	In the quantity column next to white glue
16. We now have 26 bottles for super glue and 39 bottles for white glue. How do we find out how many bottles of glue in all?	Add 26 and 39
What is your answer?	65 bottles of glue
Write that in your table and you're done.	

APPENDIX A

Direct Instruction Mathematics and Common Core State Standards

The table that follows presents the Common Core State Standards (CCSS) in math for grades K–5 and the related formats and/or teaching procedures that can be found in this text. Within each grade level, the standards are organized by domains. The domains are boldfaced and larger than the surrounding text. Groups of individual standards, called clusters, are presented under each domain. Multiple clusters of individual standards may be included within each domain. Formats and teaching procedures are listed only for the individual standards within each cluster. Because of the hierarchical organization of the standards, the formats and teaching procedures assigned to individual standards also apply to the broader cluster and domain headings.

This text was written primarily to provide direction in creating or modifying existing math curriculum to best meet the needs of students and not as a stand-alone math program. As a result, many of the formats can be directly connected to an individual standard but not all. Some of the individual standards are addressed in this text with teaching procedures described in a chapter. When possible, specific formats are listed that meet each standard. Where a specific format has not been written to address an individual standard, the chapter(s) that address the standard are included. Some individual standards require blending content and teaching procedures from multiple formats and chapters. The appropriate chapters and formats are listed when this is the case.

Grade	Standard	Format
K	**Counting and Cardinality**	**K.CC**
	A. Know number names and the count sequence.	
	1. Count to 100 by ones and by tens.	4.1, 4.4, 4.5
	2. Count forward beginning from a given number within the known sequence (instead of having to begin at 1).	4.4
	3. Write numbers from 0 to 20. Represent a number of objects with a written numeral 0–20 (with 0 representing a count of no objects).	5.1, 5.4, 5.6, 5.7
	B. Count to tell the number of objects.	
	4. Understand the relationship between numbers and quantities; connect counting to cardinality.	
	a. When counting objects, say the number names in the standard order, pairing each object with one and only one number name and each number name with one and only one object.	4.2, 4.3
	b. Understand that the last number name said tells the number of objects counted. The number of objects is the same regardless of their arrangement or the order in which they were counted.	4.3
	c. Understand that each successive number name refers to a quantity that is one larger.	4.2–4.4, 5.3, 5.4
	5. Count to answer "how many?" questions about as many as 20 things arranged in a line, a rectangular array, or a circle, or as many as 10 things in a scattered configuration; given a number from 1–20, count out that many objects.	4.2, 4.3, 5.3, 5.4

continued

Grade	Standard	Format
	C. Compare numbers.	
	6. Identify whether the numbers of objects in one group is greater than, less than, or equal to the number of objects in another group, e.g., by using matching and counting strategies.	4.2, 4.3, 5.3, 5.4
	7. Compare two numbers between 1 and 10 presented as written numerals.	4.2, 4.3, 5.3, 5.4
K	**Operations and Algebraic Thinking**	**K.OA**
	A. Understand addition as putting together and adding to, and understand subtraction as taking apart and taking from.	
	1. Represent addition and subtraction with objects, fingers, mental images, drawings, sounds (e.g. claps), acting out situations, verbal explanations, expressions, or equations.	5.2, 5.13, 6.1, 6.2, 7.2, 11.1
	2. Solve addition and subtraction word problems, and add and subtract within 10, e.g., by using objects or drawings to represent the problem.	6.1, 6.2, 6.3, 6.4, 7.1–7.4, 11.1
	3. Decompose numbers less than or equal to 10 into pairs in more than one way, e.g., by using objects or drawings, and record each decomposition by a drawing or equation (e.g., 5 = 2 + 3 and 5 = 4 + 1).	6.1–6.4, 7.1–7.4
	4. For any number from 1 to 9, find the number that makes 10 when added to the given number, e.g., by using objects or drawings, and record the answer with a drawing or equation.	6.1–6.4, 7.1–7.4
	5. Fluently add and subtract within 5.	6.1–6.4, 7.1–7.4
K	**Number and Operations in Base Ten**	**K.NBT**
	A. Work with numbers 11–19 to gain foundations for place value.	
	1. Compose and decompose numbers from 11 to 19 into ten ones and some further ones, e.g., by using objects or drawings, and record each composition or decomposition by a drawing or equation (e.g., 18 = 10 + 8); understand that these numbers are composed of ten ones and one, two, three, four, five, six, seven, eight, or nine ones.	5.3, 5.6
K	**Measurement and Data**	**K.MD**
	A. Describe and compare measurable attributes.	
	1. Describe measurable attributes of objects, such as length or weight. Describe several measurable attributes of a single object.	Chapter 12
	2. Directly compare two objects with a measurable attribute in common, to see which object has "more of"/"less of" the attribute, and describe the difference. For example, *directly compare the heights of two children and describe one child as taller/shorter.*	Chapter 12
	B. Classify objects and count the number of objects in each category.	
	3. Classify objects into given categories; count the number of objects in each category and sort the categories by count.	16.1
K	**Geometry**	**K.G**
	A. Identify and describe shapes (squares, circles, triangles, rectangles, hexagons, cubes, cones, cylinders, and spheres).	
	1. Describe objects in the environment using names of shapes, and describe the relative positions of these objects using terms such as *above, below, beside, in front of, behind,* and *next to.*	Chapters 1, 3, and 17
	2. Correctly name shapes regardless of their orientations or overall size.	17.1
	3. Identify shapes as two-dimensional (lying in a plane, "flat") or three-dimensional ("solid").	Chapter 17

B. Analyze, compare, create, and compose shapes.

    4. Analyze and compare two- and three-dimensional shapes, in different sizes and orientations, using informal language to describe their similarities, differences, parts (e.g., number of sides and vertices/"corners") and other attributes (e.g., having sides of equal length). — Chapter 17

    5. Model shapes in the world by building shapes from components (e.g. sticks and clay balls) and drawing shapes. — Chapter 17

    6. Compose simple shapes to form larger shapes. For example, *"You can join these two triangles with fill sides touching to make a rectangle?"* — Chapter 17

1   Operations and Algebraic Thinking — 1.OA

A. Represent and solve problems involving addition and subtraction.

    1. Use addition and subtraction within 20 to solve word problems involving situations of adding to, taking from, putting together, taking apart, and comparing, with unknowns in all positions, e.g. by using objects, drawings, and equations with a symbol for the unknown number to represent the problem. — 11.1–11.5

    2. Solve word problems that call for addition of three whole numbers whose sum is less than or equal to 20, e.g. by using objects, drawings, and equations with a symbol for the unknown number to represent the problem. — 7.5, 11.1–11.5

B. Understand and apply properties of operations and the relationship between addition and subtraction.

    3. Apply properties of operations as strategies to add and subtract. Examples: If $8 + 3 = 11$ is known, then $3 + 8 = 11$ is also known. (Commutative property of addition.) To add $2 + 6 + 4$, the second two numbers can be added to make a ten, so $2 + 6 + 4 = 2 + 10 = 12$ (Associative property of addition.) — 6.3, 6.4, 7.5, 7.7

    4. Understand subtraction as an unknown-addend problem. For example, subtract $10 - 8$ by finding the number that makes 10 when added to 8. — 6.4, 7.3

C. Add and subtract within 20.

    5. Relate counting to addition and subtraction (e.g., by counting on 2 to add 2). — 4.4, 7.2–7.4, 8.1

    6. Add and subtract within 20, demonstrating fluency for addition and subtraction within 10. Use strategies such as counting on; making ten (e.g., $8 + 6 = 8 + 2 + 4 = 10 + 4 = 14$); decomposing a number leading to a ten (e.g., $13 - 4 = 13 - 3 - 1 = 10 - 1 = 9$); using the relationship between addition and subtraction (e.g., knowing that $8 + 4 = 12$, one knows $12 - 8 = 4$); and creating equivalent but easier or known sums (e.g., adding $6 + 7$ by creating equivalent $6 + 6 + 1 = 12 + 1 = 13$). — 5.2, 6.1–6.4, 7.1–7.5, 7.7, 8.1

D. Work with addition and subtraction equations.

    7. Understand the meaning of the equal sign, and determine if equations are involving addition and subtraction are true or false. For example, which of the following equations are true and which are false? $6 = 6, 7 = 8 - 1, 5 + 2 = 2 + 5, 4 + 1 = 5 + 2$ — 6.2–6.4, 7.1

    8. Determine the unknown whole number in an addition or subtraction equation relating three whole numbers. For example, determine the unknown number that makes the equation true in each of the equations $8 + ? = 11, 5 = \square - 3, 6 + 6 = \square$. — 6.2–6.4, 7.2–7.4

1   Number and Operations in Base Ten — 1.NBT

A. Extend the counting sequence.

    1. Count to 120, starting at any number less than 120. In this range, read and write numerals and represent a number of objects with a written numeral. — 4.4, 5.5–5.10

continued

Grade	Standard	Format
	B. Understand place value.	
	2. Understand that the two digits of a two-digit number represent amounts of tens and ones. Understand the following as special cases:	
	a. 10 can be thought of as a bundle of ten ones—called a "ten."	5.3–5.5
	b. The numbers from 11 to 19 are composed of a ten and one, two, three, four, five, six, seven, eight, or nine ones.	5.5–5.6
	c. The numbers 10, 20, 30, 40, 50, 60, 70, 80, 90 refer to one, two, three, four, five, six, seven, eight, or nine tens (and 0 ones).	5.7–5.8
	3. Compare two two-digit numbers based on meanings of the tens and ones digits, recording the results of comparisons with the symbols $>$, $=$, and $<$.	5.3–5.8
	C. Use place value understanding and properties of operations to add and subtract.	
	4. Add within 100, including adding a two-digit number and a one-digit number, and adding a two-digit number and a multiple of 10, using concrete models or drawings and strategies based on place value, properties of operations, and/or the relationship between addition and subtraction; relate the strategy to a written method and explain the reasoning used. Understand that in adding two-digit numbers, one adds tens and tens, ones and ones; and sometimes it is necessary to compose a ten.	5.13, 7.2–7.5, 7.6–7.8
	5. Given a two-digit number, mentally find 10 more or 10 less than the number, without having to count; explain the reasoning used.	7.6–7.8
	6. Subtract multiples of 10 in the range 10–90 from multiples of 10 in the range 10–90 (positive or zero differences), using concrete models or drawings and strategies based on place value, properties of operations, and/or the relationship between addition and subtraction; relate the strategy to a written method and explain the reasoning used.	5.7–5.8, 8.3
1	**Measurement and Data**	**1.MD**
	A. Measure lengths indirectly and by iterating length units.	
	1. Order three objects by length; compare the lengths of two objects indirectly by using a third object.	Chapter 12
	2. Express the length of an object as a whole number of length units, by laying multiple copies of a shorter object (the length unit) end to end; understand that the length measurement of an object is the number of same-size length units that span it with no gaps or overlaps. *Limit to contexts where the object being measured is spanned by a whole number of length units with no gaps or overlaps.*	Chapter 12
	B. Tell and write time.	
	3. Tell and write time in hours and half-hours using analog and digital clocks.	12.6
	C. Represent and interpret data.	
	4. Organize, represent, and interpret data with up to three categories; ask and answer questions about the total number of data points, how many in each category, and how many more or less are in one category than in another.	16.1–16.4
1	**Geometry**	**1.G**
	A. Reason with shapes and their attributes.	
	1. Distinguish between defining attributes (e.g., triangles are closed and three-sided) versus non-defining attributes (e.g., color, orientation, overall size); build and draw shapes to possess defining attributes.	17.1
	2. Compose two-dimensional shapes (rectangles, squares, trapezoids, triangles, half-circles, and quarter-circles) or three-dimensional shapes (cubes, right rectangular prisms, right circular cones, and right circular cylinders) to create a composite shape, and compose new shapes from the composite shape.	Chapter 17

3. Partition circles and rectangles into two and four equal shares, describe the shares using the words *halves*, *fourths*, and *quarters*, and use the phrases *half of*, *fourth of*, and *quarter of*. Describe the whole as two of, or four of the shares. Understand for these examples that decomposing into more equal shares creates smaller shares.	13.2, 13.3, 13.5, 13.6

2	**Operations and Algebraic Thinking**	**2.OA**
	A. Represent and solve problems involving addition and subtraction.	
	1. Use addition and subtraction within 100 to solve one- and two-step word problems involving situations of adding to, taking from, putting together, taking apart, and comparing, with unknowns in all positions, e.g., by using drawings and equations with a symbol for the unknown number to represent the problem.	5.7, 5.8, 5.13, 7.5–7.8, 11.1–11.4
	B. Add and subtract within 20.	
	2. Fluently add and subtract within 20 using mental strategies. By end of Grade 2, know from memory all sums of two one-digit numbers.	6.1–6.4, 7.2–7.5, 7.7 8.1–8.2
	C. Work with equal groups of objects to gain foundations for multiplication.	
	3. Determine whether a group of objects (up to 20) has an odd or even number of members, e.g., by pairing objects or counting them by 2s; write an equation to express an even number as a sum of two equal addends.	4.5, 9.1
	4. Use addition to find the total number of objects arranged in rectangular arrays with up to 5 rows and up to 5 columns; write an equation to express the total as a sum of equal addends.	Chapter 9

2	**Number and Operations in Base Ten**	**2.NBT**
	A. Understand place value.	
	1. Understand that the three digits of a three-digit number represent amounts of hundreds, tens, and ones; e.g., 706 equals 7 hundreds, 0 tens, and 6 ones. Understand the following as special cases:	5.5–5.10
	a. 100 can be thought of as a bundle of ten tens—called a "hundred."	5.9
	b. The numbers 100, 200, 300, 400, 500, 600, 700, 800, 900 refer to one, two, three, four, five, six, seven, eight, or nine hundreds (and 0 tens and 0 ones).	5.9–5.10
	2. Count within 1000; skip-count by 5s, 10s, and 100s.	5.9–5.10, 4.5
	3. Read and write numbers to 1000 using base-ten numerals, number names, and expanded form.	5.9–5.10, 5.12
	4. Compare two three-digit numbers based on meanings of the hundreds, tens, and ones digits, using >, =, and < symbols to record the results of comparisons.	5.5–5.10, 7.1
	B. Use place value understanding and properties of operations to add and subtract.	
	5. Fluently add and subtract within 100 using strategies based on place value, properties of operations, and/or the relationship between addition and subtraction.	6.1–6.4, 7.1–7.8, 8.1–8.5
	6. Add up to four two-digit numbers using strategies based on place value and properties of operations.	7.5–7.8
	7. Add and subtract within 1000, using concrete models or drawings and strategies based on place value, properties of operations, and/or the relationship between addition and subtraction; relate the strategy to a written method. Understand that in adding or subtracting three-digit numbers, one adds or subtracts hundreds and hundreds, tens and tens, ones and ones; and sometimes it is necessary to compose or decompose tens or hundreds.	5.9–5.13, 7.6–7.8, 8.3, 8.5

continued

Grade	Standard	Format
	8. Mentally add 10 or 100 to a given number 100–900, and mentally subtract 10 or 100 from a given number 100–900.	7.8, 5.7, 5.13
	9. Explain why addition and subtraction strategies work, using place value and the properties of operations.	5.3, 5.7, 5.10, 5.13
2	**Measurement and Data**	**2.MD**
	A. Measure and estimate lengths in standard units.	
	1. Measure the length of an object by selecting and using appropriate tools such as rulers, yardsticks, meter sticks, and measuring tapes.	Chapter 12
	2. Measure the length of an object twice, using length units of different lengths for the two measurements; describe how the two measurements relate to the size of the unit chosen.	Chapter 12
	3. Estimate lengths using units of inches, feet, centimeters, and meters.	12.1–12.2
	4. Measure to determine how much longer one object is than another, expressing the length difference in terms of a standard length unit.	12.1–12.2
	B. Relate addition and subtraction to length.	
	5. Use addition and subtraction within 100 to solve word problems involving lengths that are given in the same units, e.g., by using drawings (such as drawings of rulers) and equations with a symbol for the unknown number to represent the problem.	11.1–11.2, 11.4, 12.3–12.5
	6. Represent whole numbers as lengths from 0 on a number line diagram with equally spaced points corresponding to the numbers 0, 1, 2, . . ., and represent whole-number sums and differences within 100 on a number line diagram.	13.1
	C. Work with time and money.	
	7. Tell and write time from analog and digital clocks to the nearest five minutes, using a.m. and p.m.	12.6
	8. Solve word problems involving dollar bills, quarters, dimes, nickels, and pennies, using $ and ¢ symbols appropriately. *Example: If you have 2 dimes and 3 pennies, how many cents do you have?*	12.8–12.11
	D. Represent and interpret data.	
	9. Generate measurement data by measuring lengths of several objects to the nearest whole unit, or by making repeated measurements of the same object. Show the measurements by making a line plot, where the horizontal scale is marked off in whole-number units.	Chapters 12 and 16
	10. Draw a picture graph and a bar graph (with single-unit scale) to represent a data set with up to four categories. Solve simple put together, take-apart, and compare problems 4 using information presented in a bar graph.	16.2–16.4
2	**Geometry**	**2.G**
	A. Reason with shapes and their attributes.	
	1. Recognize and draw shapes having specified attributes, such as a given number of angles or a given number of equal faces. Identify triangles, quadrilaterals, pentagons, hexagons, and cubes.	17.1
	2. Partition a rectangle into rows and columns of same-size squares and count to find the total number of them.	17.2
	3. Partition circles and rectangles into two, three, or four equal shares, describe the shares using the words *halves, thirds, half of, a third of,* etc., and describe the whole as two halves, three thirds, four fourths. Recognize that equal shares of identical wholes need not have the same shape.	13.2–13.3, 13.6

3	**Operations and Algebraic Thinking**	**3.OA**

A. Represent and solve problems involving multiplication and division.

1. Interpret products of whole numbers, e.g., interpret 5 × 7 as the total number of objects in 5 groups of 7 objects each. *For example, describe a context in which a total number of objects can be expressed as 5 × 7.*   6.3, 9.1

2. Interpret whole-number quotients of whole numbers, e.g., interpret 56 ÷ 8 as the number of objects in each share when 56 objects are partitioned equally into 8 shares, or as a number of shares when 56 objects are partitioned into equal shares of 8 objects each. *For example, describe a context in which a number of shares or a number of groups can be expressed as 56 ÷ 8.*   6.4, 10.1

3. Use multiplication and division within 100 to solve word problems in situations involving equal groups, arrays, and measurement quantities, e.g., by using drawings and equations with a symbol for the unknown number to represent the problem.   9.1–9.3, 10.1, 11.7–8

4. Determine the unknown whole number in a multiplication or division equation relating three whole numbers. *For example, determine the unknown number that makes the equation true in each of the equations 8 × ? = 48, 5 = □ ÷ 3, 6 × 6 = ?.*   9.2, 11.7–11.8

B. Understand properties of multiplication and the relationship between multiplication and division.

5. Apply properties of operations as strategies to multiply and divide. *Examples: If 6 × 4 = 24 is known, then 4 × 6 = 24 is also known. (Commutative property of multiplication.) 3 × 5 × 2 can be found by 3 × 5 = 15, then 15 × 2 = 30, or by 5 × 2 = 10, then 3 × 10 = 30. (Associative property of multiplication.) Knowing that 8 × 5 = 40 and 8 × 2 = 16, one can find 8 × 7 as 8 × (5 + 2) = (8 × 5) + (8 × 2) = 40 + 16 = 56. (Distributive property.)*   6.3–6.4, 9.1–9.3, 10.1

6. Understand division as an unknown-factor problem. *For example, find 32 ÷ 8 by finding the number that makes 32 when multiplied by 8.*   9.2, 10.1

C. Multiply and divide within 100.

7. Fluently multiply and divide within 100, using strategies such as the relationship between multiplication and division (e.g., knowing that 8 × 5 = 40, one knows 40 ÷ 5 = 8) or properties of operations. By the end of Grade 3, know from memory all products of two one-digit numbers.   6.3–6.4, 9.1–9.3, 10.1

D. Solve problems involving the four operations, and identify and explain patterns in arithmetic.

8. Solve two-step word problems using the four operations. Represent these problems using equations with a letter standing for the unknown quantity. Assess the reasonableness of answers using mental computation and estimation strategies including rounding.   11.1–11.9

9. Identify arithmetic patterns (including patterns in the addition table or multiplication table), and explain them using properties of operations. *For example, observe that 4 times a number is always even, and explain why 4 times a number can be decomposed into two equal addends.*   4.5, 6.2

3	**Number & Operations in Base Ten**	**3.NBT**

A. Use place value understanding and properties of operations to perform multi-digit arithmetic.

1. Use place value understanding to round whole numbers to the nearest 10 or 100.   10.7–10.9

continued

Grade	Standard	Format
	2. Fluently add and subtract within 1000 using strategies and algorithms based on place value, properties of operations, and/or the relationship between addition and subtraction.	7.6, 8.3–8.5
	3. Multiply one-digit whole numbers by multiples of 10 in the range 10–90 (e.g., 9 × 80, 5 × 60) using strategies based on place value and properties of operations.	6.3, 9.3
3	**Number & Operations—Fractions**	**3.NFA**
	A. Develop understanding of fractions as numbers.	
	1. Understand a fraction $1/b$ as the quantity formed by 1 part when a whole is partitioned into b equal parts; understand a fraction a/b as the quantity formed by a parts of size $1/b$.	13.1–13.2
	2. Understand a fraction as a number on the number line; represent fractions on a number line diagram.	13.1
	a. Represent a fraction $1/b$ on a number line diagram by defining the interval from 0 to 1 as the whole and partitioning it into b equal parts. Recognize that each part has size $1/b$ and that the endpoint of the part based at 0 locates the number $1/b$ on the number line.	13.1
	b. Represent a fraction a/b on a number line diagram by marking off a lengths $1/b$ from 0. Recognize that the resulting interval has size a/b and that its endpoint locates the number a/b on the number line.	13.1
	3. Explain equivalence of fractions in special cases, and compare fractions by reasoning about their size.	13.5, 13.8
	a. Understand two fractions as equivalent (equal) if they are the same size, or the same point on a number line.	13.5, 13.7–13.8
	b. Recognize and generate simple equivalent fractions, e.g., $1/2 = 2/4$, $4/6 = 2/3$. Explain why the fractions are equivalent, e.g., by using a visual fraction model.	13.8
	c. Express whole numbers as fractions, and recognize fractions that are equivalent to whole numbers. *Examples: Express 3 in the form 3 = 3/1; recognize that 6/1 = 6; locate 4/4 and 1 at the same point of a number line diagram.*	13.7–13.8
	d. Compare two fractions with the same numerator or the same denominator by reasoning about their size. Recognize that comparisons are valid only when the two fractions refer to the same whole. Record the results of comparisons with the symbols >, =, or <, and justify the conclusions, e.g., by using a visual fraction model.	13.3–13.5
3	**Measurement and Data**	**3.MD**
	A. Solve problems involving measurement and estimation.	
	1. Tell and write time to the nearest minute and measure time intervals in minutes. Solve word problems involving addition and subtraction of time intervals in minutes, e.g., by representing the problem on a number line diagram.	11.3–11.5, 12.6–12.7
	2. Measure and estimate liquid volumes and masses of objects using standard units of grams (g), kilograms (kg), and liters (l). Add, subtract, multiply, or divide to solve one-step word problems involving masses or volumes that are given in the same units, e.g., by using drawings (such as a beaker with a measurement scale) to represent the problem.	11.3–11.5, 12.1–12.5
	B. Represent and interpret data.	
	3. Draw a scaled picture graph and a scaled bar graph to represent a data set with several categories. Solve one- and two-step "how many more" and "how many less" problems using information presented in scaled bar graphs. *For example, draw a bar graph in which each square in the bar graph might represent 5 pets.*	11.3–11.5, 16.2–16.4, 11.9

4. Generate measurement data by measuring lengths using rulers marked with halves and fourths of an inch. Show the data by making a line plot, where the horizontal scale is marked off in appropriate units—whole numbers, halves, or quarters.	Chapters 12 and 16

C. Geometric measurement: understand concepts of area and relate area to multiplication and to addition.

5. Recognize area as an attribute of plane figures and understand concepts of area measurement.	17.2
a. A square with side length 1 unit, called "a unit square," is said to have "one square unit" of area, and can be used to measure area.	17.2
b. A plane figure which can be covered without gaps or overlaps by *n* unit squares is said to have an area of *n* square units.	17.2
6. Measure areas by counting unit squares (square cm, square m, square in, square ft, and improvised units).	17.2
7. Relate area to the operations of multiplication and addition.	17.2
a. Find the area of a rectangle with whole-number side lengths by tiling it, and show that the area is the same as would be found by multiplying the side lengths.	17.2
b. Multiply side lengths to find areas of rectangles with whole number side lengths in the context of solving real world and mathematical problems, and represent whole-number products as rectangular areas in mathematical reasoning.	17.2
c. Use tiling to show in a concrete case that the area of a rectangle with whole-number side lengths a and $b + c$ is the sum of $a \times b$ and $a \times c$. Use area models to represent the distributive property in mathematical reasoning.	17.2
d. Recognize area as additive. Find areas of rectilinear figures by decomposing them into non-overlapping rectangles and adding the areas of the non-overlapping parts, applying this technique to solve real world problems.	17.2

D. Geometric measurement: recognize perimeter.

8. Solve real world and mathematical problems involving perimeters of polygons, including finding the perimeter given the side lengths, finding an unknown side length, and exhibiting rectangles with the same perimeter and different areas or with the same area and different perimeters.	Chapter 17

3	**Geometry**	**3.G**

A. Reason with shapes and their attributes.

1. Understand that shapes in different categories (e.g., rhombuses, rectangles, and others) may share attributes (e.g., having four sides), and that the shared attributes can define a larger category (e.g., quadrilaterals). Recognize rhombuses, rectangles, and squares as examples of quadrilaterals, and draw examples of quadrilaterals that do not belong to any of these subcategories.	17.1
2. Partition shapes into parts with equal areas. Express the area of each part as a unit fraction of the whole. *For example, partition a shape into 4 parts with equal area, and describe the area of each part as 1/4 of the area of the shape.*	13.1–13.2, 17.2

4	**Operations and Algebraic Thinking**	**4.OA**

A. Use the four operations with whole numbers to solve problems.

1. Interpret a multiplication equation as a comparison, e.g., interpret $35 = 5 \times 7$ as a statement that 35 is 5 times as many as 7 and 7 times as many as 5. Represent verbal statements of multiplicative comparisons as multiplication equations.	6.3; 9.1

continued

Grade	Standard	Format
	2. Multiply or divide to solve word problems involving multiplicative comparison, e.g., by using drawings and equations with a symbol for the unknown number to represent the problem, distinguishing multiplicative comparison from additive comparison.	11.4, 11.7–11.8
	3. Solve multi-step word problems posed with whole numbers and having whole-number answers using the four operations, including problems in which remainders must be interpreted. Represent these problems using equations with a letter standing for the unknown quantity. Assess the reasonableness of answers using mental computation and estimation strategies including rounding.	11.9
	B. Gain familiarity with factors and multiples.	
	4. Find all factor pairs for a whole number in the range 1–100. Recognize that a whole number is a multiple of each of its factors. Determine whether a given whole number in the range 1–100 is a multiple of a given one-digit number. Determine whether a given whole number in the range 1–100 is prime or composite.	13.9, 13.15
	C. Generate and analyze patterns.	
	5. Generate a number or shape pattern that follows a given rule. Identify apparent features of the pattern that were not explicit in the rule itself. *For example, given the rule "Add 3" and the starting number 1, generate terms in the resulting sequence and observe that the terms appear to alternate between odd and even numbers. Explain informally why the numbers will continue to alternate in this way.*	18.1
4	**Number and Operations in Base Ten**	**4.NBT**
	A. Generalize place value understanding for multi-digit whole numbers.	
	1. Recognize that in a multi-digit whole number, a digit in one place represents ten times what it represents in the place to its right. *For example, recognize that 700 ÷ 70 = 10 by applying concepts of place value and division.*	5.5–5.12
	2. Read and write multi-digit whole numbers using base-ten numerals, number names, and expanded form. Compare two multi-digit numbers based on meanings of the digits in each place, using >, =, and < symbols to record the results of comparisons.	5.5–5.13
	3. Use place value understanding to round multi-digit whole numbers to any place.	5.5–5.13, 10.7–10.9
	B. Use place value understanding and properties of operations to perform multi-digit arithmetic.	
	4. Fluently add and subtract multi-digit whole numbers using the standard algorithm.	7.6, 8.3–8.5
	5. Multiply a whole number of up to four digits by a one-digit whole number, and multiply two two-digit numbers, using strategies based on place value and the properties of operations. Illustrate and explain the calculation by using equations, rectangular arrays, and/or area models.	9.3–9.4
	6. Find whole-number quotients and remainders with up to four-digit dividends and one-digit divisors, using strategies based on place value, the properties of operations, and/or the relationship between multiplication and division. Illustrate and explain the calculation by using equations, rectangular arrays, and/or area models.	10.1–10.6

4	**Number and Operation—Fractions**	**4.NF**

A. Extend understanding of fraction equivalence and ordering.

1. Explain why a fraction a/b is equivalent to a fraction $(n \times a)/(n \times b)$ by using visual fraction models, with attention to how the number and size of the parts differ even though the two fractions themselves are the same size. Use this principle to recognize and generate equivalent fractions.   13.5–13.13

2. Compare two fractions with different numerators and different denominators, e.g., by creating common denominators or numerators, or by comparing to a benchmark fraction such as 1/2. Recognize that comparisons are valid only when the two fractions refer to the same whole. Record the results of comparisons with symbols >, =, or <, and justify the conclusions, e.g., by using a visual fraction model.   13.7–13.13

B. Build fractions from unit fractions.

3. Understand a fraction a/b with $a > 1$ as a sum of fractions $1/b$.

   a. Understand addition and subtraction of fractions as joining and separating parts referring to the same whole.   13.14

   b. Decompose a fraction into a sum of fractions with the same denominator in more than one way, recording each decomposition by an equation. Justify decompositions, e.g., by using a visual fraction model. *Examples: 3/8 = 1/8 + 1/8 + 1/8; 3/8 = 1/8 + 2/8; 2 1/8 = 1 + 1 + 1/8 = 8/8 + 8/8 + 1/8.*   13.14

   c. Add and subtract mixed numbers with like denominators, e.g., by replacing each mixed number with an equivalent fraction, and/or by using properties of operations and the relationship between addition and subtraction.   13.14

   d. Solve word problems involving addition and subtraction of fractions referring to the same whole and having like denominators, e.g., by using visual fraction models and equations to represent the problem.   13.14

4. Apply and extend previous understandings of multiplication to multiply a fraction by a whole number.

   a. Understand a fraction a/b as a multiple of $1/b$. *For example, use a visual fraction model to represent 5/4 as the product 5 × (1/4), recording the conclusion by the equation 5/4 = 5 × (1/4).*   13.18

   b. Understand a multiple of a/b as a multiple of $1/b$, and use this understanding to multiply a fraction by a whole number. *For example, use a visual fraction model to express 3 × (2/5) as 6 × (1/5), recognizing this product as 6/5. (In general, n × (a/b) = (n × a)/b.)*   13.18

   c. Solve word problems involving multiplication of a fraction by a whole number, e.g., by using visual fraction models and equations to represent the problem. *For example, if each person at a party will eat 3/8 of a pound of roast beef, and there will be 5 people at the party, how many pounds of roast beef will be needed? Between what two whole numbers does your answer lie?*   11.7–11.8, 13.18

C. Understand decimal notation for fractions, and compare decimal fractions.

5. Express a fraction with denominator 10 as an equivalent fraction with denominator 100, and use this technique to add two fractions with respective denominators 10 and 100. *For example, express 3/10 as 30/100, and add 3/10 + 4/100 = 34/100.*   13.8, 13.14–13.16

6. Use decimal notation for fractions with denominators 10 or 100. *For example, rewrite 0.62 as 62/100; describe a length as 0.62 meters; locate 0.62 on a number line diagram.*   14.1–14.4

continued

Grade	Standard	Format
	7. Compare two decimals to hundredths by reasoning about their size. Recognize that comparisons are valid only when the two decimals refer to the same whole. Record the results of comparisons with the symbols >, =, or <, and justify the conclusions, e.g., by using a visual model.	14.1–14.4
4	**Measurement and Data**	**4.MD**
	A. Solve problems involving measurement and conversion of measurements.	
	1. Know relative sizes of measurement units within one system of units including km, m, cm; kg, g; lb, oz.; l, ml; hr, min, sec. Within a single system of measurement, express measurements in a larger unit in terms of a smaller unit. Record measurement equivalents in a two-column table. *For example, know that 1 ft is 12 times as long as 1 in. Express the length of a 4 ft snake as 48 in. Generate a conversion table for feet and inches listing the number pairs (1, 12), (2, 24), (3,36). . .*	12.1–12.2
	2. Use the four operations to solve word problems involving distances, intervals of time, liquid volumes, masses of objects, and money, including problems involving simple fractions or decimals, and problems that require expressing measurements given in a larger unit in terms of a smaller unit. Represent measurement quantities using diagrams such as number line diagrams that feature a measurement scale.	11.1–11.9, 12.1–12.11
	3. Apply the area and perimeter formulas for rectangles in real world and mathematical problems. *For example, find the width of a rectangular room given the area of the flooring and the length, by viewing the area formula as a multiplication equation with an unknown factor.*	17.2
	B. Represent and interpret data.	
	4. Make a line plot to display a data set of measurements in fractions of a unit (1/2, 1/4, 1/8). Solve problems involving addition and subtraction of fractions by using information presented in line plots. *For example, from a line plot find and interpret the difference in length between the longest and shortest specimens in an insect collection.*	13.1, Chapter 16
	C. Geometric measurement: understand concepts of angle and measure angles.	
	5. Recognize angles as geometric shapes that are formed wherever two rays share a common endpoint, and understand concepts of angle measurement:	17.7–17.8
	a. An angle is measured with reference to a circle with its center at the common endpoint of the rays, by considering the fraction of the circular arc between the points where the two rays intersect the circle. An angle that turns through 1/360 of a circle is called a "one-degree angle," and can be used to measure angles.	17.7
	b. An angle that turns through *n* one-degree angles is said to have an angle measure of *n* degrees.	17.7–17.8
	6. Measure angles in whole-number degrees using a protractor. Sketch angles of specified measure.	17.7–17.8
	7. Recognize angle measure as additive. When an angle is decomposed into non-overlapping parts, the angle measure of the whole is the sum of the angle measures of the parts. Solve addition and subtraction problems to find unknown angles on a diagram in real world and mathematical problems, e.g., by using an equation with a symbol for the unknown angle measure.	17.7–17.8
4	**Geometry**	**4.G**
	A. Draw and identify lines and angles, and classify shapes by properties of their lines and angles.	
	1. Draw points, lines, line segments, rays, angles (right, acute, obtuse), and perpendicular and parallel lines. Identify these in two-dimensional figures.	17.7–17.8

2. Classify two-dimensional figures based on the presence or absence of parallel or perpendicular lines, or the presence or absence of angles of a specified size. Recognize right triangles as a category, and identify right triangles. 17.1

3. Recognize a line of symmetry for a two-dimensional figure as a line across the figure such that the figure can be folded along the line into matching parts. Identify line-symmetric figures and draw lines of symmetry. Chapter 17

5 **Operations and Algebraic Thinking** **5.OA**

A. Write and interpret numerical expressions.

1. Use parentheses, brackets, or braces in numerical expressions, and evaluate expressions with these symbols. Chapter 18

2. Write simple expressions that record calculations with numbers, and interpret numerical expressions without evaluating them. *For example, express the calculation "add 8 and 7, then multiply by 2" as 2 × (8 + 7). Recognize that 3 × (18932 + 921) is three times as large as 18932 + 921, without having to calculate the indicated sum or product.* Chapter 18

B. Analyze patterns and relationships.

3. Generate two numerical patterns using two given rules. Identify apparent relationships between corresponding terms. Form ordered pairs consisting of corresponding terms from the two patterns, and graph the ordered pairs on a coordinate plane. *For example, given the rule "Add 3" and the starting number 0, and given the rule "Add 6" and the starting number 0, generate terms in the resulting sequences, and observe that the terms in one sequence are twice the corresponding terms in the other sequence. Explain informally why this is so.* 18.1

5 **Numbers and Operation in Base Ten** **5.NBT**

A. Understand the place value system.

1. Recognize that in a multi-digit number, a digit in one place represents 10 times as much as it represents in the place to its right and 1/10 of what it represents in the place to its left. 14.4

2. Explain patterns in the number of zeros of the product when multiplying a number by powers of 10, and explain patterns in the placement of the decimal point when a decimal is multiplied or divided by a power of 10. Use whole-number exponents to denote powers of 10. 14.9

3. Read, write, and compare decimals to thousandths.

   a. Read and write decimals to thousandths using base-ten numerals, number names, and expanded form, e.g., $347.392 = 3 \times 100 + 4 \times 10 + 7 \times 1 + 3 \times (1/10) + 9 \times (1/100) + 2 \times (1/1000)$. 14.1–14.3

   b. Compare two decimals to thousandths based on meanings of the digits in each place, using $>$, $=$, and $<$ symbols to record the results of comparisons. 14.1–14.3

4. Use place value understanding to round decimals to any place. 14.6

B. Perform operations with multi-digit whole numbers and with decimals to hundredths.

5. Fluently multiply multi-digit whole numbers using the standard algorithm. 9.3–9.4

6. Find whole-number quotients of whole numbers with up to four-digit dividend and two-digit divisors, using strategies based on place value, the properties of operations, and/or the relationship between multiplication and division. Illustrate and explain the calculation by using equations, rectangular arrays, and/or area models. 10.7–10.9

continued

Grade	Standard	Format
	7. Add, subtract, multiply, and divide decimals to hundredths, using concrete models or drawings and strategies based on place value, properties of operations, and/or the relationship between addition and subtraction; relate the strategy to a written method and explain the reasoning used.	14.5–14.10
5	**Numbers and Operations—Fractions**	**5.NF**
	A. Use equivalent fractions as a strategy to add and subtract fractions.	
	1. Add and subtract fractions with unlike denominators (including mixed numbers) by replacing given fractions with equivalent fractions in such a way as to produce an equivalent sum or difference of fractions with like denominators. *For example, 2/3 + 5/4 = 8/12 + 15/12 = 23/12. (In general, a/b + c/d = (ad + bc)/bd.)*	13.8–13.16
	2. Solve word problems involving addition and subtraction of fractions referring to the same whole, including cases of unlike denominators, e.g., by using visual fraction models or equations to represent the problem. Use benchmark fractions and number sense of fractions to estimate mentally and assess the reasonableness of answers. *For example, recognize an incorrect result 2/5 + 1/2 = 3/7, by observing that 3/7 < 1/2.*	11.1–11.9, 13.8–13.16
	B. Apply and extend previous understandings of multiplication and division.	
	3. Interpret a fraction as division of the numerator by the denominator $(a/b = a \div b)$. Solve word problems involving division of whole numbers leading to answers in the form of fractions or mixed numbers, e.g., by using visual fraction models or equations to represent the problem. *For example, interpret 3/4 as the result of dividing 3 by 4, noting that 3/4 multiplied by 4 equals 3, and that when 3 wholes are shared equally among 4 people each person has a share of size 3/4. If 9 people want to share a 50-pound sack of rice equally by weight, how many pounds of rice should each person get? Between what two whole numbers does your answer lie?*	11.7, 13.18
	4. Apply and extend previous understandings of multiplication to multiply a fraction or whole number by a fraction.	13.17–13.18
	a. Interpret the product $(a/b) \times q$ as *a* parts of a partition of *q* into *b* equal parts; equivalently, as the result of a sequence of operations $a \times q \div b$. *For example, use a visual fraction model to show (2/3) × 4 = 8/3, and create a story context for this equation. Do the same with (2/3) × (4/5) = 8/15. (In general, (a/b) × (c/d) = ac/bd.)*	11.7, 13.17–13.18
	b. Find the area of a rectangle with fractional side lengths by tiling it with unit squares of the appropriate unit fraction side lengths, and show that the area is the same as would be found by multiplying the side lengths. Multiply fractional side lengths to find areas of rectangles, and represent fraction products as rectangular areas.	13.17–13.18, 17.2
	5. Interpret multiplication as scaling (resizing), by:	
	a. Comparing the size of a product to the size of one factor on the basis of the size of the other factor, without performing the indicated multiplication.	9.2
	b. Explaining why multiplying a given number by a fraction greater than 1 results in a product greater than the given number (recognizing multiplication by whole numbers greater than 1 as a familiar case); explaining why multiplying a given number by a fraction less than 1 results in a product smaller than the given number; and relating the principle of fraction equivalence $a/b = (n \times a)/(n \times b)$ to the effect of multiplying a/b by 1.	13.5, 13.7, 13.18
	6. Solve real world problems involving multiplication of fractions and mixed numbers, e.g., by using visual fraction models or equations to represent the problem.	11.7, 13.17–13.18

7. Apply and extend previous understandings of division to divide unit fractions by whole numbers and whole numbers by unit fractions.1

   a. Interpret division of a unit fraction by a non-zero whole number, and   11.7, Chapter 13
      compute such quotients. *For example, create a story context for*
      (1/3) ÷ 4, and use a visual fraction model to show the quotient.
      Use the relationship between multiplication and division to explain that
      (1/3) ÷ 4 = 1/12 because (1/12) × 4 = 1/3.

   b. Interpret division of a whole number by a unit fraction, and compute   11.7, Chapter 13
      such quotients. *For example, create a story context for 4 ÷ (1/5), and*
      use a visual fraction model to show the quotient. Use the relationship
      between multiplication and division to explain that 4 ÷ (1/5) = 20
      because 20 × (1/5) = 4.

   c. Solve real world problems involving division of unit fractions by non-zero 11.7, Chapter 13
      whole numbers and division of whole numbers by unit fractions, e.g.,
      by using visual fraction models and equations to represent the problem.
      For example, how much chocolate will each person get if 3 people share
      1/2 lb of chocolate equally? How many 1/3-cup servings are in 2 cups
      of raisins?

5   Measurement and Data   5. MD

A. Convert like measurement units within a given measurement system.

   1. Convert among different-sized standard measurement units within a given   12.2
      measurement system (e.g., convert 5 cm to 0.05 m), and use these conver-
      sions in solving multi-step, real world problems.

B. Represent and interpret data.

   2. Make a line plot to display a data set of measurements in fractions of a   Chapter 16
      unit (1/2, 1/4, 1/8). Use operations on fractions for this grade to solve
      problems involving information presented in line plots. *For example, given*
      different measurements of liquid in identical beakers, find the amount of
      liquid each beaker would contain if the total amount in all the beakers
      were redistributed equally.

C. Geometric measurement: understand concepts of volume.

   3. Recognize volume as an attribute of solid figures and understand concepts   17.6
      of volume measurement.

   a. A cube with side length 1 unit, called a "unit cube," is said to have   17.6
      "one cubic unit" of volume, and can be used to measure volume.

   b. A solid figure which can be packed without gaps or overlaps using *n*   17.6
      unit cubes is said to have a volume of *n* cubic units.

   4. Measure volumes by counting unit cubes, using cubic cm, cubic in, cubic   17.6
      ft., and improvised units.

   5. Relate volume to the operations of multiplication and addition and solve   17.6
      real world and mathematical problems involving volume.

   a. Find the volume of a right rectangular prism with whole-number side   17.6
      lengths by packing it with unit cubes, and show that the volume is the
      same as would be found by multiplying the edge lengths, equivalently
      by multiplying the height by the area of the base. Represent threefold
      whole-number products as volumes, e.g., to represent the associative
      property of multiplication.

   b. Apply the formulas $V = l \times w \times h$ and $V = b \times h$ for rectangular   17.6
      prisms to find volumes of right rectangular prisms with whole-number
      edge lengths in the context of solving real world and mathematical
      problems.

continued

Grade	Standard	Format
	c. Recognize volume as additive. Find volumes of solid figures composed of two non-overlapping right rectangular prisms by adding the volumes of the non-overlapping parts, applying this technique to solve real world problems.	17.6
5	**Geometry**	**5.G**
	A. Graph points on the coordinate plane to solve real-world and mathematical problems.	
	1. Use a pair of perpendicular number lines, called axes, to define a coordinate system, with the intersection of the lines (the origin) arranged to coincide with the 0 on each line and a given point in the plane located by using an ordered pair of numbers, called its coordinates. Understand that the first number indicates how far to travel from the origin in the direction of one axis, and the second number indicates how far to travel in the direction of the second axis, with the convention that the names of the two axes and the coordinates correspond (e.g., *x*-axis and *x*-coordinate, *y*-axis and *y*-coordinate).	18.1
	2. Represent real world and mathematical problems by graphing points in the first quadrant of the coordinate plane, and interpret coordinate values of points in the context of the situation.	Chapter 16, 18.1
	B. Classify two-dimensional figures into categories based on their properties.	
	3. Understand that attributes belonging to a category of two dimensional figures also belong to all subcategories of that category. *For example, all rectangles have four right angles and squares are rectangles, so all squares have four right angles.*	17.1
	4. Classify two-dimensional figures in a hierarchy based on properties.	Chapter 17

Frequently Asked Questions About Direct Instruction Mathematics

The Direct Instruction approach has been the target of many queries, controversies, and criticisms since its inception in the 1960s. Therefore, we have included this appendix to answer questions most frequently asked about Direct Instruction, specifically pertaining to the teaching of mathematics. The appendix is organized into two distinct sections: "Instructional Questions and Issues" and "Issues of Instructional Organization and Management." Although some of the answers to the questions can be found in the research literature, some are questions of common practice. Moreover, many are not questions at all but merely instructional issues that require collective problem solving.

INSTRUCTIONAL QUESTIONS AND ISSUES

A. Doesn't Direct Instruction Mathematics Promote Only Rote Learning?

Many critics of Direct Instruction perceive that the approach consists of merely rote memorization of basic skills. These critics are confusing *rote* instruction with *explicit* instruction, and they may be misled due to the appearance of the instruction (e.g., use of scripted formats) rather than the instructional content. Because a Direct Instruction approach is characterized by teaching formats that articulate instruction in a step-by-step fashion, some educators confuse the structure of the lesson with the content of the instructional strategy. The more scripted a lesson, the stronger the perception that some form of rote instruction is being delivered.

In reality, no skills or concepts are taught by rote in a Direct Instruction mathematics approach that can be taught using an explicit strategy. Certainly, Direct Instruction mathematics includes the teaching of the counting sequence (e.g., 1 2 3 4 5) and symbol identification (6 is "six"), both of which require rote memorization. Notice, however, that the tasks of counting and symbol identification are inherently rote tasks. Programs will always contain some rote instruction, but the decision to teach something by rote is driven by the demands of the task, not the instructional designer.

Direct Instruction program designers have designed useful *strategies,* even for the teaching of basic facts. Teachers using a Direct Instruction approach are encouraged to teach fact number-family strategies that facilitate student understanding of the relationships among fact families and that reduce the number of facts that must be memorized. For example, the introduction to the fact family 4, 3, and 7 facilitates learning the following facts: $4 + 3 = 7$, $3 + 4 = 7$, $7 - 4 = 3$, and $7 - 3 = 4$. Instead of memorizing four isolated facts, students are taught a *strategy* for deriving facts when one of the family members is unknown. For example, they are taught that when the *big number* is missing they must add and when one of the *small numbers* is missing they must subtract. (Note that the language of big and small numbers is used so that the strategy may be applied to multiplication and division as well as addition and subtraction.)

The point of the above example is that, despite the fact that Direct Instruction *appears* as if it might be rote because of the way it is delivered, when teachers look closely at the *content* rather than the *form* of the lesson, they will find generalizable strategies. (See Chapter 1 for a more thorough discussion of strategy instruction and Chapter 6 for instruction on basic facts.) In this text, we provide generalizable strategies for many computation and problem-solving skills. These strategies promote conceptual understanding and develop reasoning skills.

B. How Do You Know that Direct Instruction Mathematics Strategies Are Effective?

The strategies presented in this book have been field-tested extensively with students of various ages and abilities to ensure that they are viable and useful. The underlying research basis for the design of the strategies is presented in Chapter 2. The research reviewed in Chapter 2 incorporates relevant research from mathematics instruction and the teacher effectiveness literature as well as research on specific Direct Instruction mathematics strategies. Additionally, the strategies presented in this text also have been developed with feedback from students and their teachers.

Teachers involved in field-testing the programs provided important feedback to those developing instructional strategies for the commercially available Direct Instruction mathematics programs. Student errors were carefully examined so that errors caused by a faulty strategy could be identified and the strategy rewritten. The development of effective strategies through feedback from field-testing is a unique feature of Direct Instruction mathematics. Most commercially available programs are not field-tested with students prior to their publication.

C. What Role Do Manipulatives Play in Mathematics Instruction Using a Direct Instruction Approach?

First, it is important to note that the findings of research on the use of manipulatives, or concrete objects, in elementary mathematics are inconclusive. The manipulatives themselves are neither helpful nor harmful. The way in which manipulatives are incorporated into instructional activities determines their value. Consistent with a Direct Instruction approach, manipulatives are most useful after an algorithm is taught. Concrete objects can be used as a means of demonstrating understanding of the symbolic representation. Many instructional programs do the opposite. That is, their initial instructional activities often require students to use manipulatives to generate or represent an algorithm before the students are taught the algorithm. The danger in delaying instruction on the algorithm is that students either fail to learn the algorithm or are unable to transfer the concrete representation to a symbolic one. That is, students can work the problem with manipulatives only and not understand how to compute the answer using only symbols. Another potential problem with the use of manipulatives is related to the issue of efficiency. Instruction tends to take significantly more time when initial instruction involves concrete representations.

Finally, many teachers feel that, with respect to instruction with young children, using manipulatives makes monitoring individual student performance more difficult. In Chapter 7 of this text, we recommend teaching an early addition algorithm by using line drawing instead of concrete objects. The line drawing provides students with a pictorial representation of the problem. However, even more importantly, the line-drawing strategy allows the teacher to examine individual student performance easily and remedy errors in a timely fashion.

D. Should Teachers Spend Time Teaching Memorization of Math Facts?

Chapter 6 in this text provides educators with a good rationale for teaching basic math facts along with recommendations for designing math fact instruction. The reason for teaching math facts is simply that basic fact knowledge is a prerequisite for higher-level computation and problem-solving skills. When a student must stop working a problem to figure out a fact, attention is drawn away from solving the problem and directed to computing the fact. The continuity required to learn new problem-solving routines is interrupted. Fluent knowledge of math facts facilitates not only the acquisition of higher-level skills but also independence and confidence in learning.

While we advocate teaching math facts, we understand that this instruction is time-consuming, especially with struggling students. Therefore, we suggest that instruction in math facts be supplemental to the teacher-directed lesson.

E. Should Students be Allowed to Use Calculators in Math Class?

Issues regarding the use of calculators are similar to issues of manipulatives in that it is not *whether* students use calculators but *how* and *when* they use them. Teachers must make intentional decisions about the extent to which they will allow students to rely on calculators for computation. If teachers do allow calculators, they must teach students to use them properly.

F. What Direct Instruction Mathematics Programs Are Commercially Aavailable?

Most of the commercially available Direct Instruction mathematics programs are discussed on the website of the National Institute for Direct Instruction. These programs include:

- DISTAR Arithmetic
- Connecting Math Concepts
- Corrective Math
- Essentials for Algebra
- Funnix Math

ISSUES OF INSTRUCTIONAL ORGANIZATION AND MANAGEMENT

A. Is Direct Instruction for Only Struggling Students?

Because Direct Instruction has been effective with struggling students and students receiving special education services, educators assume the strategies are appropriate *only* for students who are struggling with mathematics. On the contrary, we believe the strategies are effective for *all* students because they are well designed, generalizable, and clearly presented. The mistake many teachers make when using Direct Instruction with higher-performing students is pacing the instruction too slowly. These teachers may be providing more repetition and practice than is necessary for their students, or they may be teaching skills students already have acquired. Careful monitoring of student progress allows teachers to differentiate instruction within their classrooms to meet the needs of all of their students.

B. How Does a Direct Instruction Approach in Mathematics Work with Students with Special Needs?

The underlying philosophy of Direct Instruction is that *all* students can learn if given well-designed instruction and opportunities for practice. Students with special needs often *require* (a) well-designed, unambiguous, teacher-directed instruction and (b) *more* practice opportunities in order to master the skills presented.

As mentioned earlier, the Direct Instruction strategies in this text have been demonstrated to be effective with a range of students. But the instruction is just one part of a multi-tiered system of supports. Other essential components include assessment and service delivery. Assessment must include provisions for appropriate initial screening and diagnostic testing, in addition to continued progress monitoring that informs instructional decision-making. Service delivery in this context refers to the systematic coordination of effort by general and special educators that includes shared responsibility and collaborative problem solving.

Using the guiding principles of well-designed instruction and more practice opportunities, all teachers of students with special needs must discuss the *who, what, where,* and *how* of designing an effective program. *Who* will be responsible for teacher-directed instruction? *What* will be taught? *Where* will the student receive the instruction? *How* will the teachers orchestrate additional practice opportunities? All of the above questions are relevant to the education of students with special needs.

Glossary

Addend: The numbers of the smaller sets in an addition statement (e.g., in 4 + 3 = 7, the addends are 4 and 3).

Addition: Addition is (a) the process of combining smaller sets to form a larger set and then determining the total number of the larger set or (b) the union of two disjoint sets. Disjoint sets have no members in common.

Alternating pattern: A method for providing practice after the introduction of a new fact that involves systematically reviewing previously introduced facts interspersed with the new fact. For example, after a new numeral is introduced, a previously reviewed numeral is identified, then the new numeral is identified again, followed by two previously reviewed numerals, and so on.

Area: The number of square units it takes to cover a figure.

Base number: The number multiplied by itself when an exponent is present.

Circumference: The circumference is the distance around the outside of a circle.

Column alignment: Positioning two or more multi-digit numerals so that like place values are vertically aligned.

Commutative property: Adding or multiplying the same numbers in any order will produce the same result (5 × 3 = 15 and 3 × 5 = 15; 10 + 4 + 31 = 45, 4 + 10 + 31 = 45, and 31 + 4 + 10 = 45).

Complex addition facts: Addition facts that require a student to mentally add a single-digit number to a two-digit number.

Compound probability: The likelihood of two or more events happening together.

Decimal fractions: Fractions with a denominator of 10 or any power of 10: $1\frac{1}{10}$, $\frac{1}{100}$, $\frac{1}{1000}$, etc.

Decimals: Decimals are similar to fractions in that they both deal with something that has been divided into equal parts. Decimals are restricted, however, to situations with 10 parts or any power of 10 (10, 100, 1000, etc.). In a decimal, the number of equal parts is not indicated by a denominator but rather through place value. The position of a numeral in relation to a decimal point expresses the number of equal parts. For example, one digit after the decimal point indicates 10 equal parts; two digits after the decimal point indicate 100 equal parts. The value of the digit represents the number of parts present, used, or acted upon. For example, .5 equals $\frac{5}{10}$ and .5 represents a division into 10 equal parts with 5 parts present.

Denominator: The bottom number in a fraction.

Descriptive statistics: Statistics that summarize a data set with measures of central tendency and variability.

Diameter: The diameter is a line running from one side of the circle to the opposite side through the midpoint.

Difference: The quantity remaining after the subtrahend is taken away from the minuend.

Distractor: Information given in a word problem that is not necessary to finding the solution to the problem

Distributive property: The distributive property of multiplication over addition says that if a, b, and c are whole numbers, then

$$a \times (b + c) = (a \times b) + (a \times c)$$

This property is essential to understanding multiplication of multi-digit numbers such as 4 × 27. Expanded notation allows 27 to be rewritten as 20 + 7. The problem 4 × 27 then becomes 4 × (20 + 7), which equals (4 × 20) + (4 × 7). It is also important for later work with fractions, equations, and algebra.

Dividend: The number being divided. It corresponds to the product in a multiplication problem:

$$6 \text{ in } 2\overline{)6}$$

Division: The inverse of multiplication. When a student divides, she is finding a missing factor; 16 ÷ 8 can be expressed as 8 × □ = 16.

Divisor: The factor that is given in a division problem. It is written in front of the division sign:

$$2 \text{ in } 2\overline{)6}$$

Effect size: Quantity that allows for comparison between two groups, usually an experimental group and a control group.

Equations: A statement of equality between two expressions.

Expanded notation: Writing a number to show the value of each digit. For example, 384 = 300 + 80 + 4.

Experimental probability: The number of times a specific event occurs compared to the total number of trials.

Exponent: A numeral written above and to the right of another numeral (the base) to indicate how many times the base has been multiplied by itself ($5^3 = 5 \times 5 \times 5$).

Expressions: Mathematical phrases that may include numbers, variables, and symbols for operations.

Factors: The multiplicand and the multiplier in a multiplication problem.

Fractions: A fraction is a numeral of the form y/x where $x \neq 0$. Fractions involve division into equal-sized segments and a statement regarding the number of segments present, used, or acted upon. For example, "John ate ¼ of a pie" implies that a pie was divided into four equal parts and that John ate one of those parts.

Functions: The relationship between a set of numbers.

Graph: Visual representation of a relationship between two or more sets of data.

Greatest common factor: Largest factor of both the numerator and the denominator; e.g., the greatest common factor for ⅛ is 4.

Identity element: Any number multiplied or divided by 1 is equal to that number.

Improper fraction: A fraction whose numerator is equal to or greater than the denominator.

Interquartile range: A measure of variability consisting of the difference between the first quartile and third quartile of a set of data.

Lowest common denominator: The least common multiple of the denominators; e.g., the lowest common denominator for ⅓ + ½ + ¼ is 12.

Mean Absolute Deviation (MAD): The average distance between each data point and the mean of a set of data.

Mean: Calculated by adding a group of numbers and dividing the sum by the number of numbers that were added; often referred to as the "average."

Median: Middle number of a set of numbers that has been arranged in order of magnitude.

Minuend: Original quantity from which an amount is subtracted.

Missing addends: A problem type in which students solve for an addend (e.g., $6 + \square = 9$).

Mixed decimal: An expression consisting of a whole numeral and a decimal: e.g., 3.24, 18.05.

Mixed numeral: An improper fraction expressed as a whole number and a fraction.

Mode: The most frequently occurring value in a collection of numbers.

Multiplicand: The number of units in each equal set.

Multiplication: The process of combining a specific number of sets, each including an equal number of elements, into a single larger set.

Multiplier: The number of sets in the multiplication process.

Negative integers: Whole numbers less than zero.

Numeral: The symbol associated with a particular number.

Numerator: The top number in a fraction.

Ordinal counting: Counting associated with position (first, second, third, etc.).

Percent: The symbol % is read "percent." It represents the ratio of two quantities with the denominator being hundredths. The fraction ⅖ may be converted to an equivalent fraction, ⁴⁰/₁₀₀, which in turn may be expressed as 40%. When presenting the various forms of rational numbers, teachers must consider their interrelatedness. Problem-solving strategies designed for teaching fractions should be presented in a manner that will prepare students for decimals. Likewise, the strategies presented for decimals should prepare students for percent.

Percentage: The number obtained by finding the percent of another number.

Perimeter: The perimeter of a polygon is the sum of the length of each of its sides.

Pi: The ratio of a circle's circumference to its diameter, commonly approximated as 3.14.

Place value: Each digit has 10 times the value of the digit immediately to its right in our decimal system.

Positive integers: Whole numbers greater than zero.

Prime factors: Factors of a number that are also prime numbers.

Prime numbers: Whole numbers greater than 1 that are evenly divisible only by 1 and themselves.

Product: The answer in a multiplication problem. The number designating elements in the combined set of a multiplication problem; i.e., the sum of all the equal sets.

Proper fraction: A fraction whose numerator is less than its denominator.

Quotient: The factor solved for in a division problem. It is written above the division sign:

$$3 \text{ in } 2\overline{)6}$$

Radius: The radius of a circle is the distance between the midpoint of the circle and the edge of the circle.

Range: The difference between the smallest and largest number in a set.

Ratio: The numerical expression of the relationship between two comparable quantities. Usually the ratio is the result of dividing the first quantity by the second.

Rational counting: Coordinating counting with touching objects to determine the quantity of a group.

Ray: A portion of a line that starts at a certain point and continues in a particular direction with no end.

Regrouping: Rearranging a quantity of *objects* (not numerals) as a greater and lesser unit; for example, |||||||||||||||||||||||||| can be regrouped as ||||||| |||||||||||||||.

Renaming: Rewriting a numeral as a greater unit and a lesser unit; e.g., in 75 − 19, 75 is renamed as 60 + 15.

Rote counting: Identifying number names in sequence.

Skip counting: Counting in which students say multiples of a base number in order.

Subtrahend: The number that is subtracted from another.

Sum: The number of the new set formed by combining the smaller sets (e.g., in 4 + 3 = 7, the sum is 7).

Surface area: The total area of the surface of a three-dimensional figure.

Table: A table specifies the relationship among sets of numbers.

Term: A number or variable, or numbers and variables, multiplied by each other or separated by symbols (e.g. +, ÷, =).

Theoretical probability: Predicting the likelihood of an event using mathematics.

Volume: The number of cubic units of space inside a three-dimensional shape.

References

Adams, G. L., & Engelmann, S. (1996). *Research on Direct Instruction: 25 years beyond DISTAR*. Seattle, WA: Educational Achievement Systems.

Adelman, C. (1999). *Answers in the tool box: Academic intensity, attendance patterns, and Bachelor's degree attainment*. Washington, DC: Office of Education Research and Improvement, U.S. Department of Education. Retrieved from http://www.ed.gov/pubs/Toolbox/index.html

American Federation of Teachers. (1998a). *Seven promising schoolwide programs for raising student achievement*. Washington, DC: Author. Retrieved November 2002 from www.aft.org/edissues/downloads/seven.pdf

American Federation of Teachers. (1998b). *Six promising school wide reform programs*. Washington, DC: Author. Retrieved November 2002 from www.aft.org/edissues/rsa/promprog/wwschoolwidereform.htm

American Federation of Teachers. (1999). *Five promising remedial reading intervention programs*. Washington, DC: Author. Retrieved November 2002 from www.aft.org/edissues/whatworks/wwreading.htm

Archer, A. L., & Hughes, C. A. (2011). *Explicit instruction: Effective and efficient teaching*. New York, NY: Guilford Press.

Attewell, P., & Domina, T. (2008). Raising the bar: Curricular intensity and academic performance. *Educational Evaluation and Policy Analysis, 30*(1), 51–71.

Borman, G. D., Hewes, G. M., Overman, L. T., & Brown, S. (2002). *Comprehensive school reform and student achievement: A meta-analysis* (Report No. 59). Baltimore, MD: Center for Research on the Education of Students Placed At Risk, Johns Hopkins University. Retrieved from http://files.eric.ed.gov/fulltext/ED472569.pdf

Brophy, J., & Good, T. (1986). Teacher behavior and student achievement. In M. C. Wittrock (Ed.), *Third handbook of research on teaching* (3rd ed., pp. 328–375). New York, NY: Macmillan.

Bryant, D. P. (2005). Commentary on early identification and intervention for students with mathematics difficulties. *Journal of Learning Disabilities, 38*(4), 340–345.

Cacha, F. B. (1975). Subtraction: regrouping with flexibility. *The Arithmetic Teacher, 22*(5), 402–404.

Carnine, D. W., Silbert, J., Kame'enui, E. J., Slocum, T. A., & Travers, P. A. (2017). *Direct instruction reading*. New York, NY: Pearson.

Child Trends Databank. (2015). Mathematics proficiency. Retrieved from http://www.childtrends.org/?indicators=mathematics-proficiency

Dingman, S., Teuscher, D., Newton, J. A., & Kasmer, L. (2013). Common mathematics standards in the United States: A comparison of K–8 state and Common Core standards. *The Elementary School Journal, 113*(4), 541–564.

Dunlosky, J., Rawson, K. A., Marsh, E. J., Nathan, M. J., & Willingham, D. T. (2013). Improving students' learning with effective learning techniques: Promising directions from cognitive and educational psychology. *Psychological Science in the Public Interest, 14*(1), 4–58.

Engelmann, S. (1969). *Conceptual learning*. San Rafael, CA: Dimensions Publishing Company.

Engelmann, S. & Carnine, D. (1991). *Theory of instruction: Principles and applications*. Eugene, OR: NIFDI Press.

Engelmann, S., Carnine, D., & Steely, D. G. (1991). Making connections in mathematics. *Journal of Learning Disabilities, 24*(5), 292–303.

Engelmann, S., Becker, W. C., Carnine, D. C., & Gersten, R. (1988). The Direct Instruction model: Design and outcomes. *Education and Treatment of Children, 11*, 303–317.

Finnie, R., & Meng, R. (2006). The importance of functional literacy: Reading and math skills and labour market outcomes of high school drop-outs. *Statistics Canada*. Retrieved from http://www.statcan.gc.ca/pub/11f0019m/11f0019m2006275-eng.pdf

Fuchs, L. S., Fuchs, D., & Hamlett, C. L. (2015). Republication of "Curriculum-based measurement: A standardized, long-term goal approach to monitoring student progress." *Intervention in School and Clinic, 50*(3), 185–192.

Fuchs, L. S., Fuchs, D., Powell, S. R., Seethaler, P. M., Cirino, P. T., & Fletcher, J. M. (2008). Intensive intervention for students with mathematics disabilities: Seven principles of effective practice. *Learning Disability Quarterly, 31*, 79–92.

Gersten, R., Beckmann, S., Clarke, B., Foegen, A., Marsh, L., Star, J. R., & Witzel, B. (2009). *Assisting students struggling with mathematics: Response to intervention (RtI) for elementary and middle schools* (NCEE 2009-4060). Washington, DC: National Center for Education Evaluation and Regional Assistance, Institute of Education Sciences, U.S. Department of Education. Retrieved from http://ies.ed.gov/ncee/wwc/publications/practiceguides/

Gersten, R. Chard, D. J., Jayanthi, M., Baker, S. K., Morphy, P., & Flojo, J. (2009). Mathematics instruction for students with learning disabilities: A meta-analysis of instructional components. *Review of Educational Research, 79*(3),1202–1242.

Gersten, R., & Carnine, D. (1984). Direct Instruction mathematics: A longitudinal evaluation of low-income elementary school students. *The Elementary School Journal, 84*(4), 395–407.

Gersten, R., Clarke, B., Jordan, N. C., Newman-Gonchar, R. Haymond, K., & Wilkins, C. (2012). Universal screening in mathematics for the primary grades: Beginnings of a research base. *Exceptional Children, 78*(4), 423–445.

Herman, R., Aladjem, D., McMahon, P., Masem, E., Mulligan, I., & O'Malley, A. (1999). *An educators' guide to schoolwide reform*. Washington, DC: American Institutes for Research. Retrieved from http://files.eric.ed.gov/fulltext/ED460429.pdf

Hughes, E. M., Powell, S. R., Lembke, E. S., & Riley-Tillman, T. C. (2016). Taking the guesswork out of locating evidence-based mathematics practices for diverse learners. *Learning Disabilities Research & Practice, 31*(3), 130–141.

Jitendra, A. K., & Star, J. R. (2011). Meeting the needs of students with learning disabilities in inclusive mathematics classrooms: The role of schema-based instruction on mathematical problem-solving. *Theory Into Practice, 50,* 12–19.

Jobrack, B. (2011). *The tyranny of the textbook.* Lanham, MD: Rowman & Littlefield.

Judge, S., & Watson, S. M. R. (2011). Longitudinal outcomes for mathematics achievement for students with learning disabilities. *Journal of Educational Research, 104,* 147–157.

Kirsch, I., Jungeblut, A., Jenkins, L., & Kolstad, A. (2002). *Adult literacy in America: A first look at the findings of the National Adult Literacy Survey.* Washington, DC: National Center for Education Statistics. Retrieved from http://nces.ed.gov/pubs93/93275.pdf

Murnane, R. J., Willett, J. B., Braatz, M. J., & Duhaldeborde, Y. (2001). Do different dimensions of male high school students' skills predict labor market success a decade later? Evidence from the NLSY. *Economics of Education Review, 20,* 311–320.

Murnane, R., Willett, J., & Levy, F. (1995). The growing importance of cognitive skills in wage determination. *The Review of Economics and Statistics, 77*(2), 251–266.

National Center for Education Statistics. (2015). *The nation's report card.* Retrieved from http://www.nationsreportcard.gov/reading_math_2015/#mathematics/acl?grade=8

National Council of Teacher of Mathematics. (1980). *Agenda for action.* Retrieved from http://www.nctm.org/Standards-and-Positions/More-NCTM-Standards/An-Agenda-for-Action-(1980s)/

National Council of Teachers of Mathematics. (2000). *Executive summary: Principles and standards for school mathematics.* Retrieved from http://www.nctm.org/uploadedFiles/Standards_and_Positions/PSSM_ExecutiveSummary.pdf

National Governors Association & Council of Chief State School Officers. (2012). *Common Core State Standards for mathematics.* Retrieved from http://www.corestandards.org/assets/CCSSI_Math%20Standards.pdf

National Governors Association Center for Best Practices & Council of Chief State School Officers. (2010). *Common Core State Standards for English language arts and literacy in history/social studies, science, and technical subjects.* Washington, DC: Authors.

National Mathematics Advisory Panel. (2008). *Foundations for success: The Final report of the National Mathematics Advisory Panel,* U.S. Department of Education. Retrieved from http://www.ed.gov/about/bdscomm/list/mathpanel/report/final-report.pdf

National Mathematics Advisory Panel. (2008). *Foundations for success: The final report of the National Mathematics Advisory Panel.* Washington, DC: U.S. Department of Education.

National Research Council. (2001). *Adding it up: Helping children learn mathatics.* J. Kilpatrick, J. Swafford, & B. Findell (Eds.). Mathematics Learning Study Committee, Center for Education, Division of Behavioral and Social Sciences and Education. Washington, DC: National Academy Press.

National Science Board. (2008). Science and engineering indicators 2008 (Vol. 1, NSB 08-01; Vol. 2, NSB 08-01A). Arlington, VA: National Science Foundation.

Organization for Economic Cooperation and Development. (2014a). *PISA 2012 results in focus: What 15-year-olds know and what they can do with what they know.* Retrieved from http://www.oecd.org/pisa/keyfindings/pisa-2012-results-overview.pdf

Organization for Economic Cooperation and Development. (2014b). *United States country note results from PISA 2012.* Retrieved from http://www.oecd.org/pisa/keyfindings/PISA-2012-results-US.pdf

Organization for Economic Cooperation and Development. (2016). *Programme for International Student Assessment.* Retrieved from https://www.oecd.org/pisa/

Rasmussen, C., Heck, D., Tarr, J., Knuth, E., White, D., Lambdin, D., Baltzley, P., Quander, J., & Barnes, D. (2011). Trends and issues in high school mathematics: Research insights and needs. *Journal for Research in Mathematics Education, 42,* 204–219.

Reyna, V. F., & Brainerd, C. J. (2007). The importance of mathematics in health and human judgment: Numeracy, risk communication, and medical decision making. *Learning and Individual Differences, 17*(20), 147–159.

Reys, B. J., Reys, R. E., & Chavez, O. (2004). Why mathematics textbooks matter. *Educational Leadership, 61*(5), 61–66.

Rosenshine, B., & Stevens, R. (1986). Teaching functions. In M. C. Whittrock (Ed.), *Third handbook of research on teaching* (3rd ed., pp. 376–391). New York, NY: Macmillan.

Schmidt, W. H., & Houang, R. T. (2012). Curricular coherence and the Common Core State Standards for mathematics. *Educational Researcher, 41,* 294–308.

Schmidt, W., Houang, R., & Cogan, L. (2002). A coherent curriculum: The case of mathematics. *American Educator, 26*(2), 10–26.

Shinn, M. R., & Walker, H. M. (Eds.). (2010). *Interventions for academic and behavior problems in a three-tier model, including response-to-intervention.* Bethesda, MD: National Association of School Psychologists.

Slavin, R. E., & Lake, C. (2008). Effective programs in elementary mathematics: A best-evidence synthesis. *Review of Educational Research, 78*(3), 427–515.

Slavin, R. E., Lake, C., & Groff, C. (2009). Effective programs in middle and high school mathematics: A best-evidence synthesis. *Review of Educational Research, 79*(2), 839–911.

Snider, V. E. (2004). A comparison of spiral versus strand curriculum. *Journal of Direct Instruction, 4,* 29–40.

Stebbins, L.B., St. Pierre, R.G., Proper, E., Anderson, R.B., & Serra, T.R. (1977). Education as experimentation: A planned variation model. (Vol. IV-A, *An evaluation of Follow Through*). Cambridge, MA: ABT Associates.

Stebbins, L. B., St. Pierre, R. G., Proper, E. C., Anderson, R. B., & Cerva, T. R. (1977). *Education as experimentation: A planned variation model* (Volume IV-A: An evaluation of Follow Through). Cambridge, MA: Abt Associates.

Stein, M. L., Stuen, C., Carnine, D., & Long, R. M. (2001). Textbook evaluation and adoption practices. *Reading and Writing Quarterly, 17*(1), 5–23.

Tyler, J. H. (2004). Basic skills and the earnings of dropouts. *Economics of Education Review, 23*(3), 221–235.

Watkins, C. L. (1997). *Project Follow Through: A case study of the contingencies influencing instructional practices of the educational establishment* (Monograph). Concord, MA: Cambridge Center for Behavioral Studies.

Index

Page numbers in bold indicate definitions.